BERLITZ TRAVEL GUIDES

Africa
○ Algeria
Kenya
Morocco
South Africa
Tunisia

Asia, Middle East
○ China
Hong Kong
○ India
○ Indonesia*
○ Japan
Nepal
Singapore
Sri Lanka
Thailand
Egypt
Jerusalem/Holy Land
Saudi Arabia

Australasia
○ Australia
New Zealand

Austria/Switzerland
Tyrol
Vienna
○ Switzerland

British Isles
Channel Islands
Ireland
London
Oxford and Stratford
Scotland

Belgium/Netherlands
Brussels
Amsterdam

France
Brittany
○ France
French Riviera
Loire Valley
Normandy
Paris

Germany
Berlin
Munich
The Rhine Valley

Greece, Cyprus and Turkey
Athens
Corfu
Crete
Greek Islands Aegean
Peloponnese
Rhodes
Salonica/N. Greece
Cyprus
Istanbul/Aegean Coast
○ Turkey

Italy and Malta
Florence
Italian Adriatic
Italian Riviera
○ Italy
Naples/Amalfi Coast*
Rome
Sicily
Venice
Malta

Scandinavia
Copenhagen
Helsinki
Oslo/Bergen
Stockholm

Spain
Barcelona
Canary Islands
Costa Blanca
Costa Brava
Costa del Sol/Andalusia
Costa Dorada/Barcelona
Ibiza and Formentera
Madrid
Majorca and Minorca
Seville

Portugal
Algarve
Lisbon
Madeira

Eastern Europe
Budapest
Dubrovnik/S. Dalmatia
○ Hungary
Istria and Croatian Coast
Moscow and Leningrad

The Hermitage, Leningrad*
Prague
Split and Dalmatia
○ Yugoslavia

North America
○ U.S.A.
California
Florida
Hawaii
Miami
New York
Washington
○ Canada
Montreal
Toronto

Caribbean, Lat. Am.
Bahamas
Bermuda
French West Indies
Jamaica
Puerto Rico
Southern Caribbean
Virgin Islands
Brazil (Highlights of)
○ Mexico*
Mexico City
Rio de Janeiro

Address Books
London/New York
Paris/Rome

Blueprint Guides
Europe A-Z/France
Germany/Britain
Greece/Hungary
Italy/Spain/USSR*

More for the $
France/Italy

Cruise Guides
Alaska
Caribbean
Handbook to Cruising

Ski Guides
Austria/France
Italy/Switzerland
Skiing the Alps

Europe
Business Travel Guide
Train Travel
Pocket Guide-Europe
Cities of Europe

* in preparation / ○ country guides 192 o   2

P9-DWX-507

Berlitz Dictionaries

Dansk	Engelsk, Fransk, Italiensk, Spansk, Tysk
Deutsch	Dänisch, Englisch, Finnisch, Französisch, Italienisch, Niederländisch, Norwegisch, Portugiesisch, Schwedish, Spanisch
English	Danish, Dutch, Finnish, French, German, Italian, Norwegian, Portuguese, Spanish, Swedish, Turkish
Español	Alemán, Danés, Finlandés, Francés, Holandés, Inglés, Noruego, Sueco
Français	Allemand, Anglais, Danois, Espagnol, Finnois, Italien, Néerlandais, Norvégien, Portugais, Suédois
Italiano	Danese, Finlandese, Francese, Inglese, Norvegese, Olandese, Svedese, Tedesco
Nederlands	Duits, Engels, Frans, Italiaans, Portugees, Spaans
Norsk	Engelsk, Fransk, Italiensk, Spansk, Tysk
Português	Alemão, Francês, Holandês, Inglês, Sueco
Suomi	Englanti, Espanja, Italia, Ranska, Ruotsi, Saksa
Svenska	Engelska, Finska, Franska, Italienska, Portugisiska, Spanska, Tyska

BERLITZ®

french-english
english-french
dictionary

---

dictionnaire
français-anglais
anglais-français

By the Staff of Berlitz Guides

Revised edition 1979
Library of Congress Catalog Card Number: 78-78078

21st printing 1991
Printed in England

Contents

Table des matières

Preface

In selecting the 12.500 word-concepts in each language for this dictionary, the editors have had the traveller's needs foremost in mind. This book will prove invaluable to all the millions of travellers, tourists and business people who appreciate the reassurance a small and practical dictionary can provide. It offers them—as it does beginners and students—all the basic vocabulary they are going to encounter and to have to use, giving the key words and expressions to allow them to cope in everyday situations.

Like our successful phrase books and travel guides, these dictionaries—created with the help of a computer data bank—are designed to slip into pocket or purse, and thus have a role as handy companions at all times.

Besides just about everything you normally find in dictionaries, there are these Berlitz bonuses:

● imitated pronunciation next to each foreign-word entry, making it easy to read and enunciate words whose spelling may look forbidding

● a unique, practical glossary to simplify reading a foreign restaurant menu and to take the mystery out of complicated dishes and indecipherable names on bills of fare

● useful information on how to tell the time and how to count, on conjugating irregular verbs, commonly seen abbreviations and converting to the metric system, in addition to basic phrases.

While no dictionary of this size can pretend to completeness, we expect the user of this book will feel well armed to affront foreign travel with confidence. We should, however, be very pleased to receive comments, criticism and suggestions that you think may be of help in preparing future editions.

Préface

En choisissant 12 500 mots-concepts dans chacune des langues de ce dictionnaire, nos rédacteurs se sont souciés des besoins essentiels du voyageur. Cet ouvrage s'avérera indispensable aux millions de touristes, globe-trotters, hommes ou femmes d'affaires qui apprécient l'appoint qu'apporte un dictionnaire pratique et de format réduit. Il leur offre, ainsi qu'aux débutants et aux étudiants, tout le vocabulaire qu'ils seront amenés à rencontrer et à utiliser; il leur propose des mots-clés et des expressions leur permettant de faire face aux situations courantes.

A l'instar de nos manuels de conversation et de nos guides de voyage déjà fort appréciés, nos dictionnaires – réalisés grâce à une banque de données sur ordinateur – sont conçus pour se glisser dans une poche ou dans un sac, assumant ainsi leur rôle de compagnons à tout moment.

Outre tous les éléments contenus dans n'importe quel dictionnaire, nos ouvrages proposent:

- une transcription phonétique à côté de chaque entrée afin d'en faciliter la lecture, apport non négligeable lorsque le mot étranger semble à priori imprononçable

- un lexique pratique visant à simplifier la lecture du menu dans un restaurant et révélant tous les mystères de plats jusqu'alors inconnus

- des informations précieuses sur la façon d'exprimer le temps, de compter, sur les verbes irréguliers, sur les abréviations courantes, en plus des expressions usuelles.

Aucun dictionnaire de ce format ne peut prétendre être exhaustif, mais le but de cet ouvrage est de permettre à son utilisateur d'affronter avec confiance un voyage à l'étranger. Nous n'en serions pas moins très heureux de recevoir de nos lecteurs tous commentaires, critiques et suggestions qui nous permettraient de compléter nos futures rééditions.

french-english

_____

français-anglais

Introduction

The dictionary has been designed to take account of your practical needs. Unnecessary linguistic information has been avoided. The entries are listed in alphabetical order, regardless of whether the entry word is printed in a single word, contains an apostrophe, or is in two or more separate words. As the only exception to this rule, a few idiomatic expressions are listed alphabetically as main entries, according to the most significant word of the expression. When an entry is followed by sub-entries such as expressions and locutions, these, too, have been listed in alphabetical order.

Each main-entry word is followed by a phonetic transcription (see Guide to pronunciation). Following the transcription is the part of speech of the entry word whenever applicable. When an entry word may be used as more than one part of speech, the translations are grouped together after the respective part of speech.

The feminine or plural forms of French adjectives have been supplied whenever they diverge from the standard rule for the word-ending in question. Similarly, the plural forms of nouns are given when not in accordance with the rules for the particular word-ending.

Whenever an entry word is repeated in irregular forms, or in sub-entries, a tilde ($\sim$) is used to represent the full entry word.

In irregular feminine and plural forms, a hyphen is used to represent the part of the main-entry word that precedes the relevant word-ending.

An asterisk (*) in front of a verb indicates that the verb is irregular. For details, refer to the lists of irregular verbs.

Abbreviations

adj	adjective	*num*	numeral
adv	adverb	*p*	past tense
Am	American	*pl*	plural
art	article	*plAm*	plural (American)
conj	conjunction	*pp*	past participle
f	feminine	*pr*	present tense
fpl	feminine plural	*pref*	prefix
m	masculine	*prep*	preposition
mpl	masculine plural	*pron*	pronoun
n	noun	*v*	verb
nAm	noun (American)	*vAm*	verb (American)

Guide to Pronunciation

Each main entry in this part of the dictionary is followed by a phonetic transcription which shows you how to pronounce the words. This transcription should be read as if it were English. It is based on Standard British pronunciation, though we have tried to take account of General American pronunciation also. Below, only those letters and symbols are explained which we consider likely to be ambiguous or not immediately understood.

The syllables are separated by hyphens, and stressed syllables are printed in *italics*.

Of course, the sounds of any two languages are never exactly the same, but if you follow carefully our indications, you should be able to pronounce the foreign words in such a way that you'll be understood. To make your task easier, our transcriptions occasionally simplify slightly the sound system of the language while still reflecting the essential sound differences.

Consonants

g	always hard, as in **g**o
ñ	as in Spanish se**ñ**or, or like **ni** in o**ni**on
r	pronounced in the back of the mouth
s	always hard, as in **s**o
zh	a soft, voiced **sh**, like **s** in plea**s**ure

The sign (′) indicates a so-called aspirate h. It means that no liaison (*les huttes*—lay 'ewt) nor elision (*la hutte*—lah 'ewt) should be made.

Vowels and Diphthongs

aa	long **a,** as in c**a**r
ah	a short version of **aa**; between **a** in c**a**t and **u** in c**u**t
ai	like **air**, without any **r**-sound
eh	like **e** in g**e**t
er	as in oth**er**, without any **r**-sound
ew	a "rounded **ee**-sound". Say the vowel sound **ee** (as in s**ee**), and while saying it, round your lips as for **oo** (as in s**oo**n), without moving your tongue; when your lips are in the **oo** position, but your tongue in the **ee** position, you should be pronouncing the correct sound

igh   as in s**igh**
o   always as in h**o**t (British pronunciation)
ur   as in f**ur**, but with rounded lips and no **r**-sound

1) A bar over a vowel symbol (e.g. $\overline{\text{ew}}$) shows that this sound is long.

2) Raised letters (e.g. **oo**ᵉᵉ, ʸ**ur**) should be pronounced only fleetingly.

3) French contains nasal vowels, which we transcribe with a vowel symbol plus ~~**ng**~~ (e.g. **ah**~~**ng**~~). This ~~**ng**~~ should *not* be pronounced, and serves solely to indicate nasal quality of the preceding vowel. A nasal vowel is pronounced simultaneously through the mouth and the nose.

4) French vowels (i.e. not diphthongs) are relatively short and pure. Therefore, you should try to read a transcription like **oa** without moving tongue or lips while pronouncing the sound.

A

à (ah) *prep* to; at, on

abandonner (ah-bahng-do-*nay*) *v* desert

abat-jour (ah-bah-*zhōōr*) *m* lampshade

*abattre (ah-*bahtr*) *v* knock down; kill; dishearten

abbaye (ah-bay-*ee*) *f* abbey

abcès (ah-*psay*) *m* abscess

abeille (ah-*bay*) *f* bee

aberration (ah-beh-rah-s*Yawng*) *f* aberration

abîme (ah-*beem*) *m* abyss

abîmer (ah-bee-*may*) *v* *spoil

abolir (ah-bo-*leer*) *v* abolish

abondance (ah-bawng-*dahngss*) *f* abundance; plenty

abondant (ah-bawng-*dahng*) *adj* abundant; plentiful

abonné (ah-bo-*nay*) *m* subscriber

abonnement (ah-bon-*mahng*) *m* subscription

d'abord (dah-*bawr*) at first

abordage (ah-bor-*daazh*) *m* collision

aboutir à (ah-boo-*teer*) end at; result in

aboyer (ah-bwah-*Yay*) *v* bark, bay

abréviation (ah-bray-v*Yah*-s*Yawng*) *f* abbreviation

abri (ah-*bree*) *m* shelter; cover

abricot (ah-bree-*koa*) *m* apricot

abriter (ah-bree-*tay*) *v* shelter

abrupt (ah-*brewpt*) *adj* steep

absence (ah-*psahngss*) *f* absence

absent (ah-*psahng*) *adj* absent

absolu (ah-pso-*lew*) *adj* total, sheer

absolument (ah-pso-lew-*mahng*) *adv* absolutely

absorber (ah-psor-*bay*) *v* absorb

s'*abstenir de (ahp-ster-*neer*) abstain from

abstraction faite de (ahp-strahk-s*Yawng* feht der) apart from

abstrait (ahp-*stray*) *adj* abstract

absurde (ah-*psewrd*) *adj* absurd; foolish

abus (ah-*bew*) *m* abuse, misuse

académie (ah-kah-day-*mee*) *f* academy; ~ **des beaux-arts** art school

accélérateur (ahk-say-lay-rah-*tūrr*) *m* accelerator

accélérer (ahk-say-lay-*ray*) *v* accelerate

accent (ahk-*sahng*) *m* accent, stress

accepter (ahk-sehp-*tay*) *v* accept

accès (ahk-*say*) *m* access; approach, entrance, admittance

accessible (ahk-say-*seebl*) *adj* accessible; attainable

accessoire (ahk-say-*swaar*) *adj* additional

accessoires (ahk-say-*swaar*) *mpl* accessories *pl*

accident (ahk-see-*dahng*) m accident; ~ **d'avion** plane crash

accidenté (ahk-see-dahng-*tay*) adj hilly; uneven

accidentel (ahk-see-dahng-*tehl*) adj accidental

acclamer (ah-klah-*may*) v cheer

accommodation (ah-ko-mo-dah-s^y*awng*) f accommodation

accompagner (ah-kawng-pah-*ñay*) v accompany; conduct

accomplir (ah-kawng-*pleer*) v accomplish; perform, achieve

accomplissement (ah-kawng-plee-*smahng*) m feat

accord (ah-*kawr*) m settlement, agreement; approval; **d'accord!** all right!; okay!; *être d'accord agree; *être d'accord avec approve of

accorder (ah-kor-*day*) v grant; extend; tune in; **s'accorder avec** match

accoster (ah-ko-*stay*) v dock

accouchement (ah-koosh-*mahng*) m childbirth, delivery

accoutumé (ah-koo-tew-*may*) adj accustomed

s'accrocher (ah-kro-*shay*) *hold on

accueil (ah-*kur^{ee}*) m reception; welcome

*accueillir** (ah-kur-*^Yeer*) v welcome

accumulateur (ah-kew-mew-lah-*tūrr*) m battery

s'accumuler (ah-kew-mew-*lay*) increase

accusation (ah-kew-zah-s^y*awng*) f charge

accuser (ah-kew-*zay*) v accuse; charge

achat (ah-*shah*) m purchase; ~ **à tempérament** hire-purchase; *faire des achats shop

acheter (ahsh-*tay*) v *buy, purchase

acheteur (ahsh-*tūrr*) m buyer, purchaser

achever (ahsh-*vay*) v finish; complete, accomplish

acide (ah-*seed*) m acid

acier (ah-s^y*ay*) m steel; ~ **inoxydable** stainless steel

acné (ahk-*nay*) f acne

acompte (ah-*kawngt*) m down payment

à-coup (ah-*koo*) m tug

*acquérir** (ah-kay-*reer*) v acquire; *buy

acquisition (ah-kee-zee-s^y*awng*) f acquisition, purchase

acquittement (ah-keet-*mahng*) m acquittal

acte (ahkt) m act, deed

acteur (ahk-*tūrr*) m actor

actif (ahk-*teef*) adj active

action (ahk-s^y*awng*) f action, deed; share; **actions** stocks and shares

activité (ahk-tee-vee-*tay*) f activity; work

actrice (ahk-*treess*) f actress

actualité (ahk-twah-lee-*tay*) f current events; **actualités** news; newsreel

actuel (ahk-*twehl*) adj present; topical

actuellement (ahk-twehl-*mahng*) adv nowadays

adapter (ah-dahp-*tay*) v adapt; ~ **à** suit

addition (ah-dee-s^y*awng*) f addition; bill

additionner (ah-dee-s^yo-*nay*) v add; count

adéquat (ah-day-*kwah*) adj adequate; appropriate, proper; sufficient

adhérer à (ah-day-*ray*) join

adieu (ah-d^y*ur*) m parting

adjectif (ah-jehk-*teef*) m adjective

*admettre** (ahd-*mehtr*) v acknowledge, admit; **en admettant que** supposing that

administratif (ahd-mee-nee-strah-*teef*)

adj administrative

administration (ahd-mee-nee-strah-*s^yawng*) *f* administration; direction

administrer (ahd-mee-nee-*stray*) *v* direct; administer

admiration (ahd-mee-rah-*s^yawng*) *f* admiration

admirer (ahd-mee-*ray*) *v* admire

admission (ahd-mee-*s^yawng*) *f* admission; entry

adolescent (ah-do-leh-*sahng*) *m* teenager

adopter (ah-dop-*tay*) *v* adopt

adorable (ah-do-*rahbl*) *adj* adorable

adorer (ah-do-*ray*) *v* worship

adoucir (ah-doo-*seer*) *v* soften

adoucisseur d'eau (ah-doo-see-*sürr* doa) water-softener

adresse (ah-*drehss*) *f* address

adresser (ah-dray-*say*) *v* address; **s'adresser à** address

adroit (ah-*drwah*) *adj* skilful; smart

adulte (ah-*dewlt*) *m* adult, grown-up; *adj* adult, grown-up

adverbe (ahd-*vehrb*) *m* adverb

adversaire (ahd-vehr-*sair*) *m* opponent

aération (ah-ay-rah-*s^yawng*) *f* ventilation

aérer (ah-ay-*ray*) *v* ventilate, air; **aéré** airy

aéroport (ah-ay-ro-*pawr*) *m* airport

aérosol (ah-ay-ro-*sol*) *m* atomizer

affaire (ah-*fair*) *f* business, matter, case; affair, concern; deal; ~ **de cœur** affair

affairé (ah-fay-*ray*) *adj* busy

affaires (ah-*fair*) *fpl* business; belongings *pl*; **chiffre d'affaires** turnover; **faire des ~ avec *deal with

affamé (ah-fah-*may*) *adj* hungry

affecter (ah-fehk-*tay*) *v* affect

affection (ah-fehk-*s^yawng*) *f* affection; ailment

affectueux (ah-fehk-*twur*) *adj* affectionate

affiche (ah-*feesh*) *f* placard, poster

affiler (ah-fee-*lay*) *v* sharpen

affiliation (ah-fee-l^yah-*s^yawng*) *f* membership

s'affilier à (ah-fee-l^y*ay*) join

affirmatif (ah-feer-mah-*teef*) *adj* affirmative

affirmer (ah-feer-*may*) *v* affirm; state

affliction (ah-fleek-*s^yawng*) *f* grief, affliction

affligé (ah-flee-*zhay*) *adj* sad

affluent (ah-flew-*ahng*) *m* tributary

affranchir (ah-frahng-*sheer*) *v* stamp

affreux (ah-*frur*) *adj* dreadful, frightful

affronter (ah-frawng-*tay*) *v* face

afin de (ah-*fang* der) to, in order to; **afin que** so that

Africain (ah-free-*kang*) *m* African

africain (ah-free-*kang*) *adj* African

Afrique (ah-*freek*) *f* Africa; ~ **du Sud** South Africa

after-shave (ahf-terr-*shehv*) *m* after-shave lotion

agacer (ah-gah-*say*) *v* irritate, annoy

âge (aazh) *m* age

âgé (ah-*zhay*) *adj* aged, elderly; **le plus ~** eldest; **plus ~** elder

agence (ah-*zhahngss*) *f* agency

agenda (ah-zhang-*dah*) *m* diary

s'agenouiller (ahzh-noo-*^yay*) **kneel

agent (ah-*zhahng*) *m* agent; ~ **de police** policeman; ~ **de voyages** travel agent; ~ **immobilier** house agent

agir (ah-*zheer*) *v* act

agitation (ah-zhee-tah-*s^yawng*) *f* excitement, fuss; disturbance, unrest

agiter (ah-zhee-*tay*) *v* agitate; stir; **agité** restless

agneau (ah-*ñoa*) *m* lamb

agrafe (ah-*grahf*) *f* staple

agraire (ah-*grair*) *adj* agrarian

agrandir (ah-grahng-*deer*) *v* extend;

enlarge

agrandissement (ah-grahng-dee-smahng) *m* enlargement; extension

agréable (ah-gray-*ahbl*) *adj* pleasing, pleasant, agreeable; enjoyable

agréer (ah-gray-*ay*) *v* accept

agrément (ah-gray-*mahng*) *m* pleasure

agressif (ah-gray-*seef*) *adj* aggressive

agricole (ah-gree-*kol*) *adj* agricultural

agriculteur (ah-gree-kewl-*tūrr*) *m* farmer

agriculture (ah-gree-kewl-*tewr*) *f* agriculture

aide (ehd) *f* help, assistance, aid; *m* helper

aider (ay-*day*) *v* help, aid

aigle (aigl) *m* eagle

aiglefin (ehgl-*fang*) *m* haddock

aigre (aigr) *adj* sour

aigu (ay-*gew*) *adj* (f -guë) acute; sharp; keen

aiguille (ay-*gweeʸ*) *f* needle; spire; **travail à l'aiguille** needlework

aiguiser (ay-gee-*zay*) *v* sharpen

ail (igh) *m* (pl ails, aulx) garlic

aile (ehl) *f* wing

ailleurs (ah-ʸūrr) *adv* elsewhere; **d'ailleurs** moreover, besides

aimable (ay-*mahbl*) *adj* kind

aimer (ay-*may*) *v* like, *be fond of, love; fancy; **aimé** beloved; ~ **mieux** prefer

aine (ehn) *f* groin

aîné (ay-*nay*) *adj* elder

ainsi (ang-*see*) *adv* so, thus

air (air) *m* air; sky; tune; *avoir l'air look

aisance (eh-*zahngss*) *f* ease

aise (aiz) *f* leisure, ease

aisé (ay-*zay*) *adj* well-to-do

ajournement (ah-zhoor-ner-*mahng*) *m* delay

ajourner (ah-zhoor-*nay*) *v* adjourn, *put off, postpone

ajouter (ah-zhoo-*tay*) *v* add

ajuster (ah-zhew-*stay*) *v* adjust

alarmer (ah-lahr-*may*) *v* alarm

album (ahl-*bom*) *m* album; ~ **de collage** scrap-book

alcool (ahl-*kol*) *m* alcohol; ~ **à brûler** methylated spirits; **réchaud à ~** spirit stove

alcoolique (ahl-ko-*leek*) *adj* alcoholic

alentours (ah-lahng-*tōōr*) *mpl* surroundings *pl*; vicinity

alerte (ah-*lehrt*) *f* alarm; *adj* smart

algèbre (ahl-*zhaibr*) *f* algebra

Algérie (ahl-zhay-*ree*) *f* Algeria

Algérien (ahl-zhay-*rʸang*) *m* Algerian

algérien (ahl-zhay-*rʸang*) *adj* Algerian

alimentation (ah-lee-mahng-tah-*sʸawng*) *f* nourishment

alimenter (ah-lee-mahng-*tay*) *v* *feed

aliments (ah-lee-*mahng*) *mpl* foodstuffs *pl*; ~ **surgelés** frozen food

allaiter (ah-lay-*tay*) *v* nurse

allée (ah-*lay*) *f* avenue

Allemagne (ahl-*mahñ*) *f* Germany

Allemand (ahl-*mahng*) *m* German

allemand (ahl-*mahng*) *adj* German

*aller** (ah-*lay*) *v* *go; ~ **chercher** collect, pick up; **aller et retour** round trip *Am*; ~ **prendre** *get; **bien** ~ suit; *become; **s'en** ~ *go away; depart

allergie (ah-lehr-*zhee*) *f* allergy

alliance (ah-*lʸahngss*) *f* alliance; wedding-ring

allié (ah-*lʸay*) *m* associate; **Alliés** Allies *pl*

s'allier (ah-*lʸay*) ally

allocation (ah-lo-kah-*sʸawng*) *f* allowance

allocution (ah-lo-kew-*sʸawng*) *f* speech

allonger (ah-lawng-*zhay*) *v* lengthen; dilute

allumage (ah-lew-*maazh*) *m* ignition

allumer (ah-lew-*may*) *v* *light; switch on, turn on
allumette (ah-lew-*meht*) *f* match
allure (ah-*lewr*) *f* pace, gait
almanach (ahl-mah-*nahk*) *m* almanac
alors (ah-*lawr*) *adv* then
alouette (ah-*lweht*) *f* lark
alphabet (ahl-fah-*bay*) *m* alphabet
alpinisme (ahl-pee-*neezm*) *m* mountaineering
alternatif (ahl-tehr-nah-*teef*) *adj* alternate
alternative (ahl-tehr-nah-*teev*) *f* alternative
altitude (ahl-tee-*tewd*) *f* altitude
aluminium (ah-lew-mee-*nᵞom*) *m* aluminium
amande (ah-*mahng̱d*) *f* almond
amant (ah-*mahng̱*) *m* lover
amateur (ah-mah-*tūrr*) *m* amateur
ambassade (ahng̱-bah-*sahd*) *f* embassy
ambassadeur (ahng̱-bah-sah-*dūrr*) *m* ambassador
ambiance (ahng̱-*bᵞahng̱ss*) *f* atmosphere
ambigu (ahng̱-bee-*gew*) *adj* (f -guë) ambiguous
ambitieux (ahng̱-bee-*sᵞur*) *adj* ambitious
ambre (ahng̱br) *m* amber
ambulance (ahng̱-bew-*lahng̱ss*) *f* ambulance
ambulant (ahng̱-bew-*lahng̱*) *adj* itinerant
âme (aam) *f* soul
amélioration (ah-may-lᵞo-rah-*sᵞawng̱*) *f* improvement
améliorer (ah-may-lᵞo-*ray*) *v* improve
amende (ah-*mahng̱d*) *f* fine, penalty
amener (ahm-*nay*) *v* *bring; lower, *strike
amer (ah-*mair*) *adj* bitter
Américain (ah-may-ree-*kang̱*) *m* American

américain (ah-may-ree-*kang̱*) *adj* American
Amérique (ah-may-*reek*) *f* America; ~ **latine** Latin America
améthyste (ah-may-*teest*) *f* amethyst
ami (ah-*mee*) *m* friend
amiante (ah-*mᵞahng̱t*) *m* asbestos
amical (ah-mee-*kahl*) *adj* friendly
amidon (ah-mee-*dawng̱*) *m* starch
amidonner (ah-mee-do-*nay*) *v* starch
amie (ah-*mee*) *f* friend
amiral (ah-mee-*rahl*) *m* admiral
amitié (ah-mee-*tᵞay*) *f* friendship
ammoniaque (ah-mo-*nᵞahk*) *f* ammonia
amnistie (ahm-nee-*stee*) *f* amnesty
amoncellement (ah-mawng̱-sehl-*mahng̱*) *m* heap
en amont (ahng̱-nah-*mawng̱*) upstream
amorce (ah-*mors*) *f* bait
amortir (ah-mor-*teer*) *v* *pay off
amortisseur (ah-mor-tee-*sūrr*) *m* shock absorber
amour (ah-*mōōr*) *m* love; **mon ~** sweetheart
amoureux (ah-moo-*rur*) *adj* in love
ample (ahng̱pl) *adj* detailed; full
ampoule (ahng̱-*pool*) *f* blister; light bulb; ~ **de flash** flash-bulb
amulette (ah-mew-*leht*) *f* charm
amusant (ah-mew-*zahng̱*) *adj* funny, entertaining
amuse-gueule (ah-mewz-*gurl*) *m* appetizer
amusement (ah-mewz-*mahng̱*) *m* entertainment, amusement
amuser (ah-mew-*zay*) *v* entertain, amuse
amygdales (ah-mee-*dahl*) *fpl* tonsils *pl*
amygdalite (ah-mee-dah-*leet*) *f* tonsilitis

an (ahng) *m* year

analogue (ah-nah-*log*) *adj* similar

analyse (ah-nah-*leez*) *f* analysis

analyser (ah-nah-lee-*zay*) *v* analyse; *break down

analyste (ah-nah-*leest*) *m* analyst

ananas (ah-nah-*nah*) *m* pineapple

anarchie (ah-nahr-*shee*) *f* anarchy

anatomie (ah-nah-to-*mee*) *f* anatomy

ancêtre (ahng-*saitr*) *m* ancestor

anchois (ahng-*shwah*) *m* anchovy

ancien (ahng-s*y*a*ng*) *adj* ancient; former

ancre (ahngkr) *f* anchor

andouiller (ahng-doo-*y*ay) *m* antlers *pl*

âne (aan) *m* ass, donkey

anéantissement (ah-nay-ahng-tee-smahng) *m* destruction

anémie (ah-nay-*mee*) *f* anaemia

anesthésie (ah-neh-stay-*zee*) *f* anaesthesia

anesthésique (ah-neh-stay-*zeek*) *m* anaesthetic

ange (ahngzh) *m* angel

Anglais (ahng-*glay*) *m* Englishman; Briton

anglais (ahng-*glay*) *adj* English

angle (ahnggl) *m* angle

Angleterre (ahng-gler-*tair*) *f* England; Britain

angoisse (ahng-*gwahss*) *f* anguish

anguille (ahng-*geey*) *f* eel

animal (ah-nee-*mahl*) *m* animal; ~ **familier** pet

animateur (ah-nee-mah-*tūrr*) *m* entertainer

animer (ah-nee-*may*) *v* enliven; **animé** busy, active, crowded

anneau (ah-*noa*) *m* ring

année (ah-*nay*) *f* year; ~ **bissextile** leap-year; **par** ~ per annum

annexe (ah-*nehks*) *f* annex

annexer (ah-nehk-*say*) *v* annex

anniversaire (ah-nee-vehr-*sair*) *m* anniversary, birthday; jubilee

annonce (ah-*nawngss*) *f* announcement; advertisement; ~ **publicitaire** commercial

annoncer (ah-nawng-*say*) *v* announce

annuaire (ah-*nwair*) *m* annual; ~ **téléphonique** telephone directory; telephone book *Am*

annuel (ah-*nwehl*) *adj* yearly, annual

annulation (ah-new-lah-s*y*awng) *f* cancellation

annuler (ah-new-*lay*) *v* cancel

anonyme (ah-no-*neem*) *adj* anonymous

anormal (ah-nor-*mahl*) *adj* abnormal

antenne (ahng-*tehn*) *f* aerial

antérieur (ahng-tay-r*y*ūrr) *adj* prior, previous

antérieurement (ahng-tay-r*y*urr-mahng) *adv* formerly

anthologie (ahng-to-lo-*zhee*) *f* anthology

antialcoolique (ahng-tee-ahl-ko-*leek*) *m* teetotaller

antibiotique (ahng-tee-b*y*o-*teek*) *m* antibiotic

anticiper (ahng-tee-see-*pay*) *v* anticipate

antigel (ahng-tee-*zhehl*) *m* antifreeze

antipathie (ahng-tee-pah-*tee*) *f* dislike, antipathy

antipathique (ahng-tee-pah-*teek*) *adj* nasty; unpleasant

antiquaire (ahng-tee-*kair*) *m* antique dealer

antique (ahng-*teek*) *adj* antique, ancient

antiquité (ahng-tee-kee-*tay*) *f* antique; **Antiquité** antiquity; **antiquités** antiquities *pl*

antiseptique (ahng-tee-sehp-*teek*) *m* antiseptic

anxiété (ahng-ks*y*ay-*tay*) *f* anxiety

août (oo) August

***apercevoir** (ah-pehr-ser-*vwaar*) *v* perceive

aperçu (ah-pehr-*sew*) *m* glimpse

apéritif (ah-pay-ree-*teef*) *m* drink, aperitif

apeuré (ah-pur-*ray*) *adj* afraid

apogée (ah-po-*zhay*) *m* height, zenith; peak

***apparaître** (ah-pah-*raitr*) *v* appear

appareil (ah-pah-*ray*) *m* appliance, apparatus, machine; aircraft; ~ **à jetons** slot-machine; ~ **de chauffage** heater; ~ **photographique** camera

apparemment (ah-pah-rah-*mahng*) *adv* apparently

apparence (ah-pah-*rahngss*) *f* appearance; semblance, look

apparent (ah-pah-*rahng*) *adj* apparent

apparenté (ah-pah-rahng-*tay*) *adj* related

apparition (ah-pah-ree-*syawng*) *f* apparition

appartement (ah-pahr-ter-*mahng*) *m* flat; apartment *nAm*, suite

***appartenir** (ah-pahr-ter-*neer*) *v* belong

appel (ah-*pehl*) *m* call, cry; appeal; ~ **interurbain** trunk-call; ~ **téléphonique** telephone call

appeler (ah-*play*) *v* call, cry; **s'appeler** *be called

appendice (ah-pang-*deess*) *m* appendix

appendicite (ah-pang-dee-*seet*) *f* appendicitis

appétissant (ah-pay-tee-*sahng*) *adj* appetizing

appétit (ah-pay-*tee*) *m* appetite

applaudir (ah-ploa-*deer*) *v* clap

applaudissements (ah-ploa-dee-*smahng*) *mpl* applause

application (ah-plee-kah-*syawng*) *f* application; diligence

appliquer (ah-plee-*kay*) *v* apply; **s'appliquer à** apply

apporter (ah-por-*tay*) *v* *bring; fetch

appréciation (ah-pray-*syah-syawng*) *f* appreciation

apprécier (ah-pray-*syay*) *v* appreciate; judge

***apprendre** (ah-*prahngdr*) *v* *learn; *teach; ~ **par cœur** memorize

apprivoiser (ah-pree-vwah-*zay*) *v* tame; **apprivoisé** tame

approbation (ah-pro-bah-*syawng*) *f* approval

approche (ah-*prosh*) *f* approach

approcher (ah-pro-*shay*) *v* approach

approprié (ah-pro-pree-*ay*) *adj* appropriate, adequate, convenient; proper, suitable

approuver (ah-proo-*vay*) *v* approve; consent

approvisionner en (ah-pro-vee-z*y*o-*nay*) furnish with

approximatif (ah-prok-see-mah-*teef*) *adj* approximate

approximativement (ah-prok-see-mah-teev-*mahng*) *adv* approximately

appuyer (ah-pwee-*y*ay) *v* press; **s'appuyer** *lean

âpre (aapr) *adj* harsh

après (ah-*pray*) *adv* afterwards; *prep* after; ~ **que** after; **d'après** according to

après-midi (ah-pray-mee-*dee*) *m/f* afternoon

apte (ahpt) *adj* apt

aptitude (ahp-tee-*tewd*) *f* faculty

aquarelle (ah-kwah-*rehl*) *f* water-colour

Arabe (ah-*rahb*) *m* Arab

arabe (ah-*rahb*) *adj* Arab

Arabie Séoudite (ah-rah-bee say-oo-*deet*) Saudi Arabia

araignée (ah-ray-*ñay*) *f* spider; **toile d'araignée** spider's web

arbitraire (ahr-bee-*trair*) *adj* arbitrary

arbitre (ahr-*beetr*) *m* umpire

arbre (ahrbr) *m* tree; ~ **à cames** camshaft

arbuste (ahr-*bewst*) *m* shrub

arc (ahrk) *m* bow

arcade (ahr-*kahd*) *f* arcade

arc-en-ciel (ahr-kahng-s*Y*ehl) *m* rainbow

arche (ahrsh) *f* arch

archéologie (ahr-kay-o-lo-*zhee*) *f* archaeology

archéologue (ahr-kay-o-*log*) *m* archaeologist

archevêque (ahr-sher-*vehk*) *m* archbishop

architecte (ahr-shee-*tehkt*) *m* architect

architecture (ahr-shee-tehk-*tewr*) *f* architecture

archives (ahr-*sheev*) *fpl* archives *pl*

ardoise (ahr-*dwaaz*) *f* slate

arène (ah-*rehn*) *f* bullring

arête (ah-*reht*) *f* ridge; fishbone, bone

argent (ahr-*zhahng*) *m* silver; money; ~ **comptant** cash; ~ **liquide** cash; **en** ~ silver

argenterie (ahr-zhahng-*tree*) *f* silverware

Argentin (ahr-zhahng-*tang*) *m* Argentinian

argentin (ahr-zhahng-*tang*) *adj* Argentinian

Argentine (ahr-zhahng-*teen*) *f* Argentina

argile (ahr-*zheel*) *f* clay

argument (ahr-gew-*mahng*) *m* argument

argumenter (ahr-gew-mahng-*tay*) *v* argue

aride (ah-*reed*) *adj* arid

arithmétique (ah-reet-may-*teek*) *f* arithmetic

armateur (ahr-mah-*tūrr*) *m* shipowner

arme (ahrm) *f* weapon, arm

armée (ahr-*may*) *f* army

armer (ahr-*may*) *v* arm

armoire (ahr-*mwaar*) *f* cupboard

armure (ahr-*mewr*) *f* armour

arôme (ah-*roam*) *m* aroma

arqué (ahr-*kay*) *adj* arched

arracher (ah-rah-*shay*) *v* extract

arrangement (ah-rahngzh-*mahng*) *m* settlement

arranger (ah-rahng-*zhay*) *v* arrange; settle

arrestation (ah-reh-stah-s*Y*awng) *f* arrest

arrêt (ah-*reh*) *m* stop

arrêter (ah-ray-*tay*) *v* stop; arrest; **s'arrêter** halt; pull up

arriéré (ah-r*Y*ay-*ray*) *adj* overdue

arrière (ah-r*Y*air) *m* rear; **en** ~ backwards, back; behind

arrivée (ah-ree-*vay*) *f* coming, arrival

arriver (ah-ree-*vay*) *v* arrive; happen

arrondi (ah-rawng-*dee*) *adj* rounded

art (aar) *m* art; **arts et métiers** arts and crafts

artère (ahr-*tair*) *f* artery; thoroughfare

artichaut (ahr-tee-*shoa*) *m* artichoke

article (ahr-*teekl*) *m* article; item; **articles d'épicerie** groceries *pl*; **articles de toilette** toiletry

articulation (ahr-tee-kew-lah-s*Y*awng) *f* joint

artificiel (ahr-tee-fee-s*Y*ehl) *adj* artificial

artisan (ahr-tee-*zahng*) *m* craftsman

artisanat (ahr-tee-zah-*nah*) *m* handicraft

artiste (ahr-*teest*) *m/f* artist

artistique (ahr-tee-*steek*) *adj* artistic

ascenseur (ah-sahng-*sūrr*) *m* lift; elevator *nAm*

ascension (ah-sahng-s*Y*awng) *f* climb; ***faire l'ascension de** ascend

Asiatique (ah-z*Y*ah-*teek*) *m* Asian

asiatique (ah-z*Y*ah-*teek*) *adj* Asian

Asie (ah-*zee*) f Asia

asile (ah-*zeel*) m asylum

aspect (ah-*spay*) m aspect; appearance, look

asperge (ah-*spehrzh*) f asparagus

asphalte (ah-*sfahlt*) m asphalt

aspirateur (ah-spee-rah-*tūrr*) m vacuum cleaner; **passer l'aspirateur** hoover; vacuum *vAm*

aspirer (ah-spee-*ray*) v aspire; ~ **à** pursue, aim at

aspirine (ah-spee-*reen*) f aspirin

assaisonner (ah-say-zo-*nay*) v flavour

assassinat (ah-sah-see-*nah*) m assassination, murder

assassiner (ah-sah-see-*nay*) v murder

assécher (ah-say-*shay*) v drain

assemblée (ah-sahng-*blay*) f assembly, meeting

assembler (ah-sahng-*blay*) v assemble; join

assentiment (ah-sahng-tee-*mahng*) m consent

s'*asseoir (ah-*swaar*) *sit down

assez (ah-*say*) adv enough; fairly, pretty, rather, quite

assidu (ah-see-*dew*) adj diligent

assiette (ah-s*y*eht) f plate, dish; ~ **à soupe** soup-plate

assigner (ah-see-*ñay*) v allot; ~ **à** assign to

assistance (ah-see-*stahngss*) f assistance; attendance

assistant (ah-see-*stahng*) m assistant

assister (ah-see-*stay*) v assist, aid; ~ **à** attend, assist at

association (ah-so-s*y*ah-s*y*awng) f society, club, association

associé (ah-so-s*y*ay) m associate, partner

associer (ah-so-s*y*ay) v associate

assoiffé (ah-swah-*fay*) adj thirsty

assortiment (ah-sor-tee-*mahng*) m assortment

assurance (ah-sew-*rahngss*) f insurance; **assurance-vie** f life insurance; **assurance-voyages** f travel insurance

assurer (ah-sew-*ray*) v insure, assure; **s'assurer de** ascertain; secure

asthme (ahsm) m asthma

astronomie (ah-stro-no-*mee*) f astronomy

astucieux (ah-stew-s*y*ur) adj clever

atelier (ah-ter-l*y*ay) m workshop

athée (ah-*tay*) m atheist

athlète (ah-*tleht*) m athlete

athlétisme (ah-tlay-*teezm*) m athletics pl

atmosphère (aht-mo-*sfair*) f atmosphere

atome (ah-*tom*) m atom

atomique (ah-to-*meek*) adj atomic

atroce (ah-*tross*) adj horrible

attacher (ah-tah-*shay*) v fasten, attach; tie; **attaché à** attached to

attaque (ah-*tahk*) f fit, attack; hold-up; stroke

attaquer (ah-tah-*kay*) v attack, assault

*atteindre (ah-*tangdr*) v attain, reach

attendre (ah-*tahngdr*) v wait; expect, await; **en attendant** in the meantime

attente (ah-*tahngt*) f waiting; expectation

attentif (ah-tahng-*teef*) adj attentive, careful

attention (ah-tahng-s*y*awng) f attention, consideration; notice; ***faire ~ *pay** attention, look out; beware; ***faire ~ à** attend to, mind; **prêter ~ à** mind

atterrir (ah-tay-*reer*) v land

attestation (ah-teh-stah-s*y*awng) f certificate

attirer (ah-tee-*ray*) v attract

attitude (ah-tee-*tewd*) f attitude; position

attouchement (ah-toosh-*mahng*) *m* touch

attraction (ah-trahk-s*Yawng*) *f* attraction

attrait (ah-*tray*) *m* attraction; **attraits** charm

attraper (ah-trah-*pay*) *v* *catch; contract

attribuer à (ah-tree-*bway*) assign to

aube (ōab) *f* dawn

auberge (oa-*behrzh*) *f* inn, hostel; roadhouse; roadside restaurant; ~ **de jeunesse** youth hostel

aubergine (oa-behr-*zheen*) *f* eggplant

aubergiste (oa-behr-*zheest*) *m* innkeeper

aucun (oa-*kurng*) *adj* no; *pron* none

aucunement (oa-kewn-*mahng*) *adv* by no means

audace (oa-*dahss*) *f* nerve

audacieux (oa-dah-s*Yur*) *adj* bold

au-dessous (oa-der-*soo*) *adv* beneath; ~ **de** below

au-dessus (oa-der-*sew*) *adv* over; ~ **de** above; over

audible (oa-*deebl*) *adj* audible

auditeur (oa-dee-*tūrr*) *m* auditor, listener

auditorium (oa-dee-to-r*Yom*) *m* auditorium

augmentation (oag-mahng-tah-s*Yawng*) *f* increase, rise; ~ **de salaire** rise; raise *nAm*

augmenter (oag-mahng-*tay*) *v* increase

aujourd'hui (oa-zhoor-*dwee*) *adv* today

auparavant (oa-pah-rah-*vahng*) *adv* formerly

auprès de (oa-*pray* der) near

auriculaire (oa-ree-kew-*lair*) *m* little finger

aurore (oa-*rawr*) *f* dawn

aussi (oa-*see*) *adv* too, also; as; ~

bien as well; ~ **bien que** as well as; both ... and

aussitôt (oa-see-*toa*) *adv* at once; ~ **que** as soon as

Australie (oa-strah-*lee*) *f* Australia

Australien (oa-strah-*lYang*) *m* Australian

australien (oa-strah-*lYang*) *adj* Australian

autant (oa-*tahng*) *adv* as much

autel (oa-*tehl*) *m* altar

auteur (oa-*tūrr*) *m* author

authentique (oa-tahng-*teek*) *adj* authentic, original, genuine

auto (oa-*toa*) *f* automobile

autobus (oa-toa-*bewss*) *m* bus

autocar (oa-toa-*kaar*) *m* coach

automatique (oa-toa-mah-*teek*) *adj* automatic

automatisation (oa-toa-mah-tee-zah-s*Yawng*) *f* automation

automne (oa-*ton*) *m* autumn; fall *nAm*

automobile (oa-toa-mo-*beel*) *f* motorcar

automobilisme (oa-toa-mo-bee-*leesm*) *m* motoring

automobiliste (oa-toa-mo-bee-*leest*) *m* motorist

autonome (oa-to-*nom*) *adj* autonomous; independent

autonomie (oa-to-no-*mee*) *f* self-government

autopsie (oa-to-*psee*) *f* autopsy

autorisation (oa-to-ree-zah-s*Yawng*) *f* authorization; permission

autoriser (oa-to-ree-*zay*) *v* allow; license; ~ **à** allow to

autoritaire (oa-to-ree-*tair*) *adj* authoritarian

autorité (oa-to-ree-*tay*) *f* authority

autoroute (oa-toa-*root*) *f* motorway; highway *nAm*

auto-stoppeur (oa-toa-sto-*pūrr*) *m*

hitchhiker; ***faire de l'auto-stop** hitchhike

autour (oa-*toor*) *adv* about; around; ~ **de** around, about; round

autre (*ōatr*) *adj* other; different; **entre autres** among other things

autrefois (oa-trer-*fwah*) *adv* formerly

autrement (oa-trer-*mahng*) *adv* otherwise, else

Autriche (oa-*treesh*) *f* Austria

Autrichien (oa-tree-*sh^yang*) *m* Austrian

autrichien (oa-tree-*sh^yang*) *adj* Austrian

autruche (oa-*trewsh*) *f* ostrich

en aval (ahng-nah-*vahl*) downstream

avalanche (ah-vah-*lahngsh*) *f* avalanche

avaler (ah-vah-*lay*) *v* swallow

avance (ah-*vahngss*) *f* lead; advance; **à l'avance** in advance; **d'avance** before; in advance

avancement (ah-vahng-*smahng*) *m* advance

avancer (ah-vahng-*say*) *v* advance

avant (ah-*vahng*) *prep* before; *adv* before; ~ **que** before; **en** ~ forward; ahead, onwards

avantage (ah-vahng-*taazh*) *m* profit, advantage, benefit

avantageux (ah-vahng-tah-*zhur*) *adj* advantageous; cheap

avant-hier (ah-vahng-t^y*air*) *adv* the day before yesterday

avare (ah-*vaar*) *adj* avaricious

avec (ah-*vehk*) *prep* with

avenir (ah-*vneer*) *m* future

aventure (ah-vahng-*tewr*) *f* adventure

avenue (ah-*vnew*) *f* avenue

averse (ah-*vehrs*) *f* shower; downpour

aversion (ah-vehr-*s^yawng*) *f* aversion, dislike

avertir (ah-vehr-*teer*) *v* warn, caution; notify

avertissement (ah-vehr-tee-*smahng*) *m* warning

aveugle (ah-*vurgl*) *adj* blind

aveugler (ah-vur-*glay*) *v* blind

aviation (ah-v^yah-*s^yawng*) *f* aviation

avion (ah-*v^yawng*) *m* aeroplane; plane, aircraft; airplane *nAm*; ~ **à réaction** jet

avis (ah-*vee*) *m* advice; notice

avocat (ah-vo-*kah*) *m* solicitor, attorney, lawyer, barrister

avoine (ah-*vwahn*) *f* oats *pl*

***avoir** (ah-*vwaar*) *v* *have

avoisinant (ah-vwah-zee-*nahng*) *adj* neighbouring

avortement (ah-vort-*mahng*) *m* abortion

avoué (ah-voo-*ay*) *m* solicitor

avouer (ah-voo-*ay*) *v* admit

avril (ah-*vreel*) April

azote (ah-*zot*) *m* nitrogen

B

bâbord (bah-*bawr*) *m* port

bâche (baash) *f* tarpaulin

bactérie (bahk-tay-*ree*) *f* bacterium

bagage (bah-*gaazh*) *m* baggage; luggage; ~ **à main** hand luggage; hand baggage *Am*

bague (bahg) *f* ring; ~ **de fiançailles** engagement ring

baie (bay) *f* berry; bay, creek

se baigner (bay-*ñay*) bathe

bail (bigh) *m* (pl baux) lease

bâiller (bah-^y*ay*) *v* yawn

bain (bang) *m* bath; ~ **turc** Turkish bath; **bonnet de** ~ bathing-cap; **caleçon de** ~ bathing-trunks

baiser (bay-*zay*) *m* kiss

baisse (behss) *f* drop, decline

baisser (bay-*say*) *v* lower

bal (bahl) *m* (pl ~s) ball
balai (bah-*lay*) *m* broom
balance (bah-*lahngss*) *f* scales *pl*
balancer (bah-lahng-*say*) *v* *swing; rock
balançoire (bah-lahng-*swaar*) *f* swing; seesaw
balayer (bah-lay-*Yay*) *v* *sweep
balbutier (bahl-bew-s*Yay*) *v* falter
balcon (bahl-*kawng*) *m* balcony; circle
baleine (bah-*lehn*) *f* whale
balle (bahl) *f* ball; bullet
ballet (bah-*lay*) *m* ballet
ballon (bah-*lawng*) *m* football, ball; balloon
balustrade (bah-lew-*strahd*) *f* rail
bambin (bahng-*bang*) *m* tot, toddler
bambou (bahng-*boo*) *m* bamboo
banane (bah-*nahn*) *f* banana
banc (bahng) *m* bench; ~ **d'école** desk
bande (bahngd) *f* bunch, gang; tape, strip; **bandes dessinées** comics *pl*
bandit (bahng-*dee*) *m* bandit
banlieue (bahng-*IYur*) *f* suburb
bannière (bah-n*Yair*) *f* banner
banque (bahngk) *f* bank
banquet (bahng-*kay*) *m* banquet
baptême (bah-*tehm*) *m* christening, baptism
baptiser (bah-tee-*zay*) *v* christen, baptize
bar (baar) *m* bar
baratiner (bah-rah-tee-*nay*) *v* talk rubbish
barbe (bahrb) *f* beard
barbue (bahr-*bew*) *f* brill
baril (bah-*ree*) *m* cask, barrel; keg
bariton (bah-ree-*tawng*) *m* baritone
barmaid (bahr-*mehd*) *f* barmaid
barman (bahr-*mahn*) *m* barman; bartender
baromètre (bah-ro-*mehtr*) *m* barom-

eter
baroque (bah-*rok*) *adj* baroque
barque (bahrk) *f* boat
barrage (bah-*raazh*) *m* dam
barre (baar) *f* rod, bar, rail; helm; counter
barreau (bah-*roa*) *m* bar
barrière (bah-r*Yair*) *f* barrier; fence
bas[1] (bah) *adj* (f ~se) low; **en** ~ down; downstairs; **en** ~ **de** under, below; **vers le** ~ downwards, down
bas[2] (bah) *m* stocking; ~ **élastiques** support hose
bas-côté (bah-koa-*tay*) *m* aisle
bascule (bah-*skewl*) *f* weighing-machine
base (bahz) *f* basis, base
baser (bah-*zay*) *v* base
basilique (bah-zee-*leek*) *f* basilica
basse (bahss) *f* bass
bassin (bah-*sang*) *m* pelvis, basin
bataille (bah-*tigh*) *f* battle
bateau (bah-*toa*) *m* boat; ~ **à moteur** launch; ~ **à rames** rowing-boat; ~ **à vapeur** steamer; ~ **à voiles** sailing-boat; **bateau-citerne** *m* tanker
bâtiment (bah-tee-*mahng*) *m* building; building trade
bâtir (bah-*teer*) *v* *build; construct
bâton (bah-*tawng*) *m* stick; **bâtons de ski** ski sticks; ski poles *Am*
*battre (bahtr) *v* slap; *beat; shuffle; **se** ~ *fight
bavard (bah-*vaar*) *adj* talkative
bavardage (bah-vahr-*daazh*) *m* chat
bavarder (bah-vahr-*day*) *v* chat
beau (boa) *adj* (bel; f belle) beautiful; fair, pretty, lovely, handsome
beaucoup (boa-*koo*) *adv* much; far; ~ **de** much; many; **de** ~ by far
beau-fils (boa-*feess*) *m* son-in-law
beau-frère (boa-*frair*) *m* brother-in-law

beau-père (boa-*pair*) *m* father-in-law; stepfather

beauté (boa-*tay*) *f* beauty; **produits de ~** cosmetics *pl*

beaux-arts (boa-*zaar*) *mpl* fine arts

beaux-parents (boa-pah-*rahng*) *mpl* parents-in-law *pl*

bébé (bay-*bay*) *m* baby

bec (behk) *m* beak; nozzle

bec-de-corbin (behk-der-kor-*bang*) *m* crowbar

bêche (behsh) *f* spade

beige (baizh) *adj* beige

Belge (behlzh) *m* Belgian

belge (behlzh) *adj* Belgian

Belgique (behl-*zheek*) *f* Belgium

belle-fille (behl-*feey*) *f* daughter-in-law

belle-mère (behl-*mair*) *f* mother-in-law; stepmother

belle-sœur (behl-*sūrr*) *f* sister-in-law

bénédiction (bay-nay-deek-s*yawng*) *f* blessing

bénéfice (bay-nay-*feess*) *m* profit, benefit

bénéficiaire (bay-nay-fee-s*yair*) *m* payee

bénéficier de (bay-nay-fee-s*yay*) profit by

bénir (bay-*neer*) *v* bless

béquille (bay-*keey*) *f* crutch

berceau (behr-*soa*) *m* cradle; **~ de voyage** carry-cot

béret (bay-*ray*) *m* beret

berge (behrzh) *f* embankment

berger (behr-*zhay*) *m* shepherd

besogne (ber-*zoñ*) *f* work

besoin (ber-*zwang*) *m* need; want; **avoir ~ de* need

bétail (bay-*tigh*) *m* cattle *pl*

bête (beht) *f* beast; *adj* silly, dumb; **~ de proie** beast of prey

béton (bay-*tawng*) *m* concrete

betterave (beh-*traav*) *f* beetroot, beet

beurre (būrr) *m* butter

Bible (beebl) *f* bible

bibliothèque (bee-blee-o-*tehk*) *f* library

bicyclette (bee-see-*kleht*) *f* cycle, bicycle

bien (b*yang*) *adv* well; **bien!** well!; all right!; **~ que** though, although; **biens** *mpl* goods *pl*, possessions

bien-être (b*yang*-*naitr*) *m* welfare; comfort

bientôt (b*yang*-*toa*) *adv* soon; shortly

bienveillance (b*yang*-vay-*yahngss*) *f* goodwill

bienvenu (b*yang*-*vnew*) *adj* welcome

bière (b*yair*) *f* beer; ale

bifteck (beef-*tehk*) *m* steak

bifurcation (bee-fewr-kah-s*yawng*) *f* fork, road fork

bifurquer (bee-fewr-*kay*) *v* fork

bigorneau (bee-gor-*noa*) *m* winkle

bigoudi (bee-goo-*dee*) *m* curler

bijou (bee-*zhoo*) *m* (pl ~x) jewel; gem; **bijoux** jewellery

bijoutier (bee-zhoo-t*yay*) *m* jeweller

bilan (bee-*lahng*) *m* balance

bile (beel) *f* gall, bile

bilingue (bee-*langg*) *adj* bilingual

billard (bee-*Yaar*) *m* billiards *pl*

bille (beey) *f* marble

billet (bee-*Yay*) *m* ticket; **~ de banque** banknote; **~ de quai** platform ticket; **~ gratuit** free ticket

biologie (bee-o-lo-*zhee*) *f* biology

biscuit (bee-*skwee*) *m* biscuit; cookie *nAm*; cracker *nAm*

bistrot (bee-*stroa*) *m* pub

bizarre (bee-*zaar*) *adj* funny, odd, strange

blague (blahg) *f* joke; **~ à tabac** tobacco pouch

blaireau (bleh-*roa*) *m* shaving-brush

blâme (blaam) *m* blame

blâmer (blah-*may*) *v* blame

blanc (blahng) *adj* (f blanche) white; blank

blanchaille (blahng-*shigh*) *f* whitebait

blanchisserie (blahng-shee-*sree*) *f* laundry

blé (blay) *m* corn; wheat; grain

blesser (blay-*say*) *v* injure, *hurt, wound; offend

blessure (blay-*sewr*) *f* wound; injury

bleu (blur) *adj* (pl bleus) blue; *m* bruise

bloc (blok) *m* block

bloc-notes (blok-*not*) *m* pad, writing-pad

blond (blawng) *adj* fair

blonde (blawngd) *f* blonde

bloquer (blo-*kay*) *v* block

bobine (bo-*been*) *f* spool; ~ **d'allumage** ignition coil

bœuf (burf) *m* ox; beef

bohémien (bo-ay-m*y*ang) *m* gipsy

***boire** (bwaar) *v* *drink

bois (bwah) *m* wood; forest; ~ **d'œuvre** timber; **en** ~ wooden

boisé (bwah-*zay*) *adj* wooded

boisson (bwah-*sawng*) *f* drink, beverage; ~ **non alcoolisée** soft drink; **boissons alcoolisées** spirits

boîte (bwaht) *f* box; can, tin; ~ **à ordures** dustbin; trash can *Am*; ~ **à outils** tool kit; ~ **aux lettres** letterbox; mailbox *nAm*; ~ **d'allumettes** match-box; ~ **de couleurs** paint-box; ~ **de nuit** nightclub; ~ **de vitesse** gear-box

boiter (bwah-*tay*) *v* limp

boiteux (bwah-*tur*) *adj* lame

bol (bol) *m* basin; bowl

Bolivie (bo-lee-*vee*) *f* Bolivia

Bolivien (bo-lee-v*y*ang) *m* Bolivian

bolivien (bo-lee-v*y*ang) *adj* Bolivian

bombarder (bawng-bahr-*day*) *v* bomb

bombe (bawngb) *f* bomb

bon¹ (bawng) *adj* good; enjoyable, nice; kind

bon² (bawng) *m* voucher; ~ **de commande** order-form

bonbon (bawng-*bawng*) *m* sweet; candy *nAm*

bond (bawng) *m* jump

bondé (bawng-*day*) *adj* crowded

bondir (bawng-*deer*) *v* *leap

bonheur (bo-*nurr*) *m* happiness

bonjour! (bawng-*zhoor*) hello!

bonne (bon) *f* maid; housemaid; ~ **d'enfants** nurse

bonne-maman (bon-mah-*mahng*) *f* grandmother

bonneterie (bo-neh-*tree*) *f* hosiery

bon-papa (bawng-pah-*pah*) *m* grandfather

bonsoir! (bawng-*swaar*) good evening!

bonté (bawng-*tay*) *f* kindness

bord (bawr) *m* edge; brim, verge, border; **à** ~ aboard; ~ **de la mer** seaside, seashore; ~ **de la rivière** riverside; ~ **de la route** roadside; wayside; ~ **du trottoir** curb

bordel (bor-*dehl*) *m* brothel

borne routière (born roo-t*y*air) milestone

borné (bor-*nay*) *adj* narrow-minded

bosquet (bo-*skay*) *m* grove

bosse (boss) *f* dent, lump

botanique (bo-tah-*neek*) *f* botany

botte (bot) *f* boot

bottin (bo-*tang*) *m* telephone directory

bouc (book) *m* goat; ~ **émissaire** scapegoat

bouche (boosh) *f* mouth

bouchée (boo-*shay*) *f* bite

boucher¹ (boo-*shay*) *m* butcher

boucher² (boo-*shay*) *v* stop up

boucherie (boo-*shree*) *f* butcher's shop

bouchon (boo-*shawng*) *m* cork; stopper

boucle (bookl) f buckle; curl; loop; ~ **d'oreille** earring

boucler (boo-klay) v curl; **bouclé** curly

boue (boo) f mud; slush

bouée (boo-ay) f buoy; ~ **de sauvetage** lifebelt

boueux (boo-ur) adj muddy

bouger (boo-zhay) v move; stir

bougie (boo-zhee) f candle; ~ **d'allumage** sparking-plug

*bouillir (boo-Yeer) v boil

bouilloire (boo-Ywaar) f kettle

bouillotte (boo-Yot) f hot-water bottle

boulanger (boo-lahng-zhay) m baker

boulangerie (boo-lahng-zhree) f bakery

boule (bool) f ball

bouleau (boo-loa) m birch

bouleversé (bool-vehr-say) adj upset

boulon (boo-lawng) m bolt

boulot (boo-loa) m job

bouquet (boo-kay) m bunch, bouquet

bourg (boor) m town

bourgeois (boor-zhwah) adj bourgeois, middle-class

bourgeon (boor-zhawng) m bud

bourré (boo-ray) adj chock-full

bourreau (boo-roa) m executioner

bourse (boors) f purse; ~ **des valeurs** stock exchange; ~ **d'études** scholarship

boussole (boo-sol) f compass

bout (boo) m end; tip

bouteille (boo-tay) f bottle

boutique (boo-teek) f boutique; shop

bouton (boo-tawng) m button, knob; ~ **de col** collar stud; **boutons de manchettes** cuff-links pl

boutonner (boo-to-nay) v button

boutonnière (boo-to-nYair) f buttonhole

bowling (boa-leeng) m bowling; bowling alley

boxer (bok-say) v box

bracelet (brah-slay) m bracelet; bangle; **bracelet-montre** m wristwatch; ~ **pour montre** watch-strap

braconner (brah-ko-nay) v poach

braguette (brah-geht) f fly

branche (brahngsh) f branch; bough

brancher (brahng-shay) v connect; plug in

branchie (brahng-shee) f gill

branlant (brahng-lahng) adj unsteady

bras (brah) m arm; **bras-dessus bras-dessous** arm-in-arm

brasse (brahss) f breaststroke; ~ **papillon** butterfly stroke

brasser (brah-say) v brew

brasserie (brah-sree) f brewery

brave (brahv) adj brave, courageous; good

brèche (brehsh) f breach; gap

bref (brehf) adj (f brève) brief

brème (brehm) f bream

Brésil (bray-zeel) m Brazil

Brésilien (bray-zee-lYang) m Brazilian

brésilien (bray-zee-lYang) adj Brazilian

bretelles (brer-tehl) fpl braces pl; suspenders plAm

brevet (brer-vay) m patent

bridge (breej) m bridge

brillant (bree-Yahng) adj bright; brilliant

briller (bree-Yay) v *shine; glow

brin d'herbe (brang dehrb) blade of grass

brindille (brang-deey) f twig

brioche (bree-osh) f bun

brique (breek) f brick

briquet (bree-kay) m cigarette-lighter, lighter

brise (breez) f breeze

briser (bree-zay) v *break; **brisé** broken

Britannique (bree-tah-neek) m Briton

britannique (bree-tah-*neek*) *adj* British

broche (brosh) *f* brooch; spit

brochet (bro-*shay*) *m* pike

brochure (bro-*shewr*) *f* brochure

broder (bro-*day*) *v* embroider

broderie (bro-*dree*) *f* embroidery

bronchite (brawng-*sheet*) *f* bronchitis

bronze (brawngz) *m* bronze; **en ~** bronze

brosse (bross) *f* brush; **~ à cheveux** hairbrush; **~ à dents** toothbrush; **~ à habits** clothes-brush; **~ à ongles** nailbrush

brosser (bro-*say*) *v* brush

brouette (broo-*eht*) *f* wheelbarrow

brouillard (broo-*Yaar*) *m* fog, mist

brouiller (broo-*Yay*) *v* mix; mix up; *sow discord

bruit (brwee) *m* noise

brûler (brew-*lay*) *v* *burn

brûlure (brew-*lewr*) *f* burn; **brûlures d'estomac** heartburn

brume (brewm) *f* mist; haze

brumeux (brew-*mur*) *adj* misty; hazy, foggy

brun (brurng) *adj* brown

brunette (brew-*neht*) *f* brunette

brusque (brewsk) *adj* sudden; rude

brut (brewt) *adj* gross

brutal (brew-*tahl*) *adj* brutal

bruyant (brwee-*Yahng*) *adj* noisy

bruyère (brwee-*Yair*) *f* heather; moor

bûche (bewsh) *f* log

bûcher (bew-*shay*) *v* labour

budget (bew-*jay*) *m* budget

buffet (bew-*fay*) *m* buffet

buisson (bwee-*sawng*) *m* bush, scrub

bulbe (bewlb) *m* bulb

Bulgare (bewl-*gaar*) *m* Bulgarian

bulgare (bewl-*gaar*) *adj* Bulgarian

Bulgarie (bewl-gah-*ree*) *f* Bulgaria

bulle (bewl) *f* bubble

bulletin météorologique (bewl-tang may-tay-o-ro-lo-*zheek*) weather forecast

bureau (bew-*roa*) *m* office; bureau; desk, agency; **~ de change** exchange office; **~ de l'emploi** employment exchange; **~ de poste** post-office; **~ de renseignements** information bureau; **~ des objets trouvés** lost property office; **~ de tabac** cigar shop; **~ de voyages** travel agency; **employé de ~** clerk; **heures de ~** business hours

bureaucratie (bew-roa-krah-*see*) *f* bureaucracy

burin (bew-*rang*) *m* chisel

buste (bewst) *m* bust

but (bew) *m* purpose, aim; goal

butte (bewt) *f* mound

C

ça (sah) *pron* that

cabane (kah-*bahn*) *f* cabin

cabaret (kah-bah-*ray*) *m* cabaret

cabine (kah-*been*) *f* cabin, booth; **~ de pont** deck cabin; **~ d'essayage** fitting room; **~ téléphonique** telephone booth

cabinet (kah-bee-*nay*) *m* lavatory; cabinet; study; **~ de consultations** surgery

câble (kahbl) *m* cable

cacahuète (kah-kah-*weht*) *f* peanut

cachemire (kahsh-*meer*) *m* cashmere

cacher (kah-*shay*) *v* *hide

cachet (kah-*shay*) *m* stamp; capsule

cadavre (kah-*daavr*) *m* corpse

cadeau (kah-*doa*) *m* present, gift

cadenas (kahd-*nah*) *m* padlock

cadet (kah-*day*) *adj* junior

cadre (kaadr) *m* frame; setting; cadre

café (kah-*fay*) *m* coffee; café, public

house, saloon

caféine (kah-fay-*een*) *f* caffeine

cafétéria (kah-fay-tay-*rʸah*) *f* cafeteria

cage (kaazh) *f* cage

cahier (kah-*ʸay*) *m* notebook; ~ **de croquis** sketch-book

cahoteux (kah-o-*tur*) *adj* bumpy

caille (kigh) *f* quail

caillou (kah-*ʸoo*) *m* (pl ~x) pebble

caisse (kehss) *f* crate; pay-desk; ~ **d'épargne** savings bank

caissier (kay-*sʸay*) *m* cashier

caissière (keh-*sʸair*) *f* cashier

cal (kahl) *m* callus

calamité (kah-lah-mee-*tay*) *f* calamity, disaster

calcium (kahl-*sʸom*) *m* calcium

calcul (kahl-*kewl*) *m* calculation; ~ **biliaire** gallstone

calculatrice (kahl-kew-lah-*treess*) *f* adding-machine

calculer (kahl-kew-*lay*) *v* reckon; calculate

cale (kahl) *f* wedge, hold

caleçon (kahl-*sawng*) *m* drawers; briefs *pl*, shorts *plAm*, pants *pl*; underpants *plAm*; ~ **de bain** swimming-trunks

calendrier (kah-lahng-dree-*ay*) *m* calendar

câliner (kah-lee-*nay*) *v* cuddle

calmant (kahl-*mahng*) *m* tranquillizer

calme (kahlm) *adj* calm, quiet

calmer (kahl-*may*) *v* calm down

calomnie (kah-lom-*nee*) *f* slander

calorie (kah-lo-*ree*) *f* calorie

calvinisme (kahl-vee-*neesm*) *m* Calvinism

camarade (kah-mah-*rahd*) *m* comrade; ~ **de classe** class-mate

cambrioler (kahng-bree-o-*lay*) *v* burgle

cambrioleur (kahng-bree-o-*lūrr*) *m* burglar

camée (kah-*may*) *m* cameo

caméra (kah-may-*rah*) *f* camera

camion (kah-*mʸawng*) *m* lorry; truck *nAm*; ~ **de livraison** delivery van

camionnette (kah-mʸo-*neht*) *f* pick-up van

camp (kahng) *m* camp; ~ **de vacances** holiday camp

campagne (kahng-*pahñ*) *f* countryside, country; campaign

camper (kahng-*pay*) *v* camp

campeur (kahng-*pūrr*) *m* camper

camping (kahng-*peeng*) *m* camping; **terrain de** ~ camping site

Canada (kah-nah-*dah*) *m* Canada

Canadien (kah-nah-*dʸang*) *m* Canadian

canadien (kah-nah-*dʸang*) *adj* Canadian

canal (kah-*nahl*) *m* canal; channel

canapé (kah-nah-*pay*) *m* sofa, couch

canard (kah-*naar*) *m* duck

canari (kah-nah-*ree*) *m* canary

cancer (kahng-*sair*) *m* cancer

candélabre (kahng-day-*laabr*) *m* candelabrum

candidat (kahng-dee-*dah*) *m* candidate

candidature (kahng-dee-dah-*tūwr*) *f* application

canif (kah-*neef*) *m* penknife

caniveau (kah-nee-*voa*) *m* gutter

canne (kahn) *f* cane; walking-stick; ~ **à pêche** fishing rod

cannelle (kah-*nehl*) *f* cinnamon

canon (kah-*nawng*) *m* gun

canot (kah-*noa*) *m* canoe; dinghy; ~ **automobile** motor-boat

cantine (kahng-*teen*) *f* canteen

caoutchouc (kah-oo-*choo*) *m* rubber; ~ **mousse** foam-rubber

cap (kahp) *m* cape; course

capable (kah-*pahbl*) *adj* capable; able; *****être** ~ **de** ***be able to

capacité (kah-pah-see-*tay*) *f* ability;

capacity
cape (kahp) f cape
capitaine (kah-pee-*tehn*) m captain
capital (kah-pee-*tahl*) m capital; *adj* capital
capitale (kah-pee-*tahl*) f capital
capitalisme (kah-pee-tah-*leesm*) m capitalism
capitonner (kah-pee-to-*nay*) v upholster
capitulation (kah-pee-tew-lah-*syawng*) f capitulation
capot (kah-*poa*) m bonnet; hood *nAm*
caprice (kah-*preess*) m fancy; whim
capsule (kah-*psewl*) f capsule
capture (kahp-*tewr*) f capture
capturer (kahp-tew-*ray*) v capture
capuchon (kah-pew-*shawng*) m hood
car[1] (kaar) *conj* for
car[2] (kaar) m coach
caractère (kah-rahk-*tair*) m character
caractériser (kah-rahk-tay-ree-*zay*) v characterize; mark
caractéristique (kah-rahk-tay-ree-*steek*) f feature, characteristic, quality; *adj* characteristic, typical
carafe (kah-*rahf*) f carafe
caramel (kah-rah-*mehl*) m caramel; toffee
carat (kah-*rah*) m carat
caravane (kah-rah-*vahn*) f caravan; trailer *nAm*
carburateur (kahr-bew-rah-*tūrr*) m carburettor
cardigan (kahr-dee-*gahng*) m cardigan
cardinal (kahr-dee-*nahl*) m cardinal; *adj* cardinal
carence (kah-*rahngss*) f shortage; want
cargaison (kahr-gay-*zawng*) f cargo
carillon (kah-ree-*ʸawng*) m chimes *pl*
carnaval (kahr-nah-*vahl*) m (pl ~s) carnival

carnet (kahr-*nay*) m notebook; ~ **de chèques** cheque-book; check-book *nAm*
carotte (kah-*rot*) f carrot
carpe (kahrp) f carp
carré (kah-*ray*) m square; *adj* square
carreau (kah-*roa*) m tile; pane; **à carreaux** chequered
carrefour (kahr-*fōōr*) m junction; crossroads
carrière (kahr-*ʸair*) f career; quarry
carrosse (kah-*ross*) m carriage; coach
carrosserie (kah-ro-*sree*) f coachwork; motor body *Am*
cartable (kahr-*tahbl*) m satchel
carte (kahrt) f card; map; menu; ~ **d'abonnement** season-ticket; ~ **de crédit** credit card; charge plate *Am*; ~ **de jeu** playing-card; ~ **des vins** wine-list; ~ **de visite** visiting-card; ~ **d'identité** identity card; ~ **marine** chart; ~ **postale** card, picture postcard, postcard; ~ **routière** road map; ~ **verte** green card
carter (kahr-*tair*) m crankcase
cartilage (kahr-tee-*laazh*) m cartilage
carton (kahr-*tawng*) m cardboard; carton; **en** ~ cardboard
cartouche (kahr-*toosh*) f cartridge; carton
cas (kah) m case; instance, event; **au** ~ **où** in case; ~ **d'urgence** emergency; **en aucun** ~ by no means; **en** ~ **de** in case of
cascade (kah-*skahd*) f waterfall
case (kaaz) f section
caserne (kah-*zehrn*) f barracks *pl*
casino (kah-zee-*noa*) m casino
casque (kahsk) m helmet
casquette (kah-*skeht*) f cap
casse-croûte (kah-*skroot*) m snack
casse-noix (kah-*snwah*) m nutcrackers *pl*
casser (kah-*say*) v *break; **cassé** bro-

ken

casserole (kah-*srol*) f pan

casse-tête (kah-*steht*) m puzzle

cassis (kah-*seess*) m black-currant

castor (kah-*stawr*) m beaver

catacombe (kah-tah-*kawngb*) f catacomb

catalogue (kah-tah-*log*) m catalogue

catarrhe (kah-*taar*) m catarrh

catastrophe (kah-tah-*strof*) f calamity, disaster

catégorie (kah-tay-go-*ree*) f category; sort

cathédrale (kah-tay-*drahl*) f cathedral

catholique (kah-to-*leek*) adj catholic; Roman Catholic

cause (kōaz) f cause, reason; **à ~ de** because of; for, on account of

causer (koa-*zay*) v cause; chat

causette (koa-*zeht*) f chat

caution (koa-s*Y*awng) f bail, security, guarantee; **sujet à ~** untrustworthy

cavalier (kah-vah-*l*Yay) m horseman; rider

cave (kahv) f cellar; wine-cellar

caverne (kah-*vehrn*) f cavern

caviar (kah-v*Y*aar) m caviar

cavité (kah-vee-*tay*) f cavity

ce (ser) adj (cet; f cette, pl ces) that; this

ceci (ser-*see*) pron this

céder (say-*day*) v *give in; indulge

ceinture (sang-*te*w̄r) f belt; **~ de sécurité** safety-belt; seat-belt

cela (ser-*lah*) pron that

célébration (say-lay-brah-s*Y*awng) f celebration

célèbre (say-*lehbr*) adj famous

célébrer (say-lay-*bray*) v celebrate

célébrité (say-lay-bree-*tay*) f fame, celebrity

céleri (sehl-*ree*) m celery

célibat (say-lee-*bah*) m celibacy

célibataire (say-lee-bah-*tair*) m bachelor; adj single

cellophane (seh-lo-*fahn*) f cellophane

cellule (seh-*lewl*) f cell

celui-là (ser-lwee-*lah*) pron (f celle-là, pl ceux-là, celles-là) that

cendre (sahngdr) f ash

cendrier (sahng-dree-*ay*) m ashtray

censure (sahng-*se*w̄r) f censorship

cent (sahng) num hundred; **pour ~** percent

centigrade (sahng-tee-*grahd*) adj centigrade

centimètre (sahng-tee-*mehtr*) m centimetre; tape-measure

central (sahng-*trahl*) adj central; **~ téléphonique** telephone exchange

centrale (sahng-*trahl*) f power-station

centraliser (sahng-trah-lee-*zay*) v centralize

centre (sahngtr) m centre; **~ commercial** shopping centre; **~ de la ville** town centre; **~ de loisirs** recreation centre

cependant (ser-pahng-*dahng*) conj however; but, yet, only

céramique (say-rah-*meek*) f ceramics pl

cercle (sehrkl) m circle, ring; club

céréale (say-ray-*ahl*) f grain; corn

cérémonie (say-ray-mo-*nee*) f ceremony

cérémonieux (say-ray-mo-n*Y*ur) adj formal

cerise (ser-*reez*) f cherry

certain (sehr-*tang*) adj certain; **certains** pron some

certificat (sehr-tee-fee-*kah*) m certificate; **~ médical** health certificate

cerveau (sehr-*voa*) m brain

ces (say) adj these; those

cesser (say-*say*) v cease; discontinue, quit, stop

ceux-là (sur-*lah*) pron (f celles-là) those

chacun (shah-*kurng*) *pron* everyone; anyone

chagrin (shah-*grang*) *m* sorrow; grief

chaîne (shehn) *f* chain; ~ **de montagnes** mountain range

chair (shair) *f* flesh; ~ **de poule** goose-flesh

chaire (shair) *f* pulpit

chaise (shaiz) *f* chair; ~ **longue** deck chair

châle (shaal) *m* shawl

chalet (shah-*lay*) *m* chalet

chaleur (shah-*lūrr*) *f* heat; warmth

chambre (shahngbr) *f* room; ~ **à air** inner tube; ~ **à coucher** bedroom; ~ **d'ami** spare room, guest-room; ~ **d'enfants** nursery; ~ **et petit déjeuner** bed and breakfast; ~ **forte** vault

chameau (shah-*moa*) *m* camel

champ (shahng) *m* field; ~ **de blé** cornfield; ~ **de courses** racecourse; **sur-le-champ** immediately

champagne (shahng-*pahñ*) *m* champagne

champignon (shahng-pee-*ñawng*) *m* mushroom, toadstool

champion (shahng-*pʸawng*) *m* champion

chance (shahngss) *f* luck; fortune; chance

chanceux (shahng-*sur*) *adj* lucky

chandail (shahng-*digh*) *m* jersey, jumper, sweater

change (shahngzh) *m* change; **bureau de** ~ money exchange

changement (shahngzh-*mahng*) *m* change; variation, alteration

changer (shahng-*zhay*) *v* vary, change, alter; exchange, switch; ~ **de vitesse** change gear; ~ **en** turn into; **se** ~ change

chanson (shahng-*sawng*) *f* song; ~ **populaire** folk song

chant (shahng) *m* song, singing

chantage (shahng-*taazh*) *m* blackmail

chanter (shahng-*tay*) *v* *sing; *faire ~** blackmail

chanteur (shahng-*tūrr*) *m* singer; vocalist

chanteuse (shahng-*tūrz*) *f* singer

chantier naval (shahng-tʸay nah-*vahl*) shipyard

chanvre (shahngvr) *m* hemp

chaos (kah-*oa*) *m* chaos

chaotique (kah-o-*teek*) *adj* chaotic

chapeau (shah-*poa*) *m* hat

chapelain (shah-*plang*) *m* chaplain

chapelet (shah-*play*) *m* beads *pl*

chapelle (shah-*pehl*) *f* chapel

chapitre (shah-*peetr*) *m* chapter

chaque (shahk) *adj* each; every

charbon (shahr-*bawng*) *m* coal; ~ **de bois** charcoal

charcuterie (shahr-kew-*tree*) *f* delicatessen; butcher's shop

chardon (shahr-*dawng*) *m* thistle

charge (shahrzh) *f* charge

chargement (shahr-zher-*mahng*) *m* cargo, load, charge, freight

charger (shahr-*zhay*) *v* charge; load; **chargé de** in charge of; **se** ~ **de** *take charge of

charité (shah-ree-*tay*) *f* charity

charlatan (shahr-lah-*tahng*) *m* quack

charmant (shahr-*mahng*) *adj* graceful; glamorous

charme (shahrm) *m* charm, glamour

charmer (shahr-*may*) *v* charm, enchant

charnière (shahr-*nʸair*) *f* hinge

charrette (shah-*reht*) *f* cart

charrue (shah-*rew*) *f* plough

chasse (shahss) *f* chase; hunt

chasser (shah-*say*) *v* chase; hunt

chasseur (shah-*sūrr*) *m* hunter; bellboy

châssis (shah-*see*) *m* chassis

chaste (shahst) *adj* chaste

chat (shah) *m* cat

châtain (shah-*tang*) *adj* auburn

château (shah-*toa*) *m* castle

chatouiller (shah-too-*Yay*) *v* tickle

chaud (shoa) *adj* hot; warm

chaudière (shoa-*dYair*) *f* boiler

chauffage (shoa-*faazh*) *m* heating; ~ **central** central heating

chauffer (shoa-*fay*) *v* heat; warm

chauffeur (shoa-*fūr*) *m* chauffeur; ~ **de taxi** cab-driver

chaussée (shoa-*say*) *f* causeway; carriageway; roadway *nAm*

chaussette (shoa-*seht*) *f* sock

chaussure (shoa-*sewr*) *f* shoe; **chaussures** footwear; **chaussures de basket** plimsolls *pl*; **chaussures de gymnastique** gym shoes; **sneakers** *plAm*; **chaussures de ski** ski boots; **chaussures de tennis** tennis shoes

chauve (shōav) *adj* bald

chaux (shoa) *f* lime

chef (shehf) *m* chief; manager, boss; chieftain; ~ **cuisinier** chef; ~ **de gare** station-master; ~ **d'Etat** head of state; ~ **d'orchestre** conductor

chef-d'œuvre (sheh-*dūrvr*) *m* masterpiece

chemin (sher-*mang*) *m* lane; **à mi-chemin** halfway; ~ **de fer** railroad *nAm*; railway; ~ **du retour** way back

chemineau (sher-mee-*noa*) *m* tramp

cheminée (sher-mee-*nay*) *f* chimney; fireplace; hearth

chemise (sher-*meez*) *f* shirt; vest; ~ **de nuit** nightdress

chemisier (sher-mee-*zYay*) *m* blouse

chêne (shehn) *m* oak

chenil (sher-*nee*) *m* kennel

chèque (shehk) *m* cheque; check *nAm*; ~ **de voyage** traveller's cheque

cher (shair) *adj* dear; expensive

chercher (shehr-*shay*) *v* *seek, search; hunt for, look up, look for; *aller ~ fetch

chère (shair) *f* fare

chéri (shay-*ree*) *m* darling, sweetheart

cheval (sher-*vahl*) *m* horse; ~ **de course** race-horse; **cheval-vapeur** *m* horsepower; **chevaux de bois** merry-go-round; **monter à ~** *ride

chevalier (sher-vah-*lYay*) *m* knight

chevelu (sher-*vlew*) *adj* hairy

cheveu (sher-*vur*) *m* hair; **coupe de cheveux** haircut

cheville (sher-*veey*) *f* ankle

chèvre (shaivr) *f* goat

chevreau (sher-*vroa*) *m* kid

chez (shay) *prep* at; to; with; ~ **soi** home

chic (sheek) *adj* (f ~) smart

chichi (shee-*shee*) *m* fuss

chien (shYang) *m* dog; ~ **d'aveugle** guide-dog

chienne (shYehn) *f* bitch

chiffon (shee-*fawng*) *m* cloth; rag

chiffre (sheefr) *m* figure; digit, number

Chili (shee-*lee*) *m* Chile

Chilien (shee-*lYang*) *m* Chilean

chilien (shee-*lYang*) *adj* Chilean

chimie (shee-*mee*) *f* chemistry

chimique (shee-*meek*) *adj* chemical

Chine (sheen) *f* China

Chinois (shee-*nwah*) *m* Chinese

chinois (shee-*nwah*) *adj* Chinese

chirurgien (shee-rewr-*zhYang*) *m* surgeon

chlore (klawr) *m* chlorine

choc (shok) *m* shock

chocolat (sho-kô-*lah*) *m* chocolate

chœur (kūrr) *m* choir

choisir (shwah-*zeer*) *v* *choose; pick, select; **choisi** select

choix (shwah) *m* choice; pick, selection

chômage (shoa-*maazh*) *m* unemployment; **en ~** unemployed

chômeur (shoa-*mūrr*) *m* unemployed worker

chope (shop) *f* mug

choquer (sho-*kay*) *v* shock

chose (shōaz) *f* thing; **quelque ~** something

chou (shoo) *m* (pl ~x) cabbage; **chou-fleur** cauliflower; **choux de Bruxelles** sprouts *pl*

chouchou (shoo-*shoo*) *m* pet

chrétien (kray-t*Yang*) *m* Christian; *adj* Christian

Christ (kreest) *m* Christ

chrome (krom) *m* chromium

chronique (kro-*neek*) *adj* chronic

chronologique (kro-no-lo-*zheek*) *adj* chronological

chuchotement (shew-shot-*mahng*) *m* whisper

chuchoter (shew-sho-*tay*) *v* whisper

chute (shewt) *f* fall

cible (seebl) *f* target; mark

ciboulette (see-boo-*leht*) *f* chives *pl*

cicatrice (see-kah-*treess*) *f* scar

ciel (s*Yehl*) *m* (pl cieux) heaven; sky

cigare (see-*gaar*) *m* cigar

cigarette (see-gah-*reht*) *f* cigarette

cigogne (see-*goñ*) *f* stork

cil (seel) *m* eyelash

ciment (see-*mahng*) *m* cement

cimetière (seem-t*Yair*) *m* graveyard, cemetery, churchyard

cinéma (see-nay-*mah*) *m* cinema; pictures; movie theater *Am*, movies *Am*

cinq (sangk) *num* five

cinquante (sang-*kahngt*) *num* fifty

cinquième (sang-k*Yehm*) *num* fifth

cintre (sangtr) *m* coat-hanger, hanger

cirage (see-*raazh*) *m* shoe polish

circonstance (seer-kawng-*stahngss*) *f* circumstance; condition

circuit (seer-*kwee*) *m* circumference; circuit

circulation (seer-kew-lah-s*Yawng*) *f* circulation; traffic

cire (seer) *f* wax; **musée des figures de ~** waxworks *pl*

cirque (seerk) *m* circus

ciseaux (see-*zoa*) *mpl* scissors *pl*; **~ à ongles** nail-scissors *pl*

citation (see-tah-s*Yawng*) *f* quotation

cité (see-*tay*) *f* city

citer (see-*tay*) *v* quote

citoyen (see-twah-*Yang*) *m* citizen

citoyenneté (see-twah-*Yehn-tay*) *f* citizenship

citron (see-*trawng*) *m* lemon

civil (see-*veel*) *m* civilian; *adj* civilian, civil

civilisation (see-vee-lee-zah-s*Yawng*) *f* civilization

civilisé (see-vee-lee-*zay*) *adj* civilized

civique (see-*veek*) *adj* civic

clair (klair) *adj* clear; plain, light, serene

clairière (kleh-r*Yair*) *f* clearing

claque (klahk) *f* slap; smack, blow; **donner une ~** smack

claquer (klah-*kay*) *v* slam

clarifier (klah-ree-f*Yay*) *v* clarify

clarté (klahr-*tay*) *f* light, clearness

classe (klahss) *f* class; form; **~ moyenne** middle class; **~ touriste** tourist class

classer (klah-*say*) *v* classify; assort, grade, arrange, sort

classique (klah-*seek*) *adj* classical

clause (klōaz) *f* clause

clavecin (klahv-*sang*) *m* harpsichord

clavicule (klah-vee-*kewl*) *f* collarbone

clé (klay) *f* key; wrench; **~ à écrous** spanner; **~ de la maison** latchkey

clémence (klay-*mahngss*) *f* mercy;

grace

client (klee-ahng) m client; customer

clientèle (klee-ahng-tehl) f customers pl

clignotant (klee-ño-tahng) m indicator

climat (klee-mah) m climate

climatisation (klee-mah-tee-zah-s^{y}awng) f air-conditioning

climatisé (klee-mah-tee-zay) adj air-conditioned

clinique (klee-neek) f clinic

cloche (klosh) f bell

clocher (klo-shay) m steeple

cloison (klwah-zawng) f partition; wall

cloître (klwaatr) m cloister

cloque (klok) f blister

clos (kloa) adj closed; shut

clôture (kloa-te͞ur) f fence

clou (kloo) m nail

clown (kloon) m clown

club (klurb) m club; ~ **automobile** automobile club; ~ **de golf** golf-club

coaguler (koa-ah-gew-lay) v coagulate

cocaïne (ko-kah-een) f cocaine

cochon (ko-shawng) m pig; ~ **de lait** piglet; ~ **d'Inde** guinea-pig

cocktail (kok-tehl) m cocktail

cocotte à pression (ko-kot ah preh-s^{y}awng) pressure-cooker

code (kod) m code; ~ **postal** zip code Am

cœur (ku͞rr) m heart; core; **par** ~ by heart

coffre (kofr) m chest; boot; trunk nAm; **coffre-fort** safe

cognac (ko-ñahk) m cognac

cogner (ko-ñay) v bump; ~ **contre** knock against

cohérence (koa-ay-rahngss) f coherence

coiffeur (kwah-fu͞rr) m hairdresser; barber

coiffeuse (kwah-fu͞rz) f dressing-table

coiffure (kwah-fe͞ur) f hair-do

coin (kwang) m corner

coïncidence (koa-ang-see-dahngss) f concurrence

coïncider (koa-ang-see-day) v coincide

col (kol) m collar; mountain pass

coléoptère (ko-lay-op-tair) m bug

colère (ko-lair) f anger; temper, passion; **en** ~ angry

coléreux (ko-lay-rur) adj hot-tempered

colis (ko-lee) m parcel, package

collaboration (ko-lah-borah-s^{y}awng) f co-operation

collants (ko-lahng) mpl tights pl; panty-hose

colle (kol) f glue, gum

collectif (ko-lehk-teef) adj collective

collection (ko-lehk-s^{y}awng) f collection; ~ **d'art** art collection

collectionner (ko-lehk-s^{y}o-nay) v gather

collectionneur (ko-lehk-s^{y}o-nu͞rr) m collector

collège (ko-laizh) m college

collègue (ko-lehg) m colleague

coller (ko-lay) v paste, *stick

collier (ko-l^{y}ay) m necklace; collar, beads pl

colline (ko-leen) f hill

collision (ko-lee-z^{y}awng) f collision; crash; **entrer en** ~ collide, crash

Colombie (ko-lawng-bee) f Colombia

Colombien (ko-lawng-b^{y}ang) m Colombian

colombien (ko-lawng-b^{y}ang) adj Colombian

colonel (ko-lo-nehl) m colonel

colonie (ko-lo-nee) f colony

colonne (ko-lon) f column; pillar; ~ **de direction** steering-column

colorant (ko-lo-rahng) m colourant

coloré (ko-lo-ray) adj colourful

coma (ko-mah) m coma

combat (kawng-*bah*) *m* struggle;
fight, combat, contest, battle

*****combattre** (kawng-*bahtr*) *v* *fight;
combat, battle

combien (kawng-*b*ʸ*ang*) *adv* how
much; how many

combinaison (kawng-bee-nay-*zawng*) *f*
combination; slip

combiner (kawng-bee-*nay*) *v* combine

comble (kawngbl) *m* roof; height; *adj*
full

combler (kawng-*blay*) *v* fill up; over-
load

combustible (kawng-bew-*steebl*) *m*
fuel

comédie (ko-may-*dee*) *f* comedy; ~
musicale musical

comédien (ko-may-*d*ʸ*ang*) *m* comedian

comestible (ko-meh-*steebl*) *adj* edible

comique (ko-*meek*) *m* comedian; *adj*
comic, humorous

comité (ko-mee-*tay*) *m* committee

commandant (ko-mahng-*dahng*) *m*
commander; captain

commande (ko-*mahngd*) *f* order; **fait
sur** ~ made to order

commandement (ko-mahngd-*mahng*)
m order

commander (ko-mahng-*day*) *v* command; order

comme (kom) *conj* as; like, like;
since; ~ **si** as if

commémoration (ko-may-mo-rah-
*s*ʸ*awng*) *f* commemoration

commencement (ko-mahng-*smahng*)
m beginning

commencer (ko-mahng-*say*) *v* *begin;
commence, start

comment (ko-*mahng*) *adv* how; **n'importe** ~ anyhow; any way

commentaire (ko-mahng-*tair*) *m* comment

commenter (ko-mahng-*tay*) *v* com-

ment

commérage (ko-may-*raazh*) *m* gossip

commerçant (ko-mehr-*sahng*) *m* merchant; trader, shopkeeper

commerce (ko-*mehrs*) *m* commerce;
business, trade; ~ **de détail** retail
trade; *****faire du** ~ trade

commercial (ko-mehr-*s*ʸ*ahl*) *adj* commercial

*****commettre** (ko-*mehtr*) *v* commit

commission (ko-mee-*s*ʸ*awng*) *f* committee, commission; errand, message

commode (ko-*mod*) *f* chest of drawers; bureau *nAm*; *adj* convenient,
easy, handy

commodité (ko-mo-dee-*tay*) *f* comfort

commotion (ko-moa-*s*ʸ*awng*) *f* concussion

commun (ko-*murng*) *adj* common;
ordinary

communauté (ko-mew-noa-*tay*) *f*
community; congregation

communication (ko-mew-nee-kah-
*s*ʸ*awng*) *f* communication; information; connection; ~ **locale** local
call; *****mettre en** ~ connect

communiqué (ko-mew-nee-*kay*) *m*
communiqué

communiquer (ko-mew-nee-*kay*) *v*
communicate; inform

communisme (ko-mew-*neesm*) *m*
communism

communiste (ko-mew-*neest*) *m* communist

commutateur (ko-mew-tah-*tūrr*) *m*
switch

compact (kawng-*pahkt*) *adj* compact

compagnie (kawng-pah-*ñee*) *f* company; society; ~ **de navigation**
shipping line

compagnon (kawng-pah-*ñawng*) *m*
companion

comparaison (kawng-pah-ray-*zawng*) *f*

comparison
comparer (kawng-pah-*ray*) *v* compare
compartiment (kawng-pahr-tee-*mahng*) *m* compartment; ~ **fumeurs** smoking-compartment
compassion (kawng-pah-*s^yawng*) *f* sympathy
compatir (kawng-pah-*teer*) *v* pity
compatissant (kawng-pah-tee-*sahng*) *adj* sympathetic
compatriote (kawng-pah-tree-*ot*) *m* countryman
compensation (kawng-pahng-sah-*s^yawng*) *f* compensation
compenser (kawng-pahng-*say*) *v* compensate; *make good
compétence (kawng-pay-*tahngss*) *f* capacity
compétent (kawng-pay-*tahng*) *adj* qualified; expert
compétition (kawng-pay-tee-*s^yawng*) *f* competition
compiler (kawng-pee-*lay*) *v* compile
complémentaire (kawng-play-mahng-*tair*) *adj* further
complet[1] (kawng-*play*) *adj* (f -plète) whole, complete; total, utter; full up
complet[2] (kawng-*play*) *m* suit
complètement (kawng-pleht-*mahng*) *adv* completely
complexe (kawng-*plehks*) *m* complex; *adj* complex
complice (kawng-*pleess*) *m* accessary
compliment (kawng-plee-*mahng*) *m* compliment
complimenter (kawng-plee-mahng-*tay*) *v* compliment
compliqué (kawng-plee-*kay*) *adj* complicated
complot (kawng-*ploa*) *m* plot
comportement (kawng-por-ter-*mahng*) *m* behaviour
comporter (kawng-por-*tay*) *v* imply;

se ~ behave
composer (kawng-poa-*zay*) *v* compose
compositeur (kawng-po-zee-*tūrr*) *m* composer
composition (kawng-po-zee-*s^yawng*) *f* composition; essay
compréhension (kawng-pray-ahng-*s^yawng*) *f* understanding; insight
*****comprendre** (kawng-*prahngdr*) *v* *understand; *take, *see; conceive; comprise, include, contain
comprimé (kawng-pree-*may*) *m* tablet
compris (kawng-*pree*) *adj* inclusive; **tout** ~ all in
compromis (kawng-pro-*mee*) *m* compromise
comptable (kawng-*tahbl*) *m* bookkeeper
compte (kawngt) *m* account; ~ **en banque** bank account; ~ **rendu** report; minutes; **en fin de** ~ at last; **rendre** ~ **de** account for; **se rendre** ~ realize; *see
compter (kawng-*tay*) *v* count; ~ **sur** rely on
compteur (kawng-*tūrr*) *m* meter
comptoir (kawng-*twaar*) *m* counter
comte (kawngt) *m* count; earl
comté (kawng-*tay*) *m* county
comtesse (kawng-*tehss*) *f* countess
concéder (kawng-say-*day*) *v* grant
concentration (kawng-sahng-trah-*s^yawng*) *f* concentration
concentrer (kawng-sahng-*tray*) *v* concentrate
concept (kawng-*sehpt*) *m* idea
conception (kawng-seh-*ps^yawng*) *f* conception
concernant (kawng-sehr-*nahng*) *prep* concerning; as regards, about, regarding
concerner (kawng-sehr-*nay*) *v* concern; **en ce qui concerne** as regards, regarding

concert (kawng-*sair*) *m* concert

concession (kawng-seh-s*Yawng*) *f* concession

concessionnaire (kawng-seh-s*Y*o-*nair*) *m* distributor

*****concevoir** (kawng-*svwaar*) *v* conceive; devise, *take

concierge (kawng-s*Y*ehrzh) *m* concierge; janitor

concis (kawng-*see*) *adj* concise

*****conclure** (kawng-*klewr*) *v* finish; conclude

conclusion (kawng-klew-z*Yawng*) *f* conclusion, end; issue

concombre (kawng-*kawngbr*) *m* cucumber

concorder (kawng-kor-*day*) *v* agree

*****concourir** (kawng-koo-*reer*) *v* compete

concours (kawng-*kōōr*) *m* contest

concret (kawng-*kray*) *adj* (f -crète) concrete

concupiscence (kawng-kew-pee-*sahngss*) *f* lust

concurrence (kawng-kew-*rahngss*) *f* rivalry

concurrent (kawng-kew-*rahng*) *m* competitor; rival

condamnation (kawng-dah-nah-s*Yawng*) *f* conviction

condamné (kawng-dah-*nay*) *m* convict

condamner (kawng-dah-*nay*) *v* sentence

condition (kawng-dee-s*Yawng*) *f* condition; term

conditionnel (kawng-dee-s*Y*o-*nehl*) *adj* conditional

conducteur (kawng-dewk-*tūr*) *m* driver; conductor

*****conduire** (kawng-*dweer*) *v* conduct, guide; *drive; carry, *take; **se** ~ act

conduite (kawng-*dweet*) *f* conduct; lead

confédération (kawng-fay-day-rah-s*Yawng*) *f* federation; union

conférence (kawng-fay-*rahngss*) *f* conference; lecture; ~ **de presse** press conference

confesser (kawng-fay-*say*) *v* confess

confession (kawng-feh-s*Yawng*) *f* confession

confiance (kawng-f*Y*ahngss) *f* confidence; faith, trust; **digne de** ~ reliable, trustworthy; *****faire** ~ trust

confiant (kawng-f*Y*ahng) *adj* confident

confidentiel (kawng-fee-dahng-s*Y*ehl) *adj* confidential

confier (kawng-f*Y*ay) *v* commit

confirmation (kawng-feer-mah-s*Yawng*) *f* confirmation

confirmer (kawng-feer-*may*) *v* confirm; acknowledge

confiserie (kawng-fee-*zree*) *f* sweetshop; candy *nAm*; candy store *Am*

confiseur (kawng-fee-*zūr*) *m* confectioner

confisquer (kawng-fee-*skay*) *v* confiscate; impound

confiture (kawng-fee-*tewr*) *f* jam

conflit (kawng-*flee*) *m* conflict

confondre (kawng-*fawngdr*) *v* confuse; *mistake

*****être conforme** (aitr kawng-*form*) correspond

conformément à (kawng-for-may-*mahng*) in accordance with, according to

confort (kawng-*fawr*) *m* comfort

confortable (kawng-for-*tahbl*) *adj* comfortable; cosy

confus (kawng-*few*) *adj* confused; obscure; embarrassed

confusion (kawng-few-z*Yawng*) *f* confusion; disorder, muddle

congé (kawng-*zhay*) *m* vacation

congélateur (kawng-zhay-lah-*tūr*) *m* deep-freeze

congelé (kawng-_zhlay_) _adj_ frozen

congratuler (kawng-grah-tew-_lay_) _v_ congratulate

congrégation (kawng-gray-gah-_sᵧawng_) _f_ congregation

congrès (kawng-_gray_) _m_ congress

conifère (ko-nee-_fair_) _m_ fir-tree

conjecture (kawng-zhehk-_tewr_) _f_ guess

conjoint (kawng-_zhwang_) _adj_ joint

conjointement (kawng-zhwangt-_mahng_) _adv_ jointly

connaissance (ko-nay-_sahngss_) _f_ knowledge; acquaintance

connaisseur (ko-nay-_surr_) _m_ connoisseur

*****connaître** (ko-_naitr_) _v_ *know; **connu** well-known

connotation (ko-no-tah-_sᵧawng_) _f_ connotation

conquérant (kawng-kay-_rahng_) _m_ conqueror

*****conquérir** (kawng-kay-_reer_) _v_ conquer

conquête (kawng-_keht_) _f_ conquest

consacrer (kawng-sah-_kray_) _v_ devote

conscience (kawng-_sᵧahngss_) _f_ conscience; consciousness

conscient (kawng-_sᵧahng_) _adj_ conscious; aware

conscrit (kawng-_skree_) _m_ conscript

conseil (kawng-_say_) _m_ advice; counsel, council; board; **donner des conseils** advise

conseiller (kawng-say-_ᵧay_) _v_ advise; recommend; _m_ councillor; counsellor

consentement (kawng-sahngt-_mahng_) _m_ consent, approval

*****consentir** (kawng-sahng-_teer_) _v_ consent, agree

conséquence (kawng-say-_kahngss_) _f_ consequence; issue

par conséquent (pahr kawng-say-_kahng_) consequently

conservateur (kawng-sehr-vah-_turr_) _adj_ conservative

conservation (kawng-sehr-vah-_sᵧawng_) _f_ preservation

conservatoire (kawng-sehr-vah-_twaar_) _m_ music academy

conserver (kawng-sehr-_vay_) _v_ preserve

conserves (kawng-_sehrv_) _fpl_ tinned food; *****mettre en conserve** preserve

considérable (kawng-see-day-_rahbl_) _adj_ considerable; extensive

considération (kawng-see-day-rah-_sᵧawng_) _f_ consideration; respect

considérer (kawng-see-day-_ray_) _v_ consider; count, regard

consigne (kawng-_seeñ_) _f_ deposit; left luggage office; baggage deposit office _Am_

consister en (kawng-see-_stay_) consist of

consoler (kawng-so-_lay_) _v_ comfort

consommateur (kawng-so-mah-_turr_) _m_ consumer

consommation (kawng-so-mah-_sᵧawng_) _f_ consumption; drink

consommer (kawng-so-_may_) _v_ consume

conspiration (kawng-spee-rah-_sᵧawng_) _f_ plot

conspirer (kawng-spee-_ray_) _v_ conspire

constant (kawng-_stahng_) _adj_ constant; even

constater (kawng-stah-_tay_) _v_ ascertain; diagnose, note

constipation (kawng-stee-pah-_sᵧawng_) _f_ constipation

constipé (kawng-stee-_pay_) _adj_ constipated

constituer (kawng-stee-_tway_) _v_ constitute

constitution (kawng-stee-tew-_sᵧawng_) _f_ constitution

construction (kawng-strewk-_sᵧawng_) _f_

construction; building

***construire** (kawng-*strweer*) v construct

consul (kawng-*sewl*) m consul

consulat (kawng-sew-*lah*) m consulate

consultation (kawng-sewl-tah-*sʸawng*) f consultation

consulter (kawng-sewl-*tay*) v consult

contact (kawng-*tahkt*) m contact; touch

contacter (kawng-tahk-*tay*) v contact

contagieux (kawng-tah-*zhʸur*) adj contagious

conte (kawngt) m tale; ~ **de fées** fairytale

contempler (kawng-tahng-*play*) v view

contemporain (kawng-tahng-po-*rang*) m contemporary; adj contemporary

conteneur (kawngt-*nūrr*) m container

***contenir** (kawngt-*neer*) v contain; restrain

content (kawng-*tahng*) adj glad; pleased, joyful, happy

contenu (kawngt-*new*) m contents pl

contester (kawng-teh-*stay*) v dispute

contigu (kawng-tee-*gew*) adj (f -guë) neighbouring

continent (kawng-tee-*nahng*) m continent

continental (kawng-tee-nahng-*tahl*) adj continental

continu (kawng-tee-*new*) adj continuous

continuel (kawng-tee-*nwehl*) adj continual; continuous

continuellement (kawng-tee-nwehl-*mahng*) adv all the time, continually

continuer (kawng-tee-*nway*) v continue; carry on, *keep on, *keep, *go on, *go ahead

contour (kawng-*tōōr*) m outline, contour

contourner (kawng-toor-*nay*) v bypass

contraceptif (kawng-trah-sehp-*teef*) m contraceptive

contradictoire (kawng-trah-deek-*twaar*) adj contradictory

***contraindre** (kawng-*trangdr*) v compel

contraire (kawng-*trair*) adj opposite; m reverse, contrary; **au** ~ on the contrary

contralto (kawng-trahl-*toa*) m alto

contraste (kawng-*trahst*) m contrast

contrat (kawng-*trah*) m agreement, contract

contravention (kawng-trah-vahng-*sʸawng*) f ticket

contre (kawngtr) prep against; versus

à contrecœur (ah kawng-trer-*kūrr*) unwilling

***contredire** (kawng-trer-*deer*) v contradict

***contrefaire** (kawng-trer-*fair*) v counterfeit

contrefait (kawng-trer-*fay*) adj deformed

contremaître (kawng-trer-*maitr*) m foreman

contribution (kawng-tree-bew-*sʸawng*) f contribution

contrôle (kawng-*trōāl*) m control; inspection; ~ **des passeports** passport control

contrôler (kawng-troa-*lay*) v control; check

contrôleur (kawng-troa-*lūrr*) m ticket collector

controversé (kawng-troa-vehr-*say*) adj controversial

contusion (kawng-tew-*zʸawng*) f bruise

contusionner (kawng-tew-zʸo-*nay*) v bruise

***convaincre** (kawng-*vangkr*) v convince; persuade

convenable (kawng-*vnahbl*) *adj* proper; fit

*** convenir** (kawng-*vneer*) *v* fit, suit

conversation (kawng-vehr-sah-s*Yawng*) *f* conversation; discussion, talk

convertir (kawng-vehr-*teer*) *v* convert

conviction (kawng-veek-s*Yawng*) *f* conviction; persuasion

convocation (kawng-vo-kah-s*Yawng*) *f* summons

convulsion (kawng-vewl-s*Yawng*) *f* convulsion

coopérant (koa-o-pay-*rahng*) *adj* co-operative

coopératif (koa-o-pay-rah-*teef*) *adj* co-operative

coopération (koa-o-pay-rah-s*Yawng*) *f* co-operation

coopérative (koa-o-pay-rah-*teev*) *f* co-operative

coordination (koa-or-dee-nah-s*Yawng*) *f* co-ordination

coordonner (koa-or-do-*nay*) *v* co-ordinate

copain (ko-*pang*) *m* pal

copie (ko-*pee*) *f* copy; carbon copy

copier (ko-*pYay*) *v* copy

coq (kok) *m* cock; ~ **de bruyère** grouse

coquelicot (ko-klee-*koa*) *m* poppy

coquetier (kok-*tYay*) *m* egg-cup

coquillage (ko-kee-*Yaazh*) *m* sea-shell

coquille (ko-*keey*) *f* shell; ~ **de noix** nutshell

coquin (ko-*kang*) *m* rascal

cor (kawr) *m* horn; ~ **au pied** corn

corail (ko-*righ*) *m* (pl coraux) coral

corbeau (kor-*boa*) *m* raven

corbeille à papier (kor-bay ah pah-*pYay*) *m* wastepaper-basket

corde (kord) *f* rope; cord; string

cordial (kor-*dYahl*) *adj* hearty, cordial; sympathetic

cordon (kor-*dawng*) *m* cord; tape

cordonnier (kor-do-*nYay*) *m* shoemaker

coriace (ko-*rYahss*) *adj* tough

corne (korn) *f* horn

corneille (kor-*nay*) *f* crow

corps (kawr) *m* body

corpulent (kor-pew-*lahng*) *adj* corpulent; stout

correct (ko-*rehkt*) *adj* correct; right

correction (ko-rehk-s*Yawng*) *f* correction

correspondance (ko-reh-spawng-*dahngss*) *f* correspondence; connection

correspondant (ko-reh-spawng-*dahng*) *m* correspondent

correspondre (ko-reh-*spawngdr*) *v* correspond

corrida (ko-ree-*dah*) *f* bullfight

corridor (ko-ree-*dawr*) *m* corridor

corriger (ko-ree-*zhay*) *v* correct

*** corrompre** (ko-*rawngpr*) *v* corrupt; bribe; **corrompu** corrupt

corruption (ko-rew-ps*Yawng*) *f* corruption; bribery

corset (kor-*say*) *m* corset

cortège (kor-*taizh*) *m* procession

cosmétiques (ko-smay-*teek*) *mpl* cosmetics *pl*

costume (ko-*stewm*) *m* suit; costume; ~ **national** national dress

côte (kōat) *f* coast; rib; chop

côté (koa-*tay*) *m* side; way; **à** ~ next-door; **à** ~ **de** next to, beside; **de** ~ aside, sideways; **de l'autre** ~ **de** across; **passer à** ~ pass by

coteau (ko-*toa*) *m* hillside

côtelette (ko-*tleht*) *f* chop, cutlet

coton (ko-*tawng*) *m* cotton; **en** ~ cotton

cou (koo) *m* neck

couche (koosh) *f* layer; nappy; diaper *nAm*; **fausse** ~ miscarriage

se coucher (koo-*shay*) *lie down

couchette (koo-*sheht*) *f* bunk, berth

coucou (koo-*koo*) *m* cuckoo

coude (kood) *m* elbow

***coudre** (koodr) *v* sew

couler (koo-*lay*) *v* flow, stream

couleur (koo-*lūrr*) *f* colour; ~ **à l'eau** water-colour; **de** ~ coloured

couloir (koo-*lwaar*) *m* corridor

coup (koo) *m* blow; bump, tap, push, knock; ~ **de feu** shot; ~ **d'envoi** kick-off; ~ **de poing** punch; ~ **de téléphone** call; **jeter un** ~ **d'œil** glance

coupable (koo-*pahbl*) *adj* guilty; **déclarer** ~ convict

coupe (koop) *f* cup

coupe-papier (koop-pah-*p*^y*ay*) *m* paper-knife

couper (koo-*pay*) *v* *cut; *cut off

couple (koopl) *m* couple; ~ **marié** married couple

coupon (koo-*pawng*) *m* coupon

coupure (koo-*pewr*) *f* cut

cour (koor) *f* court; yard

courage (koo-*raazh*) *m* courage

courageux (koo-rah-*zhur*) *adj* courageous; plucky, brave

couramment (koo-rah-*mahng*) *adv* fluent

courant (koo-*rahng*) *m* current, stream; undercurrent; *adj* frequent, current; ~ **alternatif** alternating current; ~ **continu** direct current; ~ **d'air** draught; ***mettre au** ~ inform

courbe (koorb) *f* bend, curve; *adj* bent, curved, crooked

courbé (koor-*bay*) *adj* curved

courber (koor-*bay*) *v* *bend; bow

***courir** (koo-*reer*) *v* *run

couronne (koo-*ron*) *f* crown

couronner (koo-ro-*nay*) *v* crown

courrier (koo-*r*^y*ay*) *m* mail

courroie (koo-*rwah*) *f* strap; ~ **de**

ventilateur fan belt

cours (koor) *m* course; lecture; ~ **accéléré** intensive course; ~ **du change** exchange rate, rate of exchange

course (koors) *f* race; ride; ~ **de chevaux** horserace

court (koor) *adj* short; ~ **de tennis** tennis-court

court-circuit (koor-seer-*kwee*) *m* short circuit

courtepointe (koort-*pwangt*) *f* quilt

courtier (koor-*t*^y*ay*) *m* broker

courtois (koor-*twah*) *adj* courteous

cousin (koo-*zang*) *m* cousin

cousine (koo-*zeen*) *f* cousin

coussin (koo-*sang*) *m* cushion

coussinet (koo-see-*nay*) *m* pad

coût (koo) *m* cost

couteau (koo-*toa*) *m* knife; ~ **de poche** pocket-knife

coûter (koo-*tay*) *v* *cost

coûteux (koo-*tur*) *adj* expensive

coutume (koo-*tewm*) *f* custom

coutumier (koo-tew-*m*^y*ay*) *adj* customary

couture (koo-*tewr*) *f* seam; **sans** ~ seamless

couturière (koo-tew-*r*^y*air*) *f* dressmaker

couvent (koo-*vahng*) *m* convent; nunnery

couvercle (koo-*vehrkl*) *m* top, lid, cover

couvert (koo-*vair*) *m* cutlery; cover charge; *adj* cloudy

couverture (koo-vehr-*tewr*) *f* blanket; cover

couvre-lit (koo-vrer-*lee*) *m* counterpane

***couvrir** (koo-*vreer*) *v* cover

crabe (krahb) *m* crab

crachat (krah-*shah*) *m* spit

cracher (krah-*shay*) *v* *spit

crachin (krah-*shang*) *m* drizzle

craie (kray) f chalk

*craindre (krangdr) v fear, dread

crainte (krangt) f fear, dread

cramoisi (krah-mwah-zee) adj crimson

crampe (krahngp) f cramp

crampon (krahng-pawng) m clamp

cran (krahng) m guts

crâne (kraan) m skull

crapaud (krah-poa) m toad

craquement (krahk-mahng) m crack

craquer (krah-kay) v crack

cratère (krah-tair) m crater

cravate (krah-vaht) f necktie, tie

crawl (krōal) m crawl

crayon (kreh-Yawng) m pencil; ~ **à bille** Biro; ~ **pour les yeux** eye-pencil

création (kray-ah-sYawng) f creation

créature (kray-ah-tēwr) f creature

crèche (krehsh) f nursery

crédit (kray-dee) m credit

créditer (kray-dee-tay) v credit

créditeur (kray-dee-tūrr) m creditor

crédule (kray-dewl) adj credulous

créer (kray-ay) v create; design

crémation (kray-mah-sYawng) f cremation

crème (krehm) f cream; adj cream; ~ **à raser** shaving-cream; ~ **capillaire** hair cream; ~ **de beauté** face-cream; skin cream; ~ **de nuit** night-cream; ~ **fraîche** cream; ~ **glacée** ice-cream; ~ **hydratante** moisturizing cream

crémeux (kray-mur) adj creamy

crépi (kray-pee) m plaster

crépuscule (kray-pew-skewl) m dusk, twilight

cresson (kreh-sawng) m watercress

creuser (krur-zay) v *dig

creux (krur) adj hollow

crevaison (krer-vay-zawng) f puncture; blow-out

crevasse (krer-vahss) f chasm; cave

crever (krer-vay) v *burst; die; **crevé** punctured

crevette (krer-veht) f shrimp; prawn; ~ **rose** prawn

cri (kree) m shout, yell, scream, cry; **pousser des cris** shriek

cric (kreek) m jack

cricket (kree-keht) m cricket

crier (kree-ay) v cry; shout, scream

crime (kreem) m crime

criminalité (kree-mee-nah-lee-tay) f criminality

criminel (kree-mee-nehl) m criminal; adj criminal

crique (kreek) f inlet, creek

crise (kreez) f crisis; ~ **cardiaque** heart attack

cristal (kree-stahl) m crystal; **en ~** crystal

critique (kree-teek) f criticism; review; m critic; adj critical

critiquer (kree-tee-kay) v criticize

crochet (kro-shay) m hook; ***faire du ~** crochet

crocodile (kro-ko-deel) m crocodile

*croire (krwaar) v believe; guess

croisade (krwah-zahd) f crusade

croisement (krwahz-mahng) m crossing

croisière (krwah-zYair) f cruise

croissance (krwah-sahngss) f growth

*croître (krwaatr) v increase

croix (krwah) f cross

croulant (kroo-lahng) adj ramshackle

croustillant (kroo-stee-Yahng) adj crisp

croûte (kroot) f crust

croyable (krwah-Yaabl) adj credible

croyance (krwah-Yahngss) f belief

cru (krew) adj raw

cruche (krewsh) f pitcher; jug

crucifier (krew-see-fYay) v crucify

crucifix (krew-see-fee) m crucifix

crucifixion (krew-see-fee-ksYawng) f

crucifixion
cruel (krew-*ehl*) *adj* cruel; harsh
crustacé (krew-stah-*say*) *m* shellfish
Cuba (kew-*bah*) *m* Cuba
Cubain (kew-*bang*) *m* Cuban
cubain (kew-*bang*) *adj* Cuban
cube (kewb) *m* cube
*__cueillir__ (kur-*Yeer*) *v* pick
cuillère (kwee-*Yair*) *f* spoon; tablespoon; ~ **à soupe** soup-spoon; ~ **à
thé** teaspoon
cuillerée (kwee-*Yer*-ray) *f* spoonful
cuir (kweer) *m* leather; **en** ~ leather
*__cuire__ (kweer) *v* cook; ~ **au four**
bake
cuisine (kwee-*zeen*) *f* kitchen
cuisinier (kwee-zee-n*Yay*) *m* cook
cuisinière (kwee-zee-n*Yair*) *f* cooker;
stove; ~ **à gaz** gas cooker
cuisse (kweess) *f* thigh
cuivre (kweevr) *m* brass, copper; **cuivres** brassware
cul-de-sac (kewd-*sahk*) *m* cul-de-sac
culotte (kew-*lot*) *f* panties *pl*; ~ **de
gymnastique** trunks *pl*
culpabilité (kewl-pah-bee-lee-*tay*) *f*
guilt
culte (kewlt) *m* worship
cultiver (kewl-tee-*vay*) *v* cultivate;
*__grow, raise; **cultivé** cultured
culture (kewl-*tewr*) *f* culture
cupide (kew-*peed*) *adj* greedy
cupidité (kew-pee-dee-*tay*) *f* greed
cure (kewr) *f* cure
cure-dent (kewr-*dahng*) *m* toothpick
cure-pipe (kewr-*peep*) *m* pipe cleaner
curieux (kew-r*Yur*) *adj* inquisitive,
curious
curiosité (kew-r*Y*o-zee-*tay*) *f* curiosity;
curio; sight
curry (kur-*ree*) *m* curry
cycle (seekl) *m* cycle
cycliste (see-*kleest*) *m* cyclist
cygne (seeñ) *m* swan

cylindre (see-*langdr*) *m* cylinder; **tête
de** ~ cylinder head
cystite (see-*steet*) *f* cystitis

D

dactylo (dahk-tee-*loa*) *f* typist
dactylographier (dahk-tee-loa-grah-
f*Yay*) *v* type
dada (dah-*dah*) *m* hobby-horse
daim (dang) *m* deer; suede
daltonien (dahl-to-n*Yang*) *adj* colour-
blind
dame (dahm) *f* lady
damier (dah-m*Yay*) *m* draught-board;
check; **à damiers** chequered
Danemark (dahn-*mahrk*) *m* Denmark
danger (dahng-*zhay*) *m* risk, danger
dangereux (dahng-*zhrur*) *adj* dangerous; risky; unsafe
Danois (dah-*nwah*) *m* Dane
danois (dah-*nwah*) *adj* Danish
dans (dahng) *prep* into, inside, in,
within
danse (dahngss) *f* dance; ~ **folklorique** folk-dance
danser (dahng-*say*) *v* dance
date (daht) *f* date
datte (daht) *f* date
davantage (dah-vahng-*taazh*) *adv*
more
de (der) *prep* of; out of, from, off;
about; with
dé (day) *m* thimble
déballer (day-bah-*lay*) *v* unwrap, unpack
débarquer (day-bahr-*kay*) *v* disembark, land
se débarrasser de (day-bah-rah-*say*)
discard
débat (day-*bah*) *m* debate; discussion
*__débattre__ (day-*bahtr*) *v* discuss

débit (day-*bee*) *m* debit

déboucher (day-boo-*shay*) *v* uncork

debout (der-*boo*) *adv* upright; erect

déboutonner (day-boo-to-*nay*) *v* unbutton

débrancher (day-brahng-*shay*) *v* disconnect

se débrouiller avec (day-broo-*Yay*) *make do with

début (day-*bew*) *m* start, beginning; au ~ at first

débutant (day-bew-*tahng*) *m* learner, beginner

débuter (day-bew-*tay*) *v* *begin

décaféiné (day-kah-fay-ee-*nay*) *adj* decaffeinated

décédé (day-say-*day*) *adj* dead

décembre (day-*sahngbr*) December

décence (day-*sahngss*) *f* decency

décent (day-*sahng*) *adj* decent

déception (day-seh-ps*Yawng*) *f* disappointment

décerner (day-sehr-*nay*) *v* award

***décevoir** (day-*svwaar*) *v* disappoint

déchaînement (day-shehn-*mahng*) *m* outbreak

décharger (day-shahr-*zhay*) *v* discharge; unload

déchets (day-*shay*) *mpl* trash

déchirer (day-shee-*ray*) *v* rip, *tear

déchirure (day-shee-*rewr*) *f* tear

décider (day-see-*day*) *v* decide

décision (day-see-z*Yawng*) *f* decision

déclaration (day-klah-rah-s*Yawng*) *f* declaration, statement

déclarer (day-klah-*ray*) *v* declare, state

décliner (day-klee-*nay*) *v* slope

décollage (day-ko-*laazh*) *m* take-off

décoller (day-ko-*lay*) *v* *take off

décolorer (day-ko-lo-*ray*) *v* discolour; bleach

déconcerter (day-kawng-sehr-*tay*) *v* embarrass; overwhelm

décontracté (day-kawng-trahk-*tay*) *adj* easy-going

décoration (day-ko-rah-s*Yawng*) *f* decoration

décorer (day-ko-*ray*) *v* decorate

découper (day-koo-*pay*) *v* carve; *cut off

décourager (day-koo-rah-*zhay*) *v* discourage

découverte (day-koo-*vehrt*) *f* discovery

***découvrir** (day-koo-*vreer*) *v* discover; uncover

***décrire** (day-*kreer*) *v* describe

dédain (day-*dang*) *m* contempt; scorn

dedans (der-*dahng*) *adv* in; inside

dédier (day-*dYay*) *v* dedicate

dédommagement (day-do-mahzh-*mahng*) *m* indemnity

***déduire** (day-*dweer*) *v* infer, deduce; deduct

déesse (day-*ehss*) *f* goddess

défaillant (day-fah-*Yahng*) *adj* faint

***défaire** (day-*fair*) *v* *undo

défaite (day-*feht*) *f* defeat

défaut (day-*foa*) *m* fault

défavorable (day-fah-vo-*rahbl*) *adj* unfavourable

défectueux (day-fehk-*twur*) *adj* faulty, defective

défendre (day-*fahngdr*) *v* defend

défense (day-*fahngss*) *f* defence; ~ de doubler no overtaking; no passing *Am*; ~ de fumer no smoking; ~ d'entrer no entry

défi (day-*fee*) *m* challenge

défiance (day-f*Yahngss*) *f* suspicion

déficience (day-fee-s*Yahngss*) *f* deficiency

déficit (day-fee-*seet*) *m* deficit

défier (day-f*Yay*) *v* challenge, dare

définir (day-fee-*neer*) *v* determine, define

définition (day-fee-nee-s*Yawng*) *f* definition

dégel (day-*zhehl*) *m* thaw

dégeler (day-*zhlay*) *v* thaw

dégoût (day-*goo*) *m* disgust

dégoûtant (day-goo-*tahng*) *adj* disgusting, revolting

dégoûté (day-goo-*tay*) *adj* fed up with

degré (der-*gray*) *m* degree

déguisement (day-geez-*mahng*) *m* disguise

se déguiser (day-gee-*zay*) disguise

dehors (der-*awr*) *adv* outside, outdoors, out; **en ~ de** out of

déjà (day-*zhah*) *adv* already

déjeuner (day-zhur-*nay*) *m* dinner; luncheon, lunch; **petit ~** breakfast

au delà de (oa der-*lah* der) past, beyond

délabré (day-lah-*bray*) *adj* dilapidated

délai (day-*lay*) *m* set term; delay

délégation (day-lay-gah-s*Yawng*) *f* delegation

délégué (day-lay-*gay*) *m* delegate

délibération (day-lee-bay-rah-s*Yawng*) *f* deliberation; discussion

délibérer (day-lee-bay-*ray*) *v* deliberate; **délibéré** deliberate

délicat (day-lee-*kah*) *adj* tender, delicate; gentle; critical

délicatesse (day-lee-kah-*tehss*) *f* delicacy

délice (day-*leess*) *m* delight

délicieux (day-lee-s*Yur*) *adj* delightful, delicious, wonderful, lovely

délinquant (day-lang-*kahng*) *m* criminal

délivrance (day-lee-*vrahngss*) *f* delivery

délivrer (day-lee-*vray*) *v* deliver, redeem

demain (der-*mang*) *adv* tomorrow

demande (der-*mahngd*) *f* demand; application, request

demander (der-mahng-*day*) *v* ask, beg; charge; **se ~** wonder

démangeaison (day-mahng-zhay-*zawng*) *f* itch

démanger (day-mahng-*zhay*) *v* itch

démarche (day-*mahrsh*) *f* walk, pace, gait

démarreur (day-mah-*rurr*) *m* starter motor

déménagement (day-may-nahzh-*mahng*) *m* move

déménager (day-may-nah-*zhay*) *v* move

démence (day-*mahngss*) *f* madness

dément (day-*mahng*) *adj* mad

demeure (der-*murr*) *f* home

demeurer (der-mur-*ray*) *v* stay; live

demi (der-*mee*) *adj* half

démission (day-mee-s*Yawng*) *f* resignation

démissionner (day-mee-s*Yo*-nay) *v* resign

démocratie (day-mo-krah-*see*) *f* democracy

démocratique (day-mo-krah-*teek*) *adj* democratic

démodé (day-mo-*day*) *adj* out of date, old-fashioned, ancient

demoiselle (der-mwah-*zehl*) *f* miss

démolir (day-mo-*leer*) *v* demolish

démolition (day-mo-lee-s*Yawng*) *f* demolition

démonstration (day-mawng-strah-s*Yawng*) *f* demonstration

démontrer (day-mawng-*tray*) *v* *show, demonstrate, prove

dénier (day-n*Yay*) *v* deny

dénomination (day-no-mee-nah-s*Yawng*) *f* denomination

dénouer (day-*nway*) *v* untie

dense (dahngss) *adj* dense

dent (dahng) *f* tooth

dentelle (dahng-*tehl*) *f* lace

dentier (dahng-t*Yay*) *m* false teeth, denture

dentiste (dahng-*teest*) *m* dentist

dénudé (day-new-*day*) *adj* naked

dénutrition (day-new-tree-s^yawng) *f* malnutrition

départ (day-*paar*) *m* departure

département (day-pahr-ter-*mahng*) *m* division, department

dépasser (day-pah-*say*) *v* *overtake; pass

se dépêcher (day-pay-*shay*) hurry

dépendant (day-pahng-*dahng*) *adj* dependent

dépendre de (day-*pahngdr*) depend on

dépense (day-*pahngss*) *f* expense, expenditure

dépenser (day-pahng-*say*) *v* *spend

en dépit de (ahng day-*pee* der) in spite of

déplacement (day-plah-*smahng*) *m* removal

déplacer (day-plah-*say*) *v* move

*déplaire (day-*plair*) *v* displease

déplaisant (day-play-*zahng*) *adj* unpleasant

déplier (day-plee-*ay*) *v* unfold

déployer (day-plwah-*^yay*) *v* expand

déposer (day-poa-*zay*) *v* deposit, bank

dépôt (day-*poa*) *m* deposit; warehouse, depot

dépression (day-preh-s^yawng) *f* depression

déprimer (day-pree-*may*) *v* depress; **déprimé** down; blue; low

depuis (der-*pwee*) *prep* since; *adv* since; ∼ **que** since

député (day-pew-*tay*) *m* deputy; Member of Parliament

déraisonnable (day-ray-zo-*nahbl*) *adj* unreasonable

dérangement (day-rahngzh-*mahng*) *m* trouble; disturbance; **en ∼** broken, out of order

déranger (day-rahng-*zhay*) *v* disturb, upset, trouble

déraper (day-rah-*pay*) *v* slip, skid

dernier (dehr-n^yay) *adj* last; past

dernièrement (dehr-n^yehr-*mahng*) *adv* lately

derrière (deh-r^yair) *prep* after, behind; *m* bottom

dès que (day ker) as soon as

*être en désaccord (aitr ahng day-zah-*kawr*) disagree

désagréable (day-zah-gray-*ahbl*) *adj* nasty, disagreeable, unpleasant, unkind

désagrément (day-zah-gray-*mahng*) *m* inconvenience

*désapprendre (day-zah-*prahngdr*) *v* unlearn

désapprouver (day-zah-proo-*vay*) *v* disapprove

désastre (day-*zahstr*) *m* disaster

désastreux (day-zah-*strur*) *adj* disastrous

désavantage (day-zah-vahng-*taazh*) *m* disadvantage

descendance (day-sahng-*dahngss*) *f* origin

descendant (day-sahng-*dahng*) *m* descendant

descendre (day-*sahngdr*) *v* descend; *get off

descente (day-*sahngt*) *f* descent

description (day-skree-*ps^yawng*) *f* description

désenchanter (day-zahng-shahng-*tay*) *v* *let down

désert (day-*zair*) *m* desert; *adj* desert

déserter (day-zehr-*tay*) *v* desert

désespérer (day-zeh-spay-*ray*) *v* despair; **désespéré** desperate; hopeless

désespoir (day-zeh-*spwaar*) *m* despair

se déshabiller (day-zah-bee-*^yay*) undress

déshonneur (day-zo-*nūrr*) *m* disgrace, shame

désigner (day-zee-*ñay*) *v* designate;

appoint

désinfectant (day-zang-fehk-tahng) m disinfectant

désinfecter (day-zang-fehk-tay) v disinfect

désintéressé (day-zang-tay-ray-say) adj unselfish

désir (day-zeer) m desire, wish

désirable (day-zee-rahbl) adj desirable

désirer (day-zee-ray) v want, desire, wish, long for

désireux (day-zee-rur) adj eager, anxious

désobligeant (day-zo-blee-zhahng) adj unfriendly, offensive

désodorisant (day-zo-do-ree-zahng) m deodorant

désoler (day-zo-lay) v grieve; **désolé** sorry

désordonné (day-zor-do-nay) adj sloppy, untidy

désordre (day-zordr) m disorder, mess

désosser (day-zo-say) v bone

dessein (day-sang) m design

desserrer (day-say-ray) v loosen

dessert (day-sair) m dessert, sweet

dessin (day-sang) m sketch, drawing; pattern; **dessins animés** cartoon

dessiner (day-see-nay) v sketch, *draw

dessous (der-soo) adv underneath; **en ~** below; **en ~ de** beneath

dessus (der-sew) m top; **au-dessus de** on top of; **sens ~ dessous** upside-down

destin (day-stang) m destiny; fate

destinataire (day-stee-nah-tair) m addressee

destination (day-stee-nah-sYawng) f destination

destiner (day-stee-nay) v destine

destruction (day-strewk-sYawng) f destruction

détachant (day-tah-shahng) m cleaning fluid, stain remover

détacher (day-tah-shay) v unfasten, detach

détail (day-tigh) m detail; **commerce de ~** retail trade

détaillant (day-tah-Yahng) m retailer

détaillé (day-tah-Yay) adj detailed

détailler (day-tah-Yay) v retail

détecter (day-tehk-tay) v detect

détective (day-tehk-teev) m detective

*** déteindre** (day-tangdr) v fade

se détendre (day-tahngdr) relax

détente (day-tahngt) f relaxation

détention (day-tahng-sYawng) f custody

détenu (dayt-new) m prisoner

détergent (day-tehr-zhahng) m detergent

déterminer (day-tehr-mee-nay) v determine, define; **déterminé** adj definite; resolute

détester (day-teh-stay) v dislike, hate

détour (day-toor) m detour

détourner (day-toor-nay) v avert; hijack

détresse (day-trehss) f distress; misery

détritus (day-tree-tewss) m litter, garbage, rubbish

*** détruire** (day-trweer) v destroy, wreck

dette (deht) f debt

deuil (duree) m mourning

deux (dur) num two; **les ~** either, both

deuxième (dur-zYehm) num second

deux-pièces (dur-pYehss) m two-piece

dévaluation (day-vah-lwah-sYawng) f devaluation

dévaluer (day-vah-lway) v devalue

devant (der-vahng) prep in front of, ahead of, before

dévaster (day-vah-stay) v destroy

développement (day-vlop-mahng) m

development
développer (day-vlo-*pay*) *v* develop
*devenir (der-*vneer*) *v* *grow, *go, *get, *become
déviation (day-v^yah-s^y*awng*) *f* diversion, detour
dévier (day-v^y*ay*) *v* deviate
deviner (der-vee-*nay*) *v* guess
devise (der-*veez*) *f* slogan, motto
dévisser (day-vee-*say*) *v* unscrew
devoir (der-*vwaar*) *m* duty
*devoir (der-*vwaar*) *v* *be obliged to, *be bound to, *have to; need to, *should, *ought to, *shall; owe
dévorer (day-vo-*ray*) *v* devour
dévouement (day-voo-*mahng*) *m* devotion
diabète (d^yah-*beht*) *m* diabetes
diabétique (d^yah-bay-*teek*) *m* diabetic
diable (d^y*aabl*) *m* devil
diagnostic (d^yahg-no-*steek*) *m* diagnosis
diagnostiquer (d^yahg-no-stee-*kay*) *v* diagnose
diagonale (d^yah-go-*nahl*) *f* diagonal; *adj* diagonal
diagramme (d^yah-*grahm*) *m* graph, diagram
dialecte (d^yah-*lehkt*) *m* dialect
diamant (d^yah-*mahng*) *m* diamond
diapositive (d^yah-po-zee-*teev*) *f* slide
diarrhée (d^yah-*ray*) *f* diarrhoea
dictaphone (deek-tah-*fon*) *m* dictaphone
dictateur (deek-tah-*turr*) *m* dictator
dictée (deek-*tay*) *f* dictation
dicter (deek-*tay*) *v* dictate
dictionnaire (deek-s^yo-*nair*) *m* dictionary
diesel (d^yay-*zehl*) *m* diesel
dieu (d^y*ur*) *m* god
différence (dee-fay-*rahngss*) *f* distinction, difference, contrast
différent (dee-fay-*rahng*) *adj* differ-

ent; unlike
différer (dee-fay-*ray*) *v* delay; vary, differ
difficile (dee-fee-*seel*) *adj* difficult, hard
difficulté (dee-fee-kewl-*tay*) *f* difficulty
difforme (dee-*form*) *adj* deformed
digérer (dee-zhay-*ray*) *v* digest
digestible (dee-zheh-*steebl*) *adj* digestible
digestion (dee-zheh-*st^yawng*) *f* digestion
digne (deeñ) *adj* dignified; ~ **de** worthy of
digue (deeg) *f* dike, dam
diluer (dee-*lway*) *v* dissolve, dilute
dimanche (dee-*mahngsh*) *m* Sunday
dimension (dee-mahng-s^y*awng*) *f* size, extent
diminuer (dee-mee-*nway*) *v* decrease, lessen, reduce
diminution (dee-mee-new-s^y*awng*) *f* decrease
dinde (dangd) *f* turkey
dîner (dee-*nay*) *v* dine, *eat; *m* dinner
diphtérie (deef-tay-*ree*) *f* diphtheria
diplomate (dee-plo-*maht*) *m* diplomat
diplôme (dee-*ploam*) *m* certificate, diploma
*dire (deer) *v* *tell, *say
direct (dee-*rehkt*) *adj* direct
directement (dee-rehk-ter-*mahng*) *adv* straight away, straight
directeur (dee-rehk-*turr*) *m* manager, director; ~ **d'école** headmaster, head teacher
direction (dee-rehk-s^y*awng*) *f* management, direction, leadership; way; **indicateur de** ~ trafficator; directional signal *Am*
directive (dee-rehk-*teev*) *f* directive
dirigeant (dee-ree-*zhahng*) *m* leader, ruler

diriger (dee-ree-*zhay*) v direct; head, conduct, *lead; manage

discerner (dee-sehr-*nay*) v distinguish

discipline (dee-see-*pleen*) f discipline

discours (dee-*skōōr*) m speech

discret (dee-*skray*) adj (f -crète) inconspicuous

discussion (dee-skew-*s* *y* *awng*) f discussion, argument, deliberation; dispute

discuter (dee-skew-*tay*) v discuss, argue, deliberate

***disjoindre** (deess-*zhwangdr*) v disconnect

disloqué (dee-slo-*kay*) adj dislocated

***disparaître** (dee-spah-*raitr*) v vanish, disappear

disparu (dee-spah-*rew*) adj lost; m missing person

dispensaire (dee-spahng-*sair*) m health centre

dispenser (dee-spahng-*say*) v exempt; ~ **de** discharge of

disperser (dee-spehr-*say*) v scatter

disponible (dee-spo-*neebl*) adj available; obtainable; spare

disposé (dee-spoa-*zay*) adj inclined, willing

disposer de (dee-spoa-*zay*) dispose of

dispositif (dee-spoa-zee-*teef*) m apparatus

disposition (dee-spoa-zee-*s* *y* *awng*) f disposal

dispute (dee-*spewt*) f argument

disputer (dee-spew-*tay*) v argue; **se ~** dispute, quarrel

disque (deesk) m disc; record

dissertation (dee-sehr-tah-*s* *y* *awng*) f essay

dissimuler (dee-see-mew-*lay*) v *hide, conceal

***dissoudre** (dee-*soodr*) v dissolve; **se ~** dissolve

dissuader (dee-swah-*day*) v dissuade

from

distance (dee-*stahngss*) f way, distance, space

distinct (dee-*stang*) adj distinct, separate

distinction (dee-stangk-*s* *y* *awng*) f distinction, difference

distinguer (dee-stang-*gay*) v distinguish

distraction (dee-strahk-*s* *y* *awng*) f diversion; inadvertence

distrait (dee-*stray*) adj absent-minded

distribuer (dee-stree-*bway*) v distribute, *deal; issue

distributeur (dee-stree-bew-*tūrr*) m distributor; ~ **de billets** ticket machine; ~ **d'essence** fuel pump Am; ~ **de timbres** stamp machine

distribution (dee-stree-bew-*s* *y* *awng*) f distribution

district (dee-*stree*) m district

divers (dee-*vair*) adj various, several; miscellaneous

diversion (dee-vehr-*s* *y* *awng*) f diversion

divertir (dee-vehr-*teer*) v entertain, amuse

divertissant (dee-vehr-tee-*sahng*) adj entertaining

divertissement (dee-vehr-tee-*smahng*) m pleasure, fun, entertainment, amusement

divin (dee-*vang*) adj divine

diviser (dee-vee-*zay*) v divide; ~ **en deux** halve

division (dee-vee-*z* *y* *awng*) f division; department

divorce (dee-*vors*) m divorce

divorcer (dee-vor-*say*) v divorce

dix (deess) num ten

dix-huit (dee-*zweet*) num eighteen

dix-huitième (dee-zwee-*t* *y* *ehm*) num eighteenth

dixième (dee-*z* *y* *ehm*) num tenth

dix-neuf (deez-*nurf*) *num* nineteen

dix-neuvième (deez-nur-*v*y*ehm*) *num* nineteenth

dix-sept (dee-*seht*) *num* seventeen

dix-septième (dee-seh-*t*y*ehm*) *num* seventeenth

dock (dok) *m* dock

docker (do-*kair*) *m* docker

docteur (dok-*tūrr*) *m* doctor

document (do-kew-*mahng*) *m* document, certificate

doigt (dwah) *m* finger

domaine (do-*mehn*) *m* field

dôme (dōam) *m* dome

domestique (do-meh-*steek*) *adj* domestic; *m* domestic, servant

domestiqué (do-meh-stee-*kay*) *adj* tame

domicile (do-mee-*seel*) *m* domicile

domicilié (do-mee-see-*l*y*ay*) *adj* resident

domination (do-mee-nah-*s*y*awng*) *f* domination

dominer (do-mee-*nay*) *v* dominate; prevail; **dominant** leading

dommage (do-*maazh*) *m* mischief, damage; **dommage!** what a pity!

don (dawng) *m* faculty, talent; donation, gift

donateur (do-nah-*tūrr*) *m* donor

donation (do-nah-*s*y*awng*) *f* donation

donc (dawngk) *conj* therefore; so

donnée (do-*nay*) *f* data *pl*

donner (do-*nay*) *v* *give; donate; **étant donné que** because

dont (dawng) *pron* of which; of whom

doré (do-*ray*) *adj* gilt

dorénavant (do-ray-nah-*vahng*) *adv* henceforth

*dormir (dor-*meer*) *v* *sleep; ~ **trop longtemps** *oversleep

dortoir (dor-*twaar*) *m* dormitory

dos (doa) *m* back

dose (dōaz) *f* dose

dossier (do-s*y*ay*) *m* file, record

douane (dwahn) *f* Customs *pl*; **droit de** ~ Customs duty

douanier (dwah-n*y*ay*) *m* Customs officer

double (dōōbl) *adj* double

doubler (doo-*blay*) *v* pass *vAm*

doublure (doo-*blēwr*) *f* lining

douceurs (doo-*sūrr*) *fpl* sweets

douche (doosh) *f* shower

doué (doo-*ay*) *adj* talented, gifted

douille (doo^ee) *f* socket

douleur (doo-*lūrr*) *f* ache, pain; sore; sorrow, grief; **douleurs** labour; **sans** ~ painless

douloureux (doo-loo-*rur*) *adj* sore, painful

doute (doot) *m* doubt; ***mettre en** ~ query; **sans** ~ undoubtedly, without doubt

douter (doo-*tay*) *v* doubt; ~ **de** doubt

douteux (doo-*tur*) *adj* doubtful; unreliable

douve (dōōv) *f* moat

doux (doo) *adj* (*f* douce) mild; smooth, gentle

douzaine (doo-*zehn*) *f* dozen

douze (dōōz) *num* twelve

douzième (doo-z*y*ehm*) *num* twelfth

dragon (drah-*gawng*) *m* dragon

drainer (dray-*nay*) *v* drain

dramatique (drah-mah-*teek*) *adj* dramatic

dramaturge (drah-mah-*tewrzh*) *m* dramatist; playwright

drame (drahm) *m* drama

drap (drah) *m* sheet

drapeau (drah-*poa*) *m* flag

drapier (drah-p*y*ay*) *m* draper

dresser (dray-*say*) *v* *make up; train

drogue (drog) *f* drug

droguerie (dro-*gree*) *f* pharmacy, chemist's; drugstore *nAm*

droit (drwah) *m* right, law, justice; *adj* right, straight; erect, upright; ~ **administratif** administrative law; ~ **civil** civil law; ~ **commercial** commercial law; ~ **de douane** Customs duty; ~ **de stationnement** parking fee; ~ **de vote** suffrage; ~ **d'importation** duty; ~ **pénal** criminal law; **droits** dues *pl*; **tout** ~ straight ahead

de droite (der drwaht) right-hand

drôle (drōal) *adj* humorous, funny, queer

dû (dew) *adj* (f due; pl dus, dues) due

duc (dewk) *m* duke

duchesse (dew-shehss) *f* duchess

dune (dewn) *f* dune

dupe (dewp) *f* victim

duper (dew-pay) *v* cheat

dur (dewr) *adj* hard

durable (dew-rahbl) *adj* permanent, lasting

durant (dew-rahng) *prep* during

durée (dew-ray) *f* duration

durer (dew-ray) *v* continue, last

durillon (dew-ree-ᵞawng) *m* corn

duvet (dew-vay) *m* down

dynamo (dee-nah-moa) *f* dynamo

dysenterie (dee-sahng-tree) *f* dysentery

E

eau (oa) *f* water; ~ **courante** running water; ~ **de mer** sea-water; ~ **dentifrice** mouthwash; ~ **de Seltz** soda-water; ~ **douce** fresh water; ~ **gazeuse** soda-water; ~ **glacée** iced water; ~ **minérale** mineral water; ~ **oxygénée** peroxide; ~ **potable** drinking-water

eau-forte (oa-fort) *f* etching

ébène (ay-behn) *f* ebony

éblouissant (ay-bloo-ee-sahng) *adj* glaring

éblouissement (ay-bloo-ee-smahng) *m* glare

ébrécher (ay-bray-shay) *v* chip

écaille (ay-kigh) *f* scale

écarlate (ay-kahr-laht) *adj* scarlet

écarter (ay-kahr-tay) *v* *spread, part; remove; **écarté** out of the way

ecclésiastique (ay-klay-zᵞah-steek) *m* clergyman

échafaudage (ay-shah-foa-daazh) *m* scaffolding

échange (ay-shahngzh) *m* exchange

échanger (ay-shahng-zhay) *v* exchange

échantillon (ay-shahng-tee-ᵞawng) *m* sample

échappement (ay-shahp-mahng) *m* exhaust

échapper (ay-shah-pay) *v* escape; **s'échapper** slip

écharde (ay-shahrd) *f* splinter

écharpe (ay-shahrp) *f* scarf

échec (ay-shehk) *m* failure; **échec!** check!; **échecs** chess

échelle (ay-shehl) *f* ladder; scale

échiquier (ay-shee-kᵞay) *m* checkerboard *nAm*

écho (ay-koa) *m* echo

échoppe (ay-shop) *f* booth

échouer (ay-shway) *v* fail

éclabousser (ay-klah-boo-say) *v* splash

éclair (ay-klair) *m* flash; lightning

éclairage (ay-kleh-raazh) *m* lighting

éclaircir (ay-klehr-seer) *v* clarify

éclaircissement (ay-klehr-see-smahng) *m* explanation

éclairer (ay-klay-ray) *v* illuminate

éclat (ay-klah) *m* glow; glare; chip

éclatant (ay-klah-tahng) *adj* gay

éclater (ay-klah-tay) *v* *burst

éclipse (ay-kleeps) *f* eclipse

éclisse (ay-kleess) *f* splint

écluse (ay-klewz) f sluice, lock

écœurant (ay-kur-rahng) adj repellent

école (ay-kol) f school; ~ **maternelle** kindergarten; ~ **secondaire** secondary school; *faire l'école buissonnière play truant

écolier (ay-ko-lYay) m schoolboy

écolière (ay-ko-lYair) f schoolgirl

économe (ay-ko-nom) adj economical

économie (ay-ko-no-mee) f economy; **économies** savings pl

économique (ay-ko-no-meek) adj economic

économiser (ay-ko-no-mee-zay) v economize

économiste (ay-ko-no-meest) m economist

écorce (ay-kors) f bark

Ecossais (ay-ko-say) m Scot

écossais (ay-ko-say) adj Scotch; Scottish

Ecosse (ay-koss) f Scotland

s'écouler (ay-koo-lay) flow

écouter (ay-koo-tay) v listen

écouteur (ay-koo-tūrr) m receiver

écran (ay-krahng) m screen

écraser (ay-krah-zay) v mash; overwhelm; **s'écraser** crash

*écrire** (ay-kreer) v *write; **par écrit** in writing, written

écriture (ay-kree-tewr) f handwriting

écrivain (ay-kree-vang) m writer

écrou (ay-kroo) m nut

s'écrouler (ay-kroo-lay) collapse

Ecuadorien (ay-kwah-do-rYang) m Ecuadorian

écume (ay-kewm) f froth, lather

écureuil (ay-kew-rurēe) m squirrel

eczéma (ehg-zay-mah) m eczema

édification (ay-dee-fee-kah-sYawng) f construction

édifice (ay-dee-feess) m construction

édifier (ay-dee-fYay) v construct

éditeur (ay-dee-tūrr) m publisher

édition (ay-dee-sYawng) f issue, edition; ~ **du matin** morning edition

édredon (ay-drer-dawng) m eiderdown

éducation (ehr-tsee-oong) f education

éduquer (ay-dew-kay) v educate

effacer (play-fah-say) v wipe out

effectif (ay-fehk-teef) adj effective

effectivement (ay-fehk-teev-mahng) adv as a matter of fact

effectuer (ay-fehk-tway) v effect

effet (ay-fay) m result; consequence, effect; **en ~** indeed

efficace (ay-fee-kahss) adj effective; efficient

s'effilocher (ay-fee-lo-shay) fray

effondrement (ay-fawng-drer-mahng) m ruination

s'effondrer (ay-fawng-dray) collapse

s'efforcer (ay-for-say) try; bother

effort (ay-fawr) m effort, strain

effrayé (ay-fray-Yay) adj frightened, afraid

effrayer (ay-fray-Yay) v frighten; scare

effronté (ay-frawng-tay) adj bold; impertinent

égal (ay-gahl) adj even, level, equal

également (ay-gahl-mahng) adv as well, likewise, equally, also

égaler (ay-gah-lay) v equal

égaliser (ay-gah-lee-zay) v level, equalize

égalité (ay-gah-lee-tay) f equality

égard (ay-gaar) m consideration

égarer (ay-gah-ray) v *mislay

égayer (ay-gay-Yay) v cheer up

église (ay-gleez) f chapel, church

égocentrique (ay-go-sahng-treek) adj self-centred

égoïsme (ay-go-eesm) m selfishness

égoïste (ay-go-eest) adj egoistic, selfish

égout (ay-goo) m drain, sewer

égratignure (ay-grah-tee-ñēwr) f graze, scratch

Egypte (ay-*zheept*) f Egypt

Egyptien (ay-zhee-*ps*ʸ*ang*) m Egyptian

égyptien (ay-zhee-*ps*ʸ*ang*) adj Egyptian

élaborer (ay-lah-bo-*ray*) v elaborate

élan (ay-*lahng*) m diligence; moose

élargir (ay-lahr-*zheer*) v widen

élasticité (ay-lah-stee-see-*tay*) f elasticity

élastique (ay-lah-*steek*) adj elastic; m elastic, rubber band

électeur (ay-lehk-*tūrr*) m voter

élection (ay-lehk-*s*ʸ*awng*) f election

électricien (ay-lehk-tree-*s*ʸ*ang*) m electrician

électricité (ay-lehk-tree-see-*tay*) f electricity

électrique (ay-lehk-*treek*) adj electric

électronique (ay-lehk-tro-*neek*) adj electronic

élégance (ay-lay-*gahngss*) f elegance

élégant (ay-lay-*gahng*) adj smart, elegant

élément (ay-lay-*mahng*) m element

élémentaire (ay-lay-mahng-*tair*) adj primary

éléphant (ay-lay-*fahng*) m elephant

élevage (ehl-*vaazh*) m stock-farming

élévation (ay-lay-vah-*s*ʸ*awng*) f rise

élève (ay-*laiv*) m pupil, scholar

élever (ehl-*vay*) v *bring up, rear, raise; *breed

elfe (ehlf) m elf

éliminer (ay-lee-mee-*nay*) v eliminate

***élire** (ay-*leer*) v elect

elle (ehl) pron she

elle-même (ehl-*mehm*) pron herself

éloge (ay-*lozh*) m praise

éloigner (ay-lwah-*ñay*) v remove; **éloigné** distant, far-away, remote

élucider (ay-lew-see-*day*) v elucidate

émail (ay-*migh*) m (pl émaux) enamel

émaillé (ay-mah-*ʸay*) adj enamelled

émancipation (ay-mahng-see-pah-*s*ʸ*awng*) f emancipation

emballage (ahng-bah-*laazh*) m packing

emballer (ahng-bah-*lay*) v pack up, pack

embargo (ahng-bahr-*goa*) m embargo

embarquement (ahng-bahr-ker-*mahng*) m embarkation

embarquer (ahng-bahr-*kay*) v embark

embarras (ahng-bah-*rah*) m fuss

embarrassant (ahng-bah-rah-*sahng*) adj awkward, embarrassing; puzzling

embarrasser (ahng-bah-rah-*say*) v embarrass

emblème (ahng-*blehm*) m emblem

embouchure (ahng-boo-*shewr*) f mouth

embouteillage (ahng-boo-teh-ʸ*aazh*) m traffic jam, jam

embrasser (ahng-brah-*say*) v kiss

embrayage (ahng-breh-ʸ*aazh*) m clutch

embrouiller (ahng-broo-ʸ*ay*) v muddle

embuscade (ahng-bew-*skahd*) f ambush

émeraude (aym-*road*) f emerald

s'émerveiller (ay-mehr-vay-ʸ*ay*) marvel

émetteur (ay-meh-*tūrr*) m transmitter

***émettre** (ay-*mehtr*) v utter; transmit, *broadcast

émeute (ay-*mūrt*) f riot

émigrant (ay-mee-*grahng*) m emigrant

émigration (ay-mee-grah-*s*ʸ*awng*) f emigration

émigrer (ay-mee-*gray*) v emigrate

éminent (ay-mee-*nahng*) adj outstanding

émission (ay-mee-*s*ʸ*awng*) f issue; transmission, broadcast

emmagasinage (ahng-mah-gah-zee-*naazh*) m storage

emmagasiner (ahng-mah-gah-zee-*nay*) *v* store

emmener (ahng-mer-*nay*) *v* *take along

émoi (ay-*mwah*) *m* emotion

émotion (ay-moa-s*y*awng) *f* emotion

émoussé (ay-moo-*say*) *adj* dull, blunt

***émouvoir** (ay-moo-*vwaar*) *v* move

empêcher (ahng-pay-*shay*) *v* prevent

empereur (ahng-*prŭrr*) *m* emperor

empiéter (ahng-p*y*ay-*tay*) *v* trespass

empire (ahng-*peer*) *m* empire

emploi (ahng-*plwah*) *m* use; job, employment; **solliciter un ~** apply

employé (ahng-plwah-*y*ay) *m* employee; **~ de bureau** clerk

employer (ahng-plwah-*y*ay) *v* use; employ

employeur (ahng-plwah-*y*ŭrr) *m* employer

empoisonner (ahng-pwah-zo-*nay*) *v* poison

emporter (ahng-por-*tay*) *v* *take away

empreinte digitale (ahng-prangt deezhee-*tahl*) fingerprint

emprisonnement (ahng-pree-zon-*mahng*) *m* imprisonment

emprisonner (ahng-pree-zo-*nay*) *v* imprison

emprunt (ahng-*prurng*) *m* loan

emprunter (ahng-prurng-*tay*) *v* borrow

en (ahng) *prep* in; by; *pron* of it

encaisser (ahng-kay-*say*) *v* cash

enceinte (ahng-*sangt*) *adj* pregnant

encens (ahng-*sahng*) *m* incense

encercler (ahng-sehr-*klay*) *v* circle, encircle

enchantement (ahng-shahngt-*mahng*) *m* spell

enchanter (ahng-shahng-*tay*) *v* delight; bewitch

enchanteur (ahng-shahng-*tŭrr*) *adj* (f -teresse) glamorous

enclin (ahng-*klang*) *adj* inclined

encore (ahng-*kawr*) *adv* again; still, yet; **~ que** though; **~ un** another; **~ un peu** some more

encourager (ahng-koo-rah-*zhay*) *v* encourage

encre (ahngkr) *f* ink

encyclopédie (ahng-see-klo-pay-*dee*) *f* encyclopaedia

endommager (ahng-do-mah-*zhay*) *v* damage

endormi (ahng-dor-*mee*) *adj* asleep

endosser (ahng-do-*say*) *v* endorse

endroit (ahng-*drwah*) *m* spot

endurance (ahng-dew-*rahngss*) *f* stamina

endurer (ahng-dew-*ray*) *v* endure, sustain; *go through

énergie (ay-nehr-*zhee*) *f* energy; power; **~ nucléaire** nuclear energy

énergique (ay-nehr-*zheek*) *adj* energetic

énerver (ay-nehr-*vay*) *v* *get on someone's nerves; **s'énerver** *lose one's nerve

enfance (ahng-*fahngss*) *f* childhood

enfant (ahng-*fahng*) *m* child, kid

enfer (ahng-*fair*) *m* hell

enfermer (ahng-fehr-*may*) *v* lock up, *shut in

enfiler (ahng-fee-*lay*) *v* thread

enfin (ahng-*fang*) *adv* at last

enfler (ahng-*flay*) *v* *swell

enflure (ahng-*flewr*) *f* swelling

s'enfoncer (ahng-fawng-*say*) *sink

engagement (ahng-gahzh-*mahng*) *m* engagement

engager (ahng-gah-*zhay*) *v* engage; **s'engager** engage

engelure (ahng-*zhlewr*) *f* chilblain

engourdi (ahng-goor-*dee*) *adj* numb

engrais (ahng-*gray*) *m* fertilizer

énigme (ay-*neegm*) *f* mystery, riddle, puzzle, enigma

enjeu (ahng-*zhur*) *m* bet

enlacement (ahng-lah-*smah*) *m* embrace

enlever (ahngl-*vay*) *v* remove; *take away

ennemi (ehn-*mee*) *m* enemy

ennui (ahng-*nwee*) *m* annoyance, trouble; nuisance

ennuyer (ahng-nwee-ᵞ*ay*) *v* annoy, bore

ennuyeux (ahng-nwee-ᵞ*ur*) *adj* annoying; dull, unpleasant, boring

énorme (ay-*norm*) *adj* tremendous, immense, huge, enormous

enquête (ahng-*keht*) *f* inquiry; enquiry

enquêter (ahng-kay-*tay*) *v* investigate, enquire

enragé (ahng-rah-*zhay*) *adj* mad

enregistrement (ahngr-zhee-strer-*mahng*) *m* recording

enregistrer (ahngr-zhee-*stray*) *v* book; record

s'enrhumer (ahng-rew-*may*) catch a cold

enroué (ahng-roo-*ay*) *adj* hoarse

enrouler (ahng-roo-*lay*) *v* *wind

enseignement (ahng-sehñ-*mahng*) *m* tuition; **enseignements** teachings *pl*

enseigner (ahng-say-*ñay*) *v* *teach

ensemble (ahng-*sahngbl*) *adv* together; *m* whole

ensoleillé (ahng-so-lay-ᵞ*ay*) *adj* sunny

ensorceler (ahng-sor-ser-*lay*) *v* bewitch

ensuite (ahng-*sweet*) *adv* then, afterwards

entailler (ahng-tah-ᵞ*ay*) *v* carve

entasser (ahng-tah-*say*) *v* pile

entendre (ahng-*tahngdr*) *v* *hear

entente (ahng-*tahngt*) *f* agreement

enterrement (ahng-tehr-*mahng*) *m* burial

enterrer (ahng-tay-*ray*) *v* bury

enthousiasme (ahng-too-z*ᵞahsm*) *m* enthusiasm

enthousiaste (ahng-too-z*ᵞahst*) *adj* enthusiastic

entier (ahng-t*ᵞay*) *adj* whole, complete, entire

entièrement (ahng-t*ᵞ*ehr-*mahng*) *adv* wholly, completely, entirely, altogether, quite

entonnoir (ahng-to-*nwaar*) *m* funnel

entourer (ahng-too-*ray*) *v* encircle; circle, surround

entracte (ahng-*trahkt*) *m* interval, intermission

entrailles (ahng-*trigh*) *fpl* insides

entrain (ahng-*trang*) *m* zest

entraînement (ahng-trehn-*mahng*) *m* training

entraîner (ahng-tray-*nay*) *v* drill

entraîneur (ahng-treh-*nūr*) *m* coach

entrave (ahng-*traav*) *f* impediment

entraver (ahng-trah-*vay*) *v* impede

entre (ahngtr) *prep* between, among, amid

entrée (ahng-*tray*) *f* way in, entry, entrance; appearance; ~ **interdite** no admittance

entrepôt (ahng-trer-*poa*) *m* depository

***entreprendre** (ahng-trer-*prahngdr*) *v* *undertake

entrepreneur (ahng-trer-prer-*nūr*) *m* contractor

entreprise (ahng-trer-*preez*) *f* enterprise; business, concern, company, undertaking

entrer (ahng-*tray*) *v* enter, *go in

entresol (ahng-trer-*sol*) *m* mezzanine

entre-temps (ahng-trer-*tahng*) *adv* meanwhile, in the meantime

***entretenir** (ahng-trer-*tneer*) *v* maintain; support

entretien (ahng-trer-t*ᵞang*) *m* upkeep, maintenance; conversation

*entrevoir (ahng-trer-vwaar) v glimpse

entrevue (ahng-trer-vew) f interview

envahir (ahng-vah-eer) v invade

enveloppe (ahng-vlop) f envelope

envelopper (ahng-vlo-pay) v wrap

envers (ahng-vair) prep towards; **à l'envers** inside out

envie (ahng-vee) f longing, desire; envy; ***avoir ~ de** *feel like; fancy, desire

envier (ahng-vᵞay) v grudge, envy

envieux (ahng-vᵞur) adj envious

environ (ahng-vee-rawng) adv about

environnant (ahng-vee-ro-nahng) adj surrounding

environnement (ahng-vee-ron-mahng) m environment

environs (ahng-vee-rawng) mpl environment

envisager (ahng-vee-zah-zhay) v consider

envoyé (ahng-vwah-ᵞay) m envoy

*envoyer (ahng-vwah-ᵞay) v *send; dispatch

épais (ay-pay) adj (f ~se) thick

épaisseur (ay-peh-sūrr) f thickness

épaissir (ay-pay-seer) v thicken

épargner (ay-pahr-ñay) v save

épaule (ay-pōāl) f shoulder

épave (ay-paav) f wreck

épée (ay-pay) f sword

épeler (eh-play) v *spell

épice (ay-peess) f spice

épicé (ay-pee-say) adj spicy, spiced

épicerie (ay-pee-sree) f grocer's; **~ fine** delicatessen

épicier (ay-pee-sᵞay) m grocer

épidémie (ay-pee-day-mee) f epidemic

épier (ay-pᵞay) v peep

épilepsie (ay-pee-leh-psee) f epilepsy

épilogue (ay-pee-log) m epilogue

épinards (ay-pee-naar) mpl spinach

épine (ay-peen) f thorn; **~ dorsale** backbone, spine

épingle (ay-panggl) f pin; **~ à cheveux** hairpin; **~ de sûreté** safety-pin

épingler (ay-pang-glay) v pin

épique (ay-peek) adj epic

épisode (ay-pee-zod) m episode

éponge (ay-pawngzh) f sponge

époque (ay-pok) f period; **de l'époque** contemporary

épouse (ay-pōōz) f wife

épouser (ay-poo-zay) v marry

épouvantable (ay-poo-vahng-tahbl) adj terrible

épouvante (ay-poo-vahngt) f horror

époux (ay-poo) m husband

épreuve (ay-prūrv) f test, experiment; print

éprouver (ay-proo-vay) v experience; test

épuiser (ay-pwee-zay) v exhaust; use up; **épuisé** sold out

Equateur (ay-kwah-tūrr) m Ecuador

équateur (ay-kwah-tūrr) m equator

équilibre (ay-kee-leebr) m balance

équipage (ay-kee-paazh) m crew

équipe (ay-keep) f shift, team, gang; soccer team

équipement (ay-keep-mahng) m outfit, gear, equipment

équiper (ay-kee-pay) v equip

équitable (ay-kee-tahbl) adj right; reasonable

équitation (ay-kee-tah-sᵞawng) f riding

équivalent (ay-kee-vah-lahng) adj equivalent

équivoque (ay-kee-vok) adj ambiguous

érable (ay-rahbl) m maple

érafler (ay-rah-flay) v scratch

ériger (ay-ree-zhay) v erect

errer (ay-ray) v err; wander

erreur (eh-rūrr) f error; mistake

erroné (eh-ro-nay) adj mistaken

érudit (ay-rew-*dee*) *m* scholar

éruption (ay-rew-*ps^{y}awng*) *f* rash

escadrille (eh-skah-*dreey*) *f* squadron

escalier (eh-skah-*l^{y}ay*) *m* staircase; stairs *pl*; ~ **de secours** fire-escape; ~ **roulant** escalator

escargot (eh-skahr-*goa*) *m* snail

escarpé (eh-skahr-*pay*) *adj* steep

esclave (eh-*sklaav*) *m* slave

escorte (eh-*skort*) *f* escort

escorter (eh-skor-*tay*) *v* escort

****faire de l'escrime** (fair der leh-*skreem*) fence

escroc (eh-*skroa*) *m* swindler

escroquer (eh-skro-*kay*) *v* swindle

escroquerie (eh-skro-*kree*) *f* swindle

espace (eh-*spahss*) *m* space; room

espacer (eh-spah-*say*) *v* space

Espagne (eh-*spahñ*) *f* Spain

Espagnol (eh-spah-*ñol*) *m* Spaniard

espagnol (eh-spah-*ñol*) *adj* Spanish

espèce (eh-*spehss*) *f* species; breed

espérance (eh-spay-*rahngss*) *f* expectation

espérer (eh-spay-*ray*) *v* hope

espièglerie (eh-sp^{y}eh-gler-*ree*) *f* mischief

espion (eh-sp^y*awng*) *m* spy

esplanade (eh-splah-*nahd*) *f* esplanade

espoir (eh-*spwaar*) *m* hope

esprit (eh-*spree*) *m* spirit; soul, mind; ghost

esquisse (eh-*skeess*) *f* sketch

esquisser (eh-skee-*say*) *v* sketch

essai (ay-*say*) *m* trial, essay; **à l'essai** on approval

essayer (ay-say-*^{y}ay*) *v* try; attempt, test; try on

essence (ay-*sahngss*) *f* essence; petrol, fuel; gasoline *nAm*, gas *nAm*

essentiel (ay-sahng-*s^{y}ehl*) *adj* capital, essential

essentiellement (ay-sahng-s^{y}ehl-*mahng*) *adv* essentially

essieu (ay-*s^{y}ur*) *m* axle

essor (ay-*sawr*) *m* rise .

essuie-glace (ay-swee-*glahss*) *m* windscreen wiper; windshield wiper *Am*

essuyer (ay-swee-*^{y}ay*) *v* wipe; dry

est (ehst) *m* east

estampe (eh-*stahngp*) *f* print; engraving

estimation (eh-stee-mah-*s^{y}awng*) *f* estimate

estime (eh-*steem*) *f* esteem; respect

estimer (eh-stee-*may*) *v* consider, esteem, reckon; value, estimate

estomac (eh-sto-*mah*) *m* stomach

estropié (eh-stro-*p^{y}ay*) *adj* crippled

estuaire (eh-*stwair*) *m* estuary

et (ay) *conj* and

étable (ay-*tahbl*) *f* stable

établir (ay-tah-*bleer*) *v* establish; found; **s'établir** settle down

étage (ay-*taazh*) *m* floor, storey; apartment *nAm*

étagère (ay-tah-*zhair*) *f* shelf

étain (ay-*tang*) *m* pewter, tin

étal (ay-*tahl*) *m* stall

étalage (ay-tah-*laazh*) *m* shop-window

étaler (ay-tah-*lay*) *v* display

étang (ay-*tahng*) *m* pond

étape (ay-*tahp*) *f* stage

Etat (ay-*tah*) *m* state; **Etats-Unis** United States; the States

état (ay-*tah*) *m* state; condition; ~ **d'urgence** emergency

et cætera (eht-say-tay-*rah*) etcetera

été (ay-*tay*) *m* summer; **plein** ~ midsummer

****éteindre** (ay-*tangdr*) *v* *put out; switch off; extinguish

étendre (ay-*tahngdr*) *v* expand, *spread, enlarge; extend

étendu (ay-tahng-*dew*) *adj* broad, extensive; comprehensive

éternel (ay-tehr-*nehl*) *adj* eternal

éternité (ay-tehr-nee-*tay*) *f* eternity

éternuer (ay-tehr-*nway*) v sneeze

éther (ay-*tair*) m ether

Ethiopie (ay-tᶴo-*pee*) f Ethiopia

Ethiopien (ay-tᶴo-*pᶧang*) m Ethiopian

éthiopien (ay-tᶧo-*pᶧang*) adj Ethiopian

étincelle (ay-tang-*sehl*) f spark

étiqueter (ay-teek-*tay*) v label

étiquette (ay-tee-*keht*) f tag, label

étoffes (ay-*tof*) fpl drapery

étoile (ay-*twahl*) f star

étole (ay-*tol*) f stole

étonnant (ay-to-*nahng*) adj astonishing

étonnement (ay-ton-*mahng*) m astonishment, wonder, amazement

étonner (ay-to-*nay*) v amaze; astonish

étouffant (ay-too-*fahng*) adj stuffy

étouffer (ay-too-*fay*) v choke

étourdi (ay-toor-*dee*) adj dizzy, giddy

étourneau (ay-toor-*noa*) m starling

étrange (ay-*trahngzh*) adj strange; quaint, curious, queer

étranger (ay-trahng-*zhay*) m foreigner, alien, stranger; adj foreign, alien; **à l'étranger** abroad

étrangler (ay-trahng-*glay*) v choke, strangle

être (aitr) m being; creature; **~ humain** human being

*être (aitr) v *be

*étreindre (ay-*trangdr*) v hug, embrace

étreinte (ay-*trangt*) f grip; hug

étrier (ay-tree-*ay*) m stirrup

étroit (ay-*trwah*) adj narrow, tight

étude (ay-*tewd*) f study

étudiant (ay-tew-*dᶧahng*) m student

étudiante (ay-tew-*dᶧahngt*) f student

étudier (ay-tew-*dᶧay*) v study

étui (ay-*twee*) m case; **~ à cigarettes** cigarette-case

Europe (ur-*rop*) f Europe

Européen (ur-ro-pay-*ang*) m European

européen (ur-ro-pay-*ang*) adj European

eux (ur) pron them; **eux-mêmes** pron themselves

évacuer (ay-vah-*kway*) v vacate, evacuate

évaluer (ay-vah-*lway*) v evaluate; appreciate, estimate

évangile (ay-vahng-*zheel*) m gospel

s'évanouir (ay-vah-*nweer*) faint

évaporer (ay-vah-po-*ray*) v evaporate

évasion (ay-vah-*zᶧawng*) f escape

éveillé (ay-vay-*ᶧay*) adj clever

s'éveiller (ay-vay-*ᶧay*) wake up

événement (ay-vehn-*mahng*) m event; occurrence, happening

éventail (ay-vahng-*tigh*) m fan

éventuel (ay-vahng-*twehl*) adj possible, eventual

évêque (ay-*vehk*) m bishop

évidemment (ay-vee-dah-*mahng*) adv of course

évident (ay-vee-*dahng*) adj obvious, evident; self-evident

évier (ay-*vᶧay*) m sink

éviter (ay-vee-*tay*) v avoid

évolution (ay-vo-lew-*sᶧawng*) f evolution

évoquer (ay-vo-*kay*) v call to mind; evoke

exact (ehg-*zahkt*) adj just, precise, exact

exactement (ehg-zahk-ter-*mahng*) adv exactly

exactitude (ehg-zahk-tee-*tewd*) f correctness

exagérer (ehg-zah-zhay-*ray*) v exaggerate

examen (ehg-zah-*mang*) m examination; check-up

examiner (ehg-zah-mee-*nay*) v examine

excavation (ehk-skah-vah-*sᶧawng*) f

excavation

excéder (ehk-say-*day*) v exceed

excellent (ehk-seh-*lahng*) adj excellent

exceller (ehk-say-*lay*) v excel

excentrique (ehk-sahng-*treek*) adj eccentric

excepté (ehk-sehp-*tay*) prep except

exception (ehk-sehp-s^yawng) f exception

exceptionnel (ehk-sehp-s^yo-*nehl*) adj exceptional

excès (ehk-*say*) m excess; ~ **de vitesse** speeding

excessif (ehk-say-*seef*) adj excessive

excitation (ehk-see-tah-s^yawng) f excitement

exciter (ehk-see-*tay*) v excite

exclamation (ehk-sklah-mah-s^yawng) f exclamation

exclamer (ehk-sklah-*may*) v exclaim

***exclure** (ehk-*sklewr*) v exclude

exclusif (ehk-sklew-*zeef*) adj exclusive

exclusivement (ehk-sklew-zeev-*mahng*) adv solely, exclusively

excursion (ehk-skewr-s^yawng) f trip, excursion; day trip; tour

excuse (ehk-*skewz*) f excuse, apology

excuser (ehk-skew-*zay*) v excuse; **excusez-moi!** sorry!; **s'excuser** apologize

exécuter (ehg-zay-kew-*tay*) v execute

exécutif (ehg-zay-kew-*teef*) m executive; adj executive

exécution (ehg-zay-kew-s^yawng) f execution

exemplaire (ehg-zahng-*plair*) m copy

exemple (ehg-*zahng*pl) m instance, example; **par ~** for instance, for example

exempt (ehg-*zahng*) adj exempt; ~ **de droits** duty-free; ~ **d'impôts** tax-free

exempter (ehg-zahng-*tay*) v exempt

exemption (ehg-zahng-ps^yawng) f exemption

exercer (ehg-zehr-*say*) v exercise; **s'exercer** practise

exercice (ehg-zehr-*seess*) m exercise

exhiber (ehg-zee-*bay*) v exhibit

exhibition (ehg-zee-bee-s^yawng) f exhibition

exhorter (ehg-zor-*tay*) v urge

exigeant (ehg-zee-*zhahng*) adj particular

exigence (ehg-zee-*zhahng*ss) f requirement

exiger (ehg-zee-*zhay*) v demand, require

exile (ehg-*zeel*) m exile

exilé (ehg-zee-*lay*) m exile

existence (ehg-zee-*stahng*ss) f existence

exister (ehg-zee-*stay*) v exist

exotique (ehg-zo-*teek*) adj exotic

expédier (ehk-spay-*d^yay*) v dispatch, despatch, *send off, *send; ship

expédition (ehk-spay-dee-s^yawng) f expedition; consignment

expérience (ehk-spay-r^yahng ss) f experience; experiment; *faire l'**expérience de** experience

expérimenter (ehk-spay-ree-mahng-*tay*) v experiment; **expérimenté** experienced

expert (ehk-*spair*) adj skilled; m expert

expiration (ehk-spee-rah-s^yawng) f expiry

expirer (ehk-spee-*ray*) v expire, exhale

explicable (ehk-splee-*kahbl*) adj accountable

explication (ehk-splee-kah-s^yawng) f explanation

explicite (ehk-splee-*seet*) adj definite; express, explicit

expliquer (ehk-splee-*kay*) v explain

exploitation (ehk-splwah-tah-s^yawng) f exploitation; enterprise; ~ **minière**

mining
exploiter (ehk-splwah-*tay*) v exploit
explorer (ehk-splo-*ray*) v explore
exploser (ehk-sploa-*zay*) v explode
explosif (ehk-sploa-*zeef*) m explosive; *adj* explosive
explosion (ehk-sploa-z*Yawng*) f explosion, blast
exportation (ehk-spor-tah-s*Yawng*) f exports *pl*, exportation, export
exporter (ehk-spor-*tay*) v export
exposer (ehk-spoa-*zay*) v exhibit, *show
exposition (ehk-spoa-zee-s*Yawng*) f display, exposition, exhibition, show; exposure; ~ **d'art** art exhibition
exprès[1] (ehk-*spray*) *adv* on purpose
exprès[2] (ehk-*sprehss*) *adj* express; special delivery
expression (ehk-spreh-s*Yawng*) f expression
exprimer (ehk-spree-*may*) v express
expulser (ehk-spewl-*say*) v chase; expel
exquis (ehk-*skee*) *adj* delicious; exquisite; select
extase (ehk-*staaz*) m ecstasy
exténuer (ehk-stay-*nway*) v exhaust
extérieur (ehk-stay-r*Yūrr*) m exterior, outside; *adj* external, exterior; **vers l'extérieur** outwards
externe (ehk-*stehrn*) *adj* outward
extincteur (ehk-stangk-*tūrr*) m fire-extinguisher
extorquer (ehk-stor-*kay*) v extort
extorsion (ehk-stor-s*Yawng*) f extortion
extrader (ehk-strah-*day*) v extradite
*****extraire** (ehk-*strair*) v extract
extrait (ehk-*stray*) m excerpt
extraordinaire (ehk-strah-or-dee-*nair*) *adj* extraordinary, exceptional
extravagant (ehk-strah-vah-*gahng*) *adj* extravagant

extrême (ehk-*strehm*) *adj* extreme, utmost; very; m extreme
exubérant (ehg-zew-bay-*rahng*) *adj* exuberant

F

fable (*fahbl*) f fable
fabricant (fah-bree-*kahng*) m manufacturer
fabriquer (fah-bree-*kay*) v manufacture
façade (fah-*sahd*) f façade
face (*fahss*) f front; **en ~ de** facing, opposite
fâcher (fah-*shay*) v annoy; **fâché** cross
facile (fah-*seel*) *adj* easy
facilité (fah-see-lee-*tay*) f facility
façon (fah-*sawng*) f way; **de la même ~** alike; **de toute ~** anyway; at any rate
façonner (fah-so-*nay*) v model
facteur (fahk-*tūrr*) m factor; postman
facture (fahk-*tewr*) f invoice, bill
facturer (fahk-tew-*ray*) v bill
facultatif (fah-kewl-tah-*teef*) *adj* optional
faculté (fah-kewl-*tay*) f faculty
faible (*fehbl*) *adj* feeble, weak; small, slight; faint
faiblesse (feh-*blehss*) f weakness
faïence (fah-*Yahngss*) f faience; crockery
en faillite (ahng fah-*Yeet*) bankrupt
faim (*fang*) f hunger
*****faire** (*fair*) v *do; *make; cause to, *have
faisable (fer-*zahbl*) *adj* feasible, attainable
faisan (fer-*zahng*) m pheasant

fait (fay) m fact; **de ~** in fact; **en ~** as a matter of fact, in effect

falaise (fah-laiz) f cliff

*falloir (fah-lwaar) v need, *must

falsification (fahl-see-fee-kah-s^yawng) f fake

falsifier (fahl-see-f^yay) v forge

fameux (fah-mur) adj famous

familial (fah-mee-l^yahl) adj of the family

familiariser (fah-mee-l^yah-ree-zay) v accustom

familier (fah-mee-l^yay) adj familiar

famille (fah-meey) f family

fan (fahn) m fan

fanatique (fah-nah-teek) adj fanatical

se faner (fah-nay) fade

fanfare (fahng-faar) f brass band

fantaisie (fahng-tay-zee) f fantasy

fantastique (fahng-tah-steek) adj fantastic

fantôme (fahng-tōam) m phantom, ghost; spook

faon (fahng) m fawn

farce (fahrs) f farce; filling, stuffing

farci (fahr-see) adj stuffed

fardeau (fahr-doa) m burden, load

farine (fah-reen) f flour

farouche (fah-roosh) adj shy

fasciner (fah-see-nay) v fascinate

fascisme (fah-sheesm) m fascism

fasciste (fah-sheest) m fascist; adj fascist

fastidieux (fah-stee-d^yur) adj annoying; difficult

fatal (fah-tahl) adj (pl ~s) fatal, mortal

fatigant (fah-tee-gahng) adj tiring

fatigue (fah-teeg) f fatigue

fatiguer (fah-tee-gay) v tire; **fatigué** weary

faubourg (foa-boor) m outskirts pl, suburb

fauché (foa-shay) adj broke

faucon (foa-kawng) m hawk

faute (fōat) f mistake, error; fault; **donner la ~ à** blame; **sans ~** without fail

fauteuil (foa-turee) m armchair, easy chair; **~ d'orchestre** orchestra seat Am; **~ roulant** wheelchair

fauve (fōav) adj fawn

faux (foa) adj (f fausse) false; untrue

faveur (fah-vūrr) f favour; **en ~ de** on behalf of

favorable (fah-vo-rahbl) adj favourable

favori (fah-vo-ree) m (f -rite) favourite; adj pet; **favoris** whiskers pl, sideburns pl

favoriser (fah-vo-ree-zay) v favour

fédéral (fay-day-rahl) adj federal

fédération (fay-day-rah-s^yawng) f federation

fée (fay) f fairy

*feindre (fangdr) v pretend

félicitation (fay-lee-see-tah-s^yawng) f congratulation

féliciter (fay-lee-see-tay) v congratulate, compliment

femelle (fer-mehl) f female

féminin (fay-mee-nang) adj feminine, female

femme (fahm) f woman, wife; **~ de chambre** chambermaid

fendre (fahngdr) v *split; crack

fenêtre (fer-naitr) f window

fente (fahngt) f slot, cleft

féodal (fay-o-dahl) adj feudal

fer (fair) m iron; **en ~** iron; **~ à cheval** horseshoe; **~ à friser** curling-tongs pl; **~ à repasser** iron; **~ à souder** soldering-iron

ferme (fehrm) f farmhouse, farm; adj firm, steady; steadfast

fermenter (fehr-mahng-tay) v ferment

fermer (fehr-may) v close, *shut; fasten; turn off; **fermé** closed shut; **~ à clé** lock

fermeture (fehrm-*tewr*) f fastener; **~ éclair** zipper, zip

fermier (fehr-*mʸay*) m farmer

fermière (fehr-*mʸair*) f farmer's wife

féroce (fay-*ross*) adj fierce, wild

ferraille (feh-*righ*) f scrap-iron

ferry-boat (feh-ree-*boat*) m ferry-boat; train ferry

fertile (fehr-*teel*) adj fertile

fesse (fehss) f buttock

fessée (fay-*say*) f spanking

festival (feh-stee-*vahl*) m (pl ~s) festival

fête (feht) f feast

feu (fur) m fire; **~ arrière** tail-light, rear-light; **~ de circulation** traffic light; **~ de position** parking light

feuille (fur*ee*) f leaf; sheet

feuilleton (fur*ee*-*tawng*) m serial

feutre (fūrtr) m felt

février (fay-vree-*ay*) February

fiançailles (fʸahng-*sigh*) fpl engagement

fiancé (fʸahng-*say*) m fiancé; adj engaged

fiancée (fʸahng-*say*) f fiancée, bride

fibre (feebr) f fibre

ficelle (fee-*sehl*) f twine, string

fiche (feesh) f plug

fiction (feek-*sʸawng*) f fiction

fidèle (fee-*dehl*) adj faithful, true

fier (fʸair) adj proud

fièvre (fʸaivr) f fever

fiévreux (fʸay-*vrur*) adj feverish

figue (feeg) f fig

se figurer (fee-gew-*ray*) imagine

fil (feel) m thread; line, yarn; **~ de fer** wire; **~ électrique** flex; electric cord

file (feel) f file

filer (fee-*lay*) v *spin

filet (fee-*lay*) m net; **~ à bagage** luggage rack; **~ de pêche** fishing net

fille (feey) f girl; daughter; **vieille ~** spinster

film (feelm) m film, movie; **~ en couleurs** colour film

filmer (feel-*may*) v film

fils (feess) m son

filtre (feeltr) m filter; **~ à air** air-filter; **~ à huile** oil filter

filtrer (feel-*tray*) v strain

fin (fang) f finish, ending, end; issue; adj fine; sheer

final (fee-*nahl*) adj (pl ~s) final; eventual

financer (fee-nahng-*say*) v finance

finances (fee-*nahngss*) fpl finances pl

financier (fee-nahng-*sʸay*) adj financial

finir (fee-*neer*) v finish, end; **fini** finished, over

Finlandais (fang-lahng-*day*) m Finn

finlandais (fang-lahng-*day*) adj Finnish

Finlande (fang-*lahngd*) f Finland

firme (feerm) f firm

fissure (fee-*sewr*) f chink, crack

fixateur (feek-sah-*tūrr*) m setting lotion

fixe (feeks) adj fixed; permanent

fixer (feek-*say*) v attach; gaze, stare; **~ le prix** price

fjord (fʸor) m fjord

flacon (flah-*kawng*) m flask

flamant (flah-*mahng*) m flamingo

flamme (flahm) f flame

flanelle (flah-*nehl*) f flannel

flâner (flah-*nay*) v stroll

flaque (flahk) f puddle

flasque (flahsk) adj limp

fléau (flay-*oa*) m plague

flèche (flehsh) f arrow

flétan (flay-*tahng*) m halibut

fleur (flūrr) f flower

fleuriste (flur-*reest*) m flower-shop, florist

fleuve (flūrv) *m* river
flexible (flehk-*seebl*) *adj* flexible, elastic, supple
flotte (flot) *f* fleet
flotter (flo-*tay*) *v* float
flotteur (flo-*tūr*) *m* float
fluide (flew-*eed*) *adj* fluid
flûte (flewt) *f* flute
foi (fwah) *f* faith
foie (fwah) *m* liver
foin (fwang) *m* hay
foire (fwaar) *f* fair
fois (fwah) *f* time; *prep* times; **à la ~** at the same time; **deux ~** twice; **une ~** once; some time; **une ~ de plus** once more
folie (fo-*lee*) *f* lunacy
folklore (fol-*klawr*) *m* folklore
foncé (fawng-*say*) *adj* dark
foncer (fawng-*say*) *v* *speed
fonction (fawngk-s^y*awng*) *f* function; office
fonctionnaire (fawngk-s^yo-*nair*) *m* civil servant
fonctionnement (fawngk-s^yon-*mahng*) *m* working, operation
fonctionner (fawngk-s^yo-*nay*) *v* work, operate
fond (fawng) *m* ground, bottom; essence; background; **à ~** thoroughly; **au ~** fundamentally; **~ de teint** foundation cream
fondamental (fawng-dah-mahng-*tahl*) *adj* fundamental, basic, essential
fondation (fawng-dah-s^y*awng*) *f* foundation
fondement (fawngd-*mahng*) *m* base
fonder (fawng-*day*) *v* found; **bien fondé** well-founded
fonderie (fawng-*dree*) *f* ironworks
fondre (fawngdr) *v* melt; thaw
fonds (fawng) *mpl* fund
fontaine (fawng-*tehn*) *f* fountain
fonte (fawngt) *f* cast iron

football (foot-*bol*) *m* soccer
force (fors) *f* force, power, strength; **~ armée** military force; **~ motrice** driving force
forcément (for-say-*mahng*) *adv* by force
forcer (for-*say*) *v* force; strain
forer (fo-*ray*) *v* drill, bore
forestier (fo-reh-st^y*ay*) *m* forester
forêt (fo-*ray*) *f* forest
foreuse (fo-*rūrz*) *f* drill
forgeron (for-zher-*rawng*) *m* smith, blacksmith
formalité (for-mah-lee-*tay*) *f* formality
format (for-*mah*) *m* size
formation (for-mah-s^y*awng*) *f* background
forme (form) *f* shape, form; figure; condition
formel (for-*mehl*) *adj* explicit
former (for-*may*) *v* shape, form; train, educate
formidable (for-mee-*dahbl*) *adj* fine, swell; terrific
formulaire (for-mew-*lair*) *m* form; **~ d'inscription** registration form
formule (for-*mewl*) *f* formula
fort (fawr) *adj* powerful, strong; loud; *m* fort
fortement (for-ter-*mahng*) *adv* tight
forteresse (for-ter-*rehss*) *f* fortress
fortuit (for-*twee*) *adj* casual, incidental
fortune (for-*tewn*) *f* fortune
fosse (foass) *f* pit
fossé (foa-*say*) *m* ditch
fou[1] (foo) *adj* (fol; f folle) crazy, mad; insane, lunatic
fou[2] (foo) *m* fool
foudre (foodr) *f* lightning
fouet (fway) *m* whip
fouetter (fway-*tay*) *v* whip
fouille (foo^{ee}) *f* search
fouiller (foo-^y*ay*) *v* search; *dig

fouillis (foo-*Yee*) *m* muddle

foulard (foo-*laar*) *m* scarf

foule (fool) *f* crowd

fouler (foo-*lay*) *v* sprain

foulure (foo-*lewr*) *f* sprain

four (foor) *m* oven

fourbe (foorb) *adj* hypocritical

fourchette (foor-*sheht*) *f* fork

fourgon (foor-*gawng*) *m* luggage van; van

fourmi (foor-*mee*) *f* ant

fournaise (foor-*naiz*) *f* furnace

fourneau (foor-*noa*) *m* stove; ~ **à gaz** gas stove

fournir (foor-*neer*) *v* provide, furnish, supply

fourniture (foor-nee-*tewr*) *f* supply

fourreur (foo-*rŭr*) *m* furrier

fourrure (foo-*rewr*) *f* fur

foyer (fwah-*Yay*) *m* foyer, lounge; home; focus

fracas (frah-*kah*) *m* noise

fraction (frahk-*sYawng*) *f* fraction

fracture (frahk-*tewr*) *f* break, fracture

fracturer (frahk-tew-*ray*) *v* fracture

fragile (frah-*zheel*) *adj* fragile

fragment (frahg-*mahng*) *m* extract, fragment

frais[1] (fray) *adj* (f fraîche) fresh; chilly, cool

frais[2] (fray) *mpl* expenses *pl*, expenditure; ~ **de voyage** travelling expenses

fraise (fraiz) *f* strawberry

framboise (frahng-*bwaaz*) *f* raspberry

franc (frahng) *adj* (f franche) open

Français (frahng-*say*) *m* Frenchman

français (frahng-*say*) *adj* French

France (frahngss) *f* France

franchir (frahng-*sheer*) *v* cross

franc-tireur (frahng-tee-*rŭr*) *m* sniper

frange (frahngzh) *f* fringe

frappant (frah-*pahng*) *adj* striking

frappé (frah-*pay*) *m* milk-shake

frapper (frah-*pay*) *v* *beat; *hit, bump, tap, knock, *strike

fraternité (frah-tehr-nee-*tay*) *f* fraternity

fraude (frōad) *f* fraud

frayeur (freh-*Yŭr*) *f* fright

fredonner (frer-do-*nay*) *v* hum

frein (frang) *m* brake; ~ **à main** hand-brake; ~ **à pédale** foot-brake

freiner (fray-*nay*) *v* slow down, curb

fréquemment (fray-kah-*mahng*) *adv* frequently

fréquence (fray-*kahngss*) *f* frequency

fréquent (fray-*kahng*) *adj* frequent

fréquenter (fray-kahng-*tay*) *v* associate with, mix with

frère (frair) *m* brother

fret (fray) *m* freight

en friche (ahng freesh) waste

friction (freek-*sYawng*) *f* friction

frigidaire (free-zhee-*dair*) *m* refrigerator

frigo (free-*goa*) *m* fridge

fripon (free-*pawng*) *m* rascal

***frire** (freer) *v* fry

friser (free-*zay*) *v* curl

frisson (free-*sawng*) *m* shudder, chill, shiver

frissonnant (free-so-*nahng*) *adj* shivery

frissonner (free-so-*nay*) *v* tremble, shiver

froid (frwah) *m* cold; *adj* cold

froisser (frwah-*say*) *v* crease

fromage (fro-*maazh*) *m* cheese

front (frawng) *m* forehead

frontière (frawng-*tYair*) *f* border; frontier, boundary

frotter (fro-*tay*) *v* rub, scrub

fruit (frwee) *m* fruit

fugitif (few-zhee-*teef*) *m* runaway

***fuir** (fweer) *v* escape; leak

fuite (fweet) *f* flight; leak

fume-cigarettes (fewm-see-gah-*reht*)

m cigarette-holder
fumée (few-*may*) *f* smoke
fumer (few-*may*) *v* smoke
fumeur (few-*mūrr*) *m* smoker; **compartiment fumeurs** smoker
fumier (few-m*ʸay*) *m* manure; dung; **tas de ~** dunghill
fumoir (few-*mwaar*) *m* smoking-room
funérailles (few-nay-*righ*) *fpl* funeral
fureur (few-*rūrr*) *f* anger, rage
furibond (few-ree-*bawng*) *adj* furious
furieux (few-r*ʸur*) *adj* furious
furoncle (few-*rawngkl*) *m* boil
fusée (few-*zay*) *f* rocket
fusible (few-*zeebl*) *m* fuse
fusil (few-*zee*) *m* rifle, gun
fusion (few-z*ʸawng*) *f* merger
futile (few-*teel*) *adj* petty, insignificant, idle
futur (few-*tēwr*) *adj* future

G

gâcher (gah-*shay*) *v* mess up
gâchette (gah-*sheht*) *f* trigger
gâchis (gah-*shee*) *m* mess
gadget (gah-*jeht*) *m* gadget
gadoue (gah-*doo*) *f* muck
gages (gaazh) *mpl* wages *pl*; **donner en gage** pawn
gagner (gah-*ñay*) *v* *win; *make; earn, gain
gai (gay) *adj* jolly, cheerful, gay
gain (gang) *m* gain; **gains** earnings *pl*; winnings *pl*
gaine (gehn) *f* girdle
gaîté (gay-*tay*) *f* gaiety
galerie (gahl-*ree*) *f* gallery; **~ d'art** art gallery
galet (gah-*lay*) *m* pebble
galop (gah-*loa*) *m* gallop
gamin (gah-*mang*) *m* boy

gamme (gahm) *f* scale; range
gant (gahng) *m* glove
garage (gah-*raazh*) *m* garage
garagiste (gah-rah-*zheest*) *m* garage proprietor
garant (gah-*rahng*) *m* guarantor
garantie (gah-rahng-*tee*) *f* guarantee
garantir (gah-rahng-*teer*) *v* guarantee
garçon (gahr-*sawng*) *m* boy; lad; waiter
garde (gahrd) *m* guard; *f* custody; **~ du corps** bodyguard; *prendre ~** watch out
garde-boue (gahrd-*boo*) *m* mud-guard
garde-manger (gahrd-mahng-*zhay*) *m* larder
garder (gahr-*day*) *v* *keep; *hold
garde-robe (gahr-*drob*) *f* wardrobe; closet *nAm*
gardien (gahr-d*ʸang*) *m* attendant, warden; custodian; caretaker; **~ de but** goalkeeper
gardon (gahr-*dawng*) *m* roach
gare (gaar) *f* station; depot *nAm*
garer (gah-*ray*) *v* garage; **se ~** park
se gargariser (gahr-gah-ree-*zay*) gargle
gars (gah) *m* fellow
gaspillage (gah-spee-ʸ*aazh*) *m* waste
gaspiller (gah-spee-ʸ*ay*) *v* waste
gaspilleur (gah-spee-ʸ*ūrr*) *adj* wasteful
gastrique (gah-*streek*) *adj* gastric
gâteau (gah-*toa*) *m* cake
gâter (gah-*tay*) *v* *spoil
gauche (gōash) *adj* left; **de ~** left-hand
gaucher (goa-*shay*) *adj* left-handed
gaufre (gōafr) *f* waffle
gaufrette (goa-*freht*) *f* wafer
gaz (gaaz) *m* gas; **~ d'échappement** exhaust gases
gaze (gaaz) *f* gauze
gazon (gah-*zawng*) *m* lawn
géant (zhay-*ahng*) *m* giant
gel (zhehl) *m* frost

gelée (zher-*lay*) *f* jelly

geler (zher-*lay*) *v* *freeze

gémir (zhay-*meer*) *v* groan, moan

gênant (zheh-*nahng*) *adj* inconvenient, troublesome

gencive (zhahng-*seev*) *f* gum

gendre (zhahngdr) *m* son-in-law

gêner (zhay-*nay*) *v* hinder; embarrass, bother; **se ~** *be embarrassed

général (zhay-nay-*rahl*) *m* general; *adj* universal, public, general; **en ~** as a rule, in general

généralement (zhay-nay-rahl-*mahng*) *adv* as a rule

générateur (zhay-nay-rah-*türr*) *m* generator

génération (zhay-nay-rah-*syawng*) *f* generation

généreux (zhay-nay-*rur*) *adj* liberal, generous

générosité (zhay-nay-ro-zee-*tay*) *f* generosity

génie (zhay-*nee*) *m* genius

génital (zhay-nee-*tahl*) *adj* genital

genou (zher-*noo*) *m* (pl ~x) knee

genre (zhahngr) *m* kind; gender

gens (zhahng) *mpl/fpl* people *pl*

gentil (zhahng-*tee*) *adj* friendly, kind; nice; sweet

géographie (zhay-o-grah-*fee*) *f* geography

geôlier (zhoa-*lyay*) *m* jailer

géologie (zhay-o-lo-*zhee*) *f* geology

géométrie (zhay-o-may-*tree*) *f* geometry

germe (zhehrm) *m* germ

geste (zhehst) *m* sign

gesticuler (zheh-stee-kew-*lay*) *v* gesticulate

gestion (zheh-*styawng*) *f* management, administration

gibet (zhee-*bay*) *m* gallows *pl*

gibier (zhee-*byay*) *m* game

gigantesque (zhee-gahng-*tehsk*) *adj* gigantic, enormous

gilet (zhee-*lay*) *m* waistcoat; vest *nAm*

gingembre (zhang-*zhahngbr*) *m* ginger

glace (glahss) *f* ice; ice-cream

glacial (glah-*syahl*) *adj* freezing

glacier (glah-*syay*) *m* glacier

gland (glahng) *m* acorn

glande (glahngd) *f* gland

glissade (glee-*sahd*) *f* slide

glissant (glee-*sahng*) *adj* slippery

glisser (glee-*say*) *v* *slide, glide; slip

global (glo-*bahl*) *adj* broad

globe (glob) *m* globe

gloire (glwaar) *f* glory

glousser (gloo-*say*) *v* chuckle; giggle

gluant (glew-*ahng*) *adj* sticky

gobelet (go-*blay*) *m* mug, tumbler

goéland (go-ay-*lahng*) *m* seagull

golf (golf) *m* golf; **terrain de ~** golflinks

golfe (golf) *m* gulf

gomme (gom) *f* gum; rubber, eraser

gondole (gawng-*dol*) *f* gondola

gonflable (gawng-*flahbl*) *adj* inflatable

gonfler (gawng-*flay*) *v* inflate

gorge (gorzh) *f* throat; gorge, glen

gorgée (gor-*zhay*) *f* sip

gosse (goss) *m* kid, boy

goudron (goo-*drawng*) *m* tar

goulot d'étranglement (goo-lo day-trahng-gler-*mahng*) bottleneck

gourdin (goor-*dang*) *m* club, cudgel

gourmand (goor-*mahng*) *adj* greedy

gourmet (goor-*may*) *m* gourmet

goût (goo) *m* taste; ***avoir ~ de** taste

goûter (goo-*tay*) *v* taste

goutte (goot) *f* drop; gout

gouvernail (goo-vehr-*nigh*) *m* rudder

gouvernante (goo-vehr-*nahngt*) *f* governess; housekeeper

gouvernement (goo-vehr-ner-*mahng*) *m* rule, government

gouverner (goo-vehr-*nay*) *v* rule, govern

gouverneur (goo-vehr-*nūrr*) *m* governor

grâce (graass) *f* grace; pardon; ~ **à** thanks to

gracieux (grah-s*y*ur) *adj* graceful; à **titre** ~ free of charge

grade (grahd) *m* grade; degree, rank

graduel (grah-*dwehl*) *adj* gradual

graduellement (grah-dwehl-*mahng*) *adv* gradually

grain (grang) *m* corn, grain

graisse (grehss) *f* grease, fat

graisser (gray-*say*) *v* grease

graisseux (greh-*sur*) *adj* greasy

grammaire (grah-*mair*) *f* grammar

grammatical (grah-mah-tee-*kahl*) *adj* grammatical

gramme (grahm) *m* gram

grand (grahng) *adj* great; tall, big, major

Grande-Bretagne (grahngd-brer-*tahñ*) *f* Great Britain

grandeur (grahng-*dūrr*) *f* size

grandiose (grahng-d*y*ōāz) *adj* superb, magnificent

grandir (grahng-*deer*) *v* *grow

grand-mère (grahng-*mair*) *f* grandmother

grand-papa (grahng-pah-*pah*) *m* granddad

grand-père (grahng-*pair*) *m* grandfather

grands-parents (grahng-pah-*rahng*) *mpl* grandparents *pl*

grange (grahngzh) *f* barn

granit (grah-*neet*) *m* granite

graphique (grah-*feek*) *adj* graphic; *m* diagram; chart

gras (grah) *adj* (f ~se) fatty, fat

gratitude (grah-tee-*tewd*) *f* gratitude

gratte-ciel (grah-ts*y*ehl) *m* skyscraper

gratter (grah-*tay*) *v* scratch

gratuit (grah-*twee*) *adj* gratis, free of

charge, free

grave (graav) *adj* grave; bad, severe

graver (grah-*vay*) *v* engrave

graveur (grah-*vūrr*) *m* engraver

gravier (grah-v*y*ay) *m* gravel

gravillon (grah-vee-*yawng*) *m* grit

gravité (grah-vee-*tay*) *f* gravity

gravure (grah-*vewr*) *f* engraving; picture; carving

Grec (grehk) *m* Greek

grec (grehk) *adj* (f grecque) Greek

Grèce (grehss) *f* Greece

greffier (gray-f*y*ay) *m* clerk

grêle (grehl) *f* hail

grenier (grer-n*y*ay) *m* attic

grenouille (grer-noo^ee) *f* frog

grève (graiv) *f* strike; *faire ~ *strike

gréviste (gray-*veest*) *m* striker

griffe (greef) *f* claw

grill (greel) *m* grill

grille (greey) *f* gate; grate

griller (gree-*Yay*) *v* roast; grill

grillon (gree-*Yawng*) *m* cricket

grimper (grang-*pay*) *v* climb

grincer (grang-*say*) *v* creak

grippe (greep) *f* flu, influenza

gris (gree) *adj* grey

grive (greev) *f* thrush

grogner (gro-*ñay*) *v* grumble, growl

grondement (grawngd-*mahng*) *m* roar

gronder (grawng-*day*) *v* thunder; scold

gros (groa) *adj* (f -se) big; thick, fat, corpulent, stout

groseille (groa-*zay*) *f* currant; ~ **à maquereau** gooseberry

grosse (grōāss) *f* gross

grossier (groa-s*y*ay) *adj* coarse, gross, rude

grossir (gro-*seer*) *v* increase; *put on weight

grossiste (groa-*seest*) *m* wholesale dealer

grotesque (gro-*tehsk*) *adj* ludicrous

grotte (grot) f cave; grotto

groupe (groop) m group; party, set

grouper (groo-pay) v group

grue (grew) f crane

grumeau (grew-moa) m lump

grumeleux (grewm-lur) adj lumpy

gué (gay) m ford

guêpe (gehp) f wasp

ne ... guère (ner ... gair) scarcely

guérir (gay-reer) v cure; heal, recover

guérison (gay-ree-zawng) f recovery, cure

guérisseur (gay-ree-sūrr) m quack

guerre (gair) f war; **d'avant-guerre** pre-war; ~ **mondiale** world war

guetter (gay-tay) v watch for

gueule (gurl) f mouth; ~ **de bois** hangover

guichet (gee-shay) m box-office; ~ **de location** box-office

guide (geed) m guide; guidebook

guider (gee-day) v *lead

guillemets (geey-may) mpl quotation marks

guitare (gee-taar) f guitar

gymnase (zheem-naaz) m gymnasium

gymnaste (zheem-nahst) m gymnast

gymnastique (zheem-nah-steek) f gymnastics pl

gynécologue (zhee-nay-ko-log) m gynaecologist

H

habile (ah-beel) adj skilful; skilled

habileté (ah-beel-tay) f skill, art

habiller (ah-bee-Yay) v dress

habitable (ah-bee-tahbl) adj inhabitable, habitable

habitant (ah-bee-tahng) m inhabitant

habitation (ah-bee-tah-sYawng) f house

habiter (ah-bee-tay) v inhabit, live

habits (ah-bee) mpl clothes pl

habitude (ah-bee-tewd) f habit; custom; *avoir l'habitude de** would; **d'habitude** usually

habitué (ah-bee-tway) adj accustomed; *être ~ à** *be used to

habituel (ah-bee-twehl) adj common, habitual, ordinary

habituellement (ah-bee-twehl-mahng) adv usually

s'habituer *get accustomed

hache ('ahsh) f axe

hacher ('ah-shay) v chop, mince

haie ('ay) f hedge

haine ('ehn) f hatred, hate

***haïr** ('ah-eer) v hate

hâlé ('ah-lay) adj tanned

haleter ('ahl-tay) v pant

hamac ('ah-mahk) m hammock

hameau ('ah-moa) m hamlet

hameçon (ahm-sawng) m fishing hook

hanche ('ahngsh) f hip

handicapé ('ahng-dee-kah-pay) adj disabled

hardi ('ahr-dee) adj bold

hareng ('ah-rahng) m herring

haricot ('ah-ree-koa) m bean

harmonie (ahr-mo-nee) f harmony

harmonieux (ahr-mo-nYur) adj tuneful

harpe ('ahrp) f harp

hasard ('ah-zaar) m chance, luck; hazard; **par ~** by chance

hâte ('aat) f hurry, speed, haste

se hâter ('ah-tay) hasten

hausse ('ōass) f rise

haut ('oa) m top side; adj high, tall; **en ~** upstairs, above, overhead; up; **vers le ~** upwards

hautain ('oa-tang) adj haughty

hauteur ('oa-tūrr) f height; *être à la ~ de** *keep up with

haut-parleur ('oa-pahr-lūrr) m loud-speaker

havresac ('ah-vrer-*sahk*) *m* haversack; knapsack

hebdomadaire (ehb-do-mah-*dair*) *adj* weekly

hébreu (ay-*brur*) *m* Hebrew

hélas ('ay-*laass*) *adv* unfortunately

hélice (ay-*leess*) *f* propeller

hémorragie (ay-mo-rah-*zhee*) *f* haemorrhage

hémorroïdes (ay-mo-ro-*eed*) *fpl* piles *pl*, haemorrhoids *pl*

herbe (ehrb) *f* grass; herb; **mauvaise ~** weed

héréditaire (ay-ray-dee-*tair*) *adj* hereditary

hérisson ('ay-ree-*sawng*) *m* hedgehog

héritage (ay-ree-*taazh*) *m* inheritance

hériter (ay-ree-*tay*) *v* inherit

hermétique (ehr-may-*teek*) *adj* airtight

hernie ('ehr-*nee*) *f* hernia; slipped disc

héron ('ay-*rawng*) *m* heron

héros ('ay-*roa*) *m* hero

hésiter (ay-zee-*tay*) *v* hesitate

hétérosexuel (ay-tay-ro-sehk-*swehl*) *adj* heterosexual

hêtre ('aitr*) *m* beech

heure (ürr) *f* hour; **à ... heures** at ... o'clock; **~ d'arrivée** time of arrival; **~ de départ** time of departure; **~ de pointe** rush-hour; **~ d'été** summer time; **heures de bureau** office hours; **heures de consultation** consultation hours; **heures de visite** visiting hours; **heures d'ouverture** business hours; **tout à l'heure** presently; **toutes les heures** hourly

heureux (ur-*rur*) *adj* fortunate, happy

heurter ('urr-*tay*) *v* knock

hibou ('ee-*boo*) *m* (pl ~x) owl

hideux ('ee-*dur*) *adj* hideous

hier (Yair) *adv* yesterday

hiérarchie ('Yay-rahr-*shee*) *f* hierarchy

hippodrome (ee-po-*drom*) *m* racecourse

hirondelle (ee-rawng-*dehl*) *f* swallow

hisser ('ee-*say*) *v* hoist

histoire (ee-*stwaar*) *f* history; story; **~ d'amour** love-story; **~ de l'art** art history

historien (ee-sto-r^y*ang*) *m* historian

historique (ee-sto-*reek*) *adj* historic; historical

hiver (ee-*vair*) *m* winter

hobby ('o-*bee*) *m* hobby

hockey ('o-*kay*) *m* hockey

Hollandais ('o-lahng-*day*) *m* Dutchman

hollandais ('o-lahng-*day*) *adj* Dutch

Hollande ('o-*lahngd*) *f* Holland

homard ('o-*maar*) *m* lobster

hommage (o-*maazh*) *m* homage, tribute; **rendre ~** honour

homme (om) *m* man; **~ d'affaires** businessman; **~ d'Etat** statesman

homosexuel (o-mo-sehk-*swehl*) *adj* homosexual

Hongrie ('awng-*gree*) *f* Hungary

Hongrois ('awng-*grwah*) *m* Hungarian

hongrois ('awng-*grwah*) *adj* Hungarian

honnête (o-*neht*) *adj* honourable, honest; fair

honnêteté (o-neht-*tay*) *f* honesty

honneur (o-*nürr*) *m* honour, glory

honorable (o-no-*rahbl*) *adj* honourable, respectable

honoraires (o-no-*rair*) *mpl* fee

honorer (o-no-*ray*) *v* honour

honte ('awngt*) *f* shame; *avoir ~* *be ashamed; **quelle honte!** shame!

honteux ('awng-*tur*) *adj* ashamed

hôpital (o-pee-*tahl*) *m* hospital

hoquet ('o-*kay*) *m* hiccup

horaire (o-*rair*) *m* timetable, schedule

horizon (o-ree-*zawng*) *m* horizon

horizontal (o-ree-zawng-*tahl*) *adj* horizontal

horloge (or-*lawzh*) *f* clock

horloger (or-lo-*zhay*) *m* watch-maker

horreur (o-*rūrr*) *f* horror

horrible (o-*reebl*) *adj* horrible

horrifiant (o-ree-*f*y*ahng*) *adj* horrible

hors ('*awr*) *adv* out; ~ **de** outside

hors-d'œuvre ('or-*dūrvr*) *m* hors-d'œuvre

horticulture (or-tee-kewl-*tewr*) *f* horticulture

hospice (o-*speess*) *m* asylum

hospitalier (o-spee-tah-*l*y*ay*) *adj* hospitable

hospitalité (o-spee-tah-lee-*tay*) *f* hospitality

hostile (o-*steel*) *adj* hostile

hôte (ōat) *m* host; guest

hôtel (oa-*tehl*) *m* hotel; ~ **de ville** town hall

hôtesse (oa-*tehss*) *f* hostess; receptionist; ~ **de l'air** stewardess

houblon ('oo-*blawng*) *m* hop

houppette ('oo-*peht*) *f* powder-puff

housse ('*ooss*) *f* sleeve

hublot ('ew-*bloa*) *m* porthole

huile (weel) *f* oil; ~ **capillaire** hair-oil; ~ **de table** salad-oil; ~ **d'olive** olive oil; ~ **solaire** suntan oil

huiler (wee-*lay*) *v* lubricate

huileux (wee-*lur*) *adj* oily

huissier (wee-s*y*ay*) *m* bailiff

huit ('*weet*) *num* eight

huitième ('wee-*t*y*ehm*) *num* eighth

huître (weetr) *f* oyster

humain (ew-*mang*) *adj* human

humanité (ew-mah-nee-*tay*) *f* mankind, humanity

humble (urngbl) *adj* humble

humecter (ew-mehk-*tay*) *v* moisten

humeur (ew-*mūrr*) *f* mood, spirit

humide (ew-*meed*) *adj* humid; wet, damp

humidifier (ew-mee-dee-*f*y*ay*) *v* damp

humidité (ew-mee-dee-*tay*) *f* humidity, moisture, damp

humour (ew-*mōōr*) *m* humour

hurler ('ewr-*lay*) *v* yell, scream

hutte ('*ewt*) *f* hut

hydrogène (ee-dro-*zhehn*) *m* hydrogen

hygiène (ee-zh*y*ehn*) *f* hygiene

hygiénique (ee-zh*y*ay-*neek*) *adj* hygienic

hymne (eemn) *m* hymn; ~ **national** national anthem

hypocrisie (ee-po-kree-*zee*) *f* hypocrisy

hypocrite (ee-po-*kreet*) *m* hypocrite; *adj* hypocritical

hypothèque (ee-po-*tehk*) *f* mortgage

hystérique (ee-stay-*reek*) *adj* hysterical

I

ici (ee-*see*) *adv* here

icône (ee-*kōan*) *f* icon

idéal[1] (ee-day-*ahl*) *adj* (pl -aux) ideal

idéal[2] (ee-day-*ahl*) *m* (pl ~s, -aux) ideal

idée (ee-*day*) *f* idea; opinion; ~ **lumineuse** brain-wave

identification (ee-dahng-tee-fee-kah-s*y*awng*) *f* identification

identifier (ee-dahng-tee-*f*y*ay*) *v* identify

identique (ee-dahng-*teek*) *adj* identical

identité (ee-dahng-tee-*tay*) *f* identity

idiomatique (ee-d*y*o-mah-*teek*) *adj* idiomatic

idiome (ee-d*y*ōam*) *m* idiom

idiot (ee-d*y*oa*) *m* fool, idiot; *adj* idiotic

idole (ee-*dol*) f idol

idylle (ee-*deel*) f romance

ignifuge (eeg-nee-*fewzh*) adj fireproof

ignorant (ee-ño-*rahng*) adj ignorant; uneducated

ignorer (ee-ño-*ray*) v ignore; overlook

il (eel) pron he

île (eel) f island

illégal (ee-lay-*gahl*) adj illegal

illettré (ee-leh-*tray*) m illiterate

illicite (ee-lee-*seet*) adj unlawful, unauthorized

illimité (ee-lee-mee-*tay*) adj unlimited

illisible (ee-lee-*zeebl*) adj illegible

illumination (ee-lew-mee-nah-*s*ʸ*awng*) f illumination

illuminer (ee-lew-mee-*nay*) v illuminate

illusion (ee-lew-*z*ʸ*awng*) f illusion

illustration (ee-lew-strah-*s*ʸ*awng*) f illustration; picture

illustre (ee-*lewstr*) adj noted

illustré (ee-lew-*stray*) m magazine

illustrer (ee-lew-*stray*) v illustrate

ils (eel) pron they

image (ee-*maazh*) f picture, image

imaginaire (ee-mah-zhee-*nair*) adj imaginary

imagination (ee-mah-zhee-nah-*s*ʸ*awng*) f fancy, imagination

imaginer (ee-mah-zhee-*nay*) v fancy, imagine; **s'imaginer** fancy, imagine

imitation (ee-mee-tah-*s*ʸ*awng*) f imitation

imiter (ee-mee-*tay*) v imitate, copy

immaculé (ee-mah-kew-*lay*) adj stainless, spotless

immangeable (ang-mahng-*zhahbl*) adj inedible

immédiat (ee-may-*d*ʸ*ah*) adj immediate

immédiatement (ee-may-*d*ʸ*aht-mahng*) adv at once, instantly, immediately

immense (ee-*mahngss*) adj immense; vast, huge

immérité (ee-may-ree-*tay*) adj unearned

immeuble (ee-*murbl*) m house; ~ **d'habitation** block of flats; apartment house Am

immigrant (ee-mee-*grahng*) m immigrant

immigration (ee-mee-grah-*s*ʸ*awng*) f immigration

immigrer (ee-mee-*gray*) v immigrate

immobile (ee-mo-*beel*) adj motionless

immodeste (ee-mo-*dehst*) adj immodest

immondices (ee-mawng-*deess*) fpl litter

immuniser (ee-mew-nee-*zay*) v immunize

immunité (ee-mew-nee-*tay*) f immunity

impair (ang-*pair*) adj odd

imparfait (ang-pahr-*fay*) adj imperfect; faulty

impartial (ang-pahr-*s*ʸ*ahl*) adj impartial

impatient (ang-pah-*s*ʸ*ahng*) adj impatient; eager

impeccable (ang-peh-*kahbl*) adj faultless

impératrice (ang-pay-rah-*treess*) f empress

imperfection (ang-pehr-fehk-*s*ʸ*awng*) f shortcoming; fault

impérial (ang-pay-*r*ʸ*ahl*) adj imperial

imperméable (ang-pehr-may-*ahbl*) m mackintosh, raincoat; adj waterproof, rainproof

impersonnel (ang-pehr-so-*nehl*) adj impersonal

impertinence (ang-pehr-tee-*nahngss*) f impertinence

impertinent (ang-pehr-tee-*nahng*) adj

impertinent

impétueux (ang-pay-*twur*) *adj* rash

impliquer (ang-plee-*kay*) *v* involve, imply

impoli (ang-po-*lee*) *adj* impolite

impopulaire (ang-po-pew-*lair*) *adj* unpopular

importance (ang-por-*tahngss*) *f* importance; ***avoir de l'importance** matter; **sans ~** insignificant

important (ang-por-*tahng*) *adj* important; considerable, big

importateur (ang-por-tah-*tūrr*) *m* importer

importation (ang-por-tah-*syawng*) *f* import; **taxe d'importation** import duty

importer (ang-por-*tay*) *v* import

imposable (ang-poa-*zahbl*) *adj* dutiable

imposant (ang-poa-*zahng*) *adj* imposing

imposer (ang-poa-*zay*) *v* tax

impossible (ang-po-*seebl*) *adj* impossible

impôt (ang-*poa*) *m* tax; **~ sur le chiffre d'affaires** turnover tax; **~ sur le revenu** income-tax

impotence (ang-po-*tahngss*) *f* impotence

impotent (ang-po-*tahng*) *adj* impotent

impraticable (ang-prah-tee-*kahbl*) *adj* impassable

impression (ang-preh-*syawng*) *f* impression; sensation; ***faire ~ sur** impress

impressionnant (ang-preh-syo-*nahng*) *adj* impressive

impressionner (ang-preh-syo-*nay*) *v* impress

imprévu (ang-pray-*vew*) *adj* unexpected

imprimé (ang-pree-*may*) *m* printed matter

imprimer (ang-pree-*may*) *v* print

imprimerie (ang-preem-*ree*) *f* printing office

improbable (ang-pro-*bahbl*) *adj* improbable, unlikely

impropre (ang-*propr*) *adj* improper, unfit; wrong

improviser (ang-pro-vee-*zay*) *v* improvise

imprudent (ang-prew-*dahng*) *adj* unwise

impuissant (ang-pwee-*sahng*) *adj* powerless

impulsif (ang-pewl-*seef*) *adj* impulsive

impulsion (ang-pewl-*syawng*) *f* urge, impulse

inabordable (ee-nah-bor-*dahbl*) *adj* prohibitive

inacceptable (ee-nahk-sehp-*tahbl*) *adj* unacceptable

inaccessible (ee-nahk-say-*seebl*) *adj* inaccessible

inadéquat (ee-nah-day-*kwah*) *adj* inadequate, unsuitable

inadvertance (ee-nahd-vehr-*tahngss*) *f* oversight

inattendu (ee-nah-tahng-*dew*) *adj* unexpected

inattentif (ee-nah-tahng-*teef*) *adj* careless

incapable (ang-kah-*pahbl*) *adj* incapable, unable

incassable (ang-kah-*sahbl*) *adj* unbreakable

incendie (ang-sahng-*dee*) *m* fire; **alarme d'incendie** fire-alarm

incertain (ang-sehr-*tang*) *adj* doubtful, uncertain

incident (ang-see-*dahng*) *m* incident

incinérer (ang-see-nay-*ray*) *v* cremate

incision (ang-see-*zyawng*) *f* cut

inciter (ang-see-*tay*) *v* incite

inclinaison (ang-klee-neh-*zawng*) *f* gradient

inclination (ang-klee-nah-s^yawng) f
tendency; ~ **de la tête** nod

incliné (ang-klee-nay) adj slanting

s'incliner (ang-klee-nay) slant

*__**include**__ (ang-kle͞wr) v include, en-
close; comprise, count

incompétent (ang-kawng-pay-tahng)
adj incompetent, unqualified

incomplet (ang-kawng-play) adj (f -
plète) incomplete

inconcevable (ang-kawng-svahbl) adj
inconceivable

inconditionnel (ang-kawng-dee-s^yo-
nehl) adj unconditional

inconfortable (ang-kawng-for-tahbl)
adj uncomfortable

inconnu (ang-ko-new) adj unknown,
unfamiliar; m stranger

inconscient (ang-kawng-s^yahng) adj
unconscious; unaware

inconsidéré (ang-kawng-see-day-ray)
adj rash

inconvénient (ang-kawng-vay-n^yahng)
m inconvenience

incorrect (ang-ko-rehkt) adj incorrect,
inaccurate, wrong

incroyable (ang-krwah-^yahbl) adj incredible

inculte (ang-kewlt) adj uncultivated

incurable (ang-kew-rahbl) adj incurable

Inde (angd) f India

indécent (ang-day-sahng) adj indecent

indéfini (ang-day-fee-nee) adj indefinite

indemne (ang-dehmn) adj unhurt

indemnité (ang-dehm-nee-tay) f compensation, indemnity

indépendance (ang-day-pahng-
dahngss) f independence

indépendant (ang-day-pahng-dahng)
adj independent; self-employed

indésirable (ang-day-zee-rahbl) adj

undesirable

index (ang-dehks) m index finger; index

indicatif (ang-dee-kah-teef) m area
code

indication (ang-dee-kah-s^yawng) f indi-
dication

Indien (ang-d^yang) m Indian

indien (ang-d^yang) adj Indian

indifférent (ang-dee-fay-rahng) adj indifferent

indigène (ang-dee-zhehn) m native;
adj native

indigent (ang-dee-zhahng) adj poor

indigestion (ang-dee-zheh-st^yawng) f
indigestion

indignation (ang-dee-ñah-s^yawng) f
indignation

indiquer (ang-dee-kay) v point out, indicate; declare

indirect (ang-dee-rehkt) adj indirect

indispensable (ang-dee-spahng-sahbl)
adj essential

indisposé (ang-dee-spoa-zay) adj unwell

indistinct (ang-dee-stang) adj dim

individu (ang-dee-vee-dew) m individual

individuel (ang-dee-vee-dwehl) adj individual

Indonésie (ang-do-nay-zee) f Indonesia

Indonésien (ang-do-nay-z^yang) m Indonesian

indonésien (ang-do-nay-z^yang) adj Indonesian

industrie (ang-dew-stree) f industry

industriel (ang-dew-stree-ehl) adj industrial

industrieux (ang-dew-stree-ur) adj industrious

inefficace (ee-nay-fee-kahss) adj inefficient

inégal (ee-nay-gahl) adj uneven, unequal

inéquitable (ee-nay-kee-*tahbl*) *adj* unfair

inestimable (ee-neh-stee-*mahbl*) *adj* priceless

inévitable (ee-nay-vee-*tahbl*) *adj* inevitable, unavoidable

inexact (ee-nehg-*zahkt*) *adj* false, incorrect

inexpérimenté (ee-nehk-spay-ree-mahng-*tay*) *adj* inexperienced

inexplicable (ee-nehk-splee-*kahbl*) *adj* unaccountable

infâme (ang-*faam*) *adj* foul

infanterie (ang-fahng-*tree*) *f* infantry

infecter (ang-fehk-*tay*) *v* infect; **s'infecter** *become septic

infectieux (ang-fehk-*s*ʸ*ur*) *adj* infectious

infection (ang-fehk-*s*ʸ*awng*) *f* infection

inférieur (ang-fay-r*ʸ*ūrr) *adj* inferior, bottom

infidèle (ang-fee-*dehl*) *adj* unfaithful

infini (ang-fee-*nee*) *adj* infinite, endless

infinitif (ang-fee-nee-*teef*) *m* infinitive

infirme (ang-*feerm*) *m* invalid; *adj* invalid

infirmerie (ang-feer-mer-*ree*) *f* infirmary

infirmière (ang-feer-*m*ʸ*air*) *f* nurse

inflammable (ang-flah-*mahbl*) *adj* inflammable

inflammation (ang-flah-mah-*s*ʸ*awng*) *f* inflammation

inflation (ang-flah-*s*ʸ*awng*) *f* inflation

influence (ang-flew-*ahngss*) *f* influence

influencer (ang-flew-ahng-*say*) *v* influence

influent (ang-flew-*ahng*) *adj* influential

information (ang-for-mah-*s*ʸ*awng*) *f*
information; enquiry

informer (ang-for-*may*) *v* inform; **s'informer** inquire, enquire, query

infortune (ang-for-*tewn*) *f* misfortune

infortuné (ang-for-tew-*nay*) *adj* unlucky

infraction (ang-frahk-*s*ʸ*awng*) *f* offence

infrarouge (ang-frah-*rōōzh*) *adj* infrared

infructueux (ang-frewk-*twur*) *adj* unsuccessful

ingénieur (ang-zhay-n*ʸ*ūrr) *m* engineer

ingénu (ang-zhay-*new*) *adj* simple

ingérence (ang-zhay-*rahngss*) *f* interference

ingrat (ang-*grah*) *adj* ungrateful

ingrédient (ang-gray-d*ʸ*ahng) *m* ingredient

inhabitable (ee-nah-bee-*tahbl*) *adj* uninhabitable

inhabité (ee-nah-bee-*tay*) *adj* uninhabited

inhabitué (ee-nah-bee-*tway*) *adj* unaccustomed

inhabituel (ee-nah-bee-*twehl*) *adj* unusual, uncommon

inhaler (ee-nah-*lay*) *v* inhale

ininterrompu (ee-nang-teh-rawng-*pew*) *adj* continuous

initial (ee-nee-s*ʸ*ahl) *adj* initial

initiale (ee-nee-s*ʸ*ahl) *f* initial

initiative (ee-nee-s*ʸ*ah-*teev*) *f* initiative

injecter (ang-zhehk-*tay*) *v* inject

injection (ang-zhehk-*s*ʸ*awng*) *f* injection

injurier (ang-zhew-r*ʸ*ay) *v* call names

injuste (ang-*zhewst*) *adj* unjust, unfair

injustice (ang-zhew-*steess*) *f* injustice

inné (ee-*nay*) *adj* natural

innocence (ee-no-*sahngss*) *f* innocence

innocent (ee-no-*sahng*) *adj* innocent

inoculation (ee-no-kew-lah-*s*ʸ*awng*) *f*

inoculation

inoculer (ee-no-kew-*lay*) v inoculate

inoffensif (ee-no-fahng-*seef*) adj harmless

inondation (ee-nawng-dah-s*yawng*) f flood

inopportun (ee-no-por-*turng*) adj inconvenient, misplaced

inquiet (ang-k*yay*) adj (f -ète) anxious; restless

inquiétant (ang-k*yay*-*tahng*) adj scary

s'inquiéter (ang-k*yay*-*tay*) worry

inquiétude (ang-k*yay*-*tewd*) f worry; unrest

insatisfaisant (ang-sah-teess-fer-*zahng*) adj unsatisfactory

insatisfait (ang-sah-tee-*sfay*) adj dissatisfied

inscription (ang-skree-p*syawng*) f inscription; registration; entry

*** inscrire** (ang-*skreer*) v enter, book; list; **s'* inscrire** check in, register

insecte (ang-*sehkt*) m insect; bug nAm

insecticide (ang-sehk-tee-*seed*) m insecticide

insectifuge (ang-sehk-tee-*fewzh*) m insect repellent

insensé (ang-sahng-*say*) adj crazy, senseless, mad

insensible (ang-sahng-*seebl*) adj insensitive; heartless

insérer (ang-say-*ray*) v insert

insignifiant (ang-see-nee-f*yahng*) adj petty, insignificant, unimportant

insipide (ang-see-*peed*) adj tasteless

insister (ang-see-*stay*) v insist

insolation (ang-so-lah-s*yawng*) f sunstroke

insolence (ang-so-*lahngss*) f insolence

insolent (ang-so-*lahng*) adj insolent, impudent, impertinent

insolite (ang-so-*leet*) adj unusual

insomnie (ang-som-*nee*) f insomnia

insonorisé (ang-so-noa-ree-*zay*) adj soundproof

insouciant (ang-soo-s*yahng*) adj carefree

inspecter (ang-spehk-*tay*) v inspect

inspecteur (ang-spehk-*turr*) m inspector

inspection (ang-spehk-s*yawng*) f inspection

inspirer (ang-spee-*ray*) v inspire

instable (ang-*stahbl*) adj unsteady, unstable

installation (ang-stah-lah-s*yawng*) f installation

installer (ang-stah-*lay*) v install; furnish

instant (ang-*stahng*) m instant, moment; second

instantané (ang-stahng-tah-*nay*) m snapshot; adj prompt

instantanément (ang-stahng-tah-nay-*mahng*) adv instantly

instinct (ang-*stang*) m instinct

instituer (ang-stee-*tway*) v institute

institut (ang-stee-*tew*) m institute; **~ de beauté** beauty parlour

instituteur (ang-stee-tew-*turr*) m master, teacher, schoolteacher, schoolmaster

institution (ang-stee-tew-s*yawng*) f institution; institute

instructeur (ang-strewk-*turr*) m instructor

instructif (ang-strewk-*teef*) adj instructive

instruction (ang-strewk-s*yawng*) f instruction, direction

*** instruire** (ang-*strweer*) v instruct

instrument (ang-strew-*mahng*) m instrument; tool, implement; **~ de musique** musical instrument

insuffisant (ang-sew-fee-*zahng*) adj insufficient

insulte (ang-*sewlt*) f insult

insulter (ang-sewl-*tay*) v insult; scold

insupportable (ang-sew-por-*tahbl*) adj unbearable

insurrection (ang-sew-rehk-s^y*awng*) f rising

intact (ang-*tahkt*) adj whole, intact, unbroken

intellect (ang-teh-*lehkt*) m intellect

intellectuel (ang-teh-lehk-*twehl*) adj intellectual

intelligence (ang-teh-lee-*zhahngss*) f intelligence, intellect, brain

intelligent (ang-teh-lee-*zhahng*) adj intelligent, bright, clever

intense (ang-*tahngss*) adj intense; violent

intention (ang-tahng-s^y*awng*) f intention, purpose; **avoir l'intention de* intend

intentionnel (ang-tahng-s^yo-*nehl*) adj intentional, on purpose

interdiction (ang-tehr-deek-s^y*awng*) f prohibition

*interdire (ang-tehr-*deer*) v *forbid, prohibit

interdit (ang-tehr-*dee*) adj prohibited; ~ **aux piétons** no pedestrians

intéressant (ang-tay-reh-*sahng*) adj interesting

intéresser (ang-tay-ray-*say*) v interest

intérêt (ang-tay-*ray*) m interest

intérieur (ang-tay-r^y*ūr*) m interior, inside; adj internal, inside, inner; indoor; domestic; **à l'intérieur** inside; indoors, within; **à l'intérieur de** inside; **vers l'intérieur** inwards

intérim (ang-tay-*reem*) m interim

interloqué (ang-tehr-lo-*kay*) adj speechless

interlude (ang-tehr-*lewd*) m interlude

intermédiaire (ang-tehr-may-d^y*air*) m intermediary; **servir d'intermédiaire* mediate

internat (ang-tehr-*nah*) m boarding-school

international (ang-tehr-nah-s^yo-*nahl*) adj international

interne (ang-*tehrn*) adj internal, resident

interprète (ang-tehr-*preht*) m interpreter

interpréter (ang-tehr-pray-*tay*) v interpret

interrogatif (ang-teh-ro-gah-*teef*) adj interrogative

interrogatoire (ang-teh-ro-gah-*twaar*) m interrogation, examination

interroger (ang-teh-ro-*zhay*) v interrogate

*interrompre (ang-teh-*rawngpr*) v interrupt; **s'*interrompre** pause

interruption (ang-teh-rew-*ps^yawng*) f interruption

intersection (ang-tehr-sehk-s^y*awng*) f intersection

intervalle (ang-tehr-*vahl*) m interval; space

*intervenir (ang-tehr-ver-*neer*) v intervene, interfere

intervertir (ang-tehr-vehr-*teer*) v invert

intestin (ang-teh-*stang*) m intestine, gut; **intestins** bowels pl

intime (ang-*teem*) adj intimate, cosy

intimité (ang-tee-mee-*tay*) f privacy

intolérable (ang-to-lay-*rahbl*) adj intolerable

intoxication alimentaire (ang-tok-see-kah-s^yawng ah-lee-mahng-*tair*) f food poisoning

intrigue (ang-*treeg*) f intrigue; plot

introduction (ang-tro-dewk-s^y*awng*) f introduction

*introduire (ang-tro-*dweer*) v introduce

intrus (ang-*trew*) m trespasser

inutile (ee-new-*teel*) adj useless

inutilement (ee-new-teel-*mahng*) adv in vain

invalide (ang-vah-*leed*) *adj* disabled

invasion (ang-vah-z*Yawng*) *f* invasion

inventaire (ang-vahng-*tair*) *m* inventory

inventer (ang-vahng-*tay*) *v* invent

inventeur (ang-vahng-*tūrr*) *m* inventor

inventif (ang-vahng-*teef*) *adj* inventive

invention (ang-vahng-s*Yawng*) *f* invention

inverse (ang-*vehrs*) *adj* reverse

investigation (ang-veh-stee-gah-s*Yawng*) *f* investigation, enquiry

investir (ang-veh-*steer*) *v* invest

investissement (ang-veh-stee-*smahng*) *m* investment

investisseur (ang-veh-stee-*sūrr*) *m* investor

invisible (ang-vee-*zeebl*) *adj* invisible

invitation (ang-vee-tah-s*Yawng*) *f* invitation

invité (ang-vee-*tay*) *m* guest

inviter (ang-vee-*tay*) *v* invite

involontaire (ang-vo-lawng-*tair*) *adj* unintentional

iode (*Y*od) *m* iodine

Irak (ee-*rahk*) *m* Iraq

Irakien (ee-rah-k*Yang*) *m* Iraqi

irakien (ee-rah-k*Yang*) *adj* Iraqi

Iran (ee-*rahng*) *m* Iran

Iranien (ee-rah-n*Yang*) *m* Iranian

iranien (ee-rah-n*Yang*) *adj* Iranian

irascible (ee-rah-*seebl*) *adj* irascible, quick-tempered

Irlandais (eer-lahng-*day*) *m* Irishman

irlandais (eer-lahng-*day*) *adj* Irish

Irlande (eer-*lahngd*) *f* Ireland

ironie (ee-ro-*nee*) *f* irony

ironique (ee-ro-*neek*) *adj* ironical

irréel (ee-ray-*ehl*) *adj* unreal

irrégulier (ee-ray-gew-l*Yay*) *adj* irregular, uneven

irréparable (ee-ray-pah-*rahbl*) *adj* irreparable

irrétrécissable (ee-ray-tray-see-*sahbl*) *adj* shrinkproof

irrévocable (ee-ray-vo-*kahbl*) *adj* irrevocable

irritable (ee-ree-*tahbl*) *adj* irritable

irrité (ee-ree-*tay*) *adj* cross

irriter (ee-ree-*tay*) *v* irritate

Islandais (ee-slahng-*day*) *m* Icelander

islandais (ee-slahng-*day*) *adj* Icelandic

Islande (ee-*slahngd*) *f* Iceland

isolateur (ee-zo-lah-*tūrr*) *m* insulator

isolation (ee-zo-lah-s*Yawng*) *f* isolation, insulation

isolement (ee-zol-*mahng*) *m* isolation

isoler (ee-zo-*lay*) *v* isolate, insulate

Israël (ee-srah-*ehl*) *m* Israel

Israélien (ee-srah-ay-l*Yang*) *m* Israeli

israélien (ee-srah-ay-l*Yang*) *adj* Israeli

issue (ee-*sew*) *f* issue

isthme (eesm) *m* isthmus

Italie (ee-tah-*lee*) *f* Italy

Italien (ee-tah-l*Yang*) *m* Italian

italien (ee-tah-l*Yang*) *adj* Italian

italiques (ee-tah-*leek*) *mpl* italics *pl*

itinéraire (ee-tee-nay-*rair*) *m* itinerary

ivoire (ee-*vwaar*) *m* ivory

ivre (eevr) *adj* drunk; intoxicated

J

jade (zhahd) *m* jade

jadis (zhah-*deess*) *adv* formerly

jalon (zhah-*lawng*) *m* landmark

jalousie (zhah-loo-*zee*) *f* jealousy

jaloux (zhah-*loo*) *adj* jealous, envious

jamais (zhah-*may*) *adv* ever; **ne ... ~** never

jambe (zhahngb) *f* leg

jambon (zhahng-*bawng*) *m* ham

jante (zhahngt) *f* rim

janvier (zhahng-v*Yay*) January

Japon (zhah-*pawng*) *m* Japan

Japonais (zhah-po-*nay*) *m* Japanese

japonais (zhah-po-*nay*) *adj* Japanese

jaquette (zhah-*keht*) *f* jacket

jardin (zhahr-*dang*) *m* garden; ~ **potager** kitchen garden; ~ **public** public garden; ~ **zoologique** zoological gardens

jardinier (zhahr-dee-n*Yay*) *m* gardener

jarre (zhaar) *f* jar

jauge (zhōazh) *f* gauge

jaune (zhōan) *adj* yellow; ~ **d'œuf** yolk, egg-yolk

jaunisse (zhoa-*neess*) *f* jaundice

je (zher) *pron* I

jersey (zhehr-*zay*) *m* jersey

jet (zhay) *m* cast; jet, squirt, spout

jetée (zher-*kay*) *f* jetty, pier

jeter (zher-*tay*) *v* *cast, *throw; **à** ~ disposable

jeton (zher-*tawng*) *m* token, chip

jeu (zhur) *m* play, game; set; **carte de** ~ playing-card; ~ **concours** quiz; ~ **de dames** draughts; checkers *plAm*; ~ **de quilles** bowling; **terrain de jeux** playground

jeudi (zhur-*dee*) *m* Thursday

jeune (zhurn) *adj* young

jeunesse (zhur-*nehss*) *f* youth

joaillerie (zhwigh-*ree*) *f* jewellery

jockey (zho-*kay*) *m* jockey

joie (zhwah) *f* joy, gladness

***joindre** (zhwangdr) *v* join, connect; attach, enclose

jointure (zhwang-*tēwr*) *f* knuckle

joli (zho-*lee*) *adj* fine, nice, pretty, good-looking

jonc (zhawng) *m* rush

jonction (zhawngk-s*Yawng*) *f* junction

jonquille (zhawng-*keey*) *f* daffodil

Jordanie (zhor-dah-*nee*) *f* Jordan

Jordanien (zhor-dah-n*Yang*) *m* Jordanian

jordanien (zhor-dah-n*Yang*) *adj* Jordanian

joue (zhoo) *f* cheek

jouer (zhoo-*ay*) *v* play; act

jouet (zhoo-*ay*) *m* toy

joueur (zhoo-*ūrr*) *m* player

joug (zhoo) *m* yoke

jouir de (zhoo-*eer*) enjoy

jour (zhōōr) *m* day; **de** ~ by day; ~ **de fête** holiday; ~ **de la semaine** weekday; ~ **ouvrable** working day; **l'autre** ~ recently; **par** ~ per day; **un** ~ **ou l'autre** some day

journal (zhoor-*nahl*) *m* newspaper, paper; diary; ~ **du matin** morning paper

journalier (zhoor-nah-l*Yay*) *adj* daily

journalisme (zhoor-nah-*leesm*) *m* journalism

journaliste (zhoor-nah-*leest*) *m* journalist

journée (zhoor-*nay*) *f* day

joyau (zhwah-*Yoa*) *m* gem

joyeux (zhwah-*Yur*) *adj* joyful, cheerful, merry, glad

juge (zhēwzh) *m* judge

jugement (zhewzh-*mahng*) *m* judgment; sentence

juger (zhew-*zhay*) *v* judge

juif (zhweef) *adj* Jewish; *m* Jew

juillet (zhwee-*Yay*) July

juin (zhwang) June

jumeaux (zhew-*moa*) *mpl* twins *pl*

jumelles (zhew-*mehl*) *fpl* field glasses, binoculars *pl*

jument (zhew-*mahng*) *f* mare

jungle (zhawnggl) *f* jungle

jupe (zhewp) *f* skirt

jupon (zhew-*pawng*) *m* underskirt

jurer (zhew-*ray*) *v* vow, *swear; curse

juridique (zhew-ree-*deek*) *adj* legal

juriste (zhew-*reest*) *m* lawyer

juron (zhew-*rawng*) *m* curse

jury (zhew-*ree*) *m* jury

jus (zhew) *m* juice; gravy; ~ **de fruits** squash

jusque (zhewsk) *prep* to; **jusqu'à**

prep till; until; **jusqu'à ce que** till
juste (zhewst) *adj* just, righteous, right, fair; appropriate, proper, correct, exact; tight; *adv* just
justement (zhew-ster-*mahng*) *adv* rightly
justice (zhew-*steess*) *f* justice
justifier (zhew-stee-*f*ʸ*ay*) *v* justify
juteux (zhew-*tur*) *adj* juicy
juvénile (zhew-vay-*neel*) *adj* juvenile

K

kaki (kah-*kee*) *m* khaki
kangourou (kahng-goo-*roo*) *m* kangaroo
Kenya (kay-*n*ʸ*ah*) *m* Kenya
kilo (kee-*loa*) *m* kilogram
kilométrage (kee-lo-may-*traazh*) *m* distance in kilometres
kilomètre (kee-lo-*mehtr*) *m* kilometre
kiosque (kʸosk) *m* kiosk; ~ **à journaux** newsstand
klaxon (klahk-*sawng*) *m* hooter; horn
klaxonner (klahk-so-*nay*) *v* hoot; toot *vAm*, honk *vAm*

L

la (lah) *art* the; *pron* her
là (lah) *adv* there
là-bas (lah-*bah*) *adv* over there
labeur (lah-*būr*) *m* labour
laboratoire (lah-bo-rah-*twaar*) *m* laboratory; ~ **de langues** language laboratory
labourer (lah-boo-*ray*) *v* plough
labyrinthe (lah-bee-*rangt*) *m* maze, labyrinth
lac (lahk) *m* lake

lacet (lah-*say*) *m* shoe-lace, lace
lâche (laash) *m* coward; *adj* cowardly; loose
lâcher (lah-*shay*) *v* *let go
lagune (lah-*gewn*) *f* lagoon
laid (lay) *adj* ugly
laine (lehn) *f* wool; **en** ~ woollen; ~ **à repriser** darning wool; ~ **peignée** worsted
laisse (lehss) *f* leash, lead
laisser (lay-*say*) *v* *let, *leave; *leave behind
lait (lay) *m* milk
laitance (lay-*tahngss*) *f* roe
laiterie (leh-*tree*) *f* dairy
laiteux (lay-*tur*) *adj* milky
laitier (lay-*t*ʸ*ay*) *m* milkman
laiton (lay-*tawng*) *m* brass
laitue (lay-*tew*) *f* lettuce
lambrissage (lahng-bree-*saazh*) *m* panelling
lame (lahm) *f* blade; ~ **de rasoir** razor-blade
lamentable (lah-mahng-*tahbl*) *adj* lamentable
lampadaire (lahng-pah-*dair*) *m* lamp-post
lampe (lahngp) *f* lamp; ~ **de poche** torch; ~ **de travail** reading-lamp; **lampe-tempête** *f* hurricane lamp
lance (lahngss) *f* spear
lancement (lahng-*smahng*) *m* throw; launching
lancer (lahng-*say*) *v* *cast, toss, *throw; launch
lande (lahngd) *f* heath, moor
langage (lahng-*gaazh*) *m* speech
langue (lahng) *f* tongue; language; ~ **maternelle** native language, mother tongue
lanterne (lahng-*tehrn*) *f* lantern
lapin (lah-*pang*) *m* rabbit
laque (lahk) *f* varnish; ~ **capillaire** hair-spray

lard (laar) *m* bacon

large (lahrzh) *adj* wide, broad; generous, liberal

largeur (lahr-*zhūrr*) *f* width, breadth

larme (lahrm) *f* tear

laryngite (lah-rang-*zheet*) *f* laryngitis

las (lah) *adj* (f ~se) weary; ~ **de** tired of

latitude (lah-tee-*tewd*) *f* latitude

lavable (lah-*vahbl*) *adj* washable, fast-dyed

lavabo (lah-vah-*boa*) *m* wash-stand, wash-basin

lavage (lah-*vaazh*) *m* washing

laver (lah-*vay*) *v* wash

laverie automatique (lah-vree oa-toa-mah-*teek*) launderette

laxatif (lahk-sah-*teef*) *m* laxative

le[1] (ler) *art* (f la, pl les) the

le[2] (ler) *pron* (f la) him; it

leader (lee-*dair*) *m* leader

lécher (lay-*shay*) *v* lick

leçon (ler-*sawng*) *f* lesson

lecteur (lehk-*tūrr*) *m* reader

lecture (lehk-*tewr*) *f* reading

légal (lay-*gahl*) *adj* legal, lawful

légalisation (lay-gah-lee-zah-*sawng*) *f* legalization

légation (lay-gah-*sawng*) *f* legation

léger (lay-*zhay*) *adj* (f légère) slight, light; weak, gentle

légitime (lay-zhee-*teem*) *adj* legitimate, legal; just

legs (lay) *m* legacy

légume (lay-*gewm*) *m* vegetable

lendemain (lahng-dmang) *m* next day

lent (lahng) *adj* slow; slack

lentille (lahng-*teey*) *f* lens

lèpre (lehpr) *f* leprosy

lequel (ler-*kehl*) *pron* (f laquelle; pl lesquels, lesquelles) which

les (lay) *art* the; *pron* them

lésion (lay-z*awng*) *f* injury

lessive (lay-*seev*) *f* washing, laundry

lettre (lehtr) *f* letter; **boîte aux lettres** pillar-box; ~ **de crédit** letter of credit; ~ **de recommandation** letter of recommendation; ~ **recommandée** registered letter

leur (lūrr) *adj* their; *pron* them

levée (ler-*vay*) *f* collection

lever (ler-*vay*) *v* lift; ~ **du jour** daybreak; **se** ~ *rise, *get up

levier (ler-v*ay*) *m* lever; ~ **de vitesse** gear lever

lèvre (laivr) *f* lip

lévrier (lay-vr*ay*) *m* greyhound

levure (ler-*vewr*) *f* yeast

liaison (l*ay*-*zawng*) *f* affair

Liban (lee-*bahng*) *m* Lebanon

Libanais (lee-bah-*nay*) *m* Lebanese

libanais (lee-bah-*nay*) *adj* Lebanese

libéral (lee-bay-*rahl*) *adj* liberal

libération (lee-bay-rah-s*awng*) *f* liberation

libérer (lee-bay-*ray*) *v* release; liberate

Libéria (lee-bay-r*yah*) *m* Liberia

Libérien (lee-bay-r*yang*) *m* Liberian

libérien (lee-bay-r*yang*) *adj* Liberian

liberté (lee-behr-*tay*) *f* freedom, liberty

libraire (lee-*brair*) *m* bookseller

librairie (lee-bray-*ree*) *f* bookstore

libre (leebr) *adj* free

libre-service (leebr-sehr-*veess*) *m* self-service

licence (lee-*sahngss*) *f* permission, licence

licencier (lee-sahng-s*ay*) *v* fire

lien (l*yang*) *m* band; link

lier (lee-*ay*) *v* *bind

lierre (l*yair*) *m* ivy

lieu (l*yur*) *m* spot; **au** ~ **de** instead of; *avoir ~ *take place; ~ **de naissance** place of birth; ~ **de rencontre** meeting-place

lièvre (l*yaivr*) *m* hare

ligne (leeñ) *f* line; ~ **aérienne** air-

line; ~ **d'arrivée** finish; ~ **de pêche** fishing line; ~ **intérieure** extension; ~ **principale** main line
ligue (leeg) f union, league
lime (leem) f file; ~ **à ongles** nail-file
limette (lee-*meht*) f lime
limite (lee-*meet*) f limit, boundary,
bound; ~ **de vitesse** speed limit
limiter (lee-mee-*tay*) v limit
limonade (lee-mo-*nahd*) f lemonade
linge (la<del>ng</del>zh) m linen
lingerie (la<del>ng</del>-*zhree*) f lingerie
lion (l^yaw<del>ng</del>) m lion
liqueur (lee-*kürr*) f liqueur
liquide (lee-*keed*) m fluid; adj liquid
*lire (leer) v *read
lis (leess) m lily
lisible (lee-*zeebl*) adj legible
lisse (leess) adj smooth, level, even
liste (leest) f list; ~ **d'attente** waiting-list
lit (lee) m bed; ~ **de camp** camp-
bed; cot *nAm*; **lits jumeaux** twin
beds
literie (lee-*tree*) f bedding
litige (lee-*teezh*) m dispute
litre (leetr) m litre
littéraire (lee-tay-*rair*) adj literary
littérature (lee-tay-rah-te<del>w</del>r) f literature
littoral (lee-to-*rahl*) m sea-coast
livraison (lee-vreh-*zaw<del>ng</del>*) f delivery
livre[1] (leevr) m book; ~ **de cuisine**
cookery-book; cookbook *nAm*; ~
de poche paperback
livre[2] (leevr) f pound
livrer (lee-*vray*) v deliver
local (lo-*kahl*) adj local
localiser (lo-kah-lee-*zay*) v locate
localité (lo-kah-lee-*tay*) f locality
locataire (lo-kah-*tair*) m tenant
location (lo-kah-s^y*aw<del>ng</del>*) f lease; **donner en** ~ lease; ~ **de voitures** car
hire; car rental *Am*

locomotive (lo-ko-mo-*teev*) f locomotive, engine
locution (lo-kew-s^y*aw<del>ng</del>*) f phrase
loge (lozh) f dressing-room
logement (lozh-*mah<del>ng</del>*) m lodgings
pl, accommodation
loger (lo-*zhay*) v accommodate; lodge
logeur (lo-*zhürr*) m landlord
logeuse (lo-*zhürz*) f landlady
logique (lo-*zheek*) f logic; adj logical
loi (lwah) f law
loin (lwa<del>ng</del>) adv away, far; **plus** ~
further
lointain (lwa<del>ng</del>-*ta<del>ng</del>*) adj far-off, remote
loisir (lwah-*zeer*) m leisure
long (law<del>ng</del>) adj (f longue) long; **en**
~ lengthways; **le** ~ **de** past, along
longitude (law<del>ng</del>-zhee-*tewd*) f longitude
longtemps (law<del>ng</del>-*tah<del>ng</del>*) adv long
longueur (law<del>ng</del>-*gürr*) f length; ~
d'onde wave-length
lopin (lo-*pa<del>ng</del>*) m plot
lors de (lor der) at the time of
lorsque (lorsk) conj when
lot (loa) m batch
loterie (lo-*tree*) f lottery
lotion (lo-s^y*aw<del>ng</del>*) f lotion
louange (loo-*ah<del>ng</del>zh*) f glory
louche (loosh) adj cross-eyed
louer (loo-*ay*) v hire, rent, lease; *let;
engage; praise; **à** ~ for hire
loup (loo) m wolf
lourd (lo<del>o</del>r) adj heavy
loyal (lwah-^y*ahl*) adj true, loyal
loyer (lwah-^y*ay*) m rent
lubie (lew-*bee*) f whim, fad
lubrifiant (lew-bree-f^y*ah<del>ng</del>*) m lubrication oil
lubrification (lew-bree-fee-kah-s^y*aw<del>ng</del>*)
f lubrication
lubrifier (lew-bree-f^y*ay*) v lubricate
lueur (lwürr) f gleam

luge (lēwzh) *f* sleigh, sledge

lugubre (lew-*gēwbr*) *adj* creepy

lui (lwee) *pron* him; her; **lui-même** *pron* himself

luisant (lwee-*zahng*) *adj* glossy

lumbago (lawng-bah-*goa*) *m* lumbago

lumière (lew-*mʸair*) *f* light; ~ **du jour** daylight; ~ **du soleil** sunlight; ~ **latérale** sidelight

lumineux (lew-mee-*nur*) *adj* luminous

lundi (lurng-*dee*) *m* Monday

lune (lewn) *f* moon; **clair de** ~ moonlight; ~ **de miel** honeymoon

lunettes (lew-*neht*) *fpl* spectacles, glasses; ~ **de plongée** goggles *pl*; ~ **de soleil** sun-glasses *pl*

lustre (lewstr) *m* gloss

lustrer (lew-*stray*) *v* brush

lutte (lewt) *f* strife; fight, combat, battle, struggle

lutter (lew-*tay*) *v* struggle; combat

luxe (lewks) *m* luxury

luxueux (lewk-*swur*) *adj* luxurious

M

mâcher (mah-*shay*) *v* chew

machine (mah-*sheen*) *f* engine, machine; ~ **à coudre** sewing-machine; ~ **à écrire** typewriter; ~ **à laver** washing-machine

machinerie (mah-sheen-*ree*) *f* machinery

mâchoire (mah-*shwaar*) *f* jaw

maçon (mah-*sawng*) *m* bricklayer

maçonner (mah-so-*nay*) *v* *lay bricks

madame (mah-*dahm*) madam

mademoiselle (mahd-mwah-*zehl*) miss

magasin (mah-gah-*zang*) *m* store; warehouse, store-house; **grand** ~ department store; ~ **de chaussures** shoe-shop; ~ **de jouets** toyshop; ~

de spiritueux off-licence

magie (mah-*zhee*) *f* magic

magique (mah-*zheek*) *adj* magic

magistrat (mah-zhee-*strah*) *m* magistrate

magnétique (mah-ñay-*teek*) *adj* magnetic

magnéto (mah-ñay-*toa*) *f* magneto

magnétophone (mah-ñay-to-*fon*) *m* tape-recorder

magnifique (mah-ñee-*feek*) *adj* splendid, gorgeous, magnificent

mai (may) May

maigre (maigr) *adj* thin, lean

maigrir (meh-*greer*) *v* slim

maille (migh) *f* mesh

maillet (mah-*ʸay*) *m* mallet

maillon (mah-*ʸawng*) *m* link

maillot de bain (mah-*ʸoa* der bang) bathing-suit, swim-suit

main (mang) *f* hand; **fait à la** ~ hand-made

main-d'œuvre (mang-*dūfvr*) *f* manpower

maintenant (mangt-*nahng*) *adv* now; **jusqu'à** ~ so far

*maintenir (mangt-*neer*) *v* maintain

maire (mair) *m* mayor

mairie (may-*ree*) *f* town hall

mais (may) *conj* but

maïs (mah-*eess*) *m* maize; ~ **en épi** corn on the cob

maison (may-*zawng*) *f* house; home; **à la** ~ at home; **fait à la** ~ home-made; **maison-bateau** houseboat; ~ **de campagne** country house; ~ **de repos** rest-home

maître (maitr) *m* master; ~ **d'école** teacher, schoolmaster; ~ **d'hôtel** head-waiter

maîtresse (meh-*trehss*) *f* mistress; ~ **de maison** mistress

maîtriser (meh-tree-*zay*) *v* master

majeur (mah-*zhūr*) *adj* major; superior, main; of age

majorité (mah-zho-ree-*tay*) *f* bulk, majority

majuscule (mah-zhew-*skewl*) *f* capital letter

mal (mahl) *m* (pl maux) evil, harm; mischief; ***faire du ~** harm; ***faire ~** ache; *****hurt; **~ à l'aise** uneasy; **~ au cœur** sickness; **~ au dos** backache; **~ au ventre** stomach-ache; **~ aux dents** toothache; **~ de gorge** sore throat; **~ de l'air** air-sickness; **~ de mer** seasickness; **~ d'estomac** stomach-ache; **~ de tête** headache; **~ d'oreille** earache; **~ du pays** homesickness

malade (mah-*lahd*) *adj* sick, ill

maladie (mah-lah-*dee*) *f* sickness, illness, disease, ailment; **~ vénérienne** venereal disease

maladroit (mah-lah-*drwah*) *adj* clumsy, awkward

Malais (mah-*lay*) *m* Malay

malaisien (mah-lay-z*Yang*) *adj* Malaysian

malaria (mah-lah-r*Yah*) *f* malaria

malchance (mahl-*shahngss*) *f* bad luck

mâle (maal) *adj* male

malentendu (mah-lahng-tahng-*dew*) *m* misunderstanding

malgré (mahl-*gray*) *prep* in spite of, despite

malheur (mah-*lūrr*) *m* misfortune

malheureusement (mah-lur-rurz-*mahng*) *adv* unfortunately

malheureux (mah-lur-*rur*) *adj* unhappy, unfortunate; miserable, sad

malhonnête (mah-lo-*neht*) *adj* dishonest, crooked

malice (mah-*leess*) *f* mischief

malicieux (mah-lee-s*Yur*) *adj* mischievous

malin (mah-*lang*) *adj* (f maligne) malignant; sly; bright

malle (mahl) *f* trunk

mallette (mah-*leht*) *f* grip *nAm*

malodorant (mah-lo-do-*rahng*) *adj* smelly

malpropre (mahl-*propr*) *adj* foul, unclean

malsain (mahl-*sang*) *adj* unsound, unhealthy

malveillant (mahl-veh-*Yahng*) *adj* spiteful; malicious

maman (mah-*mahng*) *f* mum

mammifère (mah-mee-*fair*) *m* mammal

mammouth (mah-*moot*) *m* mammoth

manche (mahngsh) *m* handle; *f* sleeve; **La Manche** English Channel

manchette (mahng-*sheht*) *f* cuff; headline

mandarine (mahng-dah-*reen*) *f* tangerine, mandarin

mandat (mahng-*dah*) *m* mandate

mandat-poste (mahng-dah-*post*) *m* money order, postal order; mail order *Am*

manège (mah-*naizh*) *m* riding-school

mangeoire (mahng-*zhwaar*) *f* manger

manger (mahng-*zhay*) *v* *eat; *m* food

maniable (mah-n*Yahbl*) *adj* manageable

manier (mah-n*Yay*) *v* handle

manière (mah-n*Yair*) *f* way, manner; **de la même ~** likewise; **de ~ que** so that

manifestation (mah-nee-feh-stah-s*Yawng*) *f* demonstration

manifestement (mah-nee-feh-ster-*mahng*) *adv* apparently

manifester (mah-nee-feh-*stay*) *v* express; demonstrate

manipuler (mah-nee-pew-*lay*) *v* handle

mannequin (mahn-*kang*) *m* model, mannequin

manoir (mah-*nwaar*) *m* mansion,

manor-house

manquant (mahng-kahng) adj missing

manque (mahngk) m want, shortage, lack

manquer (mahng-kay) v fail, lack; miss

manteau (mahng-toa) m coat, cloak; ~ **de fourrure** fur coat

manucure (mah-new-kewr) f manicure

manuel (mah-nwehl) m textbook, handbook; adj manual; ~ **de conversation** phrase-book

manuscrit (mah-new-skree) m manuscript

maquereau (mah-kroa) m mackerel

maquillage (mah-kee-Yaazh) m make-up

marais (mah-ray) m marsh, swamp, bog

marbre (mahrbr) m marble

marchand (mahr-shahng) m merchant; tradesman, dealer; ~ **de journaux** newsagent; ~ **de légumes** greengrocer; vegetable merchant; ~ **de volaille** poulterer

marchander (mahr-shahng-day) v bargain

marchandise (mahr-shahng-deez) f merchandise; wares pl, goods pl

marche (mahrsh) f march; step; *fai-re ~ arrière reverse

marché (mahr-shay) m market; **bon ~** cheap; inexpensive; ~ **des valeurs** stock market; ~ **noir** black market; **place du ~** market-place

marcher (mahr-shay) v walk, step, *go; march; *faire ~ fool

mardi (mahr-dee) m Tuesday

marécageux (mah-ray-kah-zhur) adj marshy

marée (mah-ray) f tide; ~ **basse** low tide; ~ **haute** flood; high tide

margarine (mahr-gah-reen) f margarine

marge (mahrzh) f margin

mari (mah-ree) m husband

mariage (mah-rYaazh) m matrimony, marriage; wedding

marié (mah-rYay) m bridegroom

se marier (mah-rYay) marry

marin (mah-rang) m sailor; seaman

marinade (mah-ree-nahd) f pickles pl

marine (mah-reen) f navy; seascape

maritime (mah-ree-teem) adj maritime

marmelade (mahr-mer-lahd) f marmalade

marmite (mahr-meet) f pot

Maroc (mah-rok) m Morocco

Marocain (mah-ro-kang) m Moroccan

marocain (mah-ro-kang) adj Moroccan

marque (mahrk) f mark; sign, brand; tick; ~ **de fabrique** trademark

marquer (mahr-kay) v mark

marquise (mahr-keez) f awning

marron (mah-rawng) m chestnut

mars (mahrs) March

marteau (mahr-toa) m hammer

marteler (mahr-ter-lay) v thump

martyr (mahr-teer) m martyr

masculin (mah-skew-lang) adj masculine

masque (mahsk) m mask; ~ **de beauté** face-pack

massage (mah-saazh) m massage; ~ **facial** face massage

masse (mahss) f mass; bulk; crowd

masser (mah-say) v massage

masseur (mah-sūr) m masseur

massif (mah-seef) adj massive, solid

massue (mah-sew) f club

mat (maht) adj mat, dull, dim

mât (mah) m mast

match (mahch) m match; ~ **de boxe** boxing match; ~ **de football** football match

matelas (mah-tlah) m mattress

matériau (mah-tay-rYoa) m material

matériel (mah-tay-r*y*ehl) *m* material;
adj material; substantial
maternel (mah-tehr-*nehl*) *adj* mother-
ly
mathématique (mah-tay-mah-*teek*)
adj mathematical
mathématiques (mah-tay-mah-*teek*)
fpl mathematics
matière (mah-t*y*air) *f* matter; ~ **première** raw material
matin (mah-*tang*) *m* morning; **ce** ~
this morning
matinée (mah-tee-*nay*) *f* morning
matrimonial (mah-tree-mo-n*y*ahl) *adj*
matrimonial
maturité (mah-tew-ree-*tay*) *f* maturity
*****maudire** (moa-*deer*) *v* curse
mausolée (moa-zo-*lay*) *m* mausoleum
mauvais (moa-*vay*) *adj* bad; wicked,
ill, evil; **le plus** ~ worst
mauve (mōav) *adj* mauve
maximum (mahk-see-*mom*) *m* maximum; **au** ~ at most
mazout (mah-*zoot*) *m* fuel oil
me (mer) *pron* me; myself
mécanicien (may-kah-nee-s*y*ang) *m*
mechanic
mécanique (may-kah-*neek*) *adj* mechanical
mécanisme (may-kah-*neesm*) *m* mechanism, machinery
méchant (may-*shahng*) *adj* evil;
naughty, nasty, ill
mèche (mehsh) *f* fuse
mécontent (may-kawng-*tahng*) *adj*
discontented
médaille (may-*digh*) *f* medal
médecin (may-*dsang*) *m* physician,
doctor; ~ **généraliste** general practitioner
médecine (may-*dseen*) *f* medicine
médiateur (may-d*y*ah-*tūrr*) *m* mediator
médical (may-dee-*kahl*) *adj* medical

médicament (may-dee-kah-*mahng*) *m*
medicine, drug
médiéval (may-d*y*ay-*vahl*) *adj* mediaeval
méditer (may-dee-*tay*) *v* meditate
Méditerranée (may-dee-tay-rah-*nay*) *f*
Mediterranean
méduse (may-*dewz*) *f* jelly-fish
méfiance (may-f*y*ahngss) *f* suspicion
méfiant (may-f*y*ahng) *adj* suspicious
se méfier de (may-f*y*ay) mistrust
meilleur (meh-*y*ūrr) *adj* better; **le** ~
best
mélancolie (may-lahng-ko-*lee*) *f* melancholy
mélancolique (may-lahng-ko-*leek*) *adj*
sad
mélange (may-*lahngzh*) *m* mixture
mélanger (may-lahng-*zhay*) *v* mix
mêler (may-*lay*) *v* mix; **se** ~ **de** interfere with
mélo (may-*loa*) *m* tear-jerker
mélodie (may-lo-*dee*) *f* melody
mélodrame (may-lo-*drahm*) *m* melodrama
melon (mer-*lawng*) *m* melon
membrane (mahng-*brahn*) *f* diaphragm
membre (mahngbr) *m* member, associate; limb
mémé (may-*may*) *f* grandmother
même (mehm) *adj* same; *adv* even;
de ~ also
mémoire (may-*mwaar*) *f* memory
mémorable (may-mo-*rahbl*) *adj* memorable
mémorandum (may-mo-rahng-*dom*) *m*
memo
mémorial (may-mo-r*y*ahl) *m* memorial
menaçant (mer-nah-*sahng*) *adj* threatening
menace (mer-*nahss*) *f* threat
menacer (mer-nah-*say*) *v* threaten
ménage (may-*naazh*) *m* housekeeping,

household

ménagère (may-nah-*zhair*) f housewife

mendiant (mahng-*d*y*ahng*) m beggar

mendier (mahng-*d*y*ay*) v beg

mener (mer-*nay*) v *take, *lead

menottes (mer-*not*) fpl handcuffs pl

mensonge (mahng-*sawngzh*) m lie

menstruation (mahng-strew-ah-sy*awng*) f menstruation

mensuel (mahng-*swehl*) adj monthly

mental (mahng-*tahl*) adj mental; **aliéné** ~ lunatic

menthe (mahngt) f peppermint, mint

mention (mahng-sy*awng*) f mention

mentionner (mahng-sy*o*-*nay*) v mention

***mentir** (mahng-*teer*) v lie

menton (mahng-*tawng*) m chin

menu[1] (mer-*new*) m menu; ~ **fixe** set menu

menu[2] (mer-*new*) adj minor

menuisier (mer-nwee-z*yay*) m carpenter

mépris (may-*pree*) m contempt, scorn

méprise (may-*preez*) f mistake

mépriser (may-pree-*zay*) v despise, scorn

mer (mair) f sea

mercerie (mehr-ser-*ree*) f haberdashery

merci (mehr-*see*) thank you

mercredi (mehr-krer-*dee*) m Wednesday

mercure (mehr-*kewr*) m mercury

mère (mair) f mother

méridional (may-ree-dy*o*-*nahl*) adj southern, southerly

mérite (may-*reet*) m merit

mériter (may-ree-*tay*) v merit, deserve

merlan (mehr-*lahng*) m whiting

merle (mehrl) m blackbird

merveille (mehr-*vay*) f marvel

merveilleux (mehr-veh-*vur*) adj marvellous; fine, wonderful

mesquin (meh-*skang*) adj mean, stingy

message (meh-*saazh*) m message

messager (meh-sah-*zhay*) m messenger

messe (mehss) f Mass

mesure (mer-*zewr*) f measure; size; **en** ~ able; **fait sur** ~ tailor-made

mesurer (mer-zew-*ray*) v measure

métal (may-*tahl*) m metal

métallique (may-tah-*leek*) adj metal

méthode (may-*tod*) f method

méthodique (may-to-*deek*) adj methodical

méticuleux (may-tee-kew-*lur*) adj precise

métier (may-t*yay*) m trade, profession

mètre (mehtr) m metre

métrique (may-*treek*) adj metric

métro (may-*troa*) m underground; subway nAm

***mettre** (mehtr) v *put; *put on

meuble (murbl) m piece of furniture; **meubles** furniture

meubler (mur-*blay*) v furnish; **non meublé** unfurnished

meunier (mur-n*yay*) m miller

meurtrier (murr-tree-*ay*) m murderer

Mexicain (mehk-see-*kang*) m Mexican

mexicain (mehk-see-*kang*) adj Mexican

Mexique (mehk-*seek*) m Mexico

miche (meesh) f loaf

microbe (mee-*krob*) m germ

microphone (mee-kro-*fon*) m microphone

microsillon (mee-kro-see-y*awng*) m long-playing record

midi (mee-*dee*) m midday, noon

miel (m*y*ehl) m honey

le mien (ler m*y*ang) mine

miette (m*y*eht) f crumb

mieux (m*y*ur) adv better

migraine (mee-*grehn*) f migraine

milieu (mee-l^yur) *m* middle, midst; milieu; **au ~ de** among, amid; **du ~** middle

militaire (mee-lee-*tair*) *adj* military

mille (meel) *num* thousand; *m* mile

million (mee-l^yawng) *m* million

millionnaire (mee-l^yo-*nair*) *m* millionaire

mince (mangss[,]) *adj* slim, thin

mine¹ (meen) *f* pit, mine; **~ d'or** goldmine

mine² (meen) *f* look

minerai (meen-*ray*) *m* ore

minéral (mee-nay-*rahl*) *m* mineral

minet (mee-*nay*) *m* pussy-cat

mineur (mee-*nūrr*) *m* miner; minor; *adj* minor; under age

miniature (mee-n^yah-*tewr*) *f* miniature

minimum (mee-nee-*mom*) *m* minimum

ministère (mee-nee-*stair*) *m* ministry

ministre (mee-*neestr*) *m* minister; **premier ~** Prime Minister

minorité (mee-no-ree-*tay*) *f* minority

minuit (mee-*nwee*) midnight

minuscule (mee-new-*skewl*) *adj* tiny, minute

minute (mee-*newt*) *f* minute

minutieux (mee-new-s^yur) *adj* thorough

miracle (mee-*raakl*) *m* miracle, wonder

miraculeux (mee-rah-kew-*lur*) *adj* miraculous

miroir (mee-*rwaar*) *m* looking-glass, mirror

misaine (mee-*zehn*) *f* foresail

misérable (mee-zay-*rahbl*) *adj* miserable

misère (mee-*zair*) *f* misery

miséricorde (mee-zay-ree-*kord*) *f* mercy

miséricordieux (mee-zay-ree-kor-d^yur) *adj* merciful

mite (meet) *f* moth

mi-temps (mee-*tahng*) *f* half-time

mixeur (meek-*sūrr*) *m* mixer

mobile (mo-*beel*) *adj* mobile; movable

mode¹ (mod) *f* fashion; **à la ~** fashionable

mode² (mod) *m* fashion, manner; **~ d'emploi** directions for use

modèle (mo-*dehl*) *m* model

modeler (mo-*dlay*) *v* model

modéré (mo-day-*ray*) *adj* moderate

moderne (mo-*dehrn*) *adj* modern

modeste (mo-*dehst*) *adj* modest

modestie (mo-deh-*stee*) *f* modesty

modification (mo-dee-fee-kah-s^yawng) *f* change, alteration

modifier (mo-dee-f^yay) *v* change, modify, alter

modiste (mo-*deest*) *f* milliner

moelle (mwahl) *f* marrow

moelleux (mwah-*lur*) *adj* mellow

mœurs (murrs) *fpl* morals

mohair (mo-*air*) *m* mohair

moi (mwah) *pron* me; **moi-même** *pron* myself

moindre (mwangdr) *adj* least; inferior

moine (mwahn) *m* monk

moineau (mwah-*noa*) *m* sparrow

moins (mwang) *adv* less; *prep* minus; **à ~ que** unless; **au ~** at least

mois (mwah) *m* month

moisi (mwah-*zee*) *adj* mouldy

moisissure (mwah-zee-*sewr*) *f* mildew

moisson (mwah-*sawng*) *f* harvest

moite (mwaht) *adj* moist; damp

moitié (mwah-t^yay) *f* half; **à ~** half

molaire (mo-*lair*) *f* molar

mollet (mo-*lay*) *m* calf

moment (mo-*mahng*) *m* moment; while

momentané (mo-mahng-tah-*nay*) *adj* momentary

mon (mawng) *adj* (f ma, pl mes) my

monarchie (mo-nahr-*shee*) *f* monarchy

monarque (mo-*nahrk*) *m* monarch, ruler

monastère (mo-nah-*stair*) *m* monastery

monde (mawngd) *m* world; **tout le ~** everyone

mondial (mawng-*dᵞahl*) *adj* worldwide; global

monétaire (mo-nay-*tair*) *adj* monetary

monnaie (mo-*nay*) *f* currency; **~ étrangère** foreign currency; **petite ~** petty cash, change; **pièce de ~** coin

monologue (mo-no-*log*) *m* monologue

monopole (mo-no-*pol*) *m* monopoly

monotone (mo-no-*ton*) *adj* monotonous

monsieur (mer-*sᵞur*) *m* (pl messieurs) gentleman; mister; sir

mont (mawng) *m* mount

montagne (mawng-*tahñ*) *f* mountain

montagneux (mawng-tah-*ñur*) *adj* mountainous

montant (mawng-*tahng*) *m* amount

montée (mawng-*tay*) *f* rise; ascent

monter (mawng-*tay*) *v* *rise; ascend; *get on; assemble; mount; **se ~ à** amount to

monteur (mawng-*tūr*) *m* mechanic

monticule (mawng-tee-*kewl*) *m* hillock

montre (mawngtr) *f* watch; **~ de gousset** pocket-watch

montrer (mawng-*tray*) *v* *show; display; **~ du doigt** point

monture (mawng-*tewr*) *f* frame

monument (mo-new-*mahng*) *m* monument

se moquer de (mo-*kay*) mock

moquerie (mo-*kree*) *f* mockery

moral (mo-*rahl*) *adj* moral; *m* spirits

morale (mo-*rahl*) *f* moral

moralité (mo-rah-lee-*tay*) *f* morality

morceau (mor-*soa*) *m* piece, part; morsel, fragment, scrap, bit, lump; **~ de sucre** lump of sugar

mordache (mor-*dahsh*) *f* clamp

mordre (mordr) *v* *bite

morphine (mor-*feen*) *f* morphine, morphia

morsure (mor-*sewr*) *f* bite

mort (mawr) *f* death; *adj* dead

mortel (mor-*tehl*) *adj* fatal; mortal

morue (mo-*rew*) *f* cod

mosaïque (mo-zah-*eek*) *f* mosaic

mosquée (mo-*skay*) *f* mosque

mot (moa) *m* word; **~ de passe** password

motel (mo-*tehl*) *m* motel

moteur (mo-*tūr*) *m* motor, engine

motif (mo-*teef*) *m* cause, motive, occasion; pattern

motion (mo-*sᵞawng*) *f* motion

motocyclette (mo-to-see-*kleht*) *f* motor-cycle

mou (moo) *adj* (f molle) soft

mouche (moosh) *f* fly

mouchoir (moo-*shwaar*) *m* handkerchief; **~ de papier** tissue

***moudre** (moodr) *v* *grind

mouette (mweht) *f* gull; seagull

moufles (moofl) *fpl* mittens *pl*

mouiller (moo-*ᵞay*) *v* wet; **mouillé** wet, moist

moule (mool) *f* mussel

moulin (moo-*lang*) *m* mill; **~ à paroles** chatterbox; **~ à vent** windmill

***mourir** (moo-*reer*) *v* die

mousse (mooss) *f* foam; moss

mousseline (moo-*sleen*) *f* muslin

mousser (moo-*say*) *v* foam

mousseux (moo-*sur*) *adj* sparkling

moustache (moo-*stahsh*) *f* moustache

moustiquaire (moo-stee-*kair*) *f* mosquito-net

moustique (moo-*steek*) *m* mosquito

moutarde (moo-*tahrd*) *f* mustard
mouton (moo-*tawng*) *m* sheep; mutton
mouvement (moov-*mahng*) *m* motion, movement
se *mouvoir (moo-*vwaar*) move
moyen (mwah-*Yang*) *m* means; *adj* medium, average
moyen-âge (mwah-*Yeh-naazh*) *m* Middle Ages
moyenne (mwah-*Yehn*) *f* mean, average; **en ~** on the average
muet (mway) *adj* dumb, mute
mugir (mew-*zheer*) *v* roar
mule (mewl) *f* mule
mulet (mew-*lay*) *m* mule; mullet
multiplication (mewl-tee-plee-kah-*sYawng*) *f* multiplication
multiplier (mewl-tee-plee-*ay*) *v* multiply
municipal (mew-nee-see-*pahl*) *adj* municipal
municipalité (mew-nee-see-pah-lee-*tay*) *f* municipality
munir de (mew-*neer*) provide with
mur (mewr) *m* wall
mûr (mewr) *adj* mature, ripe
mûre (mewr) *f* blackberry; mulberry
muscade (mew-*skahd*) *f* nutmeg
muscle (mewskl) *m* muscle
musclé (mew-*sklay*) *adj* muscular
museau (mew-*zoa*) *m* snout
musée (mew-*zay*) *m* museum
musical (mew-zee-*kahl*) *adj* musical
musicien (mew-zee-*sYang*) *m* musician
musique (mew-*zeek*) *f* music; **~ pop** pop music
mutinerie (mew-teen-*ree*) *f* mutiny
mutuel (mew-*twehl*) *adj* mutual
myope (m*Y*op) *adj* short-sighted
mystère (mee-*stair*) *m* mystery
mystérieux (mee-stay-r*Y*ur) *adj* mysterious

mythe (meet) *m* myth

N

nacre (nahkr) *f* mother-of-pearl
nager (nah-*zhay*) *v* *swim
nageur (nah-*zhūrr*) *m* swimmer
naïf (nah-*eef*) *adj* naïve
nain (nang) *m* dwarf
naissance (nay-*sahngss*) *f* birth
*naître (naitr) *v* *be born
nappe (nahp) *f* table-cloth
narcose (nahr-*kōaz*) *f* narcosis
narcotique (nahr-ko-*teek*) *m* narcotic
narine (nah-*reen*) *f* nostril
natation (nah-tah-*sYawng*) *f* swimming
nation (nah-*sYawng*) *f* nation
national (nah-s*Y*o-*nahl*) *adj* national
nationaliser (nah-s*Y*o-nah-lee-*zay*) *v* nationalize
nationalité (nah-s*Y*o-nah-lee-*tay*) *f* nationality
nature (nah-*tewr*) *f* nature; essence
naturel (nah-tew-*rehl*) *adj* natural
naturellement (nah-tew-rehl-*mahng*) *adv* naturally
naufrage (noa-*fraazh*) *m* shipwreck
nausée (noa-*zay*) *f* nausea
naval (nah-*vahl*) *adj* (pl ~s) naval
navetteur (nah-veh-*tūrr*) *m* commuter
navigable (nah-vee-*gahbl*) *adj* navigable
navigation (nah-vee-gah-*sYawng*) *f* navigation
naviguer (nah-vee-*gay*) *v* navigate; sail
navire (nah-*veer*) *m* ship; boat; **~ de guerre** man-of-war
né (nay) *adj* born
néanmoins (nay-ahng-*mwang*) *adv* nevertheless

nébuleux (nay-bew-*lur*) *adj* hazy

nécessaire (nay-say-*sair*) *adj* necessary; ~ **de toilette** toilet case

nécessité (nay-say-see-*tay*) *f* need, necessity

nécessiter (nay-say-see-*tay*) *v* demand

Néerlandais (nay-ehr-lah~~ng~~-*day*) *m* Dutchman

néerlandais (nay-ehr-lah~~ng~~-*day*) *adj* Dutch

néfaste (nay-*fahst*) *adj* fatal

négatif (nay-gah-*teef*) *m* negative; *adj* negative

négligé (nay-glee-*zhay*) *m* negligee

négligence (nay-glee-*zhah~~ng~~ss*) *f* neglect

négligent (nay-glee-*zhah~~ng~~*) *adj* careless, neglectful

négliger (nay-glee-*zhay*) *v* neglect

négociant (nay-go-s*Yah~~ng~~*) *m* dealer; ~ **en vins** wine-merchant

négociation (nay-go-s*Yah*-s*Yawng*) *f* negotiation

négocier (nay-go-s*Yay*) *v* negotiate

neige (naizh) *f* snow

neiger (nay-*zhay*) *v* snow

neigeux (neh-*zhur*) *adj* snowy

néon (nay-*awng*) *m* neon

nerf (nair) *m* nerve

nerveux (nehr-*vur*) *adj* nervous

net (neht) *adj* distinct; net

nettoyage (neh-twah-*Yaazh*) *m* cleaning

nettoyer (neh-twah-*Yay*) *v* clean; ~ **à sec** dry-clean

neuf[1] (nurf) *adj* (f neuve) new

neuf[2] (nurf) *num* nine

neutre (n*ū*tr) *adj* neuter; neutral

neuvième (nur-*vYehm*) *num* ninth

neveu (ner-*vur*) *m* nephew

névralgie (nay-vrahl-*zhee*) *f* neuralgia

névrose (nay-*vrōāz*) *f* neurosis

nez (nay) *m* nose; **saignement de** ~ nosebleed

ni ... ni (nee) neither ... nor

nickel (nee-*kehl*) *m* nickel

nicotine (nee-ko-*teen*) *f* nicotine

nid (nee) *m* nest

nièce (n*Y*ehss) *f* niece

nier (nee-*ay*) *v* deny

Nigeria (nee-zhay-*rYah*) *m* Nigeria

Nigérien (nee-zhay-*rYang*) *m* Nigerian

nigérien (nee-zhay-*rYang*) *adj* Nigerian

niveau (nee-*voa*) *m* level; ~ **de vie** standard of living; **passage à** ~ level crossing

niveler (nee-*vlay*) *v* level

noble (nobl) *adj* noble

noblesse (no-*blehss*) *f* nobility

nocturne (nok-*tewrn*) *adj* nightly

Noël (no-*ehl*) Christmas, Xmas

nœud (nur) *m* knot; ~ **papillon** bow tie

noir (nwaar) *adj* black; *m* Negro

noisette (nwah-*zeht*) *f* hazelnut

noix (nwah) *f* nut; walnut; ~ **de coco** coconut

nom (naw~~ng~~) *m* name; noun; denomination; **au** ~ **de** in the name of, on behalf of; ~ **de famille** family name, surname; ~ **de jeune fille** maiden name

nombre (naw~~ng~~gbr) *m* number; quantity; numeral

nombre de milles mileage

nombreux (naw~~ng~~-*brur*) *adj* numerous

nombril (naw~~ng~~-*bree*) *m* navel

nominal (no-mee-*nahl*) *adj* nominal

nomination (no-mee-nah-s*Yawng*) *f* nomination, appointment

nommer (no-*may*) *v* name; nominate, appoint

non (naw~~ng~~) no

nord (nawr) *m* north

nord-est (no-*rehst*) *m* north-east

nord-ouest (no-*rwehst*) *m* north-west

normal (nor-*mahl*) *adj* normal, regular

norme (norm) f standard

Norvège (nor-vaizh) f Norway

Norvégien (nor-vay-zh^yang) m Norwegian

norvégien (nor-vay-zh^yang) adj Norwegian

notaire (no-tair) m notary

notamment (no-tah-mahng) adv namely

note (not) f note; mark; bill; check nAm

noter (no-tay) v note, *write down; notice

notifier (no-tee-f^yay) v notify

notion (noa-s^yawng) f notion; idea

notoire (no-twaar) adj notorious

notre (notr) adj our

nouer (noo-ay) v tie, knot

nougat (noo-gah) m nougat

nourrir (noo-reer) v *feed; **nourrissant** nourishing

nourrisson (noo-ree-sawng) m infant

nourriture (noo-ree-tewr) f food; fare

nous (noo) pron we; ourselves, us; **nous-mêmes** pron ourselves

nouveau (noo-voa) adj (nouvel; f nouvelle) new; **de ~** again; **Nouvel An** New Year

nouvelle (noo-vehl) f notice; **nouvelles** news, tidings pl

Nouvelle-Zélande (noo-vehl-zay-lahngd) f New Zealand

novembre (no-vahngbr) November

noyau (nwah-^yoa) m stone; nucleus

noyer (nwah-^yay) v drown; **se ~** *be drowned

nu (new) adj naked, nude; bare; m nude

nuage (nwaazh) m cloud; **nuages** clouds

nuageux (nwah-zhur) adj cloudy, overcast

nuance (nwahngss) f nuance; shade

nucléaire (new-klay-air) adj atomic, nuclear

***nuire** (nweer) v harm

nuisible (nwee-zeebl) adj hurtful, harmful

nuit (nwee) f night; **boîte de ~** cabaret; **cette ~** tonight; **de ~** by night, overnight; **tarif de ~** night rate

nul (newl) adj (f nulle) invalid, void

numéro (new-may-roa) m number; act; **~ d'immatriculation** registration number; licence number Am

nuque (newk) f nape of the neck

nutritif (new-tree-teef) adj nutritious

nylon (nee-lawng) m nylon

O

oasis (oa-ah-zeess) f oasis

obéir (o-bay-eer) v obey

obéissance (o-bay-ee-sahngss) f obedience

obéissant (o-bay-ee-sahng) adj obedient

obèse (o-baiz) adj stout, corpulent

obésité (o-bay-zee-tay) f fatness

objecter (ob-zhehk-tay) v object

objectif (ob-zhehk-teef) m target, objective, object, goal; adj objective

objection (ob-zhehk-s^yawng) f objection; ***faire ~ à** object to; mind

objet (ob-zhay) m object; **objets de valeur** valuables pl; **objets trouvés** lost and found

obligation (o-blee-gah-s^yawng) f bond

obligatoire (o-blee-gah-twaar) adj compulsory, obligatory

obligeant (o-blee-zhahng) adj obliging

obliger (o-blee-zhay) v oblige; force

oblique (o-bleek) adj slanting

oblong (o-blawng) adj (f oblongue) oblong

obscène (o-*psehn*) *adj* obscene
obscur (op-*skewr*) *adj* obscure; dim, dark
obscurité (op-skew-ree-*tay*) *f* dark
observation (o-psehr-vah-*s*ʸ*awng*) *f* observation
observatoire (o-psehr-vah-*twaar*) *m* observatory
observer (o-psehr-*vay*) *v* watch, observe; notice, note
obsession (o-pseh-*s*ʸ*awng*) *f* obsession
obstacle (op-*stahkl*) *m* obstacle
obstiné (op-stee-*nay*) *adj* pig-headed, obstinate; dogged
obstruer (op-strew-*ay*) *v* block
***obtenir** (op-ter-*neer*) *v* *get; obtain
occasion (o-kah-*z*ʸ*awng*) *f* chance, opportunity; occasion; **d'occasion** second-hand
occident (ok-see-*dahng*) *m* west
occidental (ok-see-dahng-*tahl*) *adj* western, westerly
occupant (o-kew-*pahng*) *m* occupant
occupation (o-kew-pah-*s*ʸ*awng*) *f* occupation; business
occuper (o-kew-*pay*) *v* occupy; *take up; **occupé** busy, engaged, occupied; **s'occuper de** attend to, look after; *take care of, see to, *deal with
océan (o-say-*ahng*) *m* ocean; **Océan Atlantique** Atlantic; **Océan Pacifique** Pacific Ocean
octobre (ok-*tobr*) October
oculiste (o-kew-*leest*) *m* oculist
odeur (o-*dŭrr*) *f* smell, odour
œil (ur*ee*) *m* (pl yeux) eye; **coup d'œil** look; glance; glimpse
œuf (urf) *m* egg; **œufs de poisson** roe
œuvre (ūrvr) *m* work; **~ d'art** work of art
offense (o-*fahngss*) *f* offence

offenser (o-fahng-*say*) *v* injure, *hurt, wound, offend; **s'offenser de** resent
offensif (o-fahng-*seef*) *adj* offensive
offensive (o-fahng-*seev*) *f* offensive
officiel (o-fee-*s*ʸ*ehl*) *adj* official
officier (o-fee-*s*ʸ*ay*) *m* officer
officieux (o-fee-*s*ʸ*ur*) *adj* unofficial
offre (ofr) *f* offer; supply
***offrir** (o-*freer*) *v* offer
oie (wah) *f* goose
oignon (o-*ñawng*) *m* onion; bulb
oiseau (wah-*zoa*) *m* bird; **~ de mer** sea-bird
oisif (wah-*zeef*) *adj* idle
olive (o-*leev*) *f* olive
ombragé (awng-brah-*zhay*) *adj* shady
ombre (awngbr) *f* shadow, shade; **~ à paupières** eye-shadow
omelette (om-*leht*) *f* omelette
***omettre** (o-*mehtr*) *v* *leave out, omit; fail
omnibus (om-nee-*bewss*) *m* stopping train
omnipotent (om-nee-po-*tahng*) *adj* omnipotent
on (awng) *pron* one
oncle (awngkl) *m* uncle
ondulation (awng-dew-lah-*s*ʸ*awng*) *f* wave
ondulé (awng-dew-*lay*) *adj* wavy, undulating
ongle (awnggl) *m* nail
onguent (awng-*gahng*) *m* ointment, salve
onyx (o-*neeks*) *m* onyx
onze (awngz) *num* eleven
onzième (awng-*z*ʸ*ehm*) *num* eleventh
opale (o-*pahl*) *f* opal
opéra (o-pay-*rah*) *m* opera; opera house
opération (o-pay-rah-*s*ʸ*awng*) *f* operation, surgery
opérer (o-pay-*ray*) *v* operate
opérette (o-pay-*reht*) *f* operetta

opiniâtre (o-pee-n^yaatr) *adj* obstinate
opinion (o-pee-n^yawng) *f* view, opinion
opposé (o-poa-zay) *adj* contrary, opposite; averse
s'opposer (o-poa-zay) oppose
opposition (o-poa-zee-s^yawng) *f* opposition
oppresser (o-pray-say) *v* oppress
opprimer (o-pree-may) *v* oppress
opticien (op-tee-s^yang) *m* optician
optimisme (op-tee-meesm) *m* optimism
optimiste (op-tee-meest) *m* optimist; *adj* optimistic
or (awr) *m* gold; **en ~** golden; **~ en feuille** gold leaf
orage (o-raazh) *m* thunderstorm
orageux (o-rah-zhur) *adj* thundery, stormy
oral (o-rahl) *adj* oral
orange (o-rahngzh) *f* orange; *adj* orange
orchestre (or-kehstr) *m* orchestra; band; **fauteuil d'orchestre** stall
ordinaire (or-dee-nair) *adj* plain, simple, usual, regular, customary; common, vulgar
ordonner (or-do-nay) *v* arrange; order; **ordonné** *adj* tidy
ordre (ordr) *m* order; method; command; **~ du jour** agenda
ordures (or-dewr) *fpl* garbage
oreille (o-ray) *f* ear
oreiller (o-ray-^yay) *m* pillow; **taie d'oreiller** pillow-case
oreillons (o-reh-^yawng) *mpl* mumps
orfèvre (or-faivr) *m* goldsmith; silversmith
organe (or-gahn) *m* organ
organique (or-gah-neek) *adj* organic
organisation (or-gah-nee-zah-s^yawng) *f* organization
organiser (or-gah-nee-zay) *v* organize

orge (orzh) *f* barley
orgue (org) *m* (pl *f*) organ; **~ de Barbarie** street-organ
orgueil (or-gur^{ee}) *m* pride
orgueilleux (or-gur-^yur) *adj* proud
orient (o-r^yahng) *m* Orient
oriental (o-r^yahng-tahl) *adj* oriental; eastern, easterly
s'orienter (o-r^yahng-tay) orientate
originairement (o-ree-zhee-nehr-mahng) *adv* originally
original (o-ree-zhee-nahl) *adj* original
origine (o-ree-zheen) *f* origin
orlon (or-lawng) *m* orlon
orme (orm) *m* elm
ornement (or-ner-mahng) *m* ornament
ornemental (or-ner-mahng-tahl) *adj* ornamental
orphelin (or-fer-lang) *m* orphan
orteil (or-tay) *m* toe
orthodoxe (or-to-doks) *adj* orthodox
orthographe (or-to-grahf) *f* spelling
os (oss) *m* (pl ~) bone
oser (oa-zay) *v* dare
otage (o-taazh) *m* hostage
ôter (oa-tay) *v* *take out; wipe
ou (oo) *conj* or; **~ ... ou** either ... or
où (oo) *adv* where; *pron* where; **n'importe ~** anywhere
ouate (waht) *f* cotton-wool
oublier (oo-blee-ay) *v* *forget
oublieux (oo-blee-ur) *adj* forgetful
ouest (wehst) *m* west
oui (wee) yes
ouïe (oo-ee) *f* hearing
ouragan (oo-rah-gahng) *m* hurricane
ourlet (oor-lay) *m* hem
ours (oors) *m* bear
oursin (oor-sang) *m* sea-urchin
outil (oo-tee) *m* tool, utensil, implement
outrage (oo-traazh) *m* outrage; offence

outrager (oo-trah-*zhay*) *v* offend
outre (ootr) *prep* beyond, besides;
d'outre-mer overseas; **en ~** furthermore, besides
ouvert (oo-*vair*) *adj* open
ouverture (oo-vehr-*tewr*) *f* opening;
overture
ouvrage (oo-*vraazh*) *m* work
ouvre-boîte (oo-vrer-*bwaht*) *m* tin-
opener; can opener
ouvre-bouteille (oo-vrer-boo-*tay*) *m*
bottle opener
ouvreur (oo-*vrūr*) *m* usher
ouvreuse (oo-*vrūz*) *f* usherette
ouvrier (oo-vree-*ay*) *m* workman,
worker
*ouvrir (oo-*vreer*) *v* open; unlock;
turn on
ovale (o-*vahl*) *adj* oval
oxygène (ok-see-*zhehn*) *m* oxygen

P

pacifisme (pah-see-*feesm*) *m* pacifism
pacifiste (pah-see-*feest*) *m* pacifist;
adj pacifist
pagaie (pah-*gay*) *f* paddle
pagaille (pah-*gigh*) *f* muddle
page (paazh) *f* page; *m* page-boy
paie (pay) *f* salary
paiement (pay-*mahng*) *m* payment;
~ à tempérament instalment
païen (pah-*Yang*) *m* pagan, heathen;
adj pagan, heathen
paille (pigh) *f* straw
pain (pang) *m* bread; **~ complet**
wholemeal bread; **petit ~** roll
pair (pair) *adj* even
paire (pair) *f* pair
paisible (pay-*zeebl*) *adj* peaceful, quiet
*paître (paitr) *v* graze
paix (pay) *f* peace

Pakistan (pah-kee-*stahng*) *m* Pakistan
Pakistanais (pah-kee-stah-*nay*) *m* Pakistani
pakistanais (pah-kee-stah-*nay*) *adj* Pakistani
palais (pah-*lay*) *m* palace; palate
pâle (paal) *adj* pale
palme (pahlm) *f* palm
palpable (pahl-*pahbl*) *adj* palpable
palper (pahl-*pay*) *v* *feel
palpitation (pahl-pee-tah-*sYawng*) *f*
palpitation
pamplemousse (pahng-pler-*mooss*) *m*
grapefruit
panier (pah-*nYay*) *m* hamper, basket
panique (pah-*neek*) *f* panic; scare
panne (pahn) *f* breakdown; **tomber
en ~** *break down
panneau (pah-*noa*) *m* panel
pansement (pahng-*smahng*) *m* bandage
panser (pahng-*say*) *v* dress
pantalon (pahng-tah-*lawng*) *m* trousers *pl*, slacks *pl*; pants *plAm*; **ensemble-pantalon** pant-suit; **~ de
ski** ski pants
pantoufle (pahng-*toofl*) *f* slipper
paon (pahng) *m* peacock
papa (pah-*pah*) *m* daddy
pape (pahp) *m* pope
papeterie (pah-peh-*tree*) *f* stationer's;
stationery
papier (pah-*pYay*) *m* paper; **en ~** paper; **~ à écrire** notepaper; **~ à lettres** notepaper, writing-paper; **~ à
machine** typing paper; **~ buvard**
blotting paper; **~ carbone** carbon
paper; **~ d'emballage** wrapping paper; **~ d'étain** tinfoil; **~ de verre**
sandpaper; **~ hygiénique** toilet-paper; **~ peint** wallpaper
papillon (pah-pee-*Yawng*) *m* butterfly
paquebot (pahk-*boa*) *m* liner
Pâques (paak) *m* Easter

paquet (pah-*kay*) *m* parcel, packet; bundle

par (pahr) *prep* by; for

parade (pah-*rahd*) *f* parade

paragraphe (pah-rah-*grahf*) *m* paragraph

*paraître (pah-*raitr*) *v* seem, appear

parallèle (pah-rah-*lehl*) *m* parallel; *adj* parallel

paralyser (pah-rah-lee-*zay*) *v* paralise; **paralysé** lame

parapher (pah-rah-*fay*) *v* initial

parapluie (pah-rah-*plwee*) *m* umbrella

parasol (pah-rah-*sol*) *m* sunshade

parc (pahrk) *m* park; ~ **de stationnement** car park; ~ **national** national park

parce que (pahr-*sker*) as, because

parcimonieux (pahr-see-mo-*n*ᵞ*ur*) *adj* economical, thrifty

parcomètre (pahr-ko-*mehtr*) *m* parking meter

*parcourir (pahr-koo-*reer*) *v* *go through; cover

parcours (pahr-*kōōr*) *m* stretch

par-dessus (pahr-der-*sew*) *prep* over

pardessus (pahr-der-*sew*) *m* coat, overcoat; topcoat

pardon (pahr-*dawng*) *m* pardon; **pardon!** sorry!

pardonner (pahr-do-*nay*) *v* *forgive

pare-brise (pahr-*breez*) *m* windscreen; windshield *nAm*

pare-choc (pahr-*shok*) *m* bumper, fender

pareil (pah-*ray*) *adj* alike, like; **sans** ~ unsurpassed

parent (pah-*rahng*) *m* relative, relation; **parents** parents *pl*; **parents nourriciers** foster-parents *pl*

paresseux (pah-reh-*sur*) *adj* lazy

parfait (pahr-*fay*) *adj* perfect; faultless

parfois (pahr-*fwah*) *adv* sometimes

parfum (pahr-*furng*) *m* scent; perfume

parfumerie (pahr-fewm-*ree*) *f* perfumery

pari (pah-*ree*) *m* bet

parier (pah-*r*ᵞ*ay*) *v* *bet

parking (pahr-*keeng*) *m* parking lot *Am*

parlement (pahr-ler-*mahng*) *m* parliament

parlementaire (pahr-ler-mahng-*tair*) *adj* parliamentary

parler (pahr-*lay*) *v* talk, *speak

parmi (pahr-*mee*) *prep* among, amid

paroisse (pah-*rwahss*) *f* parish

parole (pah-*rol*) *f* speech

parrain (pah-*rang*) *m* godfather

part (paar) *f* part, share; **à** ~ separately, apart; aside; **nulle** ~ nowhere; **quelque** ~ somewhere

partager (pahr-tah-*zhay*) *v* share

partenaire (pahr-ter-*nair*) *m* associate, partner

parti (pahr-*tee*) *m* party; side

partial (pahr-s*ʸ*ahl) *adj* partial

participant (pahr-tee-see-*pahng*) *m* participant

participer (pahr-tee-see-*pay*) *v* participate

particularité (pahr-tee-kew-lah-ree-*tay*) *f* peculiarity; detail

particulier (pahr-tee-kew-*l*ᵞ*ay*) *adj* particular, special; individual, private; peculiar; **en** ~ in particular

particulièrement (pahr-tee-kew-l*ʸ*ehr-*mahng*) *adv* specially

partie (pahr-*tee*) *f* part; **en** ~ partly

partiel (pahr-s*ʸ*ehl) *adj* partial

partiellement (pahr-s*ʸ*ehl-*mahng*) *adv* partly

*partir (pahr-*teer*) *v* *leave, *go away; *set out, depart, pull out; check out; **à partir de** as from, from; **parti** gone

partisan (pahr-tee-*zahng*) *m* advocate

partout (pahr-*too*) *adv* throughout,

everywhere; ~ **où** wherever
***parvenir à** (pahr-ver-*neer*) achieve
pas (pah) *m* step; pace, move; **faux**
~ slip; **ne ... ~** not
passablement (pah-sah-bler-*mahng*)
adv pretty, rather, quite
passage (pah-*saazh*) *m* passage;
crossing; aisle; ~ **à niveau** crossing; ~ **clouté** pedestrian crossing;
~ **pour piétons** crosswalk *nAm*
passager (pah-sah-*zhay*) *m* passenger
passant (pah-*sahng*) *m* passer-by
passé (pah-*say*) *m* past; *adj* past;
prep over
passeport (pah-*spawr*) *m* passport
passer (pah-*say*) *v* pass; *give; **en
passant** casual; ~ **à côté** pass by;
~ **en contrebande** smuggle; **se ~**
occur; **se ~ de** spare
passerelle (pah-*srehl*) *f* gangway
passe-temps (pah-*stahng*) *m* hobby
passif (pah-*seef*) *adj* passive
passion (pah-s*yawng*) *f* passion
passionnant (pah-s*y*o-*nahng*) *adj* exciting
passionné (pah-s*y*o-*nay*) *adj* passionate; keen
passoire (pah-*swaar*) *f* sieve; strainer
pastèque (pah-*stehk*) *f* watermelon
pasteur (pah-*stūrr*) *m* clergyman; parson, minister, rector
patauger (pah-toa-*zhay*) *v* wade
pâte (paat) *f* paste; dough, batter; ~
dentifrice toothpaste
patère (pah-*tair*) *f* peg
paternel (pah-tehr-*nehl*) *adj* fatherly
patience (pah-s*yahngss*) *f* patience
patient (pah-s*yahng*) *m* patient; *adj*
patient
patin (pah-*tang*) *m* skate
patinage (pah-tee-*naazh*) *m* skating;
~ **à roulettes** roller-skating
patiner (pah-tee-*nay*) *v* skate
patinette (pah-tee-*neht*) *f* scooter

patinoire (pah-tee-*nwaar*) *f* skating-rink
pâtisserie (pah-tee-*sree*) *f* cake, pastry; pastry shop
patrie (pah-*tree*) *f* fatherland, native country
patriote (pah-tree-*ot*) *m* patriot
patron (pah-*trawng*) *m* master, boss
patronne (pah-*tron*) *f* mistress
patrouille (pah-*troo*ee) *f* patrol
patrouiller (pah-troo-*Yay*) *v* patrol
patte (paht) *f* paw
pâture (pah-*tēwr*) *f* pasture
paume (pōam) *f* palm
paupière (poa-*pYair*) *f* eyelid
pause (pōaz) *f* pause; break
pauvre (pōavr) *adj* poor
pauvreté (poa-vrer-*tay*) *f* poverty
pavage (pah-*vaazh*) *m* pavement
paver (pah-*vay*) *v* pave
pavillon (pah-vee-*Yawng*) *m* pavilion;
~ **de chasse** lodge
pavot (pah-*voa*) *m* poppy
payable (pay-*Yahbl*) *adj* due
paye (pay) *f* pay
payer (pay-*Yay*) *v* *pay; ~ **à tempérament** *pay on account
pays (pay-*ee*) *m* country, land; ~ **boisé** woodland; ~ **natal** native country
paysage (pay-ee-*zaazh*) *m* landscape, scenery
paysan (pay-ee-*zahng*) *m* peasant
Pays-Bas (pay-ee-*bah*) *mpl* the Netherlands
péage (pay-*aazh*) *m* toll
peau (poa) *f* skin; hide; ~ **de porc**
pigskin; ~ **de vache** cow-hide
péché (pay-*shay*) *m* sin
pêche[1] (pehsh) *f* peach
pêche[2] (pehsh) *f* fishing industry; **attirail de** ~ fishing tackle, fishing gear
pêcher (pay-*shay*) *v* fish; ~ **à la ligne**

angle

pêcheur (peh-*shūrr*) m fisherman

pédale (pay-*dahl*) f pedal

pédicure (pay-dee-*kēwr*) m pedicure, chiropodist

peigne (pehñ) m comb; ~ **de poche** pocket-comb

peigner (pay-*ñay*) v comb

peignoir (peh-*ñwaar*) m bathrobe

*peindre (pañgdr) v paint

peine (pehn) f trouble, pains, difficulty; penalty; **à ~** hardly; just, barely, scarcely; ***avoir de la ~** grieve; **~ de mort** death penalty

peiner (pay-*nay*) v labour

peintre (pañgtr) m painter

peinture (pang-*tēwr*) f paint; picture, painting; ~ **à l'huile** oil-painting

pelage (per-*laazh*) m furs

peler (per-*lay*) v peel

pèlerin (pehl-*rang*) m pilgrim

pèlerinage (pehl-ree-*naazh*) m pilgrimage

pélican (pay-lee-*kahng*) m pelican

pelle (pehl) f spade, shovel

pellicule (peh-lee-*kewl*) f film; **pellicules** dandruff

pelouse (per-*lōōz*) f lawn

pelure (per-*lēwr*) f peel

penchant (pahng-*shahng*) m inclination

se pencher (pahng-*shay*) *bend down

pendant (pahng-*dahng*) prep for, during; ~ **que** while

pendentif (pahng-dahng-*teef*) m pendant

pendre (pahngdr) v *hang

pénétrer (pay-nay-*tray*) v penetrate

pénible (pay-*neebl*) adj laborious; painful

pénicilline (pay-nee-see-*leen*) f penicillin

péninsule (pay-nang-*sewl*) f peninsula

pensée (pahng-*say*) f thought; idea

penser (pahng-*say*) v *think; ~ **à** *think of

penseur (pahng-*sūrr*) m thinker

pensif (pahng-*seef*) adj thoughtful

pension (pahng-*syawng*) f guesthouse, pension, boarding-house; board; ~ **alimentaire** alimony; ~ **complète** room and board, full board, bed and board, board and lodging

pensionnaire (pahng-syo-*nair*) m boarder

pente (pahngt) f incline; ramp; **en ~** sloping, slanting

Pentecôte (pahngt-*kōāt*) f Whitsun

pénurie (pay-new-*ree*) f scarcity

pépé (pay-*pay*) m grandfather

pépin (pay-*pang*) m pip

pépinière (pay-pee-*nʸair*) f nursery

perceptible (pehr-sehp-*teebl*) adj noticeable, perceptible

perception (pehr-seh-*psʸawng*) f perception

percer (pehr-*say*) v pierce

*percevoir (pehr-ser-*vwaar*) v perceive; sense

perche (pehrsh) f perch, bass

percolateur (pehr-ko-lah-*tūrr*) m percolator

perdre (pehrdr) v *lose

perdrix (pehr-*dree*) f partridge

père (pair) m father; dad

perfection (pehr-fehk-*sʸawng*) f perfection

performance (pehr-for-*mahngss*) f achievement; performance

péril (pay-*reel*) m peril

périlleux (pay-ree-*ʸur*) adj perilous

périmé (pay-ree-*may*) adj expired

période (pay-*rʸod*) f period; term

périodique (pay-rʸo-*deek*) adj periodical; m journal, periodical

périr (pay-*reer*) v perish

périssable (pay-ree-*sahbl*) adj perishable

perle (pehrl) f pearl; bead

permanent (pehr-mah-*nahng*) adj permanent

permanente (pehr-mah-*nahngt*) f permanent wave

***permettre** (pehr-*mehtr*) v permit, allow; enable; **se ~** afford

permis (pehr-*mee*) m permit; permission, licence; **~ de conduire** driving licence; **~ de pêche** fishing licence; **~ de séjour** residence permit; **~ de travail** work permit; labor permit *Am*

permission (pehr-mee-*s*y*awng*) f authorization, permission; leave

perpendiculaire (pehr-pahng-dee-kew-*lair*) adj perpendicular

perroquet (peh-ro-*kay*) m parrot

perruche (peh-*rewsh*) f parakeet

perruque (peh-*rewk*) f wig

Persan (pehr-*sahng*) m Persian

persan (pehr-*sahng*) adj Persian

Perse (pehrs) f Persia

persévérer (pehr-say-vay-*ray*) v *keep up

persienne (pehr-s*y*ehn) f blind; shutter

persil (pehr-*see*) m parsley

persister (pehr-see-*stay*) v insist

personnalité (pehr-so-nah-lee-*tay*) f personality

personne (pehr-*son*) f person; **ne ... personne** nobody, no one; **par ~** per person

personnel (pehr-so-*nehl*) m personnel, staff; adj personal, private

perspective (pehr-spehk-*teev*) f perspective, prospect

persuader (pehr-swah-*day*) v persuade

perte (pehrt) f loss

pertinent (pehr-tee-*nahng*) adj proper

peser (per-*zay*) v weigh

pessimisme (peh-see-*meesm*) m pessimism

pessimiste (peh-see-*meest*) m pessimist; adj pessimistic

pétale (pay-*tahl*) m petal

pétillement (pay-teey-*mahng*) m fizz

***petit** (per-*tee*) adj small, little; petty, short, minor

petite-fille (per-teet-*feey*) f granddaughter

petit-fils (per-tee-*feess*) m grandson

pétition (pay-tee-s*y*awng) f petition

pétrole (pay-*trol*) m petroleum, oil; kerosene, paraffin; **gisement de ~** oil-well

peu (pur) adj little; m bit; **à ~ près** approximately, about; almost; **~ de** few; **quelque ~** somewhat; **sous ~** soon, shortly; **un ~** some

peuple (purpl) m people; nation; folk

peur (pūrr) f fear, fright; ***avoir ~** *be afraid

peut-être (pur-*taitr*) adv maybe, perhaps

phare (faar) m lighthouse; headlight, headlamp; **~ anti-brouillard** foglamp

pharmacie (fahr-mah-*see*) f pharmacy, chemist's; drugstore *nAm*

pharmacien (fahr-mah-s*y*ang) m chemist

pharmacologie (fahr-mah-ko-lo-*zhee*) f pharmacology

phase (faaz) f phase, stage

Philippin (fee-lee-*pang*) m Filipino

philippin (fee-lee-*pang*) adj Philippine

Philippines (fee-lee-*peen*) fpl Philippines pl

philosophe (fee-lo-*zof*) m philosopher

philosophie (fee-lo-zo-*fee*) f philosophy

phonétique (fo-nay-*teek*) adj phonetic

phonographe (fo-no-*grahf*) m gramophone

phoque (fok) m seal

photo 102 **placement**

photo (fo-*toa*) *f* photo; ~ **d'identité** passport photograph

photocopie (fo-to-ko-*pee*) *f* photostat

photographe (fo-to-*grahf*) *m* photographer

photographie (fo-to-grah-*fee*) *f* photography; photograph

photographier (fo-to-grah-*f*ʸ*ay*) *v* photograph

photomètre (fo-to-*mehtr*) *m* exposure meter

phrase (fraaz) *f* sentence

physicien (fee-zee-sʸ*ang*) *m* physicist

physiologie (fee-zʸo-lo-*zhee*) *f* physiology

physique (fee-*zeek*) *f* physics; *adj* physical; material

pianiste (pʸah-*neest*) *m* pianist

piano (pʸah-*noa*) *m* piano; ~ **à queue** grand piano

pie (pee) *f* magpie

pièce (pʸehss) *f* piece; room, chamber; ~ **de monnaie** coin; ~ **de rechange** spare part; ~ **de séjour** living-room; ~ **détachée** spare part; ~ **de théâtre** play

pied (pʸay) *m* foot; leg; **à** ~ walking, on foot

piège (pʸaizh) *m* trap

pierre (pʸair) *f* stone; **en** ~ stone; ~ **à briquet** flint; ~ **ponce** pumice stone; ~ **précieuse** gem; stone; ~ **tombale** tombstone, gravestone

piétiner (pʸay-tee-*nay*) *v* stamp

piéton (pʸay-*tawng*) *m* pedestrian

piètre (pʸehtr) *adj* poor

pieuvre (pʸūrvr) *f* octopus

pieux (pʸur) *adj* pious

pigeon (pee-*zhawng*) *m* pigeon

pignon (pee-*ñawng*) *m* gable

pile (peel) *f* stack; battery

pilier (pee-lʸ*ay*) *m* pillar

pilote (pee-*lot*) *m* pilot

pilule (pee-*lewl*) *f* pill

pin (pang) *m* pine

pince (pangss) *f* pliers *pl*, tongs *pl*; tweezers *pl*; ~ **à cheveux** hairgrip; bobby pin *Am*

pinceau (pang-*soa*) *m* brush; paintbrush

pincer (pang-*say*) *v* pinch

pincettes (pang-*seht*) *fpl* tweezers *pl*

pingouin (pang-*gwang*) *m* penguin

ping-pong (peeng-*pong*) *m* table tennis

pinson (pang-*sawng*) *m* finch

pioche (pʸosh) *f* pick-axe

pion (pʸawng) *m* pawn

pionnier (pʸo-nʸ*ay*) *m* pioneer

pipe (peep) *f* pipe

piquant (pee-*kahng*) *adj* savoury

pique-nique (peek-*neek*) *m* picnic

pique-niquer (peek-nee-*kay*) *v* picnic

piquer (pee-*kay*) *v* *sting, prick

piqûre (pee-*kewr*) *f* shot; sting, bite

pirate (pee-*raht*) *m* pirate

pire (peer) *adj* worse; **le** ~ worst

pis (pee) *adv* worse; **tant pis!** never mind!

piscine (pee-*seen*) *f* swimming pool

pissenlit (pee-sahng-*lee*) *m* dandelion

piste (peest) *f* trail; track; ring; ~ **de courses** race-track; ~ **de décollage** runway

pistolet (pee-sto-*lay*) *m* pistol

piston (pee-*stawng*) *m* piston; **segment de** ~ piston ring; **tige de** ~ piston-rod

pitié (pee-tʸ*ay*) *f* pity; ***avoir** ~ **de** pity

pittoresque (pee-to-*rehsk*) *adj* picturesque, scenic

placard (plah-*kaar*) *m* closet, cupboard

place (plahss) *f* place; seat; room; square; ~ **forte** stronghold

placement (plah-*smahng*) *m* investment

placer (plah-*say*) v place; *put, *lay; invest

plafond (plah-*fawng*) m ceiling

plage (plaazh) f beach; ~ **pour nudistes** nudist beach

plaider (pleh-*day*) v plead

plaidoyer (pleh-dwah-*Yay*) m plea

plaie (play) f wound

se *plaindre (plangdr) complain

plaine (plehn) f plain, lowlands pl

plainte (plangt) f complaint

*plaire (plair) v please; **s'il vous plaît** please

plaisant (pleh-*zahng*) adj pleasant; nice, enjoyable, amusing

plaisanter (pleh-zahng-*tay*) v joke

plaisanterie (play-zahng-*tree*) f joke

plaisir (play-*zeer*) m pleasure; joy, delight, fun, enjoyment; **avec** ~ gladly; ***prendre** ~ enjoy

plan (plahng) m plan, project; map; scheme; adj flat, level, even; **premier** ~ foreground

planche (plahngsh) f plank, board

plancher (plahng-*shay*) m floor

planétarium (plah-nay-tah-*rYom*) m planetarium

planète (plah-*neht*) f planet

planeur (plah-*nūr*) m glider

planifier (plah-nee-*fYay*) v plan

plantation (plahng-tah-*sYawng*) f plantation

plante (plahngt) f plant

planter (plahng-*tay*) v plant

plaque (plahk) f plate; sheet; ~ **d'immatriculation** registration plate; licence plate Am

plastique (plah-*steek*) adj plastic; m plastic

plat (plah) m dish; course; adj flat, plane, smooth, level

plateau (plah-*toa*) m plateau; tray

plate-bande (plaht-*bahngd*) f flower-bed

platine (plah-*teen*) m platinum

plâtre (plaatr) m plaster

plein (plang) adj full; *faire le ~ fill up; ~ à craquer chock-full; pleine saison high season

pleurer (plur-*ray*) v *weep, cry

*pleuvoir (plur-*vwaar*) v rain

pli (plee) m fold; crease; ~ **permanent** permanent press

plie (plee) f plaice

plier (plee-*ay*) v fold

plomb (plawng) m lead

plombage (plawng-*baazh*) m filling

plombier (plawng-*bYay*) m plumber

plonger (plawng-*zhay*) v dive

pluie (plwee) f rain

plume (plewm) f feather; pen

(la) plupart (plew-*paar*) most

pluriel (plew-*rYehl*) m plural

plus (plewss) adj more; prep plus; **de** ~ moreover; **le** ~ most; **ne ... ~** no longer; ~ **... plus** the ... the

plusieurs (plew-*zYūūr*) adj several

plutôt (plew-*toa*) adv fairly, pretty, rather, quite; sooner

pluvieux (plew-*vYur*) adj rainy

pneu (pnur) m (pl ~s) tyre; tire; ~ **crevé** flat tyre; ~ **de rechange** spare tyre

pneumatique (pnur-mah-*teek*) adj pneumatic

pneumonie (pnur-mo-*nee*) f pneumonia

poche (posh) f pocket; **lampe de** ~ flash-light

pochette (po-*sheht*) f pouch

poêle (pwahl) f saucepan; m stove; ~ à frire frying-pan

poème (po-*ehm*) m poem; ~ **épique** epic

poésie (po-ay-*zee*) f poetry

poète (po-*eht*) m poet

poids (pwah) m weight

poignée (pwah-*ñay*) f handle; handful; ~ **de main** handshake

poignet (pwah-*ñay*) *m* wrist

poil (pwahl) *m* hair

poing (pwang) *m* fist

point (pwang) *m* point; item; period, full stop; stitch; ~ **de congélation** freezing-point; ~ **de départ** starting-point; ~ **de repère** land-mark; ~ **de vue** view, outlook; ~ **d'interrogation** question mark; **point-virgule** *m* semi-colon

pointe (pwangt) *f* point; **heure de** ~ peak hour

pointer (pwang-*tay*) *v* tick off

pointu (pwang-*tew*) *adj* pointed

poire (pwaar) *f* pear

poireau (pwah-*roa*) *m* leek

pois (pwah) *m* pea

poison (pwah-*zawng*) *m* poison

poisson (pwah-*sawng*) *m* fish

poissonnerie (pwah-son-*ree*) *f* fish shop

poitrine (pwah-*treen*) *f* chest; bosom

poivre (pwaavr) *m* pepper

pôle nord (poal nawr) North Pole

pôle sud (poal sewd) South Pole

poli (po-*lee*) *adj* polite; civil

police (po-*leess*) *f* police *pl*; policy; **commissariat de** ~ police-station; ~ **d'assurance** insurance policy

policier (po-lee-*s*ⁱ*ay*) *m* policeman

poliomyélite (po-lⁱⁱo-m*ⁱ*ay-*leet*) *f* polio

polir (po-*leer*) *v* polish

polisson (po-lee-*sawng*) *adj* naughty

politicien (po-lee-tee-s*ⁱ*ang) *m* politician

politique (po-lee-*teek*) *f* politics; policy; *adj* political

pollution (po-lew-s*ⁱ*awng) *f* pollution

Pologne (po-*loñ*) *f* Poland

Polonais (po-lo-*nay*) *m* Pole

polonais (po-lo-*nay*) *adj* Polish

pomme (pom) *f* apple; ~ **de terre** potato; **pommes frites** chips

pommette (po-*meht*) *f* cheek-bone

pompe (pawngp) *f* pump; ~ **à eau** water pump; ~ **à essence** petrol pump; gas pump *Am*

pomper (pawng-*pay*) *v* pump

pompier (pawng-*p*ⁱ*ay*) *m* fireman; **pompiers** fire-brigade

ponctuel (pawngk-*twehl*) *adj* punctual

pondéré (pawng-day-*ray*) *adj* sober

pondre (pawngdr) *v* *lay

poney (po-*nay*) *m* pony

pont (pawng) *m* bridge; deck; **pont-levis** *m* drawbridge; ~ **principal** main deck; ~ **suspendu** suspension bridge

popeline (po-*pleen*) *f* poplin

populaire (po-pew-*lair*) *adj* popular

population (po-pew-lah-s*ⁱ*awng) *f* population

populeux (po-pew-*lur*) *adj* populous

porc (pawr) *m* pork

porcelaine (por-ser-*lehn*) *f* porcelain, china

porc-épic (por-kay-*peek*) *m* porcupine

port[1] (pawr) *m* port, harbour; ~ **de mer** seaport

port[2] (pawr) *m* postage; ~ **payé** postage paid, post-paid

portatif (por-tah-*teef*) *adj* portable

porte (port) *f* door; gate; ~ **coulissante** sliding door; ~ **tournante** revolving door

porte-bagages (port-bah-*gaazh*) *m* luggage rack

porte-bonheur (port-bo-*nūrr*) *m* lucky charm

porte-documents (port-do-kew-*mahng*) *m* attaché case

portée (por-*tay*) *f* reach; litter

portefeuille (por-ter-*fur*ᵉᵉ) *m* pocket-book, wallet

porte-jarretelles (port-zhahr-*tehl*) *m* suspender belt; garter belt *Am*

porte-manteau (port-mahng-*toa*) *m*

hat rack

porte-monnaie (port-mo-*nay*) *m* purse

porter (por-*tay*) *v* carry, *bear;
*wear; ~ **sur** concern; **se ~ bien**
*be in good health

porteur (por-*tūrr*) *m* bearer; porter

portier (por-*t*ʸ*ay*) *m* porter, doorman,
door-keeper

portion (por-*s*ʸ*awng*) *f* helping, portion

portrait (por-*tray*) *m* portrait

Portugais (por-tew-*gay*) *m* Portuguese

portugais (por-tew-*gay*) *adj* Portuguese

Portugal (por-tew-*gahl*) *m* Portugal

poser (poa-*zay*) *v* place; *put, *lay,
*set

positif (poa-zee-*teef*) *m* positive; *adj*
positive

position (poa-zee-*s*ʸ*awng*) *f* position;
site

posséder (po-say-*day*) *v* possess, own

possession (po-seh-*s*ʸ*awng*) *f* possession

possibilité (po-see-bee-lee-*tay*) *f* possibility

possible (po-*seebl*) *adj* possible

poste¹ (post) *f* post; *****mettre à la ~**
mail; ~ **aérienne** airmail; ~ **restante** poste restante

poste² (post) *m* station; post; ~ **de
secours** first-aid post; ~ **d'essence**
petrol station

poster (po-*stay*) *v* post

postérieur (po-stay-*r*ʸ*ūrr*) *m* bottom;
adj subsequent

postiche (po-*steesh*) *m* hair piece

pot (poa) *m* pot

potable (po-*tahbl*) *adj* for drinking

potage (po-*taazh*) *m* soup

poteau (po-*toa*) *m* post, pole; ~ **indicateur** milepost, signpost

potelé (po-*tlay*) *adj* plump

poterie (po-*tree*) *f* pottery, earthen-

ware, crockery

pou (poo) *m* (pl ~x) louse

poubelle (poo-*behl*) *f* rubbish-bin

pouce (pooss) *m* thumb

poudre (poodr) *f* powder; ~ **à canon**
gunpowder; ~ **dentifrice** toothpowder; ~ **de riz** face-powder; ~
pour les pieds foot powder; **savon
en ~** soap powder

poudrier (poo-dree-*ay*) *m* powder
compact

poule (pool) *f* hen

poulet (poo-*lay*) *m* chicken

poulie (poo-*lee*) *f* pulley

pouls (poo) *m* pulse

poumon (poo-*mawng*) *m* lung

poupée (poo-*pay*) *f* doll

pour (pōōr) *prep* for, to; ~ **que** so
that

pourboire (poor-*bwaar*) *m* tip, gratuity

pourcentage (poor-sahng-*taazh*) *m*
percentage

pourchasser (poor-shah-*say*) *v* chase

pourpre (poorpr) *adj* purple

pourquoi (poor-*kwah*) *adv* why; what
for

pourrir (poo-*reer*) *v* rot; **pourri** rotten

*****poursuivre** (poor-*sweevr*) *v* carry on,
continue, pursue

pourtant (poor-*tahng*) *adv* however,
yet; though

pourvu que (poor-vew ker) provided
that

poussée (poo-*say*) *f* push

pousser (poo-*say*) *v* push

poussette (poo-*seht*) *f* baby carriage
Am

poussière (poo-s*ʸ*air*) *f* dust

poussiéreux (poo-s*ʸ*ay-*rur*) *adj* dusty

poussoir (poo-*swaar*) *m* push-button

poutre (pootr) *f* beam

pouvoir (poo-*vwaar*) *m* power; authority; ~ **exécutif** executive

*****pouvoir** (poo-*vwaar*) *v* *can, *be able

to; *might, *may

praline (prah-*leen*) f chocolate

pratique (prah-*teek*) f practice; adj practical, convenient

pratiquer (prah-tee-*kay*) v practise

pré (pray) m meadow

préalable (pray-ah-*lahbl*) adj previous

précaire (pray-*kair*) adj precarious, critical

précaution (pray-koa-sʸawng) f precaution

précédemment (pray-say-dah-*mahng*) adv before

précédent (pray-say-*dahng*) adj preceding, previous, last; former

précéder (pray-say-*day*) v precede

précepteur (pray-sehp-*tūrr*) m tutor

prêcher (pray-*shay*) v preach

précieux (pray-sʸur) adj valuable; precious

précipice (pray-see-*peess*) m precipice

précipitation (pray-see-pee-tah-sʸawng) f precipitation

précipité (pray-see-pee-*tay*) adj hasty

se précipiter (pray-see-pee-*tay*) dash

précis (pray-*see*) adj precise; accurate, very

préciser (pray-see-*zay*) v specify

précision (pray-see-zʸawng) f precision; **précisions** particulars pl

prédécesseur (pray-day-seh-*sūrr*) m predecessor

***prédire** (pray-*deer*) v predict

préférable (pray-fay-*rahbl*) adj preferable

préférence (pray-fay-*rahngss*) f preference

préférer (pray-fay-*ray*) v prefer; **préféré** favourite

préfixe (pray-*feeks*) m prefix

préjudiciable (pray-zhew-dee-sʸahbl) adj harmful

préjugé (pray-zhew-*zhay*) m prejudice

prélever (prayl-*vay*) v raise

préliminaire (pray-lee-mee-*nair*) adj preliminary

prématuré (pray-mah-tew-*ray*) adj premature

premier (prer-mʸay) num first; adj foremost, primary; ~ **ministre** premier

***prendre** (prahngdr) v *take; collect; v *catch; capture; ~ **garde** look out, beware; ~ **soin de** look after

prénom (pray-*nawng*) m first name, Christian name

préparation (pray-pah-rah-sʸawng) f preparation

préparer (pray-pah-*ray*) v prepare; arrange; cook

préposition (pray-poa-zee-sʸawng) f preposition

près (pray) adv near; **à peu** ~ about; ~ **de** by, near

presbytère (prehss-bee-*tair*) m rectory; vicarage, parsonage

prescription (preh-skree-psʸawng) f prescription

***prescrire** (preh-*skreer*) v prescribe

présence (pray-*zahngss*) f presence

présent (pray-*zahng*) m present; adj present; **jusqu'à** ~ so far

présentation (pray-zahng-tah-sʸawng) f introduction

présenter (pray-zahng-*tay*) v present; introduce; **se** ~ appear; report

président (pray-zee-*dahng*) m president, chairman

présomptueux (pray-zawngp-*twur*) adj presumptuous

presque (prehsk) adv nearly, almost

pressant (preh-*sahng*) adj pressing

presse (prehss) f press

presser (pray-*say*) v press; **se** ~ hurry, rush

pression (preh-sʸawng) f pressure; ~ **atmosphérique** atmospheric pressure; ~ **des pneus** tyre pressure; ~

d'huile oil pressure

prestidigitateur (preh-stee-dee-zhee-tah-*tūr*) *m* magician

prestige (preh-*steezh*) *m* prestige

présumer (pray-zew-*may*) *v* assume

prêt (pray) *m* loan; *adj* ready; prepared

prétendre (pray-*tahngdr*) *v* claim, pretend

prétentieux (pray-tahng-*sᵧur*) *adj* conceited

prétention (pray-tahng-*sᵧawng*) *f* claim

prêter (pray-*tay*) *v* *lend; ~ **attention à** attend to, mind

prêteur sur gage (preh-turr sewr gaazh) pawnbroker

prétexte (pray-*tehkst*) *m* pretence, pretext

prêtre (praitr) *m* priest

preuve (prūrv) *f* proof, evidence; token

prévenant (preh-*vnahng*) *adj* considerate, thoughtful

***prévenir** (preh-*vneer*) *v* warn; prevent, anticipate

préventif (preh-vahng-*teef*) *adj* preventive

prévenu (pray-*vnew*) *m* accused

prévision (pray-vee-*zᵧawng*) *f* forecast, outlook

***prévoir** (pray-*vwaar*) *v* forecast; anticipate

prier (pree-*ay*) *v* pray; ask

prière (pree-*air*) *f* prayer

primaire (pree-*mair*) *adj* primary

prime (preem) *f* premium

primordial (pree-mor-*dᵧahl*) *adj* primary

prince (prangss) *m* prince

princesse (prang-*sehss*) *f* princess

principal (prang-see-*pahl*) *adj* principal; cardinal, chief, leading, main

principalement (prang-see-pahl-*mahng*) *adv* especially, mainly

principe (prang-*seep*) *m* principle

printemps (prang-*tahng*) *m* spring; springtime

priorité (pree-o-ree-*tay*) *f* priority; ~ **de passage** right of way

prise (preez) *f* grip, clutch, grasp; capture; ~ **de vue** shot

prison (pree-*zawng*) *f* prison; jail, gaol

prisonnier (pree-zo-*nᵧay*) *m* prisoner; ***faire** ~ capture; ~ **de guerre** prisoner of war

privation (pree-vah-*sᵧawng*) *f* exposure

privé (pree-*vay*) *adj* private

priver de (pree-*vay*) deprive of

privilège (pree-vee-*laizh*) *m* privilege

prix (pree) *m* price-list; charge, cost; award, prize; **prix-courant** *m* price list; ~ **d'achat** purchase price; ~ **de consolation** consolation prize; ~ **d'entrée** entrance-fee; ~ **du voyage** fare

probable (pro-*bahbl*) *adj* probable; presumable, likely

probablement (pro-bah-bler-*mahng*) *adv* probably

problème (pro-*blehm*) *m* problem; question

procédé (pro-say-*day*) *m* process

procéder (pro-say-*day*) *v* proceed

procédure (pro-say-*dēwr*) *f* procedure

procès (pro-*say*) *m* process; trial, lawsuit

procession (pro-seh-*sᵧawng*) *f* procession

processus (pro-say-*sewss*) *m* process

prochain (pro-*shang*) *adj* following, next

prochainement (pro-shehn-*mahng*) *adv* soon, shortly

proche (prosh) *adj* close, near; nearby; oncoming

proclamer (pro-klah-*may*) *v* proclaim

procurer (pro-kew-*ray*) *v* furnish; **se ~** obtain

prodigue (pro-*deeg*) *adj* lavish

producteur (pro-dewk-*tūrr*) *m* producer

production (pro-dewk-*sⁱawng*) *f* production; output; **~ en série** mass production

*produire (pro-*dweer*) *v* produce; generate; **se ~** occur, happen

produit (pro-*dwee*) *m* product; produce

profane (pro-*fahn*) *m* layman

professer (pro-fay-*say*) *v* confess

professeur (pro-feh-*sūrr*) *m* teacher; professor, master

profession (pro-feh-*sⁱawng*) *f* profession

professionnel (pro-feh-sⁱo-*nehl*) *adj* professional

profit (pro-*fee*) *m* profit, benefit

profitable (pro-fee-*tahbl*) *adj* profitable

profiter (pro-fee-*tay*) *v* profit, benefit

profond (pro-*fawng*) *adj* deep; low; profound

profondeur (pro-fawng-*dūrr*) *f* depth

programme (pro-*grahm*) *m* programme

progrès (pro-*gray*) *m* progress

progresser (pro-gray-*say*) *v* *get on

progressif (pro-gray-*seef*) *adj* progressive

progressiste (pro-gray-*seest*) *adj* progressive

projecteur (pro-zhehk-*tūrr*) *m* spotlight; searchlight

projet (pro-*zhay*) *m* project; scheme

prolongation (pro-lawng-gah-sⁱawng) *f* extension

prolonger (pro-lawng-*zhay*) *v* renew

promenade (prom-*nahd*) *f* walk, stroll; promenade; **~ en voiture** drive

se promener (prom-*nay*) walk

promeneur (prom-*nūrr*) *m* walker

promesse (pro-*mehss*) *f* promise

*promettre (pro-*mehtr*) *v* promise

promontoire (pro-mawng-*twaar*) *m* headland

promotion (pro-mo-sⁱawng) *f* promotion

*promouvoir (pro-moo-*vwaar*) *v* promote

prompt (prawng) *adj* prompt; fast

promptitude (prawng-tee-*tewd*) *f* haste

pronom (pro-*nawng*) *m* pronoun

prononcer (pro-nawng-*say*) *v* pronounce

prononciation (pro-nawng-sⁱah-sⁱawng) *f* pronunciation

propagande (pro-pah-*gahngd*) *f* propaganda

prophète (pro-*feht*) *m* prophet

proportion (pro-por-sⁱawng) *f* proportion

proportionnel (pro-por-sⁱo-*nehl*) *adj* proportional

propos (pro-*poa*) *m* intention; **à ~** by the way; **à ~ de** regarding

proposer (pro-poa-*zay*) *v* propose

proposition (pro-poa-zee-sⁱawng) *f* proposition, proposal

propre (propr) *adj* clean; own

propriétaire (pro-pree-ay-*tair*) *m* owner, proprietor; landlord

propriété (pro-pree-ay-*tay*) *f* property; estate

propulser (pro-pewl-*say*) *v* propel

prospectus (pro-spehk-*tewss*) *m* prospectus

prospère (pro-*spair*) *adj* prosperous

prospérité (pro-spay-ree-*tay*) *f* prosperity

prostituée (pro-stee-*tway*) *f* prostitute

protection (pro-tehk-sⁱawng) *f* protection

protéger (pro-tay-*zhay*) *v* protect
protéine (pro-tay-*een*) *f* protein
protestant (pro-teh-*stahng*) *adj* Protestant
protestation (pro-teh-stah-*syawng*) *f* protest
protester (pro-teh-*stay*) *v* protest
prouver (proo-*vay*) *v* prove
provenance (pro-*vnahngss*) *f* origin
***provenir de** (pro-*vneer*) *come from
proverbe (pro-*vehrb*) *m* proverb
province (pro-*vangss*) *f* province
provincial (pro-vang-*syahl*) *adj* provincial
proviseur (pro-vee-*zūrr*) *m* principal
provision (pro-vee-*zyawng*) *f* store; provisions *pl*
provisoire (pro-vee-*zwaar*) *adj* temporary, provisional
provoquer (pro-vo-*kay*) *v* cause
prudence (prew-*dahngss*) *f* caution
prudent (prew-*dahng*) *adj* careful; cautious, wary
prune (prewn) *f* plum
pruneau (prew-*noa*) *m* prune
prurit (prew-*reet*) *m* itch
psychanalyste (psee-kah-nah-*leest*) *m* psychoanalyst, analyst
psychiatre (psee-*kyaatr*) *m* psychiatrist
psychique (psee-*sheek*) *adj* psychic
psychologie (psee-ko-lo-*zhee*) *f* psychology
psychologique (psee-ko-lo-*zheek*) *adj* psychological
psychologue (psee-ko-*log*) *m* psychologist
public (pew-*bleek*) *m* audience, public; *adj* public
publication (pew-blee-kah-*syawng*) *f* publication
publicité (pew-blee-see-*tay*) *f* advertising, publicity; advertisement
publier (pew-blee-*ay*) *v* publish

puer (pway) *v* *stink
puis (pwee) *adv* then
puisque (pweesk) *conj* as
puissance (pwee-*sahngss*) *f* might, force; power, energy; capacity
puissant (pwee-*sahng*) *adj* powerful, mighty; strong
puits (pwee) *m* well; ~ **de pétrole** oil-well
pull-over (pew-lo-*vair*) *m* pullover
pulvérisateur (pewl-vay-ree-zah-*tūrr*) *m* atomizer
pulvériser (pewl-vay-ree-*zay*) *v* *grind
punaise (pew-*naiz*) *f* bug; drawing-pin; thumbtack *nAm*
punir (pew-*neer*) *v* punish
punition (pew-nee-*syawng*) *f* punishment
pupitre (pew-*peetr*) *m* desk; pulpit
pur (pēwr) *adj* pure; clean; sheer, neat
pus (pew) *m* pus
pustule (pew-*stewl*) *f* pimple
putain (pew-*tang*) *f* whore
puzzle (purzl) *m* jigsaw puzzle
pyjama (pee-zhah-*mah*) *m* pyjamas *pl*

Q

quai (kay) *m* wharf, dock, quay; platform
qualification (kah-lee-fee-kah-*syawng*) *f* qualification
qualifié (kah-lee-*fyay*) *adj* qualified; *être ~ qualify; **non** ~ unskilled
qualité (kah-lee-*tay*) *f* quality; **de première** ~ first-class; first-rate
quand (kahng) *adv* when; *conj* when; **n'importe** ~ whenever
quant à (kahng-*tah*) as regards
quantité (kahng-tee-*tay*) *f* quantity, amount; lot

quarantaine (kah-rahng-tehn) *f* quarantine

quarante (kah-rahngt) *num* forty

quart (kaar) *m* quarter; ~ **d'heure** quarter of an hour

quartier (kahr-t^yay) *m* district, quarter; **bas** ~ slum; ~ **général** headquarters *pl*

quatorze (kah-torz) *num* fourteen

quatorzième (kah-tor-z^yehm) *num* fourteenth

quatre (kahtr) *num* four

quatre-vingt-dix (kah-trer-vang-deess) *num* ninety

quatre-vingts (kah-trer-vang) *num* eighty

quatrième (kah-tr^yehm) *num* fourth

que (ker) *conj* that; as, than; *adv* how; **ce** ~ what

quel (kehl) *pron* which; **n'importe** ~ any; whichever

quelquefois (kehl-ker-fwah) *adv* sometimes

quelques (kehlk) *adj* some, some

quelqu'un (kehl-kurng) *pron* someone, somebody

querelle (ker-rehl) *f* dispute, row, quarrel

se quereller (ker-ray-lay) quarrel

question (keh-st^yawng) *f* question; inquiry, query; matter, issue, problem

quêter (kay-tay) *v* collect

quêteur (keh-tūrr) *m* collector

queue (kur) *f* tail; queue; *faire la* ~ queue; stand in line *Am*

qui (kee) *pron* who; which, that; **à** ~ whom; **n'importe** ~ anybody

quiconque (kee-kawngk) *pron* whoever

quille (keey) *f* keel

quincaillerie (kang-kigh-ree) *f* hardware; hardware store

quinine (kee-neen) *f* quinine

quinze (kangz) *num* fifteen; ~ **jours** fortnight

quinzième (kang-z^yehm) *num* fifteenth

quitter (kee-tay) *v* *leave

quoi (kwah) *pron* what; **n'importe** ~ anything

quoique (kwahk) *conj* though, although; **quoiqu'il en soit** at any rate

quote-part (kot-paar) *f* quota

quotidien (ko-tee-d^yang) *adj* everyday, daily; *m* daily

R

rabais (rah-bay) *m* discount, reduction, rebate

raccourcir (rah-koor-seer) *v* shorten

race (rahss) *f* race; breed

racial (rah-s^yahl) *adj* racial

racine (rah-seen) *f* root

racler (rah-klay) *v* scrape

raconter (rah-kawng-tay) *v* *tell

radeau (rah-doa) *m* raft

radiateur (rah-d^yah-tūrr) *m* radiator

radical (rah-dee-kahl) *adj* radical

radio (rah-d^yoa) *f* wireless, radio

radiographie (rah-d^yoa-grah-fee) *f* X-ray

radiographier (rah-d^yoa-grah-f^yay) *v* X-ray

radis (rah-dee) *m* radish

radotage (rah-do-taazh) *m* rubbish

rafale (rah-fahl) *f* gust; ~ **de pluie** cloud-burst

raffinerie (rah-feen-ree) *f* refinery; ~ **de pétrole** oil-refinery

rafraîchir (rah-fray-sheer) *v* refresh

rafraîchissement (rah-freh-shee-smahng) *m* refreshment

rage (raazh) *f* rabies; rage; craze

rager (rah-zhay) *v* rage

raide (rehd) *adj* stiff

raie (ray) *f* stripe; parting

raifort (ray-*fawr*) *m* horseradish

rail (righ) *m* rail

raisin (ray-*zang*) *m* grapes *pl*; ~ **sec** currant, raisin

raison (ray-*zawng*) *f* reason; cause; wits *pl*, sense; ***avoir** ~ * be right; **en** ~ **de** for, owing to, because of

raisonnable (ray-zo-*nahbl*) *adj* reasonable; sensible

raisonner (ray-zo-*nay*) *v* reason

ralentir (rah-lahng-*teer*) *v* slow down

rallonge (rah-*lawngzh*) *f* extension cord

ramasser (rah-mah-*say*) *v* pick up

rame (rahm) *f* oar

ramener (rahm-*nay*) *v* *bring back

ramer (rah-*may*) *v* row

rampe (rahngp) *f* banisters *pl*; railing

ramper (rahng-*pay*) *v* *creep, crawl

rance (rahngss) *adj* rancid

rançon (rahng-*sawng*) *f* ransom

rang (rahng) *m* row, rank

rangée (rahng-*zhay*) *f* line

ranger (rahng-*zhay*) *v* sort; tidy up, *put away

râpe (raap) *f* grater

râper (rah-*pay*) *v* grate

rapide (rah-*peed*) *adj* quick; fast, swift, rapid; *m* rapids *pl*

rapidement (rah-peed-*mahng*) *adv* soon

rapidité (rah-pee-dee-*tay*) *f* speed

rapiécer (rah-pᵞay-*say*) *v* patch

rappeler (rah-*play*) *v* remind; recall; **se** ~ remember, recall

rapport (rah-*pawr*) *m* report; connection, relation, reference; intercourse

rapporter (rah-por-*tay*) *v* *bring back; report

rapprocher (rah-pro-*shay*) *v* *bring closer

raquette (rah-*keht*) *f* racquet

rare (raar) *adj* rare; uncommon, scarce

rarement (rahr-*mahng*) *adv* seldom, rarely

se raser (rah-*zay*) shave

raseur (rah-*zūr*) *m* bore

rasoir (rah-*zwaar*) *m* safety-razor, razor; ~ **électrique** electric razor; shaver

rassemblement (rah-sahng-bler-*mahng*) *m* rally

rassembler (rah-sahng-*blay*) *v* assemble; collect

rassis (rah-*see*) *adj* stale

rassurer (rah-sew-*ray*) *v* reassure

rat (rah) *m* rat

râteau (rah-*toa*) *m* rake

ration (rah-sᵞ*awng*) *f* ration

rauque (rōak) *adj* hoarse

ravissant (rah-vee-*sahng*) *adj* lovely, delightful, enchanting

rayé (ray-ᵞ*ay*) *adj* striped

rayon (ray-ᵞ*awng*) *m* beam, ray; radius; spoke

rayonne (ray-ᵞ*on*) *f* rayon

rayure (ray-ᵞ*eūr*) *f* scratch

réaction (ray-ahk-sᵞ*awng*) *f* reaction

réalisable (ray-ah-lee-*zahbl*) *adj* realizable

réalisation (ray-ah-lee-zah-sᵞ*awng*) *f* realization; direction

réaliser (ray-ah-lee-*zay*) *v* realize; carry out, implement

réaliste (ray-ah-*leest*) *adj* matter-of-fact

réalité (ray-ah-lee-*tay*) *f* reality; **en** ~ actually; really

rébellion (ray-beh-lᵞ*awng*) *f* revolt, rebellion

rebord (rer-*bawr*) *m* edge, rim; ~ **de fenêtre** window-sill

rebut (rer-*bew*) *m* junk, refuse

récemment (ray-sah-*mahng*) *adv* lately, recently

récent (ray-*sahng*) *adj* recent

réception (ray-seh-*ps^yawng*) *f* receipt; reception; reception office

récession (ray-seh-*s^yawng*) *f* recession

recette (rer-*seht*) *f* recipe; **recettes** revenue

*****recevoir** (rer-*svvaar*) *v* receive; entertain

recharge (rer-*shahrzh*) *f* refill

réchauffer (ray-shoa-*fay*) *v* warm up

recherche (rer-*shehrsh*) *f* research

rechercher (rer-shehr-*shay*) *v* aim at

récif (ray-*seef*) *m* reef

récipient (ray-see-*p^yahng*) *m* container, vessel

réciproque (ray-see-*prok*) *adj* mutual

récit (ray-*see*) *m* tale; account

récital (ray-see-*tahl*) *m* (pl ~s) recital

réclamation (ray-klah-mah-*s^yawng*) *f* claim

réclame (ray-*klahm*) *f* publicity

réclamer (ray-klah-*may*) *v* claim

récolte (ray-*kolt*) *f* crop

recommandation (rer-ko-mahng-dah-*s^yawng*) *f* recommendation

recommander (rer-ko-mahng-*day*) *v* recommend; register

recommencer (rer-ko-mahng-*say*) *v* recommence

récompense (ray-kawng-*pahngss*) *f* reward, prize

récompenser (ray-kawng-pahng-*say*) *v* reward

réconciliation (ray-kawng-see-l^yah-*s^yawng*) *f* reconciliation

réconfort (ray-kawng-*fawr*) *m* comfort

reconnaissance (rer-ko-nay-*sahngss*) *f* recognition

reconnaissant (rer-ko-nay-*sahng*) *adj* thankful, grateful

*****reconnaître** (rer-ko-*naitr*) *v* recognize; acknowledge; admit, confess

record (rer-*kawr*) *m* record

*****recouvrir** (rer-koo-*vreer*) *v* upholster

récréation (ray-kray-ah-*s^yawng*) *f* recreation

recrue (rer-*krew*) *f* recruit

rectangle (rehk-*tahnggl*) *m* rectangle; oblong

rectangulaire (rehk-tahng-gew-*lair*) *adj* rectangular

rectification (rehk-tee-fee-kah-*s^yawng*) *f* correction

rectum (rehk-*tom*) *m* rectum

reçu (rer-*sew*) *m* receipt; voucher

*****recueillir** (rer-kur-^yeer*) *v* gather

reculer (rer-kew-*lay*) *v* step back; back up

récupérer (ray-kew-pay-*ray*) *v* recover

rédacteur (ray-dahk-*tūrr*) *m* editor

reddition (reh-dee-*s^yawng*) *f* surrender

rédiger (ray-dee-*zhay*) *v* *draw up

redouter (rer-doo-*tay*) *v* fear

réduction (ray-dewk-*s^yawng*) *f* discount, reduction, rebate

*****réduire** (ray-*dweer*) *v* reduce; decrease, *cut

réduit (ray-*dwee*) *m* shed

rééducation (ray-ay-dew-kah-*s^yawng*) *f* rehabilitation

réel (ray-*ehl*) *adj* real; true, factual, actual, substantial

réellement (ray-ehl-*mahng*) *adv* really

référence (ray-fay-*rahngss*) *f* reference

réfléchir (ray-flay-*sheer*) *v* *think; *think over

réflecteur (ray-flehk-*tūrr*) *m* reflector

reflet (rer-*flay*) *m* reflection

refléter (rer-flay-*tay*) *v* reflect

réforme (ray-*form*) *f* reformation

réfrigérateur (ray-free-zhay-rah-*tūrr*) *m* fridge, refrigerator

refroidir (rer-frwah-*deer*) *v* cool off

refuge (rer-*fewzh*) *m* cover

réfugié (ray-few-*zh^yay*) *m* refugee

refus (rer-*few*) *m* refusal

refuser (rer-few-*zay*) *v* refuse; deny, reject

regard (rer-*gaar*) *m* look

regarder (rer-gahr-*day*) *v* look; watch, look at; concern

régate (ray-*gaht*) *f* regatta

régime (ray-*zheem*) *m* régime; rule, government; diet

région (ray-zh^y*awng*) *f* region; district, area, zone, country

régional (ray-zh^yo-*nahl*) *adj* regional

règle (raigl) *f* rule; ruler; **en ~** in order

règlement (reh-gler-*mahng*) *m* regulation; arrangement, settlement

régler (ray-*glay*) *v* regulate; settle

réglisse (ray-*gleess*) *f* liquorice

règne (rehñ) *m* reign; dominion, rule

régner (ray-*ñay*) *v* reign; rule

regret (rer-*gray*) *m* regret

regretter (rer-gray-*tay*) *v* regret

régulier (ray-gew-l^y*ay*) *adj* regular

rein (rang) *m* kidney

reine (rehn) *f* queen

rejeter (rerzh-*tay*) *v* reject; turn down

*rejoindre (rer-zh*wangdr*) *v* rejoin

relater (rer-lah-*tay*) *v* relate; report

relatif (rer-lah-*teef*) *adj* relative; comparative; **~ à** with reference to, concerning

relation (rer-lah-s^y*awng*) *f* connection; relation

relayer (rer-lay-*^yay*) *v* relieve

relèvement (rer-lehv-*mahng*) *m* increase

relever (rerl-*vay*) *v* raise

relief (rer-l^y*ehf*) *m* relief

relier (rer-l^y*ay*) *v* link; bundle

religieuse (rer-lee-zh^y*ūrz*) *f* nun

religieux (rer-lee-zh^y*ur*) *adj* religious

religion (rer-lee-zh^y*awng*) *f* religion

relique (rer-*leek*) *f* relic

reliure (rer-l^y*ēwr*) *f* binding

remarquable (rer-mahr-*kahbl*) *adj* remarkable; noticeable, striking

remarque (rer-*mahrk*) *f* remark

remarquer (rer-mahr-*kay*) *v* notice; remark

remboursement (rahng-boor-ser-*mahng*) *m* repayment, refund

rembourser (rahng-boor-*say*) *v* *repay, reimburse, refund

remède (rer-*mehd*) *m* remedy

remerciement (rer-mehr-see-*mahng*) *m* thanks *pl*

remercier (rer-mehr-s^y*ay*) *v* thank

*remettre (rer-*mehtr*) *v* deliver; commit, hand; remit; **se ~** recover

remise (rer-*meez*) *f* delivery

remonter (rer-mawng-*tay*) *v* *wind

remorque (rer-*mork*) *f* trailer

remorquer (rer-mor-*kay*) *v* tow, tug

remorqueur (rer-mor-*kūr*) *m* tug

remplacer (rahng-plah-*say*) *v* replace

remplir (rahng-*pleer*) *v* fill; fill in; fill out *Am*

remue-ménage (rer-mew-may-*naazh*) *m* bustle

remuer (rer-*mway*) *v* stir

rémunération (ray-mew-nay-rah-s^y*awng*) *f* remuneration

rémunérer (ray-mew-nay-*ray*) *v* remunerate

renard (rer-*naar*) *m* fox

rencontre (rahng-*kawngtr*) *f* meeting, encounter; **venant à la ~** oncoming

rencontrer (rahng-kawng-*tray*) *v* *meet; *come across, run into, encounter

rendement (rahng-der-*mahng*) *m* profit

rendez-vous (rahng-day-*voo*) *m* appointment, date

rendre (rahngdr) *v* refund; *make; **~ compte de** account for; **~ visite à** call on; **se ~** surrender; *go; **se ~ compte** realize

renne (rehn) *m* reindeer

renom (rer-*nawng*) *m* reputation

renommée (rer-no-*may*) *f* fame

renoncer (rer-nawng-say) v *give up

renouveler (rer-noo-vlay) v renew

renseignement (rahng-sehñ-mahng) m information; **bureau de renseignements** inquiry office

se renseigner (rahng-say-ñay) inquire

rentable (rahng-tahbl) adj paying

rentrer (rahng-tray) v *go home; gather

renverser (rahng-vehr-say) v knock down

*renvoyer (rahng-vwah-Yay) v *send back; dismiss; ~ à refer to; postpone

répandre (ray-pahngdr) v *shed; *spill

réparation (ray-pah-rah-sYawng) f reparation, repair

réparer (ray-pah-ray) v repair; mend, fix

répartir (ray-pahr-teer) v divide

repas (rer-pah) m meal

repasser (rer-pah-say) v press, iron; **repassage permanent** drip-dry

repentir (rer-pahng-teer) m repentance

répertoire (ray-pehr-twaar) m repertory

répéter (ray-pay-tay) v repeat; rehearse

répétition (ray-pay-tee-sYawng) f repetition; rehearsal

répit (ray-pee) m respite

répondre (ray-pawngdr) v reply, answer

réponse (ray-pawngss) f reply, answer; **en ~** in reply; **sans ~** unanswered

reporter (rer-por-tay) m reporter

repos (rer-poa) m rest

reposant (rer-poa-zahng) adj restful

se reposer (rer-poa-zay) rest

repousser (rer-poo-say) v turn down; repel; **repoussant** repulsive

*reprendre (rer-prahngdr) v resume; *take over

représentant (rer-pray-zahng-tahng) m agent

représentatif (rer-pray-zahng-tah-teef) adj representative

représentation (rer-pray-zahng-tah-sYawng) f show; representation

représenter (rer-pray-zahng-tay) v represent

réprimander (ray-pree-mahng-day) v reprimand

réprimer (ray-pree-may) v suppress

reprise (rer-preez) f revival; round

repriser (rer-pree-zay) v darn

reproche (rer-prosh) m reproach

reprocher (rer-pro-shay) v reproach

reproduction (rer-pro-dewk-sYawng) f reproduction

*reproduire (rer-pro-dweer) v reproduce

reptile (rehp-teel) m reptile

républicain (ray-pew-blee-kang) adj republican

république (ray-pew-bleek) f republic

répugnance (ray-pew-ñahngss) f dislike

répugnant (ray-pew-ñahng) adj repellent; filthy, disgusting, revolting

réputation (ray-pew-tah-sYawng) f fame, reputation

*requérir (rer-kay-reer) v request

requête (rer-keht) f request

requin (rer-kang) m shark

requis (rer-kee) adj requisite

réseau (ray-zoa) m network; ~ **routier** road system

réservation (ray-zehr-vah-sYawng) f reservation; booking

réserve (ray-zehrv) f reserve; qualification; **de ~** spare; ~ **zoologique** game reserve

réserver (ray-zehr-vay) v reserve; book

réservoir (ray-zehr-vwaar) m reservoir;

tank; ~ **d'essence** petrol tank

résidence (ray-zee-*dahngss*) f residence

résident (ray-zee-*dahng*) m resident

résider (ray-zee-*day*) v reside

résille (ray-*zeey*) f hair-net

résine (ray-*zeen*) f resin

résistance (ray-zee-*stahngss*) f resistance

résister (ray-zee-*stay*) v resist

résolu (ray-zo-*lew*) adj determined, resolute

***résoudre** (ray-*zoodr*) v solve

respect (reh-*spay*) m respect; esteem, regard

respectable (reh-spehk-*tahbl*) adj respectable

respecter (reh-spehk-*tay*) v respect

respectif (reh-spehk-*teef*) adj respective

respectueux (reh-spehk-*twur*) adj respectful

respiration (reh-spee-rah-*syawng*) f breathing, respiration

respirer (reh-spee-*ray*) v breathe

resplendir (reh-splahng-*deer*) v *shine

responsabilité (reh-spawng-sah-bee-lee-*tay*) f responsibility; liability

responsable (reh-spawng-*sahbl*) adj responsible; liable

ressemblance (rer-sahng-*blahngss*) f resemblance

ressembler à (rer-sahng-*blay*) resemble

resserrer (rer-say-*ray*) v tighten; **se ~** tighten

ressort (rer-*sawr*) m spring

ressource (rer-*soors*) f expedient; **ressources** resources pl; means pl

restant (reh-*stahng*) adj remaining; m remnant, remainder

restaurant (reh-stoa-*rahng*) m restaurant; ~ **libre service** self-service restaurant

reste (rehst) m rest; remnant, remainder

rester (reh-*stay*) v stay; remain

restituer (reh-stee-*tway*) v reimburse

restriction (reh-streek-*syawng*) f restriction; qualification

résultat (ray-zewl-*tah*) m result; issue, effect, outcome

résulter (ray-zewl-*tay*) v result

résumé (ray-zew-*may*) m résumé, summary; survey

retard (rer-*taar*) m delay; **en ~** overdue, late

retarder (rer-tahr-*day*) v delay

***retenir** (rert-*neer*) v reserve, book; remember; restrain

rétine (ray-*teen*) f retina

retirer (rer-tee-*ray*) v *withdraw; *draw

retour (rer-*toor*) m return; **voyage de ~** return journey

retourner (rer-toor-*nay*) v *get back; return, turn back, *go back; turn over, turn, turn round; **se ~** turn round

retracer (rer-trah-*say*) v trace

retraite (rer-*treht*) f retirement; pension

retraité (rer-tray-*tay*) adj retired

rétrécir (ray-tray-*seer*) v *shrink

réunion (ray-ew-*nyawng*) f meeting, assembly

réunir (ray-ew-*neer*) v join; reunite; **se ~** gather

réussir (ray-ew-*seer*) v manage, succeed; pass, *make; **réussi** successful

rêve (raiv) m dream

réveil (ray-*vay*) m alarm-clock

réveiller (ray-vay-*yay*) v *awake, *wake; **réveillé** awake; **se ~** wake up

révélation (ray-vay-lah-*syawng*) f revelation

révéler (ray-vay-*lay*) v reveal; *give away; **se ~** prove

revendeur (rer-vahng-*dūrr*) m retailer

revendication (rer-vahng-dee-kah-s^y*awng*) f claim

revendiquer (rer-vahng-dee-*kay*) v claim

***revenir** (rer-*vneer*) v return

revenu (rer-*vnew*) m earnings pl, income, revenue

rêver (ray-*vay*) v *dream

revers (rer-*vair*) m reverse; lapel

revirement (rer-veer-*mahng*) m reverse, turn

reviser (rer-vee-*zay*) v revise; overhaul

révision (ray-vee-z^y*awng*) f revision

***revoir** (rer-*vwaar*) v *see again; review; **au revoir!** good-bye!

révoltant (ray-vol-*tahng*) adj revolting

révolte (ray-*volt*) f revolt, rebellion

se révolter (ray-vol-*tay*) revolt

révolution (ray-vo-lew-s^y*awng*) f revolution

révolutionnaire (ray-vo-lew-s^yo-*nair*) adj revolutionary

revolver (ray-vol-*vair*) m gun, revolver

révoquer (ray-vo-*kay*) v recall

revue (rer-*vew*) f revue; review, magazine; **~ mensuelle** monthly magazine

rez-de-chaussée (reh-dshoa-*say*) m ground floor

rhinocéros (ree-no-say-*ross*) m rhinoceros

rhubarbe (rew-*bahrb*) f rhubarb

rhumatisme (rew-mah-*teesm*) m rheumatism

rhume (rewm) m cold; **~ des foins** hay fever

riche (reesh) adj rich; wealthy

richesse (ree-*shehss*) f wealth; riches pl

ride (reed) f wrinkle

rideau (ree-*doa*) m curtain

ridicule (ree-dee-*kewl*) adj ridiculous; ludicrous

ridiculiser (ree-dee-kew-lee-*zay*) v ridicule

rien (r^y*ang*) pron nothing; nil; **ne ... ~** nothing; **~ que** only

rime (reem) f rhyme

rinçage (rang-*saazh*) m rinse

rincer (rang-*say*) v rinse

rire (reer) m laughter, laugh

***rire** (reer) v laugh

risque (reesk) m risk; chance

risquer (ree-*skay*) v venture, risk; **risqué** risky

rivage (ree-*vaazh*) m shore

rival (ree-*vahl*) m rival

rivaliser (ree-vah-lee-*zay*) v rival

rivalité (ree-vah-lee-*tay*) f rivalry

rive (reev) f bank, shore

rivière (ree-v^y*air*) f river

riz (ree) m rice

robe (rob) f dress; robe, frock, gown; **~ de chambre** dressing-gown

robinet (ro-bee-*nay*) m tap; faucet nAm

robuste (ro-*bewst*) adj solid, robust

rocher (ro-*shay*) m rock, boulder

rocheux (ro-*shur*) adj rocky

roi (rwah) m king

rôle (rōal) m role

roman (ro-*mahng*) m novel; **~ policier** detective story

romancier (ro-mahng-s^y*ay*) m novelist

romantique (ro-mahng-*teek*) adj romantic

rompre (rawngpr) v *break

rond (rawng) adj round

rond-point (rawng-*pwang*) m roundabout

ronfler (rawng-*flay*) v snore

rosaire (roa-*zair*) m rosary

rose (rōaz) f rose; adj pink, rose

roseau (roa-*zoa*) m reed

rosée (roa-*zay*) f dew

rossignol (ro-see-*ñol*) *m* nightingale
rotation (ro-tah-*s^yawng*) *f* revolution
rotin (ro-*tang*) *m* rattan
rôtir (roa-*teer*) *v* roast
rôtisserie (roa-tee-*sree*) *f* grill-room
rotule (ro-*tewl*) *f* kneecap
roue (roo) *f* wheel; ~ **de secours** spare wheel
rouge (roōzh) *adj* red; *m* rouge; ~ **à lèvres** lipstick
rouge-gorge (roozh-*gorzh*) *m* robin
rougeole (roo-*zhol*) *f* measles
rougir (roo-*zheer*) *v* blush
rouille (roo^{ee}) *f* rust
rouillé (roo-*^yay*) *adj* rusty
rouleau (roo-*loa*) *m* roll
rouler (roo-*lay*) *v* roll; *ride
roulette (roo-*leht*) *f* roulette
roulotte (roo-*lot*) *f* caravan
Roumain (roo-*mang*) *m* Rumanian
roumain (roo-*mang*) *adj* Rumanian
Roumanie (roo-mah-*nee*) *f* Rumania
route (root) *f* drive, road; route; **en ~ pour** bound for; ~ **à péage** turnpike *nAm*; ~ **d'évitement** by-pass; ~ **en réfection** road up; ~ **principale** highway, thoroughfare, main road
routine (roo-*teen*) *f* routine
royal (rwah-*^yahl*) *adj* royal
royaume (rwah-*^yoām*) *m* kingdom
ruban (rew-*bahng*) *m* ribbon; ~ **adhésif** adhesive tape, scotch tape
rubis (rew-*bee*) *m* ruby
rubrique (rew-*breek*) *f* column
ruche (rewsh) *f* beehive
rude (rewd) *adj* bleak
rue (rew) *f* street; road; ~ **principale** main street; ~ **transversale** side-street
ruelle (rwehl) *f* alley, lane
rugir (rew-*zheer*) *v* roar
rugissement (rew-zhee-*smahng*) *m* roar

rugueux (rew-*gur*) *adj* rough
ruine (rween) *f* ruins; ruin
ruiner (rwee-*nay*) *v* ruin
ruisseau (rwee-*soa*) *m* brook, stream
rumeur (rew-*mūrr*) *f* rumour
rural (rew-*rahl*) *adj* rural
ruse (rēwz) *f* ruse, artifice
rusé (rew-*zay*) *adj* cunning
Russe (rewss) *m* Russian
russe (rewss) *adj* Russian
Russie (rew-*see*) *f* Russia
rustique (rew-*steek*) *adj* rustic
rythme (reetm) *m* rhythm; pace

S

sable (sahbl) *m* sand
sableux (sah-*blur*) *adj* sandy
sabot (sah-*boa*) *m* wooden shoe; hoof
sac (sahk) *m* bag; sack; ~ **à dos** rucksack; ~ **à glace** ice-bag; ~ **à main** bag, handbag; ~ **à provisions** shopping bag; ~ **de couchage** sleeping-bag; ~ **de papier** paper bag
saccharine (sah-kah-*reen*) *f* saccharin
sacré (sah-*kray*) *adj* holy, sacred
sacrifice (sah-kree-*feess*) *m* sacrifice
sacrifier (sah-kree-*f^yay*) *v* sacrifice
sacrilège (sah-kree-*laizh*) *m* sacrilege
sacristain (sah-kree-*stang*) *m* sexton
sage (saazh) *adj* wise; good
sage-femme (sahzh-*fahm*) *f* midwife
sagesse (sah-*zhehss*) *f* wisdom
saigner (say-*ñay*) *v* *bleed
sain (sang) *adj* healthy; wholesome, well
saint (sang) *m* saint
saisir (say-*zeer*) *v* seize; *catch, grip, *take, grasp
saison (seh-*zawng*) *f* season; **hors ~** off season; **morte-saison** *f* low

season; **pleine ~** peak season
salade (sah-*lahd*) f salad
salaire (sah-*lair*) m salary, pay
salaud (sah-*loa*) m bastard
sale (sahl) adj dirty; filthy
salé (sah-*lay*) adj salty
saleté (sahl-*tay*) f dirt
salière (sah-*lʸair*) f salt-cellar
salir (sah-*leer*) v soil
salive (sah-*leev*) f spit
salle (sahl) f hall; **~ à manger**
dining-room; **~ d'attente** waiting-
room; **~ de bain** bathroom; **~ de
bal** ballroom; **~ de banquet** banqueting-hall; **~ de classe** classroom; **~ de concert** concert hall; **~
de lecture** reading-room; **~ de séjour** living-room; **~ d'exposition**
showroom
salon (sah-*lawng*) m sitting-room;
drawing-room, salon; **~ de beauté**
beauty salon; **~ de thé** tea-shop
salopette (sah-lo-*peht*) f overalls pl
saluer (sah-*lway*) v greet; salute
salut (sah-*lew*) m welfare
salutation (sah-lew-tah-*sʸawng*) f
greeting
samedi (sahm-*dee*) m Saturday
sanatorium (sah-nah-to-*rʸom*) m sanatorium
sanctuaire (sahngk-*twair*) m shrine
sandale (sahng-*dahl*) f sandal
sandwich (sahng-*dweech*) m sandwich
sang (sahng) m blood; **pur ~** thoroughbred
sanitaire (sah-nee-*tair*) adj sanitary
sans (sahng) prep without
santé (sahng-*tay*) f health
saphir (sah-*feer*) m sapphire
sapin (sah-*pang*) m fir-tree
sardine (sahr-*deen*) f sardine
satellite (sah-tay-*leet*) m satellite
satin (sah-*tang*) m satin
satisfaction (sah-teess-fahk-*sʸawng*) f

satisfaction
*****satisfaire** (sah-tee-*sfair*) v satisfy;
satisfait satisfied; content
sauce (sōass) f sauce
saucisse (soa-*seess*) f sausage
sauf (soaf) prep but
saumon (soa-*mawng*) m salmon
sauna (soa-*nah*) m sauna
saut (soa) m jump; hop, leap; **~ à
ski** ski-jump
sauter (soa-*tay*) v jump; skip; *****faire
~** fry
sauterelle (soa-*trehl*) f grasshopper
sautiller (soa-tee-*ʸay*) v hop, skip
sauvage (soa-*vaazh*) adj savage; wild,
fierce, desert
sauver (soa-*vay*) v rescue, save
sauvetage (soav-*taazh*) m rescue
sauveur (soa-*vūrr*) m saviour
savant (sah-*vahng*) m scientist
saveur (sah-*vūrr*) f flavour
*****savoir** (sah-*vwaar*) v *know; *be
able to
savoir-vivre (sah-vwahr-*veevr*) m manners pl
savon (sah-*vawng*) m soap; **~ à barbe** shaving-soap; **~ en poudre**
washing-powder
savoureux (sah-voo-*rur*) adj tasty, savoury
scandale (skahng-*dahl*) m scandal
Scandinave (skahng-dee-*naav*) m
Scandinavian
scandinave (skahng-dee-*naav*) adj
Scandinavian
Scandinavie (skahng-dee-nah-*vee*) f
Scandinavia
scarabée (skah-rah-*bay*) m beetle
sceau (soa) m seal
scélérat (say-lay-*rah*) m villain
scène (sehn) f scene; stage; **metteur
en ~** director; *****mettre en ~** direct
schéma (shay-*mah*) m diagram
scie (see) f saw

science (s^yahngss) *f* science

scientifique (s^yahng-tee-*feek*) *adj* scientific

scierie (see-*ree*) *f* saw-mill

scintillant (sang-tee-*y*ahng) *adj* sparkling

sciure (see-*ewr*) *f* sawdust

scolaire (sko-*lair*) *adj* school-

scooter (skoo-*tair*) *m* scooter

scout (skoot) *m* scout; boy scout

sculpteur (skewl-*tūrr*) *m* sculptor

sculpture (skewl-*tēwr*) *f* sculpture; ~ **sur bois** wood-carving

se (ser) *pron* himself; herself; themselves

séance (say-*ahngss*) *f* session

seau (soa) *m* bucket, pail

sec (sehk) *adj* (f sèche) dry

sèche-cheveux (sehsh-sher-*vur*) *m* hair-dryer

sécher (say-*shay*) *v* dry

sécheresse (say-*shrehss*) *f* drought

séchoir (say-*shwaar*) *m* dryer

second (ser-*gawng*) *adj* second

secondaire (ser-gawng-*dair*) *adj* secondary; subordinate

seconde (ser-*gawngd*) *f* second

secouer (ser-*kway*) *v* *shake

secours (ser-*koōr*) *m* assistance; **premier** ~ first-aid

secousse (ser-*kooss*) *f* wrench

secret[1] (ser-*kray*) *m* secret

secret[2] (ser-*kray*) *adj* (f secrète) secret

secrétaire (ser-kray-*tair*) *m* clerk, secretary

section (sehk-s^yawng) *f* section; stretch

sécurité (say-kew-ree-*tay*) *f* safety, security; **glissière de** ~ crash barrier

sédatif (say-dah-*teef*) *m* sedative

sédiment (say-dee-*mahng*) *m* deposit

***séduire** (say-*dweer*) *v* seduce

séduisant (say-dwee-*zahng*) *adj* attractive, charming

sein (sang) *m* breast; bosom

seize (saiz) *num* sixteen

seizième (seh-z^yehm) *num* sixteenth

séjour (say-*zhoōr*) *m* stay

séjourner (say-zhoor-*nay*) *v* stay

sel (sehl) *m* salt; **sels de bain** bath salts

sélection (say-lehk-s^yawng) *f* choice, selection

sélectionner (say-lehk-s^yo-*nay*) *v* select

selle (sehl) *f* saddle

selon (ser-*lawng*) *prep* according to

semaine (ser-*mehn*) *f* week

semblable (sahng-*blahbl*) *adj* alike

sembler (sahng-*blay*) *v* seem; look, appear

semelle (ser-*mehl*) *f* sole

semence (ser-*mahngss*) *f* seed

semer (ser-*may*) *v* *sow

semi- (ser-*mee*) semi-

sénat (say-*nah*) *m* senate

sénateur (say-nah-*tūrr*) *m* senator

sénile (say-*neel*) *adj* senile

sens (sahngss) *m* sense; reason; **bon** ~ sense; **en** ~ **inverse** the other way round; ~ **unique** one-way traffic

sensation (sahng-sah-s^yawng) *f* sensation; feeling

sensationnel (sahng-sah-s^yo-*nehl*) *adj* sensational

sensible (sahng-*seebl*) *adj* sensitive; considerable

sentence (sahng-*tahngss*) *f* verdict

sentier (sahng-*t*^yay) *m* path; trail; ~ **pour piétons** footpath

sentimental (sahng-tee-mahng-*tahl*) *adj* sentimental

***sentir** (sahng-*teer*) *v* *feel; *smell; ~ **mauvais** *smell

séparation (say-pah-rah-s^yawng) *f* division

séparé (say-pah-*ray*) *adj* separate

séparément (say-pah-ray-*mahng*) *adv* apart

séparer (say-pah-*ray*) *v* separate; divide, part

sept (seht) *num* seven

septembre (sehp-*tahngbr*) September

septentrional (sehp-tahng-tree-o-*nahl*) *adj* northern, north

septicémie (sehp-tee-say-*mee*) *f* blood-poisoning

septième (seh-t*Y*ehm) *num* seventh

septique (sehp-*teek*) *adj* septic

sépulture (say-pewl-*tewr*) *f* burial

serein (ser-*rang*) *adj* serene

série (say-*ree*) *f* sequence; series

sérieux (say-r*Y*ur) *adj* serious; *m* seriousness

seringue (ser-*rangg*) *f* syringe

serment (sehr-*mahng*) *m* vow, oath; **faux** ~ perjury

sermon (sehr-*mawng*) *m* sermon

serpent (sehr-*pahng*) *m* snake

serpentant (sehr-pahng-*tahng*) *adj* winding

serpenter (sehr-pahng-*tay*) *v* *wind

serre (sair) *f* greenhouse

serrer (say-*ray*) *v* tighten; **serré** tight, narrow

serrure (say-*rewr*) *f* lock; **trou de la** ~ keyhole

sérum (say-*rom*) *m* serum

serveuse (sehr-*vurz*) *f* waitress

serviable (sehr-v*Y*ahbl) *adj* helpful

service (sehr-*veess*) *m* service; service charge; section; ~ **à thé** tea-set; ~ **de table** dinner-service; ~ **d'étage** room service; **services postaux** postal service

serviette (sehr-v*Y*eht) *f* towel; napkin, serviette; briefcase; ~ **de bain** bath towel; ~ **de papier** paper napkin; ~ **hygiénique** sanitary towel

*servir (sehr-*veer*) *v* serve; attend on, wait on; *be of use; **se** ~ **de** apply

serviteur (sehr-vee-*turr*) *m* boy

seuil (sur*ee*) *m* threshold

seul (surl) *adv* alone; *adj* single, only

seulement (surl-*mahng*) *adv* only; merely

sévère (say-*vair*) *adj* strict; harsh; severe

sévir (say-*veer*) *v* rage

sexe (sehks) *m* sex

sexualité (sehk-swah-lee-*tay*) *f* sexuality

sexuel (sehk-*swehl*) *adj* sexual

shampooing (shahng-*pwang*) *m* shampoo

si (see) *conj* if; whether; *adv* so; **si ... ou** whether ... or

Siam (s*Y*ahm) *m* Siam

Siamois (s*Y*ah-*mwah*) *m* Siamese

siamois (s*Y*ah-*mwah*) *adj* Siamese

siècle (s*Y*ehkl) *m* century

siège (s*Y*aizh) *m* chair, seat; siege

le sien (ler s*Y*ang) his

siffler (see-*flay*) *v* whistle

sifflet (see-*flay*) *m* whistle

signal (see-ñahl) *m* signal; ~ **de détresse** distress signal

signalement (see-ñahl-*mahng*) *m* description

signaler (see-ñah-*lay*) *v* signal; indicate

signature (see-ñah-*tewr*) *f* signature

signe (seeñ) *m* sign; token, signal, indication; ***faire** ~ wave

signer (see-*ñay*) *v* sign

significatif (see-ñee-fee-kah-*teef*) *adj* significant

signification (see-ñee-fee-kah-s*Y*awng) *f* meaning, sense

signifier (see-ñee-f*Y*ay) *v* *mean

silence (see-*lahngss*) *m* silence; quiet, stillness

silencieux (see-lahng-s*Y*ur) *adj* silent; *m* silencer; muffler *nAm*

sillon (see-*Y*awng) *m* groove

similaire (see-mee-*lair*) *adj* similar

similitude (see-mee-lee-*tewd*) *f* similarity

simple (sangpl) *adj* simple; plain

simplement (sang-pler-*mahng*) *adv* simply

simuler (see-mew-*lay*) *v* simulate

simultané (see-mewl-tah-*nay*) *adj* simultaneous

sincère (sang-*sair*) *adj* honest, sincere

singe (sangzh) *m* monkey

singulier (sang-gew-*l*ʸ*ay*) *m* singular; *adj* peculiar, singular, queer

sinistre (see-*neestr*) *adj* sinister, ominous; *m* catastrophe

sinon (see-*nawng*) *conj* otherwise

siphon (see-*fawng*) *m* siphon, syphon

sirène (see-*rehn*) *f* siren; mermaid

sirop (see-*roa*) *m* syrup

site (seet) *m* site

situation (see-twah-*s*ʸ*awng*) *f* situation; position, location

situé (see-*tway*) *adj* situated

six (seess) *num* six

sixième (see-*z*ʸ*ehm*) *num* sixth

ski (skee) *m* ski; skiing; ~ **nautique** water ski

skier (skee-*ay*) *v* ski

skieur (skee-*ūrr*) *m* skier

slip (sleep) *m* knickers *pl*, briefs *pl*

slogan (slogahng) *m* slogan

smoking (smo-*keeng*) *m* dinnerjacket; tuxedo *nAm*

snob (snob) *adj* snooty

sobre (sobr) *adj* sober

social (so-s*ʸahl*) *adj* social

socialisme (so-s*ʸ*ah-*leesm*) *m* socialism

socialiste (so-s*ʸ*ah-*leest*) *adj* socialist; *m* socialist

société (so-s*ʸ*ay-*tay*) *f* community, society; company

sœur (sūrr) *f* sister

soi (swah) *pron* oneself; **soi-même**

pron oneself

soi-disant (swah-dee-*zahng*) *adj* socalled

soie (swah) *f* silk

soif (swahf) *f* thirst

soigné (swah-*ñay*) *adj* neat; thorough

soigner (swah-*ñay*) *v* tend; nurse

soigneux (swah-*ñur*) *adj* careful

soin (swang) *m* care; *****prendre** ~ **de** *****take care of; **soins de beauté** beauty treatment

soir (swaar) *m* night, evening; **ce** ~ tonight

soirée (swah-*ray*) *f* evening

soit … soit (swah) either … or

soixante (swah-*sahngt*) *num* sixty

soixante-dix (swah-sahngt-*deess*) *num* seventy

sol (sol) *m* floor; soil, earth, ground

soldat (sol-*dah*) *m* soldier

solde (sold) *m* balance; **soldes** sales, clearance sale

sole (sol) *f* sole

soleil (so-*lay*) *m* sun; sunshine; **coucher du** ~ sunset; **coup de** ~ sunburn; **lever du** ~ sunrise

solennel (so-lah-*nehl*) *adj* solemn

solide (so-*leed*) *adj* solid; firm, sound; *m* solid

solitaire (so-lee-*tair*) *adj* lonely

solitude (so-lee-*tewd*) *f* loneliness

soluble (so-*lewbl*) *adj* soluble

solution (so-lew-*s*ʸ*awng*) *f* solution

sombre (sawngbr) *adj* sombre, obscure; gloomy

sommaire (so-*mair*) *m* summary

somme (som) *f* sum; amount; *m* nap; ~ **globale** lump sum

sommeil (so-*may*) *m* sleep

sommelier (so-mer-*l*ʸ*ay*) *m* winewaiter

sommet (so-*may*) *m* summit; top, peak, height; ~ **de colline** hilltop

somnifère (som-nee-*fair*) *m* sleeping-pill

somnolent (som-no-*lahng*) *adj* sleepy

son[1] (*sawng*) *adj* (f sa, pl ses) his; her

son[2] (*sawng*) *m* sound

songer (sawng-*zhay*) *v* *dream; ~ à *think of

sonner (so-*nay*) *v* sound; *ring

sonnette (so-*neht*) *f* bell; doorbell

sorcière (sor-s*Y*air) *f* witch

sort (sawr) *m* fortune, lot, destiny

sorte (sort) *f* sort; **toutes sortes de** all sorts of

sortie (sor-*tee*) *f* way out, exit; ~ **de secours** emergency exit

*** sortir** (sor-*teer*) *v* *go out

sot (soa) *adj* (f sotte) foolish, silly

sottise (so-*teez*) *f* nonsense, rubbish

souche (soosh) *f* stub

souci (soo-*see*) *m* concern, worry; care

se soucier de (soo-s*Y*ay) care about

soucieux (soo-s*Y*ur) *adj* concerned, worried

soucoupe (soo-*koop*) *f* saucer

soudain (soo-*dang*) *adj* sudden; *adv* suddenly

souder (soo-*day*) *v* solder; weld

soudure (soo-*dewr*) *f* joint

souffle (soofl) *m* breath

souffler (soo-*flay*) *v* *blow

souffrance (soo-*frahngss*) *f* suffering

*** souffrir** (soo-*freer*) *v* suffer

souhait (sweh) *m* wish

souhaiter (sway-*tay*) *v* wish

souillé (soo-*Y*ay) *adj* soiled, dirty

souillure (soo-*Y*ewr) *f* blot

soulagement (soo-lahzh-*mahng*) *m* relief

soulager (soo-lah-*zhay*) *v* relieve

soulever (sool-*vay*) *v* lift; *bring up

soulier (soo-l*Y*ay) *m* shoe

souligner (soo-lee-*ñay*) *v* underline; stress, emphasize

*** soumettre** (soo-*mehtr*) *v* subject; se

~ submit

soupape (soo-*pahp*) *f* valve

soupçon (soop-*sawng*) *m* suspicion

soupçonner (soop-so-*nay*) *v* suspect

soupçonneux (soop-so-*nur*) *adj* suspicious

soupe (soop) *f* soup

souper (soo-*pay*) *m* supper

souple (soopl) *adj* supple; flexible

source (soors) *f* well; fountain, source, spring

sourcil (soor-*see*) *m* eyebrow

sourd (soor) *adj* deaf

sourire (soo-*reer*) *m* smile; ~ **forcé** grin

*** sourire** (soo-*reer*) *v* smile

souris (soo-*ree*) *f* mouse

sous (soo) *prep* under

sous-estimer (soo-zeh-stee-*may*) *v* underestimate

sous-locataire (soo-lo-kah-*tair*) *m* lodger

sous-marin (soo-mah-*rang*) *adj* underwater

soussigné (soo-see-*ñay*) *m* undersigned

sous-sol (soo-*sol*) *m* basement

sous-titre (soo-*teetr*) *m* subtitle

*** soustraire** (soo-*strair*) *v* subtract

sous-vêtements (soo-veht-*mahng*) *mpl* underwear

*** soutenir** (soot-*neer*) *v* support; *hold up

souterrain (soo-teh-*rang*) *adj* underground

soutien (soo-t*Y*ang) *m* support; relief

soutien-gorge (soo-t*Y*ang-*gorzh*) *m* brassiere, bra

souvenir (soo-*vneer*) *m* memory, remembrance; souvenir; **se *souvenir** recollect

souvent (soo-*vahng*) *adv* often; **le plus** ~ mostly

souverain (soo-*vrang*) *m* sovereign

soviétique (so-v^yay-*teek*) *adj* Soviet

soyeux (swah-*Y*ur) *adj* silken

spacieux (spah-s^yur) *adj* spacious, roomy, large

sparadrap (spah-rah-*drah*) *m* plaster, adhesive tape

spécial (spay-s^yahl) *adj* special; peculiar, particular

spécialement (spay-s^yahl-*mahng*) *adv* especially

se spécialiser (spay-s^yah-lee-*zay*) specialize

spécialiste (spay-s^yah-*leest*) *m* specialist, expert

spécialité (spay-s^yah-lee-*tay*) *f* speciality

spécifique (spay-see-*feek*) *adj* specific

spécimen (spay-see-*mehn*) *m* specimen

spectacle (spehk-*tahkl*) *m* spectacle; show; sight; ~ **de variétés** floor show, variety show

spectaculaire (spehk-tah-kew-*lair*) *adj* sensational

spectateur (spehk-tah-*tūrr*) *m* spectator

spectre (spehktr) *m* spook

spéculer (spay-kew-*lay*) *v* speculate

sphère (sfair) *f* sphere

spirituel (spee-ree-*twehl*) *adj* spiritual; witty, humorous

spiritueux (spee-ree-*twur*) *mpl* liquor, spirits

splendeur (splahng-*dūrr*) *f* splendour

splendide (splahng-*deed*) *adj* splendid; wonderful, glorious, enchanting, magnificent

sport (spawr) *m* sport; **sports d'hiver** winter sports

sportif (spor-*teef*) *m* sportsman

square (skwaar) *m* square

squelette (sker-*leht*) *m* skeleton

stable (stahbl) *adj* permanent, stable; solid, fixed

stade (stahd) *m* stadium

stand (stahng) *m* stand; ~ **de livres** bookstand

standard (stahng-*daar*) *adj* standard

standardiste (stahng-dahr-*deest*) *f* telephone operator, operator

starter (stahr-*tair*) *m* choke

station (stah-s^y*awng*) *f* station; ~ **balnéaire** seaside resort; ~ **de taxis** taxi rank; taxi stand *Am*; **station-service** *f* filling station, service station; gas station *Am*; ~ **thermale** spa

stationnaire (stah-s^yo-*nair*) *adj* stationary

stationnement (stah-s^yon-*mahng*) *m* parking; ~ **interdit** no parking

statistique (stah-tee-*steek*) *f* statistics *pl*

statue (stah-*tew*) *f* statue

stature (stah-*tēwr*) *f* figure

sténographe (stay-noa-*grahf*) *m* stenographer

sténographie (stay-noa-grah-*fee*) *f* shorthand

stérile (stay-*reel*) *adj* sterile

stériliser (stay-ree-lee-*zay*) *v* sterilize

stimulant (stee-mew-*lahng*) *m* impulse; stimulant

stimuler (stee-mew-*lay*) *v* stimulate

stipulation (stee-pew-lah-s^y*awng*) *f* stipulation

stipuler (stee-pew-*lay*) *v* stipulate

stock (stok) *m* stock; supply; *** **avoir en** ~ stock

stop! (stop) stop!

stops (stop) *mpl* brake lights

store (stawr) *m* blind

strophe (strof) *f* stanza

structure (strewk-*tēwr*) *f* structure; fabric

stupide (stew-*peed*) *adj* foolish, stupid

style (steel) *m* style

stylo (stee-*loa*) *m* fountain-pen; ~ **à**

bille ballpoint-pen

subalterne (sew-bahl-*tehrn*) *adj* minor

subir (sew-*beer*) *v* suffer

sublime (sew-*bleem*) *adj* grand

subordonné (sew-bor-do-*nay*) *adj* subordinate

subsistance (sewb-zee-*stahngss*) *f* livelihood

substance (sewb-*stahngss*) *f* substance

substantiel (sewb-stahng-s*y*ehl) *adj* substantial

substantif (sewb-stahng-*teef*) *m* noun

substituer (sewb-stee-*tway*) *v* substitute

substitut (sewb-stee-*tew*) *m* substitute; deputy

subtil (sewb-*teel*) *adj* subtle

suburbain (sew-bewr-*bang*) *adj* suburban

subvention (sewb-vahng-s*y*awng) *f* subsidy; grant

succéder (sewk-say-*day*) *v* succeed

succès (sewk-*say*) *m* success; hit

succession (sewk-seh-s*y*awng) *f* sequence

succomber (sew-kawng-*bay*) *v* succumb

succulent (sew-kew-*lahng*) *adj* tasty

succursale (sew-kewr-*sahl*) *f* branch

sucer (sew-*say*) *v* suck

sucre (sewkr) *m* sugar

sucrer (sew-*kray*) *v* sweeten; **sucré** sweet

sud (sewd) *m* south

sud-américain (sew-dah-may-ree-*kang*) *adj* Latin-American

sud-est (sew-*dehst*) *m* south-east

sud-ouest (sew-*dwehst*) *m* south-west

Suède (swehd) *f* Sweden

Suédois (sway-*dwah*) *m* Swede

suédois (sway-*dwah*) *adj* Swedish

suer (sway) *v* perspire, sweat

sueur (swūrr) *f* perspiration, sweat

*****suffire** (sew-*feer*) *v* *do, suffice

suffisant (sew-fee-*zahng*) *adj* enough, sufficient

suffoquer (sew-fo-*kay*) *v* choke

suffrage (sew-*fraazh*) *m* suffrage

suggérer (sewg-zhay-*ray*) *v* suggest

suggestion (sewg-zheh-st*y*awng) *f* suggestion

suicide (swee-*seed*) *m* suicide

Suisse (sweess) *f* Switzerland; *m* Swiss

suisse (sweess) *adj* Swiss

suite (sweet) *f* sequel; series; **et ainsi de ~** and so on; **par la ~** afterwards; **tout de ~** at once, instantly

suivant (swee-*vahng*) *adj* following, next

*****suivre** (sweevr) *v* follow; *****faire ~** forward

sujet (sew-*zhay*) *m* subject; issue, topic, theme; **~ à** liable to, subject to

superbe (sew-*pehrb*) *adj* superb

superficiel (sew-pehr-fee-s*y*ehl) *adj* superficial

superflu (sew-pehr-*flew*) *adj* superfluous; unnecessary, redundant

supérieur (sew-pay-r*y*ūrr) *adj* superior; top, upper; excellent

superlatif (sew-pehr-lah-*teef*) *adj* superlative; *m* superlative

supermarché (sew-pehr-mahr-*shay*) *m* supermarket

superstition (sew-pehr-stee-s*y*awng) *f* superstition

superviser (sew-pehr-vee-*zay*) *v* supervise

supervision (sew-pehr-vee-z*y*awng) *f* supervision

supplément (sew-play-*mahng*) *m* supplement; surcharge

supplémentaire (sew-play-mahng-*tair*) *adj* additional; extra

supplier (sew-plee-*ay*) *v* beg

supporter[1] (sew-por-*tay*) *v* *bear;

support
supporter² (sew-por-*tair*) *m* supporter
supposer (sew-poa-*zay*) *v* suppose; guess, assume, reckon
suppositoire (sew-poa-zee-*twaar*) *m* suppository
supprimer (sew-pree-*may*) *v* *do away with
suprême (sew-*prehm*) *adj* supreme
sur (sewr) *prep* upon, on; in; about
sûr (sewr) *adj* sure; safe, secure; **bien ~** naturally
surcharge (sewr-*shahrzh*) *f* overweight
sûrement (sewr-*mahng*) *adv* surely
surface (sewr-*fahss*) *f* surface; area
surgir (sewr-*zheer*) *v* *arise
surmené (sewr-mer-*nay*) *adj* overtired, overstrung
se surmener (sewr-mer-*nay*) overwork
surnom (sewr-*nawng*) *m* nickname
surpasser (sewr-pah-*say*) *v* *outdo, exceed
surplus (sewr-*plew*) *m* surplus
*surprendre (sewr-*prahngdr*) *v* surprise; amaze; *catch
surprise (sewr-*preez*) *f* surprise
surprise-partie (sewr-preez-pahr-*tee*) *f* party
surtout (sewr-*too*) *adv* most of all
surveillance (sewr-veh-*ᵞahngss*) *f* supervision
surveillant (sewr-veh-*ᵞahng*) *m* warden, supervisor
surveiller (sewr-vay-*ᵞay*) *v* watch; guard, patrol
*survenir (sewr-ver-*neer*) *v* occur
survie (sewr-*vee*) *f* survival
*survivre (sewr-*veevr*) *v* survive
suspect (sew-*spehkt*) *adj* suspicious; *m* suspect
suspecter (sew-spehk-*tay*) *v* suspect
suspendre (sew-*spahngdr*) *v* *hang; discontinue, suspend
suspension (sew-spahng-*sᵞawng*) *f* suspension

suture (sew-*tewr*) *f* stitch
suturer (sew-tew-*ray*) *v* sew up
svelte (svehlt) *adj* slender
Swahili (swah-ee-*lee*) *m* Swahili
syllabe (see-*lahb*) *f* syllable
symbole (sang-*bol*) *m* symbol
sympathie (sang-pah-*tee*) *f* sympathy
sympathique (sang-pah-*teek*) *adj* nice; pleasant
symphonie (sang-fo-*nee*) *f* symphony
symptôme (sangp-*tōam*) *m* symptom
synagogue (see-nah-*gog*) *f* synagogue
syndicat (sang-dee-*kah*) *m* trade-union; **~ d'initiative** tourist office
synonyme (see-no-*neem*) *m* synonym
synthétique (sang-tay-*teek*) *adj* synthetic
Syrie (see-*ree*) *f* Syria
Syrien (see-*rᵞang*) *m* Syrian
syrien (see-*rᵞang*) *adj* Syrian
systématique (see-stay-mah-*teek*) *adj* systematic
système (see-*stehm*) *m* system; **~ décimal** decimal system; **~ de lubrification** lubrication system; **~ de refroidissement** cooling system

T

tabac (tah-*bah*) *m* tobacco; **bureau de ~** tobacconist's; **débitant de ~** tobacconist; **~ à rouler** cigarette tobacco; **tabac pour pipe** pipe tobacco
table (tahbl) *f* table; **~ des matières** table of contents
tableau (tah-*bloa*) *m* chart; board; **~ de bord** dashboard; **~ de conversions** conversion chart; **~ de distribution** switchboard; **~ noir** blackboard

tablette (tah-*bleht*) f tablet

tablier (tah-blee-*ay*) m apron

tabou (tah-*boo*) m taboo

tache (tahsh) f speck, stain, spot, blot

tâche (taash) f duty, task

tacher (tah-*shay*) v stain

tâcher (tah-*shay*) v try

tacheté (tahsh-*tay*) adj spotted

tactique (tahk-*teek*) f tactics pl

taille (tigh) f waist; size

taille-crayon (tigh-kreh-*Yawng*) m pencil-sharpener

tailler (tah-*Yay*) v trim, chip; carve

tailleur (tah-*Yurr*) m tailor

se *taire (tair) *keep quiet, *be silent

talc (tahlk) m talc powder

talent (tah-*lahng*) m talent; faculty, gift

talon (tah-*lawng*) m heel; counterfoil

tambour (tahng-*boor*) m drum; **~ de frein** brake drum

tamiser (tah-mee-*zay*) v sift, sieve

tampon (tahng-*pawng*) m tampon

tamponner (tahng-po-*nay*) v bump

tandis que (tahng-dee ker) while; whilst

tangible (tahng-*zheebl*) adj tangible

tanière (tah-*nYair*) f den

tante (tahngt) f aunt

tapageur (tah-pah-*zhurr*) adj rowdy

taper (tah-*pay*) v *strike; **~ à la machine** type

tapis (tah-*pee*) m carpet; rug, mat

tapisserie (tah-pee-*sree*) f tapestry

taquiner (tah-kee-*nay*) v kid, tease

tard (taar) adj late

tarif (tah-*reef*) m rate

tartine (tahr-*teen*) f sandwich

tas (tah) m pile, lot, heap

tasse (tahss) f cup; **~ à thé** teacup

taureau (toa-*roa*) m bull

taux (toa) m tariff; **~ d'escompte** bank-rate

taverne (tah-*vehrn*) f tavern

taxation (tahk-sah-*sYawng*) f taxation

taxe (tahks) f tax

taxi (tahk-*see*) m taxi; cab; **chauffeur de ~** taxi-driver

taximètre (tahk-see-*mehtr*) m taximeter

Tchécoslovaquie (chay-ko-slo-vah-*kee*) f Czechoslovakia

Tchèque (chehk) m Czech

tchèque (chehk) adj Czech

te (ter) pron you; yourself

technicien (tehk-nee-s*Yang*) m technician

technique (tehk-*neek*) f technique; adj technical

technologie (tehk-no-lo-*zhee*) f technology

*teindre (tangdr) v dye

teint (tang) m complexion; **grand ~** fast-dyed

teinture (tang-*tewr*) f dye

teinturerie (tang-tewr-*ree*) f drycleaner's

tel (tehl) adj such; **~ que** such as

télégramme (tay-lay-*grahm*) m cable, telegram

télégraphier (tay-lay-grah-f*Yay*) v cable, telegraph

télémètre (tay-lay-*mehtr*) m rangefinder

télé-objectif (tay-lay-ob-zhehk-*teef*) m telephoto lens

télépathie (tay-lay-pah-*tee*) f telepathy

téléphone (tay-lay-*fon*) m telephone; phone; **coup de ~** telephone call

téléphoner (tay-lay-fo-*nay*) v phone; call, ring up; call up Am

téléphoniste (tay-lay-fo-*neest*) f telephonist

téléski (tay-lay-*skee*) m ski-lift

télévision (tay-lay-vee-z*Yawng*) f television; television set

télex (tay-*lehks*) m telex

tellement (tehl-*mahng*) adv such; so

téméraire (tay-may-*rair*) *adj* daring

témoignage (tay-mwah-*n*ʸ*aazh*) *m* testimony

témoigner (tay-mwah-*ñay*) *v* testify

témoin (tay-*mwang*) *m* witness; ~ **oculaire** eye-witness

tempe (tahŋp) *f* temple

température (tahŋ-pay-rah-*tewr*) *f* temperature; ~ **ambiante** room temperature

tempête (tahŋ-*peht*) *f* storm; tempest, gale; ~ **de neige** snowstorm, blizzard

temple (tahŋpl) *m* temple

temporaire (tahŋ-po-*rair*) *adj* temporary

temps (tahŋ) *m* time; weather; **à ~** in time; **ces derniers ~** lately; **de temps en ~** now and then, occasionally; ~ **libre** spare time

tenailles (ter-*nigh*) *fpl* pincers *pl*

tendance (tahŋ-*dahŋss*) *f* tendency; *****avoir ~** *be inclined to, tend

tendon (tahŋ-*dawng*) *m* sinew, tendon

tendre[1] (tahŋdr) *adj* delicate, tender

tendre[2] (tahŋdr) *v* stretch; ~ **à** tend to; **tendu** tense

tendresse (tahŋ-*drehss*) *f* tenderness

ténèbres (tay-*nehbr*) *fpl* dark; gloom

*****tenir** (ter-*neer*) *v* *hold; *keep; **se ~ debout** *stand; ~ **à** care for

tennis (tay-*neess*) *m* tennis; ~ **de table** ping-pong

tension (tahŋ-*s*ʸ*awng*) *f* tension; stress, strain; pressure; ~ **artérielle** blood pressure

tentation (tahŋ-tah-*s*ʸ*awng*) *f* temptation

tentative (tahŋ-tah-*teev*) *f* try, attempt

tente (tahŋt) *f* tent

tenter (tahŋ-*tay*) *v* try; attempt; tempt

tenue (ter-*new*) *f* conduct; dress; ~ **de soirée** evening dress

térébenthine (tay-ray-bahŋ-*teen*) *f* turpentine

terme (tehrm) *m* term

terminer (tehr-mee-*nay*) *v* finish; **se ~** expire

terminus (tehr-mee-*newss*) *m* terminal

terne (tehrn) *adj* dim; dull, mat

terrain (teh-*rang*) *m* terrain; grounds; ~ **d'aviation** airfield; ~ **de camping** camping site; ~ **de golf** golf-course; ~ **de jeux** recreation ground

terrasse (teh-*rahss*) *f* terrace

terre (tair) *f* earth; soil, land; **à ~** ashore; **hautes terres** uplands *pl*; **par ~** down; ~ **cuite** ceramics *pl*; ~ **ferme** mainland

terre-à-terre (teh-rah-*tair*) *adj* down-to-earth

terreur (teh-*rūr*) *f* terror; terrorism

terrible (tay-*reebl*) *adj* terrible; awful, dreadful, frightful

terrifiant (teh-ree-f*ʸahng*) *adj* terrifying; horrible, creepy

terrifier (teh-ree-f*ʸay*) *v* terrify

territoire (teh-ree-*twaar*) *m* territory

terroir (teh-*rwaar*) *m* soil

terrorisme (teh-ro-*reesm*) *m* terrorism

terroriste (teh-ro-*reest*) *m* terrorist

Térylène (tay-ree-*lehn*) *m* terylene

test (tehst) *m* test

testament (teh-stah-*mahng*) *m* will

tête (teht) *f* head

têtu (tay-*tew*) *adj* head-strong, stubborn

texte (tehkst) *m* text

textile (tehk-*steel*) *m* textile

texture (tehk-*stewr*) *f* texture

Thaïlandais (tah-ee-lahŋ-*day*) *m* Thai

thaïlandais (tah-ee-lahŋ-*day*) *adj* Thai

Thaïlande (tah-ee-*lahŋd*) *f* Thailand

thé (tay) *m* tea

théâtre (tay-*aatr*) *m* theatre; drama; ~ **de marionnettes** puppet-show; ~ **de variétés** variety theatre

théière (tay-*Yair*) *f* teapot

thème (tehm) *m* theme

théologie (tay-o-lo-*zhee*) *f* theology

théorie (tay-o-*ree*) *f* theory

théorique (tay-o-*reek*) *adj* theoretical

thérapie (tay-rah-*pee*) *f* therapy

thermomètre (tehr-mo-*mehtr*) *m* thermometer

thermoplongeur (tehr-moa-plawng-*zhūrr*) *m* immersion heater

thermos (tehr-*moss*) *m* thermos flask, vacuum flask

thermostat (tehr-mo-*stah*) *m* thermostat

thèse (taiz) *f* thesis

thon (tawng) *m* tuna

thym (tang) *m* thyme

ticket (tee-*kay*) *m* coupon

tiède (tYehd) *adj* lukewarm, tepid

le tien (ler tYang) yours

tiers (tYair) *adj* (f tierce) third

tige (teezh) *f* stem; rod

tigre (teegr) *m* tiger

tilleul (tee-*Yurl*) *m* limetree, lime

timbre (tangbr) *m* stamp; tone

timbre-poste (tang-brer-*post*) *m* postage stamp

timide (tee-*meed*) *adj* timid, shy

timidité (tee-mee-dee-*tay*) *f* timidity, shyness

timonier (tee-mo-n*Y*ay) *m* helmsman; steersman

tirage (tee-*raazh*) *m* draw; issue

tire-bouchon (teer-boo-*shawng*) *m* corkscrew

tirer (tee-*ray*) *v* *draw, pull; fire, *shoot

tiret (tee-*ray*) *m* dash

tiroir (tee-*rwaar*) *m* drawer

tisser (tee-*say*) *v* *weave

tisserand (tee-*srahng*) *m* weaver

tissu (tee-*sew*) *m* tissue; fabric, cloth, material

tissu-éponge (tee-sew-ay-*pawngz*) *m* towelling

titre (teetr) *m* title; heading

toast (toast) *m* toast

toboggan (to-bo-*gahng*) *m* slide

toi (twah) *pron* you

toile (twahl) *f* linen; **grosse** ~ canvas; ~ **d'araignée** cobweb

toilettes (twah-*leht*) *fpl* toilet, bathroom; washroom *nAm*; ~ **pour dames** ladies' room; powder-room; ~ **pour hommes** men's room

toi-même (twah-*mehm*) *pron* yourself

toit (twah) *m* roof; ~ **de chaume** *m* thatched roof

tolérable (to-lay-*rahbl*) *adj* tolerable

tolérer (to-lay-*ray*) *v* *bear

tomate (to-*maht*) *f* tomato

tombe (tawngb) *f* tomb, grave

tomber (tawng-*bay*) *v* *fall

tome (tom) *m* volume

ton¹ (tawng) *adj* (f ta, pl tes) your

ton² (tawng) *m* note, tone

tonique (to-*neek*) *m* tonic; ~ **capillaire** hair tonic

tonne (ton) *f* ton

tonneau (to-*noa*) *m* barrel; cask

tonnerre (to-*nair*) *m* thunder

torche (torsh) *f* torch

torchon (tor-*shawng*) *m* tea-cloth

tordre (tordr) *v* twist; wrench

tordu (tor-*dew*) *adj* crooked

torsion (tor-s*Y*awng) *f* twist

tort (tawr) *m* wrong; harm; *avoir ~ *be wrong; *faire du ~ wrong

tortue (tor-*tew*) *f* turtle

torture (tor-*tewr*) *f* torture

torturer (tor-tew-*ray*) *v* torture

tôt (toa) *adv* early

total (to-*tahl*) *adj* total; utter, overall; *m* total

totalement (to-tahl-*mahng*) *adv* completely

totalisateur (to-tah-lee-zah-*tūrr*) *m* totalizator

totalitaire (to-tah-lee-*tair*) *adj* totalitarian

touchant (too-*shahng*) *adj* touching

toucher (too-*shay*) *v* touch; affect; *hit; cash; *m* touch

toujours (too-*zhōōr*) *adv* always; ever; ~ **et encore** again and again

tour (tōōr) *m* turn; move; *f* tower

tourisme (too-*reesm*) *m* tourism

touriste (too-*reest*) *m* tourist

tourment (toor-*mahng*) *m* torment

tourmenter (toor-mahng-*tay*) *v* torment

tournant (toor-*nahng*) *m* turn, curve; turning-point

tourne-disque (toor-ner-*deesk*) *m* record-player

tourner (toor-*nay*) *v* turn; *spin

tournevis (toor-ner-*veess*) *m* screwdriver

tournoi (toor-*nwah*) *m* tournament

tousser (too-*say*) *v* cough

tout (too) *adj* all; every; entire; *pron* everything; **du** ~ at all; **en** ~ altogether; ~ **à fait** quite; ~ **à l'heure** presently; ~ **au plus** at most; ~ **ce que** whatever; ~ **de suite** immediately, straight away; ~ **droit** straight on; ~ **le monde** everybody

toutefois (toot-*fwah*) *adv* still

toux (too) *f* cough

toxique (tok-*seek*) *adj* toxic

tracas (trah-*kah*) *m* bother

tracasser (trah-kah-*say*) *v* bother

trace (trahss) *f* trace

tracer (trah-*say*) *v* trace

tracteur (trahk-*tūrr*) *m* tractor

tradition (trah-dee-s^y*awng*) *f* tradition

traditionnel (trah-dee-s^yo-*nehl*) *adj* traditional

traducteur (trah-dewk-*tūrr*) *m* translator

traduction (trah-dewk-s^y*awng*) *f* translation

***traduire** (trah-*dweer*) *v* translate

trafic (trah-*feek*) *m* traffic

tragédie (trah-zhay-*dee*) *f* tragedy; drama

tragique (trah-*zheek*) *adj* tragic

trahir (trah-*eer*) *v* betray

trahison (trah-ee-*zawng*) *f* treason

train (trang) *m* train; ~ **de marchandises** goods train; freight-train *nAm*; ~ **de nuit** night train; ~ **de voyageurs** passenger train; ~ **direct** through train; ~ **express** express train; ~ **local** local train

traîneau (treh-*noa*) *m* sledge; sleigh

traîner (tray-*nay*) *v* drag, haul

trait (tray) *m* line; trait; ~ **de caractère** characteristic; ~ **d'union** hyphen; ~ **du visage** feature

traite (treht) *f* draft

traité (tray-*tay*) *m* treaty

traitement (treht-*mahng*) *m* treatment

traiter (tray-*tay*) *v* treat; handle

traître (traitr) *m* traitor

trajet (trah-*zhay*) *m* way

tram (trahm) *m* tram; streetcar *nAm*

tranche (trahngsh) *f* slice

trancher (trahng-*shay*) *v* *cut off; settle

tranquille (trahng-*keel*) *adj* calm; tranquil, quiet, still

tranquillité (trahng-kee-lee-*tay*) *f* quiet

transaction (trahng-zahk-s^y*awng*) *f* transaction, deal

transatlantique (trahng-zaht-lahng-*teek*) *adj* transatlantic

transférer (trahng-sfay-*ray*) *v* transfer

transformateur (trahng-sfor-mah-*tūrr*) *m* transformer

transformer (trahng-sfor-*may*) *v* transform

transition (trahng-zee-s^yawng) f transition

transparent (trahng-spah-rahng) adj transparent; sheer

transpiration (trahng-spee-rah-s^yawng) f perspiration

transpirer (trahng-spee-ray) v perspire

transport (trahng-spawr) m transportation, transport

transporter (trahng-spor-tay) v transport

trappe (trahp) f hatch

travail (trah-vigh) m (pl travaux) work, labour, job; ~ **artisanal** handwork; ~ **manuel** handicraft; **travaux ménagers** housekeeping, housework

travailler (trah-vah-^yay) v work

travailleur (trah-vah-^yūrr) m labourer

à travers (ah trah-vair) through; across

traversée (trah-vehr-say) f passage, crossing

traverser (trah-vehr-say) v cross; pass through

trébucher (tray-bew-shay) v stumble

trèfle (trehfl) m clover; shamrock

treize (traiz) num thirteen

treizième (treh-z^yehm) num thirteenth

trembler (trahng-blay) v tremble; shiver

tremper (trahng-pay) v soak

trente (trahngt) num thirty

trentième (trahng-t^yehm) num thirtieth

trépasser (tray-pah-say) v depart

très (tray) adv very; quite

trésor (tray-zawr) m treasure; darling; **Trésor** treasury

trésorier (tray-zo-r^yay) m treasurer

triangle (tree-ahnggl) m triangle

triangulaire (tree-ahng-gew-lair) adj triangular

tribord (tree-bawr) m starboard

tribu (tree-bew) f tribe

tribunal (tree-bew-nahl) m court, law court

tribune (tree-bewn) f stand

tricher (tree-shay) v cheat

tricot (tree-koa) m knitted wear; jersey; ~ **de corps** undershirt

tricoter (tree-ko-tay) v *knit

trier (tree-ay) v sort

trimestre (tree-mehstr) m quarter

trimestriel (tree-meh-stree-ehl) adj quarterly

triomphant (tree-awng-fahng) adj triumphant

triomphe (tree-awngf) m triumph

triompher (tree-awng-fay) v triumph

triste (treest) adj sad

tristesse (tree-stehss) f sorrow, sadness

trivial (tree-v^yahl) adj vulgar

troc (trok) m exchange

trognon (tro-ñawng) m core

trois (trwah) num three; ~ **quarts** three-quarter

troisième (trwah-z^yehm) num third

trolleybus (tro-lay-bewss) m trolleybus

tromper (trawng-pay) v deceive; **se** ~ *be mistaken; err

tromperie (trawng-pree) f deceit

trompette (trawng-peht) f trumpet

tronc (trawng) m trunk

trône (trōan) m throne

trop (troa) adv too

tropical (tro-pee-kahl) adj tropical

tropiques (tro-peek) mpl tropics pl

troquer (tro-kay) v swap

trottoir (tro-twaar) m pavement; sidewalk nAm

trou (troo) m hole

trouble (troobl) adj turbid; obscure; m perturbation

troubler (troo-blay) v disturb

troupeau (troo-poa) m herd; flock

troupes (troop) fpl troops pl

trousseau (troo-*soa*) *m* kit

trousse de secours (trooss der ser-*kōōr*) first-aid kit

trouver (troò-*vay*) *v* *find; *come across; consider

truc (trewk) *m* trick

truite (trweet) *f* trout

tu (tew) *pron* you

tube (tewb) *m* tube; ~ **de plongée** snorkel

tuberculose (tew-behr-kew-*lōāz*) *f* tuberculosis

tuer (tway) *v* kill

tuile (tweel) *f* tile

tulipe (tew-*leep*) *f* tulip

tumeur (tew-*mūrr*) *f* tumour; growth

tunique (tew-*neek*) *f* tunic

Tunisie (tew-nee-*zee*) *f* Tunisia

Tunisien (tew-nee-*zᵞawng*) *m* Tunisian

tunisien (tew-nee-*zᵞawng*) *adj* Tunisian

tunnel (tew-*nehl*) *m* tunnel

turbine (tewr-*been*) *f* turbine

turboréacteur (tewr-bo-ray-ahk-*tūrr*) *m* turbojet

Turc (tewrk) *m* Turk

turc (tewrk) *adj* Turkish

Turquie (tewr-*kee*) *f* Turkey

tutelle (tew-*tehl*) *f* custody

tuteur (tew-*tūrr*) *m* guardian, tutor

tuyau (twee-ᵞ*oa*) *m* tube, pipe; ~ **d'échappement** exhaust

tympan (tang-*pahng*) *m* ear-drum

type (teep) *m* type; guy, chap

typhoïde (tee-fo-*eed*) *f* typhoid

typique (tee-*peek*) *adj* typical

tyran (tee-*rahng*) *m* tyrant

U

ulcère (ewl-*sair*) *m* sore, ulcer; ~ **à l'estomac** gastric ulcer

ultime (ewl-*teem*) *adj* ultimate

ultra-violet (ewl-trah-vᵞo-*lay*) *adj* ultraviolet

un (urng) *art* (f une) a *art*; *num* one; **l'un l'autre** each other; **l'un ou l'autre** either; **ni l'un ni l'autre** neither

unanime (ew-nah-*neem*) *adj* unanimous; like-minded

uni (ew-*nee*) *adj* joint; smooth

uniforme (ew-nee-*form*) *m* uniform; *adj* uniform

unilatéral (ew-nee-lah-tay-*rahl*) *adj* one-sided

union (ew-nᵞ*awng*) *f* union; **Union Soviétique** Soviet Union

unique (ew-*neek*) *adj* unique; sole

uniquement (ew-neek-*mahng*) *adv* exclusively

unir (ew-*neer*) *v* unite

unité (ew-nee-*tay*) *f* unity; unit; ~ **monétaire** monetary unit

univers (ew-nee-*vair*) *m* universe

universel (ew-nee-vehr-*sehl*) *adj* universal; all-round

université (ew-nee-vehr-see-*tay*) *f* university

urbain (ewr-*bang*) *adj* urban

urgence (ewr-*zhahngss*) *f* urgency; emergency

urgent (ewr-*zhahng*) *adj* pressing, urgent

urine (ew-*reen*) *f* urine

Uruguay (ew-rew-*gay*) *m* Uruguay

Uruguayen (ew-rew-gay-ᵞ*ang*) *m* Uruguayan

uruguayen (ew-rew-gay-ᵞ*ang*) *adj* Uruguayan

usage (ew-*zaazh*) *m* usage

usager (ew-zah-*zhay*) *m* user

user (ew-*zay*) *v* use up; wear out; **usé** worn; threadbare, worn-out

usine (ew-*zeen*) *f* factory; mill, plant, works *pl*; ~ **à gaz** gasworks

ustensile (ew-stahng-*seel*) *m* utensil

usuel (ew-*zwehl*) *adj* customary
utérus (ew-tay-*rewss*) *m* womb
utile (ew-*teel*) *adj* useful
utilisable (ew-tee-lee-*zahbl*) *adj* usable
utilisateur (ew-tee-lee-zah-*tŭrr*) *m* consumer
utilisation (ew-tee-lee-zah-*s*ʸ*awng*) *f* utilization
utiliser (ew-tee-lee-*zay*) *v* utilize, employ
utilité (ew-tee-lee-*tay*) *f* utility, use

V

vacance (vah-*kahngss*) *f* vacancy; **vacances** holiday
vacant (vah-*kahng*) *adj* vacant, unoccupied
vacarme (vah-*kahrm*) *m* noise, racket
vaccination (vahk-see-nah-*s*ʸ*awng*) *f* vaccination
vacciner (vahk-see-*nay*) *v* vaccinate
vache (vahsh) *f* cow
vacillant (vah-see-ʸ*ahng*) *adj* unsteady; shaky
vaciller (vah-see-ʸ*ay*) *v* falter
vagabond (vah-gah-*bawng*) *m* tramp
vagabondage (vah-gah-bawng-*daazh*) *m* vagrancy
vagabonder (vah-gah-bawng-*day*) *v* tramp, roam
vague (vahg) *f* wave; *adj* vague; faint, obscure
vaillance (vah-ʸ*ahngss*) *f* courage
vain (vang) *adj* vain; **en ~** in vain
***vaincre** (vangkr) *v* *overcome; conquer, defeat
vainqueur (vang-*kŭrr*) *m* winner
vaisseau (vay-*soa*) *m* vessel; **~ sanguin** blood-vessel
vaisselle (veh-*sehl*) *f* pottery; ***faire la ~** wash up

valable (vah-*lahbl*) *adj* valid
valet (vah-*lay*) *m* valet; knave
valeur (vah-*lŭrr*) *f* value, worth; **sans ~** worthless
valise (vah-*leez*) *f* case, bag, suitcase
vallée (vah-*lay*) *f* valley
***valoir** (vah-*lwaar*) *v* *be worth; **~ la peine** *be worth-while
valse (vahls) *f* waltz
vanille (vah-*neey*) *f* vanilla
vaniteux (vah-nee-*tur*) *adj* vain
vanneau (vah-*noa*) *m* pewit
se vanter (vahng-*tay*) boast
vapeur (vah-*pŭrr*) *f* steam; vapour
vaporisateur (vah-po-ree-zah-*tŭrr*) *m* atomizer
variable (vah-rʸ*ahbl*) *adj* variable
variation (vah-rʸah-*s*ʸ*awng*) *f* variation
varice (vah-*reess*) *f* varicose vein
varicelle (vah-ree-*sehl*) *f* chickenpox
varier (vah-rʸ*ay*) *v* vary
variété (vah-rʸay-*tay*) *f* variety
variole (vah-rʸ*ol*) *f* smallpox
vase (vaaz) *m* vase; *f* mud *m*
vaseline (vah-*zleen*) *f* vaseline
vaste (vahst) *adj* large; wide, broad, vast; extensive
vautour (voa-*tōor*) *m* vulture
veau (voa) *m* calf; veal; calf skin
végétarien (vay-zhay-tah-rʸ*ang*) *m* vegetarian
végétation (vay-zhay-tah-*s*ʸ*awng*) *f* vegetation
véhicule (vay-ee-*kewl*) *m* vehicle
veille (vāyʸ) *f* day before
veiller (vay-ʸ*ay*) *v* stay awake; **~ sur** look after
veine (vain) *f* vein
vélo (vay-*loa*) *m* bicycle, cycle
vélomoteur (vay-loa-mo-*tŭrr*) *m* motorbike *nAm*, moped
velours (ver-*lōor*) *m* velvet; **~ côtelé** corduroy; **~ de coton** velveteen

vendable (vahng-*dahbl*) *adj* saleable
vendange (vahng-*dahngzh*) *f* vintage
vendeur (vahng-*dūrr*) *m* salesman; shop assistant
vendeuse (vahng-*dūz*) *f* salesgirl
vendre (vahngdr) *v* *sell; **à** ~ for sale
vendredi (vahng-drer-*dee*) *m* Friday
vénéneux (vay-nay-*nur*) *adj* poisonous
vénérable (vay-nay-*rahbl*) *adj* venerable
Venezuela (vay-nay-zway-*lah*) *m* Venezuela
Vénézuélien (vay-nay-zway-*lYang*) *m* Venezuelan
vénézuélien (vay-nay-zway-*lYang*) *adj* Venezuelan
vengeance (vahng-*zhahngss*) *f* revenge
venger (vahng-*zhay*) *v* avenge
***venir** (ver-*neer*) *v* *come; *faire ~ *send for
vent (vahng) *m* wind; **coup de ~** blow
vente (vahngt) *f* sale; ~ **aux enchères** auction; ~ **en gros** wholesale
venteux (vahng-*tur*) *adj* windy, gusty
ventilateur (vahng-tee-lah-*tūrr*) *m* fan, ventilator
ventilation (vahng-tee-lah-*sYawng*) *f* ventilation
ventiler (vahng-tee-*lay*) *v* ventilate
ventre (vahngtr) *m* belly
venue (ver-*new*) *f* arrival
ver (vair) *m* worm
véranda (vay-rahng-*dah*) *f* veranda
verbal (vehr-*bahl*) *adj* verbal
verbe (vehrb) *m* verb
verdict (vehr-*deekt*) *m* verdict
verger (vehr-*zhay*) *m* orchard
véridique (vay-ree-*deek*) *adj* truthful
vérifier (vay-ree-*fYay*) *v* verify; check
véritable (vay-ree-*tahbl*) *adj* actual; very
vérité (vay-ree-*tay*) *f* truth

vernir (vehr-*neer*) *v* varnish; glaze
vernis (vehr-*nee*) *m* varnish; lacquer; ~ **à ongle** nail-polish
verre (vair) *m* glass; ~ **de couleur** stained glass; ~ **grossissant** magnifying glass; **verres de contact** contact lenses
verrou (veh-*roo*) *m* bolt
vers (vair) *m* verse; *prep* towards, at; ~ **le bas** downwards; ~ **le haut** up
versant (vehr-*sahng*) *m* slope
versement (vehr-ser-*mahng*) *m* deposit, remittance
verser (vehr-*say*) *v* pour; *shed
version (vehr-*sYawng*) *f* version
vert (vair) *adj* green
vertical (vehr-tee-*kahl*) *adj* vertical
vertige (vehr-*teezh*) *m* vertigo; dizziness, giddiness
vertu (vehr-*tew*) *f* virtue
vessie (vay-*see*) *f* bladder
veste (vehst) *f* jacket; ~ **de sport** blazer
vestiaire (veh-*stYair*) *m* cloakroom; checkroom *nAm*
vestibule (veh-stee-*bewl*) *m* hall, lobby
veston (veh-*stawng*) *m* jacket; ~ **sport** sports-jacket
vêtements (veht-*mahng*) *mpl* clothes *pl*; ~ **de sport** sportswear
vétérinaire (vay-tay-ree-*nair*) *m* veterinary surgeon
***vêtir** (vay-*teer*) *v* dress
veuf (vurf) *m* widower
veuve (vūrv) *f* widow
via (vee-*ah*) *prep* via
viaduc (vYah-*dewk*) *m* viaduct
viande (vYahngd) *f* meat
vibration (vee-brah-*sYawng*) *f* vibration
vibrer (vee-*bray*) *v* vibrate; tremble
vicaire (vee-*kair*) *m* vicar
vice-président (vee-spray-zee-*dahng*)

m vice-president

vicieux (vee-*s*ʸ*ur*) *adj* vicious

victime (veek-*teem*) *f* victim; casualty

victoire (veek-*twaar*) *f* victory

vide (veed) *adj* empty; *m* vacuum

vider (vee-*day*) *v* empty

vie (vee) *f* life; lifetime; **en ~** alive;
~ privée privacy

vieillard (vⁿeh-*Yaar*) *m* old man

vieillesse (vⁿeh-*Yehss*) *f* age, old age

vieilli (vⁿay-*Yee*) *adj* ancient

vieillot (vⁿeh-*Yoa*) *adj* quaint

vierge (vⁿehrzh) *f* virgin

vieux (vⁿur) *adj* (vieil; *f* vieille) old;
aged, ancient

vif (veef) *adj* vivid; intense, brisk,
lively

vigilant (vee-zhee-*lahng*) *adj* vigilant

vigne (veeñ) *f* vine

vignoble (vee-*ñobl*) *m* vineyard

vigoureux (vee-goo-*rur*) *adj* vigorous

vigueur (vee-*gūrr*) *f* strength

vilain (vee-*lang*) *adj* bad

vilebrequin (veel-brer-*kang*) *m* crankshaft

villa (vee-*lah*) *f* villa; cottage

village (vee-*laazh*) *m* village

ville (veel) *f* town

villégiature (vee-lay-zhah-*tēwr*) *f* holiday resort

vin (vang) *m* wine

vinaigre (vee-*naigr*) *m* vinegar

vingt (vang) *num* twenty

vingtième (vang-*t*ʸ*ehm*) *num* twentieth

violation (vⁿo-lah-*s*ʸ*awng*) *f* violation

violence (vⁿo-*lahngss*) *f* violence

violent (vⁿo-*lahng*) *adj* violent; fierce,
severe

violer (vⁿo-*lay*) *v* assault, rape

violet (vⁿo-*lay*) *adj* violet

violette (vⁿo-*leht*) *f* violet

violon (vⁿo-*lawng*) *m* violin

virage (vee-*raazh*) *m* turning, bend

virer (vee-*ray*) *v* turn

virgule (veer-*gewl*) *f* comma

vis (veess) *f* screw

visa (vee-*zah*) *m* visa

visage (vee-*zaazh*) *m* face

viser (vee-*zay*) *v* aim at

viseur (vee-*zūrr*) *m* view-finder

visibilité (vee-zee-bee-lee-*tay*) *f* visibility

visible (vee-*zeebl*) *adj* visible

vision (vee-*z*ʸ*awng*) *f* vision

visite (vee-*zeet*) *f* visit; call; **rendre ~
à** call on

visiter (vee-zee-*tay*) *v* visit

visiteur (vee-zee-*tūrr*) *m* visitor

vison (vee-*zawng*) *m* mink

visser (vee-*say*) *v* screw

vital (vee-*tahl*) *adj* vital

vitamine (vee-tah-*meen*) *f* vitamin

vite (veet) *adv* quickly

vitesse (vee-*tehss*) *f* speed; rate;
gear; **en ~** in a hurry; **indicateur
de ~** speedometer; **limitation de ~**
speed limit; **~ de croisière** cruising
speed

vitre (veetr) *f* window-pane

vitrine (vee-*treen*) *f* show-case, shop-
window

vivant (vee-*vahng*) *adj* alive; live

*****vivre** (veevr) *v* live; experience

vocabulaire (vo-kah-bew-*lair*) *m* vocabulary

vocal (vo-*kahl*) *adj* vocal

vœu (vur) *m* desire; vow

voici (vwah-*see*) *adv* here is

voie (vwah) *f* way; track; lane; **~
d'eau** waterway; **~ ferrée** railway;
railroad *nAm*

voilà (vwah-*lah*) *adv* there is; here you
are

voile (vwahl) *f* sail; *m* veil

*****voir** (vwaar) *v* *see

voisin (vwah-*zang*) *m* neighbour

voisinage (vwah-zee-*naazh*) *m* vicinity,

neighbourhood

voiture (vwah-*tewr*) *f* car; carriage; ~ **d'enfant** pram; ~ **de sport** sports-car; ~ **Pullman** Pullman

voix (vwah) *f* voice; **à haute** ~ aloud

vol (vol) *m* flight; robbery, theft; ~ **charter** charter flight; ~ **de nuit** night flight; ~ **de retour** return flight

volaille (vo-*ligh*) *f* poultry, fowl

volant (vo-*lahng*) *m* steering-wheel

volcan (vol-*kahng*) *m* volcano

voler (vo-*lay*) *v* *fly; *steal; rob

volet (vo-*lay*) *m* shutter

voleur (vo-*lūr*) *m* thief; robber

volontaire (vo-lawng-*tair*) *adj* voluntary; *m* volunteer

volonté (vo-lawng-*tay*) *f* will; will-power

volontiers (vo-lawng-*t^yay*) *adv* willingly, gladly

volt (volt) *m* volt

voltage (vol-*taazh*) *m* voltage

volume (vo-*lewm*) *m* volume

volumineux (voa-lew-mee-*nur*) *adj* bulky, big

vomir (vo-*meer*) *v* vomit

vote (vot) *m* vote; **droit de** ~ franchise

voter (vo-*tay*) *v* vote

***vouloir** (voo-*lwaar*) *v* want; *will; **en** ~ **à** resent; ~ **dire** *mean

vous (voo) *pron* you; yourselves; **vous-même** *pron* yourself; **vous-mêmes** *pron* yourselves

voûte (voot) *f* vault, arch

voyage (vwah-*^yaazh*) *m* journey; trip, voyage; ~ **d'affaires** business trip; ~ **de retour** return journey

voyager (vwah-*^yah-zhay*) *v* travel; ~ **en auto** motor

voyageur (vwah-*^yah-zhūr*) *m* traveller

voyelle (vwah-*^yehl*) *f* vowel

vrai (vray) *adj* true; very

vraiment (vray-*mahng*) *adv* really

vraisemblable (vray-sahng-*blahbl*) *adj* probable

vu (vew) *prep* considering

vue (vew) *f* sight; view; **point de** ~ point of view

vulgaire (vewl-*gair*) *adj* vulgar

vulnérable (vewl-nay-*rahbl*) *adj* vulnerable

W

wagon (vah-*gawng*) *m* carriage; waggon, coach; passenger car *Am*; **wagon-lit** sleeping-car; **wagon-restaurant** dining-car

Y

y (ee) *pron* there; to it

yacht (^yot) *m* yacht

Yougoslave (^yoo-go-*slahv*) *m* Jugoslav, Yugoslav

yougoslave (^yoo-go-*slahv*) *adj* Jugoslav

Yougoslavie (^yoo-go-slah-*vee*) *f* Jugoslavia, Yugoslavia

Z

zèbre (zaibr) *m* zebra

zélé (zay-*lay*) *adj* zealous; diligent

zèle (zehl) *m* zeal

zénith (zay-*neet*) *m* zenith

zéro (zay-*roa*) *m* zero; nought

zinc (zangg) *m* zinc

zodiaque (zo-*d^yahk*) *m* zodiac

zone (zōān) *f* zone; area; ~ **de stationnement** parking zone; ~ **industrielle** industrial area

zoo (zoa) *m* zoo
zoologie (zoa-o-lo-*zhee*) *f* zoology
zoom (zoom) *m* zoom lens

Menu Reader

Food

à la, à l', au, aux in the manner of, as in, with
abats, abattis giblets, innards
abricot apricot
agneau lamb
aiglefin haddock
ail garlic
ailloli garlic mayonnaise
airelle a kind of cranberry
alouette sans tête slice of veal rolled and generally stuffed with minced meat, garlic and parsley
(à l')alsacienne usually garnished with sauerkraut, ham and sausages
amande almond
amuse-gueule appetizer
ananas pineapple
anchois anchovy
(à l')ancienne old style; usually with wine-flavoured cream sauce of mushrooms, onions or shallots
(à l')andalouse usually with green peppers, aubergines and tomatoes
andouille a kind of tripe sausage
andouillette smaller kind of tripe sausage

(à l')anglaise 1) usually boiled or steamed vegetables, especially potatoes 2) breaded and fried vegetables, meat, fish or fowl
anguille eel
~ **au vert** eel braised in a white sauce served with minced parsley and other greens
anis aniseed
artichaut (globe) artichoke
asperge asparagus
assiette plate
~ **anglaise** cold meat (US cold cuts)
~ **de charcuterie** assorted pork and other meat products
assorti assorted
aubergine aubergine (US eggplant)
ballottine (de volaille) boned fowl which is stuffed, rolled, cooked and served in gelatine
banane banana
bar bass
barbue brill
basilic basil
béarnaise sauce of egg-yolk, butter, vinegar, shallots, tarragon and white wine

bécasse woodcock

béchamel white sauce

beignet fritter generally filled with fruit, vegetables or meat

(à la) Bercy butter sauce of white wine and shallots

betterave beetroot

beurre butter

~ **blanc** white butter sauce of shallots, vinegar and white wine

~ **maître d'hôtel** butter with chopped parsley and lemon juice

~ **noir** browned butter sauce of vinegar and parsley

bifteck beef steak

(à la) bigarade brown sauce generally with oranges, sugar and vinegar

biscotte rusk (US zwieback)

biscuit biscuit (US cookie)

bisque cream soup of lobster or crayfish (US chowder)

blanc de volaille boned breast of fowl

blanchaille whitebait

blanquette de veau veal stew in white sauce

(au) bleu 1) of fish (usually trout), boiled very fresh 2) of cheese, blue-veined 3) of meat, very underdone (US rare)

bœuf beef

~ **bourguignon** chunks of beef stewed in red wine with onions, bacon and mushrooms

~ **en daube** larded chunks of beef marinated in red wine with vegetables and stewed

~ **miro(n)ton** cold boiled beef or beef stew with onion sauce

~ **mode** larded chunks of beef braised in red wine with carrots and onions

~ **salé** corned beef

bolet boletus mushroom

bombe glacée moulded ice-cream dessert

(à la) bordelaise red wine sauce with shallots, beef marrow and boletus mushrooms

bouchée à la reine vol-au-vent; puff-pastry shell filled with meat, sweetbreads or seafood and sometimes mushrooms

boudin black pudding (US blood sausage)

bouillabaisse assorted fish and shellfish stewed in white wine, garlic, saffron and olive oil

bouilli 1) boiled 2) boiled beef

bouillon bouillon, broth, stock

(à la) bourguignonne button mushrooms, pearl onions or shallots braised in rich red wine

braisé braised

brandade (de morue) prepared cod with cream, oil and garlic

brie white, mellow cheese

brioche small roll or cake

(à la) broche (on a) spit

brochet pike

(en) brochette (cooked on a) skewer

cabillaud fresh cod

café glacé coffee-flavoured ice-cream dessert

caille quail

camembert soft cheese with pungent flavour

canard (caneton) duck (duckling)

~ **à l'orange** roast duck braised with oranges and orange liqueur

cannelle cinnamon

cantal smooth, firm cheese not unlike Cheddar

câpre caper

carbonnade charcoal-grilled meat
  ~ **flamande** beef slices, onions and herbs braised in beer
cardon cardoon (vegetable)
carotte carrot
carottes Vichy steamed carrots
carpe carp
carré loin, rack
  ~ **de l'Est** usually square-shaped cheese of pungent flavour
carrelet plaice
carte des vins wine list
cassis blackcurrant
cassoulet toulousain butter-bean stew of goose or with mutton, pork and sometimes sausage
céleri celery (usually celery root)
  ~ **en branche** branch celery
  ~ **-rave** celeriac, celery root
cèpe boletus mushroom
cerfeuil chervil
cerise cherry
cervelle brains
champignon mushroom
  ~ **de Paris** button mushroom
chanterelle chanterelle mushroom
charbonnade charcoal-grilled meat
charcuterie various kinds of cold pork products
charlotte fruit dessert (usually apples) made in a deep, round mould
chasse venison
chasseur hunter's style; sauce of mushrooms, tomatoes, wine and garlic herbs
chateaubriand thick slice of beef taken from the fillet
chaud warm
chaudrée fish and seafood stew, often with garlic, herbs, onions and white wine

chausson aux pommes apple dumpling (US turnover)
chevreuil deer
chicorée endive (US chicory)
chou cabbage
  ~ **de Bruxelles** brussels sprouts
  ~ **à la crème** cream puff
  ~ **-fleur** cauliflower
  ~ **rouge** red cabbage
choucroute sauerkraut
  ~ **garnie** usually with ham, bacon and sausage
ciboulette chive
citron lemon
civet de lapin (lièvre) jugged rabbit (hare)
clafoutis fruit baked in pancake batter, brandy often added
clémentine pipless (US seedless) tangerine
cochon de lait suck(l)ing pig
(en) cocotte casserole
cœur heart
  ~ **d'artichaut** artichoke heart
(à la) Colbert dipped in egg batter and breadcrumbs, fried
colin hake
concombre cucumber
confit d'oie pieces of goose preserved in its own fat
confiture jam
consommation general word for drinks
consommé clear soup served hot or cold
  ~ **Célestine** with chicken and noodles
  ~ **aux cheveux d'ange** with thin noodles
  ~ **Colbert** with poached eggs, spring vegetables
  ~ **julienne** with shredded vegetables
  ~ **madrilène** cold and fla-

voured with tomatoes

~ princesse with diced chicken and asparagus tips

~ aux vermicelles with thin noodles

contre-filet sirloin

coq au vin chicken stewed in red wine with mushrooms, bacon, onions and herbs

coquelet cockerel

coquillage shellfish

coquille Saint-Jacques scallop gratinéed in its shell

corbeille de fruits basket of assorted fruit

cornichon small gherkin (US pickle)

côte chop or rib

~ de bœuf rib of beef

~ de veau veal chop

côtelette cutlet, chop

~ d'agneau lamb chop

~ de porc pork chop

coupe a metal or glass dish usually for individual desserts

~ glacée ice-cream dessert

courgette vegetable marrow (US zucchini)

couvert cover charge

~, vin et service compris price includes wine, service and cover charges

crabe crab

crème 1) a dessert with cream or a creamy dessert

~ anglaise custard

~ caramel caramel custard

~ Chantilly whipped cream

~ glacée ice-cream

crème 2) a creamy soup

crêpe large, paper-thin pancake

~ Suzette pancake with orange sauce, flamed with brandy and often orange liqueur

cresson (water)cress

crevette shrimp

croissant crescent-shaped flaky roll (usually served for breakfast)

croque-monsieur grilled or baked ham-and-cheese sandwich

croustade pie, pastry shell filled with fish, seafood, meat or vegetables

(en) croûte (in a) pastry crust

croûton small piece of bread, toasted or fried

cru raw

crudités raw vegetables usually served sliced, grated or diced as an hors d'oeuvre

crustacé shellfish

cuisse leg or thigh

cuisses de grenouilles frogs' legs

cuit cooked

bien ~ well-done

cumin caraway, cumin

darne thick fillet of fish, usually of salmon

datte date

daurade gilt-head

déjeuner lunch

délice often used to describe a dessert speciality of the chef

demi half

~-sel soft cream cheese, slightly salty

demoiselle de Cherbourg small rock lobster

(à la) dieppoise garnish of mussels and shrimp served in white-wine sauce

dinde, dindon turkey

dindonneau young turkey

dîner dinner

diplomate moulded custard dessert with crystallized fruit and lined with sponge fingers steeped in liqueur

dodine de canard boned duck, rolled, stuffed, sometimes served cold in gelatine

(à la) du Barry garnish of cauliflower and cheese sauce, gratinéed

(aux) duxelles with minced mushrooms sautéed with butter, white wine and herbs

échalote shallot

écrevisse (freshwater) crayfish

~ **à la nage** simmered in white wine, aromatic vegetables and herbs

églefin haddock

émincé slices of cooked meat in gravy or thick cream sauce

endive chicory (US endive)

~ **à la bruxelloise** steamed chicory rolled in a slice of ham

entrecôte rib-eye steak

entrée dish served between the hors d'oeuvre or soup and the main course; the first course in a smaller dinner (US starter)

entremets small dish served before cheese; today it often means dessert

épaule shoulder

éperlan smelt

épice spice

épicé hot, peppered

épinard spinach

escalope de veau veal scallop, thin slice of veal

escalope viennoise wiener schnitzel; breaded veal cutlet

escargot snail

estouffade braised or steamed in tightly sealed vessel with minimum of cooking liquid

estragon tarragon

étuvé steamed, stewed with minimum of cooking liquid

faisan pheasant

farci stuffed

fenouil fennel

féra dace (fish)

fève broad bean

filet meat or fish fillet

~ **de bœuf** fillet of beef (US tenderloin)

~ **mignon** small round veal or pork fillet

~ **de sole** fillet of sole

(à la) financière rich sauce of pike dumplings, truffles, mushrooms, Madeira wine, sometimes with olives and crayfish

(aux) fines herbes with herbs

(à la) flamande Flemish style; usually a garnish of braised potatoes, carrots, cabbage, turnips, bacon and sausage (sometimes simmered in beer)

flambé dish flamed usually with brandy

flétan halibut

foie liver

~ **gras** goose or duck liver

fond d'artichaut artichoke heart (US bottom)

fondue (au fromage) melted-cheese mixture in a pot into which pieces of bread are dipped

fondue bourguignonne bite-size pieces of meat dipped into boiling oil at the table and eaten with a variety of sauces

fondue chinoise paper-thin slices of beef dipped into boiling bouillon and eaten with a variety of sauces

(à la) forestière forester's style; generally sautéed in butter with morel mushrooms, potatoes

and bacon
(au) four baked
frais, fraîche fresh
fraise strawberry
  ~ **des bois** wild
framboise raspberry
frappé chilled, iced
friand patty with meat filling
fricandeau braised, larded veal
fricassée browned pieces of meat braised with seasonings and vegetables and served in a thick sauce
frit fried
frites chips (US french fries)
friture (de poisson) fried fish
fromage cheese
  ~ **frais** fresh curd cheese
  ~ **de tête** brawn (US head-cheese)
fruit confit candied fruit
fruits de mer mussels, oysters, clams
fumé smoked
galette flat, plain cake
garbure thick cabbage soup made of salted pork, spices and *confit d'oie*
garni garnished
(avec) garniture (with) vegetables
gâteau cake, flan, tart
gaufre waffle
gaufrette small, crisp, sweet wafer
(en) gelée jellied
gélinotte hazel-hen, hazel-grouse (US prairie chicken)
gibelotte de lapin rabbit stew in wine sauce
gibier game
  ~ **de saison** game in season
gigot d'agneau leg of lamb
girolle chanterelle mushroom
glace ice-cream
  ~ **(à la) napolitaine** ice-cream

layers of different flavours
glacé iced, glazed
goujon gudgeon
gras-double tripe simmered in wine and onions
(au) gratin browned with bread-crumbs or cheese
gratin dauphinois sliced potatoes gratinéed in the oven with eggs, cream and cheese
gratin de fruits de mer shellfish in heavy cream sauce and gra-tinéed
grillade grilled meat
grillé grilled
grive thrush
groseille à maquereau gooseberry
groseille rouge redcurrant
gruyère a hard cheese rich in fla-vour
haché minced, hashed
hachis mince, hash
hareng herring
haricot bean
  ~ **de mouton** stew of mutton with beans and potatoes
  ~ **vert** French bean (US green bean)
Henri IV artichoke hearts gar-nished with béarnaise sauce
hollandaise sauce of egg-yolks, butter and lemon juice or vine-gar
homard lobster
  ~ **à l'américaine** (or **à l'armori-caine**) lobster flamed in brandy, simmered in white wine with garlic, tomatoes and herbs
  ~ **cardinal** flamed in brandy, diced, served in its shell with truffles and chopped mush-rooms and gratinéed
  ~ **Newburg** cut into sections, cooked in brandy and fish stock

~ **Thermidor** simmered in white wine, sautéed in butter with mushrooms, herbs, spices, mustard, flamed in brandy and gratinéed with cheese

huile oil

huître oyster

~ **belon** flat, pinkish oyster

~ **de claire** similar to bluepoint oyster

~ **portugaise** small, fat oyster

jambon ham

~ **de Bayonne** raw, with a slightly salty flavour

~ **cru** raw, cured

~ **à l'os** baked ham

jardinière cooked assorted vegetables

jarret shank, shin

julienne vegetables cut into fine strips

jus gravy, juice

lamproie lamprey

langouste spiny lobster

langoustine Norway lobster, prawn, crawfish

langue tongue

lapin rabbit

lard bacon

légume vegetable

lentille lentil

levraut young hare, leveret

lièvre hare

limande dab

livarot small, round cheese from Normandy

longe de veau loin of veal

(à la) lorraine usually braised in red wine with red cabbage

loup (de mer) (sea) bass

(à la) lyonnaise generally sautéed with onions

macédoine mixed, diced vegetables or fruit

(au) madère with Madeira wine

maigre lean

maïs maize (US corn)

maître d'hôtel sautéed in butter with chopped parsley and lemon juice

maquereau mackerel

marcassin young boar

marchand de vin red wine sauce seasoned with shallots

mariné marinated

marinière sailor's style; garnish of mussels with other seafood simmered in white wine and spices

marjolaine marjoram

maroilles strong, semi-hard cheese from Picardy

marron chestnut

matelote freshwater-fish stew (especially of eel) with wine, onions, mushrooms

médaillon small, round cut of meat

menthe mint

menu in France, generally means *menu à prix fixe*, set meal at a fixed price

merguez very spicy sausage

merlan whiting

merluche dried hake

meunière floured and sautéed in butter with lemon juice and chopped parsley

miel honey

mijoté simmered

millefeuille flaky pastry with cream filling (US napoleon)

(à la) Mirabeau with anchovies, olives, tarragon

mirabelle small yellow plum

(à la) mode in the style (of); often means made according to a local recipe

moelle marrow (bone)

144

morille morel mushroom

Mornay *béchamel* sauce with cheese

moule mussel

moules marinière mussels simmered in white wine with shallots, thyme and parsley

mousse 1) any frothy cream dish 2) chopped or pounded meat or fish with eggs and cream

mousseline 1) frothy mixture containing cream, usually whipped 2) variation of hollandaise sauce with whipped cream

moutarde mustard

mouton mutton

munster soft cheese with a pungent flavour

mûre mulberry or blackberry

myrtille bilberry (US blueberry)

nature/au naturel plain, without dressing, sauce or stuffing

navarin mutton stew with turnips

navet turnip

(à la/en) neige snow-like; i. e. with beaten egg-whites

(à la) niçoise Riviera style; usually with garlic, anchovies, olives, onions, tomatoes

(à la) nivernaise a garnish of carrots, onions, potatoes

noisette 1) hazelnut 2) boneless round piece of meat usually taken from loin or rib

noix walnut

~ **de coco** coconut

~ **(de) muscade** nutmeg

~ **de veau** pope's eye of veal

(à la) normande usually cooked with gudgeon, shrimps, mushrooms, cream and sometimes truffles

nouilles noodles

œuf egg

~ **brouillé** scrambled

~ **à la coque** soft-boiled

~ **dur** hard-boiled

~ **farci** stuffed

~ **en gelée** lightly poached and served in gelatine

~ **au jambon** ham and eggs

~ **au/sur le plat** fried

~ **poché** poached

~ **Rossini** with truffles and Madeira wine

oie goose

oignon onion

omble-chevalier freshwater fish of the char family

omelette omelet

~ **norvégienne** ice-cream dessert covered with beaten egg-whites, quickly browned in oven and served flaming (US baked Alaska)

ortolan small game bird like a finch

os bone

~ **à moelle** marrow bone

oseille sorrel

oursin sea urchin

pain bread

palourde clam

pamplemousse grapefruit

panaché mixed; two or more kinds of something

pané breaded, rolled in breadcrumbs

(en) papillote encased in greased paper and baked

parfait ice-cream dessert

Parmentier containing potatoes

pastèque watermelon

pâté 1) a moulded pastry case which holds meat or fish 2) a thickish paste often of liver (contained in an earthenware dish)

~ **ardennais** a purée of pork and seasonings encased in a loaf of bread, served in slices

 ~ **de campagne** strongly flavoured with a variety of meat

~ **en croûte** in a pastry crust

~ **de foie gras** goose (or duck) liver paste

pâtes noodles, macaroni, spaghetti

paupiette (de veau) veal bird, thin slice of veal rolled around stuffing

(à la) paysanne country style; usually containing various vegetables

pêche peach

perche perch

perdreau young partridge

perdrix partridge

(à la) périgourdine preparation with truffles

persil parsley

petit small

 ~ **déjeuner** breakfast

~ **four** small, fancy cake (US fancy cookie)

~ **pain** roll

~ **pois** green pea

~ **salé (au chou)** salt pork (with cabbage)

~**suisse** a mild-flavoured, double-cream cheese

pied de porc pig's trotter (US pig's foot)

pigeonneau squab

piment pimento

pintade guinea hen

piperade omelet with green peppers, garlic, tomatoes, ham

piquant sharp-tasting, spicy (e.g. of a sauce)

pissaladière onion and anchovy tart with black olives

plat plate

~ **du jour** speciality of the day

~ **principal** main dish

plateau de fromages cheese board

plie plaice

poché poached

(à la) poêle fried

(à) point medium

pointe d'asperge asparagus tip

poire pear

 ~ **à la Condé** served hot on a bed of vanilla-flavoured rice

~ **Belle Hélène** with vanilla ice-cream and chocolate sauce

poireau leek

pois pea

~ **chiche** chick pea

poisson fish

~ **d'eau douce** freshwater

~ **de mer** saltwater

poitrine breast, brisket

(au) poivre (with) pepper

poivron sweet pepper

pomme apple

pommes (de terre) potatoes

 ~ **allumettes** matchsticks

~ **chips** crisps (US potato chips)

~ **dauphine** mashed in butter and egg-yolks, mixed in seasoned flour and deep-fried

~ **duchesse** mashed with butter and egg-yolks

~ **en robe des champs** in their jackets

~ **frites** chips (US french fries)

~ **mousseline** mashed

~ **nature** boiled, steamed

~ **nouvelles** new

~ **vapeur** steamed, boiled

pont-l'évêque soft cheese, strong and pungent in flavour

porc pork

port-salut soft cheese, yellow in colour, mild in taste

potage soup
~ **bonne femme** potato, leek, mushroom, onion, rice and sometimes bacon
~ **cancalais** fish consommé (often with oysters or other seafood)
~ **Condé** mashed red beans
~ **Crécy** carrots
~ **cultivateur** mixed vegetables and bacon or pork
~ **du Barry** cream of cauliflower
~ **julienne** vegetables
~ **Longchamp** peas, sorrel and chervil
~ **Saint-Germain** split-pea, leek and onion
~ **soissonnais** haricot bean

pot-au-feu 1) stockpot of beef, potatoes and aromatic vegetables 2) stew

potée boiled pork or beef with vegetables, especially cabbage

potiron pumpkin

poularde fat pullet
~ **de Bresse** grain-fed; reputedly the finest available
~ **demi-deuil** with truffles inserted under the skin and simmered in broth

poule hen
~ **au pot** stewed with vegetables
~ **au riz** stewed in bouillon and served with rice

poulet chicken
~ **Marengo** sautéed in olive oil, cooked with white wine, tomatoes, garlic, shallots and mushrooms

pourboire tip (but *service* is the percentage added to the bill)

praire clam

pré-salé lamb pastured in the salt meadows on the Atlantic seashore

(à la) printanière with spring vegetables

prix price
~ **fixe** at a fixed price

profiterole au chocolat puff pastry filled with whipped cream or custard and covered with hot chocolate

(à la) provençale often with garlic, onions, herbs, olives, oil and tomatoes

prune plum

pruneau (blue) plum
~ **sec** prune

pudding blancmange, custard

puits d'amour pastry shell filled with liqueur-flavoured custard

purée pulped and strained fruit or vegetables
~ **de pommes de terre** mashed potatoes

quenelle light dumpling made of fish, fowl or meat

queue tail

quiche flan, open tart with meat or vegetable filling, eggs and cream
~ **lorraine** tart with cheese, bacon, eggs and cream

râble de lièvre saddle of hare

raclette hot, melted cheese scraped from a block of cheese; accompanied with boiled potatoes and gherkins

radis radish

(en) ragoût stew(ed)

raie skate, ray

raisin grape
~ **sec** raisin, sultana

ramequin small cheese tart

rascasse a Mediterranean fish, an

essential ingredient of *bouilla-baisse*

ratatouille Mediterranean stew of tomatoes, peppers, onions, garlic and aubergines, served hot or cold

ravigote vinegar sauce with chopped hard-boiled eggs, capers and herbs

reblochon soft, mild cheese, pale cream colour (Savoy)

(à la) reine with mince meat or fowl

reine-claude greengage

repas meal

rhubarbe rhubarb

(à la) Richelieu garnish of tomatoes, peas, bacon and potatoes

rillettes usually minced pork (sometimes goose or duck) baked in its own fat

ris de veau sweetbread

rissole fritter, pasty

riz rice

~ **pilaf** rice boiled in a bouillon, sometimes with onions

rognon kidney

romarin rosemary

roquefort blue-veined cheese made from ewe's milk; strong, salty with piquant flavour

rosbif roast beef

rôti roast(ed)

rouelle de veau shank of veal (usually a round cut)

roulade 1) a rolled slice of meat or fish with stuffing 2) dessert with cream or jam stuffing (Swiss roll)

sabayon creamy dessert of egg-yolks, sugar and white wine flavoured with a citrus fruit, served warm

safran saffron

saignant underdone (US rare)

saint-pierre John Dory (fish)

salade salad

~ **chiffonnade** shredded lettuce and sorrel in melted butter, served with a dressing

~ **de fruits** fruit salad (US fruit cocktail)

~ **niçoise** lettuce, tomatoes, green beans, hard-boiled eggs, tunny, olives, green pepper, potatoes and anchovies

~ **russe** cooked vegetables in mayonnaise

~ **verte** green

salé salted

salmis game or fowl partially roasted, then simmered in wine and vegetable *purée*

salpicon garnish or stuffing of one or various elements held together by sauce

salsifis salsify

sandre pike perch

sanglier wild boar

sarcelle teal, small freshwater duck

sauce sauce

~ **béarnaise** vinegar, egg-yolks, butter, shallots and tarragon

~ **béchamel** white sauce

~ **au beurre blanc** butter, shallots, vinegar or lemon juice

~ **au beurre noir** browned butter

~ **bordelaise** brown sauce with boletus mushrooms, red wine, shallots and beef marrow

~ **bourguignonne** red wine sauce with herbs, onions and spices (sometimes tarragon)

~ **café de Paris** cream, mustard and herbs

~ **chasseur** brown sauce with

wine, mushrooms, onions, shallots and herbs

~ **diable** hot, spicy sauce with white wine, herbs, vinegar and cayenne pepper

~ **financière** cream, Madeira wine, herbs, spices, mushrooms, truffles and olives

~ **hollandaise** butter, egg-yolks and vinegar or lemon juice

~ **lyonnaise** onions, white wine and butter

~ **madère** brown sauce with Madeira wine base

~ **Mornay** *béchamel* sauce with cheese

~ **ravigote** vinegar sauce with chopped hardboiled eggs, capers and herbs; served cold

~ **rémoulade** mayonnaise enriched with mustard and herbs

~ **suprême** chicken-stock base, thick and bland, served with fowl

~ **tartare** mayonnaise base with gherkins, chives, capers and olives

~ **vinaigrette** oil, vinegar and herbs (sometimes mustard)

saucisse sausage

~ **de Francfort** frankfurter

saucisson a large sausage

saumon salmon

sauté lightly browned in hot butter, oil or fat, sautéed

savarin sponge cake steeped in rum and usually topped with cream

sel salt

selle saddle

selon grosseur (or **grandeur**) price according to size, e.g. of a lobster, often abbreviated **s.g.**

service (non) compris service (not) included

sorbet water ice (US sherbet)

soufflé à la reine soufflé with finely chopped poultry or meat

soufflé Rothschild vanilla-flavoured soufflé with candied fruit

soupe soup

~ **au pistou** vegetables, noodles, garlic, basil and cheese

~ **à l'oignon** onion

~ **à l'oignon gratinée** onion soup topped with toast and grated cheese; gratinéed

spécialité (du chef) (chef's) speciality

steak steak

~ **haché** hamburger

~ **au poivre** broiled with crushed peppercorns (often flamed in brandy)

~ **tartare** minced beef, eaten raw, with sauce of egg-yolks, mustard, capers, onions, oil and parsley

sucre sugar

suprême de volaille boned chicken breast with creamy sauce

sur commande to your special order

(en) sus in addition, additional charge

tarte open(-faced) flan, tart

~ **Tatin** upside-down tart of caramelized apples

tartelette small tart

tendrons de veau breast of veal

(en) terrine a preparation of meat, fish, fowl or game baked in an earthenware dish called a *terrine,* served cold

tête head

thon tunny (US tuna)

(en) timbale meat, fish, seafood,

fruit or vegetables cooked in a pastry case or mould

tomate tomato

tomme a mild soft cheese

topinambour Jerusalem artichoke

tortue turtle

tournedos round cut of prime beef
~ **Rossini** garnished with foie gras and truffles, served with Madeira wine sauce

tout compris all-inclusive (price of a meal)

tranche slice
~ **napolitaine** cassata; slice of layered ice-cream and crystallized fruit

tripes tripe
~ **à la mode de Caen** baked with calf's trotters (US calf's feet), vegetables, apple brandy or cider

truffe truffle

truite trout

vacherin a mellow cheese
~ **glacé** an ice-cream dessert with meringue

vanille vanilla

(à la) vapeur steamed

varié assorted

veau veal

velouté a creamy soup (of vegetables or poultry), thickened with butter and flour

vert-pré a garnish of cress

viande meat
~ **séchée** dried beef served as hors d'oeuvre in paper-thin slices

viandes froides various cold slices of meat and ham (US cold cuts)

vinaigre vinegar

vinaigrette salad sauce of vinegar, oil, herbs and mustard

volaille fowl

vol-au-vent puff-pastry shell filled with meat, sweetbreads or fish and sometimes mushrooms

waterzooi de poulet chicken poached in white wine and shredded vegetables, cream and egg-yolks

yaourt yoghurt

Drinks

Alsace (93 communes situated on the River Rhine) produces virtually only dry white wine, notably *Gewurztraminer, Riesling, Sylvaner, Traminer;* the terms *grand vin* and *grand cru* are sometimes employed to indicate a wine of exceptional quality

Amer Picon an aperitif with wine and brandy base and quinine flavouring

Anjou a region of the Loire district producing fine rosé and white wine

apéritif often bittersweet, some aperitifs have a wine and brandy base with herbs and bitters (like *Amer Picon, Byrrh, Dubonnet*), others, called *pastis,* have an aniseed base (like *Pernod* or *Ricard*); an aperitif may also be simply vermouth (like *Noilly Prat*) or a liqueur drink like *blanc-cassis*

appellation d'origine contrôlée (A.O.C.) officially recognized wines of which there are over 250 in France; standards of quality are rigidly checked by government inspectors

armagnac a wine-distilled brandy from the Armagnac region, west of Toulouse

Beaujolais Burgundy's most southerly and extensive vineyards which produce mainly red wine, e.g., *Brouilly, Chénas, Chiroubles, Côte de Brouilly, Fleurie, Juliénas, Morgon, Moulin-à-Vent*

Belgique Belgium; though the Romans introduced wine-making to Belgium, the kingdom today only incidentally produces wine, primarily white, sometimes rosé and sparkling wine

bénédictine forest-green liqueur; brandy base, herbs and orange peel, reputedly secret formula

Berry a region of the Loire district producing red, white and rosé wine; e.g., *Châteaumeillant, Menetou-Salon, Quincy, Reuilly, Sancerre, Sauvignon*

bière beer

  ~ **blonde** light

  ~ **(en) bouteille** bottled

  ~ **brune** dark

  ~ **pression** draught (US draft)

  ~ **des Trappistes** malt beer brewed by Trappist monks

blanc-cassis white wine mixed with blackcurrant liqueur

Blayais a region of Bordeaux producing mainly red and white wine

boisson drink

Bordeaux divided into several regions: Blayais, Bourgeais, Entre-Deux-Mers, Fronsac, Graves, Médoc, Pomerol, St-Emilion, Sauternais; among the officially recognized wines are 34 reds, 23 whites and two rosés divided into three categories: general (e. g., *Bordeaux* or *Bordeaux supérieur*), regional (e. g., *Entre-Deux-Mers, Graves, Médoc*) and communal (e. g., *Margaux, Pauillac, Sauternes*); Bordeaux red wine is known as claret in America and Britain

Bourgeais a region of Bordeaux producing red and white table wine

Bourgogne Burgundy, divided into five regions: Beaujolais, Chablis, Côte Chalonnaise, Côte d'Or (which comprises the Côte de Beaune and the Côte de Nuits) and Mâconnais; Burgundy counts the largest number of officially recognized wines of France's wine-growing districts; there are four categories of wine: generic or regional (e.g., *Bourgogne* red, white or rosé), subregional (e. g., *Beaujolais, Beaujolais supérieur, Beaujolais-Villages, Côte de Beaune-Villages, Mâcon, Mâcon supérieur, Mâcon-Villages*), communal (e. g., *Beaune, Chablis, Fleurie, Meursault, Nuits-St-Georges, Volnay*) and vineyard (*climat*) (e. g., *Chambertin, Clos de Vougeot, Musigny*)

brut extra dry, refers to *Champagne*

Byrrh an aperitif with wine base and quinine, fortified with brandy

cacao cocoa

café coffee

~ **complet** with bread, roll, butter and jam; the Continental breakfast

~ **crème** with cream

~ **espresso** espresso

~ **filtre** percolated or dripped through a filter

~ **frappé** iced

~ **au lait** white (with milk)

~ **liégeois** cold with ice-cream, topped with whipped cream

~ **nature, noir** simple, black

~ **sans caféine** caffeine-free

calvados an apple brandy from Normandy

cassis blackcurrant liqueur

Chablis a region of Burgundy noted for its white wine

chambrer to bring wine gently to room *(chambre)* temperature

Champagne district divided into three large regions: Côte des Blancs, Montagne de Reims and Vallée de la Marne with some 200 kilometres (120 miles) of underground caves where the wine ferments; there are ordinary red, white and rosé wines but the production is overwhelmingly centered upon the sparkling white and rosé (usually referred to in English as pink Champagne) for which the region is universally known; vineyards are of little importance in classifying wines from Champagne since, according

to tradition, certain varieties of Champagne are produced by blending wine from different vineyards in proportions which are carefully-guarded secrets; sparkling Champagne is sold according to the amount of sugar added: *brut* (extra dry) contains up to 1.5 per cent sugar additive, *extra-sec* (very dry), 1.5–2.5 per cent, *sec* (dry), 2.5–5 per cent, *demi-sec* (slightly sweet), 5–8 per cent and *doux* (sweet), 8–15 per cent

Chartreuse a yellow or green liqueur of herbs and spices produced by monks of Grande Chartreuse in the French Alps

château castle; term employed traditionally in the district of Bordeaux to indicate a wine of exceptional quality; synonyms: *clos, domaine*

chocolat chocolate

cidre cider

citron pressé freshly squeezed lemon juice

citronnade lemon squash (US lemon drink)

claret see *Bordeaux*

clos vineyard; generally indicates a wine of exceptional quality

cognac cognac; the famed wine-distilled brandy from the Charente and Charente-Maritime regions

Cointreau orange liqueur

Corse Corsica; this Mediterranean island, a French department, produces fine wine, particularly from the hilly areas and Cape Corsica; red, white and rosé wine is characterized by a rich, full-bodied taste; the best wine, grown near Bastia, is the rosé *Patrimonio*

Côte de Beaune the southern half of Burgundy's celebrated Côte d'Or producing chiefly red wine; e.g., the prestigious *Aloxe-Corton* as well as *Beaune, Blagny, Chassagne-Montrachet, Meursault, Pernand-Vergelesses, Puligny-Montrachet, Santenay, Savigny-lès-Beaune, Volnay*

Côte de Nuits a region of Burgundy especially noted for its red wine, e.g., *Chambolle-Musigny, Fixin, Gevrey-Chambertin, Morey-St-Denis, Nuits-St-Georges, Vosne-Romanée*

Côte d'Or a famed region of Burgundy composed of the Côte de Beaune and de Nuits which is noted for its red and white wine

Côtes du Rhône extend from Vienne to Avignon along the banks of the River Rhone between the Burgundy and Provence wine districts; over a hundred communes offer a wide diversity in white, red and rosé wine of varying character; divided into a northern and southern region with notable wine: *Château-Grillet, Châteauneuf-du-Pape, Condrieu, Cornas, Côte-Rôtie, Crozes-Hermitage, Hermitage, Lirac, St-Joseph, St-Péray, Tavel*

crème 1) cream 2) sweetened liqueur like *crème de menthe, crème de cacao*

cru growth 1) refers to a particular vineyard and its wine 2) a system of grading wine; *premier cru, grand cru, cru classé*

curaçao originally from the name of the island of the Dutch Antilles, now applied to liqueur made from orange peel

cuvée a blend of wine from various vineyards, especially, according to tradition, in the making of Champagne

domaine estate; used on a wine label it indicates a wine of exceptional quality

eau water

~ **gazeuse** fizzy (US carbonated)

~ **minérale** mineral

Entre-Deux-Mers a vast Bordeaux region called "between two seas"—actually it's between two rivers—which produces white wine

extra-sec very dry (of Champagne)

framboise raspberry liqueur or brandy

frappé 1) iced 2) milk shake

Fronsac a Bordeaux region producing chiefly red wine

Gueuzelambic a strong Flemish bitter beer brewed from wheat and barley

grand cru, grand vin indicates a wine of exceptional quality

Grand Marnier an orange liqueur

Graves a Bordeaux region especially noted for its white wine but also its red

Jura a six-kilometre- (four-mile-) wide strip which runs 80 kilometres (50 miles) parallel to the western Swiss border and Burgundy; offers white, red, rosé, golden and sparkling wine; there are four formally recognized wines: *Arbois, Château-*

Chalon, Côtes du Jura and *l'Etoile*

kirsch spirit distilled from cherries

Kriekenlambic a strong Brussels bitter beer flavoured with morello cherries

lait milk

~ **écrémé** skimmed

Languedoc district, formerly a French province, to the southwest of the Rhone delta; its ordinary table wine is often referred to as *vin du Midi* but other officially recognized wines, mostly white, are produced, including *Blanquette de Limoux* (sparkling), *Clairette du Languedoc*, *Fitou* and the *Muscats* from Frontignan, Lunel, Mireval and St-Jean-de-Minervois

limonade 1) lemonade 2) soft drink

Loire a district of 200,000 hectares (80,000 acres) sprawled over the vicinity of France's longest river, the Loire; produces much fine red, white and rosé wine in four regions: Anjou (e.g., *Coteaux-de-l'Aubance*, *Coteaux-du-Layon*, *Coteaux-de-la-Loire*, *Saumur*), Berry and Nivernais *(Menetou-Salon, Pouilly-sur-Loire, Quincy, Reuilly, Sancerre)* and Touraine *(Bourgueil, Chinon, Montlouis, Vouvray)*

Lorraine a flourishing and renowned wine district up to the 18th century, today it is of minor importance; good red, white and rosé wine continue to be produced (e.g., *Vins de la Moselle, Côtes-de-Toul)*

Mâcon a region of Burgundy producing basically red wine

marc spirit distilled from grape residue

Médoc a Bordeaux region producing highly reputed red wine including *Listrac, Margaux, Moulis, Pauillac, St-Estèphe, St-Julien*

mirabelle a brandy made from small yellow plums, particularly produced in the Alsace-Lorraine area

Muscadet a white wine from the Nantes area (Loire)

muscat 1) a type of grape 2) name given to dessert wine; especially renowned is the muscat from Frontignan (Languedoc)

Nantais a region of the Loire chiefly renowned for its *Muscadet* white wine but offers other wine, e.g., *Coteaux d'Ancenis, Gros-Plant*

Neuchâtel a Swiss region producing primarily white wine (e.g., *Auvernier, Cormondrèche, Cortaillod, Hauterive*)

Noilly Prat a French vermouth

orange pressée freshly squeezed orange juice

pastis aniseed-flavoured aperitif

Pernod an aniseed-flavoured aperitif

pétillant slightly sparkling

Pomerol a Bordeaux region producing red wine (e.g., *Château Pétrus, Lalande-de-Pomerol, Néac*)

Provence France's most ancient wine-producing district; it traces its history back over two-and-a-half milleniums when Greek colonists planted the first vineyards on the Mediterranean coast of Gaul; red, white and rosé wine is produced, e.g., *Bandol, Bellet, Cassis, Coteaux-d'Aix-en-Provence, Coteaux-des-Baux, Coteaux-de-Pierrevert, Côtes-de-Provence, Palette*

quetsche spirit distilled from plums

rancio dessert wine, especially from Roussillon, which is aged in oak casks under the Midi sun

Ricard an aniseed-flavoured aperitif

Roussillon district which was a French province with Perpignan as its capital; its wine is similar in character to that of the Languedoc to the immediate north; good red, white and rosé table wine, e.g., *Corbières du Roussillon* and *Roussillon Dels Aspres;* this region produces three quarters of France's naturally sweet wine, usually referred to as *rancio*, which is aged in oak casks under the Midi sun; notable examples among them are *Banyuls, Côtes-d'Agly, Côtes-du-Haut-Roussillon; Grand-Roussillon, Muscat de Rivesaltes, Rivesaltes*

St-Emilion a Bordeaux region producing red wine including *Lussac, Montagne, Parsac, Puisseguin, St-Georges*

St-Raphaël a quinine-flavoured aperitif

Sauternais a Bordeaux region noted for its white wine *(Sauternes)*, notably the prestigious *Château d'Yquem*

Savoie Savoy; the Alpine district producing primarily dry, light and often slightly acid white wine (e.g., *Crépy, Seyssel*) but also good red, rosé and sparkling wine which is chiefly produced around Chambéry

Sud-Ouest a district in southwestern France producing quite varying types of wine, mostly white but some red and even rosé; the district includes the former province of Aquitaine, Béarn, Basque Country and Languedoc; wines of particular note are *Bergerac, Côtes-de-Duras, Gaillac, Jurançon, Madiran, Monbazillac, Montravel*

Suisse Switzerland; two-thirds of the nation's wine production consists of white wine; some 230 different vineyards are scattered over a dozen of Switzerland's 23 cantons though only four have a special significance: Neuchâtel, Tessin, Valais and Vaud

Suze an aperitif based on gentian

thé tea

Touraine for 14 centuries a celebrated wine district of the Loire producing red, white and rosé wine (e.g., *Bourgueil, Chinon, Montlouis, St-Nicolas-de-Bourgueil, Vouvray*)

Triple Sec an orange liqueur

Valais sometimes referred to as the California of Switzerland, this Swiss region produces nearly a quarter of the nation's wine; the region in the Rhone Valley is noted for providing Switzerland's best red wine (e.g., *Dôle*) and much of its finest white wine (e.g., *Arvine,*

Ermitage, Fendant, Johannis-berg, Malvoisie)

Vaud a Swiss region producing primarily white wine (e.g., *Aigle, Dézaley, Mont-sur-Rolle, Lavaux, Yvorne*)

V.D.Q.S. (vin délimité de qualité supérieure) regional wine of exceptional quality, produced according to carefully defined specifications and checked by government inspectors

Vieille Cure a wine-distilled liqueur

vin wine

~ **blanc** white

~ **chambré** wine at room temperature

~ **doux** sweet, dessert

~ **gris** pinkish

~ **mousseux** sparkling

~ **ordinaire** table

~ **du pays** local

~ **rosé** rosé (pink in reference to Champagne)

~ **rouge** red

V.S.O.P. (very special old pale) in reference to cognac, indicates that it has been aged at least 5 years

(vin de) xérès sherry

French Verbs

Three regular conjugations appear below, grouped by families according to their infinitive endings, -er, -ir and -re. Verbs with the ending -er are considered as the true regular conjugation in French. Verbs which do not follow the conjugations below are considered irregular (see irregular verb list). Note that there are some verbs which follow the regular conjugation of the category they belong to, but present some minor changes in the spelling of the stem. Example: *acheter, j'achète ; broyer, je broie*.

		1st conj.	2nd conj.	3rd conj.
Infinitive		**chant er** *(sing)*	**fin ir** *(finish)*	**vend re**[1] *(sell)*
Present	je	chant e	fin is	vend s
	tu	chant es	fin is	vend s
	il	chant e	fin it	vend –
	nous	chant ons	fin issons	vend ons
	vous	chant ez	fin issez	vend ez
	ils	chant ent	fin issent	vend ent
Imperfect	je	chant ais	fin issais	vend ais
	tu	chant ais	fin issais	vend ais
	il	chant ait	fin issait	vend ait
	nous	chant ions	fin issions	vend ions
	vous	chant iez	fin issiez	vend iez
	ils	chant aient	fin issaient	vend aient
Future	je	chant erai	fin irai	vend rai
	tu	chant eras	fin iras	vend ras
	il	chant era	fin ira	vend ra
	nous	chant erons	fin irons	vend rons
	vous	chant erez	fin irez	vend rez
	ils	chant eront	fin iront	vend ront
Conditional	je	chant erais	fin irais	vend rais
	tu	chant erais	fin irais	vend rais
	il	chant erait	fin irait	vend rait
	nous	chant erions	fin irions	vend rions
	vous	chant eriez	fin iriez	vend riez
	ils	chant eraient	fin iraient	vend raient
Pres. subj.[2]	je	chant e	fin isse	vend e
	tu	chant es	fin isses	vend es
	il	chant e	fin isse	vend e
	nous	chant ions	fin issions	vend ions
	vous	chant iez	fin issiez	vend iez
	ils	chant ent	fin issent	vend ent
Past part.		chant é(e)	fin i(e)	vend u(e)

[1] conjugated in the same way: all verbs ending in -andre, -endre, -ondre, -erdre, -ordre (except *prendre* and its compounds).

[2] French verbs are always preceded by *que* when conjugated in all tenses of subjonctive. Examples: *que je chante, que nous finissions, qu'ils aient*.

Auxiliary verbs

	avoir *(to have)*		**être** *(to be)*	
	Present	*Imperfect*	*Present*	*Imperfect*
j', je	ai	avais	suis	étais
tu	as	avais	es	étais
il	a	avait	est	était
nous	avons	avions	sommes	étions
vous	avez	aviez	êtes	étiez
ils	ont	avaient	sont	étaient
	Future	*Conditional*	*Future*	*Conditional*
j', je	aurai	aurais	serai	serais
tu	auras	aurais	seras	serais
il	aura	aurait	sera	serait
nous	aurons	aurions	serons	serions
vous	aurez	auriez	serez	seriez
ils	auront	auraient	seront	seraient
	Pres. subj. [1]	*Pres. perf*	*Pres. subj.*[1]	*Pres. perf.*
j', je	aie	ai eu	sois	ai été
tu	aies	as eu	sois	as été
il	ait	a eu	soit	a été
nous	ayons	avons eu	soyons	avons été
vous	ayez	avez eu	soyez	avez été
ils	aient	ont eu	soient	ont été

[1] French verbs are always preceded by *que* when conjugated in all tenses of subjonctive. Examples: *que je chante, que nous finissions, qu'ils aient.*

Irregular verbs

Below is a list of the verbs and tenses commonly used in spoken French. In the listing a) stands for the present tense, b) for the imperfect, c) for the future, d) for the conditional, e) for the present subjonctive and f) for the past participle. In the present tense we have given the whole conjugation, for the other tenses the first person singular, as the conjugations for tenses other than present are similar to those used in the regular verbs. Unless otherwise indicated, verbs with prefixes *(ab-, ac-, com-, con-, contre-, de-, dé-, dis-, é-, en-, entr(e)-, ex-, in-, o-, par-, pré-, pour-, re-, ré-, sous-,* etc.) are conjugated like the stem verb.

absoudre	a) absous, absous, absout, absolvons, absolvez, absolvent;
absolve	b) absolvais; c) absoudrai; d) absoudrais; e) absolve;
	f) absous, absoute
accroitre	a) accrois, accrois, accroît, accroissons, accroissez,
increase	accroissent; b) accroissais; c) accroîtrai; d) accroîtrais;
	e) accroisse; f) accru(e)

acquérir *acquire*	a) acquiers, acquiers, acquiert, acquérons, acquérez, acquièrent; b) acquérais; c) acquerrai; d) acquerrais; e) acquière; f) acquis(e)
aller *go*	a) vais, vas, va, allons, allez, vont; b) allais; c) irai; d) irais; e) aille; f) allé(e)
apercevoir *perceive*	→recevoir
apparaître *appear*	→connaître
assaillir *assail*	a) assaille, assailles, assaille, assaillons, assaillez, assaillent; b) assaillais; c) assaillirai; d) assaillirais; e) assaille; f) assailli(e)
asseoir *set*	a) assieds, assieds, assied, asseyons, asseyez, asseyent; b) asseyais; c) assiérai; d) assiérais; e) asseye; f) assis(e)
astreindre *compel*	→peindre
battre *beat*	a) bats, bats, bat, battons, battez, battent; b) battais; c) battrai; d) battrais; e) batte; f) battu(e)
boire *drink*	a) bois, bois, boit, buvons, buvez, boivent; b) buvais; c) boirai; d) boirais; e) boive; f) bu(e)
bouillir *boil*	a) bous, bous, bout, bouillons, bouillez, bouillent; b) bouillais; c) bouillirai; d) bouillirais; e) bouille; f) bouilli(e)
ceindre *gird*	→peindre
circoncire *circumcise*	→suffire
circonscrire *limit*	→écrire
clore *close*	a) je clos, tu clos, il clôt, ils closent; b) —; c) clorai; d) clorais; e) close; f) clos(e)
concevoir *conceive*	→recevoir
conclure *conclude*	a) conclus, conclus, conclut, concluons, concluez, concluent; b) concluais; c) conclurai; d) conclurais; e) conclue; f) conclu(e)
conduire *drive*	→cuire
connaître *know*	a) connais, connais, connaît, connaissons, connaissez, connaissent; b) connaissais; c) connaîtrai; d) connaîtrais; e) connaisse; f) connu(e)
conquérir *conquer*	→acquérir
construire *build*	→cuire
contraindre *constrain*	→craindre
contredire *contradict*	→médire

coudre *sew*	a) couds, couds, coud, cousons, cousez, cousent; b) cousais; c) coudrai; d) coudrais; e) couse; f) cousu(e)
courir *run*	a) cours, cours, court, courons, courez, courent; b) courais; c) courrai; d) courrais; e) coure; f) couru(e)
couvrir *cover*	a) couvre, couvres, couvre, couvrons, couvrez, couvrent; b) couvrais; c) couvrirai; d) couvrirais; e) couvre; f) couvert(e)
craindre *fear*	a) crains, crains, craint, craignons, craignez, craignent; b) craignais; c) craindrai; d) craindrais; e) craigne; f) craint(e)
croire *believe*	a) crois, crois, croit, croyons, croyez, croient; b) croyais; c) croirai; d) croirais; e) croie; f) cru(e)
croître *grow*	a) croîs, croîs, croît, croissons, croissez, croissent; b) croissais; c) croîtrai; d) croîtrais; e) croisse; f) crû, crue
cueillir *pick*	a) cueille, cueilles, cueille, cueillons, cueillez, cueillent; b) cueillais; c) cueillerai; d) cueillerais; e) cueille; f) cueilli(e)
cuire *cook*	a) cuis, cuis, cuit, cuisons, cuisez, cuisent; b) cuisais; c) cuirai; d) cuirais; e) cuise; f) cuit(e)
décevoir *deceive*	→recevoir
décrire *describe*	→écrire
déduire *deduct*	→cuire
détruire *destroy*	→cuire
devoir *have to*	a) dois, dois, doit, devons, devez, doivent; b) devais; c) devrai; d) devrais; e) doive; f) dû, due
dire *say*	a) dis, dis, dit, disons, dites, disent; b) disais; c) dirai; d) diràis; e) dise; f) dit(e)
dissoudre *dissolve*	→absoudre
dormir *sleep*	a) dors, dors, dort, dormons, dormez, dorment; b) dormais; c) dormirai; d) dormirais; e) dorme; f) dormi
échoir *fall to*	a) il échoit; b) —; c) il échoira; d) il échoirait; e) qu'il échoie; f) échu(e)
écrire *write*	a) écris, écris, écrit, écrivons, écrivez, écrivent; b) écrivais; c) écrirai; d) écrirais; e) écrive; f) écrit(e)
élire *elect*	→lire
émettre *emit*	→mettre
émouvoir *affect*	→mouvoir; f) ému(e)
empreindre *imprint*	→peindre

enduire *coat*	→cuire
enfreindre *infringe*	→craindre
envoyer *send*	a) envoie, envoies, envoie, envoyons, envoyez, envoient; b) envoyais; c) enverrai; d) enverrais; e) envoie; f) envoyé(e)
éteindre *switch off*	→peindre
étreindre *embrace*	→peindre
exclure *exclude*	→conclure
faillir *fail*	a) —; b) —; c) faillirai; d) faillirais; e) faille; f) failli
faire *do, make*	a) fais, fais, fait, faisons, faites, font; b) faisais; c) ferai; d) ferais; e) fasse; f) fait(e)
falloir *have to*	a) il faut; b) il fallait; c) il faudra; d) il faudrait; e) qu'il faille; f) il a fallu
feindre *feign*	→peindre
frire *fry*	→confire
fuir *escape*	a) fuis, fuis, fuit, fuyons, fuyez, fuient; b) fuyais; c) fuirai; d) fuirais; e) fuie; f) fui
geindre *whine*	→craindre
haïr *hate*	a) hais, hais, hait, haïssons, haïssez, haïssent; b) haïssais; c) haïrai; d) haïrais; e) haïsse; f) haï(e)
inclure *include*	→conclure
induire *induce*	→cuire
inscrire *register*	→écrire
instruire *instruct*	→cuire
interdire *forbid*	→médire
introduire *introduce*	→cuire
joindre *join*	a) joins, joins, joint, joignons, joignez, joignent; b) joignais; c) joindrai; d) joindrais; e) joigne; f) joint(e)
lire *read*	a) lis, lis, lit, lisons, lisez, lisent; b) lisais; c) lirai; d) lirais; e) lise; f) lu(e)

luire *shine*	a) luis, luis, luit, luisons, luisez, luisent; b) luisais; c) luirai; d) luirais; e) luise; f) lui
maudire *curse*	a) maudis, maudis, maudit, maudissons, maudissez, maudissent; b) maudissais; c) maudirai; d) maudirais; e) maudisse; f) maudit(e)
médire *speak ill of*	a) médis, médis, médit, médisons, médisez, médisent; b) médisais; c) médirai; d) médirais; e) médise; f) médit(e)
mentir *lie*	a) mens, mens, ment, mentons, mentez, mentent; b) mentais; c) mentirai; d) mentirais; e) mente; f) menti
mettre *put*	a) mets, mets, met, mettons, mettez, mettent; b) mettais; c) mettrai; d) mettrais; e) mette; f) mis(e)
moudre *grind*	a) mouds, mouds, moud, moulons, moulez, moulent; b) moulais; c) moudrai; d) moudrais; e) moule; f) moulu(e)
mourir *die*	a) meurs, meurs, meurt, mourons, mourez, meurent; b) mourais; c) mourrai; d) mourrais; e) meure; f) mort(e)
mouvoir *set in motion*	a) meus, meus, meut, mouvons, mouvez, meuvent; b) mouvais; c) mouvrai; d) mouvrais; e) meuve; f) mû, mue
naître *be born*	a) nais, nais, naît, naissons, naissez, naissent; b) naissais; c) naîtrai; d) naîtrais; e) naisse; f) né(e)
nuire *harm*	→cuire; f) nui
offrir *offer*	→couvrir
ouvrir *open*	→couvrir
paître *graze*	a) pais, pais, paît, paissons, paissez, paissent; b) paissais; c) paîtrai; d) paîtrais; e) paisse; f) —
paraître *appear*	→connaître
partir *leave*	→mentir; f) parti(e)
peindre *paint*	a) peins, peins, peint, peignons, peignez, peignent; b) peignais; c) peindrai; d) peindrais; e) peigne; f) peint(e)
percevoir *perceive*	→recevoir
plaindre *pity*	→craindre
plaire *please*	a) plais, plais, plaît, plaisons, plaisez, plaisent; b) plaisais; c) plairai; d) plairais; e) plaise; f) plu
pleuvoir *rain*	a) il pleut; b) il pleuvait; c) il pleuvra; d) il pleuvrait; e) qu'il pleuve; f) il a plu
pourvoir *provide*	a) pourvois, pourvois, pourvoit, pourvoyons, pourvoyez, pourvoient; b) pourvoyais; c) pourvoirai; d) pourvoirais; e) pourvoie; f) pourvu(e)

pouvoir *be able to*	a) peux (puis), peux, peut, pouvons, pouvez, peuvent; b) pouvais, c) pourrai; d) pourrais; e) puisse; f) pu
prédire *foretell*	a) prédis, prédis, prédit, prédisons, prédisez, prédisent; b) prédisais; c) prédirai; d) prédirais; e) prédise; f) prédit(e)
prendre *take*	a) prends, prends, prend, prenons, prenez, prennent; b) prenais; c) prendrai; d) prendrais; e) prenne; f) pris(e)
prescrire *prescribe*	→écrire
prévoir *foresee*	a) prévois, prévois, prévoit, prévoyons, prévoyez, prévoient; b) prévoyais; c) prévoirai; d) prévoirais; e) prévoie; f) prévu(e)
produire *produce*	→cuire
proscrire *outlaw*	→écrire
recevoir *receive*	a) reçois, reçois, reçoit, recevons, recevez, reçoivent; b) recevais; c) recevrai; d) recevrais; e) reçoive; f) reçu(e)
requérir *require*	→acquérir
restreindre *restrict*	→peindre
rire *laugh*	a) ris, ris, rit, rions, riez, rient; b) riais; c) rirai; d) rirais; e) rie; f) ri
savoir *know*	a) sais, sais, sait, savons, savez, savent; b) savais; c) saurai; d) saurais; e) sache; f) su(e)
séduire *seduce*	→cuire
sentir *feel*	→mentir; f) senti(e)
servir *serve*	a) sers, sers, sert, servons, servez, servent; b) servais; c) servirai; d) servirais; e) serve; f) servi(e)
sortir *go out*	→mentir; f) sorti(e)
souffrir *suffer*	→couvrir
souscrire *subscribe*	→écrire
suffire *be enough*	a) suffis, suffis, suffit, suffisons, suffisez, suffisent; b) suffisais; c) suffirai; d) suffirais; e) suffise; e) suffi
suivre *follow*	a) suis, suis, suit, suivons, suivez, suivent; b) suivais; c) suivrai; d) suivrais; e) suive; f) suivi(e)
taire *be silent*	a) tais, tais, tait, taisons, taisez, taisent; b) taisais; c) tairai; d) tairais; e) taise; f) tu(e)
teindre *dye*	→peindre

tenir
hold

a) tiens, tiens, tient, tenons, tenez, tiennent; b) tenais;
c) tiendrai; d) tiendrais; e) tienne; f) tenu(e)

traduire
translate

→cuire

traire
milk (cow)

a) trais, trais, trait, trayons, trayez, traient; b) trayais;
c) trairai; d) trairais; e) traie; f) trait(e)

transcrire
transcribe

→écrire

tressaillir
startle

→assaillir

vaincre
defeat

a) vaincs, vaincs, vainc, vainquons, vainquez, vainquent;
b) vainquais; c) vaincrai; d) vaincrais; e) vainque; f) vaincu(e)

valoir
be worth

a) vaux, vaux, vaut, valons, valez, valent; b) valais; c) vaudrai;
d) vaudrais; e) vaille; f) valu(e)

venir
come

→tenir

vêtir
dress

a) vêts, vêts, vêt, vêtons, vêtez, vêtent; b) vêtais; c) vêtirai;
d) vêtirais; e) vête; f) vêtu(e)

vivre
live

a) vis, vis, vit, vivons, vivez, vivent; b) vivais; c) vivrai;
d) vivrais; e) vive; f) vécu(e)

voir
see

a) vois, vois, voit, voyons, voyez, voient; b) voyais; c) verrai;
d) verrais; e) voie; f) vu(e)

vouloir
want

a) veux, veux, veut, voulons, voulez, veulent; b) voulais;
c) voudrai; d) voudrais; e) veuille; f) voulu(e)

French Abbreviations

ACF	*Automobile-Club de France*	Automobile Association of France
ACS	*Automobile-Club de Suisse*	Swiss Automobile Association
AELE	*Association européenne de libre-échange*	EFTA, European Free Trade Association
apr. J.-C.	*après Jésus-Christ*	A.D.
av. J.-C.	*avant Jésus-Christ*	B.C.
bd	*boulevard*	boulevard
c.-à-d.	*c'est-à-dire*	i.e.
c/c	*compte courant*	current account
CCP	*compte de chèques postaux*	postal account
CEE	*Communauté économique européenne*	EEC, European Economic Community (Common Market)
CFF	*Chemins de fer fédéraux*	Swiss Federal Railways
ch	*chevaux-vapeur*	horsepower
Cie, Co.	*compagnie*	company
CRS	*Compagnies républicaines de sécurité*	French order and riot police
ct	*courant ; centime*	of the month ; 1/100 of a franc
CV	*chevaux-vapeur*	horsepower
EU	*Etats-Unis*	United States
exp.	*expéditeur*	sender
F(F)	*franc français*	French franc
FB	*franc belge*	Belgian franc
Fs/Fr.s.	*franc suisse*	Swiss franc
h.	*heure*	hour, o'clock
hab.	*habitants*	inhabitants, population
M.	*Monsieur*	Mr.
Me	*Maître*	title for barrister or lawyer
Mgr	*Monseigneur*	ecclesiastic title for the rank of bishop
Mlle	*Mademoiselle*	Miss
MM.	*Messieurs*	gentlemen, Messrs.
Mme	*Madame*	Mrs.
n°	*numéro*	number
ONU	*Organisation des Nations Unies*	UN
OTAN	*Organisation du Traité de l'Atlantique Nord*	NATO, North Atlantic Treaty Organization

PCV	*payable chez vous*	transfer-charge call (collect call)
PDG	*président-directeur général*	chairman of the board
p.ex.	*par exemple*	e.g.
PJ	*police judiciaire*	criminal investigation department
PMU	*pari mutuel urbain*	off-track betting
p.p.	*port payé*	postage paid
P & T	*Postes et Télé-communications*	post and telecommunications (France)
PTT	*Postes, Télégraphes, Téléphones*	Post, Telegraph, Telephone (Belgium and Switzerland)
RATP	*Régie autonome des transports parisiens*	Parisian transport authority
RF	*République française*	the French Republic
RN	*route nationale*	national highway
RP	*Révérend Père*	Reverend Father
RSVP	*répondez, s'il vous plaît*	RSVP, please reply
s/	*sur*	on, at
SA	*société anonyme*	Ltd., Inc.
S. à r.l.	*société à responsabilité limitée*	limited liability company
SE	*Son Eminence; Son Excellence*	His Eminence; His/Her Excellency
SI	*Syndicat d'Initiative*	tourist office
SM	*Sa Majesté*	His/Her Majesty
SNCB	*Société nationale des chemins de fer belges*	Belgian National Railways
SNCF	*Société nationale des chemins de fer français*	French National Railways
St, Ste	*saint, sainte*	saint
succ.	*successeur; succursale*	successor; branch office
s.v.p.	*s'il vous plaît*	please
TCB	*Touring-Club royal de Belgique*	Royal Touring Club of Belgium
TCF	*Touring-Club de France*	Touring Club of France
TCS	*Touring-Club Suisse*	Swiss Touring Club
TEE	*Trans Europ Express*	luxury train, first-class only
t.s.v.p.	*tournez, s'il vous plaît*	please turn over
TVA	*taxe à la valeur ajoutée*	VAT, value added tax
Vve	*veuve*	widow

Numerals

Cardinal numbers		Ordinal numbers	
0	zéro	1er	premier
1	un	2^e	deuxième (second)
2	deux	3^e	troisième
3	trois	4^e	quatrième
4	quatre	5^e	cinquième
5	cinq	6^e	sixième
6	six	7^e	septième
7	sept	8^e	huitième
8	huit	9^e	neuvième
9	neuf	10^e	dixième
10	dix	11^e	onzième
11	onze	12^e	douzième
12	douze	13^e	treizième
13	treize	14^e	quatorzième
14	quatorze	15^e	quinzième
15	quinze	16^e	seizième
16	seize	17^e	dix-septième
17	dix-sept	18^e	dix-huitième
18	dix-huit	19^e	dix-neuvième
19	dix-neuf	20^e	vingtième
20	vingt	21^e	vingt et unième
21	vingt et un	22^e	vingt-deuxième
22	vingt-deux	23^e	vingt-troisième
30	trente	30^e	trentième
40	quarante	40^e	quarantième
50	cinquante	50^e	cinquantième
60	soixante	60^e	soixantième
70	soixante-dix	70^e	soixante-dixième
71	soixante et onze	71^e	soixante et onzième
72	soixante-douze	72^e	soixante-douzième
80	quatre-vingts	80^e	quatre-vingtième
81	quatre-vingt-un	81^e	quatre-vingt-unième
90	quatre-vingt-dix	90^e	quatre-vingt-dixième
100	cent	100^e	centième
101	cent un	101^e	cent unième
230	deux cent trente	200^e	deux centième
1 000	mille	330^e	trois cent trentième
1 107	onze cent sept	1 000^e	millième
2 000	deux mille	1 107^e	onze cent septième
1 000 000	un million	2 000^e	deux millième

Time

Although official time in France is based on the 24-hour clock, the 12-hour system is used in conversation.

If you have to indicate that it is a.m. or p.m., add *du matin, de l'après-midi* or *du soir*.

Thus:

huit heures du matin	8 a.m.
deux heures de l'après-midi	2 p.m.
huit heures du soir	8 p.m.

Days of the Week

dimanche	Sunday	*jeudi*	Thursday
lundi	Monday	*vendredi*	Friday
mardi	Tuesday	*samedi*	Saturday
mercredi	Wednesday		

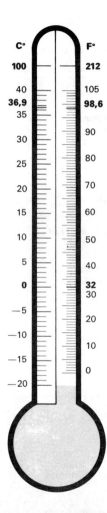

Conversion tables/
Tables de conversion

Metres and feet
The figure in the middle stands for both metres and feet, e.g. 1 metre = 3.281 ft. and 1 foot = 0.30 m.

Mètres et pieds
Le chiffre du milieu représente à la fois des mètres et des pieds. Par ex.: 1 mètre = 3,281 pieds et 1 pied = 0,30 m.

Metres/Mètres		Feet/Pieds
0.30	**1**	3.281
0.61	**2**	6.563
0.91	**3**	9.843
1.22	**4**	13.124
1.52	**5**	16.403
1.83	**6**	19.686
2.13	**7**	22.967
2.44	**8**	26.248
2.74	**9**	29.529
3.05	**10**	32.810
3.66	**12**	39.372
4.27	**14**	45.934
6.10	**20**	65.620
7.62	**25**	82.023
15.24	**50**	164.046
22.86	**75**	246.069
30.48	**100**	328.092

Temperature
To convert Centigrade to Fahrenheit, multiply by 1.8 and add 32.
To convert Fahrenheit to Centigrade, subtract 32 from Fahrenheit and divide by 1.8.

Température
Pour convertir les degrés centigrades en degrés Fahrenheit, multipliez les premiers par 1,8 et ajoutez 32 au total obtenu.
Pour convertir les degrés Fahrenheit en degrés centigrades, soustrayez 32 et divisez le résultat par 1,8.

Some Basic Phrases

Quelques expressions utiles

Please.	S'il vous plaît.
Thank you very much.	Merci beaucoup.
Don't mention it.	Il n'y a pas de quoi.
Good morning.	Bonjour *(matin)*.
Good afternoon.	Bonjour *(après-midi)*.
Good evening.	Bonsoir.
Good night.	Bonne nuit.
Good-bye.	Au revoir.
See you later.	A bientôt.
Where is/Where are...?	Où se trouve/Où se trouvent...?
What do you call this?	Comment appelez-vous ceci?
What does that mean?	Que veut dire cela?
Do you speak English?	Parlez-vous anglais?
Do you speak German?	Parlez-vous allemand?
Do you speak French?	Parlez-vous français?
Do you speak Spanish?	Parlez-vous espagnol?
Do you speak Italian?	Parlez-vous italien?
Could you speak more slowly, please?	Pourriez-vous parler plus lentement, s'il vous plaît?
I don't understand.	Je ne comprends pas.
Can I have...?	Puis-je avoir...?
Can you show me...?	Pouvez-vous m'indiquer...?
Can you tell me...?	Pouvez-vous me dire...?
Can you help me, please?	Pouvez-vous m'aider, s'il vous plaît?
I'd like...	Je voudrais...
We'd like...	Nous voudrions...
Please give me...	S'il vous plaît, donnez-moi...
Please bring me...	S'il vous plaît, apportez-moi...
I'm hungry.	J'ai faim.
I'm thirsty.	J'ai soif.
I'm lost.	Je me suis perdu.
Hurry up!	Dépêchez-vous!

| There is/There are… | Il y a… |
| There isn't/There aren't… | Il n'y a pas… |

Arrival / Arrivée

Your passport, please.	Votre passeport, s'il vous plaît.
Have you anything to declare?	Avez-vous quelque chose à déclarer?
No, nothing at all.	Non, rien du tout.
Can you help me with my luggage, please?	Pouvez-vous prendre mes bagages, s'il vous plaît?
Where's the bus to the centre of town, please?	Où est le bus pour le centre de la ville, s'il vous plaît?
This way, please.	Par ici, s'il vous plaît.
Where can I get a taxi?	Où puis-je trouver un taxi?
What's the fare to…?	Quel est le tarif pour…?
Take me to this address, please.	Conduisez-moi à cette adresse, s'il vous plaît.
I'm in a hurry.	Je suis pressé.

Hotel / Hôtel

My name is…	Je m'appelle…
Have you a reservation?	Avez-vous réservé?
I'd like a room with a bath.	J'aimerais une chambre avec bains.
What's the price per night?	Quel est le prix pour une nuit?
May I see the room?	Puis-je voir la chambre?
What's my room number, please?	Quel est le numéro de ma chambre, s'il vous plaît?
There's no hot water.	Il n'y a pas d'eau chaude.
May I see the manager, please?	Puis-je voir le directeur, s'il vous plaît?
Did anyone telephone me?	Y a-t-il eu des appels pour moi?
Is there any mail for me?	Y a-t-il du courrier pour moi?
May I have my bill (check), please?	Puis-je avoir ma note, s'il vous plaît?

Eating out

Do you have a fixed-price menu?

May I see the menu?

May we have an ashtray, please?

Where's the toilet, please?

I'd like an hors d'œuvre (starter).

Have you any soup?

I'd like some fish.

What kind of fish do you have?

I'd like a steak.

What vegetables have you got?

Nothing more, thanks.

What would you like to drink?

I'll have a beer, please.

I'd like a bottle of wine.

May I have the bill (check), please?

Is service included?

Thank you, that was a very good meal.

Restaurant

Avez-vous un menu?

Puis-je voir la carte?

Pouvons-nous avoir un cendrier, s'il vous plaît?

Où sont les toilettes, s'il vous plaît?

Je voudrais un hors-d'œuvre.

Avez-vous du potage?

J'aimerais du poisson.

Qu'avez-vous comme poisson?

Je voudrais un steak.

Quels légumes servez-vous?

Je suis servi, merci.

Qu'aimeriez-vous boire?

J'aimerais une bière, s'il vous plaît.

Je voudrais une bouteille de vin.

Puis-je avoir l'addition, s'il vous plaît?

Le service est-il compris?

Merci, c'était très bon.

Travelling

Where's the railway station, please?

Where's the ticket office, please?

I'd like a ticket to...

First or second class?

First class, please.

Single or return (one way or roundtrip)?

Do I have to change trains?

What platform does the train for... leave from?

Voyages

Où se trouve la gare, s'il vous plaît?

Où est le guichet, s'il vous plaît?

J'aimerais un billet pour...

Première ou deuxième classe?

Première classe, s'il vous plaît.

Aller simple ou aller et retour?

Est-ce que je dois changer de train?

De quel quai part le train pour...?

Where's the nearest underground (subway) station?	Où est la station de métro la plus proche?
Where's the bus station, please?	Où est la gare routière, s'il vous plaît?
When's the first bus to...?	A quelle heure part le premier autobus pour...?
Please let me off at the next stop.	S'il vous plaît, déposez-moi au prochain arrêt.

Relaxing

Distractions

What's on at the cinema (movies)?	Que joue-t-on au cinéma?
What time does the film begin?	A quelle heure commence le film?
Are there any tickets for tonight?	Reste-t-il encore des places pour ce soir?
Where can we go dancing?	Où pouvons-nous aller danser?

Meeting people

Rencontres

How do you do.	Bonjour madame/mademoiselle/ monsieur.
How are you?	Comment allez-vous?
Very well, thank you. And you?	Très bien, merci. Et vous?
May I introduce...?	Puis-je vous présenter...?
My name is...	Je m'appelle...
I'm very pleased to meet you.	Enchanté de faire votre connaissance.
How long have you been here?	Depuis combien de temps êtes-vous ici?
It was nice meeting you.	Enchanté d'avoir fait votre connaissance.
Do you mind if I smoke?	Est-ce que ça vous dérange que je fume?
Do you have a light, please?	Avez-vous du feu, s'il vous plaît?
May I get you a drink?	Puis-je vous offrir un verre?
May I invite you for dinner tonight?	Puis-je vous inviter à dîner ce soir?
Where shall we meet?	Où nous retrouverons-nous?

Shops, stores and services

Where's the nearest bank, please?

Where can I cash some travellers' cheques?

Can you give me some small change, please?

Where's the nearest chemist's (pharmacy)?

How do I get there?

Is it within walking distance?

Can you help me, please?

How much is this? And that?

It's not quite what I want.

I like it.

Can you recommend something for sunburn?

I'd like a haircut, please.

I'd like a manicure, please.

Street directions

Can you show me on the map where I am?

You are on the wrong road.

Go/Walk straight ahead.

It's on the left/on the right.

Emergencies

Call a doctor quickly.

Call an ambulance.

Please call the police.

Magasins et services

Où se trouve la banque la plus proche, s'il vous plaît?

Où puis-je changer des chèques de voyage?

Pouvez-vous me donner de la monnaie, s'il vous plaît?

Où est la pharmacie la plus proche?

Comment puis-je m'y rendre?

Peut-on y aller à pied?

Pouvez-vous m'aider, s'il vous plaît?

Combien coûte ceci? Et cela?

Ce n'est pas exactement ce que je désire.

Cela me plaît.

Pouvez-vous me conseiller quelque chose contre les coups de soleil?

Je voudrais me faire couper les cheveux, s'il vous plaît.

Je voudrais une manucure, s'il vous plaît.

Directions

Pouvez-vous me montrer sur la carte où je me trouve?

Vous n'êtes pas sur la bonne route.

Continuez tout droit.

C'est à gauche/à droite.

Urgences

Appelez vite un médecin.

Appelez une ambulance.

Appelez la police, s'il vous plaît.

anglais-français

english-french

Introduction

Ce dictionnaire a été conçu dans un but pratique. Vous n'y trouverez donc pas d'information linguistique inutile. Les adresses sont classées par ordre alphabétique, sans tenir compte du fait qu'un mot peut être simple ou composé, avec ou sans trait d'union. Seule exception à cette règle: quelques expressions idiomatiques qui ont été classées en fonction du terme le plus significatif.

Lorsqu'une adresse est suivie d'adresses secondaires (p. ex. expressions usuelles ou locutions), ces dernières sont également rangées par ordre alphabétique sous le mot vedette.

Chaque mot souche est suivi d'une transcription phonétique (voir le Guide de prononciation) et, s'il y a lieu, de l'indication de la catégorie grammaticale (substantif, verbe, adjectif, etc.). Lorsqu'un mot souche peut appartenir à plusieurs catégories grammaticales, les traductions qui s'y réfèrent sont groupées derrière chacune d'elles.

Les pluriels irréguliers des substantifs sont toujours donnés, de même que certains pluriels pouvant prêter à hésitation.

Pour éviter toute répétition, nous avons utilisé un tilde (~) en lieu et place de l'adresse principale.

Dans le pluriel des mots composés, le tiret (-) remplace la partie du mot qui demeure inchangée.

Un astérisque (*) signale les verbes irréguliers. Pour plus de détails, consulter la liste de ces verbes.

Ce dictionnaire tient compte de l'épellation anglaise. Les mots et les définitions des termes typiquement américains ont été indiqués comme tels (voir la liste des abréviations utilisées dans le texte).

Abréviations

adj	adjectif	*num*	numéral
adv	adverbe	*p*	imparfait
Am	américain	*pl*	pluriel
art	article	*plAm*	pluriel (américain)
conj	conjonction	*pp*	participe passé
f	féminin	*pr*	présent
fpl	féminin pluriel	*pref*	préfixe
m	masculin	*prep*	préposition
mpl	masculin pluriel	*pron*	pronom
n	nom	*v*	verbe
nAm	nom (américain)	*vAm*	verbe (américain)

Guide de prononciation

Chaque article de cette partie du dictionnaire est accompagné d'une transcription phonétique qui vous indique la prononciation des mots. Vous la lirez comme si chaque lettre ou groupe de lettres avait la même valeur qu'en français. Au-dessous figurent uniquement les lettres et les symboles ambigus ou particulièrement difficiles à comprendre. *Toutes* les consonnes, y compris celles placées à la fin d'une syllabe ou d'un mot, doivent être prononcées.

Les traits d'union séparent chaque syllabe. Celles que l'on doit accentuer sont imprimées en *italique*.

Les sons de deux langues ne coïncident jamais parfaitement; mais si vous suivez soigneusement nos indications, vous pourrez prononcer les mots étrangers de façon à vous faire comprendre. Pour faciliter votre tâche, nos transcriptions simplifient parfois légèrement le système phonétique de la langue, mais elles reflètent néanmoins les différences de son essentielles.

Consonnes

ð	le **th** anglais de **th**e; **z** dit en zézayant
gh	comme **g** dans **g**ai
h	doit être prononcé en expirant fortement; rappelle le **h** de l'interjection **h**ue!
ng/nng	comme dans campi**ng**; ou comme le dernier son de pai**n**, prononcé avec l'accent du Midi
s	toujours comme dans **s**i
θ	le **th** anglais de **th**ink; **s** dit en zézayant
y	toujours comme dans **y**eux

Au début ou à la fin d'un mot anglais, **b**, **d**, **v**, **z** sont moins sonores qu'en français. C'est également le cas avec **gh** et **ð**.

Voyelles et diphtongues

æ	entre **a** et **è**
i	entre **i** et **é**
ii	comme **i** dans l**i**re
o	proche du **o** de p**o**mme, mais avec la langue placée plus bas et plus retirée dans la bouche et avec les lèvres plus arrondies

1) Les voyelles longues sont indiquées par un dédoublement (p.ex. **oo**) ou par un accent circonflexe placé sur le second élément (p.ex. **eû**).

2) Nos transcriptions comprenant un **i** doivent être lues comme des diphtongues; le **i** ne doit pas être séparé de la voyelle qui le précède (comme dans tr**ahi**), mais doit se fondre dans celle-ci (comme dans **ai**l).

3) Les lettres imprimées en petits caractères et dans une position surélevée doivent être prononcées d'une façon assez faible et rapide (p.ex. ^{ou}i, i^{eu}).

Prononciation américaine

Notre transcription correspond à la prononciation anglaise habituelle. Si la langue américaine varie grandement d'une région à l'autre, elle présente tout de même quelques différences marquantes par rapport à l'anglais de Grande-Bretagne. Ainsi par exemple:

1) Le **r**, qu'il soit placé devant une consonne ou à la fin d'un mot, se prononce toujours (contrairement à l'habitude anglaise).

2) Le **ââ** devient **ææ** dans certains mots, tels que *ask*, *castle*, *laugh*, etc.

3) Le **o** anglais se prononce **a** ou souvent **oo**.

4) Placé devant **oû**, le son **y** est fréquemment omis (ainsi: *duty*, *tune*, *new*, etc.)

5) Enfin, l'accent tonique de certains mots peut varier considérablement.

A

a (éï,eu) *art* (an) un *art*

abbey (æ-bi) *n* abbaye *f*

abbreviation (eu-brii-vi-*éï*-cheunn) *n* abréviation *f*

aberration (æ-beu-*réï*-cheunn) *n* aberration *f*

ability (eu-*bi*-leu-ti) *n* capacité *f*

able (*éï*-beul) *adj* en mesure; capable; **be ~ to *être capable de; *savoir, *pouvoir

abnormal (æb-*noo*-meul) *adj* anormal

aboard (eu-*bood*) *adv* à bord

abolish (eu-*bo*-lich) *v* abolir

abortion (eu-*boo*-cheunn) *n* avortement *m*

about (eu-*baout*) *prep* de; concernant, sur; autour de; *adv* à peu près; autour

above (eu-*bav*) *prep* au-dessus de; *adv* en haut

abroad (eu-*brood*) *adv* à l'étranger

abscess (æb-sèss) *n* abcès *m*

absence (*æb*-seunns) *n* absence *f*

absent (*æb*-seunnt) *adj* absent

absolutely (*æb*-seu-loût-li) *adv* absolument

abstain from (eub-*stéïn*) s'*abstenir de

abstract (*æb*-strækt) *adj* abstrait

absurd (eub-*seúd*) *adj* absurde

abundance (eu-*bann*-deunns) *n* abondance *f*

abundant (eu-*bann*-deunnt) *adj* abondant

abuse (eu-*byoûss*) *n* abus *m*

abyss (eu-*biss*) *n* abîme *m*

academy (eu-*kæ*-deu-mi) *n* académie *f*

accelerate (euk-*sè*-leu-réït) *v* accélérer

accelerator (euk-*sè*-leu-réï-teu) *n* accélérateur *m*

accent (*æk*-seunnt) *n* accent *m*

accept (euk-*sèpt*) *v* accepter

access (*æk*-sèss) *n* accès *m*

accessary (euk-*sè*-seu-ri) *n* complice *m*

accessible (euk-*sè*-seu-beul) *adj* accessible

accessories (euk-*sè*-seu-riz) *pl* accessoires *mpl*

accident (*æk*-si-deunnt) *n* accident *m*

accidental (æk-si-*dèn*-teul) *adj* accidentel

accommodate (eu-*ko*-meu-déït) *v* loger

accommodation (eu-ko-meu-*déï*-cheunn) *n* accommodation *f*, logement *m*

accompany (eu-*kamm*-peu-ni) *v* accompagner

accomplish (eu-*kamm*-plich) *v* achever; accomplir

in accordance with (inn eu-*koo*-deunns ᵒᵘið) conformément à

according to (eu-*koo*-dinng toû) d'après, selon; conformément à

account (eu-*kaount*) *n* compte *m*; récit *m*; ~ **for** rendre compte de; **on** ~ **of** à cause de

accountable (eu-*kaoun*-teu-beul) *adj* explicable

accurate (*æ*-kyou-reut) *adj* précis

accuse (eu-*kyoûz*) *v* accuser

accused (eu-*kyoûzd*) *n* prévenu *m*

accustom (eu-*ka*-steumm) *v* familiariser; **accustomed** accoutumé, habitué

ache (éïk) *v* *faire mal; *n* douleur *f*

achieve (eu-*tchiiv*) *v* *parvenir à; accomplir

achievement (eu-*tchiiv*-meunnt) *n* performance *f*

acid (*æ*-sid) *n* acide *m*

acknowledge (euk-*no*-lidj) *v* *reconnaître; *admettre; confirmer

acne (*æk*-ni) *n* acné *f*

acorn (*éï*-koon) *n* gland *m*

acquaintance (eu-*kᵒᵘéïn*-teunns) *n* connaissance *f*

acquire (eu-*kᵒᵘaïᵉᵘ*) *v* *acquérir

acquisition (æ-kᵒᵘi-*zi*-cheunn) *n* acquisition *f*

acquittal (eu-*kᵒᵘi*-teul) *n* acquittement *m*

across (eu-*kross*) *prep* à travers; de l'autre côté de; *adv* de l'autre côté

act (ækt) *n* acte *m*; numéro *m*; *v* agir; se *conduire; jouer

action (*æk*-cheunn) *n* action *f*

active (*æk*-tiv) *adj* actif; animé

activity (æk-*ti*-veu-ti) *n* activité *f*

actor (*æk*-teu) *n* acteur *m*

actress (*æk*-triss) *n* actrice *f*

actual (*æk*-tchou-eul) *adj* véritable, réel

actually (*æk*-tchou-eu-li) *adv* en réalité

acute (eu-*kyoût*) *adj* aigu

adapt (eu-*dæpt*) *v* adapter

add (æd) *v* additionner; ajouter

adding-machine (*æ*-dinng-meu-chiin) *n* calculatrice *f*

addition (eu-*di*-cheunn) *n* addition *f*

additional (eu-*di*-cheu-neul) *adj* supplémentaire; accessoire

address (eu-*drèss*) *n* adresse *f*; *v* adresser; s'adresser à

addressee (æ-drè-*sii*) *n* destinataire *m*

adequate (*æ*-di-kᵒᵘeut) *adj* adéquat; approprié

adjective (*æ*-djik-tiv) *n* adjectif *m*

adjourn (eu-*djeûnn*) *v* ajourner

adjust (eu-*djast*) *v* ajuster

administer (eud-*mi*-ni-steu) *v* administrer

administration (eud-mi-ni-*stréï*-cheunn) *n* administration *f*; gestion *f*

administrative (eud-*mi*-ni-streu-tiv) *adj* administratif; ~ **law** droit administratif

admiral (*æd*-meu-reul) *n* amiral *m*

admiration (æd-meu-*réï*-cheunn) *n* admiration *f*

admire (eud-*maïᵉᵘ*) *v* admirer

admission (eud-*mi*-cheunn) *n* admission *f*

admit (eud-*mit*) *v* *admettre; *reconnaître

admittance (eud-*mi*-teunns) *n* accès *m*; **no** ~ entrée interdite

adopt (eu-*dopt*) *v* adopter

adorable (eu-*doo*-reu-beul) *adj* adorable

adult (*æ*-dalt) *n* adulte *m*; *adj* adulte

advance (eud-*vââns*) *n* avancement *m*; avance *f*; *v* avancer; **in** ~ à l'avance, d'avance

advanced (eud-*vâânst*) *adj* avancé

advantage (eud-*vâân*-tidj) *n* avantage *m*

advantageous (æd-veunn-*téï*-djeuss) *adj* avantageux

adventure (eud-*vèn*-tcheu) *n* aventure *f*

adverb (*æd*-veûb) *n* adverbe *m*

advertisement (eud-*veû*-tiss-meunnt) *n* annonce *f*; publicité *f*

advertising (*æd*-veu-taï-zinng) *n* publicité *f*

advice (eud-*vaïss*) *n* avis *m*, conseil *m*

advise (eud-*vaïz*) *v* donner des conseils, conseiller

advocate (*æd*-veu-keut) *n* partisan *m*

aerial (*è*ᵉᵘ-ri-eul) *n* antenne *f*

aeroplane (*è*ᵉᵘ-reu-pléïn) *n* avion *m*

affair (eu-*fê*ᵉᵘ) *n* affaire *f*; liaison *f*, affaire de cœur

affect (eu-*fèkt*) *v* affecter; toucher

affected (eu-*fèk*-tid) *adj* affecté

affection (eu-*fèk*-cheunn) *n* affection *f*

affectionate (eu-*fèk*-cheu-nit) *adj* affectueux

affiliated (eu-*fi*-li-éï-tid) *adj* affilié

affirmative (eu-*feû*-meu-tiv) *adj* affirmatif

affliction (eu-*flik*-cheunn) *n* affliction *f*

afford (eu-*food*) *v* se *permettre

afraid (eu-*fréïd*) *adj* apeuré, effrayé; *be ~ *avoir peur

Africa (*æ*-fri-keu) Afrique *f*

African (*æ*-fri-keunn) *adj* africain; *n* Africain *m*

after (*ââf*-teu) *prep* après; derrière; *conj* après que

afternoon (ââf-teu-*noûn*) *n* après-midi *m/f*

afterwards (*ââf*-teu-ᵒᵘeudz) *adv* après; par la suite, ensuite

again (eu-*ghèn*) *adv* encore; de nouveau; *~ and again* toujours et encore

against (eu-*ghènst*) *prep* contre

age (éïdj) *n* âge *m*; vieillesse *f*; *of ~* majeur; *under ~* mineur

aged (*éï*-djid) *adj* âgé; vieux

agency (*éï*-djeunn-si) *n* agence *f*; bureau *m*

agenda (eu-*djèn*-deu) *n* ordre du jour

agent (*éï*-djeunnt) *n* agent *m*, représentant *m*

aggressive (eu-*ghrè*-siv) *adj* agressif

ago (eu-*ghô*ᵒᵘ) *adv* il y a

agrarian (eu-*ghrè*ᵉᵘ-ri-eunn) *adj* agraire

agree (eu-*ghrii*) *v* *être d'accord; *consentir; concorder

agreeable (eu-*ghrii*-eu-beul) *adj* agréable

agreement (eu-*ghrii*-meunnt) *n* contrat *m*; accord *m*; entente *f*

agriculture (*æ*-ghri-kal-tcheu) *n* agriculture *f*

ahead (eu-*hèd*) *adv* en avant; *~ of* devant; *go ~* continuer; *straight ~* tout droit

aid (éïd) *n* aide *f*; *v* assister, aider

ailment (*éïl*-meunnt) *n* affection *f*; maladie *f*

aim (éïm) *n* but *m*; *~ at* viser; rechercher, aspirer à

air (è*ᵉᵘ*) *n* air *m*; *v* aérer

air-conditioning (*è*ᵉᵘ-keunn-di-cheu-ninng) *n* climatisation *f*; **air-conditioned** *adj* climatisé

aircraft (*è*ᵉᵘ-krââft) *n* (pl ~) avion *m*; appareil *m*

airfield (*è*ᵉᵘ-fiild) *n* terrain d'aviation

air-filter (*è*ᵉᵘ-fil-teu) *n* filtre à air

airline (*è*ᵉᵘ-laïn) *n* ligne aérienne

airmail (*è*ᵉᵘ-méïl) *n* poste aérienne

airplane (*è*ᵉᵘ-pléïn) *nAm* avion *m*

airport (*è*ᵉᵘ-poot) *n* aéroport *m*

air-sickness (*è*ᵉᵘ-sik-neuss) *n* mal de l'air

airtight (*è*ᵉᵘ-taït) *adj* hermétique

airy (è*eu*-ri) *adj* aéré

aisle (aïl) *n* bas-côté *m* ; passage *m*

alarm (eu-*lââm*) *n* alerte *f* ; *v* alarmer

alarm-clock (eu-*lââm*-klok) *n* réveil *m*

album (*æl*-beumm) *n* album *m*

alcohol (*æl*-keu-hol) *n* alcool *m*

alcoholic (æl-keu-*ho*-lik) *adj* alcoolique

ale (éïl) *n* bière *f*

algebra (*æl*-dji-breu) *n* algèbre *f*

Algeria (æl-*dji*eu-ri-eu) Algérie *f*

Algerian (æl-*dji*eu-ri-eunn) *adj* algérien ; *n* Algérien *m*

alien (*éï*-li-eunn) *n* étranger *m* ; *adj* étranger

alike (eu-*laïk*) *adj* pareil, semblable ; *adv* de la même façon

alimony (*æ*-li-meu-ni) *n* pension alimentaire

alive (eu-*laïv*) *adj* en vie, vivant

all (ool) *adj* tout ; ~ **in** tout compris ; ~ **right!** bien! ; **at** ~ du tout

allergy (*æ*-leu-dji) *n* allergie *f*

alley (*æ*-li) *n* ruelle *f*

alliance (eu-*laï*-eunns) *n* alliance *f*

Allies (*æ*-laïz) *pl* Alliés

allot (eu-*lot*) *v* assigner

allow (eu-*laou*) *v* autoriser, *permettre ; ~ **to** autoriser à ; *be allowed *être autorisé

allowance (eu-*laou*-eunns) *n* allocation *f*

all-round (ool-*raound*) *adj* universel

almanac (*ool*-meu-næk) *n* almanach *m*

almond (*ââ*-meunnd) *n* amande *f*

almost (*ool*-mô*ou*st) *adv* presque ; à peu près

alone (eu-*lô*ou*n*) *adv* seul

along (eu-*lonng*) *prep* le long de

aloud (eu-*laoud*) *adv* à haute voix

alphabet (*æl*-feu-bèt) *n* alphabet *m*

already (ool-*rè*-di) *adv* déjà

also (*ool*-sô*ou*) *adv* aussi ; de même, également

altar (*ool*-teu) *n* autel *m*

alter (*ool*-teu) *v* changer, modifier

alteration (ool-teu-*réï*-cheunn) *n* changement *m*, modification *f*

alternate (ool-*teû*-neut) *adj* alternatif

alternative (ool-*teû*-neu-tiv) *n* alternative *f*

although (ool-*ðô*ou) *conj* quoique, bien que

altitude (*æl*-ti-tyoûd) *n* altitude *f*

alto (*æl*-tô*ou*) *n* (pl ~s) contralto *m*

altogether (ool-teu-*ghè*-ðeu) *adv* entièrement ; en tout

always (*ool*-*ou*éïz) *adv* toujours

am (æm) *v* (pr be)

amaze (eu-*méïz*) *v* étonner, *surprendre

amazement (eu-*méïz*-meunnt) *n* étonnement *m*

ambassador (æm-*bæ*-seu-deu) *n* ambassadeur *m*

amber (*æm*-beu) *n* ambre *m*

ambiguous (æm-*bi*-ghyou-euss) *adj* ambigu ; équivoque

ambitious (æm-*bi*-cheuss) *adj* ambitieux

ambulance (*æm*-byou-leunns) *n* ambulance *f*

ambush (*æm*-bouch) *n* embuscade *f*

America (eu-*mè*-ri-keu) Amérique *f*

American (eu-*mè*-ri-keunn) *adj* américain ; *n* Américain *m*

amethyst (*æ*-mi-θist) *n* améthyste *f*

amid (eu-*mid*) *prep* entre ; parmi, au milieu de

ammonia (eu-*mô*ou-ni-eu) *n* ammoniaque *f*

amnesty (*æm*-ni-sti) *n* amnistie *f*

among (eu-*manng*) *prep* parmi ; au milieu de, entre ; ~ **other things** entre autres

amount (eu-*maount*) *n* quantité *f* ; montant *m*, somme *f* ; ~ **to** se monter à

amuse (eu-*myoûz*) v divertir, amuser

amusement (eu-*myoûz*-meunnt) *n* amusement *m*, divertissement *m*

amusing (eu-*myoû*-zinng) *adj* plaisant

anaemia (eu-*nii*-mi-eu) *n* anémie *f*

anaesthesia (æ-niss-*θii*-zi-eu) *n* anesthésie *f*

anaesthetic (æ-niss-*θè*-tik) *n* anesthésique *m*

analyse (æ-neu-laïz) v analyser

analysis (eu-*næ*-leu-siss) *n* (pl -ses) analyse *f*

analyst (æ-neu-list) *n* analyste *m*; psychanalyste *m*

anarchy (æ-neu-ki) *n* anarchie *f*

anatomy (eu-*næ*-teu-mi) *n* anatomie *f*

ancestor (æn-sè-steu) *n* ancêtre *m*

anchor (æng-keu) *n* ancre *f*

anchovy (æn-tcheu-vi) *n* anchois *m*

ancient (éïn-cheunnt) *adj* vieux, ancien; démodé, vieilli; antique

and (ænd, eunnd) *conj* et

angel (éïn-djeul) *n* ange *m*

anger (æng-gheu) *n* colère *f*; fureur *f*

angle (æng-gheul) v pêcher à la ligne; *n* angle *m*

angry (æng-ghri) *adj* en colère

animal (æ-ni-meul) *n* animal *m*

ankle (æng-keul) *n* cheville *f*

annex[1] (æ-nèks) *n* annexe *f*

annex[2] (eu-*nèks*) v annexer

anniversary (æ-ni-*veû*-seu-ri) *n* anniversaire *m*

announce (eu-*naouns*) v annoncer

announcement (eu-*naouns*-meunnt) *n* annonce *f*

annoy (eu-*noï*) v agacer, fâcher; ennuyer

annoyance (eu-*noï*-eunns) *n* ennui *m*

annoying (eu-*noï*-inng) *adj* fastidieux, ennuyeux

annual (æ-nyou-eul) *adj* annuel; *n* annuaire *m*

per annum (peur æ-neumm) par année

anonymous (eu-*no*-ni-meuss) *adj* anonyme

another (eu-*na*-ðeu) *adj* encore un; un autre

answer (âân-seu) v répondre à; *n* réponse *f*

ant (ænt) *n* fourmi *f*

anthology (æn-*θo*-leu-dji) *n* anthologie *f*

antibiotic (æn-ti-baï-*o*-tik) *n* antibiotique *m*

anticipate (æn-*ti*-si-péït) v *prévoir, anticiper; *prévenir

antifreeze (æn-ti-friiz) *n* antigel *m*

antipathy (æn-*ti*-peu-θi) *n* antipathie *f*

antique (æn-*tiik*) *adj* antique; *n* antiquité *f*; ~ **dealer** antiquaire *m*

antiquity (æn-*ti*-k^{ou}eu-ti) *n* Antiquité; **antiquities** *pl* antiquités

antiseptic (æn-ti-*sèp*-tik) *n* antiseptique *m*

antlers (ænt-leuz) *pl* andouiller *m*

anxiety (æng-*zaï*-eu-ti) *n* anxiété *f*

anxious (ængk-cheuss) *adj* désireux; inquiet

any (è-ni) *adj* n'importe quel

anybody (è-ni-bo-di) *pron* n'importe qui

anyhow (è-ni-haou) *adv* n'importe comment

anyone (è-ni-^{ou}ann) *pron* chacun

anything (è-ni-θinng) *pron* n'importe quoi

anyway (è-ni-^{ou}éï) *adv* de toute façon

anywhere (è-ni-^{ou}è^{eu}) *adv* n'importe où

apart (eu-*pâât*) *adv* à part, séparément; ~ **from** abstraction faite de

apartment (eu-*pâât*-meunnt) *nAm* appartement *m*; étage *m*; ~ **house** *Am* immeuble d'habitation

aperitif (eu-*pè*-reu-tiv) *n* apéritif *m*

apologize (eu-*po*-leu-djaïz) v s'excuser

apology (eu-*po*-leu-dji) n excuse f

apparatus (æ-peu-*réi*-teuss) n dispositif m, appareil m

apparent (eu-*pæ*-reunnt) adj apparent

apparently (eu-*pæ*-reunnt-li) adv apparemment ; manifestement

apparition (æ-peu-*ri*-cheunn) n apparition f

appeal (eu-*piil*) n appel m

appear (eu-*pieu*) v sembler, *paraître ; *apparaître ; se présenter

appearance (eu-*pieu*-reunns) n apparence f ; aspect m ; entrée f

appendicitis (eu-pèn-di-*saï*-tiss) n appendicite f

appendix (eu-*pèn*-diks) n (pl -dices, -dixes) appendice m

appetite (æ-peu-taït) n appétit m

appetizer (æ-peu-taï-zeu) n amuse-gueule m

appetizing (æ-peu-taï-zinng) adj appétissant

applause (eu-*plooz*) n applaudissements mpl

apple (æ-peul) n pomme f

appliance (eu-*plaï*-eunns) n appareil m

application (æ-pli-*kéi*-cheunn) n application f ; demande f ; candidature f

apply (eu-*plaï*) v appliquer ; se *servir de ; solliciter un emploi ; s'appliquer à

appoint (eu-*point*) v désigner, nommer

appointment (eu-*point*-meunnt) n rendez-vous m ; nomination f

appreciate (eu-*prii*-chi-éït) v évaluer ; apprécier

appreciation (eu-prii-chi-*éi*-cheunn) n appréciation f

approach (eu-*prôou*tch) v approcher ; n approche f ; accès m

appropriate (eu-*prôou*-pri-eut) adj jus-te, approprié, adéquat

approval (eu-*proû*-veul) n approbation f ; consentement m, accord m ; **on** ~ à l'essai

approve (eu-*proûv*) v approuver ; ~ **of** *être d'accord avec

approximate (eu-*prok*-si-meut) adj approximatif

approximately (eu-*prok*-si-meut-li) adv à peu près, approximativement

apricot (*éi*-pri-kot) n abricot m

April (*éi*-preul) n avril

apron (*éi*-preunn) n tablier m

Arab (æ-reub) adj arabe ; n Arabe m

arbitrary (ââ-bi-treu-ri) adj arbitraire

arcade (ââ-*kéid*) n arcade f

arch (ââtch) n arche f ; voûte f

archaeologist (ââ-ki-*o*-leu-djist) n archéologue m

archaeology (ââ-ki-*o*-leu-dji) n archéologie f

archbishop (ââtch-*bi*-cheup) n archevêque m

arched (ââtcht) adj arqué

architect (*ââ*-ki-tèkt) n architecte m

architecture (*ââ*-ki-tèk-tcheu) n architecture f

archives (ââ-kaïvz) pl archives fpl

are (ââ) v (pr be)

area (*èeu*-ri-eu) n région f ; zone f ; surface f ; ~ **code** indicatif m

Argentina (ââ-djeunn-*tii*-neu) Argentine f

Argentinian (ââ-djeunn-*ti*-ni-eunn) adj argentin ; n Argentin m

argue (*ââ*-ghyoû) v argumenter, discuter ; disputer

argument (*ââ*-ghyou-meunnt) n argument m ; discussion f ; dispute f

arid (æ-rid) adj aride

***arise** (eu-*raïz*) v surgir

arithmetic (eu-*ri*θ-meu-tik) n arithmétique f

arm (ââm) n bras m ; arme f ; v armer

armchair (ââm-tchè^{eu}) *n* fauteuil *m*

armed (ââmd) *adj* armé; ~ **forces** forces armées

armour (ââ-meu) *n* armure *f*

army (ââ-mi) *n* armée *f*

aroma (eu-rô^{ou}-meu) *n* arôme *m*

around (eu-raound) *prep* autour de; *adv* autour

arrange (eu-réïndj) *v* classer, arranger; préparer

arrangement (eu-réïndj-meunnt) *n* règlement *m*

arrest (eu-rèst) *v* arrêter; *n* arrestation *f*

arrival (eu-raï-veul) *n* arrivée *f*; venue *f*

arrive (eu-raïv) *v* arriver

arrow (æ-rô^{ou}) *n* flèche *f*

art (âât) *n* art *m*; habileté *f*; ~ **collection** collection d'art; ~ **exhibition** exposition d'art; ~ **gallery** galerie d'art; ~ **history** histoire de l'art; **arts and crafts** arts et métiers; ~ **school** académie des beaux-arts

artery (ââ-teu-ri) *n* artère *f*

artichoke (ââ-ti-tchô^{ou}k) *n* artichaut *m*

article (ââ-ti-keul) *n* article *m*

artifice (ââ-ti-fiss) *n* ruse *f*

artificial (ââ-ti-fi-cheul) *adj* artificiel

artist (ââ-tist) *n* artiste *m/f*

artistic (ââ-ti-stik) *adj* artistique

as (æz) *conj* comme; aussi; que; puisque, parce que; ~ **from** à partir de; ~ **if** comme si

asbestos (æz-bè-stoss) *n* amiante *m*

ascend (eu-sènd) *v* monter; *faire l'ascension de

ascent (eu-sènt) *n* montée *f*

ascertain (æ-seu-téïn) *v* constater; s'assurer de

ash (æch) *n* cendre *f*

ashamed (eu-chéïmd) *adj* honteux;

*be ~ *avoir honte

ashore (eu-choo) *adv* à terre

ashtray (æch-tréï) *n* cendrier *m*

Asia (éï-cheu) Asie *f*

Asian (éï-cheunn) *adj* asiatique; *n* Asiatique *m*

aside (eu-saïd) *adv* de côté, à part

ask (âsk) *v* demander; prier

asleep (eu-sliip) *adj* endormi

asparagus (eu-spæ-reu-gheuss) *n* asperge *f*

aspect (æ-spèkt) *n* aspect *m*

asphalt (æss-fælt) *n* asphalte *m*

aspire (eu-spaï^{eu}) *v* aspirer

aspirin (æ-speu-rinn) *n* aspirine *f*

ass (æss) *n* âne *m*

assassination (eu-sæ-si-néï-cheunn) *n* assassinat *m*

assault (eu-soolt) *v* attaquer; violer

assemble (eu-sèm-beul) *v* rassembler; monter, assembler

assembly (eu-sèm-bli) *n* réunion *f*, assemblée *f*

assignment (eu-saïn-meunnt) *n* tâche assignée

assign to (eu-saïn) assigner à; attribuer à

assist (eu-sist) *v* assister

assistance (eu-si-steunns) *n* secours *m*; aide *f*, assistance *f*

assistant (eu-si-steunnt) *n* assistant *m*

associate (eu-sô^{ou}-chi-eut) *n* partenaire *m*, associé *m*; allié *m*; membre *m*; *v* associer; ~ **with** fréquenter

association (eu-sô^{ou}-si-éï-cheunn) *n* association *f*

assort (eu-soot) *v* classer

assortment (eu-soot-meunnt) *n* assortiment *m*

assume (eu-syoûm) *v* supposer, présumer

assure (eu-chou^{eu}) *v* assurer

asthma (æss-meu) *n* asthme *m*

astonish (eu-sto-nich) *v* étonner

astonishing (eu-*sto*-ni-chinng) *adj* étonnant

astonishment (eu-*sto*-nich-meunnt) *n* étonnement *m*

astronomy (eu-*stro*-neu-mi) *n* astronomie *f*

asylum (eu-*saï*-leumm) *n* asile *m* ; hospice *m*

at (æt) *prep* à, chez ; vers

ate (èt) *v* (p eat)

atheist (*éï*-θi-ist) *n* athée *m*

athlete (*æθ*-liit) *n* athlète *m*

athletics (æθ-*lè*-tiks) *pl* athlétisme *m*

Atlantic (eut-*læn*-tik) Océan Atlantique

atmosphere (*æt*-meuss-fi^eu) *n* atmosphère *f* ; ambiance *f*

atom (*æ*-teumm) *n* atome *m*

atomic (eu-*to*-mik) *adj* atomique ; nucléaire

atomizer (*æ*-teu-maï-zeu) *n* vaporisateur *m* ; aérosol *m*, pulvérisateur *m*

attach (eu-*tætch*) *v* attacher ; fixer ; *joindre

attack (eu-*tæk*) *v* attaquer ; *n* attaque *f*

attain (eu-*téïn*) *v* *atteindre

attainable (eu-*téï*-neu-beul) *adj* faisable ; accessible

attempt (eu-*tèmpt*) *v* tenter ; essayer ; *n* tentative *f*

attend (eu-*tènd*) *v* assister à ; ~ **on** *servir ; ~ **to** s'occuper de ; *faire attention à, prêter attention à

attendance (eu-*tèn*-deunns) *n* assistance *f*

attendant (eu-*tèn*-deunnt) *n* gardien *m*

attention (eu-*tèn*-cheunn) *n* attention *f* ; ***pay** ~ *faire attention

attentive (eu-*tèn*-tiv) *adj* attentif

attic (*æ*-tik) *n* grenier *m*

attitude (*æ*-ti-tyoûd) *n* attitude *f*

attorney (eu-*teû*-ni) *n* avocat *m*

attract (eu-*trækt*) *v* attirer

attraction (eu-*træk*-cheunn) *n* attraction *f* ; attrait *m*

attractive (eu-*træk*-tiv) *adj* séduisant

auburn (*oo*-beunn) *adj* châtain

auction (*ook*-cheunn) *n* vente aux enchères

audible (*oo*-di-beul) *adj* audible

audience (*oo*-di-eunns) *n* public *m*

auditor (*oo*-di-teu) *n* auditeur *m*

auditorium (oo-di-*too*-ri-eumm) *n* auditorium *m*

August (*oo*-gheust) août

aunt (âânt) *n* tante *f*

Australia (o-*stréï*-li-eu) Australie *f*

Australian (o-*stréï*-li-eunn) *adj* australien ; *n* Australien *m*

Austria (*o*-stri-eu) Autriche *f*

Austrian (*o*-stri-eunn) *adj* autrichien ; *n* Autrichien *m*

authentic (oo-*θèn*-tik) *adj* authentique

author (*oo*-θeu) *n* auteur *m*

authoritarian (oo-θo-ri-*tè*^eu-ri-eunn) *adj* autoritaire

authority (oo-*θo*-reu-ti) *n* autorité *f* ; pouvoir *m*

authorization (oo-θeu-raï-*zéï*-cheunn) *n* autorisation *f* ; permission *f*

automatic (oo-teu-*mæ*-tik) *adj* automatique

automation (oo-teu-*méï*-cheunn) *n* automatisation *f*

automobile (*oo*-teu-meu-biil) *n* auto *f* ; ~ **club** club automobile

autonomous (oo-*to*-neu-meuss) *adj* autonome

autopsy (*oo*-to-psi) *n* autopsie *f*

autumn (*oo*-teumm) *n* automne *m*

available (eu-*véï*-leu-beul) *adj* disponible

avalanche (*æ*-veu-lâânch) *n* avalanche *f*

avaricious (æ-veu-*ri*-cheuss) *adj* avare

avenue (*æ*-veu-nyoû) *n* avenue *f*

average (*æ*-veu-ridj) *adj* moyen; *n* moyenne *f*; **on the** ~ en moyenne

averse (eu-*veûss*) *adj* opposé

aversion (eu-*veû*-cheunn) *n* aversion *f*

avert (eu-*veût*) *v* détourner

avoid (eu-*voïd*) *v* éviter

await (eu-ᵒᵘ*éit*) *v* attendre

awake (eu-ᵒᵘ*éïk*) *adj* réveillé

*awake (eu-ᵒᵘ*éïk*) *v* réveiller

award (eu-ᵒᵘ*ood*) *n* prix *m*; *v* décerner

aware (eu-ᵒᵘ*è*eu) *adj* conscient

away (eu-ᵒᵘ*éï*) *adv* loin; ***go** ~ s'en ***aller**

awful (*oo*-feul) *adj* terrible

awkward (*oo*-kᵒᵘeud) *adj* embarrassant; maladroit

awning (*oo*-ninng) *n* marquise *f*

axe (æks) *n* hache *f*

axle (*æk*-seul) *n* essieu *m*

B

baby (*béï*-bi) *n* bébé *m*; ~ **carriage** *Am* poussette *f*

babysitter (*béï*-bi-si-steu) *n* baby-sitter *m*

bachelor (*bæ*-tcheu-leu) *n* célibataire *m*

back (bæk) *n* dos *m*; *adv* en arrière; ***go** ~ retourner

backache (*bæ*-kéïk) *n* mal au dos

backbone (*bæk*-bôᵒᵘn) *n* épine dorsale

background (*bæk*-ghraound) *n* fond *m*; formation *f*

backwards (*bæk*-ᵒᵘeudz) *adv* en arrière

bacon (*béï*-keunn) *n* lard *m*

bacterium (bæk-*tii*-ri-eumm) *n* (pl -ria) bactérie *f*

bad (bæd) *adj* mauvais; grave; vilain

bag (bægh) *n* sac *m*; sac à main; valise *f*

baggage (*bæ*-ghidj) *n* bagage *m*; ~ **deposit office** *Am* consigne *f*; **hand** ~ *Am* bagage à main

bail (béïl) *n* caution *f*

bailiff (*béï*-lif) *n* huissier *m*

bait (béït) *n* amorce *f*

bake (béïk) *v* *cuire au four

baker (*béï*-keu) *n* boulanger *m*

bakery (*béï*-keu-ri) *n* boulangerie *f*

balance (*bæ*-leunns) *n* équilibre *m*; bilan *m*; solde *m*

balcony (*bæl*-keu-ni) *n* balcon *m*

bald (boold) *adj* chauve

ball (bool) *n* ballon *m*, balle *f*; bal *m*

ballet (*bæ*-léï) *n* ballet *m*

balloon (beu-*loûn*) *n* ballon *m*

ballpoint-pen (*bool*-point-pèn) *n* stylo à bille

ballroom (*bool*-roûm) *n* salle de bal

bamboo (bæm-*boû*) *n* (pl ~s) bambou *m*

banana (beu-*nââ*-neu) *n* banane *f*

band (bænd) *n* orchestre *m*; lien *m*

bandage (*bæn*-didj) *n* pansement *m*

bandit (*bæn*-dit) *n* bandit *m*

bangle (*bæng*-gheul) *n* bracelet *m*

banisters (*bæ*-ni-steuz) *pl* rampe *f*

bank (bængk) *n* rive *f*; banque *f*; *v* déposer; ~ **account** compte en banque

banknote (*bængk*-nôᵒᵘt) *n* billet de banque

bank-rate (*bængk*-réït) *n* taux d'escompte

bankrupt (*bængk*-rapt) *adj* en faillite

banner (*bæ*-neu) *n* bannière *f*

banquet (*bæng*-kᵒᵘit) *n* banquet *m*

banqueting-hall (*bæng*-kᵒᵘi-tinng-hool) *n* salle de banquet

baptism (*bæp*-ti-zeumm) *n* baptême *m*

baptize (bæp-*taïz*) *v* baptiser

bar (bââ) n bar m; barre f; bárreau m

barber (bââ-beu) n coiffeur m

bare (bè^{eu}) adj nu

barely (bè^{eu}-li) adv à peine

bargain (bââ-ghinn) n bonne affaire; v marchander

baritone (bæ-ri-tô^{ou}n) n bariton m

bark (bââk) n écorce f; v aboyer

barley (bââ-li) n orge f

barmaid (bââ-méïd) n barmaid f

barman (bââ-meunn) n (pl -men) barman m

barn (bâân) n grange f

barometer (beu-ro-mi-teu) n baromètre m

baroque (beu-rok) adj baroque

barracks (bæ-reuks) pl caserne f

barrel (bæ-reul) n tonneau m, baril m

barrier (bæ-ri-eu) n barrière f

barrister (bæ-ri-steu) n avocat m

bartender (bââ-tèn-deu) n barman m

base (béïss) n base f; fondement m; v baser

baseball (béïss-bool) n base-ball m

basement (béïss-meunnt) n sous-sol m

basic (béï-sik) adj fondamental

basilica (beu-zi-li-keu) n basilique f

basin (béï-seunn) n bol m, bassin m

basis (béï-siss) n (pl bases) base f

basket (bââ-skit) n panier m

bass[1] (béïss) n basse f

bass[2] (bæss) n (pl ~) perche f

bastard (bââ-steud) n bâtard m; salaud m

batch (bætch) n lot m

bath (bââθ) n bain m; ~ **salts** sels de bain; ~ **towel** serviette de bain

bathe (béïð) v se baigner

bathing-cap (béï-ðinng-kæp) n bonnet de bain

bathing-suit (béï-ðinng-soût) n maillot de bain

bathing-trunks (béï-ðinng-tranngks) n caleçon de bain

bathrobe (bââθ-rô^{ou}b) n peignoir m

bathroom (bââθ-roûm) n salle de bain; toilettes fpl

batter (bæ-teu) n pâte f

battery (bæ-teu-ri) n pile f; accumulateur m

battle (bæ-teul) n bataille f; lutte, combat m; v *combattre

bay (béï) n baie f; v aboyer

***be** (bii) v *être

beach (biitch) n plage f; **nudist ~** plage pour nudistes

bead (biid) n perle f; **beads** pl collier m; chapelet m

beak (biik) n bec m

beam (biim) n rayon m; poutre f

bean (biin) n haricot m

bear (bè^{eu}) n ours m

***bear** (bè^{eu}) v porter; tolérer; supporter

beard (bi^{eu}d) n barbe f

bearer (bè^{eu}-reu) n porteur m

beast (biist) n bête f; ~ **of prey** bête de proie

***beat** (biit) v frapper; *battre

beautiful (byoû-ti-feul) adj beau

beauty (byoû-ti) n beauté f; ~ **parlour** institut de beauté; ~ **salon** salon de beauté; ~ **treatment** soins de beauté

beaver (bii-veu) n castor m

because (bi-koz) conj parce que; étant donné que; ~ **of** en raison de, à cause de

***become** (bi-kamm) v *devenir; bien *aller

bed (bèd) n lit m; ~ **and board** pension complète; ~ **and breakfast** chambre et petit déjeuner

bedding (bè-dinng) n literie f

bedroom (bèd-roûm) n chambre à coucher

bee (bii) n abeille f

beech (bii-tch) n hêtre m

beef (biif) n bœuf m

beehive (bii-haïv) n ruche f

been (biin) v (pp be)

beer (bi^{eu}) n bière f

beet (biit) n betterave f

beetle (bii-teul) n scarabée m

beetroot (biit-roût) n betterave f

before (bi-foo) prep avant; devant; conj avant que; adv d'avance; précédemment, avant

beg (bègh) v mendier; supplier; demander

beggar (bè-gheu) n mendiant m

*****begin** (bi-ghinn) v commencer; débuter

beginner (bi-ghi-neu) n débutant m

beginning (bi-ghi-ninng) n commencement m; début m

on behalf of (onn bi-hââf ov) au nom de; en faveur de

behave (bi-héïv) v se comporter

behaviour (bi-héï-vyeu) n comportement m

behind (bi-haïnd) prep derrière; adv en arrière

beige (béïj) adj beige

being (bii-inng) n être m

Belgian (bèl-djeunn) adj belge; n Belge m

Belgium (bèl-djeumm) Belgique f

belief (bi-liif) n croyance f

believe (bi-liiv) v *croire

bell (bèl) n cloche f; sonnette f

bellboy (bèl-boï) n chasseur m

belly (bè-li) n ventre m

belong (bi-lonng) v *appartenir

belongings (bi-lonng-inngz) pl affaires fpl

beloved (bi-lavd) adj aimé

below (bi-lô^{ou}) prep au-dessous de; en bas de; adv en dessous

belt (bèlt) n ceinture f; **garter ~** Am

porte-jarretelles m

bench (bèntch) n banc m

bend (bènd) n virage m, courbe f

*****bend** (bènd) v courber; **~ down** se pencher

beneath (bi-niiθ) prep en dessous de; adv au-dessous

benefit (bè-ni-fit) n profit m, bénéfice m; avantage m; v profiter

bent (bènt) adj (pp bend) courbe

beret (bè-réï) n béret m

berry (bè-ri) n baie f

berth (beûθ) n couchette f

beside (bi-saïd) prep à côté de

besides (bi-saïdz) adv en outre; d'ailleurs; prep outre

best (bèst) adj le meilleur

bet (bèt) n pari m; enjeu m

*****bet** (bèt) v parier

betray (bi-tréï) v trahir

better (bè-teu) adj meilleur

between (bi-t^{ou}iin) prep entre

beverage (bè-veu-ridj) n boisson f

beware (bi-^{ou}è^{eu}) v *prendre garde, *faire attention

bewitch (bi-^{ou}itch) v ensorceler, enchanter

beyond (bi-yonnd) prep au delà de; outre; adv au delà

bible (baï-beul) n Bible f

bicycle (baï-si-keul) n bicyclette f; vélo m

big (bigh) adj grand; volumineux; gros; important

bile (baïl) n bile f

bilingual (baï-linng-gh^{ou}eul) adj bilingue

bill (bil) n facture f; addition f, note f; v facturer

billiards (bil-yeudz) pl billard m

*****bind** (baïnd) v lier

binding (baïn-dinng) n reliure f

binoculars (bi-no-kyeu-leuz) pl jumelles fpl

biology (baï-*o*-leu-dji) n biologie f
birch (beûtch) n bouleau m
bird (beûd) n oiseau m
Biro (*baï*-rô^{ou}) n crayon à bille
birth (beûθ) n naissance f
birthday (*beûθ*-déï) n anniversaire m
biscuit (*biss*-kit) n biscuit m
bishop (*bi*-cheup) n évêque m
bit (bit) n morceau m; peu m
bitch (bitch) n chienne f
bite (baït) n bouchée f; morsure f; piqûre f
*****bite** (baït) v mordre
bitter (*bi*-teu) adj amer
black (blæk) adj noir; ~ **market** marché noir
blackberry (*blæk*-beu-ri) n mûre f
blackbird (*blæk*-beûd) n merle m
blackboard (*blæk*-bood) n tableau noir
black-currant (blæk-*ka*-reunnt) n cassis m
blackmail (*blæk*-méïl) n chantage m; v *faire chanter
blacksmith (*blæk*-smiθ) n forgeron m
bladder (*blæ*-deu) n vessie f
blade (bléïd) n lame f; ~ **of grass** brin d'herbe
blame (bléïm) n blâme m; v donner la faute à, blâmer
blank (blængk) adj blanc
blanket (*blæng*-kit) n couverture f
blast (blââst) n explosion f
blazer (*bléï*-zeu) n veste de sport, blazer m
bleach (bliitch) v décolorer
bleak (bliik) adj rude
*****bleed** (bliid) v saigner
bless (blèss) v bénir
blessing (*blè*-sinng) n bénédiction f
blind (blaïnd) n store m, persienne f; adj aveugle; v aveugler
blister (*bli*-steu) n ampoule f, cloque f
blizzard (*bli*-zeud) n tempête de neige

block (blok) v obstruer, bloquer; n bloc m; ~ **of flats** immeuble d'habitation
blonde (blonnd) n blonde f
blood (blad) n sang m; ~ **pressure** tension artérielle
blood-poisoning (*blad*-poï-zeu-ninng) n septicémie f
blood-vessel (*blad*-vè-seul) n vaisseau sanguin
blot (blot) n tache f; souillure f; **blotting paper** papier buvard
blouse (blaouz) n chemisier m
blow (blô^{ou}) n claque f, coup m; coup de vent
*****blow** (blô^{ou}) v souffler
blow-out (*blô^{ou}*-aout) n crevaison f
blue (bloû) adj bleu; déprimé
blunt (blannt) adj émoussé
blush (blach) v rougir
board (bood) n planche f; tableau m; pension f; conseil m; ~ **and lodging** pension complète
boarder (*boo*-deu) n pensionnaire m
boarding-house (*boo*-dinng-haouss) n pension f
boarding-school (*boo*-dinng-skoûl) n internat m
boast (bô^{ou}st) v se vanter
boat (bô^{ou}t) n navire m, bateau m
body (*bo*-di) n corps m
bodyguard (*bo*-di-ghââd) n garde du corps
bog (bogh) n marais m
boil (boïl) v *bouillir; n furoncle m
bold (bô^{ou}ld) adj audacieux; effronté, hardi
Bolivia (beu-*li*-vi-eu) Bolivie f
Bolivian (beu-*li*-vi-eunn) adj bolivien; n Bolivien m
bolt (bô^{ou}lt) n verrou m; boulon m
bomb (bomm) n bombe f; v bombarder
bond (bonnd) n obligation f

bone (bô^{ou}n) *n* os *m*; arête *f*; *v* désosser

bonnet (*bo*-nit) *n* capot *m*

book (bouk) *n* livre *m*; *v* *retenir, réserver; *inscrire, enregistrer

booking (*bou*-kinng) *n* réservation *f*

bookseller (*bouk*-sè-leu) *n* libraire *m*

bookstand (*bouk*-stænd) *n* stand de livres

bookstore (*bouk*-stoo) *n* librairie *f*

boot (boût) *n* botte *f*; coffre *m*

booth (boûð) *n* échoppe *f*; cabine *f*

border (*boo*-deu) *n* frontière *f*; bord *m*

bore¹ (boo) *v* ennuyer; forer; *n* raseur *m*

bore² (boo) *v* (p bear)

boring (*boo*-rinng) *adj* ennuyeux

born (boon) *adj* né

borrow (*bo*-rô^{ou}) *v* emprunter

bosom (*bou*-zeumm) *n* poitrine *f*; sein *m*

boss (boss) *n* chef *m*, patron *m*

botany (*bo*-teu-ni) *n* botanique *f*

both (bô^{ou}θ) *adj* les deux; **both … and** aussi bien que

bother (*bo*-ðeu) *v* gêner, tracasser; s'efforcer; *n* tracas *m*

bottle (*bo*-teul) *n* bouteille *f*; ~ **opener** ouvre-bouteille *m*; **hot-water** ~ bouillotte *f*

bottleneck (*bo*-teul-nèk) *n* goulot d'étranglement

bottom (*bo*-teumm) *n* fond *m*; postérieur *m*, derrière *m*; *adj* inférieur

bough (baou) *n* branche *f*

bought (boot) *v* (p, pp buy)

boulder (*bô^{ou}l*-deu) *n* rocher *m*

bound (baound) *n* limite *f*; ***be ~ to** *devoir; ~ **for** en route pour

boundary (*baoun*-deu-ri) *n* limite *f*; frontière *f*

bouquet (bou-*kéï*) *n* bouquet *m*

bourgeois (*bou^{eu}*-j^{ou}ââ) *adj* bourgeois

boutique (bou-*tiik*) *n* boutique *f*

bow¹ (baou) *v* courber

bow² (bô^{ou}) *n* arc *m*; ~ **tie** nœud papillon

bowels (baou^{eu}lz) *pl* intestins

bowl (bô^{ou}l) *n* bol *m*

bowling (*bô^{ou}*-linng) *n* bowling *m*, jeu de quilles; ~ **alley** bowling *m*

box¹ (boks) *v* boxer; **boxing match** match de boxe

box² (boks) *n* boîte *f*

box-office (*boks*-o-fiss) *n* guichet de location, guichet *m*

boy (boï) *n* garçon *m*; gamin *m*, gosse *m*; serviteur *m*; ~ **scout** scout *m*

bra (brââ) *n* soutien-gorge *m*

bracelet (*bréïss*-lit) *n* bracelet *m*

braces (*bréï*-siz) *pl* bretelles *fpl*

brain (bréïn) *n* cerveau *m*; intelligence *f*

brain-wave (*bréïn*-^{ou}éïv) *n* idée lumineuse

brake (bréïk) *n* frein *m*; ~ **drum** tambour de frein; ~ **lights** stops *mpl*

branch (brâântch) *n* branche *f*; succursale *f*

brand (brænd) *n* marque *f*

brand-new (brænd-*nyou*) *adj* flambant neuf

brass (brââss) *n* laiton *m*; cuivre *m*, cuivre jaune; ~ **band** fanfare *f*

brassiere (*bræ*-zi^{eu}) *n* soutien-gorge *m*

brassware (*brââss*-^{ou}è^{eu}) *n* cuivres

brave (bréïv) *adj* courageux, brave

Brazil (breu-*zil*) Brésil *m*

Brazilian (breu-*zil*-yeunn) *adj* brésilien; *n* Brésilien *m*

breach (briitch) *n* brèche *f*

bread (brèd) *n* pain *m*; **wholemeal** ~ pain complet

breadth (brèdθ) *n* largeur *f*

break (bréïk) *n* fracture *f*; pause *f*

*break (bréïk) v rompre, casser; ~
 down tomber en panne; analyser
breakdown (bréïk-daoun) n panne f
breakfast (brèk-feust) n petit déjeuner
bream (briim) n (pl ~) brème f
breast (brèst) n sein m
breaststroke (brèst-strôᵒᵘk) n brasse f
breath (brèθ) n souffle m
breathe (briið) v respirer
breathing (brii-ðinng) n respiration f
breed (briid) n race f; espèce f
*breed (briid) v élever
breeze (briiz) n brise f
brew (broû) v brasser
brewery (broû-eu-ri) n brasserie f
bribe (braïb) v *corrompre
bribery (braï-beu-ri) n corruption f
brick (brik) n brique f
bricklayer (brik-léïᵉᵘ) n maçon m
bride (braïd) n fiancée f
bridegroom (braïd-ghroûm) n marié m
bridge (bridj) n pont m; bridge m
brief (briif) adj bref
briefcase (bril-kéïss) n serviette f
briefs (briifs) pl slip m, caleçon m
bright (braït) adj brillant; malin, intelligent
brill (bril) n barbue f
brilliant (bril-yeunnt) adj brillant
brim (brimm) n bord m
*bring (brinng) v apporter; amener;
 ~ back rapporter, ramener; ~ up
 élever; soulever
brisk (brisk) adj vif
Britain (bri-teunn) Angleterre f
British (bri-tich) adj britannique
Briton (bri-teunn) n Britannique m;
 Anglais m
broad (brood) adj large; vaste, étendu; global
broadcast (brood-kââst) n émission f
*broadcast (brood-kââst) v *émettre
brochure (brôᵒᵘ-chouᵉᵘ) n brochure f
broke¹ (brôᵒᵘk) v (p break)

broke² (brôᵒᵘk) adj fauché
broken (brôᵒᵘ-keunn) adj (pp break)
 cassé, brisé; en dérangement
broker (brôᵒᵘ-keu) n courtier m
bronchitis (bronng-kaï-tiss) n bronchite f
bronze (bronnz) n bronze m; adj en
 bronze
brooch (brôᵒᵘtch) n broche f
brook (brouk) n ruisseau m
broom (broûm) n balai m
brothel (bro-θeul) n bordel m
brother (bra-ðeu) n frère m
brother-in-law (bra-ðeu-rinn-loo) n (pl
 brothers-) beau-frère m
brought (broot) v (p, pp bring)
brown (braoun) adj brun
bruise (broûz) n bleu m, contusion f;
 v contusionner
brunette (broû-nèt) n brunette f
brush (brach) n brosse f; pinceau m;
 v lustrer, brosser
brutal (broû-teul) adj brutal
bubble (ba-beul) n bulle f
bucket (ba-kit) n seau m
buckle (ba-keul) n boucle f
bud (bad) n bourgeon m
budget (ba-djit) n budget m
buffet (bou-féï) n buffet m
bug (bagh) n punaise f; coléoptère
 m; nAm insecte m
*build (bild) v bâtir
building (bil-dinng) n construction f
bulb (balb) n bulbe m; oignon m;
 light ~ ampoule f
Bulgaria (bal-ghèᵉᵘ-ri-eu) Bulgarie f
Bulgarian (bal-ghèᵉᵘ-ri-eunn) adj bulgare; n Bulgare m
bulk (balk) n masse f; majorité f
bulky (bal-ki) adj volumineux
bull (boul) n taureau m
bullet (bou-lit) n balle f
bullfight (boul-faït) n corrida f
bullring (boul-rinng) n arène f

bump (bammp) *v* cogner; tamponner; frapper; *n* coup *m*

bumper (*bamm*-peu) *n* pare-choc *m*

bumpy (*bamm*-pi) *adj* cahoteux

bun (bann) *n* brioche *f*

bunch (banntch) *n* bouquet *m*; bande *f*

bundle (*bann*-deul) *n* paquet *m*; *v* relier, lier ensemble

bunk (banngk) *n* couchette *f*

buoy (boï) *n* bouée *f*

burden (*beû*-deunn) *n* fardeau *m*

bureau (*byou*^{eu}-rô^{ou}) *n* (pl ~x, ~s) bureau *m*; *nAm* commode *f*

bureaucracy (byou^{eu}-*ro*-kreu-si) *n* bureaucratie *f*

burglar (*beû*-ghleu) *n* cambrioleur *m*

burgle (*beû*-gheul) *v* cambrioler

burial (*bè*-ri-eul) *n* sépulture *f*, enterrement *m*

burn (beûnn) *n* brûlure *f*

***burn** (beûnn) *v* brûler

***burst** (beûst) *v* éclater

bury (*bè*-ri) *v* enterrer

bus (bass) *n* autobus *m*

bush (bouch) *n* buisson *m*

business (*biz*-neuss) *n* affaires *fpl*, commerce *m*; entreprise *f*, affaire *f*; occupation *f*; ~ **hours** heures d'ouverture, heures de bureau; ~ **trip** voyage d'affaires; **on** ~ pour affaires

businessman (*biz*-neuss-meunn) *n* (pl -men) homme d'affaires

bust (bast) *n* buste *m*

bustle (*ba*-seul) *n* remue-ménage *m*

busy (*bi*-zi) *adj* occupé; animé, affairé

but (bat) *conj* mais; cependant; *prep* sauf

butcher (*bou*-tcheu) *n* boucher *m*

butter (*ba*-teu) *n* beurre *m*

butterfly (*ba*-teu-flaï) *n* papillon *m*; ~ **stroke** brasse papillon

buttock (*ba*-teuk) *n* fesse *f*

button (*ba*-teunn) *n* bouton *m*; *v* boutonner

buttonhole (*ba*-teunn-hô^{ou}l) *n* boutonnière *f*

***buy** (baï) *v* acheter; *acquérir

buyer (*baï*-eu) *n* acheteur *m*

by (baï) *prep* par; en; près de

by-pass (*baï*-pââss) *n* route d'évitement; *v* contourner

C

cab (kæb) *n* taxi *m*

cabaret (*kæ*-beu-réï) *n* cabaret *m*; boîte de nuit

cabbage (*kæ*-bidj) *n* chou *m*

cab-driver (*kæb*-draï-veu) *n* chauffeur de taxi

cabin (*kæ*-binn) *n* cabine *f*; cabane *f*

cabinet (*kæ*-bi-neut) *n* cabinet *m*

cable (*kéï*-beul) *n* câble *m*; télégramme *m*; *v* télégraphier

cadre (*kââ*-deu) *n* cadre *m*

café (*kæ*-féï) *n* café *m*

cafeteria (kæ-feu-*ti*^{eu}-ri-eu) *n* cafétéria *f*

caffeine (*kæ*-fiin) *n* caféine *f*

cage (kéïdj) *n* cage *f*

cake (kéïk) *n* gâteau *m*; pâtisserie *f*

calamity (keu-*læ*-meu-ti) *n* calamité *f*, catastrophe *f*

calcium (*kæl*-si-eumm) *n* calcium *m*

calculate (*kæl*-kyou-léït) *v* calculer

calculation (kæl-kyou-*léï*-cheunn) *n* calcul *m*

calendar (*kæ*-leunn-deu) *n* calendrier *m*

calf (kââf) *n* (pl calves) veau *m*; mollet *m*; ~ **skin** veau *m*

call (kool) *v* appeler; téléphoner; *n* appel *m*; visite *f*; coup de téléphone; ***be called** s'appeler; ~ **names** injurier; ~ **on** rendre visite à; ~ **up** *Am* téléphoner

callus (*kæ*-leuss) *n* cal *m*

calm (kââm) *adj* tranquille, calme; ~ **down** calmer

calorie (*kæ*-leu-ri) *n* calorie *f*

Calvinism (*kæl*-vi-ni-zeumm) *n* calvinisme *m*

came (kéïm) *v* (p come)

camel (*kæ*-meul) *n* chameau *m*

cameo (*kæ*-mi-ô^ou^) *n* (pl ~s) camée *m*

camera (*kæ*-meu-reu) *n* appareil photographique; caméra *f*; ~ **shop** magasin de photographe

camp (kæmp) *n* camp *m*; *v* camper

campaign (kæm-*péïn*) *n* campagne *f*

camp-bed (kæmp-*bèd*) *n* lit de camp

camper (*kæm*-peu) *n* campeur *m*

camping (*kæm*-pinng) *n* camping *m*; ~ **site** terrain de camping

camshaft (*kæm*-chââft) *n* arbre à cames

can (kæn) *n* boîte *f*; ~ **opener** ouvre-boîte *m*

*can (kæn) *v* *pouvoir

Canada (*kæ*-neu-da) Canada *m*

Canadian (keu-*néï*-di-eunn) *adj* canadien; *n* Canadien *m*

canal (keu-*næl*) *n* canal *m*

canary (keu-*nè^eu^*-ri) *n* canari *m*

cancel (*kæn*-seul) *v* annuler

cancellation (kæn-seu-*léï*-cheunn) *n* annulation *f*

cancer (*kæn*-seu) *n* cancer *m*

candelabrum (kæn-deu-*lââ*-breumm) *n* (pl -bra) candélabre *m*

candidate (*kæn*-di-deut) *n* candidat *m*

candle (*kæn*-deul) *n* bougie *f*

candy (*kæn*-di) *nAm* bonbon *m*; confiserie *f*; ~ **store** *Am* confiserie *f*

cane (kéïn) *n* canne *f*

canister (*kæ*-ni-steu) *n* boîte métalli-

que

canoe (keu-*noû*) *n* canot *m*

canteen (kæn-*tiin*) *n* cantine *f*

canvas (*kæn*-veuss) *n* grosse toile

cap (kæp) *n* casquette *f*

capable (*kéï*-peu-beul) *adj* capable

capacity (keu-*pæ*-seu-ti) *n* capacité *f*; puissance *f*; compétence *f*

cape (kéïp) *n* cape *f*; cap *m*

capital (*kæ*-pi-teul) *n* capitale *f*; capital *m*; *adj* capital, essentiel; ~ **letter** majuscule *f*

capitalism (*kæ*-pi-teu-li-zeumm) *n* capitalisme *m*

capitulation (keu-pi-tyou-*léï*-cheunn) *n* capitulation *f*

capsule (*kæp*-syoûl) *n* capsule *f*

captain (*kæp*-tinn) *n* capitaine *m*; commandant *m*

capture (*kæp*-tcheu) *v* *faire prisonnier, capturer; *prendre; *n* capture *f*; prise *f*

car (kââ) *n* voiture *f*; ~ **hire** location de voitures; ~ **park** parc de stationnement; ~ **rental** *Am* location de voitures

carafe (keu-*ræf*) *n* carafe *f*

caramel (*kæ*-reu-meul) *n* caramel *m*

carat (*kæ*-reut) *n* carat *m*

caravan (*kæ*-reu-væn) *n* caravane *f*; roulotte *f*

carburettor (kââ-byou-*rè*-teu) *n* carburateur *m*

card (kââd) *n* carte *f*; carte postale

cardboard (*kââd*-bood) *n* carton *m*; *adj* en carton

cardigan (*kââ*-di-gheunn) *n* cardigan *m*

cardinal (*kââ*-di-neul) *n* cardinal *m*; *adj* cardinal, principal

care (kè^eu^) *n* soin *m*; souci *m*; ~ **about** se soucier de; ~ **for** *tenir à; *take ~ of *prendre soin de, s'occuper de

career (keu-*ri*^{eu}) *n* carrière *f*

carefree (kè^{eu}-frii) *adj* insouciant

careful (kè^{eu}-feul) *adj* prudent; soigneux, attentif

careless (kè^{eu}-leuss) *adj* inattentif, négligent

caretaker (kè^{eu}-téï-keu) *n* gardien *m*

cargo (kââ-ghô^{ou}) *n* (pl ~es) chargement *m*, cargaison *f*

carnival (kââ-ni-veul) *n* carnaval *m*

carp (kââp) *n* (pl ~) carpe *f*

carpenter (kââ-pinn-teu) *n* menuisier *m*

carpet (kââ-pit) *n* tapis *m*

carriage (kæ-ridj) *n* wagon *m*; carrosse *m*, voiture *f*

carriageway (kæ-ridj-^{ou}éï) *n* chaussée *f*

carrot (kæ-reut) *n* carotte *f*

carry (kæ-ri) *v* porter; *conduire; ~ on** continuer; *poursuivre; ~ out** réaliser

carry-cot (kæ-ri-kot) *n* berceau de voyage

cart (kâât) *n* charrette *f*

cartilage (kââ-ti-lidj) *n* cartilage *m*

carton (kââ-teunn) *n* carton *m*; cartouche *f*

cartoon (kââ-*toûn*) *n* dessins animés *m*

cartridge (kââ-tridj) *n* cartouche *f*

carve (kââv) *v* découper; entailler, tailler

carving (kââ-vinng) *n* gravure *f*

case (kéïss) *n* cas *m*; affaire *f*; valise *f*; étui *m*; **attaché ~** porte-documents *m*; **in ~** au cas où; **in ~ of** en cas de

cash (kæch) *n* argent liquide, argent comptant; *v* toucher, encaisser

cashier (kæ-*chi*^{eu}) *n* caissier *m*; caissière *f*

cashmere (kæch-mi^{eu}) *n* cachemire *m*

casino (keu-*sii*-nô^{ou}) *n* (pl ~s) casino *m*

cask (kââsk) *n* baril *m*, tonneau *m*

cast (kâast) *n* jet *m*

*****cast** (kâast) *v* lancer, jeter; **cast iron** fonte *f*

castle (kââ-seul) *n* château *m*

casual (kæ-jou-eul) *adj* sans façons; en passant, fortuit

casualty (kæ-jou-eul-ti) *n* victime *f*

cat (kæt) *n* chat *m*

catacomb (kæ-teu-kô^{ou}m) *n* catacombe *f*

catalogue (kæ-teu-logh) *n* catalogue *m*

catarrh (keu-*tââ*) *n* catarrhe *m*

catastrophe (keu-*tæ*-streu-fi) *n* sinistre *m*

*****catch** (kætch) *v* attraper; saisir; *surprendre; *prendre**

category (kæ-ti-gheu-ri) *n* catégorie *f*

cathedral (keu-*θii*-dreul) *n* cathédrale *f*

catholic (kæ-θeu-lik) *adj* catholique

cattle (kæ-teul) *pl* bétail *m*

caught (koot) *v* (p, pp catch)

cauliflower (ko-li-flaou^{eu}) *n* chou-fleur

cause (kooz) *v* causer; provoquer; *n* cause *f*; raison *f*, motif *m*; **~ to** *faire

causeway (kooz-^{ou}éï) *n* chaussée *f*

caution (koo-cheunn) *n* prudence *f*; *v* avertir

cautious (koo-cheuss) *adj* prudent

cave (kéïv) *n* grotte *f*; crevasse *f*

cavern (kæ-veunn) *n* caverne *f*

caviar (kæ-vi-ââ) *n* caviar *m*

cavity (kæ-veu-ti) *n* cavité *f*

cease (siiss) *v* cesser

ceiling (*sii*-linng) *n* plafond *m*

celebrate (sè-li-bréït) *v* célébrer

celebration (sè-li-bréï-cheunn) *n* célébration *f*

celebrity (si-*lè*-breu-ti) *n* célébrité *f*

celery (*sè*-leu-ri) *n* céleri *m*

celibacy (*sè*-li-beu-si) *n* célibat *m*

cell (sèl) *n* cellule *f*

cellar (*sè*-leu) *n* cave *f*

cellophane (*sè*-leu-féïn) *n* cellophane *f*

cement (si-*mènt*) *n* ciment *m*

cemetery (*sè*-mi-tri) *n* cimetière *m*

censorship (*sèn*-seu-chip) *n* censure *f*

centigrade (*sèn*-ti-ghréïd) *adj* centigrade

centimetre (*sèn*-ti-mii-teu) *n* centimètre *m*

central (*sèn*-treul) *adj* central; ~ **heating** chauffage central; ~ **station** gare centrale

centralize (*sèn*-treu-laïz) *v* centraliser

centre (*sèn*-teu) *n* centre *m*

century (*sèn*-tcheu-ri) *n* siècle *m*

ceramics (si-*ræ*-miks) *pl* terre cuite, céramique *f*

ceremony (*sè*-reu-meu-ni) *n* cérémonie *f*

certain (*seû*-teunn) *adj* certain

certificate (seu-*ti*-fi-keut) *n* certificat *m*; attestation *f*, document *m*, diplôme *m*

chain (tchéïn) *n* chaîne *f*

chair (tchè^eu) *n* chaise *f*; siège *m*

chairman (*tchè^eu*-meunn) *n* (pl -men) président *m*

chalet (*chæ*-léï) *n* chalet *m*

chalk (tchook) *n* craie *f*

challenge (*tchæ*-leunndj) *v* défier; *n* défi *m*

chamber (*tchéïm*-beu) *n* pièce *f*

chambermaid (*tchéïm*-beu-méïd) *n* femme de chambre

champagne (chæm-*péïn*) *n* champagne *m*

champion (*tchæm*-pyeunn) *n* champion *m*; défenseur *m*

chance (tchââns) *n* hasard *m*; chance *f*, occasion *f*; risque *m*; **by** ~ par hasard

change (tchéïndj) *v* modifier, changer; se changer; *n* modification *f*, changement *m*; petite monnaie, change *m*

channel (*tchæ*-neul) *n* canal *m*; **English Channel** La Manche

chaos (*kéï*-oss) *n* chaos *m*

chaotic (kéï-*o*-tik) *adj* chaotique

chap (tchæp) *n* type *m*

chapel (*tchæ*-peul) *n* église *f*, chapelle *f*

chaplain (*tchæ*-plinn) *n* chapelain *m*

character (*kæ*-reuk-teu) *n* caractère *m*

characteristic (kæ-reuk-teu-*ri*-stik) *adj* caractéristique; *n* caractéristique *f*; trait de caractère

characterize (*kæ*-reuk-teu-raïz) *v* caractériser

charcoal (*tchââ*-kô^oul) *n* charbon de bois

charge (tchââdj) *v* demander; charger; accuser; *n* prix *m*; charge *f*, chargement *m*; accusation *f*; ~ **plate** *Am* carte de crédit; **free of** ~ à titre gracieux; **in** ~ **of** chargé de; ***take** ~ **of** se charger de

charity (*tchæ*-reu-ti) *n* charité *f*

charm (tchââm) *n* attraits, charme *m*; amulette *f*

charming (*tchââ*-minng) *adj* séduisant

chart (tchâât) *n* tableau *m*; graphique *m*; carte marine; **conversion** ~ tableau de conversions

chase (tchéïss) *v* pourchasser; expulser, chasser; *n* chasse *f*

chasm (*kæ*-zeumm) *n* crevasse *f*

chassis (*chæ*-si) *n* (pl ~) châssis *m*

chaste (tchéïst) *adj* chaste

chat (tchæt) *v* bavarder, causer; *n* causette *f*, bavardage *m*

chatterbox (*tchæ*-teu-boks) *n* moulin à paroles

cheap (tchiip) *adj* bon marché; avantageux

cheat (tchiit) v tricher; duper

check (tchèk) v contrôler, vérifier; n damier m; nAm note f; chèque m; **check!** échec!; ~ **in** s'*inscrire; ~ **out** *partir

check-book (tchèk-bouk) nAm carnet de chèques

checkerboard (tchè-keu-bood) nAm échiquier m

checkers (tchè-keuz) plAm jeu de dames

checkroom (tchèk-roûm) nAm vestiaire m

check-up (tchè-kap) n examen m

cheek (tchiik) n joue f

cheek-bone (tchiik-bôoun) n pommette f

cheer (tchieu) v acclamer; ~ **up** égayer

cheerful (tchieu-feul) adj joyeux, gai

cheese (tchiiz) n fromage m

chef (chèf) n chef cuisinier

chemical (kè-mi-keul) adj chimique

chemist (kè-mist) n pharmacien m; **chemist's** pharmacie f; droguerie f

chemistry (kè-mi-stri) n chimie f

cheque (tchèk) n chèque m

cheque-book (tchèk-bouk) n carnet de chèques

chequered (tchè-keud) adj à carreaux, à damiers

cherry (tchè-ri) n cerise f

chess (tchèss) n échecs

chest (tchèst) n poitrine f; coffre m; ~ **of drawers** commode f

chestnut (tchèss-nat) n marron m

chew (tchoû) v mâcher

chewing-gum (tchoû-inng-ghamm) n chewing-gum m

chicken (tchi-kinn) n poulet m

chickenpox (tchi-kinn-poks) n varicelle f

chief (tchiif) n chef m; adj principal

chieftain (tchiif-teunn) n chef m

chilblain (tchil-bléïn) n engelure f

child (tchaïld) n (pl children) enfant m

childbirth (tchaïld-beûθ) n accouchement m

childhood (tchaïld-houd) n enfance f

Chile (tchi-li) Chili m

Chilean (tchi-li-eunn) adj chilien; n Chilien m

chill (tchil) n frisson m

chilly (tchi-li) adj frais

chimes (tchaïmz) pl carillon m

chimney (tchimm-ni) n cheminée f

chin (tchinn) n menton m

China (tchaï-neu) Chine f

china (tchaï-neu) n porcelaine f

Chinese (tchaï-niiz) adj chinois; n Chinois m

chink (tchinngk) n fissure f

chip (tchip) n éclat m; jeton m; v tailler, ébrécher; **chips** pommes frites

chiropodist (ki-ro-peu-dist) n pédicure m

chisel (tchi-zeul) n burin m

chives (tchaïvz) pl ciboulette f

chlorine (kloo-riin) n chlore m

chock-full (tchok-foul) adj plein à craquer, bourré

chocolate (tcho-kleut) n chocolat m; praline f

choice (tchoïss) n choix m; sélection f

choir (kouaïeu) n chœur m

choke (tchôouk) v suffoquer; étrangler, étouffer; n starter m

*choose (tchoûz) v choisir

chop (tchop) n côte f, côtelette f; v hacher

Christ (kraïst) Christ m

christen (kri-seunn) v baptiser

christening (kri-seu-ninng) n baptême m

Christian (kriss-tcheunn) adj chrétien;

~ **name** prénom *m*

Christmas (*kriss*-meuss) Noël

chromium (*krô*ᵒᵘ-mi-eumm) *n* chrome *m*

chronic (*kro*-nik) *adj* chronique

chronological (kro-neu-*lo*-dji-keul) *adj* chronologique

chuckle (*tcha*-keul) *v* glousser

chunk (tchanngk) *n* gros morceau *m*

church (tcheûtch) *n* église *f*

churchyard (*tcheûtch*-yââd) *n* cimetière *m*

cigar (si-*ghââ*) *n* cigare *m*; ~ **shop** bureau de tabac

cigarette (si-gheu-*rèt*) *n* cigarette *f*

cigarette-case (si-gheu-*rèt*-kéïss) *n* étui à cigarettes

cigarette-holder (si-gheu-*rèt*-hôᵒᵘl-deu) *n* fume-cigarettes *m*

cigarette-lighter (si-gheu-*rèt*-laï-teu) *n* briquet *m*

cinema (*si*-neu-meu) *n* cinéma *m*

cinnamon (*si*-neu-meunn) *n* cannelle *f*

circle (*seû*-keul) *n* cercle *m*; balcon *m*; *v* encercler, entourer

circulation (seû-kyou-*léï*-cheunn) *n* circulation *f*

circumstance (*seû*-keumm-stæns) *n* circonstance *f*

circus (*seû*-keuss) *n* cirque *m*

citizen (*si*-ti-zeunn) *n* citoyen *m*

citizenship (*si*-ti-zeunn-chip) *n* citoyenneté *f*

city (*si*-ti) *n* cité *f*

civic (*si*-vik) *adj* civique

civil (*si*-veul) *adj* civil; poli; ~ **law** droit civil; ~ **servant** fonctionnaire *m*

civilian (si-*vil*-yeunn) *adj* civil; *n* civil *m*

civilization (si-veu-laï-*zéï*-cheunn) *n* civilisation *f*

civilized (*si*-veu-laïzd) *adj* civilisé

claim (kléïm) *v* revendiquer, récla-

mer; prétendre; *n* revendication *f*, prétention *f*

clamp (klæmp) *n* mordache *f*; crampon *m*

clap (klæp) *v* applaudir

clarify (*klæ*-ri-faï) *v* éclaircir, clarifier

class (klââss) *n* classe *f*

classical (*klæ*-si-keul) *adj* classique

classify (*klæ*-si-faï) *v* classer

class-mate (*klââss*-méit) *n* camarade de classe

classroom (*klââss*-roûm) *n* salle de classe

clause (klooz) *n* clause *f*

claw (kloo) *n* griffe *f*

clay (kléï) *n* argile *f*

clean (kliin) *adj* pur, propre; *v* nettoyer

cleaning (*klii*-ninng) *n* nettoyage *m*; ~ **fluid** détachant *m*

clear (kli*ᵉᵘ*) *adj* clair; *v* nettoyer

clearing (*kli*ᵉᵘ-rinng) *n* clairière *f*

cleft (klèft) *n* fente *f*

clergyman (*kleû*-dji-meunn) *n* (pl -men) pasteur *m*; ecclésiastique *m*

clerk (klââk) *n* employé de bureau; greffier *m*; secrétaire *m*

clever (*klè*-veu) *adj* intelligent; astucieux, éveillé

client (*klaï*-eunnt) *n* client *m*

cliff (klif) *n* falaise *f*

climate (*klaï*-mit) *n* climat *m*

climb (klaïm) *v* grimper; *n* ascension *f*

clinic (*kli*-nik) *n* clinique *f*

cloak (klôᵒᵘk) *n* manteau *m*

cloakroom (*klô*ᵒᵘk-roûm) *n* vestiaire *m*

clock (klok) *n* horloge *f*; **at ... o'-clock** à ... heures

cloister (*kloï*-steu) *n* cloître *m*

close¹ (klôᵒᵘz) *v* fermer; **closed** *adj* fermé, clos

close² (klôᵒᵘss) *adj* proche

closet (*klo*-zit) *n* placard *m*; *nAm* garde-robe *f*

cloth (kloθ) *n* tissu *m*; chiffon *m*

clothes (klô^{ou}ðz) *pl* habits *mpl*, vêtements *mpl*

clothes-brush (*klô^{ou}ðz*-brach) *n* brosse à habits

clothing (*klô^{ou}*-ðinng) *n* habillement *m*

cloud (klaoud) *n* nuage *m*

cloud-burst (*klaoud*-beûst) *n* rafale de pluie

cloudy (*klaou*-di) *adj* couvert, nuageux

clover (*klô^{ou}*-veu) *n* trèfle *m*

clown (klaoun) *n* clown *m*

club (klab) *n* club *m*; cercle *m*, association *f*; gourdin *m*, massue *f*

clumsy (*klamm*-zi) *adj* maladroit

clutch (klatch) *n* embrayage *m*; prise *f*

coach (kô^{ou}tch) *n* car *m*; wagon *m*; carrosse *m*; entraîneur *m*

coachwork (*kô^{ou}tch*-^{ou}eûk) *n* carrosserie *f*

coagulate (kô^{ou}-*æ*-ghyou-léït) *v* coaguler

coal (kô^{ou}l) *n* charbon *m*

coarse (kooss) *adj* grossier

coast (kô^{ou}st) *n* côte *f*

coat (kô^{ou}t) *n* pardessus *m*, manteau *m*

coat-hanger (*kô^{ou}t*-hæng-eu) *n* cintre *m*

cobweb (*kob*-^{ou}èb) *n* toile d'araignée

cocaine (kô^{ou}-*kéïn*) *n* cocaïne *f*

cock (kok) *n* coq *m*

cocktail (*kok*-téïl) *n* cocktail *m*

coconut (*kô^{ou}*-keu-nat) *n* noix de coco

cod (kod) *n* (pl ~) morue *f*

code (kô^{ou}d) *n* code *m*

coffee (*ko*-fi) *n* café *m*

coherence (kô^{ou}-*hi^{eu}*-reunns) *n* cohérence *f*

coin (koïn) *n* pièce de monnaie

coincide (kô^{ou}-inn-*saïd*) *v* coïncider

cold (kô^{ou}ld) *adj* froid; *n* froid *m*; rhume *m*; **catch a ~** s'enrhumer

collapse (keu-*læps*) *v* s'effondrer, s'écrouler

collar (*ko*-leu) *n* collier *m*; col *m*; **~ stud** bouton de col

collarbone (*ko*-leu-bô^{ou}n) *n* clavicule *f*

colleague (*ko*-liigh) *n* collègue *m*

collect (keu-*lèkt*) *v* rassembler; *prendre, *aller chercher; quêter

collection (keu-*lèk*-cheunn) *n* collection *f*; levée *f*

collective (keu-*lèk*-tiv) *adj* collectif

collector (keu-*lèk*-teu) *n* collectionneur *m*; quêteur *m*

college (*ko*-lidj) *n* collège *m*

collide (keu-*laïd*) *v* entrer en collision

collision (keu-*li*-jeunn) *n* collision *f*; abordage *m*

Colombia (keu-*lomm*-bi-eu) Colombie *f*

Colombian (keu-*lomm*-bi-eunn) *adj* colombien; *n* Colombien *m*

colonel (*keû*-neul) *n* colonel *m*

colony (*ko*-leu-ni) *n* colonie *f*

colour (*ka*-leu) *n* couleur *f*; *v* colorer; **~ film** film en couleurs

colourant (*ka*-leu-reunnt) *n* colorant *m*

colour-blind (*ka*-leu-blaïnd) *adj* daltonien

coloured (*ka*-leud) *adj* de couleur

colourful (*ka*-leu-feul) *adj* coloré

column (*ko*-leumm) *n* colonne *f*; rubrique *f*

coma (*kô^{ou}*-meu) *n* coma *m*

comb (kô^{ou}m) *v* peigner; *n* peigne *m*

combat (*komm*-bæt) *n* lutte *f*, combat *m*; *v* *combattre, lutter

combination (komm-bi-*néï*-cheunn) *n* combinaison *f*

combine (keumm-*baïn*) *v* combiner

*come (kamm) v *venir; ~ **across** rencontrer; trouver

comedian (keu-*mii*-di-eunn) n comédien m; comique m

comedy (*ko*-meu-di) n comédie f; **musical** ~ comédie musicale

comfort (*kamm*-feut) n bien-être m, commodité f, confort m; réconfort m; v consoler

comfortable (*kamm*-feu-teu-beul) adj confortable

comic (*ko*-mik) adj comique

comics (*ko*-miks) pl bandes dessinées

coming (*ka*-minng) n arrivée f

comma (*ko*-meu) n virgule f

command (keu-*mâând*) v commander; n ordre m

commander (keu-*mâân*-deu) n commandant m

commemoration (keu-mè-meu-*réï*-cheunn) n commémoration f

commence (keu-*mèns*) v commencer

comment (*ko*-mènt) n commentaire m; v commenter

commerce (*ko*-meûss) n commerce m

commercial (keu-*meû*-cheul) adj commercial; n annonce publicitaire; ~ **law** droit commercial

commission (keu-*mi*-cheunn) n commission f

commit (keu-*mit*) v *remettre, confier; *commettre

committee (keu-*mi*-ti) n commission f, comité m

common (*ko*-meunn) adj commun; habituel; ordinaire

commune (*ko*-myoûn) n commune f

communicate (keu-*myoû*-ni-kéït) v communiquer

communication (keu-myoû-ni-*kéï*-cheunn) n communication f

communism (*ko*-myou-ni-zeumm) n communisme m

communist (*ko*-myou-nist) n commu-

niste m

community (keu-*myoû*-neu-ti) n société f, communauté f

commuter (keu-*myoû*-teu) n navetteur m

compact (*komm*-pækt) adj compact

companion (keumm-*pæ*-nyeunn) n compagnon m

company (*kamm*-peu-ni) n compagnie f; entreprise f, société f

comparative (keumm-*pæ*-reu-tiv) adj relatif

compare (keumm-*pè^{eu}*) v comparer

comparison (keumm-*pæ*-ri-seunn) n comparaison f

compartment (keumm-*pâât*-meunnt) n compartiment m

compass (*kamm*-peuss) n boussole f

compel (keumm-*pèl*) v *contraindre

compensate (*komm*-peunn-séït) v compenser

compensation (komm-peunn-*séï*-cheunn) n compensation f; indemnité f

compete (keumm-*piit*) v *concourir

competition (komm-peu-*ti*-cheunn) n compétition f

competitor (keumm-*pè*-ti-teur) n concurrent m

compile (keumm-*païl*) v compiler

complain (keumm-*pléïn*) v se *plaindre

complaint (keumm-*pléïnt*) n plainte f; **complaints book** cahier de doléances

complete (keumm-*pliit*) adj entier, complet; v achever

completely (keumm-*pliit*-li) adv entièrement, totalement, complètement

complex (*komm*-plèks) n complexe m; adj complexe

complexion (keumm-*plèk*-cheunn) n teint m

complicated (*komm*-pli-kéï-tid) adj

compliqué

compliment (*komm*-pli-meunnt) *n* compliment *m* ; *v* complimenter, féliciter

compose (keumm-*pô°ᵘz*) *v* composer

composer (keumm-*pô°ᵘ*-zeu) *n* compositeur *m*

composition (komm-peu-*zi*-cheunn) *n* composition *f*

comprehensive (komm-pri-*hèn*-siv) *adj* étendu

comprise (keumm-*praïz*) *v* *comprendre, *inclure

compromise (*komm*-preu-maïz) *n* compromis *m*

compulsory (keumm-*pal*-seu-ri) *adj* obligatoire

comrade (*komm*-réïd) *n* camarade *m*

conceal (keunn-*siil*) *v* dissimuler

conceited (keunn-*sii*-tid) *adj* prétentieux

conceive (keunn-*siiv*) *v* *concevoir, *comprendre

concentrate (*konn*-seunn-tréït) *v* concentrer

concentration (konn-seunn-*tréï*-cheunn) *n* concentration *f*

conception (keunn-*sèp*-cheunn) *n* conception *f*

concern (keunn-*seûnn*) *v* regarder, concerner ; *n* souci *m* ; affaire *f* ; entreprise *f*

concerned (keunn-*seûnnd*) *adj* soucieux ; concerné

concerning (keunn-*seû*-ninng) *prep* relatif à, concernant

concert (*konn*-seut) *n* concert *m* ; ~ **hall** salle de concert

concession (keunn-*sè*-cheunn) *n* concession *f*

concierge (kon-si-*è°ᵘj*) *n* concierge *m*

concise (keunn-*saïss*) *adj* concis

conclusion (keunng-*kloû*-jeunn) *n* conclusion *f*

concrete (*konng*-kriit) *adj* concret ; *n* béton *m*

concurrence (keunng-*ka*-reunns) *n* coïncidence *f*

concussion (keunng-*ka*-cheunn) *n* commotion *f*

condition (keunn-*di*-cheunn) *n* condition *f* ; état *m*, forme *f* ; circonstance *f*

conditional (keunn-*di*-cheu-neul) *adj* conditionnel

conduct¹ (*konn*-dakt) *n* conduite *f*

conduct² (keunn-*dakt*) *v* *conduire ; accompagner ; diriger

conductor (keunn-*dak*-teu) *n* conducteur *m* ; chef d'orchestre

confectioner (keunn-*fèk*-cheu-neu) *n* confiseur *m*

conference (*konn*-feu-reunns) *n* conférence *f*

confess (keunn-*fèss*) *v* *reconnaître ; confesser ; professer

confession (keunn-*fè*-cheunn) *n* confession *f*

confidence (*konn*-fi-deunns) *n* confiance *f*

confident (*konn*-fi-deunnt) *adj* confiant

confidential (konn-fi-*dèn*-cheul) *adj* confidentiel

confirm (keunn-*feûmm*) *v* confirmer

confirmation (konn-feu-*méï*-cheunn) *n* confirmation *f*

confiscate (*konn*-fi-skéït) *v* confisquer

conflict (*konn*-flikt) *n* conflit *m*

confuse (keunn-*fyoûz*) *v* confondre ; **confused** *adj* confus

confusion (keunn-*fyoû*-jeunn) *n* confusion *f*

congratulate (keunng-*ghræ*-tchou-léït) *v* congratuler, féliciter

congratulation (keunng-ghræ-tchou-*léï*-cheunn) *n* félicitation *f*, félicitation *m*

congregation (konng-ghri-*ghéï*-cheunn) *n* communauté *f*, congrégation *f*

congress (*konng*-ghrèss) *n* congrès *m*

connect (keu-*nèkt*) *v* *joindre; *mettre en communication; brancher

connection (keu-*nèk*-cheunn) *n* relation *f*; rapport *m*; communication *f*, correspondance *f*

connoisseur (ko-neu-*seû*) *n* connaisseur *m*

connotation (ko-neu-*téï*-cheunn) *n* connotation *f*

conquer (*konng*-keu) *v* *conquérir; *vaincre

conqueror (*konng*-keu-reu) *n* conquérant *m*

conquest (*konng*-k^{ou}èst) *n* conquête *f*

conscience (*konn*-cheunns) *n* conscience *f*

conscious (*konn*-cheuss) *adj* conscient

consciousness (*konn*-cheuss-neuss) *n* conscience *f*

conscript (*konn*-skript) *n* conscrit *m*

consent (keunn-*sènt*) *v* *consentir; approuver; *n* assentiment *m*, consentement *m*

consequence (*konn*-si-k^{ou}eunns) *n* effet *m*, conséquence *f*

consequently (*konn*-si-k^{ou}eunnt-li) *adv* par conséquent

conservative (keunn-*seû*-veu-tiv) *adj* conservateur

consider (keunn-*si*-deu) *v* considérer; envisager; trouver, estimer

considerable (keunn-*si*-deu-reu-beul) *adj* considérable; important, sensible

considerate (keunn-*si*-deu-reut) *adj* prévenant

consideration (keunn-si-deu-*réï*-cheunn) *n* considération *f*; égard *m*, attention *f*

considering (keunn-*si*-deu-rinng) *prep* vu

consignment (keunn-*saïn*-meunnt) *n* expédition *f*

consist of (keunn-*sist*) consister en

conspire (keunn-*spai*^{eu}) *v* conspirer

constant (*konn*-steunnt) *adj* constant

constipated (*konn*-sti-péï-tid) *adj* constipé

constipation (konn-sti-*péï*-cheunn) *n* constipation *f*

constituency (keunn-*sti*-tchou-eunn-si) *n* circonscription électorale

constitution (konn-sti-*tyoû*-cheunn) *n* constitution *f*

construct (keunn-*strakt*) *v* *construire; bâtir, édifier

construction (keunn-*strak*-cheunn) *n* construction *f*; édification *f*; édifice *m*

consul (*konn*-seul) *n* consul *m*

consulate (*konn*-syou-leut) *n* consulat *m*

consult (keunn-*salt*) *v* consulter

consultation (konn-seul-*téï*-cheunn) *n* consultation *f*; ~ **hours** *n* heures de consultation

consumer (keunn-*syoû*-meu) *n* utilisateur *m*, consommateur *m*

contact (*konn*-tækt) *n* contact *m*; *v* contacter; ~ **lenses** verres de contact

contagious (keunn-*téï*-djeuss) *adj* contagieux

contain (keunn-*téïn*) *v* *contenir; *comprendre

container (keunn-*téï*-neu) *n* récipient *m*; conteneur *m*

contemporary (keunn-*tèm*-peu-reu-ri) *adj* contemporain; de l'époque; *n* contemporain *m*

contempt (keunn-*tèmpt*) *n* dédain *m*, mépris *m*

content (keunn-*tènt*) *adj* satisfait

contents (*konn*-tènts) *pl* contenu *m*

contest (*konn*-tèst) *n* combat *m*; concours *m*

continent (*konn*-ti-neunnt) *n* continent *m*

continental (konn-ti-*nèn*-teul) *adj* continental

continual (keunn-*ti*-nyou-eul) *adj* continuel

continue (keunn-*ti*-nyoû) *v* continuer; *poursuivre, durer

continuous (keunn-*ti*-nyou-euss) *adj* continuel, continu, ininterrompu

contour (*konn*-tou^{eu}) *n* contour *m*

contraceptive (konn-treu-*sèp*-tiv) *n* contraceptif *m*

contract[1] (*konn*-trækt) *n* contrat *m*

contract[2] (keunn-*trækt*) *v* attraper

contractor (keunn-*træk*-teu) *n* entrepreneur *m*

contradict (konn-treu-*dikt*) *v* *contredire

contradictory (konn-treu-*dik*-teu-ri) *adj* contradictoire

contrary (*konn*-treu-ri) *n* contraire *m*; *adj* opposé; **on the ~** au contraire

contrast (*konn*-trâast) *n* contraste *m*; différence *f*

contribution (konn-tri-*byoû*-cheunn) *n* contribution *f*

control (keunn-*trô*^{ou}*l*) *n* contrôle *m*; *v* contrôler

controversial (konn-treu-*veû*-cheul) *adj* discuté, controversé

convenience (keunn-*vii*-nyeunns) *n* commodité *f*

convenient (keunn-*vii*-nyeunnt) *adj* pratique; approprié, qui convient, commode

convent (*konn*-veunnt) *n* couvent *m*

conversation (konn-veu-*séï*-cheunn) *n* entretien *m*, conversation *f*

convert (keunn-*veût*) *v* convertir

convict[1] (keunn-*vikt*) *v* déclarer coupable

convict[2] (*konn*-vikt) *n* condamné *m*

conviction (keunn-*vik*-cheunn) *n* conviction *f*; condamnation *f*

convince (keunn-*vinns*) *v* *convaincre

convulsion (keunn-*val*-cheunn) *n* convulsion *f*

cook (kouk) *n* cuisinier *m*; *v* *cuire; préparer

cookbook (*kouk*-bouk) *nAm* livre de cuisine

cooker (*kou*-keu) *n* cuisinière *f*; **gas ~** cuisinière à gaz

cookery-book (*kou*-keu-ri-bouk) *n* livre de cuisine

cookie (*kou*-ki) *nAm* biscuit *m*

cool (koûl) *adj* frais; **cooling system** système de refroidissement

co-operation (kô^{ou}-o-peu-*réï*-cheunn) *n* coopération *f*; collaboration *f*

co-operative (kô^{ou}-o-peu-reu-tiv) *adj* coopératif; coopérant; *n* coopérative *f*

co-ordinate (kô^{ou}-*oo*-di-néït) *v* coordonner

co-ordination (kô^{ou}-oo-di-*néï*-cheunn) *n* coordination *f*

copper (*ko*-peu) *n* cuivre *m*

copy (*ko*-pi) *n* copie *f*; exemplaire *m*; *v* copier; imiter; **carbon ~** copie *f*

coral (*ko*-reul) *n* corail *m*

cord (kood) *n* corde *f*; cordon *m*

cordial (*koo*-di-eul) *adj* cordial

corduroy (*koo*-deu-roï) *n* velours côtelé

core (koo) *n* cœur *m*; trognon *m*

cork (kook) *n* bouchon *m*

corkscrew (*kook*-skroû) *n* tire-bouchon *m*

corn (koon) *n* grain *m*; céréale *f*, blé *m*; durillon *m*, cor au pied; **~ on the cob** maïs en épi

corner (*koo*-neu) *n* coin *m*

cornfield (*koon*-fiild) *n* champ de blé

corpse (koops) *n* cadavre *m*

corpulent (*koo*-pyou-leunnt) *adj* corpulent; gros, obèse

correct (keu-*rèkt*) adj juste, correct; v corriger

correction (keu-*rèk*-cheunn) n correction f; rectification f

correctness (keu-*rèkt*-neuss) n exactitude f

correspond (ko-ri-*sponnd*) v correspondre; *être conforme

correspondence (ko-ri-*sponn*-deunns) n correspondance f

correspondent (ko-ri-*sponn*-deunnt) n correspondant m

corridor (*ko*-ri-doo) n corridor m

corrupt (keu-*rapt*) adj corrompu; v *corrompre

corruption (keu-*rap*-cheunn) n corruption f

corset (*koo*-sit) n corset m

cosmetics (koz-*mè*-tiks) pl cosmétiques mpl, produits de beauté

cost (kost) n coût m; prix m

*cost (kost) v coûter

cosy (*kô*ou-zi) adj intime, confortable

cot (kot) nAm lit de camp

cottage (*ko*-tidj) n villa f

cotton (*ko*-teunn) n coton m; en coton

cotton-wool (*ko*-teunn-ououl) n ouate f

couch (kaoutch) n canapé m

cough (kof) n toux f; v tousser

could (koud) v (p can)

council (*kaoun*-seul) n conseil m

councillor (*kaoun*-seu-leu) n conseiller m

counsel (*kaoun*-seul) n conseil m

counsellor (*kaoun*-seu-leu) n conseiller m

count (kaount) v compter; additionner; *inclure; considérer; n comte m

counter (*kaoun*-teu) n comptoir m; barre f

counterfeit (*kaoun*-teu-fiit) v *contrefaire

counterfoil (*kaoun*-teu-foïl) n talon m

counterpane (*kaoun*-teu-péïn) n couvre-lit m

countess (*kaoun*-tiss) n comtesse f

country (*kann*-tri) n pays m; campagne f; région f; ~ **house** maison de campagne

countryman (*kann*-tri-meunn) n (pl -men) compatriote m

countryside (*kann*-tri-saïd) n campagne f

county (*kaoun*-ti) n comté m

couple (*ka*-peul) n couple m

coupon (*koû*-ponn) n ticket m, coupon m

courage (*ka*-ridj) n vaillance f, courage m

courageous (keu-*réï*-djeuss) adj brave, courageux

course (kooss) n cap m; plat m; cours m; **intensive** ~ cours accéléré; **of** ~ évidemment

court (koot) n tribunal m; cour f

courteous (*keû*-ti-euss) adj courtois

cousin (*ka*-zeunn) n cousine f, cousin m

cover (*ka*-veu) v *couvrir; n refuge m, abri m; couvercle m; couverture f

cow (kaou) n vache f

coward (*kaou*-eud) n lâche m

cowardly (*kaou*-eud-li) adj lâche

cow-hide (*kaou*-haïd) n peau de vache f

crab (kræb) n crabe m

crack (kræk) n craquement m; fissure f; v craquer; fendre

cracker (*kræ*-keu) nAm biscuit m

cradle (*kréi*-deul) n berceau m

cramp (kræmp) n crampe f

crane (kréïn) n grue f

crankcase (*krængk*-kéïss) n carter m

crankshaft (*krængk*-chââft) n vilebrequin m

crash (kræch) n collision f; v entrer en collision; s'écraser; ~ **barrier** glissière de sécurité

crate (kréit) n caisse f

crater (kréï-teu) n cratère m

crawl (krool) v ramper; n crawl m

craze (kréiz) n rage f

crazy (kréï-zi) adj fou; insensé

creak (kriik) v grincer

cream (kriim) n crème f; crème fraîche; adj crème

creamy (krii-mi) adj crémeux

crease (kriiss) v froisser; n pli m; faux pli

create (kri-éït) v créer

creature (krii-tcheu) n créature f; être m

credible (krè-di-beul) adj croyable

credit (krè-dit) n crédit m; v créditer; ~ **card** carte de crédit

creditor (krè-di-teu) n créditeur m

credulous (krè-dyou-leuss) adj crédule

creek (kriik) n baie f, crique f

*creep (kriip) v ramper

creepy (krii-pi) adj lugubre, terrifiant

cremate (kri-méit) v incinérer

cremation (kri-méï-cheunn) n crémation f

crew (kroû) n équipage m

cricket (kri-kit) n cricket m; grillon m

crime (kraïm) n crime m

criminal (kri-mi-neul) n délinquant m, criminel m; adj criminel; ~ **law** droit pénal

criminality (kri-mi-næ-leu-ti) n criminalité f

crimson (krimm-zeunn) adj cramoisi

crippled (kri-peuld) adj estropié

crisis (kraï-siss) n (pl crises) crise f

crisp (krisp) adj croustillant

critic (kri-tik) n critique m

critical (kri-ti-keul) adj critique; précaire, délicat

criticism (kri-ti-si-zeumm) n critique f

criticize (kri-ti-saïz) v critiquer

crochet (krôᵒᵘ-chéï) v *faire du crochet

crockery (kro-keu-ri) n poterie f, faïence f

crocodile (kro-keu-daïl) n crocodile m

crooked (krou-kid) adj tordu, courbe; malhonnête

crop (krop) n récolte f

cross (kross) v traverser; adj irrité, fâché; n croix f

cross-eyed (kross-aïd) adj louche

crossing (kro-sinng) n traversée f; croisement m; passage m; passage à niveau

crossroads (kross-rôᵒᵘdz) n carrefour m

crosswalk (kross-ᵒᵘook) nAm passage pour piétons

crow (krôᵒᵘ) n corneille f

crowbar (krôᵒᵘ-bââ) n bec-de-corbin m

crowd (kraoud) n masse f, foule f

crowded (kraou-did) adj animé; bondé

crown (kraoun) n couronne f; v couronner

crucifix (kroû-si-fiks) n crucifix m

crucifixion (kroû-si-fik-cheunn) n crucifixion f

crucify (kroû-si-faï) v crucifier

cruel (krouᵉᵘl) adj cruel

cruise (kroûz) n croisière f

crumb (kramm) n miette f

crusade (kroû-séïd) n croisade f

crust (krast) n croûte f

crutch (kratch) n béquille f

cry (kraï) v pleurer; crier; appeler; n cri m; appel m

crystal (kri-steul) n cristal m; adj en cristal

Cuba (kyoû-beu) Cuba m

Cuban (kyoû-beunn) adj cubain; n

Cubain *m*

cube (kyoûb) *n* cube *m*

cuckoo (*kou*-koû) *n* coucou *m*

cucumber (*kyoû*-keumm-beu) *n* concombre *m*

cuddle (*ka*-deul) *v* câliner

cudgel (*ka*-djeul) *n* gourdin *m*

cuff (kaf) *n* manchette *f*

cuff-links (*kaf*-linngks) *pl* boutons de manchettes

cultivate (*kal*-ti-véït) *v* cultiver

culture (*kal*-tcheu) *n* culture *f*

cultured (*kal*-tcheud) *adj* cultivé

cunning (*ka*-ninng) *adj* rusé

cup (kap) *n* tasse *f*; coupe *f*

cupboard (*ka*-beud) *n* placard *m*

curb (keûb) *n* bord du trottoir; *v* freiner

cure (kyou^eu) *v* guérir; *n* cure *f*; guérison *f*

curio (*kyou^eu*-ri-ô^ou) *n* (pl ~s) curiosité *f*

curiosity (kyou^eu-ri-*o*-seu-ti) *n* curiosité *f*

curious (*kyou^eu*-ri-euss) *adj* curieux; étrange

curl (keûl) *v* boucler; friser; *n* boucle *f*

curler (*keû*-leu) *n* bigoudi *m*

curling-tongs (*keû*-linng-tonngz) *pl* fer à friser

curly (*keû*-li) *adj* bouclé

currant (*ka*-reunnt) *n* raisin sec; groseille *f*

currency (*ka*-reunn-si) *n* monnaie *f*; **foreign ~** monnaie étrangère

current (*ka*-reunnt) *n* courant *m*; *adj* courant; **alternating ~** courant alternatif; **direct ~** courant continu

curry (*ka*-ri) *n* curry *m*

curse (keûss) *v* jurer; *maudire; *n* juron *m*

curtain (*keû*-teunn) *n* rideau *m*

curve (keûv) *n* courbe *f*; tournant *m*

curved (keûvd) *adj* courbe, courbé

cushion (*kou*-cheunn) *n* coussin *m*

custodian (ka-*stô^ou*-di-eunn) *n* gardien *m*

custody (*ka*-steu-di) *n* détention *f*; garde *f*; tutelle *f*

custom (*ka*-steumm) *n* coutume *f*; habitude *f*

customary (*ka*-steu-meu-ri) *adj* usuel, coutumier, ordinaire

customer (*ka*-steu-meu) *n* client *m*

Customs (*ka*-steummz) *pl* douane *f*; ~ **duty** droit de douane; ~ **officer** douanier *m*

cut (kat) *n* incision *f*; coupure *f*

***cut** (kat) *v* couper; *réduire; ~ **off** découper; couper

cutlery (*kat*-leu-ri) *n* couvert *m*

cutlet (*kat*-leut) *n* côtelette *f*

cycle (*saï*-keul) *n* vélo *m*; bicyclette *f*; cycle *m*

cyclist (*saï*-klist) *n* cycliste *m*

cylinder (*si*-linn-deu) *n* cylindre *m*; ~ **head** tête de cylindre

cystitis (si-*staï*-tiss) *n* cystite *f*

Czech (tchèk) *adj* tchèque; *n* Tchèque *m*

Czechoslovakia (tchè-keu-sleu-*vââ*-ki-eu) Tchécoslovaquie *f*

D

dad (dæd) *n* père *m*

daddy (*dæ*-di) *n* papa *m*

daffodil (*dæ*-feu-dil) *n* jonquille *f*

daily (*déï*-li) *adj* journalier, quotidien; *n* quotidien *m*

dairy (*dè^eu*-ri) *n* laiterie *f*

dam (dæm) *n* barrage *m*; digue *f*

damage (*dæ*-midj) *n* dommage *m*; *v* endommager

damp (dæmp) *adj* humide; moite; *n*

humidité f; v humidifier

dance (dââns) v danser; n danse f

dandelion (dæn-di-laï-eunn) n pissen-lit m

dandruff (dæn-dreuf) n pellicules

Dane (déïn) n Danois m

danger (déïn-djeu) n danger m

dangerous (déïn-djeu-reuss) adj dangereux

Danish (déï-nich) adj danois

dare (dè^{eu}) v oser; défier

daring (dè^{eu}-rinng) adj téméraire

dark (dââk) adj obscur; n obscurité f, ténèbres fpl

darling (dââ-linng) n trésor m, chéri m

darn (dâân) v repriser

dash (dæch) v se précipiter; n tiret m

dashboard (dæch-bood) n tableau de bord

data (déï-teu) pl donnée f

date¹ (déït) n date f; rendez-vous m; v dater; **out of ~** démodé

date² (déït) n datte f

daughter (doo-teu) n fille f

dawn (doon) n aube f; aurore f

day (déï) n jour m; **by ~** de jour; **~ trip** excursion f; **per ~** par jour; **the ~ before yesterday** avant-hier

daybreak (déï-bréïk) n lever du jour

daylight (déï-laït) n lumière du jour

dead (dèd) adj mort; décédé

deaf (dèf) adj sourd

deal (diil) n transaction f, affaire f

***deal** (diil) v distribuer; **~ with** v s'occuper de; *faire des affaires avec

dealer (dii-leu) n négociant m, marchand m

dear (di^{eu}) adj cher

death (dèθ) n mort f; **~ penalty** peine de mort

debate (di-béït) n débat m

debit (dè-bit) n débit m

debt (dèt) n dette f

decaffeinated (dii-kæ-fi-néï-tid) adj décaféiné

deceit (di-siit) n tromperie f

deceive (di-siiv) v tromper

December (di-sèm-beu) décembre

decency (dii-seunn-si) n décence f

decent (dii-seunnt) adj décent

decide (di-saïd) v décider

decision (di-si-jeunn) n décision f

deck (dèk) n pont m; **~ cabin** cabine de pont; **~ chair** chaise longue

declaration (dè-kleu-réï-cheunn) n déclaration f

declare (di-klè^{eu}) v déclarer; indiquer

decoration (dè-keu-réï-cheunn) n décoration f

decrease (dii-kriiss) v *réduire; diminuer; n diminution f

dedicate (dè-di-kéït) v dédier

deduce (di-dyoûss) v *déduire

deduct (di-dakt) v *déduire

deed (diid) n action f, acte m

deep (diip) adj profond

deep-freeze (diip-friiz) n congélateur m

deer (di^{eu}) n (pl ~) daim m

defeat (di-fiit) v *vaincre; n défaite f

defective (di-fèk-tiv) adj défectueux

defence (di-fèns) n défense f

defend (di-fènd) v défendre

deficiency (di-fi-cheunn-si) n déficience f

deficit (dè-fi-sit) n déficit m

define (di-faïn) v définir, déterminer

definite (dè-fi-nit) adj déterminé; explicite

definition (dè-fi-ni-cheunn) n définition f

deformed (di-foomd) adj contrefait, difforme

degree (di-ghrii) n degré m; grade m

delay (di-léï) v retarder; différer; n retard m; ajournement m

delegate (*dè*-li-gheut) *n* délégué *m*

delegation (dè-li-*ghéï*-cheunn) *n* délégation *f*

deliberate[1] (di-*li*-beu-réït) *v* discuter, délibérer

deliberate[2] (di-*li*-beu-reut) *adj* délibéré

deliberation (di-li-beu-*réï*-cheunn) *n* discussion *f*, délibération *f*

delicacy (*dè*-li-keu-si) *n* délicatesse *f*

delicate (*dè*-li-keut) *adj* délicat; tendre

delicatessen (dè-li-keu-*tè*-seunn) *n* épicerie fine

delicious (di-*li*-cheuss) *adj* exquis, délicieux

delight (di-*laït*) *n* délice *m*, plaisir *m*; *v* enchanter

delightful (di-*laït*-feul) *adj* délicieux, ravissant

deliver (di-*li*-veu) *v* *remettre, livrer; délivrer

delivery (di-*li*-veu-ri) *n* remise *f*, livraison *f*; accouchement *m*; délivrance *f*; ~ **van** camion de livraison

demand (di-*mâând*) *v* nécessiter, exiger; *n* demande *f*

democracy (di-*mo*-kreu-si) *n* démocratie *f*

democratic (dè-meu-*kræ*-tik) *adj* démocratique

demolish (di-*mo*-lich) *v* démolir

demolition (dè-meu-*li*-cheunn) *n* démolition *f*

demonstrate (*dè*-meunn-stréït) *v* démontrer; manifester

demonstration (dè-meunn-*stréï*-cheunn) *n* démonstration *f*; manifestation *f*

den (dèn) *n* tanière *f*

Denmark (*dèn*-mââk) Danemark *m*

denomination (di-no-mi-*néï*-cheunn) *n* dénomination *f*

dense (dèns) *adj* dense

dent (dènt) *n* bosse *f*

dentist (*dèn*-tist) *n* dentiste *m*

denture (*dèn*-tcheu) *n* dentier *m*

deny (di-*naï*) *v* nier; dénier, refuser

deodorant (dii-*ô*^{ou}-deu-reunnt) *n* désodorisant *m*

depart (di-*pâât*) *v* s'en *aller, *partir; trépasser

department (di-*pâât*-meunnt) *n* division *f*, département *m*; ~ **store** grand magasin

departure (di-*pââ*-tcheu) *n* départ *m*

dependant (di-*pèn*-deunnt) *adj* dépendant

depend on (di-*pènd*) dépendre de

deposit (di-*po*-zit) *n* versement *m*; consigne *f*; sédiment *m*, dépôt *m*; *v* déposer

depository (di-*po*-zi-teu-ri) *n* entrepôt *m*

depot (*dè*-pô^{ou}) *n* dépôt *m*; *nAm* gare *f*

depress (di-*prèss*) *v* déprimer

depression (di-*prè*-cheunn) *n* dépression *f*

deprive of (di-*praïv*) priver de

depth (dèpθ) *n* profondeur *f*

deputy (*dè*-pyou-ti) *n* député *m*; substitut *m*

descend (di-*sènd*) *v* descendre

descendant (di-*sèn*-deunnt) *n* descendant *m*

descent (di-*sènt*) *n* descente *f*

describe (di-*skraïb*) *v* *décrire

description (di-*skrip*-cheunn) *n* description *f*; signalement *m*

desert[1] (*dè*-zeut) *n* désert *m*; *adj* sauvage, désert

desert[2] (di-*zeût*) *v* déserter; abandonner

deserve (di-*zeûv*) *v* mériter

design (di-*zaïn*) *v* créer; *n* dessein *m*

designate (*dè*-zigh-néït) *v* désigner

desirable (di-*zaï*^{eu}-reu-beul) *adj* dési-

rable
desire (di-*zaï^{eu}*) *n* vœu *m*; envie *f*, désir *m*; *v* *avoir envie de, désirer
desk (dèsk) *n* bureau *m*; pupitre *m*; banc d'école
despair (di-*spè^{eu}*) *n* désespoir *m*; *v* désespérer
despatch (di-*spætch*) *v* expédier
desperate (*dè*-speu-reut) *adj* désespéré
despise (di-*spaïz*) *v* mépriser
despite (di-*spaït*) *prep* malgré
dessert (di-*zeût*) *n* dessert *m*
destination (dè-sti-*néï*-cheunn) *n* destination *f*
destine (*dè*-stinn) *v* destiner
destiny (*dè*-sti-ni) *n* destin *m*, sort *m*
destroy (di-*stroï*) *v* dévaster, *détruire
destruction (di-*strak*-cheunn) *n* destruction *f*; anéantissement *m*
detach (di-*tætch*) *v* détacher
detail (*dii*-téïl) *n* particularité *f*, détail *m*
detailed (*dii*-téïld) *adj* détaillé
detect (di-*tèkt*) *v* détecter
detective (di-*tèk*-tiv) *n* détective *m*; ~ **story** roman policier
detergent (di-*teû*-djeunnt) *n* détergent *m*
determine (di-*teû*-minn) *v* définir, déterminer
determined (di-*teû*-minnd) *adj* résolu
detour (*dii*-tou^{eu}) *n* détour *m*; déviation *f*
devaluation (dii-væl-you-*éï*-cheunn) *n* dévaluation *f*
devalue (dii-*væl*-yoû) *v* dévaluer
develop (di-*vè*-leup) *v* développer
development (di-*vè*-leup-meunnt) *n* développement *m*
deviate (*dii*-vi-éït) *v* dévier
devil (*dè*-veul) *n* diable *m*
devise (di-*vaïz*) *v* *concevoir
devote (di-*vô^{ou}t*) *v* consacrer

dew (dyoû) *n* rosée *f*
diabetes (daï-eu-*bii*-tiiz) *n* diabète *m*
diabetic (daï-eu-*bè*-tik) *n* diabétique *m*
diagnose (daï-eugh-*nô^{ou}z*) *v* diagnostiquer; constater
diagnosis (daï-eugh-*nô^{ou}*-siss) *n* (pl -ses) diagnostic *m*
diagonal (daï-*æ*-gheu-neul) *n* diagonale *f*; *adj* diagonale
diagram (*daï*-eu-græm) *n* diagramme *m*; schéma *m*, graphique *m*
dialect (*daï*-eu-lèkt) *n* dialecte *m*
diamond (*daï*-eu-meunnd) *n* diamant *m*
diaper (*daï*-eu-peu) *nAm* couche *f*
diaphragm (*daï*-eu-fræm) *n* membrane *f*
diarrhoea (daï-eu-*ri*-eu) *n* diarrhée *f*
diary (*daï*-eu-ri) *n* agenda *m*; journal *m*
dictaphone (*dik*-teu-fô^{ou}n) *n* dictaphone *m*
dictate (dik-*téït*) *v* dicter
dictation (dik-*téï*-cheunn) *n* dictée *f*
dictator (dik-*téï*-teu) *n* dictateur *m*
dictionary (*dik*-cheu-neu-ri) *n* dictionnaire *m*
did (did) *v* (p do)
die (daï) *v* *mourir
diesel (*dii*-zeul) *n* diesel *m*
diet (*daï*-eut) *n* régime *m*
differ (*di*-feu) *v* différer
difference (*di*-feu-reunns) *n* différence *f*; distinction *f*
different (*di*-feu-reunnt) *adj* différent; autre
difficult (*di*-fi-keult) *adj* difficile; fastidieux
difficulty (*di*-fi-keul-ti) *n* difficulté *f*; peine *f*
*dig (digh) *v* creuser; fouiller
digest (di-*djèst*) *v* digérer
digestible (di-*djè*-steu-beul) *adj* diges-

tible

digestion (di-*djèss*-tcheunn) *n* digestion *f*

digit (*di*-djit) *n* chiffre *m*

dignified (*digh*-ni-faïd) *adj* digne

dike (daïk) *n* digue *f*

dilapidated (di-*læ*-pi-déï-tid) *adj* délabré

diligence (*di*-li-djeunns) *n* élan *m*, application *f*

diligent (*di*-li-djeunnt) *adj* zélé, assidu

dilute (daï-*lyoût*) *v* allonger, diluer

dim (dimm) *adj* terne, mat ; obscur, indistinct

dine (daïn) *v* dîner

dinghy (*dinng*-daï) *n* canot *m*

dining-car (*daï*-ninng-kââ) *n* wagon-restaurant

dining-room (*daï*-ninng-roûm) *n* salle à manger

dinner (*di*-neu) *n* dîner *m* ; déjeuner *m*

dinner-jacket (*di*-neu-djæ-kit) *n* smoking *m*

dinner-service (*di*-neu-seû-viss) *n* service de table

diphtheria (dif-θ^{ieu}-ri-eu) *n* diphtérie *f*

diploma (di-*plô^{ou}*-meu) *n* diplôme *m*

diplomat (*di*-pleu-mæt) *n* diplomate *m*

direct (di-*rèkt*) *adj* direct ; *v* diriger ; administrer ; *mettre en scène

direction (di-*rèk*-cheunn) *n* direction *f* ; instruction *f* ; réalisation *f* ; administration *f* ; **directional signal** *Am* indicateur de direction ; **directions for use** mode d'emploi

directive (di-*rèk*-tiv) *n* directive *f*

director (di-*rèk*-teu) *n* directeur *m* ; metteur en scène

dirt (deût) *n* saleté *f*

dirty (*deû*-ti) *adj* sale, souillé

disabled (di-*séï*-beuld) *adj* handicapé, invalide

disadvantage (di-seud-*vâân*-tidj) *n* désavantage *m*

disagree (di-seu-*ghrii*) *v* *être en désaccord

disagreeable (di-seu-*ghrii*-eu-beul) *adj* désagréable

disappear (di-seu-*p^{ieu}*) *v* *disparaître

disappoint (di-seu-*poïnt*) *v* *décevoir

disappointment (di-seu-*poïnt*-meunnt) *n* déception *f*

disapprove (di-seu-*proûv*) *v* désapprouver

disaster (di-*zââ*-steu) *n* désastre *m* ; catastrophe *f*, calamité *f*

disastrous (di-*zââ*-streuss) *adj* désastreux

disc (disk) *n* disque *m* ; **slipped ~** hernie *f*

discard (di-*skââd*) *v* se débarrasser de

discharge (diss-*tchââdj*) *v* décharger ; **~ of** dispenser de

discipline (*di*-si-plinn) *n* discipline *f*

discolour (di-*ska*-leu) *v* décolorer

disconnect (di-skeu-*nèkt*) *v* *disjoindre ; débrancher

discontented (di-skeunn-*tèn*-tid) *adj* mécontent

discontinue (di-skeunn-*ti*-nyoû) *v* suspendre, cesser

discount (*di*-skaount) *n* réduction *f*, rabais *m*

discover (di-*ska*-veu) *v* *découvrir

discovery (di-*ska*-veu-ri) *n* découverte *f*

discuss (di-*skass*) *v* discuter ; *débattre

discussion (di-*ska*-cheunn) *n* discussion *f* ; conversation *f*, délibération *f*, débat *m*

disease (di-*ziiz*) *n* maladie *f*

disembark (di-simm-*bââk*) *v* débarquer

disgrace (diss-*ghréïss*) *n* déshonneur

m

disguise (diss-*ghaïz*) *v* se déguiser; *n* déguisement *m*

disgusting (diss-*gha*-stinng) *adj* répugnant, dégoûtant

dish (dich) *n* assiette *f*; plat *m*

dishonest (di-*so*-nist) *adj* malhonnête

disinfect (di-sinn-*fèkt*) *v* désinfecter

disinfectant (di-sinn-*fèk*-teunnt) *n* désinfectant *m*

dislike (di-*slaïk*) *v* détester, ne pas aimer; *n* répugnance *f*, aversion *f*, antipathie *f*

dislocated (*di*-sleu-kéï-tid) *adj* disloqué

dismiss (diss-*miss*) *v* *renvoyer

disorder (di-*soo*-deu) *n* désordre *m*; confusion *f*

dispatch (di-*spætch*) *v* *envoyer, expédier

display (di-*spléï*) *v* étaler; montrer; *n* exposition *f*

displease (di-*spliiz*) *v* *déplaire

disposable (di-spô*ou*-zeu-beul) *adj* à jeter

disposal (di-spô*ou*-zeul) *n* disposition *f*

dispose of (di-spô*ou*z) disposer de

dispute (di-*spyoût*) *n* discussion *f*; querelle *f*, litige *m*; *v* se disputer, contester

dissatisfied (di-*sæ*-tiss-faïd) *adj* insatisfait

dissolve (di-*zolv*) *v* *dissoudre, diluer

dissuade from (di-s*ou*éïd) dissuader

distance (*di*-steunns) *n* distance *f*; ~ **in kilometres** kilométrage *m*

distant (*di*-steunnt) *adj* éloigné

distinct (di-*stinngkt*) *adj* net; distinct

distinction (di-*stinngk*-cheunn) *n* distinction *f*, différence *f*

distinguish (di-*stinng*-gh*ou*ich) *v* distinguer, discerner

distinguished (di-*stinng*-gh*ou*icht) *adj*

distingué

distress (di-*strèss*) *n* détresse *f*; ~ **signal** signal de détresse

distribute (di-*stri*-byoût) *v* distribuer

distributor (di-*stri*-byou-teu) *n* concessionnaire *m*; distributeur *m*

district (*di*-strikt) *n* district *m*; région *f*; quartier *m*

disturb (di-*steûb*) *v* déranger

disturbance (di-*steû*-beunns) *n* dérangement *m*; agitation *f*

ditch (ditch) *n* fossé *m*

dive (daïv) *v* plonger

diversion (daï-*veû*-cheunn) *n* déviation *f*; diversion *f*

divide (di-*vaïd*) *v* diviser; répartir; séparer

divine (di-*vaïn*) *adj* divin

division (di-*vi*-jeunn) *n* division *f*; séparation *f*; département *m*

divorce (di-*vooss*) *n* divorce *m*; *v* divorcer

dizziness (*di*-zi-neuss) *n* vertige *m*

dizzy (*di*-zi) *adj* étourdi

***do** (doû) *v* *faire; *suffire

dock (dok) *n* dock *m*; quai *m*; *v* accoster

docker (*do*-keu) *n* docker *m*

doctor (*dok*-teu) *n* médecin *m*, docteur *m*

document (*do*-kyou-meunnt) *n* document *m*

dog (dogh) *n* chien *m*

dogged (*do*-ghid) *adj* obstiné

doll (dol) *n* poupée *f*

dome (dô*ou*m) *n* dôme *m*

domestic (deu-*mè*-stik) *adj* domestique; intérieur; *n* domestique *m*

domicile (*do*-mi-saïl) *n* domicile *m*

domination (do-mi-*néï*-cheunn) *n* domination *f*

dominion (deu-*mi*-nyeunn) *n* règne *m*

donate (dô*ou*-*néït*) *v* donner

donation (dô*ou*-*néï*-cheunn) *n* don *m*,

donation f

done (dann) v (pp do)

donkey (*donng*-ki) n âne m

donor (*dô*ᵒᵘ-neu) n donateur m

door (doo) n porte f; **revolving ~** porte tournante; **sliding ~** porte coulissante

doorbell (*doo*-bèl) n sonnette f

door-keeper (*doo*-kii-peu) n portier m

doorman (*doo*-meunn) n (pl -men) portier m

dormitory (*doo*-mi-tri) n dortoir m

dose (dôᵒᵘss) n dose f

dot (dot) n point m

double (*da*-beul) adj double

doubt (daout) v douter de, douter; n doute m; **without ~** sans doute

doubtful (*daout*-feul) adj douteux; incertain

dough (dôᵒᵘ) n pâte f

down¹ (daoun) adv en bas; vers le bas, par terre; adj déprimé; prep le long de, en bas de; **~ payment** acompte m

down² (daoun) n duvet m

downpour (*daoun*-poo) n averse f

downstairs (daoun-*stè*ᵉᵘz) adv en bas

downstream (daoun-*striim*) adv en aval

down-to-earth (daoun-tou-*eû*θ) adj terre-à-terre

downwards (*daoun*-ᵒᵘeudz) adv vers le bas

dozen (*da*-zeunn) n (pl ~, ~s) douzaine f

draft (drââft) n traite f

drag (drægh) v traîner

dragon (*dræ*-gheunn) n dragon m

drain (dréïn) v assécher; drainer; n égout m

drama (*drââ*-meu) n drame m; tragédie f; théâtre m

dramatic (dreu-*mæ*-tik) adj dramatique

dramatist (*dræ*-meu-tist) n dramaturge m

drank (drængk) v (p drink)

draper (*dréï*-peu) n drapier m

drapery (*dréï*-peu-ri) n étoffes fpl

draught (drââft) n courant d'air; **draughts** jeu de dames

draught-board (*drââft*-bood) n damier m

draw (droo) n tirage m

*draw (droo) v dessiner; tirer; retirer; **~ up** rédiger

drawbridge (*droo*-bridj) n pont-levis m

drawer (*droo*-eu) n tiroir m; **drawers** caleçon m

drawing (*droo*-inng) n dessin m

drawing-pin (*droo*-inng-pinn) n punaise f

drawing-room (*droo*-inng-roûm) n salon m

dread (drèd) v *craindre; n crainte f

dreadful (*drèd*-feul) adj terrible, affreux

dream (driim) n rêve m

*dream (driim) v rêver, songer

dress (drèss) v habiller; se *vêtir, s'habiller, *vêtir; panser; n robe f

dressing-gown (*drè*-sinng-ghaoun) n robe de chambre

dressing-room (*drè*-sinng-roûm) n loge f

dressing-table (*drè*-sinng-téï-beul) n coiffeuse f

dressmaker (*drèss*-méï-keu) n couturière f

drill (dril) v forer; entraîner; n foreuse f

drink (drinngk) n apéritif m, boisson f

*drink (drinngk) v *boire

drinking-water (*drinng*-kinng-ᵒᵘoo-teu) n eau potable

drip-dry (drip-*draï*) adj repassage permanent, sans repassage

drive (draïv) n route f ; promenade en voiture

*****drive** (draïv) v *conduire

driver (draï-veu) n conducteur m

drizzle (dri-zeul) n crachin m

drop (drop) v laisser tomber ; n goutte f

drought (draout) n sécheresse f

drown (draoun) v noyer ; *be drowned se noyer

drug (dragh) n drogue f ; médicament m

drugstore (dragh-stoo) nAm droguerie f, pharmacie f ; bazar m

drum (dramm) n tambour m

drunk (dranngk) adj (pp drink) ivre

dry (draï) adj sec ; v sécher ; essuyer

dry-clean (draï-kliin) v nettoyer à sec

dry-cleaner's (draï-klii-neuz) n teinturerie f

dryer (draï-eu) n séchoir m

duchess (da-tchiss) n duchesse f

duck (dak) n canard m

due (dyoû) adj attendu ; payable ; dû

dues (dyoûz) pl droits

dug (dagh) v (p, pp dig)

duke (dyoûk) n duc m

dull (dal) adj ennuyeux ; terne, mat ; émoussé

dumb (damm) adj muet ; bête

dune (dyoûn) n dune f

dung (danng) n fumier m

dunghill (danng-hil) n tas de fumier

duration (dyou-réï-cheunn) n durée f

during (dyou eu-rinng) prep durant, pendant

dusk (dask) n crépuscule m

dust (dast) n poussière f

dustbin (dast-binn) n boîte à ordures

dusty (da-sti) adj poussiéreux

Dutch (datch) adj néerlandais, hollandais

Dutchman (datch-meunn) n (pl -men) Néerlandais m, Hollandais m

dutiable (dyoû-ti-eu-beul) adj imposable

duty (dyoû-ti) n devoir m ; tâche f ; droit d'importation ; **Customs** ~ droit de douane

duty-free (dyoû-ti-frii) adj exempt de droits

dwarf (d^ooof) n nain m

dye (daï) v *teindre ; n teinture f

dynamo (daï-neu-mô^ou) n (pl ~s) dynamo f

dysentery (di-seunn-tri) n dysenterie f

E

each (iitch) adj chaque ; ~ **other** l'un l'autre

eager (ii-gheu) adj désireux, impatient

eagle (ii-gheul) n aigle m

ear (i^eu) n oreille f

earache (i^eu-réïk) n mal d'oreille

ear-drum (i^eu-dramm) n tympan m

earl (eûl) n comte m

early (eû-li) adj tôt

earn (eûnn) v gagner

earnest (eû-nist) n sérieux m

earnings (eû-ninngz) pl revenu m, gains

earring (i^eu-rinng) n boucle d'oreille

earth (eûθ) n terre f ; sol m

earthenware (eû-θeunn-^ouè^eu) n poterie f

earthquake (eûθ-k^ouéïk) n tremblement de terre

ease (iiz) n aisance f ; aise f

east (iist) n est m

Easter (ii-steu) Pâques

easterly (ii-steu-li) adj oriental

eastern (ii-steunn) adj oriental

easy (ii-zi) adj facile ; commode ; ~ **chair** fauteuil m

easy-going (*ii*-zi-ghô^{ou}-inng) *adj* décontracté

* **eat** (iit) *v* manger; dîner

eavesdrop (*iivz*-drop) *v* écouter aux portes

ebony (*è*-beu-ni) *n* ébène *f*

eccentric (ik-*sèn*-trik) *adj* excentrique

echo (è-kô^{ou}) *n* (pl ~es) écho *m*

eclipse (i-*klips*) *n* éclipse *f*

economic (ii-keu-*no*-mik) *adj* économique

economical (ii-keu-*no*-mi-keul) *adj* parcimonieux, économe

economist (i-*ko*-neu-mist) *n* économiste *m*

economize (i-*ko*-neu-maïz) *v* économiser

economy (i-*ko*-neu-mi) *n* économie *f*

ecstasy (*èk*-steu-zi) *n* extase *m*

Ecuador (è-k^{ou}eu-doo) Equateur *m*

Ecuadorian (è-k^{ou}eu-*doo*-ri-eunn) *n* Ecuadorien *m*

eczema (*èk*-si-meu) *n* eczéma *m*

edge (èdj) *n* rebord *m*, bord *m*

edible (è-di-beul) *adj* comestible

edition (i-*di*-cheunn) *n* édition *f*; **morning ~** édition du matin

editor (è-di-teu) *n* rédacteur *m*

educate (è-djou-kéït) *v* former, éduquer

education (è-djou-*kéï*-cheunn) *n* éducation *f*

eel (iil) *n* anguille *f*

effect (i-*fèkt*) *n* résultat *m*, effet *m*; *v* effectuer; **in ~** en fait

effective (i-*fèk*-tiv) *adj* efficace, effectif

efficient (i-*fi*-cheunnt) *adj* efficace

effort (è-feut) *n* effort *m*

egg (ègh) *n* œuf *m*

egg-cup (*ègh*-kap) *n* coquetier *m*

eggplant (*ègh*-plâânt) *n* aubergine *f*

egg-yolk (*ègh*-yô^{ou}k) *n* jaune d'œuf

egoistic (è-ghô^{ou}-*i*-stik) *adj* égoïste

Egypt (*ii*-djipt) Egypte *f*

Egyptian (i-*djip*-cheunn) *adj* égyptien; *n* Egyptien *m*

eiderdown (*aï*-deu-daoun) *n* édredon *m*

eight (éït) *num* huit

eighteen (*éï*-tiin) *num* dix-huit

eighteenth (*éï*-*tiin*θ) *num* dix-huitième

eighth (éïtθ) *num* huitième

eighty (*éï*-ti) *num* quatre-vingts

either (*aï*-ðeu) *pron* l'un ou l'autre; **either ... or** ou ... ou, soit ... soit

elaborate (i-*læ*-beu-réït) *v* élaborer

elastic (i-*læ*-stik) *adj* élastique; flexible; élastique *m*

elasticity (è-læ-*sti*-seu-ti) *n* élasticité *f*

elbow (*èl*-bô^{ou}) *n* coude *m*

elder (*èl*-deu) *adj* plus âgé

elderly (*èl*-deu-li) *adj* âgé

eldest (*èl*-dist) *adj* le plus âgé

elect (i-*lèkt*) *v* *élire

election (i-*lèk*-cheunn) *n* élection *f*

electric (i-*lèk*-trik) *adj* électrique; **~ razor** rasoir électrique; **~ cord** fil électrique

electrician (i-lèk-*tri*-cheunn) *n* électricien *m*

electricity (i-lèk-*tri*-seu-ti) *n* électricité *f*

electronic (i-lèk-*tro*-nik) *adj* électronique

elegance (è-li-gheunns) *n* élégance *f*

elegant (è-li-gheunnt) *adj* élégant

element (è-li-meunnt) *n* élément *m*

elephant (è-li-feunnt) *n* éléphant *m*

elevator (è-li-véï-teu) *nAm* ascenseur *m*

eleven (i-*lè*-veunn) *num* onze

eleventh (i-*lè*-veunnθ) *num* onzième

elf (èlf) *n* (pl elves) elfe *m*

eliminate (i-*li*-mi-néït) *v* éliminer

elm (èlm) *n* orme *m*

else (èls) *adv* autrement

elsewhere (èl-s^{ou}è^{eu}) adv ailleurs

elucidate (i-lou-si-déït) v élucider

emancipation (i-mæn-si-péï-cheunn) n émancipation f

embankment (imm-bængk-meunnt) n berge f

embargo (èm-bââ-ghô^{ou}) n (pl ~es) embargo m

embark (imm-bââk) v embarquer

embarkation (èm-bââ-kéï-cheunn) n embarquement m

embarrass (imm-bæ-reuss) v embarrasser; déconcerter; gêner; **embarrassed** confus

embassy (èm-beu-si) n ambassade f

emblem (èm-bleumm) n emblème m

embrace (imm-bréïss) v *étreindre; n enlacement m

embroider (imm-broï-deu) v broder

embroidery (imm-broï-deu-ri) n broderie f

emerald (è-meu-reuld) n émeraude f

emergency (i-meû-djeunn-si) n cas d'urgence, urgence f; état d'urgence; ~ **exit** sortie de secours

emigrant (è-mi-ghreunnt) n émigrant m

emigrate (è-mi-ghréït) v émigrer

emigration (è-mi-ghréï-cheunn) n émigration f

emotion (i-mô^{ou}-cheunn) n émoi m, émotion f

emperor (èm-peu-reu) n empereur m

emphasize (èm-feu-saïz) v souligner

empire (èm-paï^{eu}) n empire m

employ (imm-ploï) v employer; utiliser

employee (èm-ploï-ii) n employé m

employer (imm-ploï-eu) n employeur m

employment (imm-ploï-meunnt) n emploi m; ~ **exchange** bureau de l'emploi

empress (èm-priss) n impératrice f

empty (èmp-ti) adj vide; v vider

enable (i-néï-beul) v *permettre

enamel (i-næ-meul) n émail m

enamelled (i-næ-meuld) adj émaillé

enchanting (inn-tchâân-tinng) adj splendide, ravissant

encircle (inn-seû-keul) v encercler, entourer

enclose (inng-klô^{ou}z) v *inclure, *joindre

enclosure (inng-klô^{ou}-jeu) n pièce jointe

encounter (inng-kaoun-teu) v rencontrer; n rencontre f

encourage (inng-ka-ridj) v encourager

encyclopaedia (èn-saï-kleu-pii-di-eu) n encyclopédie f

end (ènd) n fin f, bout m; conclusion f; v finir

ending (èn-dinng) n fin f

endless (ènd-leuss) adj infini

endorse (inn-dooss) v endosser

endure (inn-dyou^{eu}) v endurer

enemy (è-neu-mi) n ennemi m

energetic (è-neu-djè-tik) adj énergique

energy (è-neu-dji) n énergie f; puissance f

engage (inng-ghéïdj) v engager; louer; s'engager; **engaged** fiancé; occupé

engagement (inng-ghéïdj-meunnt) n fiançailles fpl; engagement m; ~ **ring** bague de fiançailles

engine (èn-djinn) n machine f, moteur m; locomotive f

engineer (èn-dji-ni^{eu}) n ingénieur m

England (inng-ghleunnd) Angleterre f

English (inng-ghlich) adj anglais

Englishman (inng-ghlich-meunn) n (pl -men) Anglais m

engrave (inng-ghréïv) v graver

engraver (inng-ghréï-veu) n graveur m

engraving (inng-ghréï-vinng) n estampe f; gravure f

enigma (i-*nigh*-meu) n énigme f

enjoy (inn-*djoï*) v jouir de, *prendre plaisir

enjoyable (inn-*djoï*-eu-beul) adj agréable, plaisant; bon

enjoyment (inn-*djoï*-meunnt) n plaisir m

enlarge (inn-*lââdj*) v agrandir; étendre

enlargement (inn-*lââdj*-meunnt) n agrandissement m

enormous (i-*noo*-meuss) adj gigantesque, énorme

enough (i-*naf*) adv assez; adj suffisant

enquire (inng-*k*ᵒᵘ*aï*ᵉᵘ) v s'informer; enquêter

enquiry (inng-*k*ᵒᵘ*aï*ᵉᵘ-ri) n information f; investigation f; enquête f

enter (*èn*-teu) v entrer; *inscrire

enterprise (*èn*-teu-praïz) n entreprise f

entertain (èn-teu-*téïn*) v divertir, amuser; *recevoir

entertainer (èn-teu-*téï*-neu) n animateur m

entertaining (èn-teu-*téï*-ninng) adj amusant, divertissant

entertainment (èn-teu-*téïn*-meunnt) n amusement m, divertissement m

enthusiasm (inn-θyoû-zi-æ-zeumm) n enthousiasme m

enthusiastic (inn-θyoû-zi-æ-stik) adj enthousiaste

entire (inn-*taï*ᵉᵘ) adj tout, entier

entirely (inn-*taï*ᵉᵘ-li) adv entièrement

entrance (*èn*-treunns) n entrée f; accès m

entrance-fee (*èn*-treunns-fii) n prix d'entrée

entry (*èn*-tri) n entrée f; admission f; inscription f; **no** ~ défense d'entrer

envelope (*èn*-veu-lôᵒᵘp) n enveloppe f

envious (*èn*-vi-euss) adj envieux, jaloux

environment (inn-*vaï*ᵉᵘ-reunn-meunnt) n environnement m; environs mpl

envoy (*èn*-voï) n envoyé m

envy (*èn*-vi) n envie f; v envier

epic (*è*-pik) n poème épique; adj épique

epidemic (è-pi-*dè*-mik) n épidémie f

epilepsy (*è*-pi-lèp-si) n épilepsie f

epilogue (*è*-pi-logh) n épilogue m

episode (*è*-pi-sôᵒᵘd) n épisode m

equal (*ii*-kᵒᵘeul) adj égal; v égaler

equality (i-*k*ᵒᵘo-leu-ti) n égalité f

equalize (*ii*-kᵒᵘeu-laïz) v égaliser

equally (*ii*-kᵒᵘeu-li) adv également

equator (i-*k*ᵒᵘ*éï*-teu) n équateur m

equip (i-*k*ᵒᵘip) v équiper

equipment (i-*k*ᵒᵘip-meunnt) n équipement m

equivalent (i-*k*ᵒᵘi-veu-leunnt) adj équivalent

eraser (i-*réï*-zeu) n gomme f

erect (i-*rèkt*) v ériger; adj debout, droit

err (eû) v se tromper, errer

errand (*è*-reunnd) n commission f

error (*è*-reu) n faute f, erreur f

escalator (*è*-skeu-léï-teu) n escalier roulant

escape (i-*skéïp*) v échapper; *fuir; n évasion f

escort[1] (*è*-skoot) n escorte f

escort[2] (i-*skoot*) v escorter

especially (i-*spè*-cheu-li) adv principalement, spécialement

esplanade (è-spleu-*néïd*) n esplanade f

essay (*è*-séï) n essai m; dissertation f, composition f

essence (*è*-seunns) n essence f; fond m, nature f

essential (i-*sèn*-cheul) adj indispensable; fondamental, essentiel

essentially (i-*sèn*-cheu-li) *adv* essentiellement

establish (i-*stæ*-blich) *v* établir

estate (i-*stéït*) *n* propriété *f*

esteem (i-*stiim*) *n* respect *m*, estime *f*; *v* estimer

estimate¹ (*è*-sti-méït) *v* évaluer, estimer

estimate² (*è*-sti-meut) *n* estimation *f*

estuary (*èss*-tchou-eu-ri) *n* estuaire *m*

etcetera (èt-sè-teu-reu) et cætera

etching (*è*-tchinng) *n* eau-forte *f*

eternal (i-*teû*-neul) *adj* éternel

eternity (i-*teû*-neu-ti) *n* éternité *f*

ether (*ii*-θeu) *n* éther *m*

Ethiopia (i-θi-*ô*-pi-eu) Ethiopie *f*

Ethiopian (i-θi-*ô*[ou]-pi-eunn) *adj* éthiopien; *n* Ethiopien *m*

Europe (*you*[eu]-reup) Europe *f*

European (you[eu]-reu-*pii*-eunn) *adj* européen; *n* Européen *m*

evacuate (i-*væ*-kyou-éït) *v* évacuer

evaluate (i-*væl*-you-éït) *v* évaluer

evaporate (i-*væ*-peu-réït) *v* évaporer

even (*ii*-veunn) *adj* lisse, plan, égal; constant; pair; *adv* même

evening (*iiv*-ninng) *n* soir *m*; ~ **dress** tenue de soirée

event (i-*vènt*) *n* événement *m*; cas *m*

eventual (i-*vèn*-tchou-eul) *adj* éventuel; final

ever (*è*-veu) *adv* jamais; toujours

every (*èv*-ri) *adj* tout, chaque

everybody (*èv*-ri-bo-di) *pron* tout le monde

everyday (*èv*-ri-déï) *adj* quotidien

everyone (*èv*-ri-[ou]ann) *pron* chacun, tout le monde

everything (*èv*-ri-θinng) *pron* tout

everywhere (*èv*-ri-[ou]è[eu]) *adv* partout

evidence (*è*-vi-deunns) *n* preuve *f*

evident (*è*-vi-deunnt) *adj* évident

evil (*ii*-veul) *n* mal *m*; *adj* méchant,

mauvais

evolution (ii-veu-*loû*-cheunn) *n* évolution *f*

exact (igh-*zækt*) *adj* juste, exact

exactly (igh-*zækt*-li) *adv* exactement

exaggerate (igh-*zæ*-djeu-réït) *v* exagérer

examination (igh-zæ-mi-*néï*-cheunn) *n* examen *m*; interrogatoire *m*

examine (igh-*zæ*-minn) *v* examiner

example (igh-*zââm*-peul) *n* exemple *m*; **for** ~ par exemple

excavation (èks-keu-*véï*-cheunn) *n* excavation *f*

exceed (ik-*siid*) *v* excéder; surpasser

excel (ik-*sèl*) *v* exceller

excellent (*èk*-seu-leunnt) *adj* excellent

except (ik-*sèpt*) *prep* excepté

exception (ik-*sèp*-cheunn) *n* exception *f*

exceptional (ik-*sèp*-cheu-neul) *adj* extraordinaire, exceptionnel

excerpt (*èk*-seûpt) *n* extrait *m*

excess (ik-*sèss*) *n* excès *m*

excessive (ik-*sè*-siv) *adj* excessif

exchange (iks-*tchéïndj*) *v* échanger, changer; *n* troc *m*; bourse *f*; ~ **office** bureau de change; ~ **rate** cours du change

excite (ik-*saït*) *v* exciter

excitement (ik-*saït*-meunnt) *n* agitation *f*, excitation *f*

exciting (ik-*saï*-tinng) *adj* passionnant

exclaim (ik-*skléïm*) *v* exclamer

exclamation (èk-skleu-*méï*-cheunn) *n* exclamation *f*

exclude (ik-*skloûd*) *v* *exclure

exclusive (ik-*skloû*-siv) *adj* exclusif

exclusively (ik-*skloû*-siv-li) *adv* exclusivement, uniquement

excursion (ik-*skeû*-cheunn) *n* excursion *f*

excuse¹ (ik-*skyoûss*) *n* excuse *f*

excuse² (ik-*skyoûz*) *v* excuser

execute (èk-si-kyoût) v exécuter

execution (èk-si-*kyoû*-cheunn) n exécution f

executioner (èk-si-*kyoû*-cheu-neu) n bourreau m

executive (igh-*zè*-kyou-tiv) adj exécutif; n pouvoir exécutif; exécutif m

exempt (igh-*jèmpt*) v dispenser, exempter; adj exempt

exemption (igh-*zèmp*-cheunn) n exemption f

exercise (*èk*-seu-saïz) n exercice m; v exercer

exhale (èks-*héïl*) v expirer

exhaust (igh-*zoost*) n tuyau d'échappement, échappement m; v exténuer; ~ **gases** gaz d'échappement

exhibit (igh-*zi*-bit) v exposer; exhiber

exhibition (èk-si-*bi*-cheunn) n exhibition f, exposition f

exile (*èk*-saïl) n exile m; exilé m

exist (igh-*zist*) v exister

existence (igh-*zi*-steunns) n existence f

exit (*èk*-sit) n sortie f

exotic (igh-*zo*-tik) adj exotique

expand (ik-*spænd*) v étendre; déployer

expect (ik-*spèkt*) v attendre

expectation (èk-spèk-*téï*-cheunn) n espérance f

expedition (èk-speu-*di*-cheunn) n expédition f

expel (ik-*spèl*) v expulser

expenditure (ik-*spèn*-di-tcheu) n dépense f

expense (ik-*spèns*) n dépense f; **expenses** pl frais mpl

expensive (ik-*spèn*-siv) adj cher; coûteux

experience (ik-*spi*^{eu}-ri-eunns) n expérience f; v éprouver, *vivre, *faire l'expérience de; **experienced** expérimenté

experiment (ik-*spè*-ri-meunnt) n épreuve f, expérience f; v expérimenter

expert (*èk*-speût) n spécialiste m, expert m; adj compétent

expire (ik-*spaï*^{eu}) v *venir à échéance, se terminer, expirer; **expired** périmé

expiry (ik-*spaï*^{eu}-ri) n expiration f

explain (ik-*spléïn*) v expliquer

explanation (èk-spleu-*néï*-cheunn) n éclaircissement m, explication f

explicit (ik-*spli*-sit) adj formel, explicite

explode (ik-*splô*^{ou}d) v exploser

exploit (ik-*sploït*) v exploiter

explore (ik-*sploo*) v explorer

explosion (ik-*splô*^{ou}-jeunn) n explosion f

explosive (ik-*splô*^{ou}-siv) adj explosif; n explosif m

export[1] (ik-*spoot*) v exporter

export[2] (*èk*-spoot) n exportation f

exportation (èk-spoo-*téï*-cheunn) n exportation f

exports (*èk*-spoots) pl exportation f

exposition (èk-speu-*zi*-cheunn) n exposition f

exposure (ik-*spô*^{ou}-jeu) n privation f; exposition f; ~ **meter** photomètre m

express (ik-*sprèss*) v exprimer; manifester; adj exprès; explicite; ~ **train** train express

expression (ik-*sprè*-cheunn) n expression f

exquisite (ik-*sk*^{ou}*i*-zit) adj exquis

extend (ik-*stènd*) v étendre; agrandir; accorder

extension (ik-*stèn*-cheunn) n prolongation f; agrandissement m; ligne intérieure; ~ **cord** rallonge f

extensive (ik-*stèn*-siv) adj considérable; vaste, étendu

extent (ik-*stènt*) n dimension f

exterior (èk-*sti*eu-ri-eu) *adj* extérieur;
n extérieur *m*

external (èk-*steû*-neul) *adj* extérieur

extinguish (ik-*stinng*-ghouich) *v*
*éteindre

extort (ik-*stoot*) *v* extorquer

extortion (ik-*stoo*-cheunn) *n* extorsion
f

extra (*èk*-streu) *adj* supplémentaire

extract¹ (ik-*strækt*) *v* arracher, *extraire

extract² (*èk*-strækt) *n* fragment *m*

extradite (*èk*-streu-daït) *v* extrader

extraordinary (ik-*stroo*-deunn-ri) *adj*
extraordinaire

extravagant (ik-*stræ*-veu-gheunnt) *adj*
exagéré, extravagant

extreme (ik-*striim*) *adj* extrême; *n* extrême *m*

exuberant (igh-*zyoû*-beu-reunnt) *adj*
exubérant

eye (aï) *n* œil *m*

eyebrow (*aï*-braou) *n* sourcil *m*

eyelash (*aï*-læch) *n* cil *m*

eyelid (*aï*-lid) *n* paupière *f*

eye-pencil (*aï*-pèn-seul) *n* crayon pour
les yeux

eye-shadow (*aï*-chæ-dôou) *n* ombre à
paupières

eye-witness (*aï*-ouit-neuss) *n* témoin
oculaire

F

fable (*féï*-beul) *n* fable *f*

fabric (*fæ*-brik) *n* tissu *m*; structure *f*

façade (feu-*sââd*) *n* façade *f*

face (féïss) *n* visage *m*; *v* affronter;
~ **massage** massage facial; **facing**
en face de

face-cream (*féïss*-kriim) *n* crème de
beauté

face-pack (*féïss*-pæk) *n* masque de
beauté

face-powder (*féïss*-paou-deu) *n* poudre de riz

facility (feu-*si*-leu-ti) *n* facilité *f*

fact (fækt) *n* fait *m*; **in** ~ de fait

factor (*fæk*-teu) *n* facteur *m*

factory (*fæk*-teu-ri) *n* usine *f*

factual (*fæk*-tchou-eul) *adj* réel

faculty (*fæ*-keul-ti) *n* faculté *f*; don
m, talent *m*, aptitude *f*

fad (fæd) *n* lubie *f*

fade (féïd) *v* se faner, *déteindre

faience (faï-*anss*) *n* faïence *f*

fail (féïl) *v* échouer; manquer; *omettre; **without** ~ sans faute

failure (*féïl*-yeu) *n* échec *m*

faint (féïnt) *v* s'évanouir; *adj* faible,
vague, défaillant

fair (fèeu) *n* foire *f*; *adj* honnête, juste; blond; beau

fairly (*fèeu*-li) *adv* assez, plutôt

fairy (*fèeu*-ri) *n* fée *f*

fairytale (*fèeu*-ri-téïl) *n* conte de fées

faith (féïθ) *n* foi *f*; confiance *f*

faithful (*féïθ*-foul) *adj* fidèle

fake (féïk) *n* falsification *f*

fall (fool) *n* chute *f*; *nAm* automne *m*
*fall (fool) *v* tomber

false (fools) *adj* faux; inexact; ~
teeth dentier *m*

falter (*fool*-teu) *v* vaciller; balbutier

fame (féïm) *n* renommée *f*, célébrité
f; réputation *f*

familiar (feu-*mil*-yeu) *adj* familier

family (*fæ*-meu-li) *n* famille *f*; ~
name nom de famille

famous (*féï*-meuss) *adj* fameux

fan (fæn) *n* ventilateur *m*; éventail
m; fan *m*; ~ **belt** courroie de ventilateur

fanatical (feu-*næ*-ti-keul) *adj* fanatique

fancy (*fæn*-si) *v* aimer, *avoir envie

de; s'imaginer, imaginer; *n* caprice *m*; imagination *f*

fantastic (fæn-tæ-stik) *adj* fantastique

fantasy (fæn-teu-zi) *n* fantaisie *f*

far (fââ) *adj* loin; *adv* beaucoup; **by ~** de beaucoup; **so ~** jusqu'à maintenant

far-away (fââ-reu-ᵒᵘéï) *adj* éloigné

farce (fââss) *n* farce *f*

fare (fèᵉᵘ) *n* prix du voyage; chère *f*, nourriture *f*

farm (fââm) *n* ferme *f*

farmer (fââ-meu) *n* fermier *m*; **farmer's wife** fermière *f*

farmhouse (fââm-haouss) *n* ferme *f*

far-off (fââ-rof) *adj* lointain

fascinate (fæ-si-néït) *v* fasciner

fascism (fæ-chi-zeumm) *n* fascisme *m*

fascist (fæ-chist) *adj* fasciste

fashion (fæ-cheunn) *n* mode *f*; mode *m*

fashionable (fæ-cheu-neu-beul) *adj* à la mode

fast (fââst) *adj* prompt, rapide; ferme

fast-dyed (fââst-daïd) *adj* lavable, grand teint

fasten (fââ-seunn) *v* attacher; fermer

fastener (fââ-seu-neu) *n* fermeture *f*

fat (fæt) *adj* gras, gros; *n* graisse *f*

fatal (féï-teul) *adj* néfaste, mortel, fatal

fate (féït) *n* destin *m*

father (fââ-ðeu) *n* père *m*

father-in-law (fââ-ðeu-rinn-loo) *n* (pl fathers-) beau-père *m*

fatherland (fââ-ðeu-leunnd) *n* patrie *f*

fatness (fæt-neuss) *n* obésité *f*

fatty (fæ-ti) *adj* gras

faucet (foo-sit) *nAm* robinet *m*

fault (foolt) *n* faute *f*; imperfection *f*, défaut *m*

faultless (foolt-leuss) *adj* impeccable; parfait

faulty (fool-ti) *adj* imparfait, défec-

tueux

favour (féï-veu) *n* faveur *f*; *v* favoriser

favourable (féï-veu-reu-beul) *adj* favorable

favourite (féï-veu-rit) *n* favori *m*; *adj* préféré

fawn (foon) *adj* fauve; *n* faon *m*

fear (fiᵉᵘ) *n* crainte *f*, peur *f*; *v* *craindre

feasible (fii-zeu-beul) *adj* faisable

feast (fiist) *n* fête *f*

feat (fiit) *n* accomplissement *m*

feather (fè-ðeu) *n* plume *f*

feature (fii-tcheu) *n* caractéristique *f*; trait du visage

February (fè-brou-eu-ri) février

federal (fè-deu-reul) *adj* fédéral

federation (fè-deu-réï-cheunn) *n* fédération *f*; confédération *f*

fee (fii) *n* honoraires *mpl*

feeble (fii-beul) *adj* faible

*feed (fiid) *v* nourrir; **fed up with** dégoûté

*feel (fiil) *v* *sentir; palper; **~ like** *avoir envie de

feeling (fii-linng) *n* sensation *f*

fell (fèl) *v* (p fall)

fellow (fè-lôᵒᵘ) *n* gars *m*

felt¹ (fèlt) *n* feutre *m*

felt² (fèlt) *v* (p, pp feel)

female (fii-méïl) *adj* féminin

feminine (fè-mi-ninn) *adj* féminin

fence (fèns) *n* clôture *f*; barrière *f*; *v* *faire de l'escrime

fender (fèn-deu) *n* pare-choc *m*

ferment (feû-mènt) *v* fermenter

ferry-boat (fè-ri-bôᵒᵘt) *n* ferry-boat *m*

fertile (feû-taïl) *adj* fertile

festival (fè-sti-veul) *n* festival *m*

festive (fè-stiv) *adj* de fête

fetch (fètch) *v* apporter; *aller chercher

feudal (fyoû-deul) *adj* féodal

fever (*fii*-veu) *n* fièvre *f*

feverish (*fii*-veu-rich) *adj* fiévreux

few (fyoû) *adj* peu de

fiancé (fi-*an*-séï) *n* fiancé *m*

fiancée (fi-*an*-séï) *n* fiancée *f*

fibre (*faï*-beu) *n* fibre *f*

fiction (*fik*-cheunn) *n* fiction *f*

field (fiild) *n* champ *m*; domaine *m*; ~ **glasses** jumelles *fpl*

fierce (fi^{eu}ss) *adj* féroce; sauvage, violent

fifteen (fif-*tiin*) *num* quinze

fifteenth (fif-*tiin*θ) *num* quinzième

fifth (fifθ) *num* cinquième

fifty (*fif*-ti) *num* cinquante

fig (figh) *n* figue *f*

fight (faït) *n* lutte *f*, combat *m*

*fight (faït) *v* se *battre, *combattre

figure (*fi*-gheu) *n* stature *f*, forme *f*; chiffre *m*

file (faïl) *n* lime *f*; dossier *m*; file *f*

Filipino (fi-li-*pii*-nô^{ou}) *n* Philippin *m*

fill (fil) *v* remplir; ~ **in** remplir; **filling station** station-service *f*; ~ **out** *Am* remplir; ~ **up** *faire le plein

filling (*fi*-linng) *n* plombage *m*; farce *f*

film (film) *n* film *m*; pellicule *f*; *v* filmer

filter (*fil*-teu) *n* filtre *m*

filthy (*fil*-θi) *adj* répugnant, sale

final (*faï*-neul) *adj* final

finance (faï-*næns*) *v* financer

finances (faï-*næn*-siz) *pl* finances *fpl*

financial (faï-*næn*-cheul) *adj* financier

finch (finntch) *n* pinson *m*

*find (faïnd) *v* trouver

fine (faïn) *n* amende *f*; *adj* fin; joli; formidable, merveilleux; ~ **arts** beaux-arts *mpl*

finger (*finng*-gheu) *n* doigt *m*; **little** ~ auriculaire *m*

fingerprint (*finng*-gheu-prinnt) *n* empreinte digitale

finish (*fi*-nich) *v* achever, finir; terminer; *n* fin *f*; ligne d'arrivée

Finland (*finn*-leunnd) Finlande *f*

Finn (finn) *n* Finlandais *m*

Finnish (*fi*-nich) *adj* finlandais

fire (faï^{eu}) *n* feu *m*; incendie *m*; *v* tirer; licencier

fire-alarm (*faï^{eu}*-reu-lââm) *n* alarme d'incendie

fire-brigade (*faï^{eu}*-bri-ghéïd) *n* pompiers

fire-escape (*faï^{eu}*-ri-skéïp) *n* escalier de secours

fire-extinguisher (*faï^{eu}*-rik-stinng-gh^{ou}i-cheu) *n* extincteur *m*

fireplace (*faï^{eu}*-pléïss) *n* cheminée *f*

fireproof (*faï^{eu}*-proûf) *adj* ignifuge; qui va au four

firm (feûmm) *adj* ferme; solide; *n* firme *f*

first (feûst) *num* premier; **at** ~ d'abord; au début; ~ **name** prénom *m*

first-aid (feûst-*éïd*) *n* premier secours; ~ **kit** trousse de secours; ~ **post** poste de secours

first-class (feûst-*klââss*) *adj* de première qualité

first-rate (feûst-*réït*) *adj* de premier ordre, de première qualité

fir-tree (*feû*-trii) *n* conifère *m*, sapin *m*

fish¹ (fich) *n* (pl ~, ~es) poisson *m*; ~ **shop** poissonnerie *f*

fish² (fich) *v* pêcher; **fishing gear** attirail de pêche; **fishing hook** hameçon *m*; **fishing industry** pêche *f*; **fishing licence** permis de pêche; **fishing line** ligne de pêche; **fishing net** filet de pêche; **fishing rod** canne à pêche; **fishing tackle** attirail de pêche

fishbone (*fich*-bô^{ou}n) *n* arête *f*

fisherman (*fi*-cheu-meunn) *n* (pl -men)

pêcheur *m*

fist (fist) *n* poing *m*

fit (fit) *adj* convenable; *n* attaque *f*; *v* *convenir; **fitting room** cabine d'essayage

five (faïv) *num* cinq

fix (fiks) *v* réparer

fixed (fikst) *adj* fixe

fizz (fiz) *n* pétillement *m*

fjord (fyood) *n* fjord *m*

flag (flægh) *n* drapeau *m*

flame (fléïm) *n* flamme *f*

flamingo (fleu-*minng*-ghô^ou) *n* (pl ~s, ~es) flamant *m*

flannel (*flæ*-neul) *n* flanelle *f*

flash (flæch) *n* éclair *m*

flash-bulb (*flæch*-balb) *n* ampoule de flash

flash-light (*flæch*-laït) *n* lampe de poche

flask (flââsk) *n* flacon *m*; **thermos ~** thermos *m*

flat (flæt) *adj* plan, plat; *n* appartement *m*; **~ tyre** pneu crevé

flavour (*fléï*-veu) *n* saveur *f*; *v* assaisonner

fleet (fliit) *n* flotte *f*

flesh (flèch) *n* chair *f*

flew (floû) *v* (p fly)

flex (flèks) *n* fil électrique

flexible (*flèk*-si-beul) *adj* flexible; souple

flight (flaït) *n* vol *m*; **charter ~** vol charter

flint (flinnt) *n* pierre à briquet

float (flô^out) *v* flotter; *n* flotteur *m*

flock (flok) *n* troupeau *m*

flood (flad) *n* inondation *f*; marée haute

floor (floo) *n* sol *m*; étage *m*; **~ show** spectacle de variétés

florist (*flo*-rist) *n* fleuriste *m*

flour (flaou^eu) *n* farine *f*

flow (flô^ou) *v* s'écouler, couler

flower (flaou^eu) *n* fleur *f*

flowerbed (*flaou^eu*-bèd) *n* plate-bande *f*

flower-shop (*flaou^eu*-chop) *n* fleuriste *m*

flown (flô^oun) *v* (pp fly)

flu (floû) *n* grippe *f*

fluent (*floû*-eunnt) *adj* couramment

fluid (*floû*-id) *adj* fluide; *n* liquide *m*

flute (floût) *n* flûte *f*

fly (flaï) *n* mouche *f*; braguette *f*

* fly (flaï) *v* voler

foam (fô^oum) *n* mousse *f*; *v* mousser

foam-rubber (*fô^oum*-ra-beu) *n* caoutchouc mousse

focus (*fô^ou*-keuss) *n* foyer *m*

fog (fogh) *n* brouillard *m*

foggy (*fo*-ghi) *adj* brumeux

foglamp (*fogh*-læmp) *n* phare anti-brouillard

fold (fô^ould) *v* plier; *n* pli *m*

folk (fô^ouk) *n* peuple *m*; **~ song** chanson populaire

folk-dance (*fô^ouk*-dââns) *n* danse folklorique

folklore (*fô^ouk*-loo) *n* folklore *m*

follow (*fo*-lô^ou) *v* *suivre; **following** *adj* prochain, suivant

* be fond of (bii fonnd ov) aimer

food (foûd) *n* nourriture *f*; manger *m*; **~ poisoning** intoxication alimentaire

foodstuffs (*foûd*-stafs) *pl* aliments *mpl*

fool (foûl) *n* idiot *m*, fou *m*; *v* *faire marcher

foolish (*foû*-lich) *adj* sot, stupide; absurde

foot (fout) *n* (pl feet) pied *m*; **~ powder** poudre pour les pieds; **on ~** à pied

football (*fout*-bool) *n* ballon *m*; **~ match** match de football

foot-brake (*fout*-bréïk) *n* frein à pédale

footpath (fout-pââθ) *n* sentier pour piétons

footwear (fout-^{ou}è^{eu}) *n* chaussures

for (foo, feu) *prep* pour; pendant; à cause de, en raison de, par; *conj* car

*****forbid** (feu-*bid*) *v* *interdire

force (fooss) *v* obliger, forcer; *n* puissance *f*, force *f*; **by ~** forcément; **driving ~** force motrice

ford (food) *n* gué *m*

forecast (foo-kââst) *n* prévision *f*; *v* *prévoir

foreground (foo-ghraound) *n* premier plan

forehead (fo-rèd) *n* front *m*

foreign (fo-rinn) *adj* étranger

foreigner (fo-ri-neu) *n* étranger *m*

foreman (foo-meunn) *n* (pl -men) contremaître *m*

foremost (foo-mô^{ou}st) *adj* premier

foresail (foo-séïl) *n* misaine *f*

forest (fo-rist) *n* bois *m*, forêt *f*

forester (fo-ri-steu) *n* forestier *m*

forge (foodj) *v* falsifier

*****forget** (feu-*ghèt*) *v* oublier

forgetful (feu-*ghèt*-feul) *adj* oublieux

*****forgive** (feu-*ghiv*) *v* pardonner

fork (fook) *n* fourchette *f*; bifurcation *f*; *v* bifurquer

form (foom) *n* forme *f*; formulaire *m*; classe *f*; *v* former

formal (foo-meul) *adj* cérémonieux

formality (foo-*mæ*-leu-ti) *n* formalité *f*

former (foo-meu) *adj* ancien; précédent; **formerly** antérieurement, auparavant

formula (foo-myou-leu) *n* (pl ~e, ~s) formule *f*

fort (foot) *n* fort *m*

fortnight (foot-naït) *n* quinze jours

fortress (foo-triss) *n* forteresse *f*

fortunate (foo-tcheu-neut) *adj* heureux

fortune (foo-tchoûn) *n* fortune *f*; sort

m, chance *f*

forty (foo-ti) *num* quarante

forward (foo-^{ou}eud) *adv* en avant; *v* *faire suivre

foster-parents (fo-steu-pè^{eu}-reunnts) *pl* parents nourriciers

fought (foot) *v* (p, pp fight)

foul (faoul) *adj* malpropre; infâme

found¹ (faound) *v* (p, pp find)

found² (faound) *v* fonder, établir

foundation (faoun-*déï*-cheunn) *n* fondation *f*; **~ cream** fond de teint

fountain (faoun-tinn) *n* fontaine *f*; source *f*

fountain-pen (faoun-tinn-pèn) *n* stylo *m*

four (foo) *num* quatre

fourteen (foo-tiin) *num* quatorze

fourteenth (foo-*tiin*θ) *num* quatorzième

fourth (fooθ) *num* quatrième

fowl (faoul) *n* (pl ~s, ~) volaille *f*

fox (foks) *n* renard *m*

fraction (*fræk*-cheunn) *n* fraction *f*

fracture (*fræk*-tcheu) *v* fracturer; *n* fracture *f*

fragile (*fræ*-djaïl) *adj* fragile

fragment (*frægh*-meunnt) *n* fragment *m*; morceau *m*

frame (fréïm) *n* cadre *m*; monture *f*

France (frââns) France *f*

franchise (*fræn*-tchaïz) *n* droit de vote

fraternity (freu-*teû*-neu-ti) *n* fraternité *f*

fraud (frood) *n* fraude *f*

fray (fréï) *v* s'effilocher

free (frii) *adj* libre; gratuit; **~ of charge** gratuit; **~ ticket** billet gratuit

freedom (*frii*-deumm) *n* liberté *f*

*****freeze** (friiz) *v* geler

freezing (*frii*-zinng) *adj* glacial

freezing-point (*frii*-zinng-poïnt) *n* point de congélation

freight (fréït) *n* fret *m*, chargement *m*

freight-train (fréït-tréïn) *nAm* train de marchandises

French (frèntch) *adj* français

Frenchman (frèntch-meunn) *n* (pl -men) Français *m*

frequency (frii-k^{ou}eunn-si) *n* fréquence *f*

frequent (frii-k^{ou}eunnt) *adj* courant, fréquent

fresh (frèch) *adj* frais; ~ **water** eau douce

friction (frik-cheunn) *n* friction *f*

Friday (fraï-di) vendredi *m*

fridge (fridj) *n* réfrigérateur *m*, frigo *m*

friend (frènd) *n* ami *m*; amie *f*

friendly (frènd-li) *adj* gentil; amical

friendship (frènd-chip) *n* amitié *f*

fright (fraït) *n* peur *f*, frayeur *f*

frighten (fraï-teunn) *v* effrayer

frightened (fraï-teunnd) *adj* effrayé; ***be** ~ *être effrayé

frightful (fraït-feul) *adj* terrible, affreux

fringe (frinndj) *n* frange *f*

frock (frok) *n* robe *f*

frog (frogh) *n* grenouille *f*

from (fromm) *prep* de; à partir de

front (frannt) *n* face *f*; **in** ~ **of** devant

frontier (frann-ti^{eu}) *n* frontière *f*

frost (frost) *n* gel *m*

froth (froθ) *n* écume *f*

frozen (frô^{ou}-zeunn) *adj* congelé; ~ **food** aliments surgelés

fruit (froût) *n* fruits; fruit *m*

fry (fraï) *v* *faire sauter; *frire

frying-pan (fraï-inng-pæn) *n* poêle à frire

fuel (fyoû-eul) *n* combustible *m*; essence *f*; ~ **pump** *Am* distributeur d'essence

full (foul) *adj* plein; ~ **board** pension complète; ~ **stop** point *m*; ~ **up** complet

fun (fann) *n* divertissement *m*, plaisir *m*

function (fanngk-cheunn) *n* fonction *f*

fund (fannd) *n* fonds *mpl*

fundamental (fann-deu-*mèn*-teul) *adj* fondamental

funeral (fyoû-neu-reul) *n* funérailles *fpl*

funnel (fa-neul) *n* entonnoir *m*

funny (fa-ni) *adj* drôle, amusant; bizarre

fur (feû) *n* fourrure *f*; ~ **coat** manteau de fourrure; **furs** pelage *m*

furious (fyou^{eu}-ri-euss) *adj* furibond, furieux

furnace (feû-niss) *n* fournaise *f*

furnish (feû-nich) *v* fournir, procurer; installer, meubler; ~ **with** approvisionner en

furniture (feû-ni-tcheu) *n* meubles

furrier (fa-ri-eu) *n* fourreur *m*

further (feû-ðeu) *adj* plus loin; complémentaire

furthermore (feû-ðeu-moo) *adv* en outre

furthest (feû-ðist) *adj* le plus éloigné

fuse (fyoûz) *n* fusible *m*; mèche *f*

fuss (fass) *n* agitation *f*; embarras *m*, chichi *m*

future (fyoû-tcheu) *n* avenir *m*; *adj* futur

G

gable (ghéï-beul) *n* pignon *m*

gadget (ghæ-djit) *n* gadget *m*

gaiety (ghéï-eu-ti) *n* gaîté *f*

gain (ghéïn) *v* gagner; *n* gain *m*

gait (ghéït) *n* allure *f*, démarche *f*

gale (ghéïl) *n* tempête *f*

gall (ghool) *n* bile *f*; ~ **bladder** vésicule biliaire

gallery (*ghæ*-leu-ri) *n* galerie *f*

gallop (*ghæ*-leup) *n* galop *m*

gallows (*ghæ*-lô^{ou}z) *pl* gibet *m*

gallstone (*ghool*-stô^{ou}n) *n* calcul biliaire

game (ghéïm) *n* jeu *m*; gibier *m*; ~ **reserve** réserve zoologique

gang (ghæng) *n* bande *f*; équipe *f*

gangway (*ghæng*-^{ou}éï) *n* passerelle *f*

gaol (djéïl) *n* prison *f*

gap (ghæp) *n* brèche *f*

garage (*ghæ*-râaj) *n* garage *m*; *v* garer

garbage (*ghââ*-bidj) *n* détritus *m*, ordures *fpl*

garden (*ghââ*-deunn) *n* jardin *m*; **public** ~ jardin public; **zoological gardens** jardin zoologique

gardener (*ghââ*-deu-neu) *n* jardinier *m*

gargle (*ghââ*-gheul) *v* se gargariser

garlic (*ghââ*-lik) *n* ail *m*

gas (ghæss) *n* gaz *m*; *nAm* essence *f*; ~ **cooker** cuisinière à gaz; ~ **pump** *Am* pompe à essence; ~ **station** *Am* station-service *f*; ~ **stove** fourneau à gaz

gasoline (*ghæ*-seu-liin) *nAm* essence *f*

gastric (*ghæ*-strik) *adj* gastrique; ~ **ulcer** ulcère à l'estomac

gasworks (*ghæss*-^{ou}eûks) *n* usine à gaz

gate (ghéït) *n* porte *f*; grille *f*

gather (*ghæ*-ðeu) *v* collectionner; se réunir; rentrer

gauge (ghéïdj) *n* jauge *f*

gauze (ghooz) *n* gaze *f*

gave (ghéïv) *v* (p give)

gay (ghéï) *adj* gai; éclatant

gaze (ghéïz) *v* fixer

gear (ghi^{eu}) *n* vitesse *f*; équipement *m*; **change** ~ changer de vitesse; ~ **lever** levier de vitesse

gear-box (*ghi^{eu}*-boks) *n* boîte de vitesse

gem (djèm) *n* joyau *m*, pierre précieuse; bijou *m*

gender (*djèn*-deu) *n* genre *m*

general (*djè*-neu-reul) *adj* général; *n* général *m*; ~ **practitioner** médecin généraliste; **in** ~ en général

generate (*djè*-neu-réït) *v* *produire

generation (djè-neu-*réï*-cheunn) *n* génération *f*

generator (*djè*-neu-réï-teur) *n* générateur *m*

generosity (djè-neu-*ro*-seu-ti) *n* générosité *f*

generous (*djè*-neu-reuss) *adj* large, généreux

genital (*djè*-ni-teul) *adj* génital

genius (*djii*-ni-euss) *n* génie *m*

gentle (*djèn*-teul) *adj* doux; léger; délicat

gentleman (*djèn*-teul-meunn) *n* (pl -men) monsieur *m*

genuine (*djè*-nyou-inn) *adj* authentique

geography (dji-*o*-ghreu-fi) *n* géographie *f*

geology (dji-*o*-leu-dji) *n* géologie *f*

geometry (dji-*o*-meu-tri) *n* géométrie *f*

germ (djeûmm) *n* microbe *m*; germe *m*

German (*djeû*-meunn) *adj* allemand; *n* Allemand *m*

Germany (*djeû*-meu-ni) Allemagne *f*

gesticulate (dji-*sti*-kyou-léït) *v* gesticuler

***get** (ghèt) *v* *obtenir; *aller prendre; *devenir; ~ **back** retourner; ~ **off** descendre; ~ **on** monter; progresser; ~ **up** se lever

ghost (ghô^{ou}st) *n* fantôme *m*; esprit *m*

giant (*djaï*-eunnt) *n* géant *m*

giddiness (*ghi*-di-neuss) *n* vertige *m*

giddy (*ghi*-di) *adj* étourdi

gift (ghift) *n* don *m*, cadeau *m*; talent *m*

gifted (*ghif*-tid) *adj* doué

gigantic (djaï-*ghæn*-tik) *adj* gigantesque

giggle (*ghi*-gheul) *v* glousser

gill (ghil) *n* branchie *f*

gilt (ghilt) *adj* doré

ginger (*djinn*-djeu) *n* gingembre *m*

gipsy (*djip*-si) *n* bohémien *m*

girdle (*gheû*-deul) *n* gaine *f*

girl (gheûl) *n* fille *f*; ~ **guide** scout *m*

*give (ghiv) *v* donner; passer; ~ **away** révéler; ~ **in** céder; ~ **up** renoncer

glacier (*ghlæ*-si-eu) *n* glacier *m*

glad (ghlæd) *adj* joyeux, content; **gladly** avec plaisir, volontiers

gladness (*ghlæd*-neuss) *n* joie *f*

glamorous (*ghlæ*-meu-reuss) *adj* enchanteur, charmant

glamour (*ghlæ*-meu) *n* charme *m*

glance (ghlââns) *n* coup d'œil; *v* jeter un coup d'œil

gland (ghlænd) *n* glande *f*

glare (ghlè[eu]) *n* éclat *m*; éblouissement *m*

glaring (*ghlè[eu]*-rinng) *adj* éblouissant

glass (ghlââss) *n* verre *m*; de verre; **glasses** lunettes *fpl*; **magnifying** ~ verre grossissant

glaze (ghléïz) *v* vernir

glen (ghlèn) *n* gorge *f*

glide (ghlaïd) *v* glisser

glider (*ghlaï*-deu) *n* planeur *m*

glimpse (ghlimmps) *n* aperçu *m*; coup d'œil; *v* *entrevoir

global (*ghlô[ou]*-beul) *adj* mondial

globe (ghlô[ou]b) *n* globe *m*

gloom (ghloûm) *n* ténèbres *fpl*

gloomy (*ghloû*-mi) *adj* sombre

glorious (*ghloo*-ri-euss) *adj* splendide

glory (*ghloo*-ri) *n* gloire *f*; honneur *m*, louange *f*

gloss (ghloss) *n* lustre *m*

glossy (*ghlo*-si) *adj* luisant

glove (ghlav) *n* gant *m*

glow (ghlô[ou]) *v* briller; *n* éclat *m*

glue (ghloû) *n* colle *f*

*go (ghô[ou]) *v* se rendre, *aller; marcher; *devenir; ~ **ahead** continuer; ~ **away** *partir; ~ **back** retourner; ~ **home** rentrer; ~ **in** entrer; ~ **on** continuer; ~ **out** *sortir; ~ **through** endurer

goal (ghô[ou]l) *n* objectif *m*, but *m*

goalkeeper (*ghô[ou]l*-kii-peu) *n* gardien de but

goat (ghô[ou]t) *n* bouc *m*, chèvre *f*

god (ghod) *n* dieu *m*

goddess (*gho*-diss) *n* déesse *f*

godfather (*ghod*-fââ-ðeu) *n* parrain *m*

goggles (*gho*-gheulz) *pl* lunettes de plongée

gold (ghô[ou]ld) *n* or *m*; ~ **leaf** or en feuille

golden (*ghô[ou]l*-deunn) *adj* en or

goldmine (*ghô[ou]ld*-maïn) *n* mine d'or

goldsmith (*ghô[ou]ld*-smiθ) *n* orfèvre *m*

golf (gholf) *n* golf *m*

golf-club (*gholf*-klab) *n* club de golf

golf-course (*gholf*-kooss) *n* terrain de golf

golf-links (*gholf*-linngks) *n* terrain de golf

gondola (*ghonn*-deu-leu) *n* gondole *f*

gone (ghonn) *adv* (pp go) parti

good (ghoud) *adj* bon; sage, brave

good-bye! (ghoud-*baï*) au revoir!

good-humoured (ghoud-*hyoû*-meud) *adj* de bonne humeur

good-looking (ghoud-*lou*-kinng) *adj* joli

good-natured (ghoud-*néï*-tcheud) *adj* de bon caractère

goods (ghoudz) *pl* marchandise *f*, biens *mpl*; ~ **train** train de marchandises

good-tempered (ghoud-*tèm*-peud) *adj* de bonne humeur

goodwill (ghoud-*ou*il) *n* bienveillance *f*

goose (ghoûss) *n* (pl geese) oie *f*

gooseberry (*ghouz*-beu-ri) *n* groseille à maquereau

goose-flesh (*ghoûss*-flèch) *n* chair de poule

gorge (ghoodj) *n* gorge *f*

gorgeous (*ghoo*-djeuss) *adj* magnifique

gospel (*gho*-speul) *n* évangile *m*

gossip (*gho*-sip) *n* commérage *m*; *v* *faire des commérages

got (ghot) *V* (p, pp get)

gout (ghaout) *n* goutte *f*

govern (*gha*-veunn) *V* gouverner

governess (*gha*-veu-niss) *n* gouvernante *f*

government (*gha*-veunn-meunnt) *n* régime *m*, gouvernement *m*

governor (*gha*-veu-neu) *n* gouverneur *m*

gown (ghaoun) *n* robe *f*

grace (ghréïss) *n* grâce *f*; clémence *f*

graceful (*ghréïss*-feul) *adj* charmant, gracieux

grade (ghréïd) *n* grade *m*; *v* classer

gradient (*ghréï*-di-eunnt) *n* inclinaison *f*

gradual (*ghræ*-djou-eul) *adj* graduel

graduate (*ghræ*-djou-éït) *v* *obtenir un diplôme

grain (ghréïn) *n* grain *m*, blé *m*, céréale *f*

gram (ghræm) *n* gramme *m*

grammar (*ghræ*-meu) *n* grammaire *f*

grammatical (ghreu-*mæ*-ti-keul) *adj* grammatical

gramophone (*ghræ*-meu-fôoun) *n* phonographe *m*

grand (ghrænd) *adj* sublime

granddad (*ghræn*-dæd) *n* grand-papa *m*

granddaughter (*ghræn*-doo-teu) *n* petite-fille *f*

grandfather (*ghræn*-fââ-ðeu) *n* grand-père *m*; pépé *m*, bon-papa *m*

grandmother (*ghræn*-ma-ðeu) *n* grand-mère *f*; mémé *f*, bonne-maman *f*

grandparents (*ghræn*-pèeu-reunnts) *pl* grands-parents *mpl*

grandson (*ghræn*-sann) *n* petit-fils *m*

granite (*ghræ*-nit) *n* granit *m*

grant (ghrâânt) *v* accorder; concéder; *n* subvention *f*, bourse *f*

grapefruit (*ghréïp*-froût) *n* pamplemousse *m*

grapes (ghréïps) *pl* raisin *m*

graph (ghræf) *n* diagramme *m*

graphic (*ghræ*-fik) *adj* graphique

grasp (ghrââsp) *v* saisir; *n* prise *f*

grass (ghrââss) *n* herbe *f*

grasshopper (*ghrââss*-ho-peu) *n* sauterelle *f*

grate (ghréït) *n* grille *f*; *v* râper

grateful (*ghréït*-feul) *adj* reconnaissant

grater (*ghréï*-teu) *n* râpe *f*

gratis (*ghræ*-tiss) *adj* gratuit

gratitude (*ghræ*-ti-tyoûd) *n* gratitude *f*

gratuity (ghreu-*tyoû*-eu-ti) *n* pourboire *m*

grave (ghréïv) *n* tombe *f*; *adj* grave

gravel (*ghræ*-veul) *n* gravier *m*

gravestone (*ghréïv*-stôoun) *n* pierre tombale

graveyard (*ghréïv*-yââd) *n* cimetière *m*

gravity (*ghræ*-veu-ti) *n* gravité *f*

gravy (*ghréï*-vi) *n* jus *m*

graze (ghréïz) *v* *paître; *n* égratignure *f*

grease (ghriiss) *n* graisse *f*; *v* graisser

greasy (*ghrii*-si) *adj* graisseux

great (ghréit) *adj* grand; **Great Britain** Grande-Bretagne *f*

Greece (ghriiss) Grèce *f*

greed (ghriid) *n* cupidité *f*

greedy (ghrii-di) *adj* cupide; gourmand

Greek (ghriik) *adj* grec; *n* Grec *m*

green (ghriin) *adj* vert; ~ **card** carte verte

greengrocer (ghriin-ghrô ᵒᵘ-seu) *n* marchand de légumes

greenhouse (ghriin-haouss) *n* serre *f*

greens (ghriinz) *pl* légumes *mpl*

greet (ghriit) *v* saluer

greeting (ghrii-tinng) *n* salutation *f*

grey (ghréï) *adj* gris

greyhound (ghréï-haound) *n* lévrier *m*

grief (ghriif) *n* chagrin *m*; affliction *f*, douleur *f*

grieve (ghriiv) *v* *avoir de la peine

grill (ghril) *n* grill *m*; *v* griller

grill-room (ghril-roûm) *n* rôtisserie *f*

grin (ghrinn) *n* sourire forcé

***grind** (ghraïnd) *v* *moudre; pulvériser

grip (ghrip) *v* saisir; *n* prise *f*, étreinte *f*; *nAm* mallette *f*

grit (ghrit) *n* gravillon *m*

groan (ghrô ᵒᵘn) *v* gémir

grocer (ghrô ᵒᵘ-seu) *n* épicier *m*; **grocer's** épicerie *f*

groceries (ghrô ᵒᵘ-seu-riz) *pl* articles d'épicerie

groin (ghroïn) *n* aine *f*

groove (ghroûv) *n* sillon *m*

gross¹ (ghrô ᵒᵘss) *n* (pl ~) grosse *f*

gross² (ghrô ᵒᵘss) *adj* grossier; brut

grotto (ghro-tô ᵒᵘ) *n* (pl ~es, ~s) grotte *f*

ground¹ (ghraound) *n* fond *m*, sol *m*; ~ **floor** rez-de-chaussée *m*; **grounds** terrain *m*

ground² (ghraound) *v* (p, pp grind)

group (ghroûp) *n* groupe *m*

grouse (ghraouss) *n* (pl ~) coq de bruyère

grove (ghrô ᵒᵘv) *n* bosquet *m*

***grow** (ghrô ᵒᵘ) *v* grandir; cultiver; *devenir

growl (ghraoul) *v* grogner

grown-up (ghrô ᵒᵘn-ap) *adj* adulte; *n* adulte *m*

growth (ghrô ᵒᵘθ) *n* croissance *f*; tumeur *f*

grudge (ghradj) *v* envier

grumble (ghramm-beul) *v* grogner

guarantee (ghæ-reunn-tii) *n* garantie *f*; caution *f*; *v* garantir

guarantor (ghæ-reunn-too) *n* garant *m*

guard (ghââd) *n* garde *m*; *v* surveiller

guardian (ghââ-di-eunn) *n* tuteur *m*

guess (ghèss) *v* deviner; *croire, supposer; *n* conjecture *f*

guest (ghèst) *n* hôte *m*, invité *m*

guest-house (ghèst-haouss) *n* pension *f*

guest-room (ghèst-roûm) *n* chambre d'ami

guide (ghaïd) *n* guide *m*; *v* *conduire

guidebook (ghaïd-bouk) *n* guide *m*

guide-dog (ghaïd-dogh) *n* chien d'aveugle

guilt (ghilt) *n* culpabilité *f*

guilty (ghil-ti) *adj* coupable

guinea-pig (ghi-ni-pigh) *n* cochon d'Inde

guitar (ghi-tââ) *n* guitare *f*

gulf (ghalf) *n* golfe *m*

gull (ghal) *n* mouette *f*

gum (ghamm) *n* gencive *f*; gomme *f*; colle *f*

gun (ghann) *n* fusil *m*, revolver *m*; canon *m*

gunpowder (ghann-paou-deu) *n* poudre à canon

gust (ghast) *n* rafale *f*

gusty (gha-sti) *adj* venteux

gut (ghat) *n* intestin *m*; **guts** cran *m*

gutter (*gha*-teu) *n* caniveau *m*

guy (ghaï) *n* type *m*

gymnasium (djimm-*néï*-zi-eumm) *n* (pl ~s, -sia) gymnase *m*

gymnast (*djimm*-næst) *n* gymnaste *m*

gymnastics (djimm-*næ*-stiks) *pl* gymnastique *f*

gynaecologist (ghaï-neu-*ko*-leu-djist) *n* gynécologue *m*

H

haberdashery (*hæ*-beu-dæ-cheu-ri) *n* mercerie *f*

habit (*hæ*-bit) *n* habitude *f*

habitable (*hæ*-bi-teu-beul) *adj* habitable

habitual (heu-*bi*-tchou-eul) *adj* habituel

had (hæd) *v* (p, pp have)

haddock (*hæ*-deuk) *n* (pl ~) aiglefin *m*

haemorrhage (*hè*-meu-ridj) *n* hémorragie *f*

haemorrhoids (*hè*-meu-roïdz) *pl* hémorroïdes *fpl*

hail (héïl) *n* grêle *f*

hair (hè^{eu}) *n* cheveu *m*; ~ **cream** crème capillaire; ~ **piece** postiche *m*; ~ **rollers** bigoudis *mpl*; ~ **tonic** tonique capillaire

hairbrush (*hè^{eu}*-brach) *n* brosse à cheveux

haircut (*hè^{eu}*-kat) *n* coupe de cheveux

hair-do (*hè^{eu}*-doû) *n* coiffure *f*

hairdresser (*hè^{eu}*-drè-seu) *n* coiffeur *m*

hair-dryer (*hè^{eu}*-draï-eu) *n* sèche-cheveux *m*

hair-grip (*hè^{eu}*-ghrip) *n* pince à cheveux

hair-net (*hè^{eu}*-nèt) *n* résille *f*

hair-oil (*hè^{eu}*-roïl) *n* huile capillaire

hairpin (*hè^{eu}*-pinn) *n* épingle à cheveux

hair-spray (*hè^{eu}*-spréï) *n* laque capillaire

hairy (*hè^{eu}*-ri) *adj* chevelu

half¹ (hââf) *adj* demi; *adv* à moitié

half² (hââf) *n* (pl halves) moitié *f*

half-time (hââf-*taïm*) *n* mi-temps *f*

halfway (hââf-*^{ou}éï*) *adv* à mi-chemin

halibut (*hæ*-li-beut) *n* (pl ~) flétan *m*

hall (hool) *n* vestibule *m*; salle *f*

halt (hoolt) *v* s'arrêter

halve (hââv) *v* diviser en deux

ham (hæm) *n* jambon *m*

hamlet (*hæm*-leut) *n* hameau *m*

hammer (*hæ*-meu) *n* marteau *m*

hammock (*hæ*-meuk) *n* hamac *m*

hamper (*hæm*-peu) *n* panier *m*

hand (hænd) *n* main *f*; *v* *remettre; ~ **cream** crème pour les mains

handbag (*hænd*-bægh) *n* sac à main

handbook (*hænd*-bouk) *n* manuel *m*

hand-brake (*hænd*-bréïk) *n* frein à main

handcuffs (*hænd*-kafs) *pl* menottes *fpl*

handful (*hænd*-foul) *n* poignée *f*

handicraft (*hæn*-di-krââft) *n* travail manuel; artisanat *m*

handkerchief (*hæng*-keu-tchif) *n* mouchoir *m*

handle (*hæn*-deul) *n* manche *m*, poignée *f*; *v* manipuler; traiter

hand-made (hænd-*méïd*) *adj* fait à la main

handshake (*hænd*-chéïk) *n* poignée de main

handsome (*hæn*-seumm) *adj* beau

handwork (*hænd*-^{ou}eûk) *n* travail artisanal

handwriting (*hænd*-raï-tinng) *n* écriture *f*

handy (*hæn*-di) *adj* commode

*hang (hæng) *v* suspendre; pendre

hanger (*hæng*-eu) *n* cintre *m*

hangover (*hæng*-ô^{ou}-veu) *n* gueule de bois

happen (*hæ*-peunn) *v* se *produire, arriver

happening (*hæ*-peu-ninng) *n* événement *m*

happiness (*hæ*-pi-neuss) *n* bonheur *m*

happy (*hæ*-pi) *adj* content, heureux

harbour (*hââ*-beu) *n* port *m*

hard (hââd) *adj* dur; difficile; **hardly** à peine

hardware (*hââd*-^{ou}è^{eu}) *n* quincaillerie *f*; ~ **store** quincaillerie *f*

hare (hè^{eu}) *n* lièvre *m*

harm (hââm) *n* mal *m*; tort *m*; *v* *faire du mal

harmful (*hââm*-feul) *adj* préjudiciable, nuisible

harmless (*hââm*-leuss) *adj* inoffensif

harmony (*hââ*-meu-ni) *n* harmonie *f*

harp (hââp) *n* harpe *f*

harpsichord (*hââp*-si-kood) *n* clavecin *m*

harsh (hââch) *adj* âpre; sévère; cruel

harvest (*hââ*-vist) *n* moisson *f*

has (hæz) *v* (pr have)

haste (héïst) *n* promptitude *f*, hâte *f*

hasten (*héï*-seunn) *v* se hâter

hasty (*héï*-sti) *adj* précipité

hat (hæt) *n* chapeau *m*; ~ **rack** porte-manteau *m*

hatch (hætch) *n* trappe *f*

hate (héït) *v* détester; *haïr; *n* haine *f*

hatred (*héï*-trid) *n* haine *f*

haughty (*hoo*-ti) *adj* hautain

haul (hool) *v* traîner

*have (hæv) *v* *avoir; *faire; ~ **to** *devoir

haversack (*hæ*-veu-sæk) *n* havresac *m*

hawk (hook) *n* faucon *m*

hay (héï) *n* foin *m*; ~ **fever** rhume des foins

hazard (*hæ*-zeud) *n* hasard *m*

haze (héïz) *n* brume *f*

hazelnut (*héï*-zeul-nat) *n* noisette *f*

hazy (*héï*-zi) *adj* brumeux; nébuleux

he (hii) *pron* il

head (hèd) *n* tête *f*; *v* diriger; ~ **of state** chef d'Etat; ~ **teacher** directeur d'école

headache (*hè*-déïk) *n* mal de tête

heading (*hè*-dinng) *n* titre *m*

headlamp (*hèd*-læmp) *n* phare *m*

headland (*hèd*-leunnd) *n* promontoire *m*

headlight (*hèd*-laït) *n* phare *m*

headline (*hèd*-laïn) *n* manchette *f*

headmaster (hèd-*mââ*-steu) *n* directeur d'école

headquarters (hèd-*k*^{ou}*oo*-teuz) *pl* quartier général

head-strong (*hèd*-stronng) *adj* têtu

head-waiter (hèd-^{ou}*éï*-teu) *n* maître d'hôtel

heal (hiil) *v* guérir

health (hèlθ) *n* santé *f*; ~ **centre** dispensaire *m*; ~ **certificate** certificat médical

healthy (*hèl*-θi) *adj* sain

heap (hiip) *n* amoncellement *m*, tas *m*

*hear (hi^{eu}) *v* entendre

hearing (*hi*^{eu}-rinng) *n* ouïe *f*

heart (hâât) *n* cœur *m*; **by** ~ par cœur; ~ **attack** crise cardiaque

heartburn (*hâât*-beunn) *n* brûlures d'estomac

hearth (hââθ) *n* cheminée *f*

heartless (*hâât*-leuss) *adj* insensible

hearty (*hââ*-ti) *adj* cordial

heat (hiit) *n* chaleur *f*; *v* chauffer; **heating pad** coussin chauffant

heater (*hii*-teu) *n* appareil de chauffage; **immersion** ~ thermoplongeur *m*

heath (hiiθ) *n* lande *f*

heathen (*hii*-ðeunn) *n* païen *m*

heather (*hè*-ðeu) *n* bruyère *f*

heating (*hii*-tinng) *n* chauffage *m*

heaven (*hè*-veunn) *n* ciel *m*

heavy (*hè*-vi) *adj* lourd

Hebrew (*hii*-broû) *n* hébreu *m*

hedge (hèdj) *n* haie *f*

hedgehog (*hèdj*-hogh) *n* hérisson *m*

heel (hiil) *n* talon *m*

height (haït) *n* hauteur *f*; sommet *m*, apogée *m*

hell (hèl) *n* enfer *m*

hello! (hè-*lô*ou) bonjour!

helm (hèlm) *n* barre *f*

helmet (*hèl*-mit) *n* casque *m*

helmsman (*hèlmz*-meunn) *n* timonier *m*

help (hèlp) *v* aider; *n* aide *f*

helper (*hèl*-peu) *n* aide *m*

helpful (*hèlp*-feul) *adj* serviable

helping (*hèl*-pinng) *n* portion *f*

hem (hèm) *n* ourlet *m*

hemp (hèmp) *n* chanvre *m*

hen (hèn) *n* poule *f*

henceforth (hèns-*foo*θ) *adv* dorénavant

her (heû) *pron* la *art/pron*, lui; *adj* son

herb (heûb) *n* herbe *f*

herd (heûd) *n* troupeau *m*

here (hi*eu*) *adv* ici; ~ **you are** voilà

hereditary (hi-*rè*-di-teu-ri) *adj* héréditaire

hernia (*heû*-ni-eu) *n* hernie *f*

hero (*hi*eu-rôou) *n* (pl ~es) héros *m*

heron (*hè*-reunn) *n* héron *m*

herring (*hè*-rinng) *n* (pl ~, ~s) hareng *m*

herself (heû-*sèlf*) *pron* se; elle-même

hesitate (*hè*-zi-téït) *v* hésiter

heterosexual (hè-teu-reu-*sèk*-chou-eul) *adj* hétérosexuel

hiccup (*hi*-kap) *n* hoquet *m*

hide (haïd) *n* peau *f*

*hide** (haïd) *v* cacher; dissimuler

hideous (*hi*-di-euss) *adj* hideux

hierarchy (*hai*eu-râa-ki) *n* hiérarchie *f*

high (haï) *adj* haut

highway (*haï*-ouéï) *n* route principale; *nAm* autoroute *f*

hijack (*haï*-djæk) *v* détourner

hike (haïk) *v* faire des randonnées

hill (hil) *n* colline *f*

hillock (*hi*-leuk) *n* monticule *m*

hillside (*hil*-saïd) *n* coteau *m*

hilltop (*hil*-top) *n* sommet de colline *m*

hilly (*hi*-li) *adj* accidenté

him (himm) *pron* le, lui

himself (himm-*sèlf*) *pron* se; lui-même

hinder (*hinn*-deu) *v* gêner

hinge (hinndj) *n* charnière *f*

hip (hip) *n* hanche *f*

hire (haï*eu*) *v* louer; **for** ~ à louer

hire-purchase (haï*eu*-*peû*-tcheuss) *n* achat à tempérament

his (hiz) *adj* son

historian (hi-*stoo*-ri-eunn) *n* historien *m*

historic (hi-*sto*-rik) *adj* historique

historical (hi-*sto*-ri-keul) *adj* historique

history (*hi*-steu-ri) *n* histoire *f*

hit (hit) *n* succès *m*

*hit** (hit) *v* frapper; toucher

hitchhike (*hitch*-haïk) *v* *faire de l'auto-stop

hitchhiker (*hitch*-haï-keu) *n* auto-stoppeur *m*

hoarse (hooss) *adj* rauque, enroué

hobby (*ho*-bi) *n* hobby *m*, passe-temps *m*

hobby-horse (*ho*-bi-hooss) *n* dada *m*

hockey (*ho*-ki) *n* hockey *m*

hoist (hoïst) *v* hisser

hold (hôᵒuld) *n* cale *f*

hold (hôᵒuld) *v* *tenir; garder; ~ **on** s'accrocher; ~ **up** *soutenir

hold-up (*hôᵒul*-dap) *n* attaque *f*

hole (hôᵒul) *n* trou *m*

holiday (*ho*-leu-di) *n* vacances; jour de fête; ~ **camp** camp de vacances; ~ **resort** villégiature *f*; **on** ~ en vacances

Holland (*ho*-leunnd) Hollande *f*

hollow (ho-lôᵒu) *adj* creux

holy (hôᵒu-li) *adj* sacré

homage (*ho*-midj) *n* hommage *m*

home (hôᵒum) *n* maison *f*; foyer *m*, demeure *f*; *adv* chez soi; **at** ~ à la maison

home-made (hôᵒum-*méïd*) *adj* fait à la maison

homesickness (*hôᵒu*m-sik-neuss) *n* mal du pays

homosexual (hôᵒu-meu-*sèk*-chou-eul) *adj* homosexuel

honest (*o*-nist) *adj* honnête; sincère

honesty (*o*-ni-sti) *n* honnêteté *f*

honey (*ha*-ni) *n* miel *m*

honeymoon (*ha*-ni-moûn) *n* lune de miel

honk (hanngk) *vAm* klaxonner

honour (*o*-neu) *n* honneur *m*; *v* honorer, rendre hommage

honourable (*o*-neu-reu-beul) *adj* honorable; honnête

hood (houd) *n* capuchon *m*; *nAm* capot *m*

hoof (hoûf) *n* sabot *m*

hook (houk) *n* crochet *m*

hoot (hoût) *v* klaxonner

hooter (*hoû*-teu) *n* klaxon *m*

hoover (*hoû*-veu) *v* passer l'aspirateur

hop¹ (hop) *v* sautiller; *n* saut *m*

hop² (hop) *n* houblon *m*

hope (hôᵒup) *n* espoir *m*; *v* espérer

hopeful (*hôᵒu*p-feul) *adj* plein d'espoir

hopeless (*hôᵒu*p-leuss) *adj* désespéré

horizon (heu-*raï*-zeunn) *n* horizon *m*

horizontal (ho-ri-*zonn*-teul) *adj* horizontal

horn (hoon) *n* corne *f*; cor *m*; klaxon *m*

horrible (*ho*-ri-beul) *adj* horrible; terrifiant, atroce, horrifiant

horror (*ho*-reu) *n* épouvante *f*, horreur *f*

horse (hooss) *n* cheval *m*

horseman (*hooss*-meunn) *n* (pl -men) cavalier *m*

horsepower (*hooss*-paouᵉu) *n* cheval-vapeur *m*

horserace (*hooss*-réïss) *n* course de chevaux

horseradish (*hooss*-ræ-dich) *n* raifort *m*

horseshoe (*hooss*-choû) *n* fer à cheval

horticulture (*hoo*-ti-kal-tcheu) *n* horticulture *f*

hosiery (*hôᵒu*-jeu-ri) *n* bonneterie *f*

hospitable (*ho*-spi-teu-beul) *adj* hospitalier

hospital (*ho*-spi-teul) *n* hôpital *m*

hospitality (ho-spi-*tæ*-leu-ti) *n* hospitalité *f*

host (hôᵒust) *n* hôte *m*

hostage (*ho*-stidj) *n* otage *m*

hostel (*ho*-steul) *n* auberge *f*

hostess (*hôᵒu*-stiss) *n* hôtesse *f*

hostile (*ho*-staïl) *adj* hostile

hot (hot) *adj* chaud

hotel (hôᵒu-*tèl*) *n* hôtel *m*

hot-tempered (hot-*tèm*-peud) *adj* coléreux

hour (aouᵉu) *n* heure *f*

hourly (*aou*ᵉu-li) *adj* toutes les heures

house (haouss) *n* maison *f*; habitation *f*; immeuble *m*; ~ **agent** agent immobilier; ~ **block** *Am* pâté de maisons; **public** ~ café *m*

houseboat (*haouss*-bôᵒut) *n* maison-bateau

household (*haouss*-hôᵒᵘld) *n* ménage *m*

housekeeper (*haouss*-kii-peu) *n* gouvernante *f*

housekeeping (*haouss*-kii-pinng) *n* travaux ménagers, ménage *m*

housemaid (*haouss*-méïd) *n* bonne *f*

housewife (*haouss*-ᵒᵘaïf) *n* ménagère *f*

housework (*haouss*-ᵒᵘeûk) *n* travaux ménagers

how (haou) *adv* comment; que; ~ **many** combien; ~ **much** combien

however (haou-è-veu) *conj* pourtant, cependant

hug (hagh) *v* *étreindre; *n* étreinte *f*

huge (hyoûdj) *adj* immense, énorme

hum (hamm) *v* fredonner

human (hyoû-meunn) *adj* humain; ~ **being** être humain

humanity (hyou-*mæ*-neu-ti) *n* humanité *f*

humble (*hamm*-beul) *adj* humble

humid (*hyoû*-mid) *adj* humide

humidity (hyou-*mi*-deu-ti) *n* humidité *f*

humorous (*hyoû*-meu-reuss) *adj* comique, spirituel, drôle

humour (*hyoû*-meu) *n* humour *m*

hundred (*hann*-dreud) *n* cent

Hungarian (hanng-*ghè*ᵉᵘ-ri-eunn) *adj* hongrois; *n* Hongrois *m*

Hungary (*hanng*-gheu-ri) Hongrie *f*

hunger (*hanng*-gheu) *n* faim *f*

hungry (*hanng*-ghri) *adj* affamé

hunt (hannt) *v* chasser; *n* chasse *f*; ~ **for** chercher

hunter (*hann*-teu) *n* chasseur *m*

hurricane (*ha*-ri-keunn) *n* ouragan *m*; ~ **lamp** lampe-tempête *f*

hurry (*ha*-ri) *v* se dépêcher, se presser; *n* hâte *f*; **in a** ~ en vitesse

***hurt** (heût) *v* *faire mal, blesser; offenser

hurtful (*heût*-feul) *adj* nuisible

husband (*haz*-beunnd) *n* époux *m*, mari *m*

hut (hat) *n* hutte *f*

hydrogen (*haï*-dreu-djeunn) *n* hydrogène *m*

hygiene (*haï*-djiin) *n* hygiène *f*

hygienic (haï-*djii*-nik) *adj* hygiénique

hymn (himm) *n* hymne *m*

hyphen (*haï*-feunn) *n* trait d'union

hypocrisy (hi-*po*-kreu-si) *n* hypocrisie *f*

hypocrite (*hi*-peu-krit) *n* hypocrite *m*

hypocritical (hi-peu-*kri*-ti-keul) *adj* hypocrite, fourbe

hysterical (hi-*stè*-ri-keul) *adj* hystérique

I

I (aï) *pron* je

ice (aïss) *n* glace *f*

ice-bag (*aïss*-bægh) *n* sac à glace

ice-cream (*aïss*-kriim) *n* crème glacée, glace *f*

Iceland (*aïss*-leunnd) Islande *f*

Icelander (*aïss*-leunn-deu) *n* Islandais *m*

Icelandic (aïss-*læn*-dik) *adj* islandais

icon (*aï*-konn) *n* icône *f*

idea (aï-*di*ᵉᵘ) *n* idée *f*; pensée *f*; notion *f*, concept *m*

ideal (aï-*di*ᵉᵘl) *adj* idéal; *n* idéal *m*

identical (aï-*dèn*-ti-keul) *adj* identique

identification (aï-dèn-ti-fi-*kéï*-cheunn) *n* identification *f*

identify (aï-*dèn*-ti-faï) *v* identifier

identity (aï-*dèn*-teu-ti) *n* identité *f*; ~ **card** carte d'identité

idiom (*i*-di-eumm) *n* idiome *m*

idiomatic (i-di-eu-*mæ*-tik) *adj* idiomatique

idiot (*i*-di-eut) *n* idiot *m*

idiotic (i-di-*o*-tik) *adj* idiot

idle (aï-deul) *adj* oisif; futile

idol (aï-deul) *n* idole *f*

if (if) *conj* si

ignition (igh-*ni*-cheunn) *n* allumage *m*; ~ **coil** bobine d'allumage

ignorant (*igh*-neu-reunnt) *adj* ignorant

ignore (igh-*noo*) *v* ignorer

ill (il) *adj* malade; mauvais; méchant

illegal (i-*lii*-gheul) *adj* illégal

illegible (i-*lè*-djeu-beul) *adj* illisible

illiterate (i-*li*-teu-reut) *n* illettré *m*

illness (*il*-neuss) *n* maladie *f*

illuminate (i-*loû*-mi-néït) *v* illuminer

illumination (i-loû-mi-*néï*-cheunn) *n* illumination *f*

illusion (i-*loû*-jeunn) *n* illusion *f*

illustrate (*i*-leu-stréït) *v* illustrer

illustration (i-leu-*stréï*-cheunn) *n* illustration *f*

image (*i*-midj) *n* image *f*

imaginary (i-*mæ*-dji-neu-ri) *adj* imaginaire

imagination (i-mæ-dji-*néï*-cheunn) *n* imagination *f*

imagine (i-*mæ*-djinn) *v* imaginer; s'imaginer; se figurer

imitate (*i*-mi-téït) *v* imiter

imitation (i-mi-*téï*-cheunn) *n* imitation *f*

immediate (i-*mii*-dyeut) *adj* immédiat

immediately (i-*mii*-dyeut-li) *adv* sur-le-champ, tout de suite, immédiatement

immense (i-*mèns*) *adj* immense, énorme

immigrant (*i*-mi-ghreunnt) *n* immigrant *m*

immigrate (*i*-mi-ghréït) *v* immigrer

immigration (i-mi-*ghréï*-cheunn) *n* immigration *f*

immodest (i-*mo*-dist) *adj* immodeste

immunity (i-*myoû*-neu-ti) *n* immunité *f*

immunize (*i*-myou-naïz) *v* immuniser

impartial (imm-*pââ*-cheul) *adj* impartial

impassable (imm-*pââ*-seu-beul) *adj* impraticable

impatient (imm-*péï*-cheunnt) *adj* impatient

impede (imm-*piid*) *v* entraver

impediment (imm-*pè*-di-meunnt) *n* entrave *f*

imperfect (imm-*peû*-fikt) *adj* imparfait

imperial (imm-*piºu*-ri-eul) *adj* impérial

impersonal (imm-*peû*-seu-neul) *adj* impersonnel

impertinence (imm-*peû*-ti-neunns) *n* impertinence *f*

impertinent (imm-*peû*-ti-neunnt) *adj* insolent, effronté, impertinent

implement[1] (*imm*-pli-meunnt) *n* instrument *m*, outil *m*

implement[2] (*imm*-pli-mènt) *v* réaliser

imply (imm-*plaï*) *v* impliquer; comporter

impolite (imm-peu-*laït*) *adj* impoli

import[1] (imm-*poot*) *v* importer

import[2] (*imm*-poot) *n* importation *f*; ~ **duty** taxe d'importation

importance (imm-*poo*-teunns) *n* importance *f*

important (imm-*poo*-teunnt) *adj* important

importer (imm-*poo*-teu) *n* importateur *m*

imposing (imm-*pôºu*-zinng) *adj* imposant

impossible (imm-*po*-seu-beul) *adj* impossible

impotence (*imm*-peu-teunns) *n* impotence *f*

impotent (*imm*-peu-teunnt) *adj* impotent

impound (imm-*paound*) *v* confisquer

impress (imm-*prèss*) *v* *faire impression sur, impressionner

impression (imm-*prè*-cheunn) *n* impression *f*

impressive (imm-*prè*-siv) *adj* impressionnant

imprison (imm-*pri*-zeunn) *v* emprisonner

imprisonment (imm-*pri*-zeunn-meunnt) *n* emprisonnement *m*

improbable (imm-*pro*-beu-beul) *adj* improbable

improper (imm-*pro*-peu) *adj* impropre

improve (imm-*proûv*) *v* améliorer

improvement (imm-*proûv*-meunnt) *n* amélioration *f*

improvise (*imm*-preu-vaïz) *v* improviser

impudent (*imm*-pyou-deunnt) *adj* insolent

impulse (*imm*-pals) *n* impulsion *f*; stimulant *m*

impulsive (imm-*pal*-siv) *adj* impulsif

in (inn) *prep* en; dans, sur; *adv* dedans

inaccessible (i-næk-*sè*-seu-beul) *adj* inaccessible

inaccurate (i-*næ*-kyou-reut) *adj* incorrect

inadequate (i-*næ*-di-k^ou-eut) *adj* inadéquat

incapable (inng-*kéï*-peu-beul) *adj* incapable

incense (*inn*-sèns) *n* encens *m*

incident (*inn*-si-deunnt) *n* incident *m*

incidental (inn-si-*dèn*-teul) *adj* fortuit

incite (inn-*saït*) *v* inciter

inclination (inng-kli-*néï*-cheunn) *n* penchant *m*

incline (inng-*klaïn*) *n* pente *f*

inclined (inng-*klaïnd*) *adj* disposé, enclin; *be ~ to* *v* *avoir tendance

include (inng-*kloûd*) *v* *comprendre, *inclure

inclusive (inng-*kloû*-siv) *adj* compris

income (*inng*-keumm) *n* revenu *m*

income-tax (*inng*-keumm-tæks) *n* impôt sur le revenu

incompetent (inng-*komm*-peu-teunnt) *adj* incompétent

incomplete (inn-keumm-*pliit*) *adj* incomplet

inconceivable (inng-keunn-*sii*-veu-beul) *adj* inconcevable

inconspicuous (inng-keunn-*spi*-kyou-euss) *adj* discret

inconvenience (inng-keunn-*vii*-nyeunns) *n* désagrément *m*, inconvénient *m*

inconvenient (inng-keunn-*vii*-nyeunnt) *adj* inopportun; gênant

incorrect (inng-keu-*rèkt*) *adj* inexact, incorrect

increase¹ (inng-*kriiss*) *v* augmenter; s'accumuler, *croître

increase² (*inng*-kriiss) *n* augmentation *f*; relèvement *m*

incredible (inng-*krè*-deu-beul) *adj* incroyable

incurable (inng-*kyou^eu*-reu-beul) *adj* incurable

indecent (inn-*dii*-seunnt) *adj* indécent

indeed (inn-*diid*) *adv* en effet

indefinite (inn-*dè*-fi-nit) *adj* indéfini

indemnity (inn-*dèm*-neu-ti) *n* dédommagement *m*, indemnité *f*

independence (inn-di-*pèn*-deunns) *n* indépendance *f*

independent (inn-di-*pèn*-deunnt) *adj* indépendant; autonome

index (*inn*-dèks) *n* index *m*; *~ finger* index *m*

India (*inn*-di-eu) Inde *f*

Indian (*inn*-di-eunn) *adj* indien; *n* Indien *m*

indicate (*inn*-di-kéït) *v* signaler, indiquer

indication (inn-di-*kéï*-cheunn) *n* signe *m*, indication *f*

indicator (*inn*-di-kéï-teu) *n* clignotant *m*

indifferent (inn-*di*-feu-reunnt) *adj* indifférent

indigestion (inn-di-*djèss*-tcheunn) *n* indigestion *f*

indignation (inn-digh-*néï*-cheunn) *n* indignation *f*

indirect (inn-di-*rèkt*) *adj* indirect

individual (inn-di-*vi*-djou-eul) *adj* particulier, individuel; *n* individu *m*

Indonesia (inn-deu-*nii*-zi-eu) Indonésie *f*

Indonesian (inn-deu-*nii*-zi-eunn) *adj* indonésien; *n* Indonésien *m*

indoor (*inn*-doo) *adj* intérieur

indoors (inn-*dooz*) *adv* à l'intérieur

indulge (inn-*daldj*) *v* céder

industrial (inn-*da*-stri-eul) *adj* industriel; ~ **area** zone industrielle

industrious (inn-*da*-stri-euss) *adj* industrieux

industry (*inn*-deu-stri) *n* industrie *f*

inedible (i-*nè*-di-beul) *adj* immangeable

inefficient (i-ni-*fi*-cheunnt) *adj* inefficace

inevitable (i-*nè*-vi-teu-beul) *adj* inévitable

inexpensive (i-nik-*spèn*-siv) *adj* bon marché

inexperienced (i-nik-*spieu*-ri-eunnst) *adj* inexpérimenté

infant (*inn*-feunnt) *n* nourrisson *m*

infantry (*inn*-feunn-tri) *n* infanterie *f*

infect (inn-*fèkt*) *v* infecter

infection (inn-*fèk*-cheunn) *n* infection *f*

infectious (inn-*fèk*-cheuss) *adj* infectieux

infer (inn-*feû*) *v* *déduire

inferior (inn-*fieu*-ri-eu) *adj* moindre, inférieur

infinite (*inn*-fi-neut) *adj* infini

infinitive (inn-*fi*-ni-tiv) *n* infinitif *m*

infirmary (inn-*feû*-meu-ri) *n* infirmerie *f*

inflammable (inn-*flæ*-meu-beul) *adj* inflammable

inflammation (inn-fleu-*méï*-cheunn) *n* inflammation *f*

inflatable (inn-*fléï*-teu-beul) *adj* gonflable

inflate (inn-*fléït*) *v* gonfler

inflation (inn-*fléï*-cheunn) *n* inflation *f*

influence (*inn*-flou-eunns) *n* influence *f*; *v* influencer

influential (inn-flou-*èn*-cheul) *adj* influent

influenza (inn-flou-*èn*-zeu) *n* grippe *f*

inform (inn-*foom*) *v* informer; *mettre au courant, communiquer

informal (inn-*foo*-meul) *adj* sans cérémonie

information (inn-feu-*méï*-cheunn) *n* information *f*; renseignement *m*, communication *f*; ~ **bureau** bureau de renseignements

infra-red (inn-freu-*rèd*) *adj* infrarouge

infrequent (inn-*frii*-k^{ou}eunnt) *adj* peu fréquent

ingredient (inng-*ghrii*-di-eunnt) *n* ingrédient *m*

inhabit (inn-*hæ*-bit) *v* habiter

inhabitable (inn-*hæ*-bi-teu-beul) *adj* habitable

inhabitant (inn-*hæ*-bi-teunnt) *n* habitant *m*

inhale (inn-*héïl*) *v* inhaler

inherit (inn-*hè*-rit) *v* hériter

inheritance (inn-*hè*-ri-teunns) *n* héritage *m*

initial (i-*ni*-cheul) *adj* initial; *n* initiale *f*; *v* parapher

initiative (i-*ni*-cheu-tiv) *n* initiative *f*

inject (inn-*djèkt*) *v* injecter

injection (inn-*djèk*-cheunn) *n* injection *f*

injure (*inn*-djeu) *v* blesser; offenser
injury (*inn*-djeu-ri) *n* blessure *f*; lésion *f*
injustice (inn-*dja*-stiss) *n* injustice *f*
ink (inngk) *n* encre *f*
inlet (*inn*-lèt) *n* crique *f*
inn (inn) *n* auberge *f*
inner (*i*-neu) *adj* intérieur; ~ **tube** chambre à air
inn-keeper (*inn*-kii-peu) *n* aubergiste *m*
innocence (*i*-neu-seunns) *n* innocence *f*
innocent (*i*-neu-seunnt) *adj* innocent
inoculate (i-*no*-kyou-léit) *v* inoculer
inoculation (i-no-kyou-*léï*-cheunn) *n* inoculation *f*
inquire (inng-*k*ᵒᵘ*aï*ᵉᵘ) *v* se renseigner, s'informer
inquiry (inng-*k*ᵒᵘ*aï*ᵉᵘ-ri) *n* question *f*, enquête *f*; ~ **office** bureau de renseignements
inquisitive (inng-*k*ᵒᵘ*i*-zeu-tiv) *adj* curieux
insane (inn-*séïn*) *adj* fou
inscription (inn-*skrip*-cheunn) *n* inscription *f* ·
insect (*inn*-sèkt) *n* insecte *m*; ~ **repellent** insectifuge *m*
insecticide (inn-*sèk*-ti-saïd) *n* insecticide *m*
insensitive (inn-*sèn*-seu-tiv) *adj* insensible
insert (inn-*seût*) *v* insérer
inside (inn-*saïd*) *n* intérieur *m*; *adj* intérieur; *adv* à l'intérieur; dedans; *prep* dans, à l'intérieur de; ~ **out** à l'envers; **insides** entrailles *fpl*
insight (*inn*-saït) *n* compréhension *f*
insignificant (inn-sigh-*ni*-fi-keunnt) *adj* insignifiant; sans importance; futile
insist (inn-*sist*) *v* insister; persister
insolence (*inn*-seu-leunns) *n* insolence *f*

insolent (*inn*-seu-leunnt) *adj* insolent
insomnia (inn-*somm*-ni-eu) *n* insomnie *f*
inspect (inn-*spèkt*) *v* inspecter
inspection (inn-*spèk*-cheunn) *n* inspection *f*; contrôle *m*
inspector (inn-*spèk*-teu) *n* inspecteur *m*
inspire (inn-*spaï*ᵉᵘ) *v* inspirer
install (inn-*stool*) *v* installer
installation (inn-steu-*léï*-cheunn) *n* installation *f*
instalment (inn-*stool*-meunnt) *n* paiement à tempérament
instance (*inn*-steunns) *n* exemple *m*; cas *m*; **for** ~ par exemple
instant (*inn*-steunnt) *n* instant *m*
instantly (*inn*-steunnt-li) *adv* instantanément, tout de suite, immédiatement
instead of (inn-*stèd* ov) au lieu de
instinct (*inn*-stinngkt) *n* instinct *m*
institute (*inn*-sti-tyoût) *n* institut *m*; institution *f*; *v* instituer
institution (inn-sti-*tyoû*-cheunn) *n* institution *f*
instruct (inn-*strakt*) *v* *instruire
instruction (inn-*strak*-cheunn) *n* instruction *f*
instructive (inn-*strak*-tiv) *adj* instructif
instructor (inn-*strak*-teu) *n* instructeur *m*
instrument (*inn*-strou-meunnt) *n* instrument *m*; **musical** ~ instrument de musique
insufficient (*inn*-seu-*fi*-cheunnt) *adj* insuffisant
insulate (*inn*-syou-léit) *v* isoler
insulation (inn-syou-*léï*-cheunn) *n* isolation *f*
insulator (*inn*-syou-léï-teu) *n* isolateur *m*
insult[1] (inn-*salt*) *v* insulter

insult² (*inn*-salt) *n* insulte *f*

insurance (inn-*chou^eu*-reunns) *n* assurance *f*; ~ **policy** police d'assurance

insure (inn-*chou^eu*) *v* assurer

intact (inn-*tækt*) *adj* intact

intellect (*inn*-teu-lèkt) *n* intellect *m*, intelligence *f*

intellectual (inn-teu-*lèk*-tchou-eul) *adj* intellectuel

intelligence (inn-*tè*-li-djeunns) *n* intelligence *f*

intelligent (inn-*tè*-li-djeunnt) *adj* intelligent

intend (inn-*tènd*) *v* *avoir l'intention de

intense (inn-*tèns*) *adj* intense; vif

intention (inn-*tèn*-cheunn) *n* intention *f*

intentional (inn-*tèn*-cheu-neul) *adj* intentionnel

intercourse (*inn*-teu-kooss) *n* rapport *m*

interest (*inn*-treust) *n* intérêt *m*; *v* intéresser

interesting (*inn*-treu-stinng) *adj* intéressant

interfere (inn-teu-*fi^eu*) *v* *intervenir; ~ **with** se mêler de

interference (inn-teu-*fi^eu*-reunns) *n* ingérence *f*

interim (*inn*-teu-rimm) *n* intérim *m*

interior (inn-*ti^eu*-ri-eu) *n* intérieur *m*

interlude (*inn*-teu-loûd) *n* interlude *m*

intermediary (inn-teu-*mii*-dyeu-ri) *n* intermédiaire *m*

intermission (inn-teu-*mi*-cheunn) *n* entracte *m*

internal (inn-*teû*-neul) *adj* intérieur, interne

international (inn-teu-*næ*-cheu-neul) *adj* international

interpret (inn-*teû*-prit) *v* interpréter

interpreter (inn-*teû*-pri-teu) *n* interprète *m*

interrogate (inn-*tè*-reu-ghéït) *v* interroger

interrogation (inn-tè-reu-*ghéi*-cheunn) *n* interrogatoire *m*

interrogative (inn-teu-*ro*-gheu-tiv) *adj* interrogatif

interrupt (inn-teu-*rapt*) *v* *interrompre

interruption (inn-teu-*rap*-cheunn) *n* interruption *f*

intersection (inn-teu-*sèk*-cheunn) *n* intersection *f*

interval (*inn*-teu-veul) *n* entracte *m*; intervalle *m*

intervene (inn-teu-*viin*) *v* *intervenir

interview (*inn*-teu-vyoû) *n* entrevue *f*, interview *f*

intestine (inn-*tè*-stinn) *n* intestin *m*

intimate (*inn*-ti-meut) *adj* intime

into (*inn*-tou) *prep* dans

intolerable (inn-*to*-leu-reu-beul) *adj* intolérable

intoxicated (inn-*tok*-si-kéï-tid) *adj* ivre

intrigue (inn-*triigh*) *n* intrigue *f*

introduce (inn-treu-*dyoûss*) *v* présenter; *introduire

introduction (inn-treu-*dak*-cheunn) *n* présentation *f*; introduction *f*

invade (inn-*véïd*) *v* envahir

invalid¹ (*inn*-veu-liid) *n* infirme *m*; *adj* infirme

invalid² (inn-*væ*-lid) *adj* nul

invasion (inn-*véï*-jeunn) *n* invasion *f*

invent (inn-*vènt*) *v* inventer

invention (inn-*vèn*-cheunn) *n* invention *f*

inventive (inn-*vèn*-tiv) *adj* inventif

inventor (inn-*vèn*-teu) *n* inventeur *m*

inventory (*inn*-veunn-tri) *n* inventaire *m*

invert (inn-*veût*) *v* intervertir

invest (inn-*vèst*) *v* investir; placer

investigate (inn-*vè*-sti-ghéït) *v* enquêter

investigation (inn-vè-sti-*ghéï*-cheunn) *n* investigation *f*

investment (inn-*vèst*-meunnt) *n* investissement *m* ; placement *m*

investor (inn-*vè*-steu) *n* investisseur *m*

invisible (inn-*vi*-zeu-beul) *adj* invisible

invitation (inn-vi-*téï*-cheunn) *n* invitation *f*

invite (inn-*vaït*) *v* inviter

invoice (*inn*-voïss) *n* facture *f*

involve (inn-*volv*) *v* impliquer

inwards (*inn*-^{ou}eudz) *adv* vers l'intérieur

iodine (*aï*-eu-diin) *n* iode *m*

Iran (i-*râân*) Iran *m*

Iranian (i-*réï*-ni-eunn) *adj* iranien ; *n* Iranien *m*

Iraq (i-*rââk*) Irak *m*

Iraqi (i-*rââ*-ki) *adj* irakien ; *n* Irakien *m*

irascible (i-*ræ*-si-beul) *adj* irascible

Ireland (*aï^{eu}*-leunnd) Irlande *f*

Irish (*aï^{eu}*-rich) *adj* irlandais

Irishman (*aï^{eu}*-rich-meunn) *n* (pl -men) Irlandais *m*

iron (*aï*-eunn) *n* fer *m* ; fer à repasser ; en fer ; *v* repasser

ironical (aï-*ro*-ni-keul) *adj* ironique

ironworks (*aï*-eunn-^{ou}eûks) *n* fonderie *f*

irony (*aï^{eu}*-reu-ni) *n* ironie *f*

irregular (i-*rè*-ghyou-leu) *adj* irrégulier

irreparable (i-*rè*-peu-reu-beul) *adj* irréparable

irrevocable (i-*rè*-veu-keu-beul) *adj* irrévocable

irritable (*i*-ri-teu-beul) *adj* irritable

irritate (*i*-ri-téït) *v* agacer, irriter

is (iz) *v* (pr be)

island (*aï*-leunnd) *n* île *f*

isolate (*aï*-seu-léït) *v* isoler

isolation (aï-seu-*léï*-cheunn) *n* isolement *m* ; isolation *f*

Israel (*iz*-réïl) Israël *m*

Israeli (iz-*réï*-li) *adj* israélien ; *n* Israélien *m*

issue (*i*-choû) *v* distribuer ; *n* émission *f*, tirage *m*, édition *f* ; question *f*, sujet *m* ; conséquence *f*, issue *f*, résultat *m*, conclusion *f*, fin *f*

isthmus (*iss*-meuss) *n* isthme *m*

it (it) *pron* le

Italian (i-*tæl*-yeunn) *adj* italien ; *n* Italien *m*

italics (i-*tæ*-liks) *pl* italiques *mpl*

Italy (*i*-teu-li) Italie *f*

itch (itch) *n* démangeaison *f* ; prurit *m* ; *v* démanger

item (*aï*-teumm) *n* article *m* ; point *m*

itinerant (aï-*ti*-neu-reunnt) *adj* ambulant

itinerary (aï-*ti*-neu-reu-ri) *n* itinéraire *m*

ivory (*aï*-veu-ri) *n* ivoire *m*

ivy (*aï*-vi) *n* lierre *m*

J

jack (djæk) *n* cric *m*

jacket (*djæ*-kit) *n* veste *f*, veston *m* ; jaquette *f*

jade (djéïd) *n* jade *m*

jail (djéïl) *n* prison *f*

jailer (*djéï*-leu) *n* geôlier *m*

jam (djæm) *n* confiture *f* ; embouteillage *m*

janitor (*djæ*-ni-teu) *n* concierge *m*

January (*djæ*-nyou-eu-ri) janvier

Japan (djeu-*pæn*) Japon *m*

Japanese (djæ-peu-*niiz*) *adj* japonais ; *n* Japonais *m*

jar (djââ) *n* jarre *f*

jaundice (*djoon*-diss) *n* jaunisse *f*

jaw (djoo) *n* mâchoire *f*

jealous (*djè*-leuss) *adj* jaloux

jealousy (*djè*-leu-si) *n* jalousie *f*

jeans (djiinz) *pl* blue-jean *m*

jelly (*djè*-li) *n* gelée *f*

jelly-fish (*djè*-li-fich) *n* méduse *f*

jersey (*djeû*-zi) *n* jersey *m*; chandail *m*

jet (djèt) *n* jet *m*; avion à réaction

jetty (*djè*-ti) *n* jetée *f*

Jew (djoû) *n* juif *m*

jewel (*djoû*-eul) *n* bijou *m*

jeweller (*djoû*-eu-leu) *n* bijoutier *m*

jewellery (*djoû*-eul-ri) *n* bijoux; joaillerie *f*

Jewish (*djoû*-ich) *adj* juif

job (djob) *n* boulot *m*; emploi *m*, travail *m*

jockey (*djo*-ki) *n* jockey *m*

join (djoïn) *v* *joindre; s'affilier à, adhérer à; assembler, réunir

joint (djoïnt) *n* articulation *f*; soudure *f*; *adj* uni, conjoint

jointly (*djoïnt*-li) *adv* conjointement

joke (djô^{ou}k) *n* blague *f*, plaisanterie *f*

jolly (*djo*-li) *adj* gai

Jordan (*djoo*-deunn) Jordanie *f*

Jordanian (djoo-*déï*-ni-eunn) *adj* jordanien; *n* Jordanien *m*

journal (*djeû*-neul) *n* périodique *m*

journalism (*djeû*-neu-li-zeumm) *n* journalisme *m*

journalist (*djeû*-neu-list) *n* journaliste *m*

journey (*djeû*-ni) *n* voyage *m*

joy (djoï) *n* plaisir *m*, joie *f*

joyful (*djoï*-feul) *adj* content, joyeux

jubilee (*djoû*-bi-lii) *n* anniversaire *m*

judge (djadj) *n* juge *m*; *v* juger; apprécier

judgment (*djadj*-meunnt) *n* jugement *m*

jug (djagh) *n* cruche *f*

Jugoslav (yoû-gheu-*slââv*) *adj* yougoslave; *n* Yougoslave *m*

Jugoslavia (yoû-gheu-*slââ*-vi-eu) Yougoslavie *f*

juice (djoûss) *n* jus *m*

juicy (*djoû*-si) *adj* juteux

July (djou-*laï*) juillet

jump (djammp) *v* sauter; *n* bond *m*, saut *m*

jumper (*djamm*-peu) *n* chandail *m*

junction (*djanngk*-cheunn) *n* carrefour *m*; jonction *f*

June (djoûn) juin

jungle (*djanng*-gheul) *n* jungle *f*

junior (*djoû*-nyeu) *adj* cadet

junk (djanngk) *n* rebut *m*

jury (*djou^{eu}*-ri) *n* jury *m*

just (djast) *adj* légitime, juste; exact; *adv* à peine; juste

justice (*dja*-stiss) *n* droit *m*; justice *f*

juvenile (*djoû*-veu-naïl) *adj* juvénile

K

kangaroo (kæng-gheu-*roû*) *n* kangourou *m*

keel (kiil) *n* quille *f*

keen (kiin) *adj* passionné; aigu

*keep (kiip) *v* *tenir; garder; continuer; ~ **away from** se *tenir éloigné de; ~ **off** ne pas toucher; ~ **on** continuer; ~ **quiet** se *taire; ~ **up** persévérer; ~ **up with** *être à la hauteur de

keg (kègh) *n* baril *m*

kennel (*kè*-neul) *n* chenil *m*

Kenya (*kè*-nyeu) Kenya *m*

kerosene (*kè*-reu-siin) *n* pétrole *m*

kettle (*kè*-teul) *n* bouilloire *f*

key (kii) *n* clé *f*

keyhole (*kii*-hô^{ou}l) *n* trou de la serrure

khaki (*kââ*-ki) *n* kaki *m*

kick (kik) *v* donner des coups de pied; *n* coup de pied

kick-off (ki-*kof*) *n* coup d'envoi

kid (kid) *n* enfant *m*, gosse *m*; chevreau *m*; *v* taquiner

kidney (*kid*-ni) *n* rein *m*

kill (kil) *v* tuer

kilogram (*ki*-leu-ghræm) *n* kilo *m*

kilometre (*ki*-leu-mii-teu) *n* kilomètre *m*

kind (kaïnd) *adj* gentil, aimable; bon; *n* genre *m*

kindergarten (*kinn*-deu-ghââ-teunn) *n* école maternelle

king (kinng) *n* roi *m*

kingdom (*kinng*-deumm) *n* royaume *m*

kiosk (*kii*-osk) *n* kiosque *m*

kiss (kiss) *n* baiser *m*; *v* embrasser

kit (kit) *n* trousseau *m*

kitchen (*ki*-tchinn) *n* cuisine *f*; ~ **garden** jardin potager

knapsack (*næp*-sæk) *n* havresac *m*

knave (néïv) *n* valet *m*

knee (nii) *n* genou *m*

kneecap (*nii*-kæp) *n* rotule *f*

*****kneel** (niil) *v* s'agenouiller

knew (nyoû) *v* (p know)

knickers (*ni*-keuz) *pl* slip *m*

knife (naïf) *n* (pl knives) couteau *m*

knight (naït) *n* chevalier *m*

*****knit** (nit) *v* tricoter

knob (nob) *n* bouton *m*

knock (nok) *v* frapper; *n* coup *m*; ~ **against** cogner contre; ~ **down** renverser

knot (not) *n* nœud *m*; *v* nouer

*****know** (nô°ᵘ) *v* *savoir, *connaître

knowledge (*no*-lidj) *n* connaissance *f*

knuckle (*na*-keul) *n* jointure *f*

L

label (*léï*-beul) *n* étiquette *f*; *v* étiqueter

laboratory (leu-*bo*-reu-teu-ri) *n* laboratoire *m*

labour (*léï*-beu) *n* travail *m*, labeur *m*; douleurs; *v* bûcher, peiner; **labor permit** *Am* permis de travail

labourer (*léï*-beu-reu) *n* travailleur *m*

labour-saving (*léï*-beu-séï-vinng) *adj* qui économise du travail

labyrinth (*læ*-beu-rinnθ) *n* labyrinthe *m*

lace (léïss) *n* dentelle *f*; lacet *m*

lack (læk) *n* manque *m*; *v* manquer

lacquer (*læ*-keu) *n* vernis *m*

lad (læd) *n* garçon *m*

ladder (*læ*-deu) *n* échelle *f*

lady (*léï*-di) *n* dame *f*; **ladies' room** toilettes pour dames

lagoon (leu-*ghoûn*) *n* lagune *f*

lake (léïk) *n* lac *m*

lamb (læm) *n* agneau *m*

lame (léïm) *adj* paralysé, boiteux

lamentable (*læ*-meunn-teu-beul) *adj* lamentable

lamp (læmp) *n* lampe *f*

lamp-post (*læmp*-pô°ᵘst) *n* lampadaire *m*

lampshade (*læmp*-chéïd) *n* abat-jour *m*

land (lænd) *n* pays *m*, terre *f*; *v* atterrir; débarquer

landlady (*lænd*-léï-di) *n* logeuse *f*

landlord (*lænd*-lood) *n* propriétaire *m*; logeur *m*

landmark (*lænd*-mââk) *n* point de repère; jalon *m*

landscape (*lænd*-skéïp) *n* paysage *m*

lane (léïn) *n* ruelle *f*, chemin *m*; voie *f*

language (*læng*-gh^{ou}idj) *n* langue *f*;
~ **laboratory** laboratoire de langues

lantern (*læn*-teunn) *n* lanterne *f*

lapel (leu-*pèl*) *n* revers *m*

larder (*lââ*-deu) *n* garde-manger *m*

large (lââdj) *adj* vaste; spacieux

lark (lâàk) *n* alouette *f*

laryngitis (læ-rinn-*djaï*-tiss) *n* laryngite
f

last (lââst) *adj* dernier; précédent; *v*
durer; **at** ~ enfin; en fin de compte

lasting (*lââ*-stinng) *adj* durable

latchkey (*lætch*-kii) *n* clé de la maison

late (léit) *adj* tard; en retard

lately (*léit*-li) *adv* ces derniers temps,
dernièrement, récemment

lather (*lââ*-ðeu) *n* écume *f*

Latin America (*læ*-tinn eu-*mè*-ri-keu)
Amérique latine

Latin-American (læ-tinn-eu-*mè*-ri-
keunn) *adj* sud-américain

latitude (*læ*-ti-tyoûd) *n* latitude *f*

laugh (lââf) *v* *rire; *n* rire *m*

laughter (*lââf*-teu) *n* rire *m*

launch (loontch) *v* lancer; *n* bateau à
moteur

launching (*loon*-tchinng) *n* lancement
m

launderette (loon-deu-*rèt*) *n* laverie
automatique

laundry (*loon*-dri) *n* blanchisserie *f*;
lessive *f*

lavatory (*læ*-veu-teu-ri) *n* cabinet *m*

lavish (*læ*-vich) *adj* prodigue

law (loo) *n* loi *f*; droit *m*; ~ **court**
tribunal *m*

lawful (*loo*-feul) *adj* légal

lawn (loon) *n* gazon *m*, pelouse *f*

lawsuit (*loo*-soût) *n* procès *m*

lawyer (*loo*-yeu) *n* avocat *m*; juriste
m

laxative (*læk*-seu-tiv) *n* laxatif *m*

*lay** (léï) *v* placer, poser; ~ **bricks**
maçonner

layer (*léï*^{eu}) *n* couche *f*

layman (*léï*-meunn) *n* profane *m*

lazy (*léï*-zi) *adj* paresseux

lead[1] (liid) *n* avance *f*; conduite *f*;
laisse *f*

lead[2] (lèd) *n* plomb *m*

*lead** (liid) *v* diriger

leader (*lii*-deu) *n* leader *m*, dirigeant
m

leadership (*lii*-deu-chip) *n* direction *f*

leading (*lii*-dinng) *adj* dominant, principal

leaf (liif) *n* (pl leaves) feuille *f*

league (liigh) *n* ligue *f*

leak (liik) *v* *fuir; *n* fuite *f*

leaky (*lii*-ki) *adj* ayant une fuite

lean (liin) *adj* maigre

*lean** (liin) *v* s'appuyer

leap (liip) *n* saut *m*

*leap** (liip) *v* bondir

leap-year (*liip*-yi^{eu}) *n* année bissextile

*learn** (leûnn) *v* *apprendre

learner (*leû*-neu) *n* débutant *m*

lease (liiss) *n* location *f*; bail *m*; *v*
donner en location, louer

leash (liich) *n* laisse *f*

least (liist) *adj* moindre; **at** ~ au
moins

leather (*lè*-ðeu) *n* cuir *m*; en cuir

leave (liiv) *n* permission *f*

*leave** (liiv) *v* *partir, quitter; laisser; ~ **out** *omettre

Lebanese (lè-beu-*niiz*) *adj* libanais; *n*
Libanais *m*

Lebanon (*lè*-beu-neunn) Liban *m*

lecture (*lèk*-tcheu) *n* cours *m*, conférence *f*

left[1] (lèft) *adj* gauche

left[2] (lèft) *v* (p, pp leave)

left-hand (*lèft*-hænd) *adj* à gauche, de
gauche

left-handed (lèft-*hæn*-did) *adj* gaucher

leg (lègh) *n* pied *m*, jambe *f*

legacy (*lè*-gheu-si) *n* legs *m*

legal (*lii*-gheul) *adj* légitime, légal ; juridique

legalization (lii-gheu-laï-*zéï*-cheunn) *n* légalisation *f*

legation (li-*ghéï*-cheunn) *n* légation *f*

legible (*lè*-dji-beul) *adj* lisible

legitimate (li-*dji*-ti-meut) *adj* légitime

leisure (*lè*-jeu) *n* loisir *m* ; aise *f*

lemon (*lè*-meunn) *n* citron *m*

lemonade (lè-meu-*néïd*) *n* limonade *f*

***lend** (lènd) *v* prêter

length (lèngθ) *n* longueur *f*

lengthen (*lèng*-θeunn) *v* allonger

lengthways (*lèngθ*-ᵒᵘéïz) *adv* en long

lens (lènz) *n* lentille *f* ; **telephoto ~** télé-objectif *m* ; **zoom ~** zoom *m*

leprosy (*lè*-preu-si) *n* lèpre *f*

less (lèss) *adv* moins

lessen (*lè*-seunn) *v* diminuer

lesson (*lè*-seunn) *n* leçon *f*

***let** (lèt) *v* laisser ; louer ; **~ down** désenchanter

letter (*lè*-teu) *n* lettre *f* ; **~ of credit** lettre de crédit ; **~ of recommendation** lettre de recommandation

letter-box (*lè*-teu-boks) *n* boîte aux lettres

lettuce (*lè*-tiss) *n* laitue *f*

level (*lè*-veul) *adj* égal ; plat, lisse, plan ; *n* niveau *m* ; *v* égaliser, niveler ; **~ crossing** passage à niveau

lever (*lii*-veu) *n* levier *m*

Levis (*lii*-vaïz) *pl* blue-jean *m*

liability (laï-eu-*bi*-leu-ti) *n* responsabilité *f*

liable (*laï*-eu-beul) *adj* responsable ; **~ to** sujet à

liberal (*li*-beu-reul) *adj* libéral ; généreux, large

liberation (li-beu-*réï*-cheunn) *n* libération *f*

Liberia (laï-*biᵉᵘ*-ri-eu) Libéria *m*

Liberian (laï-*biᵉᵘ*-ri-eunn) *adj* libérien ; *n* Libérien *m*

liberty (*li*-beu-ti) *n* liberté *f*

library (*laï*-breu-ri) *n* bibliothèque *f*

licence (*laï*-seunns) *n* licence *f* ; permis *m* ; **driving ~** permis de conduire ; **~ number** *Am* numéro d'immatriculation ; **~ plate** *Am* plaque d'immatriculation

license (*laï*-seunns) *v* autoriser

lick (lik) *v* lécher

lid (lid) *n* couvercle *m*

lie (laï) *v* *mentir ; *n* mensonge *m*

***lie** (laï) *v* *être couché ; **~ down** se coucher

life (laïf) *n* (pl lives) vie *f* ; **~ insurance** assurance-vie *f*

lifebelt (*laïf*-bèlt) *n* bouée de sauvetage

lifetime (*laïf*-taïm) *n* vie *f*

lift (lift) *v* soulever, lever ; *n* ascenseur *m*

light (laït) *n* lumière *f* ; *adj* léger ; clair ; **~ bulb** ampoule *f*

***light** (laït) *v* allumer

lighter (*laï*-teu) *n* briquet *m*

lighthouse (*laït*-haouss) *n* phare *m*

lighting (*laï*-tinng) *n* éclairage *m*

lightning (*laït*-ninng) *n* éclair *m*

like (laïk) *v* aimer ; bien aimer ; *adj* pareil ; *conj* comme

likely (*laï*-kli) *adj* probable

like-minded (laïk-*maïn*-did) *adj* unanime

likewise (*laïk*-ᵒᵘaïz) *adv* de la même manière, également

lily (*li*-li) *n* lis *m*

limb (limm) *n* membre *m*

lime (laïm) *n* chaux *f* ; tilleul *m* ; limette *f*

limetree (*laïm*-trii) *n* tilleul *m*

limit (*li*-mit) *n* limite *f* ; *v* limiter

limp (limmp) *v* boiter ; *adj* flasque

line (laïn) *n* ligne *f* ; trait *m* ; fil *m* ; rangée *f* ; **stand in ~** *Am* *faire la queue

linen (*li*-ninn) *n* toile *f*; linge *m*

liner (*laï*-neu) *n* paquebot *m*

lining (*laï*-ninng) *n* doublure *f*

link (linngk) *v* relier; *n* lien *m*; maillon *m*

lion (*laï*-eunn) *n* lion *m*

lip (lip) *n* lèvre *f*

lipsalve (*lip*-sââv) *n* pommade pour les lèvres

lipstick (*lip*-stik) *n* rouge à lèvres

liqueur (li-*kyou^{eu}*) *n* liqueur *f*

liquid (*li*-k^{ou}id) *adj* liquide; *n* liquide *m*

liquor (*li*-keu) *n* spiritueux *mpl*

liquorice (*li*-keu-riss) *n* réglisse *f*

list (list) *n* liste *f*; *v* *inscrire

listen (*li*-seunn) *v* écouter

listener (*liss*-neu) *n* auditeur *m*

literary (*li*-treu-ri) *adj* littéraire

literature (*li*-treu-tcheu) *n* littérature *f*

litre (*lii*-teu) *n* litre *m*

litter (*li*-teu) *n* détritus *m*; immondices *fpl*; portée *f*

little (*li*-teul) *adj* petit; peu

live[1] (liv) *v* *vivre; habiter

live[2] (laïv) *adj* vivant

livelihood (*laïv*-li-houd) *n* subsistance *f*

lively (*laïv*-li) *adj* vif

liver (*li*-veu) *n* foie *m*

living-room (*li*-vinng-roûm) *n* pièce de séjour, salle de séjour

load (lô^{ou}d) *n* chargement *m*; fardeau *m*; *v* charger

loaf (lô^{ou}f) *n* (pl loaves) miche *f*

loan (lô^{ou}n) *n* prêt *m*

lobby (*lo*-bi) *n* vestibule *m*

lobster (*lob*-steu) *n* homard *m*

local (lô^{ou}-keul) *adj* local; ~ **call** communication locale; ~ **train** train local

locality (lô^{ou}-*kæ*-leu-ti) *n* localité *f*

locate (lô^{ou}-*kéït*) *v* localiser

location (lô^{ou}-*kéï*-cheunn) *n* situation *f*

lock (lok) *v* fermer à clé; *n* serrure *f*; écluse *f*; ~ **up** enfermer

locomotive (lô^{ou}-keu-*mô^{ou}*-tiv) *n* locomotive *f*

lodge (lodj) *v* loger; *n* pavillon de chasse

lodger (*lo*-djeu) *n* sous-locataire *m*

lodgings (*lo*-djinngz) *pl* logement *m*

log (logh) *n* bûche *f*

logic (*lo*-djik) *n* logique *f*

logical (*lo*-dji-keul) *adj* logique

lonely (*lô^{ou}n*-li) *adj* solitaire

long (lonng) *adj* long; ~ **for** désirer; **no longer** ne … plus

longing (*lonng*-inng) *n* envie *f*

longitude (*lonn*-dji-tyoûd) *n* longitude *f*

look (louk) *v* regarder; sembler, *avoir l'air; *n* coup d'œil, regard *m*; apparence *f*, aspect *m*; ~ **after** s'occuper de, *prendre soin de, veiller sur; ~ **at** regarder; ~ **for** chercher; ~ **out** *prendre garde, *faire attention; ~ **up** chercher

looking-glass (*lou*-kinng-ghlââss) *n* miroir *m*

loop (loûp) *n* boucle *f*

loose (loûss) *adj* lâche

loosen (*loû*-seunn) *v* desserrer

lord (lood) *n* lord *m*

lorry (*lo*-ri) *n* camion *m*

***lose** (loûz) *v* perdre

loss (loss) *n* perte *f*

lost (lost) *adj* égaré; disparu; ~ **and found** objets trouvés; ~ **property office** bureau des objets trouvés

lot (lot) *n* sort *m*; tas *m*, quantité *f*

lotion (*lô^{ou}*-cheunn) *n* lotion *f*; **after-shave** ~ after-shave *m*

lottery (*lo*-teu-ri) *n* loterie *f*

loud (laoud) *adj* fort

loud-speaker (laoud-*spii*-keu) *n* haut-parleur *m*

lounge (laoundj) *n* foyer *m*

louse (laouss) *n* (pl lice) pou *m*

love (lav) *v* aimer; *n* amour *m*; **in ~** amoureux

lovely (*lav*-li) *adj* délicieux, ravissant, beau

lover (*la*-veu) *n* amant *m*

love-story (*lav*-stoo-ri) *n* histoire d'amour

low (lôᵒᵘ) *adj* bas; profond; déprimé; **~ tide** marée basse

lower (*lô*ᵒᵘ-eu) *v* baisser; amener; *adj* inférieur, bas

lowlands (*lô*ᵒᵘ-leunndz) *pl* plaine *f*

loyal (*loï*-eul) *adj* loyal

lubricate (*loû*-bri-kéït) *v* huiler, lubrifier

lubrication (loû-bri-*kéï*-cheunn) *n* lubrification *f*; **~ oil** lubrifiant *m*; **~ system** système de lubrification

luck (lak) *n* chance *f*; hasard *m*; **bad ~** malchance *f*

lucky (*la*-ki) *adj* chanceux; **~ charm** porte-bonheur *m*

ludicrous (*loû*-di-kreuss) *adj* ridicule, grotesque

luggage (*la*-ghidj) *n* bagage *m*; **hand ~** bagage à main; **left ~ office** consigne *f*; **~ rack** porte-bagages *m*, filet à bagage; **~ van** fourgon *m*

lukewarm (*loûk*-ᵒᵘoom) *adj* tiède

lumbago (lamm-*béï*-ghôᵒᵘ) *n* lumbago *m*

luminous (*loû*-mi-neuss) *adj* lumineux

lump (lammp) *n* morceau *m*, grumeau *m*; bosse *f*; **~ of sugar** morceau de sucre; **~ sum** somme globale

lumpy (*lamm*-pi) *adj* grumeleux

lunacy (*loû*-neu-si) *n* folie *f*

lunatic (*loû*-neu-tik) *adj* fou; *n* aliéné mental

lunch (lanntch) *n* lunch *m*, déjeuner *m*

luncheon (*lann*-tcheunn) *n* déjeuner *m*

lung (lanng) *n* poumon *m*

lust (last) *n* concupiscence *f*

luxurious (lagh-*jou*ᵉᵘ-ri-euss) *adj* luxueux

luxury (*lak*-cheu-ri) *n* luxe *m*

M

machine (meu-*chiin*) *n* appareil *m*, machine *f*

machinery (meu-*chii*-neu-ri) *n* machinerie *f*; mécanisme *m*

mackerel (*mæ*-kreul) *n* (pl ~) maquereau *m*

mackintosh (*mæ*-kinn-toch) *n* imperméable *m*

mad (mæd) *adj* dément, insensé, fou; enragé

madam (*mæ*-deumm) *n* madame *f*

madness (*mæd*-neuss) *n* démence *f*

magazine (mæ-gheu-*ziin*) *n* revue *f*

magic (*mæ*-djik) *n* magie *f*; *adj* magique

magician (meu-*dji*-cheunn) *n* prestidigitateur *m*

magistrate (*mæ*-dji-stréït) *n* magistrat *m*

magnetic (mægh-*nè*-tik) *adj* magnétique

magneto (mægh-*nii*-tôᵒᵘ) *n* (pl ~s) magnéto *f*

magnificent (mægh-*ni*-fi-seunnt) *adj* magnifique; grandiose, splendide

magpie (*mægh*-paï) *n* pie *f*

maid (méïd) *n* bonne *f*

maiden name (*méï*-deunn néïm) nom de jeune fille

mail (méïl) *n* courrier *m*; *v* *mettre à la poste; **~ order** Am mandat-poste *m*

mailbox (*méïl*-boks) *nAm* boîte aux lettres

main (méïn) *adj* principal; majeur; ~ **deck** pont principal; ~ **line** ligne principale; ~ **road** route principale; ~ **street** rue principale

mainland (méïn-leunnd) *n* terre ferme

mainly (méïn-li) *adv* principalement

mains (méïnz) *pl* secteur *m*

maintain (méïn-téïn) *v* *maintenir

maintenance (méïn-teu-neunns) *n* entretien *m*

maize (méïz) *n* maïs *m*

major (méi-djeu) *adj* grand; majeur

majority (meu-djo-reu-ti) *n* majorité *f*

***make** (méïk) *v* *faire, rendre; gagner; réussir; ~ **do with** se débrouiller avec; ~ **good** compenser; ~ **up** dresser

make-up (méï-kap) *n* maquillage *m*

malaria (meu-lèᵉᵘ-ri-eu) *n* malaria *f*

Malay (meu-léï) *n* Malais *m*

Malaysia (meu-léï-zi-eu) Malaysia *m*

Malaysian (meu-léï-zi-eunn) *adj* malaisien

male (méïl) *adj* mâle

malicious (meu-li-cheuss) *adj* malveillant

malignant (meu-ligh-neunnt) *adj* malin

mallet (mæ-lit) *n* maillet *m*

malnutrition (mæl-nyou-tri-cheunn) *n* dénutrition *f*

mammal (mæ-meul) *n* mammifère *m*

mammoth (mæ-meuθ) *n* mammouth *m*

man (mæn) *n* (pl men) homme *m*; **men's room** toilettes pour hommes

manage (mæ-nidj) *v* diriger; réussir

manageable (mæ-ni-djeu-beul) *adj* maniable

management (mæ-nidj-meunnt) *n* direction *f*; gestion *f*

manager (mæ-ni-djeu) *n* chef *m*, directeur *m*

mandarin (mæn-deu-rinn) *n* mandarine *f*

mandate (mæn-déït) *n* mandat *m*

manger (méïn-djeu) *n* mangeoire *f*

manicure (mæ-ni-kyouᵉᵘ) *n* manucure *f*; *v* soigner les ongles

mankind (mæn-kaïnd) *n* humanité *f*

mannequin (mæ-neu-kinn) *n* mannequin *m*

manner (mæ-neu) *n* mode *m*, manière *f*; **manners** *pl* savoir-vivre *m*

man-of-war (mæ-neuv-ᵒᵘoo) *n* navire de guerre

manor-house (mæ-neu-haouss) *n* manoir *m*

mansion (mæn-cheunn) *n* manoir *m*

manual (mæ-nyou-eul) *adj* manuel

manufacture (mæ-nyou-fæk-tcheu) *v* fabriquer

manufacturer (mæ-nyou-fæk-tcheu-reu) *n* fabricant *m*

manure (meu-nyouᵉᵘ) *n* fumier *m*

manuscript (mæ-nyou-skript) *n* manuscrit *m*

many (mè-ni) *adj* beaucoup de

map (mæp) *n* carte *f*; plan *m*

maple (méï-peul) *n* érable *m*

marble (mââ-beul) *n* marbre *m*; bille *f*

March (mââtch) mars

march (mââtch) *v* marcher; *n* marche *f*

mare (mèᵉᵘ) *n* jument *f*

margarine (mââ-djeu-riin) *n* margarine *f*

margin (mââ-djinn) *n* marge *f*

maritime (mæ-ri-taïm) *adj* maritime

mark (mââk) *v* marquer; caractériser; *n* marque *f*; note *f*; cible *f*

market (mââ-kit) *n* marché *m*

market-place (mââ-kit-pléïss) *n* place du marché

marmalade (mââ-meu-léïd) *n* marmelade *f*

marriage (mæ-ridj) *n* mariage *m*

marrow (*mæ*-rô^ou) *n* moelle *f*

marry (*mæ*-ri) *v* épouser, se marier

marsh (mââch) *n* marais *m*

marshy (*mââ*-chi) *adj* marécageux

martyr (*mââ*-teu) *n* martyr *m*

marvel (*mââ*-veul) *n* merveille *f*; *v* s'émerveiller

marvellous (*mââ*-veu-leuss) *adj* merveilleux

mascara (mæ-*skââ*-reu) *n* cosmétique pour les cils

masculine (*mæ*-skyou-linn) *adj* masculin

mash (mæch) *v* écraser

mask (mââsk) *n* masque *m*

Mass (mæss) *n* messe *f*

mass (mæss) *n* masse *f*; ~ **production** production en série

massage (*mæ*-sââj) *n* massage *m*; *v* masser

masseur (mæ-*seû*) *n* masseur *m*

massive (*mæ*-siv) *adj* massif

mast (mââst) *n* mât *m*

master (*mââ*-steu) *n* maître *m*; patron *m*; professeur *m*, instituteur *m*; *v* maîtriser

masterpiece (*mââ*-steu-piiss) *n* chef-d'œuvre *m*

mat (mæt) *n* tapis *m*; *adj* mat, terne

match (mætch) *n* allumette *f*; match *m*; *v* s'accorder avec

match-box (*mætch*-boks) *n* boîte d'allumettes

material (meu-*tieu*-ri-eul) *n* matériel *m*; tissu *m*; *adj* physique, matériel

mathematical (mæ-θeu-*mæ*-ti-keul) *adj* mathématique

mathematics (mæ-θeu-*mæ*-tiks) *n* mathématiques *fpl*

matrimonial (mæ-tri-*môou*-ni-eul) *adj* matrimonial

matrimony (*mæ*-tri-meu-ni) *n* mariage *m*

matter (*mæ*-teu) *n* matière *f*; affaire *f*, question *f*; *v* *avoir de l'importance; **as a** ~ **of fact** effectivement, en fait

matter-of-fact (mæ-teu-reuv-*fækt*) *adj* réaliste

mattress (*mæ*-treuss) *n* matelas *m*

mature (meu-*tyou*^eu) *adj* mûr

maturity (meu-*tyou*^eu-reu-ti) *n* maturité *f*

mausoleum (moo-seu-*lii*-eumm) *n* mausolée *m*

mauve (môou v) *adj* mauve

May (méï) mai

***may** (méï) *v* *pouvoir

maybe (*méï*-bii) *adv* peut-être

mayor (mè^eu) *n* maire *m*

maze (méïz) *n* labyrinthe *m*

me (mii) *pron* moi; me

meadow (*mè*-dô^ou) *n* pré *m*

meal (miil) *n* repas *m*

mean (miin) *adj* mesquin; *n* moyenne *f*

***mean** (miin) *v* signifier; *vouloir dire

meaning (*mii*-ninng) *n* signification *f*

meaningless (*mii*-ninng-leuss) *adj* dénué de sens

means (miinz) *n* moyen *m*; **by no** ~ aucunement, en aucun cas

in the meantime (inn ðeu *miin*-taïm) en attendant, entre-temps

meanwhile (*miin*-^ouaïl) *adv* entre-temps

measles (*mii*-zeulz) *n* rougeole *f*

measure (*mè*-jeu) *v* mesurer; *n* mesure *f*

meat (miit) *n* viande *f*

mechanic (mi-*kæ*-nik) *n* monteur *m*, mécanicien *m*

mechanical (mi-*kæ*-ni-keul) *adj* mécanique

mechanism (*mè*-keu-ni-zeumm) *n* mécanisme *m*

medal (*mè*-deul) *n* médaille *f*

mediaeval (mè-di-*ii*-veul) *adj* médiéval

mediate (*mii*-di-éït) *v* *servir d'intermédiaire

mediator (*mii*-di-éï-teu) *n* médiateur *m*

medical (mè-di-keul) *adj* médical

medicine (*mèd*-sinn) *n* médicament *m*; médecine *f*

meditate (mè-di-téït) *v* méditer

Mediterranean (mè-di-teu-*réï*-ni-eunn) Méditerranée *f*

medium (*mii*-di-eumm) *adj* moyen

***meet** (miit) *v* rencontrer

meeting (*mii*-tinng) *n* assemblée *f*, réunion *f*; rencontre *f*

meeting-place (*mii*-tinng-pléïss) *n* lieu de rencontre

melancholy (mè-leunng-keu-li) *n* mélancolie *f*

mellow (mè-lôᵒᵘ) *adj* moelleux

melodrama (mè-leu-drââ-meu) *n* mélodrame *m*

melody (mè-leu-di) *n* mélodie *f*

melon (mè-leunn) *n* melon *m*

melt (mèlt) *v* fondre

member (*mèm*-beu) *n* membre *m*; **Member of Parliament** député *m*

membership (*mèm*-beu-chip) *n* affiliation *f*

memo (mè-môᵒᵘ) *n* (pl ~s) mémorandum *m*

memorable (mè-meu-reu-beul) *adj* mémorable

memorial (meu-*moo*-ri-eul) *n* mémorial *m*

memorize (mè-meu-raïz) *v* *apprendre par cœur

memory (mè-meu-ri) *n* mémoire *f*; souvenir *m*

mend (mènd) *v* réparer

menstruation (mèn-strou-*éï*-cheunn) *n* menstruation *f*

mental (*mèn*-teul) *adj* mental

mention (*mèn*-cheunn) *v* mentionner; *n* mention *f*

menu (mè-nyoû) *n* carte *f*, menu *m*

merchandise (*meû*-tcheunn-daïz) *n* marchandise *f*

merchant (*meû*-tcheunnt) *n* commerçant *m*, marchand *m*

merciful (*meû*-si-feul) *adj* miséricordieux

mercury (*meû*-kyou-ri) *n* mercure *m*

mercy (*meû*-si) *n* miséricorde *f*, clémence *f*

mere (miᵉᵘ) *adj* pur

merely (*miᵉᵘ*-li) *adv* seulement

merger (*meû*-djeu) *n* fusion *f*

merit (mè-rit) *v* mériter; *n* mérite *m*

mermaid (*meû*-méïd) *n* sirène *f*

merry (mè-ri) *adj* joyeux

merry-go-round (*mè*-ri-ghôᵒᵘ-raound) *n* chevaux de bois

mesh (mèch) *n* maille *f*

mess (mèss) *n* désordre *m*, gâchis *m*; ~ **up** gâcher

message (mè-sidj) *n* commission *f*, message *m*

messenger (mè-sinn-djeu) *n* messager *m*

metal (mè-teul) *n* métal *m*; métallique

meter (*mii*-teu) *n* compteur *m*

method (mè-θeud) *n* méthode *f*; ordre *m*

methodical (meu-θo-di-keul) *adj* méthodique

methylated spirits (mè-θeu-léï-tid *spi*-rits) alcool à brûler

metre (*mii*-teu) *n* mètre *m*

metric (mè-trik) *adj* métrique

Mexican (*mèk*-si-keunn) *adj* mexicain; *n* Mexicain *m*

Mexico (*mèk*-si-kôᵒᵘ) Mexique *m*

mezzanine (*mè*-zeu-niin) *n* entresol *m*

microphone (*maï*-kreu-fôᵒᵘn) *n* microphone *m*

midday (*mid*-déï) *n* midi *m*

middle (*mi*-deul) *n* milieu *m*; *adj* du milieu; **Middle Ages** moyen-âge *m*; ~ **class** classe moyenne; **middle-class** *adj* bourgeois

midnight (*mid*-naït) *n* minuit *m*

midst (midst) *n* milieu *m*

midsummer (*mid*-sa-meu) *n* plein été

midwife (*mid*-ᵒᵘaïf) *n* (pl -wives) sage-femme *f*

might (maït) *n* puissance *f*

might (maït) *v* *pouvoir

mighty (*maï*-ti) *adj* puissant

mild (maïld) *adj* doux

mildew (*mil*-dyou) *n* moisissure *f*

mile (maïl) *n* mille *m*

mileage (*maï*-lidj) *n* nombre de milles

milepost (*maïl*-pôᵒᵘst) *n* poteau indicateur

milestone (*maïl*-stôᵒᵘn) *n* borne routière

milieu (*mii*-lyeû) *n* milieu *m*

military (*mi*-li-teu-ri) *adj* militaire; ~ **force** force armée

milk (milk) *n* lait *m*

milkman (*milk*-meunn) *n* (pl -men) laitier *m*

milk-shake (*milk*-chéïk) *n* frappé *m*

milky (*mil*-ki) *adj* laiteux

mill (mil) *n* moulin *m*; usine *f*

miller (*mi*-leu) *n* meunier *m*

milliner (*mi*-li-neu) *n* modiste *f*

million (*mil*-yeunn) *n* million *m*

millionaire (mil-yeu-*nè*ᵉᵘ) *n* millionnaire *m*

mince (minns) *v* hacher

mind (maïnd) *n* esprit *m*; *v* *faire objection à; prêter attention à, *faire attention à

mine (maïn) *n* mine *f*

miner (*maï*-neu) *n* mineur *m*

mineral (*mi*-neu-reul) *n* minéral *m*; ~ **water** eau minérale

miniature (*minn*-yeu-tcheu) *n* miniature *f*

minimum (*mi*-ni-meumm) *n* minimum *m*

mining (*maï*-ninng) *n* exploitation minière

minister (*mi*-ni-steu) *n* ministre *m*; pasteur *m*; **Prime Minister** premier ministre

ministry (*mi*-ni-stri) *n* ministère *m*

mink (minngk) *n* vison *m*

minor (*maï*-neu) *adj* petit, menu, mineur; subalterne; *n* mineur *m*

minority (maï-*no*-reu-ti) *n* minorité *f*

mint (minnt) *n* menthe *f*

minus (*maï*-neuss) *prep* moins

minute¹ (*mi*-nit) *n* minute *f*; **minutes** compte rendu

minute² (maï-*nyoût*) *adj* minuscule

miracle (*mi*-reu-keul) *n* miracle *m*

miraculous (mi-*ræ*-kyou-leuss) *adj* miraculeux

mirror (*mi*-reu) *n* miroir *m*

misbehave (miss-bi-*héïv*) *v* se *conduire mal

miscarriage (miss-*kæ*-ridj) *n* fausse couche

miscellaneous (mi-seu-*léï*-ni-euss) *adj* divers

mischief (*miss*-tchif) *n* espièglerie *f*; mal *m*, dommage *m*, malice *f*

mischievous (*miss*-tchi-veuss) *adj* malicieux

miserable (*mi*-zeu-reu-beul) *adj* misérable, malheureux

misery (*mi*-zeu-ri) *n* détresse *f*, misère *f*

misfortune (miss-*foo*-tchèn) *n* infortune *f*, malheur *m*

mislay (miss-*léï*) *v* égarer

misplaced (miss-*pléïst*) *adj* inopportun; mal placé

mispronounce (miss-preu-*naouns*) *v* mal prononcer

miss¹ (miss) mademoiselle, demoiselle

f

miss² (miss) v manquer

missing (*mi*-sinng) *adj* manquant; ~ **person** disparu *m*

mist (mist) *n* brume *f*, brouillard *m*

mistake (mi-*stéïk*) *n* méprise *f*, faute *f*, erreur *f*

*****mistake** (mi-*stéïk*) v confondre

mistaken (mi-*stéï*-keunn) *adj* erroné; *****be** ~ se tromper

mister (*mi*-steu) monsieur *m*

mistress (*mi*-streuss) *n* maîtresse de maison; patronne *f*; maîtresse *f*

mistrust (miss-*trast*) v se méfier de

misty (*mi*-sti) *adj* brumeux

*****misunderstand** (mi-sann-deu-*stænd*) v mal *comprendre

misunderstanding (mi-sann-deu-*stæn*-dinng) *n* malentendu *m*

misuse (miss-*youss*) *n* abus *m*

mittens (*mi*-teunnz) *pl* moufles *fpl*

mix (miks) v mélanger, mêler; ~ **with** fréquenter

mixed (mikst) *adj* mêlé, mélangé

mixer (*mik*-seu) *n* mixeur *m*

mixture (*miks*-tcheu) *n* mélange *m*

moan (môᵒᵘn) v gémir

moat (môᵒᵘt) *n* douve *f*

mobile (*môᵒᵘ*-baïl) *adj* mobile

mock (mok) v se moquer de

mockery (*mo*-keu-ri) *n* moquerie *f*

model (*mo*-deul) *n* modèle *m*; mannequin *m*; v façonner, modeler

moderate (*mo*-deu-reut) *adj* modéré

modern (*mo*-deunn) *adj* moderne

modest (*mo*-dist) *adj* modeste

modesty (*mo*-di-sti) *n* modestie *f*

modify (*mo*-di-faï) v modifier

mohair (*môᵒᵘ*-hèᵉᵘ) *n* mohair *m*

moist (moïst) *adj* mouillé, moite

moisten (*moï*-seunn) v humecter

moisture (*moïss*-tcheu) *n* humidité *f*; **moisturizing cream** crème hydratante

molar (*môᵒᵘ*-leu) *n* molaire *f*

moment (*môᵒᵘ*-meunnt) *n* instant *m*, moment *m*

momentary (*môᵒᵘ*-meunn-teu-ri) *adj* momentané

monarch (*mo*-neuk) *n* monarque *m*

monarchy (*mo*-neu-ki) *n* monarchie *f*

monastery (*mo*-neu-stri) *n* monastère *m*

Monday (*mann*-di) lundi *m*

monetary (*ma*-ni-teu-ri) *adj* monétaire; ~ **unit** unité monétaire

money (*ma*-ni) *n* argent *m*; ~ **exchange** bureau de change; ~ **order** mandat-poste *m*

monk (manngk) *n* moine *m*

monkey (*manng*-ki) *n* singe *m*

monologue (*mo*-no-logh) *n* monologue *m*

monopoly (meu-*no*-peu-li) *n* monopole *m*

monotonous (meu-*no*-teu-neuss) *adj* monotone

month (mannθ) *n* mois *m*

monthly (*mannθ*-li) *adj* mensuel; ~ **magazine** revue mensuelle

monument (*mo*-nyou-meunnt) *n* monument *m*

mood (moûd) *n* humeur *f*

moon (moûn) *n* lune *f*

moonlight (*moûn*-laït) *n* clair de lune

moor (mouᵉᵘ) *n* bruyère *f*, lande *f*

moose (moûss) *n* (pl ~, ~s) élan *m*

moped (*môᵒᵘ*-pèd) *n* vélomoteur *m*

moral (*mo*-reul) *n* morale *f*; *adj* moral; **morals** mœurs *fpl*

morality (meu-*ræ*-leu-ti) *n* moralité *f*

more (moo) *adj* plus; **once** ~ une fois de plus

moreover (moo-*rôᵒᵘ*-veu) *adv* d'ailleurs, de plus

morning (*moo*-ninng) *n* matin *m*; ~ **paper** journal du matin

Moroccan (meu-*ro*-keunn) *adj* marocain; *n* Marocain *m*

Morocco (meu-*ro*-kôᵒᵘ) Maroc *m*

morphia (*moo*-fi-eu) *n* morphine *f*

morphine (*moo*-fiin) *n* morphine *f*

morsel (*moo*-seul) *n* morceau *m*

mortal (*moo*-teul) *adj* fatal, mortel

mortgage (*moo*-ghidj) *n* hypothèque *f*

mosaic (meu-*zéï*-ik) *n* mosaïque *f*

mosque (mosk) *n* mosquée *f*

mosquito (meu-*skii*-tôᵒᵘ) *n* (pl ~es) moustique *m*

mosquito-net (meu-*skii*-tôᵒᵘ-nèt) *n* moustiquaire *f*

moss (moss) *n* mousse *f*

most (môᵒᵘst) *adj* le plus; **at ~** au maximum, tout au plus; **~ of all** surtout

mostly (*môᵒᵘst*-li) *adv* le plus souvent

motel (môᵒᵘ-*tèl*) *n* motel *m*

moth (moθ) *n* mite *f*

mother (*ma*-ðeu) *n* mère *f*; **~ tongue** langue maternelle

mother-in-law (*ma*-ðeu-rinn-loo) *n* (pl mothers-) belle-mère *f*

mother-of-pearl (ma-ðeu-reuv-*peûl*) *n* nacre *f*

motion (*môᵒᵘ*-cheunn) *n* mouvement *m*; motion *f*

motive (*môᵒᵘ*-tiv) *n* motif *m*

motor (*môᵒᵘ*-teu) *n* moteur *m*; *v* voyager en auto; **~ body** *Am* carrosserie *f*; **starter ~** démarreur *m*

motorbike (*môᵒᵘ*-teu-baïk) *nAm* vélomoteur *m*

motor-boat (*môᵒᵘ*-teu-bôᵒᵘt) *n* canot automobile

motor-car (*môᵒᵘ*-teu-kââ) *n* automobile *f*

motor-cycle (*môᵒᵘ*-teu-saï-keul) *n* motocyclette *f*

motoring (*môᵒᵘ*-teu-rinng) *n* automobilisme *m*

motorist (*môᵒᵘ*-teu-rist) *n* automobiliste *m*

motorway (*môᵒᵘ*-teu-ᵒᵘéï) *n* autoroute *f*

motto (mo-tôᵒᵘ) *n* (pl ~es, ~s) devise *f*

mouldy (*môᵒᵘl*-di) *adj* moisi

mound (maound) *n* butte *f*

mount (maount) *v* monter; *n* mont *m*

mountain (*maoun*-tinn) *n* montagne *f*; **~ pass** col *m*; **~ range** chaîne de montagnes

mountaineering (maoun-ti-*ni*ᵉᵘ-rinng) *n* alpinisme *m*

mountainous (*maoun*-ti-neuss) *adj* montagneux

mourning (*moo*-ninng) *n* deuil *m*

mouse (maouss) *n* (pl mice) souris *f*

moustache (meu-*stââch*) *n* moustache *f*

mouth (maouθ) *n* bouche *f*; gueule *f*; embouchure *f*

mouthwash (*maou*θ-ᵒᵘoch) *n* eau dentifrice

movable (*moû*-veu-beul) *adj* mobile

move (moûv) *v* bouger; déplacer; se *mouvoir; déménager; *émouvoir; *n* tour *m*, pas *m*; déménagement *m*

movement (*moûv*-meunnt) *n* mouvement *m*

movie (*moû*-vi) *n* film *m*; **movies** *Am* cinéma *m*; **~ theater** *Am* cinéma *m*

much (match) *adj* beaucoup de; *adv* beaucoup; **as ~** autant

muck (mak) *n* gadoue *f*

mud (mad) *n* boue *f*

muddle (*ma*-deul) *n* fouillis *m*, pagaille *f*, confusion *f*; *v* embrouiller

muddy (*ma*-di) *adj* boueux

mud-guard (*mad*-ghââd) *n* garde-boue *m*

muffler (*maf*-leu) *nAm* silencieux *m*

mug (magh) *n* gobelet *m*, chope *f*

mulberry (*mal*-beu-ri) *n* mûre *f*

mule (myoûl) *n* mulet *m*, mule *f*

mullet (*ma*-lit) *n* mulet *m*
multiplication (mal-ti-pli-*kéï*-cheunn) *n* multiplication *f*
multiply (*mal*-ti-plaï) *v* multiplier
mumps (mammps) *n* oreillons *mpl*
municipal (myoû-*ni*-si-peul) *adj* municipal
municipality (myoû-ni-si-*pæ*-leu-ti) *n* municipalité *f*
murder (*meû*-deu) *n* assassinat *m*; *v* assassiner
murderer (*meû*-deu-reu) *n* meurtrier *m*
muscle (*ma*-seul) *n* muscle *m*
muscular (*ma*-skyou-leu) *adj* musclé
museum (myoû-*zii*-eumm) *n* musée *m*
mushroom (*mach*-roûm) *n* champignon *m*
music (*myoû*-zik) *n* musique *f*; ~ **academy** conservatoire *m*
musical (*myoû*-zi-keul) *adj* musical; *n* comédie musicale
music-hall (*myoû*-zik-hool) *n* music-hall *m*
musician (myoû-*zi*-cheunn) *n* musicien *m*
muslin (*maz*-linn) *n* mousseline *f*
mussel (*ma*-seul) *n* moule *f*
*** must** (mast) *v* *falloir
mustard (*ma*-steud) *n* moutarde *f*
mute (myoût) *adj* muet
mutiny (*myoû*-ti-ni) *n* mutinerie *f*
mutton (*ma*-teunn) *n* mouton *m*
mutual (*myoû*-tchou-eul) *adj* mutuel, réciproque
my (maï) *adj* mon
myself (maï-*sèlf*) *pron* me; moi-même
mysterious (mi-*stiᵉᵘ*-ri-euss) *adj* mystérieux
mystery (*mi*-steu-ri) *n* énigme *f*, mystère *m*
myth (miθ) *n* mythe *m*

N

nail (néïl) *n* ongle *m*; clou *m*
nailbrush (*néïl*-brach) *n* brosse à ongles
nail-file (*néïl*-faïl) *n* lime à ongles
nail-polish (*néïl*-po-lich) *n* vernis à ongle
nail-scissors (*néïl*-si-zeuz) *pl* ciseaux à ongles
naïve (nââ-*iïv*) *adj* naïf
naked (*néï*-kid) *adj* nu; dénudé
name (néïm) *n* nom *m*; *v* nommer; **in the** ~ **of** au nom de
namely (*néïm*-li) *adv* notamment
nap (næp) *n* somme *m*
napkin (*næp*-kinn) *n* serviette *f*
nappy (*næ*-pi) *n* couche *f*
narcosis (nââ-*kôᵒᵘ*-siss) *n* (pl -ses) narcose *f*
narcotic (nââ-*ko*-tik) *n* narcotique *m*
narrow (*næ*-rôᵒᵘ) *adj* serré, étroit
narrow-minded (næ-rôᵒᵘ-*maïn*-did) *adj* borné
nasty (*nââ*-sti) *adj* antipathique, désagréable; méchant
nation (*néï*-cheunn) *n* nation *f*; peuple *m*
national (*næ*-cheu-neul) *adj* national; de l'Etat; ~ **anthem** hymne national; ~ **dress** costume national; ~ **park** parc national
nationality (næ-cheu-*næ*-leu-ti) *n* nationalité *f*
nationalize (*næ*-cheu-neu-laïz) *v* nationaliser
native (*néï*-tiv) *n* indigène *m*; *adj* indigène; ~ **country** patrie *f*, pays natal; ~ **language** langue maternelle
natural (*næ*-tcheu-reul) *adj* naturel; inné

naturally (*næ*-tcheu-reu-li) *adv* bien sûr, naturellement

nature (*néï*-tcheu) *n* nature *f*

naughty (*noo*-ti) *adj* polisson, méchant

nausea (*noo*-si-eu) *n* nausée *f*

naval (*néï*-veul) *adj* naval

navel (*néï*-veul) *n* nombril *m*

navigable (*næ*-vi-gheu-beul) *adj* navigable

navigate (*næ*-vi-ghéït) *v* naviguer

navigation (*næ*-vi-*ghéï*-cheunn) *n* navigation *f*

navy (*néï*-vi) *n* marine *f*

near (ni*eu*) *prep* près de; *adj* proche, près

nearby (*ni*eu-baï) *adj* proche

nearly (*ni*eu-li) *adv* presque

neat (niit) *adj* soigné; pur

necessary (*nè*-seu-seu-ri) *adj* nécessaire

necessity (neu-*sè*-seu-ti) *n* nécessité *f*

neck (nèk) *n* cou *m*; **nape of the ~** nuque *f*

necklace (*nèk*-leuss) *n* collier *m*

necktie (*nèk*-taï) *n* cravate *f*

need (niid) *v* *falloir, *avoir besoin de; *n* besoin *m*; nécessité *f*; **~ to** *devoir

needle (*nii*-deul) *n* aiguille *f*

needlework (*nii*-deul-ou eûk) *n* travail à l'aiguille

negative (*nè*-gheu-tiv) *adj* négatif; *n* négatif *m*

neglect (ni-*ghlèkt*) *v* négliger; *n* négligence *f*

neglectful (ni-*ghlèkt*-feul) *adj* négligent

negligee (*nè*-ghli-jéï) *n* négligé *m*

negotiate (ni-*ghô*ou-chi-éït) *v* négocier

negotiation (ni-ghô ou-chi-*éï*-cheunn) *n* négociation *f*

Negro (*nii*-ghrô ou) *n* (pl ~es) noir *m*

neighbour (*néï*-beu) *n* voisin *m*

neighbourhood (*néï*-beu-houd) *n* voisinage *m*

neighbouring (*néï*-beu-rinng) *adj* contigu, avoisinant

neither (*naï*-ðeu) *pron* ni l'un ni l'autre; **neither ... nor** ni ... ni

neon (*nii*-onn) *n* néon *m*

nephew (*nè*-fyou) *n* neveu *m*

nerve (neûv) *n* nerf *m*; audace *f*

nervous (*neû*-veuss) *adj* nerveux

nest (nèst) *n* nid *m*

net (nèt) *n* filet *m*; *adj* net

the Netherlands (*nè*-ðeu-leunndz) Pays-Bas *mpl*

network (*nèt*-ou eûk) *n* réseau *m*

neuralgia (nyou eu-*ræl*-djeu) *n* névralgie *f*

neurosis (nyou eu-*rô*ou-siss) *n* névrose *f*

neuter (*nyoû*-teu) *adj* neutre

neutral (*nyoû*-treul) *adj* neutre

never (*nè*-veu) *adv* ne ... jamais

nevertheless (nè-veu-ðeu-*lèss*) *adv* néanmoins

new (nyoû) *adj* nouveau; **New Year** Nouvel An

news (nyoûz) *n* nouvelles, nouvelle *f*; actualités

newsagent (*nyoû*-zéï-djeunnt) *n* marchand de journaux

newspaper (*nyoûz*-péï-peu) *n* journal *m*

newsreel (*nyoûz*-riil) *n* actualités

newsstand (*nyoûz*-stænd) *n* kiosque à journaux

New Zealand (nyoû *zii*-leunnd) Nouvelle-Zélande *f*

next (nèkst) *adj* prochain, suivant; **~ to** à côté de

next-door (nèkst-*doo*) *adv* à côté

nice (naïss) *adj* gentil, joli, plaisant; bon; sympathique

nickel (*ni*-keul) *n* nickel *m*

nickname (*nik*-néïm) *n* surnom *m*

nicotine (*ni*-keu-tiin) *n* nicotine *f*

niece (niiss) *n* nièce *f*

Nigeria (naï-*djie*u-ri-eu) Nigeria *m*

Nigerian (naï-*djie*u-ri-eunn) *adj* nigérien; *n* Nigérien *m*

night (naït) *n* nuit *f*; soir *m*; **by ~** de nuit; **~ flight** vol de nuit; **~ rate** tarif de nuit; **~ train** train de nuit

nightclub (*naït*-klab) *n* boîte de nuit

night-cream (*naït*-kriim) *n* crème de nuit

nightdress (*naït*-drèss) *n* chemise de nuit

nightingale (*naï*-tinng-ghéïl) *n* rossignol *m*

nightly (*naït*-li) *adj* nocturne

nil (nil) rien

nine (naïn) *num* neuf

nineteen (naïn-*tiin*) *num* dix-neuf

nineteenth (naïn-*tiin*θ) *num* dix-neuvième

ninety (*naïn*-ti) *num* quatre-vingt-dix

ninth (naïnθ) *num* neuvième

nitrogen (*naï*-treu-djeunn) *n* azote *m*

no (nôou) *n* non; *adj* aucun; **~ one** ne ... personne

nobility (nôou-*bi*-leu-ti) *n* noblesse *f*

noble (*nôou*-beul) *adj* noble

nobody (*nôou*-bo-di) *pron* ne ... personne

nod (nod) *n* inclination de la tête; *v* opiner de la tête

noise (noïz) *n* bruit *m*; fracas *m*, vacarme *m*

noisy (*noï*-zi) *adj* bruyant; sonore

nominal (*no*-mi-neul) *adj* nominal

nominate (*no*-mi-néït) *v* nommer

nomination (no-mi-*néï*-cheunn) *n* nomination *f*

none (nann) *pron* aucun

nonsense (*nonn*-seunns) *n* sottise *f*

noon (noûn) *n* midi *m*

normal (*noo*-meul) *adj* normal

north (nooθ) *n* nord *m*; *adj* septen-

trional; **North Pole** pôle nord

north-east (nooθ-*iist*) *n* nord-est *m*

northerly (*noo*-ðeu-li) *adj* du nord

northern (*noo*-ðeunn) *adj* septentrional

north-west (nooθ-*ouèst*) *n* nord-ouest *m*

Norway (*noo*-ouéï) Norvège *f*

Norwegian (noo-*ouii*-djeunn) *adj* norvégien; *n* Norvégien *m*

nose (nôouz) *n* nez *m*

nosebleed (*nôou*z-bliid) *n* saignement de nez

nostril (*no*-stril) *n* narine *f*

not (not) *adv* ne ... pas

notary (*nôou*-teu-ri) *n* notaire *m*

note (nôout) *n* note *f*; ton *m*; *v* noter; observer, constater

notebook (*nôou*t-bouk) *n* carnet *m*

noted (*nôou*-tid) *adj* illustre

notepaper (*nôou*t-péï-peu) *n* papier à écrire, papier à lettres

nothing (*na*-θinng) *n* rien, ne ... rien

notice (*nôou*-tiss) *v* observer, noter, remarquer; *n* avis *m*, nouvelle *f*; attention *f*

noticeable (*nôou*-ti-seu-beul) *adj* perceptible; remarquable

notify (*nôou*-ti-faï) *v* notifier; avertir

notion (*nôou*-cheunn) *n* notion *f*

notorious (nôou-*too*-ri-euss) *adj* notoire

nougat (*noû*-ghââ) *n* nougat *m*

nought (noot) *n* zéro *m*

noun (naoun) *n* nom *m*, substantif *m*

nourishing (*na*-ri-chinng) *adj* nourrissant

novel (*no*-veul) *n* roman *m*

novelist (*no*-veu-list) *n* romancier *m*

November (nôou-*vèm*-beu) novembre

now (naou) *adv* maintenant; à l'heure actuelle; **~ and then** de temps en temps

nowadays (*naou*-eu-déïz) *adv* actuel-

lement
nowhere (*nôᵒᵘ-ouᵉᵘ*) *adv* nulle part
nozzle (*no-zeul*) *n* bec *m*
nuance (nyoû-*anss*) *n* nuance *f*
nuclear (*nyoû*-kli-eu) *adj* nucléaire; ~ **energy** énergie nucléaire
nucleus (*nyoû*-kli-euss) *n* noyau *m*
nude (nyoûd) *adj* nu; *n* nu *m*
nuisance (*nyoû*-seunns) *n* ennui *m*
numb (namm) *adj* engourdi
number (*namm*-beu) *n* numéro *m*; chiffre *m*, nombre *m*
numeral (*nyoû*-meu-reul) *n* nombre *m*
numerous (*nyoû*-meu-reuss) *adj* nombreux
nun (nann) *n* religieuse *f*
nunnery (*na*-neu-ri) *n* couvent *m*
nurse (neûss) *n* infirmière *f*; bonne d'enfants; *v* soigner; allaiter
nursery (*neû*-seu-ri) *n* chambre d'enfants; crèche *f*; pépinière *f*
nut (nat) *n* noix *f*; écrou *m*
nutcrackers (*nat*-kræ-keuz) *pl* casse-noix *m*
nutmeg (*nat*-mègh) *n* muscade *f*
nutritious (nyoû-*tri*-cheuss) *adj* nutritif
nutshell (*nat*-chèl) *n* coquille de noix
nylon (*naï*-lònn) *n* nylon *m*

O

oak (ôᵒᵘk) *n* chêne *m*
oar (oo) *n* rame *f*
oasis (ôᵒᵘ-*éï*-siss) *n* (pl oases) oasis *f*
oath (ôᵒᵘθ) *n* serment *m*
oats (ôᵒᵘts) *pl* avoine *f*
obedience (eu-*bii*-di-eunns) *n* obéissance *f*
obedient (eu-*bii*-di-eunnt) *adj* obéissant
obey (eu-*béï*) *v* obéir

object¹ (*ob*-djikt) *n* objet *m*; objectif *m*
object² (eub-*djèkt*) *v* objecter; ~ **to** *faire objection à
objection (eub-*djèk*-cheunn) *n* objection *f*
objective (eub-*djèk*-tiv) *adj* objectif; *n* objectif *m*
obligatory (eu-*bli*-gheu-teu-ri) *adj* obligatoire
oblige (eu-*blaïdj*) *v* obliger; *be obliged to *être obligé de; *devoir
obliging (eu-*blaï*-djinng) *adj* obligeant
oblong (*ob*-lonng) *adj* oblong; *n* rectangle *m*
obscene (eub-*siin*) *adj* obscène
obscure (eub-*skyou*ᵉᵘ) *adj* confus, vague, sombre, obscur
observation (ob-zeu-*véï*-cheunn) *n* observation *f*
observatory (eub-*zeû*-veu-tri) *n* observatoire *m*
observe (eub-*zeûv*) *v* observer
obsession (eub-*sè*-cheunn) *n* obsession *f*
obstacle (*ob*-steu-keul) *n* obstacle *m*
obstinate (*ob*-sti-neut) *adj* obstiné; opiniâtre
obtain (eub-*téïn*) *v* se procurer, *obtenir
obtainable (eub-*téï*-neu-beul) *adj* disponible
obvious (*ob*-vi-euss) *adj* évident
occasion (eu-*kéï*-jeunn) *n* occasion *f*; motif *m*
occasionally (eu-*kéï*-jeu-neu-li) *adv* de temps en temps
occupant (*o*-kyou-peunnt) *n* occupant *m*
occupation (o-kyou-*péï*-cheunn) *n* occupation *f*
occupy (*o*-kyou-païh) *v* occuper
occur (eu-*keû*) *v* se passer, se *produire, *survenir

occurrence (eu-*ka*-reunns) *n* événement *m*

ocean (*ô*^{ou}-cheunn) *n* océan *m*

October (ok-*tô*^{ou}-beu) octobre

octopus (*ok*-teu-peuss) *n* pieuvre *f*

oculist (*o*-kyou-list) *n* oculiste *m*

odd (od) *adj* bizarre; impair

odour (*ô*^{ou}-deu) *n* odeur *f*

of (ov, euv) *prep* de

off (of) *prep* de

offence (eu-*fèns*) *n* infraction *f*; offense *f*, outrage *m*

offend (eu-*fènd*) *v* blesser, offenser; outrager

offensive (eu-*fèn*-siv) *adj* offensif; désobligeant; *n* offensive *f*

offer (*o*-feu) *v* *offrir; *n* offre *f*

office (*o*-fiss) *n* bureau *m*; fonction *f*; ~ **hours** heures de bureau

officer (*o*-fi-seu) *n* officier *m*

official (eu-*fi*-cheul) *adj* officiel

off-licence (*of*-laï-seunns) *n* magasin de spiritueux

often (*o*-feunn) *adv* souvent

oil (oïl) *n* huile *f*; pétrole *m*; **fuel** ~ mazout *m*; ~ **filter** filtre à huile; ~ **pressure** pression d'huile

oil-painting (oïl-*péin*-tinng) *n* peinture à l'huile

oil-refinery (*oïl*-ri-faï-neu-ri) *n* raffinerie de pétrole

oil-well (*oïl*-^{ou}èl) *n* gisement de pétrole, puits de pétrole

oily (*oï*-li) *adj* huileux

ointment (*oïnt*-meunnt) *n* onguent *m*

okay! (ô^{ou}-*kéï*) d'accord!

old (ô^{ou}ld) *adj* vieux; ~ **age** vieillesse *f*

old-fashioned (ô^{ou}ld-*fæ*-cheunnd) *adj* démodé

olive (*o*-liv) *n* olive *f*; ~ **oil** huile d'olive

omelette (*omm*-leut) *n* omelette *f*

ominous (*o*-mi-neuss) *adj* sinistre

omit (eu-*mit*) *v* *omettre

omnipotent (omm-*ni*-peu-teunnt) *adj* omnipotent

on (onn) *prep* sur; à

once (^{ou}anns) *adv* une fois; **at** ~ immédiatement, tout de suite; ~ **more** une fois de plus

oncoming (*onn*-ka-minng) *adj* venant à la rencontre, proche

one (^{ou}ann) *num* un; *pron* on

oneself (^{ou}ann-*sèlf*) *pron* soi-même

onion (*a*-nyeunn) *n* oignon *m*

only (ô^{ou}n-li) *adj* seul; *adv* rien que, seulement; *conj* cependant

onwards (*onn*-^{ou}eudz) *adv* en avant

onyx (*o*-niks) *n* onyx *m*

opal (ô^{ou}-peul) *n* opale *f*

open (ô^{ou}-peunn) *v* *ouvrir; *adj* ouvert; franc

opening (ô^{ou}-peu-ninng) *n* ouverture *f*

opera (*o*-peu-reu) *n* opéra *m*; ~ **house** opéra *m*

operate (*o*-peu-réit) *v* opérer, fonctionner

operation (o-peu-*réï*-cheunn) *n* fonctionnement *m*; opération *f*

operator (*o*-peu-réï-teu) *n* standardiste *f*

operetta (o-peu-*rè*-teu) *n* opérette *f*

opinion (eu-*pi*-nyeunn) *n* idée *f*, opinion *f*

opponent (eu-*pô*^{ou}-neunnt) *n* adversaire *m*

opportunity (o-peu-*tyoû*-neu-ti) *n* occasion *f*

oppose (eu-*pô*^{ou}z) *v* s'opposer

opposite (*o*-peu-zit) *prep* en face de; *adj* opposé, contraire

opposition (o-peu-*zi*-cheunn) *n* opposition *f*

oppress (eu-*prèss*) *v* oppresser, opprimer

optician (op-*ti*-cheunn) *n* opticien *m*

optimism (*op*-ti-mi-zeumm) *n* optimisme *m*

optimist (*op*-ti-mist) *n* optimiste *m*

optimistic (op-ti-*mi*-stik) *adj* optimiste

optional (*op*-cheu-neul) *adj* facultatif

or (oo) *conj* ou

oral (*oo*-reul) *adj* oral

orange (*o*-rinndj) *n* orange *f*; *adj* orange

orchard (*oo*-tcheud) *n* verger *m*

orchestra (*oo*-ki-streu) *n* orchestre *m*; ~ **seat** *Am* fauteuil d'orchestre

order (*oo*-deu) *v* commander; *n* ordre *m*; commandement *m*; commande *f*; **in** ~ en règle; **in** ~ **to** afin de; **made to** ~ fait sur commande; **out of** ~ en dérangement; **postal** ~ mandat-poste *m*

order-form (*oo*-deu-foom) *n* bon de commande

ordinary (*oo*-deunn-ri) *adj* commun, habituel

ore (oo) *n* minerai *m*

organ (*oo*-gheunn) *n* organe *m*; orgue *m*

organic (oo-*ghæ*-nik) *adj* organique

organization (oo-gheu-naï-*zéï*-cheunn) *n* organisation *f*

organize (*oo*-gheu-naïz) *v* organiser

Orient (*oo*-ri-eunnt) *n* orient *m*

oriental (oo-ri-*èn*-teul) *adj* oriental

orientate (*oo*-ri-eunn-téït) *v* s'orienter

origin (*o*-ri-djinn) *n* origine *f*; descendance *f*, provenance *f*

original (eu-*ri*-dji-neul) *adj* authentique, original

originally (eu-*ri*-dji-neu-li) *adv* originairement

orlon (*oo*-lonn) *n* orlon *m*

ornament (*oo*-neu-meunnt) *n* ornement *m*

ornamental (oo-neu-*mèn*-teul) *adj* ornemental

orphan (*oo*-feunn) *n* orphelin *m*

orthodox (*oo*-θeu-doks) *adj* orthodoxe

ostrich (*o*-stritch) *n* autruche *f*

other (*a*-ðeu) *adj* autre

otherwise (*a*-ðeu-ᵒᵘaïz) *conj* sinon; *adv* autrement

*ought to (oot) **devoir*

our (aouᵉᵘ) *adj* notre

ourselves (aouᵉᵘ-*sèlvz*) *pron* nous; nous-mêmes

out (aout) *adv* dehors, hors; ~ **of** en dehors de, de

outbreak (*aout*-bréïk) *n* déchaînement *m*

outcome (*aout*-kamm) *n* résultat *m*

*outdo (aout-*doú*) *v* surpasser

outdoors (aout-*dooz*) *adv* dehors

outer (*aou*-teu) *adj* extérieur

outfit (*aout*-fit) *n* équipement *m*

outline (*aout*-laïn) *n* contour *m*; *v* esquisser

outlook (*aout*-louk) *n* prévision *f*; point de vue

output (*aout*-pout) *n* production *f*

outrage (*aout*-réïdj) *n* outrage *m*

outside (aout-*saïd*) *adv* dehors; *prep* hors de; *n* extérieur *m*

outsize (*aout*-saïz) *n* hors série

outskirts (*aout*-skeûts) *pl* faubourg *m*

outstanding (aout-*stæn*-dinng) *adj* éminent

outward (*aout*-ᵒᵘeud) *adj* externe

outwards (*aout*-ᵒᵘeudz) *adv* vers l'extérieur

oval (*ô*ᵒᵘ-veul) *adj* ovale

oven (*a*-veunn) *n* four *m*

over (*ô*ᵒᵘ-veu) *prep* au-dessus de, par-dessus; passé; *adv* au-dessus; *adj* fini; ~ **there** là-bas

overall (*ô*ᵒᵘ-veu-rool) *adj* total

overalls (*ô*ᵒᵘ-veu-roolz) *pl* salopette *f*

overcast (*ô*ᵒᵘ-veu-kââst) *adj* nuageux

overcoat (*ô*ᵒᵘ-veu-kôᵒᵘt) *n* pardessus *m*

*overcome (ô*ᵒᵘ*-veu-*kamm*) *v* *vaincre

overdue (ô^{ou}-veu-*dyoù*) *adj* en retard ; arriéré

overgrown (ô^{ou}-veu-*ghrô^{ou}n*) *adj* couvert de verdure

overhaul (ô^{ou}-veu-*hool*) *v* reviser

overhead (ô^{ou}-veu-*hèd*) *adv* en haut

overlook (ô^{ou}-veu-*louk*) *v* ignorer

overnight (ô^{ou}-veu-*naït*) *adv* de nuit

overseas (ô^{ou}-veu-*siiz*) *adj* d'outre-mer

oversight (ô^{ou}-veu-saït) *n* inadvertance *f*

***oversleep** (ô^{ou}-veu-*sliip*) *v* *dormir trop longtemps

overstrung (ô^{ou}-veu-*stranng*) *adj* surmené

***overtake** (ô^{ou}-veu-*téïk*) *v* dépasser ; **no overtaking** défense de doubler

over-tired (ô^{ou}-veu-*taï^{eu}d*) *adj* surmené

overture (ô^{ou}-veu-tcheu) *n* ouverture *f*

overweight (ô^{ou}-veu-^{ou}éït) *n* surcharge *f*

overwhelm (ô^{ou}-veu-^{ou}èlm) *v* déconcerter, écraser

overwork (ô^{ou}-veu-^{ou}eûk) *v* se surmener

owe (ô^{ou}) *v* *devoir ; **owing to** en raison de

owl (aoul) *n* hibou *m*

own (ô^{ou}n) *v* posséder ; *adj* propre

owner (ô^{ou}-neu) *n* propriétaire *m*

ox (oks) *n* (pl oxen) bœuf *m*

oxygen (*ok*-si-djeunn) *n* oxygène *m*

oyster (*oï*-steu) *n* huître *f*

P

pace (péïss) *n* allure *f* ; démarche *f*, pas *m* ; rythme *m*

Pacific Ocean (peu-*si*-fik ô^{ou}-cheunn) Océan Pacifique

pacifism (*pæ*-si-fi-zeumm) *n* pacifisme *m*

pacifist (*pæ*-si-fist) *n* pacifiste *m*

pack (pæk) *v* emballer ; ~ **up** emballer

package (*pæ*-kidj) *n* colis *m*

packet (*pæ*-kit) *n* paquet *m*

packing (*pæ*-kinng) *n* emballage *m*

pad (pæd) *n* coussinet *m* ; bloc-notes *m*

paddle (*pæ*-deul) *n* pagaie *f*

padlock (*pæd*-lok) *n* cadenas *m*

pagan (*péï*-gheunn) *adj* païen ; *n* païen *m*

page (péïdj) *n* page *f*

page-boy (*péïdj*-boï) *n* page *m*

pail (péïl) *n* seau *m*

pain (péïn) *n* douleur *f* ; **pains** peine *f*

painful (*péïn*-feul) *adj* douloureux

painless (*péïn*-leuss) *adj* sans douleur

paint (péïnt) *n* peinture *f* ; *v* *peindre

paint-box (*péïnt*-boks) *n* boîte de couleurs

paint-brush (*péïnt*-brach) *n* pinceau *m*

painter (*péïn*-teu) *n* peintre *m*

painting (*péïn*-tinng) *n* peinture *f*

pair (pè^{eu}) *n* paire *f*

Pakistan (pââ-ki-*stâân*) Pakistan *m*

Pakistani (pââ-ki-*stââ*-ni) *adj* pakistanais ; *n* Pakistanais *m*

palace (*pæ*-leuss) *n* palais *m*

pale (péïl) *adj* pâle

palm (pââm) *n* palme *f* ; paume *f*

palpable (*pæl*-peu-beul) *adj* palpable

palpitation (pæl-pi-*téï*-cheunn) *n* palpitation *f*

pan (pæn) *n* casserole *f*

pane (péïn) *n* carreau *m*

panel (*pæ*-neul) *n* panneau *m*

panelling (*pæ*-neu-linng) *n* lambrissage *m*

panic (*pæ*-nik) *n* panique *f*

pant (pænt) *v* haleter

panties (*pæn*-tiz) *pl* culotte *f*

pants (pænts) *pl* caleçon *m*; *plAm* pantalon *m*

pant-suit (*pænt*-soût) *n* ensemble-pantalon

panty-hose (*pæn*-ti-hô^{ou}z) *n* collants *mpl*

paper (*péi*-peu) *n* papier *m*; journal *m*; en papier; **carbon** ~ papier carbone; ~ **bag** sac en papier; ~ **napkin** serviette de papier; **typing** ~ papier à machine; **wrapping** ~ papier d'emballage

paperback (*péi*-peu-bæk) *n* livre de poche

paper-knife (*péi*-peu-naïf) *n* coupe-papier *m*

parade (peu-*réïd*) *n* parade *f*

paraffin (*pæ*-reu-finn) *n* pétrole *m*

paragraph (*pæ*-reu-ghrââf) *n* paragraphe *m*

parakeet (*pæ*-reu-kiit) *n* perruche *f*

paralise (*pæ*-reu-laïz) *v* paralyser

parallel (*pæ*-reu-lèl) *adj* parallèle; *n* parallèle *f*

parcel (*pââ*-seul) *n* colis *m*, paquet *m*

pardon (*pââ*-deunn) *n* pardon *m*; grâce *f*

parents (*pè^{eu}*-reunnts) *pl* parents

parents-in-law (*pè^{eu}*-reunnts-inn-loo) *pl* beaux-parents *mpl*

parish (*pæ*-rich) *n* paroisse *f*

park (pââk) *n* parc *m*; *v* se garer

parking (*pââ*-kinng) *n* stationnement *m*; **no** ~ stationnement interdit; ~ **fee** droit de stationnement; ~ **light** feu de position; ~ **lot** *Am* parking *m*; ~ **meter** parcomètre *m*; ~ **zone** zone de stationnement

parliament (*pââ*-leu-meunnt) *n* parlement *m*

parliamentary (pââ-leu-*mèn*-teu-ri) *adj* parlementaire

parrot (*pæ*-reut) *n* perroquet *m*

parsley (*pââ*-sli) *n* persil *m*

parson (*pââ*-seunn) *n* pasteur *m*

parsonage (*pââ*-seu-nidj) *n* presbytère *m*

part (pâât) *n* part *f*, partie *f*; morceau *m*; *v* séparer; **spare** ~ pièce de rechange

partial (*pââ*-cheul) *adj* partiel; partial

participant (pââ-*ti*-si-peunnt) *n* participant *m*

participate (pââ-*ti*-si-péït) *v* participer

particular (peu-*ti*-kyou-leu) *adj* spécial, particulier; exigeant; **in** ~ en particulier

parting (*pââ*-tinng) *n* adieu *m*; raie *f*

partition (pââ-*ti*-cheunn) *n* cloison *f*

partly (*pâât*-li) *adv* en partie, partiellement

partner (*pâât*-neu) *n* partenaire *m*; associé *m*

partridge (*pââ*-tridj) *n* perdrix *f*

party (*pââ*-ti) *n* parti *m*; surprise-partie *f*; groupe *m*

pass (pââss) *v* passer, dépasser; réussir; *vAm* doubler; **no passing** *Am* défense de doubler; ~ **by** passer à côté; ~ **through** traverser

passage (*pæ*-sidj) *n* passage *m*; traversée *f*

passenger (*pæ*-seunn-djeu) *n* passager *m*; ~ **car** *Am* wagon *m*; ~ **train** train de voyageurs

passer-by (pââ-seu-*baï*) *n* passant *m*

passion (*pæ*-cheunn) *n* passion *f*; colère *f*

passionate (*pæ*-cheu-neut) *adj* passionné

passive (*pæ*-siv) *adj* passif

passport (*pââss*-poot) *n* passeport *m*; ~ **control** contrôle des passeports; ~ **photograph** photo d'identité

password (*pââss*-^{ou}eûd) *n* mot de passe

past (pâât) *n* passé *m*; *adj* passé, dernier; *prep* le long de, au delà de

paste (péïst) *n* pâte *f*; *v* coller

pastry (péï-stri) *n* pâtisserie *f*; ~ **shop** pâtisserie *f*

pasture (pââss-tcheu) *n* pâture *f*

patch (pætch) *v* rapiécer

patent (péï-teunnt) *n* brevet *m*

path (pââθ) *n* sentier *m*

patience (péï-cheunns) *n* patience *f*

patient (péï-cheunnt) *adj* patient; *n* patient *m*

patriot (péï-tri-eut) *n* patriote *m*

patrol (peu-trôᵒᵘl) *n* patrouille *f*; *v* patrouiller; surveiller

pattern (pæ-teunn) *n* motif *m*, dessin *m*

pause (pooz) *n* pause *f*; *v* s'*interrompre

pave (péïv) *v* paver

pavement (péïv-meunnt) *n* trottoir *m*; pavage *m*

pavilion (peu-*vil*-yeunn) *n* pavillon *m*

paw (poo) *n* patte *f*

pawn (poon) *v* donner en gage, *mettre en gage; *n* pion *m*

pawnbroker (poon-brôᵒᵘ-keu) *n* prêteur sur gage

pay (péï) *n* salaire *m*, paye *f*

*****pay** (péï) *v* payer; ~ **attention to** *faire attention à; **paying** rentable; ~ **off** amortir; ~ **on account** payer à tempérament

pay-desk (péï-dèsk) *n* caisse *f*

payee (péï-*ii*) *n* bénéficiaire *m*

payment (péï-meunnt) *n* paiement *m*

pea (pii) *n* pois *m*

peace (piiss) *n* paix *f*

peaceful (*piiss*-feul) *adj* paisible

peach (piitch) *n* pêche *f*

peacock (*pii*-kok) *n* paon *m*

peak (piik) *n* sommet *m*; apogée *m*; ~ **hour** heure de pointe; ~ **season** pleine saison

peanut (*pii*-nat) *n* cacahuète *f*

pear (pèᵉᵘ) *n* poire *f*

pearl (peûl) *n* perle *f*

peasant (pè-zeunnt) *n* paysan *m*

pebble (pè-beul) *n* galet *m*

peculiar (pi-*kyoûl*-yeu) *adj* singulier; spécial, particulier

peculiarity (pi-kyoû-li-*æ*-reu-ti) *n* particularité *f*

pedal (pè-deul) *n* pédale *f*

pedestrian (pi-*dè*-stri-eunn) *n* piéton *m*; **no pedestrians** interdit aux piétons; ~ **crossing** passage clouté

pedicure (pè-di-kyouᵉᵘ) *n* pédicure *m*

peel (piil) *v* peler; *n* pelure *f*

peep (piip) *v* épier

peg (pègh) *n* patère *f*

pelican (pè-li-keunn) *n* pélican *m*

pelvis (*pèl*-viss) *n* bassin *m*

pen (pèn) *n* plume *f*

penalty (pè-neul-ti) *n* amende *f*; peine *f*; ~ **kick** penalty *m*

pencil (*pèn*-seul) *n* crayon *m*

pencil-sharpener (*pèn*-seul-chââp-neu) *n* taille-crayon *m*

pendant (*pèn*-deunnt) *n* pendentif *m*

penetrate (pè-ni-tréït) *v* pénétrer

penguin (*pèng*-ghᵒᵘinn) *n* pingouin *m*

penicillin (pè-ni-*si*-linn) *n* pénicilline *f*

peninsula (peu-*ninn*-syou-leu) *n* péninsule *f*

penknife (*pèn*-naïf) *n* (pl -knives) canif *m*

pension¹ (*pan*-si-on) *n* pension *f*

pension² (*pèn*-cheunn) *n* pension *f*

people (*pii*-peul) *pl* gens *mpl/fpl*; *n* peuple *m*

pepper (pè-peu) *n* poivre *m*

peppermint (*pè*-peu-minnt) *n* menthe *f*

perceive (peu-*siiv*) *v* *percevoir

percent (peu-*sènt*) *n* pour cent

percentage (peu-*sèn*-tidj) *n* pourcentage *m*

perceptible (peu-*sèp*-ti-beul) *adj* perceptible

perception (peu-*sèp*-cheunn) *n* perception *f*

perch (peûtch) (pl ~) perche *f*

percolator (*peû*-keu-léï-teu) *n* percolateur *m*

perfect (*peû*-fikt) *adj* parfait

perfection (peu-*fèk*-cheunn) *n* perfection *f*

perform (peu-*foom*) *v* accomplir

performance (peu-*foo*-meunns) *n* performance *f*

perfume (*peû*-fyoûm) *n* parfum *m*

perhaps (peu-*hæps*) *adv* peut-être

peril (*pè*-ril) *n* péril *m*

perilous (*pè*-ri-leuss) *adj* périlleux

period (*pi*eu-ri-eud) *n* époque *f*, période *f*; point *m*

periodical (pi*eu*-ri-*o*-di-keul) *n* périodique *m*; *adj* périodique

perish (*pè*-rich) *v* périr

perishable (*pè*-ri-cheu-beul) *adj* périssable

perjury (*peû*-djeu-ri) *n* faux serment

permanent (*peû*-meu-neunnt) *adj* durable, permanent; stable, fixe; ~ **press** pli permanent; ~ **wave** permanente *f*

permission (peu-*mi*-cheunn) *n* permission *f*, autorisation *f*; permis *m*, licence *f*

permit[1] (peu-*mit*) *v* *permettre

permit[2] (*peû*-mit) *n* permis *m*

peroxide (peu-*rok*-saïd) *n* eau oxygénée

perpendicular (peû-peunn-*di*-kyou-leu) *adj* perpendiculaire

Persia (*peû*-cheu) Perse *f*

Persian (*peû*-cheunn) *adj* persan; *n* Persan *m*

person (*peû*-seunn) *n* personne *f*; **per ~** par personne

personal (*peû*-seu-neul) *adj* personnel

personality (peû-seu-*næ*-leu-ti) *n* personnalité *f*

personnel (peû-seu-*nèl*) *n* personnel *m*

perspective (peu-*spèk*-tiv) *n* perspective *f*

perspiration (peû-speu-*réï*-cheunn) *n* transpiration *f*, sueur *f*

perspire (peu-*spaï*eu) *v* transpirer, suer

persuade (peu-s*ou*éïd) *v* persuader; *convaincre

persuasion (peu-s*ou*éï-jeunn) *n* conviction *f*

pessimism (*pè*-si-mi-zeumm) *n* pessimisme *m*

pessimist (*pè*-si-mist) *n* pessimiste *m*

pessimistic (pè-si-*mi*-stik) *adj* pessimiste

pet (pèt) *n* animal familier; chouchou *m*; favori

petal (*pè*-teul) *n* pétale *m*

petition (pi-*ti*-cheunn) *n* pétition *f*

petrol (*pè*-treul) *n* essence *f*; ~ **pump** pompe à essence; ~ **station** poste d'essence; ~ **tank** réservoir d'essence

petroleum (pi-*trô*ou-li-eumm) *n* pétrole *m*

petty (*pè*-ti) *adj* petit, futile, insignifiant; ~ **cash** petite monnaie

pewit (*pii*-ou it) *n* vanneau *m*

pewter (*pyoû*-teu) *n* étain *m*

phantom (*fæn*-teumm) *n* fantôme *m*

pharmacology (fââ-meu-*ko*-leu-dji) *n* pharmacologie *f*

pharmacy (*fââ*-meu-si) *n* pharmacie *f*; droguerie *f*

phase (féïz) *n* phase *f*

pheasant (*fè*-zeunnt) *n* faisan *m*

Philippine (*fi*-li-païn) *adj* philippin

Philippines (*fi*-li-piinz) *pl* Philippines *fpl*

philosopher (fi-*lo*-seu-feu) *n* philosophe *m*

philosophy (fi-*lo*-seu-fi) *n* philosophie

f

phone (fô^{ou}n) *n* téléphone *m*; *v* téléphoner

phonetic (feu-*nè*-tik) *adj* phonétique

photo (fô^{ou}-tô^{ou}) *n* (pl ~s) photo *f*

photograph (fô^{ou}-teu-ghrââf) *n* photographie *f*; *v* photographier

photographer (feu-*to*-ghreu-feu) *n* photographe *m*

photography (feu-*to*-ghreu-fi) *n* photographie *f*

photostat (fô^{ou}-teu-stæt) *n* photocopie *f*

phrase (fréïz) *n* locution *f*

phrase-book (*fréïz*-bouk) *n* manuel de conversation

physical (*fi*-zi-keul) *adj* physique

physician (fi-*zi*-cheunn) *n* médecin *m*

physicist (*fi*-zi-sist) *n* physicien *m*

physics (*fi*-ziks) *n* physique *f*

physiology (fi-zi-*o*-leu-dji) *n* physiologie *f*

pianist (*pii*-eu-nist) *n* pianiste *m*

piano (pi-*æ*-nô^{ou}) *n* piano *m*; **grand ~** piano à queue

pick (pik) *v* *cueillir; choisir; *n* choix *m*; **~ up** ramasser; *aller chercher; **pick-up van** camionnette *f*

pick-axe (*pi*-kæks) *n* pioche *f*

pickles (*pi*-keulz) *pl* conserves au vinaigre, marinade *f*

picnic (*pik*-nik) *n* pique-nique *m*; *v* pique-niquer

picture (*pik*-tcheu) *n* peinture *f*; illustration *f*, gravure *f*; image *f*; **~ postcard** carte postale, carte postale illustrée; **pictures** cinéma *m*

picturesque (pik-tcheu-*rèsk*) *adj* pittoresque

piece (piiss) *n* morceau *m*, pièce *f*

pier (pi^{eu}) *n* jetée *f*

pierce (pi^{eu}ss) *v* percer

pig (pigh) *n* cochon *m*

pigeon (*pi*-djeunn) *n* pigeon *m*

pig-headed (pigh-*hè*-did) *adj* obstiné

piglet (*pigh*-leut) *n* cochon de lait

pigskin (*pigh*-skinn) *n* peau de porc

pike (païk) (pl ~) brochet *m*

pile (païl) *n* tas *m*; *v* entasser; **piles** *pl* hémorroïdes *fpl*

pilgrim (*pil*-ghrimm) *n* pèlerin *m*

pilgrimage (*pil*-ghri-midj) *n* pèlerinage *m*

pill (pil) *n* pilule *f*

pillar (*pi*-leu) *n* colonne *f*, pilier *m*

pillar-box (*pi*-leu-boks) *n* boîte aux lettres

pillow (*pi*-lô^{ou}) *n* oreiller *m*

pillow-case (*pi*-lô^{ou}-kéïss) *n* taie d'oreiller

pilot (*paï*-leut) *n* pilote *m*

pimple (*pimm*-peul) *n* pustule *f*

pin (pinn) *n* épingle *f*; *v* épingler; **bobby ~** *Am* pince à cheveux

pincers (*pinn*-seuz) *pl* tenailles *fpl*

pinch (pinntch) *v* pincer

pineapple (*paï*-næ-peul) *n* ananas *m*

ping-pong (*pinng*-ponng) *n* tennis de table

pink (pinngk) *adj* rose

pioneer (paï"-eu-*ni*^{eu}) *n* pionnier *m*

pious (*paï*-euss) *adj* pieux

pip (pip) *n* pépin *m*

pipe (païp) *n* pipe *f*; tuyau *m*; **~ cleaner** cure-pipe *m*; **~ tobacco** tabac pour pipe

pirate (*païeu*-reut) *n* pirate *m*

pistol (*pi*-steul) *n* pistolet *m*

piston (*pi*-steunn) *n* piston *m*; **~ ring** segment de piston

piston-rod (*pi*-steunn-rod) *n* tige de piston

pit (pit) *n* fosse *f*; mine *f*

pitcher (*pi*-tcheu) *n* cruche *f*

pity (*pi*-ti) *n* pitié *f*; *v* *avoir pitié de, compatir; **what a pity!** dommage!

placard (*plæ*-kââd) *n* affiche *f*

place (pléïss) *n* place *f*; *v* poser, pla-

cer; ~ **of birth** lieu de naissance;
*take ~ *avoir lieu

plague (pléigh) n fléau m

plaice (pléïss) (pl ~) plie f

plain (pléïn) adj clair; ordinaire, simple; n plaine f

plan (plæn) n plan m; v planifier

plane (pléïn) adj plat; n avion m; ~
crash accident d'avion

planet (plæ-nit) n planète f

planetarium (plæ-ni-tè⁽ᵉᵘ⁾-ri-eumm) n
planétarium m

plank (plængk) n planche f

plant (plâânt) n plante f; usine f; v
planter

plantation (plæn-téï-cheunn) n plantation f

plaster (plââ-steu) n crépi m, plâtre
m; sparadrap m

plastic (plæ-stik) adj plastique; n
plastique m

plate (pléït) n assiette f; plaque f

plateau (plæ-tô⁽ᵒᵘ⁾) n (pl ~x, ~s) plateau m

platform (plæt-foom) n quai m; ~
ticket billet de quai

platinum (plæ-ti-neumm) n platine m

play (pléï) v jouer; n jeu m; pièce de
théâtre; **one-act** ~ pièce en un acte; ~ **truant** *faire l'école buissonnière

player (pléï⁽ᵉᵘ⁾) n joueur m

playground (pléï-ghraound) n terrain
de jeux

playing-card (pléï-inng-kââd) n carte
de jeu

playwright (pléï-raït) n dramaturge m

plea (plii) n plaidoyer m

plead (pliid) v plaider

pleasant (plè-zeunnt) adj plaisant,
sympathique, agréable

please (pliiz) s'il vous plaît; v *plaire;
pleased content; **pleasing** agréable

pleasure (plè-jeu) n agrément m, divertissement m, plaisir m

plentiful (plèn-ti-feul) adj abondant

plenty (plèn-ti) n abondance f

pliers (plaï⁽ᵉᵘ⁾z) pl pince f

plimsolls (plimm-seulz) pl chaussures
de basket

plot (plot) n conspiration f, complot
m; intrigue f; lopin m

plough (plaou) n charrue f; v labourer

plucky (pla-ki) adj courageux

plug (plagh) n fiche f; ~ **in** brancher

plum (plamm) n prune f

plumber (pla-meu) n plombier m

plump (plammp) adj potelé

plural (plou⁽ᵉᵘ⁾-reul) n pluriel m

plus (plass) prep plus

pneumatic (nyoû-mæ-tik) adj pneumatique

pneumonia (nyoû-mô⁽ᵒᵘ⁾-ni-eu) n pneumonie f

poach (pô⁽ᵒᵘ⁾tch) v braconner

pocket (po-kit) n poche f

pocket-book (po-kit-bouk) n portefeuille m

pocket-comb (po-kit-kô⁽ᵒᵘ⁾m) n peigne
de poche

pocket-knife (po-kit-naïf) n (pl
-knives) couteau de poche

pocket-watch (po-kit-⁽ᵒᵘ⁾otch) n montre de gousset

poem (pô⁽ᵒᵘ⁾-imm) n poème m

poet (pô⁽ᵒᵘ⁾-it) n poète m

poetry (pô⁽ᵒᵘ⁾-i-tri) n poésie f

point (poïnt) n point m; pointe f; v
montrer du doigt; ~ **of view** point
de vue; ~ **out** indiquer

pointed (poïn-tid) adj pointu

poison (poï-zeunn) n poison m; v empoisonner

poisonous (poï-zeu-neuss) adj vénéneux

Poland (pô⁽ᵒᵘ⁾-leunnd) Pologne f

Pole (pô⁽ᵒᵘ⁾l) n Polonais m

pole (pô^{ou}l) *n* poteau *m*

police (peu-*liss*) *pl* police *f*

policeman (peu-*liiss*-meunn) *n* (pl -men) agent de police, policier *m*

police-station (peu-*liiss*-stéï-cheunn) *n* commissariat de police

policy (*po*-li-si) *n* politique *f*; police *f*

polio (*pô^{ou}*-li-ô^{ou}) *n* poliomyélite *f*

Polish (*pô^{ou}*-lich) *adj* polonais

polish (*po*-lich) *v* polir

polite (peu-*laït*) *adj* poli

political (peu-*li*-ti-keul) *adj* politique

politician (po-li-*ti*-cheunn) *n* politicien *m*

politics (*po*-li-tiks) *n* politique *f*

pollution (peu-*loû*-cheunn) *n* pollution *f*

pond (ponnd) *n* étang *m*

pony (*pô^{ou}*-ni) *n* poney *m*

poor (pou^{eu}) *adj* pauvre; indigent; piètre

pope (pô^{ou}p) *n* pape *m*

poplin (*po*-plinn) *n* popeline *f*

pop music (pop *myoû*-zik) musique pop

poppy (*po*-pi) *n* coquelicot *m*; pavot *m*

popular (*po*-pyou-leu) *adj* populaire

population (po-pyou-*léï*-cheunn) *n* population *f*

populous (*po*-pyou-leuss) *adj* populeux

porcelain (*poo*-seu-linn) *n* porcelaine *f*

porcupine (*poo*-kyou-païn) *n* porc-épic *m*

pork (pook) *n* porc *m*

port (poot) *n* port *m*; bâbord *m*

portable (*poo*-teu-beul) *adj* portatif

porter (*poo*-teu) *n* porteur *m*; portier *m*

porthole (*poot*-hô^{ou}l) *n* hublot *m*

portion (*poo*-cheunn) *n* portion *f*

portrait (*poo*-trit) *n* portrait *m*

Portugal (*poo*-tyou-gheul) Portugal *m*

Portuguese (poo-tyou-*ghiiz*) *adj* portugais; *n* Portugais *m*

position (peu-*zi*-cheunn) *n* position *f*; situation *f*; attitude *f*

positive (*po*-zeu-tiv) *adj* positif; *n* positif *m*

possess (peu-*zèss*) *v* posséder; **possessed** *adj* possédé

possession (peu-*zè*-cheunn) *n* possession *f*; **possessions** biens *mpl*

possibility (po-seu-*bi*-leu-ti) *n* possibilité *f*

possible (*po*-seu-beul) *adj* possible; éventuel

post (pô^{ou}st) *n* poteau *m*; poste *m*; poste *f*; *v* poster; **post-office** bureau de poste

postage (*pô^{ou}*-stidj) *n* port *m*; ~ **paid** port payé; ~ **stamp** timbre-poste *m*

postcard (*pô^{ou}st*-kâad) *n* carte postale

poster (*pô^{ou}*-steu) *n* affiche *f*

poste restante (pô^{ou}st rè-*stant*) poste restante

postman (*pô^{ou}st*-meunn) *n* (pl -men) facteur *m*

post-paid (pô^{ou}st-*péïd*) *adj* port payé

postpone (peu-spô^{ou}n) *v* ajourner, *renvoyer à

pot (pot) *n* pot *m*

potato (peu-*téï*-tô^{ou}) *n* (pl ~es) pomme de terre *f*

pottery (*po*-teu-ri) *n* poterie *f*; vaisselle *f*

pouch (paoutch) *n* pochette *f*

poulterer (*pô^{ou}l*-teu-reu) *n* marchand de volaille

poultry (*pô^{ou}l*-tri) *n* volaille *f*

pound (paound) *n* livre *f*

pour (poo) *v* verser

poverty (*po*-veu-ti) *n* pauvreté *f*

powder (*paou*-deu) *n* poudre *f*; ~ **compact** poudrier *m*; **talc** ~ talc *m*

powder-puff (*paou*-deu-paf) *n* houppette f

powder-room (*paou*-deu-roûm) n toilettes pour dames

power (*paou*ᵉᵘ) n force f, puissance f; énergie f; pouvoir m

powerful (*paou*ᵉᵘ-feul) adj puissant; fort

powerless (*paou*ᵉᵘ-leuss) adj impuissant

power-station (*paou*ᵉᵘ-stéï-cheunn) n centrale f

practical (*præk*-ti-keul) adj pratique

practically (*præk*-ti-kli) adv pratiquement

practice (*præk*-tiss) n pratique f

practise (*præk*-tiss) v pratiquer; s'exercer

praise (préïz) v louer; n éloge m

pram (præm) n voiture d'enfant

prawn (proon) n crevette f, crevette rose

pray (préï) v prier

prayer (*prè*ᵉᵘ) n prière f

preach (priitch) v prêcher

precarious (pri-*kè*ᵉᵘ-ri-euss) adj précaire

precaution (pri-*koo*-cheunn) n précaution f

precede (pri-siid) v précéder

preceding (pri-*sii*-dinng) adj précédent

precious (*prè*-cheuss) adj précieux

precipice (*prè*-si-piss) n précipice m

precipitation (pri-si-pi-*téï*-cheunn) n précipitation f

precise (pri-*saïss*) adj précis, exact; méticuleux

predecessor (*prii*-di-sè-seu) n prédécesseur m

predict (pri-*dikt*) v *prédire

prefer (pri-*feû*) v aimer mieux, préférer

preferable (*prè*-feu-reu-beul) adj préférable

preference (*prè*-feu-reunns) n préférence f

prefix (*prii*-fiks) n préfixe m

pregnant (*prègh*-neunnt) adj enceinte

prejudice (*prè*-djeu-diss) n préjugé m

preliminary (pri-*li*-mi-neu-ri) adj préliminaire

premature (*prè*-meu-tchou°) adj prématuré

premier (*prèm*-iᵉᵘ) n premier ministre

premises (*prè*-mi-siz) pl locaux mpl

premium (*prii*-mi-eumm) n prime f

prepaid (prii-*péïd*) adj payé d'avance

preparation (prè-peu-*réï*-cheunn) n préparation f

prepare (pri-*pè*ᵉᵘ) v préparer

prepared (pri-*pè*ᵉᵘd) adj prêt

preposition (prè-peu-*zi*-cheunn) n préposition f

prescribe (pri-*skraïb*) v *prescrire

prescription (pri-*skrip*-cheunn) n prescription f

presence (*prè*-zeunns) n présence f

present¹ (*prè*-zeunnt) n cadeau m; présent m; adj actuel; présent

present² (pri-*zènt*) v présenter

presently (*prè*-zeunnt-li) adv tout à l'heure

preservation (prè-zeu-*véï*-cheunn) n conservation f

preserve (pri-*zeûv*) v conserver; *mettre en conserve

president (*prè*-zi-deunnt) n président m

press (prèss) n presse f; v appuyer, presser; repasser; ~ **conference** conférence de presse

pressing (*prè*-sinng) adj pressant, urgent

pressure (*prè*-cheu) n pression f; tension f; **atmospheric** ~ pression atmosphérique

pressure-cooker (*prè*-cheu-kou-keu) n cocotte à pression

prestige (prè-*stiij*) n prestige m

presumable (pri-*zyoû*-meu-beul) adj probable

presumptuous (pri-*zammp*-cheuss) adj présomptueux

pretence (pri-*tèns*) n prétexte m

pretend (pri-*tènd*) v *feindre, prétendre

pretext (*prii*-tèkst) n prétexte m

pretty (*pri*-ti) adj beau, joli; adv assez, plutôt, passablement

prevent (pri-*vènt*) v empêcher; *prévenir

preventive (pri-*vèn*-tiv) adj préventif

previous (*prii*-vi-euss) adj précédent, antérieur, préalable

pre-war (prii-*ou*oo) adj d'avant-guerre

price (praïss) v fixer le prix; ~ **list** prix-courant m

priceless (*praïss*-leuss) adj inestimable

price-list (*praïss*-list) n prix m

prick (prik) v piquer

pride (praïd) n orgueil m

priest (priist) n prêtre m

primary (*praï*-meu-ri) adj primaire; premier, primordial; élémentaire

prince (prinns) n prince m

princess (prinn-sèss) n princesse f

principal (*prinn*-seu-peul) adj principal; n proviseur m, directeur m

principle (*prinn*-seu-peul) n principe m

print (prinnt) v imprimer; n épreuve f; estampe f; **printed matter** imprimé m

prior (praï*eu*) adj antérieur

priority (praï-*o*-reu-ti) n priorité f

prison (*pri*-zeunn) n prison f

prisoner (*pri*-zeu-neu) n détenu m, prisonnier m; ~ **of war** prisonnier de guerre

privacy (*praï*-veu-si) n intimité f, vie privée

private (*praï*-vit) adj particulier, privé; personnel

privilege (*pri*-vi-lidj) n privilège m

prize (praïz) n prix m; récompense f

probable (*pro*-beu-beul) adj vraisemblable, probable

probably (*pro*-beu-bli) adv probablement

problem (*pro*-bleumm) n problème m; question f

procedure (preu-*sii*-djeu) n procédure f

proceed (preu-*siid*) v procéder

process (*prô*ou-sèss) n processus m, procédé m; procès m

procession (preu-*sè*-cheunn) n procession f, cortège m

proclaim (preu-*klé*ïm) v proclamer

produce[1] (preu-*dyoûss*) v *produire

produce[2] (*prod*-yoûss) n produit m

producer (preu-*dyoû*-seu) n producteur m

product (*pro*-dakt) n produit m

production (preu-*dak*-cheunn) n production f

profession (preu-*fè*-cheunn) n métier m, profession f

professional (preu-*fè*-cheu-neul) adj professionnel

professor (preu-*fè*-seu) n professeur m

profit (*pro*-fit) n bénéfice m, profit m; avantage m; v profiter

profitable (*pro*-fi-teu-beul) adj profitable

profound (preu-*faound*) adj profond

programme (*prô*ou-ghræm) n programme m

progress[1] (*prô*ou-ghrèss) n progrès m

progress[2] (preu-*ghrèss*) v avancer

progressive (preu-*ghrè*-siv) adj progressiste; progressif

prohibit (preu-*hi*-bit) v *interdire

prohibition (prô*ou*-i-*bi*-cheunn) n interdiction f

prohibitive (preu-*hi*-bi-tiv) *adj* inabordable

project (*pro*-djèkt) *n* plan *m*, projet *m*

promenade (pro-meu-*nââd*) *n* promenade *f*

promise (*pro*-miss) *n* promesse *f*; *v* *promettre

promote (preu-*môᵒᵘt*) *v* *promouvoir

promotion (preu-*môᵒᵘ*-cheunn) *n* promotion *f*

prompt (prommpt) *adj* instantané, prompt

pronoun (*prôᵒᵘ*-naoun) *n* pronom *m*

pronounce (preu-*naouns*) *v* prononcer

pronunciation (preu-nann-si-*éï*-cheunn) *n* prononciation *f*

proof (proûf) *n* preuve *f*

propaganda (pro-peu-*ghæn*-deu) *n* propagande *f*

propel (preu-*pèl*) *v* propulser

propeller (preu-*pè*-leu) *n* hélice *f*

proper (*pro*-peu) *adj* juste; convenable, pertinent, adéquat, approprié

property (*pro*-peu-ti) *n* propriété *f*

prophet (*pro*-fit) *n* prophète *m*

proportion (preu-*poo*-cheunn) *n* proportion *f*

proportional (preu-*poo*-cheu-neul) *adj* proportionnel

proposal (preu-*pôᵒᵘ*-zeul) *n* proposition *f*

propose (preu-*pôᵒᵘz*) *v* proposer

proposition (pro-peu-*zi*-cheunn) *n* proposition *f*

proprietor (preu-*praï*-eu-teu) *n* propriétaire *m*

prospect (*pro*-spèkt) *n* perspective *f*

prospectus (preu-*spèk*-teuss) *n* prospectus *m*

prosperity (pro-*spè*-reu-ti) *n* prospérité *f*

prosperous (*pro*-speu-reuss) *adj* prospère

prostitute (*pro*-sti-tyoût) *n* prostituée

f

protect (preu-*tèkt*) *v* protéger

protection (preu-*tèk*-cheunn) *n* protection *f*

protein (*prôᵒᵘ*-tiin) *n* protéine *f*

protest¹ (*prôᵒᵘ*-tèst) *n* protestation *f*

protest² (preu-*tèst*) *v* protester

Protestant (*pro*-ti-steunnt) *adj* protestant

proud (praoud) *adj* fier; orgueilleux

prove (proûv) *v* démontrer, prouver; se révéler

proverb (*pro*-veûb) *n* proverbe *m*

provide (preu-*vaïd*) *v* fournir; **provided that** pourvu que

province (*pro*-vinns) *n* province *f*

provincial (preu-*vinn*-cheul) *adj* provincial

provisional (preu-*vi*-jeu-neul) *adj* provisoire

provisions (preu-*vi*-jeunnz) *pl* provision *f*

prune (proûn) *n* pruneau *m*

psychiatrist (saï-*kaï*-eu-trist) *n* psychiatre *m*

psychic (*saï*-kik) *adj* psychique

psychoanalyst (saï-kôᵒᵘ-*æ*-neu-list) *n* psychanalyste *m*

psychological (saï-ko-*lo*-dji-keul) *adj* psychologique

psychologist (saï-*ko*-leu-djist) *n* psychologue *m*

psychology (saï-*ko*-leu-dji) *n* psychologie *f*

pub (pab) *n* bistrot *m*

public (*pa*-blik) *adj* public; général; *n* public *m*; ~ **garden** jardin public; ~ **house** café *m*

publication (pa-bli-*kéï*-cheunn) *n* publication *f*

publicity (pa-*bli*-seu-ti) *n* publicité *f*

publish (*pa*-blich) *v* publier

publisher (*pa*-bli-cheu) *n* éditeur *m*

puddle (*pa*-deul) *n* flaque *f*

pull (poul) *v* tirer; ~ **out** *partir; ~ **up** s'arrêter

pulley (*pou*-li) *n* (pl ~s) poulie *f*

Pullman (*poul*-meunn) *n* voiture Pullman

pullover (pou-lô^{ou}-veu) *n* pull-over *m*

pulpit (*poul*-pit) *n* pupitre *m*, chaire *f*

pulse (pals) *n* pouls *m*

pump (pammp) *n* pompe *f*; *v* pomper

punch (panntch) *v* donner des coups de poing; *n* coup de poing

punctual (*panngk*-tchou-eul) *adj* ponctuel

puncture (*panngk*-tcheu) *n* crevaison *f*

punctured (*panngk*-tcheud) *adj* crevé

punish (*pa*-nich) *v* punir

punishment (*pa*-nich-meunnt) *n* punition *f*

pupil (*pyoû*-peul) *n* élève *m*

puppet-show (*pa*-pit-chô^{ou}) *n* théâtre de marionnettes

purchase (*peû*-tcheuss) *v* acheter; *n* acquisition *f*, achat *m*; ~ **price** prix d'achat

purchaser (*peû*-tcheu-seu) *n* acheteur *m*

pure (pyou^{eu}) *adj* pur

purple (*peû*-peul) *adj* pourpre

purpose (*peû*-peuss) *n* intention *f*, but *m*; **on** ~ intentionnel

purse (peûss) *n* bourse *f*, porte-monnaie *m*

pursue (peu-*syoû*) *v* *poursuivre; aspirer à

pus (pass) *n* pus *m*

push (pouch) *n* poussée *f*, coup *m*; *v* pousser

push-button (*pouch*-ba-teunn) *n* poussoir *m*

*put (pout) *v* placer, poser, *mettre; ~ **away** ranger; ~ **off** ajourner; ~ **on** *mettre; ~ **out** *éteindre

puzzle (*pa*-zeul) *n* casse-tête *m*; énigme *f*; *v* embarrasser; **jigsaw** ~ puzzle *m*

puzzling (*paz*-linng) *adj* embarrassant

pyjamas (peu-*djââ*-meuz) *pl* pyjama *m*

Q

quack (k^{ou}æk) *n* guérisseur *m*, charlatan *m*

quail (k^{ou}éïl) *n* (pl ~, ~s) caille *f*

quaint (k^{ou}éïnt) *adj* étrange; vieillot

qualification (k^{ou}o-li-fi-*kéï*-cheunn) *n* qualification *f*; réserve *f*, restriction *f*

qualified (*k^{ou}o*-li-faïd) *adj* qualifié; compétent

qualify (*k^{ou}o*-li-faï) *v* *être qualifié

quality (*k^{ou}o*-leu-ti) *n* qualité *f*; caractéristique *f*

quantity (*k^{ou}onn*-teu-ti) *n* quantité *f*; nombre *m*

quarantine (*k^{ou}o*-reunn-tiin) *n* quarantaine *f*

quarrel (*k^{ou}o*-reul) *v* se quereller, se disputer; *n* querelle *f*

quarry (*k^{ou}o*-ri) *n* carrière *f*

quarter (*k^{ou}oo*-teu) *n* quart *m*; trimestre *m*; quartier *m*; ~ **of an hour** quart d'heure

quarterly (*k^{ou}oo*-teu-li) *adj* trimestriel

quay (kii) *n* quai *m*

queen (k^{ou}iin) *n* reine *f*

queer (k^{ou}i^{eu}) *adj* singulier, étrange; drôle

query (*k^{ou}i^{eu}*-ri) *n* question *f*; *v* s'informer; *mettre en doute

question (*k^{ou}èss*-tcheunn) *n* question *f*; problème *m*; *v* interroger; *mettre en doute; ~ **mark** point d'interrogation

queue (kyoû) *n* queue *f*; *v* *faire la queue

quick (k^{ou}ik) *adj* rapide

quick-tempered (k^ouik-tèm-peud) *adj* irascible

quiet (k^ouaï-eut) *adj* paisible, calme, tranquille; *n* silence *m*, tranquillité *f*

quilt (k^ouilt) *n* courtepointe *f*

quinine (k^oui-niin) *n* quinine *f*

quit (k^ouit) *v* cesser

quite (k^ouaït) *adv* entièrement, tout à fait; passablement, assez, plutôt; très

quiz (k^ouiz) *n* (pl ~zes) jeu concours

quota (k^ouô^ou-teu) *n* quote-part *f*

quotation (k^ouô^ou-téï-cheunn) *n* citation *f*; ~ **marks** guillemets *mpl*

quote (k^ouô^out) *v* citer

R

rabbit (ræ-bit) *n* lapin *m*

rabies (réï-biz) *n* rage *f*

race (réïss) *n* course *f*; race *f*

race-course (réïss-kooss) *n* champ de courses, hippodrome *m*

race-horse (réïss-hooss) *n* cheval de course

race-track (réïss-træk) *n* piste de courses

racial (réï-cheul) *adj* racial

racket (ræ-kit) *n* vacarme *m*

racquet (ræ-kit) *n* raquette *f*

radiator (réï-di-éï-teu) *n* radiateur *m*

radical (ræ-di-keul) *adj* radical

radio (réï-di-ô^ou) *n* radio *f*

radish (ræ-dich) *n* radis *m*

radius (réï-di-euss) *n* (pl radii) rayon *m*

raft (rââft) *n* radeau *m*

rag (rægh) *n* chiffon *m*

rage (réïdj) *n* fureur *f*, rage *f*; *v* rager, sévir

raid (réïd) *n* raid *m*

rail (réïl) *n* balustrade *f*, barre *f*

railing (réï-linng) *n* rampe *f*

railroad (réïl-rô^oud) *nAm* voie ferrée, chemin de fer

railway (réïl-^ouéï) *n* chemin de fer, voie ferrée

rain (réïn) *n* pluie *f*; *v* *pleuvoir

rainbow (réïn-bô^ou) *n* arc-en-ciel *m*

raincoat (réïn-kô^out) *n* imperméable *m*

rainproof (réïn-prouf) *adj* imperméable

rainy (réï-ni) *adj* pluvieux

raise (réïz) *v* élever; relever; cultiver; prélever; *nAm* augmentation de salaire

raisin (réï-zeunn) *n* raisin sec

rake (réïk) *n* râteau *m*

rally (ræ-li) *n* rassemblement *m*

ramp (ræmp) *n* pente *f*

ramshackle (ræm-chæ-keul) *adj* croulant

rancid (ræn-sid) *adj* rance

rang (ræng) *v* (p ring)

range (réïndj) *n* gamme *f*

range-finder (réïndj-faïn-deu) *n* télémètre *m*

rank (rængk) *n* grade *m*; rang *m*

ransom (ræn-seumm) *n* rançon *f*

rape (réïp) *v* violer

rapid (ræ-pid) *adj* rapide

rapids (ræ-pidz) *pl* rapide *m*

rare (rè^eu) *adj* rare

rarely (rè^eu-li) *adv* rarement

rascal (rââ-skeul) *n* coquin *m*, fripon *m*

rash (ræch) *n* éruption *f*; *adj* impétueux, inconsidéré

raspberry (rââz-beu-ri) *n* framboise *f*

rat (ræt) *n* rat *m*

rate (réït) *n* tarif *m*; vitesse *f*; **at any ~** de toute façon, quoiqu'il en soit; **~ of exchange** cours du change

rather (rââ-ðeu) *adv* assez, passablement, plutôt

ration (*ræ*-cheunn) *n* ration *f*

rattan (ræ-*tæn*) *n* rotin *m*

raven (*réï*-veunn) *n* corbeau *m*

raw (roo) *adj* cru; ~ **material** matière première

ray (réï) *n* rayon *m*

rayon (*réï*-onn) *n* rayonne *f*

razor (*réï*-zeu) *n* rasoir *m*

razor-blade (*réï*-zeu-bléïd) *n* lame de rasoir

reach (riitch) *v* *atteindre; *n* portée *f*

reaction (ri-*æk*-cheunn) *n* réaction *f*

***read** (riid) *v* *lire

reading (*rii*-dinng) *n* lecture *f*

reading-lamp (*rii*-dinng-læmp) *n* lampe de travail

reading-room (*rii*-dinng-roûm) *n* salle de lecture

ready (*rè*-di) *adj* prêt

ready-made (rè-di-*méïd*) *adj* de confection

real (ri*eu*l) *adj* réel

reality (ri-*æ*-leu-ti) *n* réalité *f*

realizable (*ri*eu-laï-zeu-beul) *adj* réalisable

realize (*ri*eu-laïz) *v* se rendre compte; réaliser

really (*ri*eu-li) *adv* vraiment, réellement; en réalité

rear (ri*eu*) *n* arrière *m*; *v* élever

rear-light (ri*eu*-*laït*) *n* feu arrière

reason (*rii*-zeunn) *n* cause *f*, raison *f*; sens *m*; *v* raisonner

reasonable (*rii*-zeu-neu-beul) *adj* raisonnable; équitable

reassure (rii-eu-*chou*eu) *v* rassurer

rebate (*rii*-béït) *n* réduction *f*, rabais *m*

rebellion (ri-*bèl*-yeunn) *n* révolte *f*, rébellion *f*

recall (ri-*kool*) *v* se rappeler; rappeler; révoquer

receipt (ri-*siit*) *n* reçu *m*; réception *f*

receive (ri-*siiv*) *v* *recevoir

receiver (ri-*sii*-veu) *n* écouteur *m*

recent (*rii*-seunnt) *adj* récent

recently (*rii*-seunnt-li) *adv* l'autre jour, récemment

reception (ri-*sèp*-cheunn) *n* réception *f*; accueil *m*; ~ **office** réception *f*

receptionist (ri-*sèp*-cheu-nist) *n* hôtesse *f*

recession (ri-*sè*-cheunn) *n* récession *f*

recipe (*rè*-si-pi) *n* recette *f*

recital (ri-*saï*-teul) *n* récital *m*

reckon (*rè*-keunn) *v* calculer; estimer; supposer

recognition (rè-keugh-*ni*-cheunn) *n* reconnaissance *f*

recognize (*rè*-keugh-naïz) *v* *reconnaître

recollect (rè-keu-*lèkt*) *v* se *souvenir

recommence (rii-keu-*mèns*) *v* recommencer

recommend (rè-keu-*mènd*) *v* recommander; conseiller

recommendation (rè-keu-mèn-*déï*-cheunn) *n* recommandation *f*

reconciliation (rè-keunn-si-li-*éï*-cheunn) *n* réconciliation *f*

record[1] (*rè*-kood) *n* disque *m*; record *m*; dossier *m*; **long-playing** ~ microsillon *m*

record[2] (ri-*kood*) *v* enregistrer

recorder (ri-*koo*-deu) *n* magnétophone *m*

recording (ri-*koo*-dinng) *n* enregistrement *m*

record-player (*rè*-kood-pléï*eu*) *n* tourne-disque *m*

recover (ri-*ka*-veu) *v* récupérer; se *remettre, guérir

recovery (ri-*ka*-veu-ri) *n* guérison *f*

recreation (rè-kri-*éï*-cheunn) *n* récréation *f*; ~ **centre** centre de loisirs; ~ **ground** terrain de jeux

recruit (ri-*kroût*) *n* recrue *f*

rectangle (*rèk*-tæng-gheul) *n* rectangle *m*

rectangular (rèk-*tæng*-ghiou-leu) *adj* rectangulaire

rector (*rèk*-teu) *n* pasteur *m*, recteur *m*

rectory (*rèk*-teu-ri) *n* presbytère *m*

rectum (*rèk*-teumm) *n* rectum *m*

red (rèd) *adj* rouge

redeem (ri-*diim*) *v* délivrer

reduce (ri-*dyouss*) *v* *réduire, diminuer

reduction (ri-*dak*-cheunn) *n* rabais *m*, réduction *f*

redundant (ri-*dann*-deunnt) *adj* superflu

reed (riid) *n* roseau *m*

reef (riif) *n* récif *m*

reference (*rèf*-reunns) *n* référence *f*; rapport *m*; **with ~ to** relatif à

refer to (ri-*feû*) *v* *renvoyer à

refill (*rii*-fil) *n* recharge *f*

refinery (ri-*faï*-neu-ri) *n* raffinerie *f*

reflect (ri-*flèkt*) *v* refléter

reflection (ri-*flèk*-cheunn) *n* reflet *m*

reflector (ri-*flèk*-teu) *n* réflecteur *m*

reformation (rè-feu-*méï*-cheunn) *n* réforme *f*

refresh (ri-*frèch*) *v* rafraîchir

refreshment (ri-*frèch*-meunnt) *n* rafraîchissement *m*

refrigerator (ri-*fri*-djeu-réï-teu) *n* frigidaire *m*, réfrigérateur *m*

refund[1] (ri-*fannd*) *v* rendre, rembourser

refund[2] (*rii*-fannd) *n* remboursement *m*

refusal (ri-*fyou*-zeul) *n* refus *m*

refuse[1] (ri-*fyoûz*) *v* refuser

refuse[2] (*rè*-fyoûss) *n* rebut *m*

regard (ri-*ghâad*) *v* considérer; *n* respect *m*; **as regards** quant à, concernant, en ce qui concerne

regarding (ri-*ghââ*-dinng) *prep* en ce qui concerne, concernant; à propos de

regatta (ri-*ghæ*-teu) *n* régate *f*

régime (réï-*jiim*) *n* régime *m*

region (*rii*-djeunn) *n* région *f*

regional (*rii*-djeu-neul) *adj* régional

register (*rè*-dji-steu) *v* s'*inscrire; recommander; **registered letter** lettre recommandée

registration (rè-dji-*stréï*-cheunn) *n* inscription *f*; ~ **form** formulaire d'inscription; ~ **number** numéro d'immatriculation; ~ **plate** plaque d'immatriculation

regret (ri-*ghrèt*) *v* regretter; *n* regret *m*

regular (*rè*-ghyou-leu) *adj* régulier; ordinaire, normal

regulate (*rè*-ghyou-léït) *v* régler

regulation (rè-ghyou-*léï*-cheunn) *n* règlement *m*

rehabilitation (rii-heu-bi-li-*téï*-cheunn) *n* rééducation *f*

rehearsal (ri-*heû*-seul) *n* répétition *f*

rehearse (ri-*heûss*) *v* répéter

reign (réïn) *n* règne *m*; *v* régner

reimburse (rii-imm-*beûss*) *v* restituer, rembourser

reindeer (*réïn*-di[eu]) *n* (pl ~) renne *m*

reject (ri-*djèkt*) *v* refuser, rejeter

relate (ri-*léït*) *v* relater

related (ri-*léï*-tid) *adj* apparenté

relation (ri-*léï*-cheunn) *n* rapport *m*, relation *f*; parent *m*

relative (*rè*-leu-tiv) *n* parent *m*; *adj* relatif

relax (ri-*læks*) *v* se détendre

relaxation (ri-læk-*séï*-cheunn) *n* détente *f*

reliable (ri-*laï*-eu-beul) *adj* digne de confiance

relic (*rè*-lik) *n* relique *f*

relief (ri-*liif*) *n* soulagement *m*; soutien *m*; relief *m*

relieve (ri-*liiv*) *v* soulager; relayer

religion (ri-*li*-djeunn) *n* religion *f*

religious (ri-*li*-djeuss) *adj* religieux

rely on (ri-*laï*) compter sur

remain (ri-*méïn*) *v* rester

remainder (ri-*méïn*-deu) *n* restant *m*, reste *m*

remaining (ri-*méï*-ninng) *adj* restant

remark (ri-*mââk*) *n* remarque *f*; *v* remarquer

remarkable (ri-*mââ*-keu-beul) *adj* remarquable

remedy (*rè*-meu-di) *n* remède *m*

remember (ri-*mèm*-beu) *v* se rappeler; *retenir

remembrance (ri-*mèm*-breunns) *n* souvenir *m*

remind (ri-*maïnd*) *v* rappeler

remit (ri-*mit*) *v* *remettre

remittance (ri-*mi*-teunns) *n* versement *m*

remnant (*rèm*-neunnt) *n* reste *m*, restant *m*

remote (ri-*môout*) *adj* éloigné, lointain

removal (ri-*moû*-veul) *n* déplacement *m*

remove (ri-*moûv*) *v* enlever

remunerate (ri-*myoû*-neu-réït) *v* rémunérer

remuneration (ri-myoû-neu-*réï*-cheunn) *n* rémunération *f*

renew (ri-*nyoû*) *v* renouveler; prolonger

rent (rènt) *v* louer; *n* loyer *m*

repair (ri-*pèeu*) *v* réparer; *n* réparation *f*

reparation (rè-peu-*réï*-cheunn) *n* réparation *f*

***repay** (ri-*péï*) *v* rembourser

repayment (ri-*péï*-meunnt) *n* remboursement *m*

repeat (ri-*piit*) *v* répéter

repellent (ri-*pè*-leunnt) *adj* écœurant, répugnant

repentance (ri-*pèn*-teunns) *n* repentir *m*

repertory (*rè*-peu-teu-ri) *n* répertoire *m*

repetition (rè-peu-*ti*-cheunn) *n* répétition *f*

replace (ri-*pléïss*) *v* remplacer

reply (ri-*plaï*) *v* répondre; *n* réponse *f*; **in ~** en réponse

report (ri-*poot*) *v* relater; rapporter; se présenter; *n* compte rendu, rapport *m*

reporter (ri-*poo*-teu) *n* reporter *m*

represent (rè-pri-*zènt*) *v* représenter

representation (rè-pri-zèn-*téï*-cheunn) *n* représentation *f*

representative (rè-pri-*zèn*-teu-tiv) *adj* représentatif

reprimand (*rè*-pri-mâând) *v* réprimander

reproach (ri-*prôoutch*) *n* reproche *m*; *v* reprocher

reproduce (rii-preu-*dyoûss*) *v* *reproduire

reproduction (rii-preu-*dak*-cheunn) *n* reproduction *f*

reptile (*rèp*-taïl) *n* reptile *m*

republic (ri-*pa*-blik) *n* république *f*

republican (ri-*pa*-bli-keunn) *adj* républicain

repulsive (ri-*pal*-siv) *adj* repoussant

reputation (rè-pyou-*téï*-cheunn) *n* réputation *f*; renom *m*

request (ri-*kouèst*) *n* requête *f*; demande *f*; *v* *requérir

require (ri-*kouaïeu*) *v* exiger

requirement (ri-*kouaïeu*-meunnt) *n* exigence *f*

requisite (*rè*-koui-zit) *adj* requis

rescue (*rè*-skyoû) *v* sauver; *n* sauvetage *m*

research (ri-*seûtch*) *n* recherche *f*

resemblance (ri-*zèm*-bleunns) *n* ressemblance *f*

resemble (ri-*zèm*-beul) *v* ressembler à
resent (ri-*zènt*) *v* s'offenser de, en *vouloir à
reservation (rè-zeu-*véï*-cheunn) *n* réservation *f*
reserve (ri-*zeûv*) *v* réserver; *retenir; *n* réserve *f*
reserved (ri-*zeûvd*) *adj* réservé
reservoir (*rè*-zeu-v*ouâ*â) *n* réservoir *m*
reside (ri-*zaïd*) *v* résider
residence (*rè*-zi-deunns) *n* résidence *f*; ~ **permit** permis de séjour
resident (*rè*-zi-deunnt) *n* résident *m*; *adj* domicilié; interne
resign (ri-*zaïn*) *v* démissionner
resignation (rè-zigh-*néï*-cheunn) *n* démission *f*
resin (*rè*-zinn) *n* résine *f*
resist (ri-*zist*) *v* résister
resistance (ri-*zi*-steunns) *n* résistance *f*
resolute (*rè*-zeu-loût) *adj* résolu, déterminé
respect (ri-*spèkt*) *n* respect *m*; estime *f*, considération *f*; *v* respecter
respectable (ri-*spèk*-teu-beul) *adj* honorable, respectable
respectful (ri-*spèkt*-feul) *adj* respectueux
respective (ri-*spèk*-tiv) *adj* respectif
respiration (rè-speu-*réï*-cheunn) *n* respiration *f*
respite (*rè*-spaït) *n* répit *m*
responsibility (ri-sponn-seu-*bi*-leu-ti) *n* responsabilité *f*
responsible (ri-*sponn*-seu-beul) *adj* responsable
rest (rèst) *n* repos *m*; reste *m*; *v* se reposer
restaurant (*rè*-steu-ron) *n* restaurant *m*
restful (*rèst*-feul) *adj* reposant
rest-home (*rèst*-hô*ou*m) *n* maison de repos

restless (*rèst*-leuss) *adj* agité; inquiet
restrain (ri-*stréïn*) *v* *contenir, *retenir
restriction (ri-*strik*-cheunn) *n* restriction *f*
result (ri-*zalt*) *n* résultat *m*; effet *m*; *v* résulter
resume (ri-*zyoûm*) *v* *reprendre
résumé (*rè*-zyou-méï) *n* résumé *m*
retail (*rii*-téïl) *v* détailler; ~ **trade** commerce de détail
retailer (*rii*-téï-leu) *n* détaillant *m*; revendeur *m*
retina (*rè*-ti-neu) *n* rétine *f*
retired (ri-*taïeu*d) *adj* retraité
return (ri-*teûnn*) *v* *revenir, retourner; *n* retour *m*; ~ **flight** vol de retour; ~ **journey** voyage de retour
reunite (rii-you-*naït*) *v* réunir
reveal (ri-*viil*) *v* révéler
revelation (rè-veu-*léï*-cheunn) *n* révélation *f*
revenge (ri-*vèndj*) *n* vengeance *f*
revenue (*rè*-veu-nyou) *n* recettes, revenu *m*
reverse (ri-*veûss*) *n* contraire *m*; revers *m*; marche arrière; revirement *m*; *adj* inverse; *v* *faire marche arrière
review (ri-*vyoû*) *n* critique *f*; revue *f*
revise (ri-*vaïz*) *v* reviser
revision (ri-*vi*-jeunn) *n* révision *f*
revival (ri-*vaï*-veul) *n* reprise *f*
revolt (ri-*vôoul*t) *v* se révolter; *n* rébellion *f*, révolte *f*
revolting (ri-*vôoul*-tinng) *adj* dégoûtant, révoltant, répugnant
revolution (rè-veu-*loû*-cheunn) *n* révolution *f*; rotation *f*
revolutionary (rè-veu-*loû*-cheu-neu-ri) *adj* révolutionnaire
revolver (ri-*vol*-veu) *n* revolver *m*
revue (ri-*vyoû*) *n* revue *f*
reward (ri-*ou*ood) *n* récompense *f*; *v*

récompenser

rheumatism (*roú*-meu-ti-zeumm) *n* rhumatisme *m*

rhinoceros (raï-*no*-seu-reuss) *n* (pl ~, ~es) rhinocéros *m*

rhubarb (*roû*-bââb) *n* rhubarbe *f*

rhyme (raïm) *n* rime *f*

rhythm (*ri*-ðeumm) *n* rythme *m*

rib (rib) *n* côte *f*

ribbon (*ri*-beunn) *n* ruban *m*

rice (raïss) *n* riz *m*

rich (ritch) *adj* riche

riches (*ri*-tchiz) *pl* richesse *f*

riddle (*ri*-deul) *n* énigme *f*

ride (raïd) *n* course *f*

*****ride** (raïd) *v* rouler; monter à cheval

rider (*raï*-deu) *n* cavalier *m*

ridge (ridj) *n* arête *f*

ridicule (*ri*-di-kyoûl) *v* ridiculiser

ridiculous (ri-*di*-kyou-leuss) *adj* ridicule

riding (*raï*-dinng) *n* équitation *f*

riding-school (*raï*-dinng-skoûl) *n* manège *m*

rifle (*raï*-feul) *v* fusil *m*

right (raït) *n* droit *m*; *adj* correct, juste; droit; équitable; **all right!** d'accord! ; * **be** = *avoir raison; ~ **of way** priorité de passage

righteous (*raï*-tcheuss) *adj* juste

right-hand (*raït*-hænd) *adj* à droite, de droite

rightly (*raït*-li) *adv* justement

rim (rimm) *n* jante *f*; rebord *m*

ring (rinng) *n* bague *f*; cercle *m*; piste *f*

*****ring** (rinng) *v* sonner; ~ **up** téléphoner

rinse (rinns) *v* rincer; *n* rinçage *m*

riot (*raï*-eut) *n* émeute *f*

rip (rip) *v* déchirer

ripe (raïp) *adj* mûr

rise (raïz) *n* augmentation de salaire, augmentation *f*; élévation *f*; montée *f*; essor *m*

*****rise** (raïz) *v* se lever; monter

rising (*raï*-zinng) *n* insurrection *f*

risk (risk) *n* risque *m*; danger *m*; *v* risquer

risky (*ri*-ski) *adj* dangereux, risqué

rival (*raï*-veul) *n* rival *m*; concurrent *m*; *v* rivaliser

rivalry (*raï*-veul-ri) *n* rivalité *f*; concurrence *f*

river (*ri*-veu) *n* fleuve *m*; ~ **bank** rive *f*

riverside (*ri*-veu-saïd) *n* bord de la rivière

roach (rôôtch) *n* (pl ~) gardon *m*

road (rôᵒud) *n* rue *f*, route *f*; ~ **fork** *n* bifurcation *f*; ~ **map** carte routière; ~ **system** réseau routier; ~ **up** route en réfection

roadhouse (*rôᵒu*d-haouss) *n* auberge *f*

roadside (*rôᵒu*d-saïd) *n* bord de la route; ~ **restaurant** auberge *f*

roadway (*rôᵒu*d-ᵒuéï) *nAm* chaussée *f*

roam (rôᵒum) *v* vagabonder

roar (roo) *v* mugir, rugir; *n* rugissement *m*, grondement *m*

roast (rôᵒust) *v* griller, rôtir

rob (rob) *v* voler

robber (*ro*-beu) *n* voleur *m*

robbery (*ro*-beu-ri) *n* vol *m*

robe (rôᵒub) *n* robe *f*

robin (*ro*-binn) *n* rouge-gorge *m*

robust (rôᵒu-*bast*) *adj* robuste

rock (rok) *n* rocher *m*; *v* balancer

rocket (*ro*-kit) *n* fusée *f*

rocky (*ro*-ki) *adj* rocheux

rod (rod) *n* barre *f*, tige *f*

roe (rôᵒu) *n* œufs de poisson, laitance *f*

roll (rôᵒul) *v* rouler; *n* rouleau *m*; petit pain

roller-skating (*rôᵒu*-leu-skéï-tinng) *n* patinage à roulettes

Roman Catholic (*rôᵒu*-meunn kæ-θeu-lik) catholique

romance (reu-*mæns*) *n* idylle *f*

romantic (reu-*mæn*-tik) *adj* romantique

roof (roûf) *n* toit *m*; **thatched** ~ toit de chaume *m*

room (roûm) *n* pièce *f*, chambre *f*; espace *m*, place *f*; ~ **and board** pension complète; ~ **service** service d'étage; ~ **temperature** température ambiante

roomy (*roû*-mi) *adj* spacieux

root (roût) *n* racine *f*

rope (rô*ou*p) *n* corde *f*

rosary (*rô*ou-zeu-ri) *n* rosaire *m*

rose (rô*ou*z) *n* rose *f*; *adj* rose

rotten (*ro*-teunn) *adj* pourri

rouge (roûj) *n* rouge *m*

rough (raf) *adj* rugueux

roulette (roû-*lèt*) *n* roulette *f*

round (raound) *adj* rond; *prep* autour de; *n* reprise *f*; ~ **trip** *Am* aller et retour

roundabout (*raoun*-deu-baout) *n* rond-point *m*

rounded (*raoun*-did) *adj* arrondi

route (roût) *n* route *f*

routine (roû-*tiin*) *n* routine *f*

row[1] (rô*ou*) *n* rang *m*; *v* ramer

row[2] (raou) *n* querelle *f*

rowdy (*raou*-di) *adj* tapageur

rowing-boat (*rô*ou-inng-bô*ou*t) *n* bateau à rames

royal (*roï*-eul) *adj* royal

rub (rab) *v* frotter

rubber (*ra*-beu) *n* caoutchouc *m*; gomme *f*; ~ **band** élastique *m*

rubbish (*ra*-bich) *n* détritus *m*; radotage *m*, sottise *f*; **talk** ~ baratiner

rubbish-bin (*ra*-bich-binn) *n* poubelle *f*

ruby (*roû*-bi) *n* rubis *m*

rucksack (*rak*-sæk) *n* sac à dos

rudder (*ra*-deu) *n* gouvernail *m*

rude (roûd) *adj* grossier

rug (ragh) *n* tapis *m*

ruin (*roû*-inn) *v* ruiner; *n* ruine *f*

ruination (roû-i-*néï*-cheunn) *n* effondrement *m*

rule (roûl) *n* règle *f*; régime *m*, gouvernement *m*, règne *m*; *v* régner, gouverner; **as a** ~ généralement, en général

ruler (*roû*-leu) *n* monarque *m*, dirigeant *m*; règle *f*

Rumania (roû-*méï*-ni-eu) Roumanie *f*

Rumanian (roû-*méï*-ni-eunn) *adj* roumain; *n* Roumain *m*

rumour (*roû*-meu) *n* rumeur *f*

***run** (rann) *v* *courir; ~ **into** rencontrer

runaway (*ra*-neu-*ou*éï) *n* fugitif *m*

rung (rann) *v* (pp ring)

runway (*rann*-*ou*éï) *n* piste de décollage

rural (*rou*eu-reul) *adj* rural

ruse (roûz) *n* ruse *f*

rush (rach) *v* se presser; *n* jonc *m*

rush-hour (*rach*-aou*eu*) *n* heure de pointe

Russia (*ra*-cheu) Russie *f*

Russian (*ra*-cheunn) *adj* russe; *n* Russe *m*

rust (rast) *n* rouille *f*

rustic (*ra*-stik) *adj* rustique

rusty (*ra*-sti) *adj* rouillé

S

saccharin (*sæ*-keu-rinn) *n* saccharine *f*

sack (sæk) *n* sac *m*

sacred (*séï*-krid) *adj* sacré

sacrifice (*sæ*-kri-faïss) *n* sacrifice *m*; *v* sacrifier

sacrilege (*sæ*-kri-lidj) *n* sacrilège *m*

sad (sæd) *adj* triste; malheureux, affligé, mélancolique

saddle (*sæ*-deul) *n* selle *f*

sadness (*sæd*-neuss) *n* tristesse *f*

safe (séïf) *adj* sûr; *n* coffre-fort

safety (*séïf*-ti) *n* sécurité *f*

safety-belt (*séïf*-ti-bèlt) *n* ceinture de sécurité

safety-pin (*séïf*-ti-pinn) *n* épingle de sûreté

safety-razor (*séïf*-ti-réï-zeu) *n* rasoir *m*

sail (séïl) *v* naviguer; *n* voile *f*

sailing-boat (*séï*-linng-bôᵒᵘt) *n* bateau à voiles

sailor (*séï*-leu) *n* marin *m*

saint (séïnt) *n* saint *m*

salad (*sæ*-leud) *n* salade *f*

salad-oil (*sæ*-leud-oïl) *n* huile de table

salary (*sæ*-leu-ri) *n* paie *f*, salaire *m*

sale (séïl) *n* vente *f*; **clearance ~** soldes; **for ~** à vendre; **sales** soldes

saleable (*séï*-leu-beul) *adj* vendable

salesgirl (*séïlz*-gheul) *n* vendeuse *f*

salesman (*séïlz*-meunn) *n* (pl -men) vendeur *m*

salmon (*sæ*-meunn) *n* (pl ~) saumon *m*

salon (*sæ*-lon) *n* salon *m*

saloon (seu-*loûn*) *n* café *m*

salt (soolt) *n* sel *m*

salt-cellar (*soolt*-sè-leu) *n* salière *f*

salty (*sool*-ti) *adj* salé

salute (seu-*loût*) *v* saluer

salve (sââv) *n* onguent *m*

same (séïm) *adj* même

sample (*sââm*-peul) *n* échantillon *m*

sanatorium (sæ-neu-*too*-ri-eumm) *n* (pl ~s, -ria) sanatorium *m*

sand (sænd) *n* sable *m*

sandal (*sæn*-deul) *n* sandale *f*

sandpaper (*sænd*-péï-peu) *n* papier de verre

sandwich (*sæn*-ᵒᵘidj) *n* sandwich *m*; tartine *f*

sandy (*sæn*-di) *adj* sableux

sanitary (*sæ*-ni-teu-ri) *adj* sanitaire; **~ towel** serviette hygiénique

sapphire (*sæ*-faïᵉᵘ) *n* saphir *m*

sardine (sââ-*diin*) *n* sardine *f*

satchel (*sæ*-tcheul) *n* cartable *m*

satellite (*sæ*-teu-laït) *n* satellite *m*

satin (*sæ*-tinn) *n* satin *m*

satisfaction (sæ-tiss-*fæk*-cheunn) *n* satisfaction *f*

satisfy (*sæ*-tiss-faï) *v* *satisfaire

Saturday (*sæ*-teu-di) *n* samedi *m*

sauce (sooss) *n* sauce *f*

saucepan (*sooss*-peunn) *n* poêle *f*

saucer (*soo*-seu) *n* soucoupe *f*

Saudi Arabia (saou-di-eu-*réï*-bi-eu) Arabie Séoudite

sauna (*soo*-neu) *n* sauna *m*

sausage (*so*-sidj) *n* saucisse *f*

savage (*sæ*-vidj) *adj* sauvage

save (séïv) *v* sauver; épargner

savings (*séï*-vinngz) *pl* économies; **~ bank** caisse d'épargne

saviour (*séï*-vyeu) *n* sauveur *m*

savoury (*séï*-veu-ri) *adj* savoureux; piquant

saw¹ (soo) *v* (p see)

saw² (soo) *n* scie *f*

sawdust (*soo*-dast) *n* sciure *f*

saw-mill (*soo*-mil) *n* scierie *f*

***say** (séï) *v* *dire

scaffolding (*skæ*-feul-dinng) *n* échafaudage *m*

scale (skéïl) *n* échelle *f*; gamme *f*; écaille *f*; **scales** *pl* balance *f*

scandal (*skæn*-deul) *n* scandale *m*

Scandinavia (skæn-di-*néï*-vi-eu) Scandinavie *f*

Scandinavian (skæn-di-*néï*-vi-eunn) *adj* scandinave; *n* Scandinave *m*

scapegoat (*skéïp*-ghôᵒᵘt) *n* bouc émissaire

scar (skââ) *n* cicatrice *f*

scarce (skeᵉᵘss) *adj* rare

scarcely (*skèᵉᵘ*-sli) *adv* à peine

scarcity (*skè^{eu}*-seu-ti) *n* pénurie *f*

scare (*skè^{eu}*) *v* effrayer; *n* panique *f*

scarf (*skââf*) *n* (pl ~s, scarves) écharpe *f*

scarlet (*skââ*-leut) *adj* écarlate

scary (*skè^{eu}*-ri) *adj* inquiétant

scatter (*skæ*-teu) *v* disperser

scene (siin) *n* scène *f*

scenery (*sii*-neu-ri) *n* paysage *m*

scenic (*sii*-nik) *adj* pittoresque

scent (sènt) *n* parfum *m*

schedule (*chè*-dyoûl) *n* horaire *m*

scheme (skiim) *n* plan *m*; projet *m*

scholar (*sko*-leu) *n* érudit *m*; élève *m*

scholarship (*sko*-leu-chip) *n* bourse d'études

school (skoûl) *n* école *f*

schoolboy (*skoûl*-boï) *n* écolier *m*

schoolgirl (*skoûl*-gheûl) *n* écolière *f*

schoolmaster (*skoûl*-mââ-steu) *n* instituteur *m*, maître d'école

schoolteacher (*skoûl*-tii-tcheu) *n* instituteur *m*

science (*saï*-eunns) *n* science *f*

scientific (saï-eunn-*ti*-fik) *adj* scientifique

scientist (*saï*-eunn-tist) *n* savant *m*

scissors (*si*-zeuz) *pl* ciseaux *mpl*

scold (skô^{ou}ld) *v* gronder; insulter

scooter (*skoû*-teu) *n* scooter *m*; patinette *f*

score (skoo) *n* nombre de points; *v* marquer

scorn (skoon) *n* dédain *m*, mépris *m*; *v* mépriser

Scot (skot) *n* Ecossais *m*

Scotch (skotch) *adj* écossais; **scotch tape** ruban adhésif

Scotland (*skot*-leunnd) Ecosse *f*

Scottish (*sko*-tich) *adj* écossais

scout (skaout) *n* scout *m*

scrap (skræp) *n* morceau *m*

scrap-book (*skræp*-bouk) *n* album de collage

scrape (skréïp) *v* racler

scrap-iron (*skræ*-païeun) *n* ferraille *f*

scratch (skrætch) *v* érafler, gratter; *n* rayure *f*, égratignure *f*

scream (skriim) *v* hurler, crier; *n* cri *m*

screen (skriin) *n* écran *m*

screw (skroû) *n* vis *f*; *v* visser

screw-driver (*skroû*-draï-veu) *n* tournevis *m*

scrub (skrab) *v* frotter; *n* buisson *m*

sculptor (*skalp*-teu) *n* sculpteur *m*

sculpture (*skalp*-tcheu) *n* sculpture *f*

sea (sii) *n* mer *f*

sea-bird (*sii*-beûd) *n* oiseau de mer

sea-coast (*sii*-kô^{ou}st) *n* littoral *m*

seagull (*sii*-ghal) *n* mouette *f*, goéland *m*

seal (siil) *n* sceau *m*; phoque *m*

seam (siim) *n* couture *f*

seaman (*sii*-meunn) *n* (pl -men) marin *m*

seamless (*siim*-leuss) *adj* sans couture

seaport (*sii*-poot) *n* port de mer

search (seûtch) *v* chercher; fouiller; *n* fouille *f*

searchlight (*seûtch*-laït) *n* projecteur *m*

seascape (*sii*-skéïp) *n* marine *f*

sea-shell (*sii*-chèl) *n* coquillage *m*

seashore (*sii*-choo) *n* bord de la mer

seasick (*sii*-sik) *adj* souffrant du mal de mer

seasickness (*sii*-sik-neuss) *n* mal de mer

seaside (*sii*-saïd) *n* bord de la mer; ~ **resort** station balnéaire

season (*sii*-zeunn) *n* saison *f*; **high** ~ pleine saison; **low** ~ morte-saison *f*; **off** ~ hors saison

season-ticket (*sii*-zeunn-ti-kit) *n* carte d'abonnement

seat (siit) *n* siège *m*; place *f*

seat-belt (*siit*-bèlt) *n* ceinture de sécurité

sea-urchin (sii-eû-tchinn) n oursin m

sea-water (sii-ᵒᵘoo-teu) n eau de mer

second (sè-keunnd) num deuxième; n seconde f; instant m

secondary (sè-keunn-deu-ri) adj secondaire; ~ **school** école secondaire

second-hand (sè-keunnd-hænd) adj d'occasion

secret (sii-kreut) n secret m; adj secret

secretary (sè-kreu-tri) n secrétaire f; secrétaire m

section (sèk-cheunn) n section f; case f, service m

secure (si-kyouᵉᵘ) adj sûr; v s'assurer de

security (si-kyouᵉᵘ-reu-ti) n sécurité f; caution f

sedate (si-déït) adj posé

sedative (sè-deu-tiv) n sédatif m

seduce (si-dyoûss) v *séduire

*see (sii) v *voir; *comprendre, se rendre compte; ~ **to** s'occuper de

seed (siid) n semence f

*seek (siik) v chercher

seem (siim) v *paraître, sembler

seen (siin) v (pp see)

seesaw (sii-soo) n balançoire f

seize (siiz) v saisir

seldom (sèl-deumm) adv rarement

select (si-lèkt) v sélectionner, choisir; adj exquis, choisi

selection (si-lèk-cheunn) n choix m, sélection f

self-centred (sèlf-sèn-teud) adj égocentrique

self-employed (sèl-fimm-ploïd) adj indépendant

self-evident (sèl-fè-vi-deunnt) adj évident

self-government (sèlf-gha-veu-meunnt) n autonomie f

selfish (sèl-fich) adj égoïste

selfishness (sèl-fich-neuss) n égoïsme m

self-service (sèlf-seû-viss) n libre-service m

*sell (sèl) v vendre

semblance (sèm-bleunns) n apparence f

semi- (sè-mi) semi-

semicircle (sè-mi-seû-keul) n demi-cercle m

semi-colon (sè-mi-kôᵒᵘ-leunn) n point-virgule m

senate (sè-neut) n sénat m

senator (sè-neu-teu) n sénateur m

*send (sènd) v expédier, *envoyer; ~ **back** *renvoyer; ~ **for** *faire venir; ~ **off** expédier

senile (sii-naïl) adj sénile

sensation (sèn-séï-cheunn) n sensation f; impression f

sensational (sèn-séï-cheu-neul) adj spectaculaire, sensationnel

sense (sèns) n sens m; bon sens, raison f; signification f; v *percevoir; ~ **of honour** sens de l'honneur

senseless (sèns-leuss) adj insensé

sensible (sèn-seu-beul) adj raisonnable

sensitive (sèn-si-tiv) adj sensible

sentence (sèn-teunns) n phrase f; jugement m; v condamner

sentimental (sèn-ti-mèn-teul) adj sentimental

separate¹ (sè-peu-réït) v séparer

separate² (sè-peu-reut) adj distinct, séparé

separately (sè-peu-reut-li) adv à part

September (sèp-tèm-beu) septembre

septic (sèp-tik) adj septique; *be-come ~ s'infecter

sequel (sii-kᵒᵘeul) n suite f

sequence (sii-kᵒᵘeunns) n succession f; série f

serene (seu-*riin*) *adj* serein; clair

serial (*si*ᵉᵘ-ri-eul) *n* feuilleton *m*

series (*si*ᵉᵘ-riiz) *n* (pl ~) suite *f*, série *f*

serious (*si*ᵉᵘ-ri-euss) *adj* sérieux

seriousness (*si*ᵉᵘ-ri-euss-neuss) *n* sérieux *m*

sermon (*seû*-meunn) *n* sermon *m*

serum (*si*ᵉᵘ-reumm) *n* sérum *m*

servant (*seû*-veunnt) *n* domestique *m*

serve (seûv) *v* *servir

service (*seû*-viss) *n* service *m*; ~ **charge** service *m*; ~ **station** station-service *f*

serviette (seû-vi-*èt*) *n* serviette *f*

session (*sè*-cheunn) *n* séance *f*

set (sèt) *n* jeu *m*, groupe *m*

*set** (sèt) *v* poser; ~ **menu** menu fixe; ~ **out** *partir

setting (*sè*-tinng) *n* cadre *m*; ~ **lotion** fixateur *m*

settle (*sè*-teul) *v* régler, arranger; ~ **down** s'établir

settlement (*sè*-teul-meunnt) *n* règlement *m*, arrangement *m*, accord *m*

seven (*sè*-veunn) *num* sept

seventeen (sè-veunn-*tiin*) *num* dix-sept

seventeenth (sè-veunn-*tiin*θ) *num* dix-septième

seventh (*sè*-veunnθ) *num* septième

seventy (*sè*-veunn-ti) *num* soixante-dix

several (*sè*-veu-reul) *adj* divers, plusieurs

severe (si-*vi*ᵉᵘ) *adj* violent, sévère, grave

sew (sôᵒᵘ) *v* *coudre; ~ **up** suturer

sewer (*soû*-eu) *n* égout *m*

sewing-machine (*sô*ᵒᵘ-inng-meu-chiin) *n* machine à coudre

sex (sèks) *n* sexe *m*

sexton (*sèk*-steunn) *n* sacristain *m*

sexual (*sèk*-chou-eul) *adj* sexuel

sexuality (sèk-chou-æ-leu-ti) *n* sexualité *f*

shade (chéid) *n* ombre *f*; nuance *f*

shadow (*chæ*-dôᵒᵘ) *n* ombre *f*

shady (*chéi*-di) *adj* ombragé

*shake** (chéïk) *v* secouer

shaky (*chéï*-ki) *adj* vacillant

*shall** (chæl) *v* *devoir

shallow (*chæ*-lôᵒᵘ) *adj* peu profond

shame (chéïm) *n* honte *f*; déshonneur *m*; **shame!** quelle honte!

shampoo (chæm-*poû*) *n* shampooing *m*

shamrock (*chæm*-rok) *n* trèfle *m*

shape (chéïp) *n* forme *f*; *v* former

share (chèᵉᵘ) *v* partager; *n* part *f*; action *f*

shark (châak) *n* requin *m*

sharp (châap) *adj* aigu

sharpen (*chââ*-peunn) *v* affiler, aiguiser

shave (chéïv) *v* se raser

shaver (*chéi*-veu) *n* rasoir électrique

shaving-brush (*chéi*-vinng-brach) *n* blaireau *m*

shaving-cream (*chéi*-vinng-kriim) *n* crème à raser

shaving-soap (*chéi*-vinng-sôᵒᵘp) *n* savon à barbe

shawl (chool) *n* châle *m*

she (chii) *pron* elle

shed (chèd) *n* réduit *m*

*shed** (chèd) *v* verser; répandre

sheep (chiip) *n* (pl ~) mouton *m*

sheer (chiᵉᵘ) *adj* absolu, pur; fin, transparent

sheet (chiit) *n* drap *m*; feuille *f*; plaque *f*

shelf (chèlf) *n* (pl shelves) étagère *f*

shell (chèl) *n* coquille *f*

shellfish (*chèl*-fich) *n* crustacé *m*

shelter (*chèl*-teu) *n* abri *m*; *v* abriter

shepherd (*chè*-peud) *n* berger *m*

shift (chift) *n* équipe *f*

*shine (chaïn) v briller; resplendir

ship (chip) n navire m; v expédier; **shipping line** compagnie de navigation

shipowner (chi-pô^{ou}-neu) n armateur m

shipyard (chip-yââd) n chantier naval

shirt (cheût) n chemise f

shiver (chi-veu) v trembler, frissonner; n frisson m

shivery (chi-veu-ri) adj frissonnant

shock (chok) n choc m; v choquer; ~ **absorber** amortisseur m

shocking (cho-kinng) adj choquant

shoe (choû) n chaussure f; **gym shoes** chaussures de gymnastique; ~ **polish** cirage m

shoe-lace (choû-léïss) n lacet m

shoemaker (choû-méï-keu) n cordonnier m

shoe-shop (choû-chop) n magasin de chaussures

shook (chouk) v (p shake)

*shoot (choût) v tirer

shop (chop) n boutique f; v *faire des achats; ~ **assistant** vendeur m; **shopping bag** sac à provisions; **shopping centre** centre commercial

shopkeeper (chop-kii-peu) n commerçant m

shop-window (chop-^{ou}inn-dô^{ou}) n vitrine f

shore (choo) n rive f, rivage m

short (choot) adj court; petit; ~ **circuit** court-circuit m

shortage (choo-tidj) n carence f, manque m

shortcoming (choot-ka-minng) n imperfection f

shorten (choo-teunn) v raccourcir

shorthand (choot-hænd) n sténographie f

shortly (choot-li) adv sous peu, prochainement, bientôt

shorts (choots) pl short m; plAm caleçon m

short-sighted (choot-saï-tid) adj myope

shot (chot) n coup de feu; piqûre f; prise de vue

*should (choud) v *devoir

shoulder (chô^{ou}l-deu) n épaule f

shout (chaout) v crier; n cri m

shovel (cha-veul) n pelle f

show (chô^{ou}) n représentation f, spectacle m; exposition f

*show (chô^{ou}) v montrer; exposer; démontrer

show-case (chô^{ou}-kéïss) n vitrine f

shower (chaou^{eu}) n douche f; averse f

showroom (chô^{ou}-roûm) n salle d'exposition

shriek (chriik) v pousser des cris; n cri aigu

shrimp (chrimmp) n crevette f

shrine (chraïn) n sanctuaire m

*shrink (chrinngk) v rétrécir

shrinkproof (chrinngk-proûf) adj irrétrécissable

shrub (chrab) n arbuste m

shudder (cha-deu) n frisson m

shuffle (cha-feul) v *battre

*shut (chat) v fermer; **shut** clos, fermé; ~ **in** enfermer

shutter (cha-teu) n persienne f, volet m

shy (chaï) adj farouche, timide

shyness (chaï-neuss) n timidité f

Siam (saï-æm) Siam m

Siamese (saï-eu-miiz) adj siamois; n Siamois m

sick (sik) adj malade; ayant mal au cœur

sickness (sik-neuss) n maladie f; mal au cœur

side (saïd) n côté m; parti m; **one-sided** adj unilatéral

sideburns (*saïd*-beûnnz) *pl* favoris
sidelight (*saïd*-laït) *n* lumière latérale
side-street (*saïd*-striit) *n* rue transversale
sidewalk (*saïd*-^{ou}ook) *n Am* trottoir *m*
sideways (*saïd*-^{ou}éïz) *adv* de côté
siege (siidj) *n* siège *m*
sieve (siv) *n* passoire *f*; *v* tamiser
sift (sift) *v* tamiser
sight (saït) *n* vue *f*; spectacle *m*; curiosité *f*
sign (saïn) *n* marque *f*, signe *m*; geste *m*; *v* signer
signal (*sigh*-neul) *n* signal *m*; signe *m*; *v* signaler
signature (*sigh*-neu-tcheu) *n* signature *f*
significant (sigh-*ni*-fi-keunnt) *adj* significatif
signpost (*saïn*-pô^{ou}st) *n* poteau indicateur
silence (*saï*-leunns) *n* silence *m*; *v* *faire taire
silencer (*saï*-leunn-seu) *n* silencieux *m*
silent (*saï*-leunnt) *adj* silencieux; *be ~* se *taire
silk (silk) *n* soie *f*
silken (*sil*-keunn) *adj* soyeux
silly (*si*-li) *adj* bête, sot
silver (*sil*-veu) *n* argent *m*; en argent
silversmith (*sil*-veu-smiθ) *n* orfèvre *m*
silverware (*sil*-veu-^{ou}è^{eu}) *n* argenterie *f*
similar (*si*-mi-leu) *adj* analogue, similaire
similarity (si-mi-*læ*-reu-ti) *n* similitude *f*
simple (*simm*-peul) *adj* ingénu, simple; ordinaire
simply (*simm*-pli) *adv* simplement
simulate (*si*-myou-léït) *v* simuler
simultaneous (si-meul-*téï*-ni-euss) *adj* simultané
sin (sinn) *n* péché *m*

since (sinns) *prep* depuis; *adv* depuis; *conj* depuis que; comme
sincere (sinn-*si^{eu}*) *adj* sincère
sinew (*si*-nyoû) *n* tendon *m*
***sing** (sinng) *v* chanter
singer (*sinng*-eu) *n* chanteur *m*; chanteuse *f*
single (*sinng*-gheul) *adj* seul; célibataire
singular (*sinng*-ghyou-leu) *n* singulier *m*; *adj* singulier
sinister (*si*-ni-steu) *adj* sinistre
sink (sinngk) *n* évier *m*
***sink** (sinngk) *v* s'enfoncer
sip (sip) *n* gorgée *f*
siphon (*saï*-feunn) *n* siphon *m*
sir (seû) *n* monsieur *m*
siren (*saï^{eu}*-reunn) *n* sirène *f*
sister (*si*-steu) *n* sœur *f*
sister-in-law (*si*-steu-rinn-loo) *n* (pl sisters-) belle-sœur *f*
***sit** (sit) *v* *être assis; *~ down* s'*asseoir
site (saït) *n* site *m*; position *f*
sitting-room (*si*-tinng-roûm) *n* salon *m*
situated (*si*-tchou-éï-tid) *adj* situé
situation (si-tchou-*éï*-cheunn) *n* situation *f*
six (siks) *num* six
sixteen (siks-*tiin*) *num* seize
sixteenth (siks-*tiin*θ) *num* seizième
sixth (siksθ) *num* sixième
sixty (*siks*-ti) *num* soixante
size (saïz) *n* taille *f*, mesure *f*; dimension *f*, grandeur *f*; format *m*
skate (skéït) *v* patiner; *n* patin *m*
skating (*skéï*-tinng) *n* patinage *m*
skating-rink (*skéï*-tinng-rinngk) *n* patinoire *f*
skeleton (*skè*-li-teunn) *n* squelette *m*
sketch (skètch) *n* dessin *m*, esquisse *f*; *v* dessiner, esquisser
sketch-book (*skètch*-bouk) *n* cahier de

croquis

ski[1] (skii) v skier

ski[2] (skii) n (pl ~, ~s) ski m; ~
boots chaussures de ski; ~ **pants**
pantalon de ski; ~ **poles** Am bâtons de ski; ~ **sticks** bâtons de ski

skid (skid) v déraper

skier (skii-eu) n skieur m

skiing (skii-inng) n ski m

ski-jump (skii-djammp) n saut à ski

skilful (skil-feul) adj habile, adroit

ski-lift (skii-lift) n téléski m

skill (skil) n habileté f

skilled (skild) adj habile; expert

skin (skinn) n peau f; ~ **cream** crème
de beauté

skip (skip) v sautiller; sauter

skirt (skeût) n jupe f

skull (skal) n crâne m

sky (skaï) n ciel m; air m

skyscraper (skaï-skréï-peu) n gratte-
ciel m

slack (slæk) adj lent

slacks (slæks) pl pantalon m

slam (slæm) v claquer

slander (slâân-deu) n calomnie f

slant (slâânt) v s'incliner

slanting (slâân-tinng) adj oblique, en
pente, incliné

slap (slæp) v *battre; n claque f

slate (sléit) n ardoise f

slave (sléïv) n esclave m

sledge (slèdj) n luge f, traîneau m

sleep (sliip) n sommeil m

***sleep** (sliip) v *dormir

sleeping-bag (slii-pinng-bægh) n sac
de couchage

sleeping-car (slii-pinng-kââ) n wagon-
lit

sleeping-pill (slii-pinng-pil) n somnifère m

sleepless (sliip-leuss) adj sans sommeil

sleepy (slii-pi) adj somnolent

sleeve (sliiv) n manche f; housse f

sleigh (sléï) n luge f, traîneau m

slender (slèn-deu) adj svelte

slice (slaïss) n tranche f

slide (slaïd) n glissade f; toboggan
m; diapositive f

***slide** (slaïd) v glisser

slight (slaït) adj léger; faible

slim (slimm) adj mince; v maigrir

slip (slip) v déraper, glisser; s'échapper; n faux pas; combinaison f

slipper (sli-peu) n pantoufle f

slippery (sli-peu-ri) adj glissant

slogan (slô[ou]-gheunn) n devise f, slogan m

slope (slô[ou]p) n versant m; v décliner

sloping (slô[ou]-pinng) adj en pente

sloppy (slo-pi) adj désordonné

slot (slot) n fente f

slot-machine (slot-meu-chiin) n appareil à jetons

slovenly (sla-veunn-li) adj mal soigné

slow (slô[ou]) adj lent; ~ **down** ralentir; freiner

sluice (slouss) n écluse f

slum (slamm) n bas quartier

slump (slammp) n baisse des prix

slush (slach) n boue f

sly (slaï) adj malin

smack (smæk) v donner une claque;
n claque f

small (smool) adj petit; faible

smallpox (smool-poks) n variole f

smart (smâât) adj élégant; adroit,
alerte

smell (smèl) n odeur f

***smell** (smèl) v *sentir; *sentir mau-
vais

smelly (smè-li) adj malodorant

smile (smaïl) v *sourire; n sourire m

smith (şmiθ) n forgeron m

smoke (smô[ou]k) v fumer; n fumée f;
no smoking défense de fumer

smoker (smô[ou]-keu) n fumeur m;

compartiment fumeurs

smoking-compartment (*smô^ou*-kinng-keumm-pâât-meunnt) *n* compartiment fumeurs

smoking-room (*smô^ou*-kinng-roûm) *n* fumoir *m*

smooth (smoûð) *adj* uni, plat, lisse; doux

smuggle (*sma*-gheul) *v* passer en contrebande

snack (snæk) *n* casse-croûte *m*

snack-bar (*snæk*-bââ) *n* snack-bar *m*

snail (snéïl) *n* escargot *m*

snake (snéïk) *n* serpent *m*

snapshot (*snæp*-chot) *n* instantané *m*

sneakers (*snii*-keuz) *plAm* chaussures de gymnastique

sneeze (sniiz) *v* éternuer

sniper (*snaï*-peu) *n* franc-tireur *m*

snooty (snoû-ti) *adj* snob

snore (snoo) *v* ronfler

snorkel (*snoo*-keul) *n* tube de plongée

snout (snaout) *n* museau *m*

snow (snô^ou) *n* neige *f*; *v* neiger

snowstorm (*snô^ou*-stoom) *n* tempête de neige

snowy (*snô^ou*-i) *adj* neigeux

so (sô^ou) *conj* donc; *adv* ainsi; tellement, si; **and ~ on** et ainsi de suite; **~ far** jusqu'à présent; **~ that** de manière que, pour que, afin que

soak (sô^ouk) *v* tremper

soap (sô^oup) *n* savon *m*; **~ powder** savon en poudre

sober (*sô^ou*-beu) *adj* sobre; pondéré

so-called (sô^ou-*koold*) *adj* soi-disant

soccer (*so*-keu) *n* football *m*; **~ team** équipe *f*

social (*sô^ou*-cheul) *adj* social

socialism (*sô^ou*-cheu-li-zeumm) *n* socialisme *m*

socialist (*sô^ou*-cheu-list) *adj* socialiste; *n* socialiste *m*

society (seu-*saï*-eu-ti) *n* société *f*; as-sociation *f*; compagnie *f*

sock (sok) *n* chaussette *f*

socket (*so*-kit) *n* douille *f*

soda-water (*sô^ou*-deu-^ou oo-teu) *n* eau de Seltz, eau gazeuse

sofa (*sô^ou*-feu) *n* canapé *m*

soft (soft) *adj* mou; **~ drink** boisson non alcoolisée

soften (so-feunn) *v* adoucir

soil (soïl) *n* sol *m*; terroir *m*, terre *f*

soiled (soïld) *adj* souillé

sold (sô^ould) *v* (p, pp sell); **~ out** épuisé

solder (*sol*-deu) *v* souder

soldering-iron (*sol*-deu-rinng-aï^eu n) *n* fer à souder

soldier (*sô^ou*l-djeu) *n* soldat *m*

sole[1] (sô^oul) *adj* unique

sole[2] (sô^oul) *n* semelle *f*; sole *f*

solely (*sô^ou*l-li) *adv* exclusivement

solemn (*so*-leumm) *adj* solennel

solicitor (seu-*li*-si-teu) *n* avoué *m*, avocat *m*

solid (*so*-lid) *adj* robuste, solide; massif; *n* solide *m*

soluble (*so*-lyou-beul) *adj* soluble

solution (seu-*loû*-cheunn) *n* solution *f*

solve (solv) *v* *résoudre

sombre (*somm*-beu) *adj* sombre

some (samm) *adj* quelques; *pron* certains, quelques; un peu; **~ day** un jour ou l'autre; **~ more** encore un peu; **~ time** une fois

somebody (*samm*-beu-di) *pron* quelqu'un

somehow (*samm*-haou) *adv* d'une manière ou d'une autre

someone (*samm*-^ou ann) *pron* quelqu'un

something (*samm*-θinng) *pron* quelque chose

sometimes (*samm*-taïmz) *adv* parfois

somewhat (*samm*-^ou ot) *adv* quelque peu

somewhere (*samm*-⁻ᵒᵘèᵉᵘ) *adv* quelque part

son (sann) *n* fils *m*

song (sonng) *n* chanson *f*

son-in-law (*sa*-ninn-loo) *n* (pl sons-) gendre *m*

soon (soûn) *adv* rapidement, sous peu, prochainement, bientôt; **as ~ as** dès que

sooner (*soû*-neu) *adv* plutôt

sore (soo) *adj* douloureux; *n* douleur *f*; ulcère *m*; **~ throat** mal de gorge

sorrow (*so*-rôᵒᵘ) *n* tristesse *f*, douleur *f*, chagrin *m*

sorry (*so*-ri) *adj* désolé; **sorry!** excusez-moi!, pardon!

sort (soot) *v* classer, ranger; *n* catégorie *f*, sorte *f*; **all sorts of** toutes sortes de

soul (sôᵒᵘl) *n* âme *f*; esprit *m*

sound (saound) *n* son *m*; *v* sonner; *adj* solide

soundproof (*saound*-proûf) *adj* insonorisé

soup (soûp) *n* soupe *f*

soup-plate (*soûp*-pléït) *n* assiette à soupe

soup-spoon (*soûp*-spoûn) *n* cuillère à soupe

sour (saouᵉᵘ) *adj* aigre

source (sooss) *n* source *f*

south (saouθ) *n* sud *m*; **South Pole** pôle sud

South Africa (saouθ æ-fri-keu) Afrique du Sud

south-east (saouθ-*iist*) *n* sud-est *m*

southerly (*sa*-ðeu-li) *adj* méridional

southern (*sa*-ðeunn) *adj* méridional

south-west (saouθ-ᵒᵘ*èst*) *n* sud-ouest *m*

souvenir (*soû*-veu-niᵉᵘ) *n* souvenir *m*

sovereign (*sov*-rinn) *n* souverain *m*

Soviet (*sô*ᵒᵘ-vi-eut) *adj* soviétique

Soviet Union (*sô*ᵒᵘ-vi-eut *you*-nyeunn) Union Soviétique

*sow (sôᵒᵘ) *v* semer

spa (spââ) *n* station thermale

space (spéïss) *n* espace *m*; distance *f*, intervalle *m*; *v* espacer

spacious (*spéï*-cheuss) *adj* spacieux

spade (spéïd) *n* bêche *f*, pelle *f*

Spain (spéïn) Espagne *f*

Spaniard (*spæ*-nyeud) *n* Espagnol *m*

Spanish (*spæ*-nich) *adj* espagnol

spanking (*spæng*-kinng) *n* fessée *f*

spanner (*spæ*-neu) *n* clé à écrous

spare (spèᵉᵘ) *adj* de réserve, disponible; *v* se passer de; **~ part** pièce détachée; **~ room** chambre d'ami; **~ time** temps libre; **~ tyre** pneu de rechange; **~ wheel** roue de secours

spark (spââk) *n* étincelle *f*

sparking-plug (*spââ*-kinng-plagh) *n* bougie d'allumage

sparkling (*spââ*-klinng) *adj* scintillant; mousseux

sparrow (*spæ*-rôᵒᵘ) *n* moineau *m*

*speak (spiik) *v* parler

spear (spiᵉᵘ) *n* lance *f*

special (*spè*-cheul) *adj* particulier, spécial; **~ delivery** exprès

specialist (*spè*-cheu-list) *n* spécialiste *m*

speciality (spè-chi-*æ*-leu-ti) *n* spécialité *f*

specialize (*spè*-cheu-laïz) *v* se spécialiser

specially (*spè*-cheu-li) *adv* particulièrement

species (*spii*-chiiz) *n* (pl ~) espèce *f*

specific (speu-*si*-fik) *adj* spécifique

specimen (*spè*-si-meunn) *n* spécimen *m*

speck (spèk) *n* tache *f*

spectacle (*spèk*-teu-keul) *n* spectacle *m*; **spectacles** lunettes *fpl*

spectator (spèk-*téï*-teu) *n* spectateur *m*

speculate (*spè*-kyou-léït) *v* spéculer

speech (spiitch) *n* parole *f*; allocution *f*, discours *m*; langage *m*

speechless (*spiitch*-leuss) *adj* interloqué

speed (spiid) *n* vitesse *f*; rapidité *f*, hâte *f*; **cruising ~** vitesse de croisière; **~ limit** limite de vitesse, limitation de vitesse

** **speed** (spiid) *v* foncer; rouler trop vite

speeding (*spii*-dinng) *n* excès de vitesse

speedometer (spii-*do*-mi-teu) *n* indicateur de vitesse

spell (spèl) *n* enchantement *m*

** **spell** (spèl) *v* épeler

spelling (*spè*-linng) *n* orthographe *f*

** **spend** (spènd) *v* dépenser; employer

sphere (sfi^{eu}) *n* sphère *f*

spice (spaïss) *n* épice *f*

spiced (spaïst) *adj* épicé

spicy (*spaï*-si) *adj* épicé

spider (*spaï*-deu) *n* araignée *f*; **spider's web** toile d'araignée

** **spill** (spil) *v* répandre

** **spin** (spinn) *v* filer; tourner

spinach (*spi*-nidj) *n* épinards *mpl*

spine (spaïn) *n* épine dorsale

spinster (*spinn*-steu) *n* vieille fille

spire (spaï^{eu}) *n* aiguille *f*

spirit (*spi*-rit) *n* esprit *m*; humeur *f*; **spirits** boissons alcoolisées, spiritueux *mpl*; moral *m*; **~ stove** réchaud à alcool

spiritual (*spi*-ri-tchou-eul) *adj* spirituel

spit (spit) *n* crachat *m*, salive *f*; broche *f*

** **spit** (spit) *v* cracher

in spite of (inn spaït ov) en dépit de, malgré

spiteful (*spaït*-feul) *adj* malveillant

splash (splæch) *v* éclabousser

splendid (*splèn*-did) *adj* magnifique, splendide

splendour (*splèn*-deu) *n* splendeur *f*

splint (splinnt) *n* éclisse *f*

splinter (*splinn*-teu) *n* écharde *f*

** **split** (split) *v* fendre

** **spoil** (spoïl) *v* gâter

spoke¹ (spô^{ou}k) *v* (p speak)

spoke² (spô^{ou}k) *n* rayon *m*

sponge (spanndj) *n* éponge *f*

spook (spoûk) *n* spectre *m*, fantôme *m*

spool (spoûl) *n* bobine *f*

spoon (spoûn) *n* cuillère *f*

spoonful (*spoûn*-foul) *n* cuillerée *f*

sport (spoot) *n* sport *m*

sports-car (*spoots*-kââ) *n* voiture de sport

sports-jacket (*spoots*-djæ-kit) *n* veston sport

sportsman (*spoots*-meunn) *n* (pl -men) sportif *m*

sportswear (*spoots*-^{ou}è^{eu}) *n* vêtements de sport

spot (spot) *n* tache *f*; lieu *m*, endroit *m*

spotless (*spot*-leuss) *adj* immaculé

spotlight (*spot*-laït) *n* projecteur *m*

spotted (*spo*-tid) *adj* tacheté

spout (spaout) *n* jet *m*

sprain (spréïn) *v* fouler; *n* foulure *f*

** **spread** (sprèd) *v* étendre

spring (sprinng) *n* printemps *m*; ressort *m*; source *f*

springtime (*sprinng*-taïm) *n* printemps *m*

sprouts (spraouts) *pl* choux de Bruxelles

spy (spaï) *n* espion *m*

squadron (*sk^{ou}o*-dreunn) *n* escadrille *f*

square (sk^{ou}è^{eu}) *adj* carré; *n* carré *m*; square *m*, place *f*

squash (sk^{ou}och) *n* jus de fruits

squirrel (*sk^{ou}i*-reul) *n* écureuil *m*

squirt (sk^{ou}eût) *n* jet *m*

stable (*stéï*-beul) *adj* stable; *n* étable *f*

stack (stæk) *n* pile *f*

stadium (*stéï*-di-eumm) *n* stade *m*

staff (stââf) *n* personnel *m*

stage (stéïdj) *n* scène *f*; phase *f*, étape *f*

stain (stéïn) *v* tacher; *n* tache *f*; **stained glass** verre de couleur; ~ **remover** détachant *m*

stainless (*stéïn*-leuss) *adj* immaculé; ~ **steel** acier inoxydable

staircase (*stè^{eu}*-kéïss) *n* escalier *m*

stairs (stè^{eu}z) *pl* escalier *m*

stale (stéïl) *adj* rassis

stall (stool) *n* étal *m*; fauteuil d'orchestre

stamina (*stæ*-mi-neu) *n* endurance *f*

stamp (stæmp) *n* timbre *m*; *v* affranchir; piétiner; ~ **machine** distributeur de timbres

stand (stænd) *n* stand *m*; tribune *f*

*****stand** (stænd) *v* se *tenir debout

standard (*stæn*-deud) *n* norme *f*; standard; ~ **of living** niveau de vie

stanza (*stæn*-zeu) *n* strophe *f*

staple (*stéï*-peul) *n* agrafe *f*

star (stââ) *n* étoile *f*

starboard (*stââ*-beud) *n* tribord *m*

starch (stââtch) *n* amidon *m*; *v* amidonner

stare (stè^{eu}) *v* fixer

starling (*stââ*-linng) *n* étourneau *m*

start (stâât) *v* commencer; *n* début *m*; **starter motor** démarreur *m*

starting-point (*stââ*-tinng-poïnt) *n* point de départ

state (stéït) *n* Etat *m*; état *m*; *v* déclarer

the States Etats-Unis

statement (*stéït*-meunnt) *n* déclaration *f*

statesman (*stéïts*-meunn) *n* (pl -men) homme d'Etat

station (*stéï*-cheunn) *n* gare *f*; poste *m*

stationary (*stéï*-cheu-neu-ri) *adj* stationnaire

stationer's (*stéï*-cheu-neuz) *n* papeterie *f*

stationery (*stéï*-cheu-neu-ri) *n* papeterie *f*

station-master (*stéï*-cheunn-mââ-steu) *n* chef de gare

statistics (steu-*ti*-stiks) *pl* statistique *f*

statue (*stæ*-tchou) *n* statue *f*

stay (stéï) *v* rester; séjourner; *n* séjour *m*

steadfast (*stèd*-fââst) *adj* ferme

steady (*stè*-di) *adj* ferme

steak (stéïk) *n* bifteck *m*

*****steal** (stiil) *v* voler

steam (stiim) *n* vapeur *f*

steamer (*stii*-meu) *n* bateau à vapeur

steel (stiil) *n* acier *m*

steep (stiip) *adj* abrupt, escarpé

steeple (*stii*-peul) *n* clocher *m*

steering-column (*sti^{eu}*-rinng-ko-leumm) *n* colonne de direction

steering-wheel (*sti^{eu}*-rinng-^{ou}iil) *n* volant *m*

steersman (*sti^{eu}z*-meunn) *n* (pl -men) timonier *m*

stem (stèm) *n* tige *f*

stenographer (stè-*no*-greu-feu) *n* sténographe *m*

step (stèp) *n* pas *m*; marche *f*; *v* marcher

stepchild (*stèp*-tchaïld) *n* (pl -children) enfant d'un autre lit

stepfather (*stèp*-fââ-ðeu) *n* beau-père *m*

stepmother (*stèp*-ma-ðeu) *n* belle-mère *f*

sterile (*stè*-raïl) *adj* stérile

sterilize (*stè*-ri-laïz) *v* stériliser

steward (*styoù*-eud) *n* steward *m*

stewardess (*styoù*-eu-dèss) *n* hôtesse

de l'air

stick (stik) n bâton m

*stick (stik) v coller

sticky (sti-ki) adj gluant

stiff (stif) adj raide

still (stil) adv encore; toutefois; adj tranquille

stillness (stil-neuss) n silence m

stimulant (sti-myou-leunnt) n stimulant m

stimulate (sti-myou-léit) v stimuler

sting (stinng) n piqûre f

*sting (stinng) v piquer

stingy (stinn-dji) adj mesquin

*stink (stinngk) v puer

stipulate (sti-pyou-léit) v stipuler

stipulation (sti-pyou-léi-cheunn) n stipulation f

stir (steû) v bouger; remuer

stirrup (sti-reup) n étrier m

stitch (stitch) n point m, point de côté; suture f

stock (stok) n stock m; v *avoir en stock; ~ **exchange** bourse des valeurs, bourse f; ~ **market** marché des valeurs; **stocks and shares** actions

stocking (sto-kinng) n bas m

stole[1] (stô^{ou}l) v (p steal)

stole[2] (stô^{ou}l) n étole f

stomach (sta-meuk) n estomac m

stomach-ache (sta-meu-kéïk) n mal au ventre, mal d'estomac

stone (stô^{ou}n) n pierre f; pierre précieuse; noyau m; en pierre; **pumice** ~ pierre ponce

stood (stoud) v (p, pp stand)

stop (stop) v arrêter; cesser; n arrêt m; **stop!** stop!

stopper (sto-peu) n bouchon m

storage (stoo-ridj) n emmagasinage m

store (stoo) n provision f; magasin m; v emmagasiner

store-house (stoo-haouss) n magasin m

storey (stoo-ri) n étage m

stork (stook) n cigogne f

storm (stoom) n tempête f

stormy (stoo-mi) adj orageux

story (stoo-ri) n histoire f

stout (staout) adj gros, obèse, corpulent

stove (stô^{ou}v) n fourneau m; cuisinière f

straight (stréït) adj droit; adv directement; ~ **ahead** tout droit; ~ **away** directement, tout de suite; ~ **on** tout droit

strain (stréïn) n effort m; tension f; v forcer; filtrer

strainer (stréï-neu) n passoire f

strange (stréïndj) adj étrange; bizarre

stranger (stréïn-djeu) n étranger m; inconnu m

strangle (stræng-gheul) v étrangler

strap (stræp) n courroie f

straw (stroo) n paille f

strawberry (stroo-beu-ri) n fraise f

stream (striim) n ruisseau m; courant m; v couler

street (striit) n rue f

streetcar (striit-kââ) nAm tram m

street-organ (strii-too-gheunn) n orgue de Barbarie

strength (strèngθ) n vigueur f, force f

stress (strèss) n tension f; accent m; v souligner

stretch (strètch) v tendre; n section f

strict (strikt) adj sévère

strife (straïf) n lutte f

strike (straïk) n grève f

*strike (straïk) v frapper; *faire grève; amener

striking (straï-kinng) adj frappant, remarquable

string (strinng) n ficelle f; corde f

strip (strip) n bande f

stripe (straïp) n raie f

striped (straïpt) *adj* rayé

stroke (strô^{ou}k) *n* attaque *f*

stroll (strô^{ou}l) *v* flâner; *n* promenade *f*

strong (stronng) *adj* fort; puissant

stronghold (*stronng*-hô^{ou}ld) *n* place forte

structure (*strak*-tcheu) *n* structure *f*

struggle (*stra*-gheul) *n* combat *m*, lutte *f*; *v* lutter

stub (stab) *n* souche *f*

stubborn (*sta*-beunn) *adj* têtu

student (*styoû*-deunnt) *n* étudiant *m*; étudiante *f*

study (*sta*-di) *v* étudier; *n* étude *f*; cabinet *m*

stuff (staf) *n* substance *f*; fatras *m*

stuffed (staft) *adj* farci

stuffing (*sta*-finng) *n* farce *f*

stuffy (*sta*-fi) *adj* étouffant

stumble (*stamm*-beul) *v* trébucher

stung (stanng) *v* (p, pp sting)

stupid (*styoû*-pid) *adj* stupide

style (staïl) *n* style *m*

subject[1] (*sab*-djikt) *n* sujet *m*; ~ **to** sujet à

subject[2] (seub-*djèkt*) *v* *soumettre

submit (seub-*mit*) *v* se *soumettre

subordinate (seu-*boo*-di-neut) *adj* subordonné; secondaire

subscriber (seub-*skraï*-beu) *n* abonné *m*

subscription (seub-*skrip*-cheunn) *n* abonnement *m*

subsequent (*sab*-si-k^{ou}eunnt) *adj* postérieur

subsidy (*sab*-si-di) *n* subvention *f*

substance (*sab*-steunns) *n* substance *f*

substantial (seub-*stæn*-cheul) *adj* matériel; réel; substantiel

substitute (*sab*-sti-tyoût) *v* substituer; *n* substitut *m*

subtitle (*sab*-taï-teul) *n* sous-titre *m*

subtle (*sa*-teul) *adj* subtil

subtract (seub-*trækt*) *v* *soustraire

suburb (*sa*-beub) *n* banlieue *f*, faubourg *m*

suburban (seu-*beû*-beunn) *adj* suburbain

subway (*sab*-^{ou}éï) *nAm* métro *m*

succeed (seuk-*siid*) *v* réussir; succéder

success (seuk-*sèss*) *n* succès *m*

successful (seuk-*sèss*-feul) *adj* réussi

succumb (seu-*kamm*) *v* succomber

such (satch) *adj* tel; *adv* tellement; ~ **as** tel que

suck (sak) *v* sucer

sudden (*sa*-deunn) *adj* soudain

suddenly (*sa*-deunn-li) *adv* soudain

suede (s^{ou}éïd) *n* daim *m*

suffer (*sa*-feu) *v* *souffrir; subir

suffering (*sa*-feu-rinng) *n* souffrance *f*

suffice (seu-*faïss*) *v* *suffire

sufficient (seu-*fi*-cheunnt) *adj* adéquat, suffisant

suffrage (*sa*-fridj) *n* droit de vote, suffrage *m*

sugar (*chou*-gheu) *n* sucre *m*

suggest (seu-*djèst*) *v* suggérer

suggestion (seu-*djèss*-tcheunn) *n* suggestion *f*

suicide (*soû*-i-saïd) *n* suicide *m*

suit (soût) *v* *convenir; adapter à; bien *aller; *n* complet *m*

suitable (*soû*-teu-beul) *adj* qui convient, approprié

suitcase (*soût*-kéïss) *n* valise *f*

suite (s^{ou}iit) *n* appartement *m*

sum (samm) *n* somme *f*

summary (*sa*-meu-ri) *n* sommaire *m*, résumé *m*

summer (*sa*-meu) *n* été *m*; ~ **time** heure d'été

summit (*sa*-mit) *n* sommet *m*

summons (*sa*-meunnz) *n* (pl ~es) convocation *f*

sun (sann) *n* soleil *m*

sunbathe (*sann*-béïð) v *prendre un bain de soleil

sunburn (*sann*-beunn) n coup de soleil

Sunday (*sann*-di) dimanche m

sun-glasses (*sann*-ghlââ-siz) pl lunettes de soleil

sunlight (*sann*-laït) n lumière du soleil

sunny (*sa*-ni) adj ensoleillé

sunrise (*sann*-raïz) n lever du soleil

sunset (*sann*-sèt) n coucher du soleil

sunshade (*sann*-chéïd) n parasol m

sunshine (*sann*-chaïn) n soleil m

sunstroke (*sann*-strô ᵒᵘk) n insolation f

suntan oil (*sann*-tæn-oïl) huile solaire

superb (sou-*peûb*) adj grandiose, superbe

superficial (soû-peu-*fi*-cheul) adj superficiel

superfluous (sou-*peû*-flou-euss) adj superflu

superior (sou-*piᵉᵘ*-ri-eu) adj supérieur, majeur

superlative (sou-*peû*-leu-tiv) adj superlatif; n superlatif m

supermarket (*soû*-peu-mââ-kit) n supermarché m

superstition (soû-peu-*sti*-cheunn) n superstition f

supervise (*soû*-peu-vaïz) v superviser

supervision (soû-peu-*vi*-jeunn) n supervision f, surveillance f

supervisor (*soû*-peu-vaï-zeu) n surveillant m

supper (*sa*-peu) n souper m

supple (*sa*-peul) adj souple, flexible

supplement (*sa*-pli-meunnt) n supplément m

supply (seu-*plaï*) n fourniture f; stock m; offre f; v fournir

support (seu-*poot*) v supporter, *soutenir; n soutien m; ~ **hose** bas élastiques

supporter (seu-*poo*-teu) n supporter

suppose (seu-*pôᵒᵘz*) v supposer; **supposing that** en admettant que

suppository (seu-*po*-zi-teu-ri) n suppositoire m

suppress (seu-*press*) v réprimer

surcharge (*seû*-tchââdj) n supplément m

sure (chou ᵉᵘ) adj sûr

surely (*chou*ᵉᵘ-li) adv sûrement

surface (*seû*-fiss) n surface f

surgeon (*seû*-djeunn) n chirurgien m; **veterinary** ~ vétérinaire m

surgery (*seû*-djeu-ri) n opération f; cabinet de consultations

surname (*seû*-néïm) n nom de famille

surplus (*seû*-pleuss) n surplus m

surprise (seu-*praïz*) n surprise f; v *surprendre

surrender (seu-*rèn*-deu) v se rendre; n reddition f

surround (seu-*raound*) v entourer

surrounding (seu-*raoun*-dinng) adj environnant

surroundings (seu-*raoun*-dinngz) pl alentours mpl

survey (*seû*-véï) n résumé m

survival (seu-*vaï*-veul) n survie f

survive (seu-*vaïv*) v *survivre

suspect[1] (seu-*spèkt*) v soupçonner; suspecter

suspect[2] (*sa*-spèkt) n suspect m

suspend (seu-*spènd*) v suspendre

suspenders (seu-*spèn*-deuz) plAm bretelles fpl; **suspender belt** porte-jarretelles m

suspension (seu-*spèn*-cheunn) n suspension f; ~ **bridge** pont suspendu

suspicion (seu-*spi*-cheunn) n soupçon m; défiance f, méfiance f

suspicious (seu-*spi*-cheuss) adj suspect; soupçonneux, méfiant

sustain (seu-*stéïn*) v endurer

Swahili (sᵒᵘeu-*hii*-li) n Swahili m

swallow ($s^{ou}o$-lô^{ou}) v avaler; n hirondelle f

swam (s^{ou}æm) v (p swim)

swamp (s^{ou}ommp) n marais m

swan (s^{ou}onn) n cygne m

swap (s^{ou}op) v troquer

***swear** (s^{ou}è^{eu}) v jurer

sweat (s^{ou}èt) n sueur f; v suer

sweater (s^{ou}è-teu) n chandail m

Swede (s^{ou}iid) n Suédois m

Sweden (s^{ou}ii-deunn) Suède f

Swedish (s^{ou}ii-dich) adj suédois

***sweep** (s^{ou}iip) v balayer

sweet (s^{ou}iit) adj sucré; gentil; n bonbon m; dessert m; **sweets** douceurs fpl, bonbons

sweeten (s^{ou}ii-teunn) v sucrer

sweetheart (s^{ou}iit-hâât) n mon amour, chéri m

sweetshop (s^{ou}ii-chop) n confiserie f

swell (s^{ou}èl) adj formidable

***swell** (s^{ou}èl) v enfler

swelling (s^{ou}è-linng) n enflure f

swift (s^{ou}ift) adj rapide

***swim** (s^{ou}imm) v nager

swimmer (s^{ou}i-meu) n nageur m

swimming (s^{ou}i-minng) n natation f; ~ **pool** piscine f

swimming-trunks (s^{ou}i-minng-tranngks) n caleçon de bain

swim-suit (s^{ou}imm-soût) n maillot de bain

swindle (s^{ou}inn-deul) v escroquer; n escroquerie f

swindler (s^{ou}inn-dleu) n escroc m

swing (s^{ou}inng) n balançoire f

***swing** (s^{ou}inng) v balancer

Swiss (s^{ou}iss) adj suisse; n Suisse m

switch (s^{ou}itch) n commutateur m; v changer; ~ **off** *éteindre; ~ **on** allumer

switchboard (s^{ou}itch-bood) n tableau de distribution

Switzerland (s^{ou}it-seu-leunnd) Suisse f

sword (sood) n épée f

swum (s^{ou}amm) v (pp swim)

syllable (si-leu-beul) n syllabe f

symbol (simm-beul) n symbole m

sympathetic (simm-peu-θè-tik) adj cordial, compatissant

sympathy (simm-peu-θi) n sympathie f; compassion f

symphony (simm-feu-ni) n symphonie f

symptom (simm-teumm) n symptôme m

synagogue (si-neu-ghogh) n synagogue f

synonym (si-neu-nimm) n synonyme m

synthetic (sinn-θè-tik) adj synthétique

syphon (sai-feunn) n siphon m

Syria (si-ri-eu) Syrie f

Syrian (si-ri-eunn) adj syrien; n Syrien m

syringe (si-rinndj) n seringue f

syrup (si-reup) n sirop m

system (si-steumm) n système m; **decimal** ~ système décimal

systematic (si-steu-mæ-tik) adj systématique

T

table (téi-beul) n table f; ~ **of contents** table des matières; ~ **tennis** ping-pong m

table-cloth (téi-beul-kloθ) n nappe f

tablespoon (téi-beul-spoûn) n cuillère f

tablet (tæ-blit) n tablette f

taboo (teu-boû) n tabou m

tactics (tæk-tiks) pl tactique f

tag (tægh) n étiquette f

tail (téil) n queue f

tail-light (téil-laït) n feu arrière

tailor (*téi*-leu) *n* tailleur *m*

tailor-made (*téi*-leu-méïd) *adj* fait sur mesure

*****take** (téïk) *v* *prendre; saisir; *conduire; *concevoir, *comprendre; ~ **away** emporter; enlever; ~ **off** décoller; ~ **out** ôter; ~ **over** *reprendre; ~ **place** *avoir lieu; ~ **up** occuper

take-off (*téi*-kof) *n* décollage *m*

tale (téïl) *n* conte *m*, récit *m*

talent (*tæ*-leunnt) *n* don *m*, talent *m*

talented (*tæ*-leunn-tid) *adj* doué

talk (took) *v* parler; *n* conversation *f*

talkative (*too*-keu-tiv) *adj* bavard

tall (tool) *adj* haut; grand

tame (téïm) *adj* domestique, apprivoisé; *v* apprivoiser

tampon (*tæm*-peunn) *n* tampon *m*

tangerine (tæn-djeu-*riin*) *n* mandarine *f*

tangible (*tæn*-dji-beul) *adj* tangible

tank (tæng k) *n* réservoir *m*

tanker (*tæng*-keu) *n* bateau-citerne *m*

tanned (tænd) *adj* hâlé

tap (tæp) *n* robinet *m*; coup *m*; *v* frapper

tape (téïp) *n* bande *f*; cordon *m*; **adhesive** ~ ruban adhésif; sparadrap *m*

tape-measure (*téïp*-mè-jeu) *n* centimètre *m*

tape-recorder (*téïp*-ri-koo-deu) *n* magnétophone *m*

tapestry (*tæ*-pi-stri) *n* tapisserie *f*

tar (tââ) *n* goudron *m*

target (*tââ*-ghit) *n* objectif *m*, cible *f*

tariff (*tæ*-rif) *n* taux *m*

tarpaulin (tââ-*poo*-linn) *n* bâche *f*

task (tââsk) *n* tâche *f*

taste (téïst) *n* goût *m*; *v* *avoir goût de; goûter

tasteless (*téïst*-leuss) *adj* insipide

tasty (*téï*-sti) *adj* succulent, savoureux

taught (toot) *v* (p, pp teach)

tavern (*tæ*-veunn) *n* taverne *f*

tax (tæks) *n* impôt *m*; *v* imposer

taxation (tæk-*séï*-cheunn) *n* taxation *f*

tax-free (*tæks*-frii) *adj* exempt d'impôts

taxi (*tæk*-si) *n* taxi *m*; ~ **rank** station de taxis; ~ **stand** *Am* station de taxis

taxi-driver (*tæk*-si-draï-veu) *n* chauffeur de taxi

taxi-meter (*tæk*-si-mii-teu) *n* taximètre *m*

tea (tii) *n* thé *m*

*****teach** (tiitch) *v* *apprendre, enseigner

teacher (*tii*-tcheu) *n* professeur *m*, maître *m*; instituteur *m*, maître d'école

teachings (*tii*-tchinngz) *pl* enseignements

tea-cloth (*tii*-kloθ) *n* torchon *m*

teacup (*tii*-kap) *n* tasse à thé

team (tiim) *n* équipe *f*

teapot (*tii*-pot) *n* théière *f*

tear[1] (ti^{eu}) *n* larme *f*

tear[2] (tè^{eu}) *n* déchirure *f*; *****tear** *v* déchirer

tear-jerker (*ti^{eu}*-djeù-keu) *n* mélo *m*

tease (tiiz) *v* taquiner

tea-set (*tii*-sèt) *n* service à thé

tea-shop (*tii*-chop) *n* salon de thé

teaspoon (*tii*-spoûn) *n* cuillère à thé

teaspoonful (*tii*-spoûn-foul) *n* cuillerée à thé

technical (*tèk*-ni-keul) *adj* technique

technician (tèk-*ni*-cheunn) *n* technicien *m*

technique (tèk-*niik*) *n* technique *f*

technology (tèk-*no*-leu-dji) *n* technologie *f*

teenager (*tii*-néï-djeu) *n* adolescent *m*

teetotaller (tii-*tô^{ou}*-teu-leu) *n* antialcoolique *m*

telegram (*tè*-li-ghræm) *n* télégramme *m*

telegraph (*tè*-li-ghrââf) *v* télégraphier

telepathy (ti-*lè*-peu-θi) *n* télépathie *f*

telephone (*tè*-li-fôᵒᵘn) *n* téléphone *m*; ~ **book** *Am* annuaire téléphonique; ~ **booth** cabine téléphonique; ~ **call** coup de téléphone, appel téléphonique; ~ **directory** annuaire téléphonique, bottin *m*; ~ **exchange** central téléphonique; ~ **operator** standardiste *f*

telephonist (ti-*lè*-feu-nist) *n* téléphoniste *f*

television (*tè*-li-vi-jeunn) *n* télévision *f*; ~ **set** télévision *f*

telex (*tè*-lèks) *n* télex *m*

*****tell** (tèl) *v* *dire; raconter

temper (*tèm*-peu) *n* colère *f*

temperature (*tèm*-preu-tcheu) *n* température *f*

tempest (*tèm*-pist) *n* tempête *f*

temple (*tèm*-peul) *n* temple *m*; tempe *f*

temporary (*tèm*-peu-reu-ri) *adj* provisoire, temporaire

tempt (tèmpt) *v* tenter

temptation (tèmp-*téï*-cheunn) *n* tentation *f*

ten (tèn) *num* dix

tenant (*tè*-neunnt) *n* locataire *m*

tend (tènd) *v* *avoir tendance; soigner; ~ **to** tendre à

tendency (*tèn*-deunn-si) *n* inclination *f*, tendance *f*

tender (*tèn*-deu) *adj* tendre, délicat

tendon (*tèn*-deunn) *n* tendon *m*

tennis (*tè*-niss) *n* tennis *m*; ~ **shoes** chaussures de tennis

tennis-court (*tè*-niss-koot) *n* court de tennis

tense (tèns) *adj* tendu

tension (*tèn*-cheunn) *n* tension *f*

tent (tènt) *n* tente *f*

tenth (tènθ) *num* dixième

tepid (*tè*-pid) *adj* tiède

term (teûmm) *n* terme *m*; période *f*; condition *f*

terminal (*teû*-mi-neul) *n* terminus *m*

terrace (*tè*-reuss) *n* terrasse *f*

terrain (tè-*réín*) *n* terrain *m*

terrible (*tè*-ri-beul) *adj* épouvantable, terrible

terrific (teu-*ri*-fik) *adj* formidable

terrify (*tè*-ri-faï) *v* terrifier

territory (*tè*-ri-teu-ri) *n* territoire *m*

terror (*tè*-reu) *n* terreur *f*

terrorism (*tè*-reu-ri-zeumm) *n* terrorisme *m*, terreur *f*

terrorist (*tè*-reu-rist) *n* terroriste *m*

terylene (*tè*-reu-liin) *n* Térylène *m*

test (tèst) *n* test *m*, épreuve *f*; *v* essayer, éprouver

testify (*tè*-sti-faï) *v* témoigner

text (tèkst) *n* texte *m*

textbook (*tèks*-bouk) *n* manuel *m*

textile (*tèk*-staïl) *n* textile *m*

texture (*tèks*-tcheu) *n* texture *f*

Thai (taï) *adj* thaïlandais; *n* Thaïlandais *m*

Thailand (*taï*-lænd) Thaïlande *f*

than (ðæn) *conj* que

thank (θængk) *v* remercier; ~ **you** merci

thankful (*θ*ængk-feul) *adj* reconnaissant

that (ðæt) *adj* ce; *pron* celui-là, cela, qui; *conj* que

thaw (θoo) *v* dégeler, fondre; *n* dégel *m*

the (ðeu,ði) *art* le *art*; **the ... the** plus ... plus

theatre (*θiᵉᵘ*-teu) *n* théâtre *m*

theft (θèft) *n* vol *m*

their (ðèᵉᵘ) *adj* leur

them (ðèm) *pron* les; leur

theme (θiim) *n* thème *m*, sujet *m*

themselves (ðeumm-*sèlvz*) *pron* se;

eux-mêmes

then (ðèn) *adv* alors; ensuite, puis

theology (θi-*o*-leu-dji) *n* théologie *f*

theoretical (θi*eu*-rè-ti-keul) *adj* théorique

theory (θi*eu*-ri) *n* théorie *f*

therapy (θè-reu-pi) *n* thérapie *f*

there (ðè*eu*) *adv* là

therefore (ðè*eu*-foo) *conj* donc

thermometer (θeu-*mo*-mi-teu) *n* thermomètre *m*

thermostat (*θeû*-meu-stæt) *n* thermostat *m*

these (ðiiz) *adj* ces

thesis (*θii*-siss) *n* (pl theses) thèse *f*

they (ðéi) *pron* ils

thick (θik) *adj* gros; épais

thicken (*θi*-keunn) *v* épaissir

thickness (*θik*-neuss) *n* épaisseur *f*

thief (θiif) *n* (pl thieves) voleur *m*

thigh (θaï) *n* cuisse *f*

thimble (*θimm*-beul) *n* dé *m*

thin (θinn) *adj* mince; maigre

thing (θinng) *n* chose *f*

*****think** (θinngk) *v* penser; réfléchir; ~ **of** penser à; songer à; ~ **over** réfléchir

thinker (*θinng*-keu) *n* penseur *m*

third (θeûd) *num* troisième

thirst (θeûst) *n* soif *f*

thirsty (*θeû*-sti) *adj* assoiffé

thirteen (θeû-*tiin*) *num* treize

thirteenth (θeû-*tiinθ*) *num* treizième

thirtieth (*θeû*-ti-euθ) *num* trentième

thirty (*θeû*-ti) *num* trente

this (ðiss) *adj* ce; *pron* ceci

thistle (*θi*-seul) *n* chardon *m*

thorn (θoon) *n* épine *f*

thorough (*θa*-reu) *adj* minutieux, soigné

thoroughbred (*θa*-reu-brèd) *adj* pur sang

thoroughfare (*θa*-reu-fè*eu*) *n* route principale, artère *f*

those (ðô*eu*z) *adj* ces; *pron* ceux-là

though (ðô*ou*) *conj* bien que, encore que, quoique; *adv* pourtant

thought¹ (θoot) *v* (p, pp think)

thought² (θoot) *n* pensée *f*

thoughtful (*θoot*-feul) *adj* pensif; prévenant

thousand (*θaou*-zeunnd) *num* mille

thread (θrèd) *n* fil *m*; *v* enfiler

threadbare (*θrèd*-bè*eu*) *adj* usé

threat (θrèt) *n* menace *f*

threaten (*θrè*-teunn) *v* menacer; **threatening** menaçant

three (θrii) *num* trois

three-quarter (θrii-*k*°*oo*-teu) *adj* trois quarts

threshold (*θrè*-chô*ou*ld) *n* seuil *m*

threw (θroû) *v* (p throw)

thrifty (*θrif*-ti) *adj* parcimonieux

throat (θrô*ou*t) *n* gorge *f*

throne (θrô*ou*n) *n* trône *m*

through (θroû) *prep* à travers

throughout (θroû-*aout*) *adv* partout

throw (θrô*ou*) *n* lancement *m*

*****throw** (θrô*ou*) *v* jeter, lancer

thrush (θrach) *n* grive *f*

thumb (θamm) *n* pouce *m*

thumbtack (*θamm*-tæk) *nAm* punaise *f*

thump (θammp) *v* marteler

thunder (*θann*-deu) *n* tonnerre *m*; *v* gronder

thunderstorm (*θann*-deu-stoom) *n* orage *m*

thundery (*θann*-deu-ri) *adj* orageux

Thursday (*θeûz*-di) jeudi *m*

thus (ðass) *adv* ainsi

thyme (taïm) *n* thym *m*

tick (tik) *n* marque *f*; ~ **off** pointer

ticket (*ti*-kit) *n* billet *m*; contravention *f*; ~ **collector** contrôleur *m*; ~ **machine** distributeur de billets

tickle (*ti*-keul) *v* chatouiller

tide (taïd) *n* marée *f*; **high** ~ marée

haute; **low** ~ marée basse

tidings (*taï*-dinngz) *pl* nouvelles

tidy (*taï*-di) *adj* ordonné; ~ **up** ranger

tie (taï) *v* nouer, attacher; *n* cravate *f*

tiger (*taï*-gheu) *n* tigre *m*

tight (taït) *adj* serré; étroit, juste; *adv* fortement

tighten (*taï*-teunn) *v* serrer; resserrer; se resserrer

tights (taïts) *pl* collants *mpl*

tile (taïl) *n* carreau *m*; tuile *f*

till (til) *prep* jusqu'à; *conj* jusqu'à ce que

timber (*timm*-beu) *n* bois d'œuvre

time (taïm) *n* temps *m*; fois *f*; **all the** ~ continuellement; **in** ~ à temps; ~ **of arrival** heure d'arrivée; ~ **of departure** heure de départ

time-saving (*taïm*-séï-vinng) *adj* qui fait gagner du temps

timetable (*taïm*-téï-beul) *n* horaire *m*

timid (*ti*-mid) *adj* timide

timidity (ti-*mi*-deu-ti) *n* timidité *f*

tin (tinn) *n* étain *m*; boîte *f*; **tinned food** conserves *fpl*

tinfoil (*tinn*-foïl) *n* papier d'étain

tin-opener (*ti*-nô⁰ᵘ-peu-neu) *n* ouvre-boîte *m*

tiny (*taï*-ni) *adj* minuscule

tip (tip) *n* bout *m*; pourboire *m*

tire¹ (*taï*ᵉᵘ) *n* pneu *m*

tire² (*taï*ᵉᵘ) *v* fatiguer

tired (*taï*ᵉᵘd) *adj* fatigué; ~ **of** las de

tiring (*taï*ᵉᵘ-rinng) *adj* fatigant

tissue (*ti*-choù) *n* tissu *m*; mouchoir de papier

title (*taï*-teul) *n* titre *m*

to (toù) *prep* jusque; à, pour, chez; afin de

toad (tô⁰ᵘd) *n* crapaud *m*

toadstool (*tô⁰ᵘd*-stoùl) *n* champignon *m*

toast (tô⁰ᵘst) *n* toast *m*

tobacco (teu-*bæ*-kô⁰ᵘ) *n* (pl ~s) tabac *m*; ~ **pouch** blague à tabac

tobacconist (teu-*bæ*-keu-nist) *n* débitant de tabac; **tobacconist's** bureau de tabac

today (teu-*déï*) *adv* aujourd'hui

toddler (*tod*-leu) *n* bambin *m*

toe (tô⁰ᵘ) *n* orteil *m*

toffee (*to*-fi) *n* caramel *m*

together (teu-*ghè*-ðeu) *adv* ensemble

toilet (*toï*-leut) *n* toilettes *fpl*; ~ **case** nécessaire de toilette

toilet-paper (*toï*-leut-péï-peu) *n* papier hygiénique

toiletry (*toï*-leu-tri) *n* articles de toilette

token (*tô⁰ᵘ*-keunn) *n* signe *m*; preuve *f*; jeton *m*

told (tô⁰ᵘld) *v* (p, pp tell)

tolerable (*to*-leu-reu-beul) *adj* tolérable

toll (tô⁰ᵘl) *n* péage *m*

tomato (teu-*mââ*-tô⁰ᵘ) *n* (pl ~es) tomate *f*

tomb (toùm) *n* tombe *f*

tombstone (*toùm*-stô⁰ᵘn) *n* pierre tombale

tomorrow (teu-*mo*-rô⁰ᵘ) *adv* demain

ton (tann) *n* tonne *f*

tone (tô⁰ᵘn) *n* ton *m*; timbre *m*

tongs (tonngz) *pl* pince *f*

tongue (tanng) *n* langue *f*

tonic (*to*-nik) *n* tonique *m*

tonight (teu-*naït*) *adv* cette nuit, ce soir

tonsilitis (tonn-seu-*laï*-tiss) *n* amygdalite *f*

tonsils (*tonn*-seulz) *pl* amygdales *fpl*

too (toù) *adv* trop; aussi

took (touk) *v* (p take)

tool (toùl) *n* instrument *m*, outil *m*; ~ **kit** boîte à outils

toot (toùt) *vAm* klaxonner

tooth (toùθ) *n* (pl teeth) dent *f*

toothache (*toù*-θéïk) *n* mal aux dents

toothbrush (*toûθ*-brach) *n* brosse à dents

toothpaste (*toûθ*-péïst) *n* pâte dentifrice

toothpick (*toûθ*-pik) *n* cure-dent *m*

toothpowder (*toûθ*-paou-deu) *n* poudre dentifrice

top (top) *n* sommet *m*; dessus *m*; couvercle *m*; supérieur; **on ~ of** au-dessus de; **~ side** haut *m*

topcoat (*top*-kô^{ou}t) *n* pardessus *m*

topic (*to*-pik) *n* sujet *m*

topical (*to*-pi-keul) *adj* actuel

torch (tootch) *n* torche *f*; lampe de poche

torment¹ (too-*mènt*) *v* tourmenter

torment² (*too*-mènt) *n* tourment *m*

torture (*too*-tcheu) *n* torture *f*; *v* torturer

toss (toss) *v* lancer

tot (tot) *n* bambin *m*

total (*tô^{ou}*-teul) *adj* total; complet, absolu; *n* total *m*

totalitarian (tô^{ou}-tæ-li-*tè^{eu}*-ri-eunn) *adj* totalitaire

totalizator (*tô^{ou}*-teu-laï-zéï-teu) *n* totalisateur *m*

touch (tatch) *v* toucher; *n* contact *m*, attouchement *m*; toucher *m*

touching (*ta*-tchinng) *adj* touchant

tough (taf) *adj* coriace

tour (tou^{eu}) *n* excursion *f*

tourism (*tou^{eu}*-ri-zeumm) *n* tourisme *m*

tourist (*tou^{eu}*-rist) *n* touriste *m*; **~ class** classe touriste; **~ office** syndicat d'initiative

tournament (*tou^{eu}*-neu-meunnt) *n* tournoi *m*

tow (tô^{ou}) *v* remorquer

towards (teu-^{ou}*oodz*) *prep* vers; envers

towel (taou^{eu}l) *n* serviette *f*

towelling (*taou^{eu}*-linng) *n* tissu-éponge *m*

tower (taou^{eu}) *n* tour *f*

town (taoun) *n* ville *f*; **~ centre** centre de la ville; **~ hall** hôtel de ville

townspeople (*taounz*-pii-peul) *pl* citadins *mpl*

toxic (*tok*-sik) *adj* toxique

toy (toï) *n* jouet *m*

toyshop (*toï*-chop) *n* magasin de jouets

trace (tréïss) *n* trace *f*; *v* tracer, retracer

track (træk) *n* voie *f*; piste *f*

tractor (*træk*-teu) *n* tracteur *m*

trade (tréïd) *n* commerce *m*; métier *m*; *v* *faire du commerce

trademark (*tréïd*-mââk) *n* marque de fabrique

trader (*tréï*-deu) *n* commerçant *m*

tradesman (*tréïdz*-meunn) *n* (pl -men) marchand *m*

trade-union (tréïd-*you*-nyeunn) *n* syndicat *m*

tradition (treu-*di*-cheunn) *n* tradition *f*

traditional (treu-*di*-cheu-neul) *adj* traditionnel

traffic (*træ*-fik) *n* circulation *f*; **~ jam** embouteillage *m*; **~ light** feu de circulation

trafficator (*træ*-fi-kéï-teu) *n* indicateur de direction

tragedy (*træ*-djeu-di) *n* tragédie *f*

tragic (*træ*-djik) *adj* tragique

trail (tréïl) *n* piste *f*, sentier *m*

trailer (*tréï*-leu) *n* remorque *f*; *nAm* caravane *f*

train (tréïn) *n* train *m*; *v* dresser, former; **stopping ~** omnibus *m*; **through ~** train direct; **~ ferry** ferry-boat *m*

training (*tréï*-ninng) *n* entraînement *m*

trait (tréït) *n* trait *m*

traitor (*tréï*-teu) *n* traître *m*

tram (træm) *n* tram *m*

tramp (træmp) *n* chemineau *m*, vagabond *m*; *v* vagabonder

tranquil (træng-k^ou il) *adj* tranquille

tranquillizer (træng-k^ou i-laï-zeu) *n* calmant *m*

transaction (træn-*zæk*-cheunn) *n* transaction *f*

transatlantic (træn-zeut-*læn*-tik) *adj* transatlantique

transfer (træns-*feû*) *v* transférer

transform (træns-*foom*) *v* transformer

transformer (træns-*foo*-meu) *n* transformateur *m*

transition (træn-*si*-cheunn) *n* transition *f*

translate (træns-*léit*) *v* *traduire

translation (træns-*léi*-cheunn) *n* traduction *f*

translator (træns-*léi*-teu) *n* traducteur *m*

transmission (trænz-*mi*-cheunn) *n* émission *f*

transmit (trænz-*mit*) *v* *émettre

transmitter (trænz-*mi*-teu) *n* émetteur *m*

transparent (træn-*spè^eu*-reunnt) *adj* transparent

transport[1] (*træn*-spoot) *n* transport *m*

transport[2] (træn-*spoot*) *v* transporter

transportation (træn-spoo-*téi*-cheunn) *n* transport *m*

trap (træp) *n* piège *m*

trash (træch) *n* déchets *mpl*; ~ **can** *Am* boîte à ordures

travel (*træ*-veul) *v* voyager; ~ **agency** bureau de voyages; ~ **agent** agent de voyages; ~ **insurance** assurance-voyages *f*; **travelling expenses** frais de voyage

traveller (*træ*-veu-leu) *n* voyageur *m*; **traveller's cheque** chèque de voyage

tray (tréï) *n* plateau *m*

treason (*trii*-zeunn) *n* trahison *f*

treasure (*trè*-jeu) *n* trésor *m*

treasurer (*trè*-jeu-reu) *n* trésorier *m*

treasury (*trè*-jeu-ri) *n* Trésor

treat (triit) *v* traiter

treatment (*triit*-meunnt) *n* traitement *m*

treaty (*trii*-ti) *n* traité *m*

tree (trii) *n* arbre *m*

tremble (*trèm*-beul) *v* frissonner, trembler; vibrer

tremendous (tri-*mèn*-deuss) *adj* énorme

trespass (*trèss*-peuss) *v* empiéter

trespasser (*trèss*-peu-seu) *n* intrus *m*

trial (traï^eu l) *n* procès *m*; essai *m*

triangle (*traï*-æng-gheul) *n* triangle *m*

triangular (traï-*æng*-ghyou-leu) *adj* triangulaire

tribe (traïb) *n* tribu *f*

tributary (*tri*-byou-teu-ri) *n* affluent *m*

tribute (*tri*-byoût) *n* hommage *m*

trick (trik) *n* truc *m*

trigger (*tri*-gheu) *n* gâchette *f*

trim (trimm) *v* tailler

trip (trip) *n* excursion *f*, voyage *m*

triumph (*traï*-eummf) *n* triomphe *m*; *v* triompher

triumphant (traï-*amm*-feunnt) *adj* triomphant

trolley-bus (*tro*-li-bass) *n* trolleybus *m*

troops (troûps) *pl* troupes *fpl*

tropical (*tro*-pi-keul) *adj* tropical

tropics (*tro*-piks) *pl* tropiques *mpl*

trouble (*tra*-beul) *n* ennui *m*, peine *f*, dérangement *m*; *v* déranger

troublesome (*tra*-beul-seumm) *adj* gênant

trousers (*traou*-zeuz) *pl* pantalon *m*

trout (traout) *n* (pl ~) truite *f*

truck (trak) *nAm* camion *m*

true (troû) *adj* vrai; réel; loyal, fidèle

trumpet (*tramm*-pit) *n* trompette *f*

trunk (tranngk) *n* malle *f*; tronc *m*;

nAm coffre *m*; **trunks** *pl* culotte de gymnastique

trunk-call (*tranngk*-kool) *n* appel interurbain

trust (trast) *v* *faire confiance; *n* confiance *f*

trustworthy (*trast*-ᵒᵘeû-ði) *adj* digne de confiance

truth (troûθ) *n* vérité *f*

truthful (*troûθ*-feul) *adj* véridique

try (traï) *v* essayer; tenter, s'efforcer; *n* tentative *f*; ~ **on** essayer

tube (tyoûb) *n* tuyau *m*, tube *m*

tuberculosis (tyoû-beû-kyou-*lôᵒᵘ*-siss) *n* tuberculose *f*

Tuesday (*tyoûz*-di) mardi *m*

tug (tagh) *v* remorquer; *n* remorqueur *m*; à-coup *m*

tuition (tyoû-*i*-cheunn) *n* enseignement *m*

tulip (*tyoû*-lip) *n* tulipe *f*

tumbler (*tamm*-bleu) *n* gobelet *m*

tumour (*tyoû*-meu) *n* tumeur *f*

tuna (*tyoû*-neu) *n* (pl ~, ~s) thon *m*

tune (tyoûn) *n* air *m*; ~ **in** accorder

tuneful (*tyoûn*-feul) *adj* harmonieux

tunic (*tyoû*-nik) *n* tunique *f*

Tunisia (tyoû-*ni*-zi-eu) Tunisie *f*

Tunisian (tyoû-*ni*-zi-eunn) *adj* tunisien; *n* Tunisien *m*

tunnel (*ta*-neul) *n* tunnel *m*

turbine (*teû*-baïn) *n* turbine *f*

turbojet (teû-bô ᵒᵘ-*djèt*) *n* turboréacteur *m*

Turk (teûk) *n* Turc *m*

Turkey (*teû*-ki) Turquie *f*

turkey (*teû*-ki) *n* dinde *f*

Turkish (*teû*-kich) *adj* turc; ~ **bath** bain turc

turn (teûnn) *v* tourner; retourner, virer; *n* revirement *m*, tour *m*; tournant *m*; ~ **back** retourner; ~ **down** rejeter; ~ **into** changer en; ~ **off** fermer; ~ **on** allumer; *ouvrir;

~ **over** retourner; ~ **round** retourner; se retourner

turning (*teû*-ninng) *n* virage *m*

turning-point (*teû*-ninng-poïnt) *n* tournant *m*

turnover (*teû*-nôᵒᵘ-veu) *n* chiffre d'affaires; ~ **tax** impôt sur le chiffre d'affaires

turnpike (*teûnn*-païk) *nAm* route à péage

turpentine (*teû*-peunn-taïn) *n* térébenthine *f*

turtle (*teû*-teul) *n* tortue *f*

tutor (*tyoû*-teu) *n* précepteur *m*; tuteur *m*

tuxedo (tak-*sii*-dôᵒᵘ) *nAm* (pl ~s, ~es) smoking *m*

tweed (tᵒᵘiid) *n* tweed *m*

tweezers (*tᵒᵘii*-zeuz) *pl* pince *f*

twelfth (tᵒᵘèlfθ) *num* douzième

twelve (tᵒᵘèlv) *num* douze

twentieth (*tᵒᵘèn*-ti-euθ) *num* vingtième

twenty (*tᵒᵘèn*-ti) *num* vingt

twice (tᵒᵘaïss) *adv* deux fois

twig (tᵒᵘigh) *n* brindille *f*

twilight (*tᵒᵘaï*-laït) *n* crépuscule *m*

twine (tᵒᵘaïn) *n* ficelle *f*

twins (tᵒᵘinnz) *pl* jumeaux *mpl*; **twin beds** lits jumeaux

twist (tᵒᵘist) *v* tordre; *n* torsion *f*

two (toû) *num* deux

two-piece (toû-piiss) *adj* deux-pièces *m*

type (taïp) *v* taper à la machine, dactylographier; *n* type *m*

typewriter (*taïp*-raï-teu) *n* machine à écrire

typewritten (*taïp*-ri-teunn) dactylographié

typhoid (*taï*-foïd) *n* typhoïde *f*

typical (*ti*-pi-keul) *adj* caractéristique, typique

typist (*taï*-pist) *n* dactylo *f*

tyrant (*tai^{eu}*-reunnt) *n* tyran *m*

tyre (taï^{eu}) *n* pneu *m*; ~ **pressure** pression des pneus

U

ugly (*a*-ghli) *adj* laid

ulcer (*al*-seu) *n* ulcère *m*

ultimate (*al*-ti-meut) *adj* ultime

ultraviolet (al-treu-*vai^{eu}*-leut) *adj* ultra-violet

umbrella (amm-*brè*-leu) *n* parapluie *m*

umpire (*amm*-paï^{eu}) *n* arbitre *m*

unable (a-*néï*-beul) *adj* incapable

unacceptable (a-neuk-*sèp*-teu-beul) *adj* inacceptable

unaccountable (a-neu-*kaoun*-teu-beul) *adj* inexplicable

unaccustomed (a-neu-*ka*-steummd) *adj* inhabitué

unanimous (yoû-*næ*-ni-meuss) *adj* unanime

unanswered (a-*nâân*-seud) *adj* sans réponse

unauthorized (a-*noo*-θeu-raïzd) *adj* illicite

unavoidable (a-neu-*voï*-deu-beul) *adj* inévitable

unaware (a-neu-^{ou}*è*^{eu}) *adj* inconscient

unbearable (ann-*bè*^{eu}-reu-beul) *adj* insupportable

unbreakable (ann-*bréï*-keu-beul) *adj* incassable

unbroken (ann-*brô*^{ou}-keunn) *adj* intact

unbutton (ann-*ba*-teunn) *v* déboutonner

uncertain (ann-*seû*-teunn) *adj* incertain

uncle (*anng*-keul) *n* oncle *m*

unclean (ann-*kliin*) *adj* malpropre

uncomfortable (ann-*kamm*-feu-teu-beul) *adj* inconfortable

uncommon (ann-*ko*-meunn) *adj* inhabituel, rare

unconditional (ann-keunn-*di*-cheu-neul) *adj* inconditionnel

unconscious (ann-*konn*-cheuss) *adj* inconscient

uncork (ann-*kook*) *v* déboucher

uncover (ann-*ka*-veu) *v* *découvrir

uncultivated (ann-*kal*-ti-véï-tid) *adj* inculte

under (ann-*deu*) *prep* en bas de, sous

undercurrent (*ann*-deu-ka-reunnt) *n* courant *m*

underestimate (ann-deu-*rè*-sti-méït) *v* sous-estimer

underground (*ann*-deu-ghraound) *adj* souterrain; *n* métro *m*

underline (ann-deu-*laïn*) *v* souligner

underneath (ann-deu-*niiθ*) *adv* dessous

underpants (*ann*-deu-pænts) *plAm* caleçon *m*

undershirt (*ann*-deu-cheût) *n* tricot de corps

undersigned (*ann*-deu-saïnd) *n* soussigné *m*

* **understand** (ann-deu-*stænd*) *v* *comprendre

understanding (ann-deu-*stæn*-dinng) *n* compréhension *f*

* **undertake** (ann-deu-*téïk*) *v* *entreprendre

undertaking (ann-deu-*téï*-kinng) *n* entreprise *f*

underwater (*ann*-deu-^{ou}oo-teu) *adj* sous-marin

underwear (*ann*-deu-^{ou}è^{eu}) *n* sous-vêtements *mpl*

undesirable (ann-di-*zaï^{eu}*-reu-beul) *adj* indésirable

* **undo** (ann-*doû*) *v* *défaire

undoubtedly (ann-*daou*-tid-li) *adv*

sans doute

undress (ann-*drèss*) *v* se déshabiller

undulating (*ann*-dyou-*léï*-tinng) *adj* ondulé

unearned (a-*neûnnd*) *adj* immérité

uneasy (a-*nii*-zi) *adj* mal à l'aise

uneducated (a-*nè*-dyou-*kéï*-tid) *adj* ignorant

unemployed (a-nimm-*ploïd*) *adj* en chômage

unemployment (a-nimm-*ploï*-meunnt) *n* chômage *m*

unequal (a-*nii*-k^oueul) *adj* inégal

uneven (a-*nii*-veunn) *adj* inégal, accidenté; irrégulier

unexpected (a-nik-*spèk*-tid) *adj* imprévu, inattendu

unfair (ann-*fè^eu*) *adj* inéquitable, injuste

unfaithful (ann-*féïθ*-feul) *adj* infidèle

unfamiliar (ann-feu-*mil*-yeu) *adj* inconnu

unfasten (ann-*fââ*-seunn) *v* détacher

unfavourable (ann-*féï*-veu-reu-beul) *adj* défavorable

unfit (ann-*fit*) *adj* impropre

unfold (ann-*fô^ou*ld) *v* déplier

unfortunate (ann-*foo*-tcheu-neut) *adj* malheureux

unfortunately (ann-*foo*-tcheu-neut-li) *adv* hélas, malheureusement

unfriendly (ann-*frènd*-li) *adj* désobligeant

unfurnished (ann-*feû*-nicht) *adj* non meublé

ungrateful (ann-*ghréït*-feul) *adj* ingrat

unhappy (ann-*hæ*-pi) *adj* malheureux

unhealthy (ann-*hèl*-θi) *adj* malsain

unhurt (ann-*heût*) *adj* indemne

uniform (*yoû*-ni-foom) *n* uniforme *m*; *adj* uniforme

unimportant (a-nimm-*poo*-teunnt) *adj* insignifiant

uninhabitable (a-ninn-*hæ*-bi-teu-beul)

adj inhabitable

uninhabited (a-ninn-*hæ*-bi-tid) *adj* inhabité

unintentional (a-ninn-*tèn*-cheu-neul) *adj* involontaire

union (*yoû*-nyeunn) *n* union *f*; ligue *f*, confédération *f*

unique (yoû-*niik*) *adj* unique

unit (*yoû*-nit) *n* unité *f*

unite (yoû-*naït*) *v* unir

United States (yoû-*naï*-tid stéïts) Etats-Unis

unity (*yoû*-neu-ti) *n* unité *f*

universal (yoû-ni-*veû*-seul) *adj* général, universel

universe (*yoû*-ni-veûss) *n* univers *m*

university (yoû-ni-*veû*-seu-ti) *n* université *f*

unjust (ann-*djast*) *adj* injuste

unkind (ann-*kaïnd*) *adj* désagréable, peu aimable

unknown (ann-*nô^ou*n) *adj* inconnu

unlawful (ann-*loo*-feul) *adj* illicite

unlearn (ann-*leûnn*) *v* *désapprendre

unless (eunn-*lèss*) *conj* à moins que

unlike (ann-*laïk*) *adj* différent

unlikely (ann-*laï*-kli) *adj* improbable

unlimited (ann-*li*-mi-tid) *adj* illimité

unload (ann-*lô^ou*d) *v* décharger

unlock (ann-*lok*) *v* *ouvrir

unlucky (ann-*la*-ki) *adj* infortuné

unnecessary (ann-*nè*-seu-seu-ri) *adj* superflu

unoccupied (a-*no*-kyou-païd) *adj* vacant

unofficial (a-neu-*fi*-cheul) *adj* officieux

unpack (ann-*pæk*) *v* déballer

unpleasant (ann-*plè*-zeunnt) *adj* ennuyeux, déplaisant; désagréable, antipathique

unpopular (ann-*po*-pyou-leu) *adj* peu aimé, impopulaire

unprotected (ann-preu-*tèk*-tid) *adj* non protégé

unqualified (ann-k^{ou}o-li-faïd) *adj* incompétent

unreal (ann-$ri^{eu}l$) *adj* irréel

unreasonable (ann-*rii*-zeu-neu-beul) *adj* déraisonnable

unreliable (ann-ri-*laï*-eu-beul) *adj* douteux

unrest (ann-*rèst*) *n* agitation *f*; inquiétude *f*

unsafe (ann-*séïf*) *adj* dangereux

unsatisfactory (ann-sæ-tiss-*fæk*-teu-ri) *adj* insatisfaisant

unscrew (ann-*skroû*) *v* dévisser

unselfish (ann-*sèl*-fich) *adj* désintéressé

unskilled (ann-*skild*) *adj* non qualifié

unsound (ann-*saound*) *adj* malsain

unstable (ann-*stéï*-beul) *adj* instable

unsteady (ann-*stè*-di) *adj* branlant, instable; vacillant

unsuccessful (ann-seuk-*sèss*-feul) *adj* infructueux

unsuitable (ann-*soû*-teu-beul) *adj* inadéquat

unsurpassed (ann-seu-*pââst*) *adj* sans pareil

untidy (ann-*taï*-di) *adj* désordonné

untie (ann-*taï*) *v* dénouer

until (eunn-*til*) *prep* jusqu'à

untrue (ann-*troû*) *adj* faux

untrustworthy (ann-*trast*-^{ou}eû-ði) *adj* sujet à caution

unusual (ann-*yoû*-jou-eul) *adj* inhabituel, insolite

unwell (ann-^{ou}èl) *adj* indisposé

unwilling (ann-^{ou}i-linng) *adj* à contrecœur

unwise (ann-^{ou}aïz) *adj* imprudent

unwrap (ann-*ræp*) *v* déballer

up (ap) *adv* vers le haut, en haut

upholster (ap-*hô^{ou}l*-steu) *v* capitonner, *recouvrir

upkeep (*ap*-kiip) *n* entretien *m*

uplands (*ap*-leunndz) *pl* hautes terres

upon (eu-*ponn*) *prep* sur

upper (*a*-peu) *adj* supérieur

upright (*ap*-raït) *adj* droit; *adv* debout

upset (ap-*sèt*) *v* déranger; *adj* bouleversé

upside-down (ap-saïd-*daoun*) *adv* sens dessus dessous

upstairs (ap-*stè^{eu}z*) *adv* en haut

upstream (ap-*striim*) *adv* en amont

upwards (*ap*-^{ou}eudz) *adv* vers le haut

urban (*eû*-beunn) *adj* urbain

urge (eûdj) *v* exhorter; *n* impulsion *f*

urgency (*eû*-djeunn-si) *n* urgence *f*

urgent (*eû*-djeunnt) *adj* urgent

urine (*you^{eu}*-rinn) *n* urine *f*

Uruguay (*you^{eu}*-reu-gh^{ou}aï) Uruguay *m*

Uruguayan (you^{eu}-reu-*gh^{ou}aï*-eunn) *adj* uruguayen; *n* Uruguayen *m*

us (ass) *pron* nous

usable (*yoû*-zeu-beul) *adj* utilisable

usage (*yoû*-zidj) *n* usage *m*

use[1] (yoûz) *v* employer; *be used to *être habitué à; ~ **up** user *f*

use[2] (yoûss) *n* emploi *m*; utilité *f*; *be of ~ *servir

useful (*yoûss*-feul) *adj* utile

useless (*yoûss*-leuss) *adj* inutile

user (*yoû*-zeu) *n* usager *m*

usher (*a*-cheu) *n* ouvreur *m*

usherette (a-cheu-*rèt*) *n* ouvreuse *f*

usual (*yoû*-jou-eul) *adj* ordinaire

usually (*yoû*-jou-eu-li) *adv* habituellement

utensil (you-*tèn*-seul) *n* outil *m*, ustensile *m*

utility (yoû-*ti*-leu-ti) *n* utilité *f*

utilize (*yoû*-ti-laïz) *v* utiliser

utmost (*at*-mô^{ou}st) *adj* extrême

utter (*a*-teu) *adj* complet, total; *v* *émettre

V

vacancy (*véï*-keunn-si) *n* vacance *f*

vacant (*véï*-keunnt) *adj* vacant

vacate (veu-*kéït*) *v* évacuer

vacation (veu-*kéï*-cheunn) *n* congé *m*

vaccinate (*væk*-si-néït) *v* vacciner

vaccination (væk-si-*néï*-cheunn) *n* vaccination *f*

vacuum (*væ*-kyou-eumm) *n* vide *m*; *vAm* passer l'aspirateur; ~ **cleaner** aspirateur *m*; ~ **flask** thermos *m*

vagrancy (*véï*-ghreunn-si) *n* vagabondage *m*

vague (véïgh) *adj* vague

vain (véïn) *adj* vaniteux; vain; **in** ~ inutilement, en vain

valet (væ-lit) *n* valet *m*

valid (*væ*-lid) *adj* valable

valley (*væ*-li) *n* vallée *f*

valuable (*væ*-lyou-beul) *adj* de valeur, précieux; **valuables** *pl* objets de valeur

value (*væ*-lyoû) *n* valeur *f*; *v* estimer

valve (vælv) *n* soupape *f*

van (væn) *n* fourgon *m*

vanilla (veu-*ni*-leu) *n* vanille *f*

vanish (*væ*-nich) *v* *disparaître

vapour (*véï*-peu) *n* vapeur *f*

variable (vè*eu*-ri-eu-beul) *adj* variable

variation (vè*eu*-ri-*éï*-cheunn) *n* variation *f*; changement *m*

varied (vè*eu*-rid) *adj* varié

variety (veu-*raï*-eu-ti) *n* variété *f*; ~ **show** spectacle de variétés; ~ **theatre** théâtre de variétés

various (vè*eu*-ri-euss) *adj* divers

varnish (*vââ*-nich) *n* laque *f*, vernis *m*; *v* vernir

vary (vè*eu*-ri) *v* varier; changer; différer

vase (vââz) *n* vase *m*

vaseline (*væ*-seu-liin) *n* vaseline *f*

vast (vââst) *adj* immense, vaste

vault (voolt) *n* voûte *f*; chambre forte

veal (viil) *n* veau *m*

vegetable (*vè*-djeu-teu-beul) *n* légume *m*; ~ **merchant** marchand de légumes

vegetarian (vè-dji-*tè*eu-ri-eunn) *n* végétarien *m*

vegetation (vè-dji-*téï*-cheunn) *n* végétation *f*

vehicle (*vii*-eu-keul) *n* véhicule *m*

veil (véïl) *n* voile *m*

vein (véïn) *n* veine *f*; **varicose** ~ varice *f*

velvet (*vèl*-vit) *n* velours *m*

velveteen (vèl-vi-*tiin*) *n* velours de coton

venerable (*vè*-neu-reu-beul) *adj* vénérable

venereal disease (vi-*ni*eu-ri-eul di-*ziiz*) maladie vénérienne

Venezuela (vè-ni-z*ou*éï-leu) Venezuela *m*

Venezuelan (vè-ni-z*ou*éï-leunn) *adj* vénézuélien; *n* Vénézuélien *m*

ventilate (*vèn*-ti-léït) *v* ventiler; aérer

ventilation (vèn-ti-*léï*-cheunn) *n* ventilation *f*; aération *f*

ventilator (*vèn*-ti-léï-teu) *n* ventilateur *m*

venture (*vèn*-tcheu) *v* risquer

veranda (veu-*ræn*-deu) *n* véranda *f*

verb (veûb) *n* verbe *m*

verbal (*veû*-beul) *adj* verbal

verdict (*veû*-dikt) *n* sentence *f*, verdict *m*

verge (veûdj) *n* bord *m*

verify (*vè*-ri-faï) *v* vérifier

verse (veûss) *n* vers *m*

version (*veû*-cheunn) *n* version *f*

versus (*veû*-seuss) *prep* contre

vertical (*veû*-ti-keul) *adj* vertical

vertigo (*veû*-ti-ghô ou) *n* vertige *m*

very (*vè*-ri) *adv* très; *adj* vrai, véritable, précis; extrême

vessel (*vè*-seul) *n* vaisseau *m*; récipient *m*

vest (vèst) *n* chemise *f*; *nAm* gilet *m*

veterinary surgeon (*vè*-tri-neu-ri seû-djeunn) vétérinaire *m*

via (vaï*eu*) *prep* via

viaduct (*vaï*eu-dakt) *n* viaduc *m*

vibrate (vaï-*bréït*) *v* vibrer

vibration (vaï-*bréï*-cheunn) *n* vibration *f*

vicar (*vi*-keu) *n* vicaire *m*

vicarage (*vi*-keu-ridj) *n* presbytère *m*

vice-president (vaïss-*prè*-zi-deunnt) *n* vice-président *m*

vicinity (vi-*si*-neu-ti) *n* alentours *mpl*, voisinage *m*

vicious (*vi*-cheuss) *adj* vicieux

victim (*vik*-timm) *n* victime *f*; dupe *f*

victory (*vik*-teu-ri) *n* victoire *f*

view (vyoû) *n* vue *f*; point de vue, opinion *f*; *v* contempler

view-finder (*vyoû*-faïn-deu) *n* viseur *m*

vigilant (*vi*-dji-leunnt) *adj* vigilant

villa (*vi*-leu) *n* villa *f*

village (*vi*-lidj) *n* village *m*

villain (*vi*-leunn) *n* scélérat *m*

vine (vaïn) *n* vigne *f*

vinegar (*vi*-ni-gheu) *n* vinaigre *m*

vineyard (vinn-yeud) *n* vignoble *m*

vintage (vinn-tidj) *n* vendange *f*

violation (vaïeu-*léï*-cheunn) *n* violation *f*

violence (*vaï*eu-leunns) *n* violence *f*

violent (*vaï*eu-leunnt) *adj* violent; intense

violet (*vaï*eu-leut) *n* violette *f*; *adj* violet

violin (vaïeu-*linn*) *n* violon *m*

virgin (*veû*-djinn) *n* vierge *f*

virtue (*veû*-tchoû) *n* vertu *f*

visa (*vii*-zeu) *n* visa *m*

visibility (vi-zeu-*bi*-leu-ti) *n* visibilité *f*

visible (*vi*-zeu-beul) *adj* visible

vision (*vi*-jeunn) *n* vision *f*

visit (*vi*-zit) *v* visiter; *n* visite *f*; **visiting hours** heures de visite

visiting-card (*vi*-zi-tinng-kââd) *n* carte de visite

visitor (*vi*-zi-teu) *n* visiteur *m*

vital (*vaï*-teul) *adj* vital

vitamin (*vi*-teu-minn) *n* vitamine *f*

vivid (*vi*-vid) *adj* vif

vocabulary (veu-*kæ*-byou-leu-ri) *n* vocabulaire *m*

vocal (*vô*ou-keul) *adj* vocal

vocalist (*vô*ou-keu-list) *n* chanteur *m*

voice (voïss) *n* voix *f*

void (voïd) *adj* nul

volcano (vol-*kéï*-nôou) *n* (pl ~es, ~s) volcan *m*

volt (vôoult) *n* volt *m*

voltage (*vô*ou/-tidj) *n* voltage *m*

volume (*vo*-lyoum) *n* volume *m*; tome *m*

voluntary (*vo*-leunn-teu-ri) *adj* volontaire

volunteer (vo-leunn-*ti*eu) *n* volontaire *m*

vomit (*vo*-mit) *v* vomir

vote (vôoult) *v* voter; *n* vote *m*

voucher (*vaou*-tcheu) *n* reçu *m*, bon *m*

vow (vaou) *n* vœu *m*, serment *m*; *v* jurer

vowel (*vaou*eul) *n* voyelle *f*

voyage (*voï*-idj) *n* voyage *m*

vulgar (*val*-gheu) *adj* vulgaire; ordinaire, trivial

vulnerable (*val*-neu-reu-beul) *adj* vulnérable

vulture (*val*-tcheu) *n* vautour *m*

W

wade (ᵒᵘéïd) *v* patauger

wafer (ᵒᵘéï-feu) *n* gaufrette *f*

waffle (ᵒᵘo-feul) *n* gaufre *f*

wages (ᵒᵘéï-djiz) *pl* gages *mpl*

waggon (ᵒᵘæ-gheunn) *n* wagon *m*

waist (ᵒᵘéïst) *n* taille *f*

waistcoat (ᵒᵘéïss-kôᵒᵘt) *n* gilet *m*

wait (ᵒᵘéït) *v* attendre; ~ **on** *servir

waiter (ᵒᵘéï-teu) *n* garçon *m*

waiting (ᵒᵘéï-tinng) *n* attente *f*

waiting-list (ᵒᵘéï-tinng-list) *n* liste d'attente

waiting-room (ᵒᵘéï-tinng-roûm) *n* salle d'attente

waitress (ᵒᵘéï-triss) *n* serveuse *f*

***wake** (ᵒᵘéïk) *v* réveiller; ~ **up** s'éveiller, se réveiller

walk (ᵒᵘook) *v* marcher; se promener; *n* promenade *f*; démarche *f*; walking à pied

walker (ᵒᵘoo-keu) *n* promeneur *m*

walking-stick (ᵒᵘoo-kinng-stik) *n* canne *f*

wall (ᵒᵘool) *n* mur *m*; cloison *f*

wallet (ᵒᵘo-lit) *n* portefeuille *m*

wallpaper (ᵒᵘool-péï-peu) *n* papier peint

walnut (ᵒᵘool-nat) *n* noix *f*

waltz (ᵒᵘools) *n* valse *f*

wander (ᵒᵘonn-deu) *v* errer

want (ᵒᵘonnt) *v* *vouloir; désirer; *n* besoin *m*; carence *f*, manque *m*

war (ᵒᵘoo) *n* guerre *f*

warden (ᵒᵘoo-deunn) *n* surveillant *m*, gardien *m*

wardrobe (ᵒᵘoo-drôᵒᵘb) *n* garde-robe *f*

warehouse (ᵒᵘèᵉᵘ-haouss) *n* magasin *m*, dépôt *m*

wares (ᵒᵘèᵉᵘz) *pl* marchandise *f*

warm (ᵒᵘoom) *adj* chaud; *v* chauffer

warmth (ᵒᵘoomθ) *n* chaleur *f*

warn (ᵒᵘoon) *v* *prévenir, avertir

warning (ᵒᵘoo-ninng) *n* avertissement *m*

wary (ᵒᵘèᵉᵘ-ri) *adj* prudent

was (ᵒᵘoz) *v* (p be)

wash (ᵒᵘoch) *v* laver; ~ **and wear** sans repassage; ~ **up** *faire la vaisselle

washable (ᵒᵘo-cheu-beul) *adj* lavable

wash-basin (ᵒᵘoch-béï-seunn) *n* lavabo *m*

washing (ᵒᵘo-chinng) *n* lavage *m*; lessive *f*

washing-machine (ᵒᵘo-chinng-meuchiin) *n* machine à laver

washing-powder (ᵒᵘo-chinng-paoudeu) *n* savon en poudre

washroom (ᵒᵘoch-roûm) *nAm* toilettes *fpl*

wash-stand (ᵒᵘoch-stænd) *n* lavabo *m*

wasp (ᵒᵘosp) *n* guêpe *f*

waste (ᵒᵘéïst) *v* gaspiller; *n* gaspillage *m*; *adj* en friche

wasteful (ᵒᵘéïst-feul) *adj* gaspilleur

wastepaper-basket (ᵒᵘéïst-péï-peubââ-skit) *n* corbeille à papier

watch (ᵒᵘotch) *v* regarder, observer; surveiller; *n* montre *f*; ~ **for** guetter; ~ **out** *prendre garde

watch-maker (ᵒᵘotch-méï-keu) *n* horloger *m*

watch-strap (ᵒᵘotch-stræp) *n* bracelet pour montre

water (ᵒᵘoo-teu) *n* eau *f*; **iced** ~ eau glacée; **running** ~ eau courante; ~ **pump** pompe à eau; ~ **ski** ski nautique

water-colour (ᵒᵘoo-teu-ka-leu) *n* couleur à l'eau; aquarelle *f*

watercress (ᵒᵘoo-teu-krèss) *n* cresson *m*

waterfall (ᵒᵘoo-teu-fool) *n* cascade *f*

watermelon (^{ou}oo-teu-mè-leunn) *n* pastèque *f*

waterproof (^{ou}oo-teu-proûf) *adj* imperméable

water-softener (^{ou}oo-teu-sof-neu) *n* adoucisseur d'eau

waterway (^{ou}oo-teu-^{ou}éï) *n* voie d'eau

watt (^{ou}ot) *n* watt *m*

wave (^{ou}éïv) *n* ondulation *f*, vague *f*; *v* *faire signe

wave-length (^{ou}éïv-lèngθ) *n* longueur d'onde

wavy (^{ou}éï-vi) *adj* ondulé

wax (^{ou}æks) *n* cire *f*

waxworks (^{ou}æks-^{ou}eûks) *pl* musée des figures de cire

way (^{ou}éï) *n* manière *f*, façon *f*; voie *f*; côté *m*, direction *f*; distance *f*; **any ~** n'importe comment; **by the ~** à propos; **one-way traffic** sens unique; **out of the ~** écarté; **the other ~ round** en sens inverse; **~ back** chemin du retour; **~ in** entrée *f*; **~ out** sortie *f*

wayside (^{ou}éï-saïd) *n* bord de la route

we (^{ou}ii) *pron* nous

weak (^{ou}iik) *adj* faible; léger

weakness (^{ou}iik-neuss) *n* faiblesse *f*

wealth (^{ou}èlθ) *n* richesse *f*

wealthy (^{ou}èl-θi) *adj* riche

weapon (^{ou}è-peunn) *n* arme *f*

***wear** (^{ou}èeu) *v* porter; **~ out** user

weary (^{ou}ieu-ri) *adj* las, fatigué

weather (^{ou}è-ðeu) *n* temps *m*; **~ forecast** bulletin météorologique

***weave** (^{ou}iiv) *v* tisser

weaver (^{ou}ii-veu) *n* tisserand *m*

wedding (^{ou}è-dinng) *n* mariage *m*

wedding-ring (^{ou}è-dinng-rinng) *n* alliance *f*

wedge (^{ou}èdj) *n* cale *f*

Wednesday (^{ou}ènz-di) mercredi *m*

weed (^{ou}iid) *n* mauvaise herbe

week (^{ou}iik) *n* semaine *f*

weekday (^{ou}iik-déï) *n* jour de la semaine

weekly (^{ou}ii-kli) *adj* hebdomadaire

***weep** (^{ou}iip) *v* pleurer

weigh (^{ou}éï) *v* peser

weighing-machine (^{ou}éï-inng-meu-chiin) *n* bascule *f*

weight (^{ou}éït) *n* poids *m*

welcome (^{ou}èl-keumm) *adj* bienvenu; *n* accueil *m*; *v* *accueillir

weld (^{ou}èld) *v* souder

welfare (^{ou}èl-fèeu) *n* bien-être *m*

well[1] (^{ou}èl) *adv* bien; *adj* sain; **as ~** également, aussi bien; **as ~ as** aussi bien que; **well!** bien!

well[2] (^{ou}èl) *n* source *f*, puits *m*

well-founded (^{ou}èl-*faoun*-did) *adj* bien fondé

well-known (^{ou}èl-nô^{ou}n) *adj* connu

well-to-do (^{ou}èl-teu-*doû*) *adj* aisé

went (^{ou}ènt) *v* (p go)

were (^{ou}eû) *v* (p be)

west (^{ou}èst) *n* occident *m*, ouest *m*

westerly (^{ou}è-steu-li) *adj* occidental

western (^{ou}è-steunn) *adj* occidental

wet (^{ou}èt) *adj* mouillé; humide

whale (^{ou}éïl) *n* baleine *f*

wharf (^{ou}oof) *n* (pl ~s, wharves) quai *m*

what (^{ou}ot) *pron* quoi; ce que; **~ for** pourquoi

whatever (^{ou}o-*tè*-veu) *pron* tout ce que

wheat (^{ou}iit) *n* blé *m*

wheel (^{ou}iil) *n* roue *f*

wheelbarrow (^{ou}iil-bæ-rô^{ou}) *n* brouette *f*

wheelchair (^{ou}iil-tchè^{eu}) *n* fauteuil roulant

when (^{ou}èn) *adv* quand; *conj* quand, lorsque

whenever (^{ou}è-*nè*-veu) *conj* n'importe quand

where (^{ou}è^{eu}) *adv* où; *conj* où

wherever (ᵒᵘè-ᵉᵘ-_rè_-veu) _conj_ partout où

whether (ᵒᵘè-ðeu) _conj_ si; **whether ... or** si ... ou

which (ᵒᵘitch) _pron_ quel; qui

whichever (ᵒᵘi-_tchè_-veu) _adj_ n'importe quel

while (ᵒᵘaïl) _conj_ tandis que; _n_ moment _m_

whilst (ᵒᵘaïlst) _conj_ tandis que

whim (ᵒᵘimm) _n_ lubie _f_, caprice _m_

whip (ᵒᵘip) _n_ fouet _m_; _v_ fouetter

whiskers (ᵒᵘi-skeuz) _pl_ favoris

whisper (ᵒᵘi-speu) _v_ chuchoter; _n_ chuchotement _m_

whistle (ᵒᵘi-seul) _v_ siffler; _n_ sifflet _m_

white (ᵒᵘaït) _adj_ blanc

whitebait (ᵒᵘaït-béït) _n_ blanchaille _f_

whiting (ᵒᵘaï-tinng) _n_ (pl ~) merlan _m_

Whitsun (ᵒᵘit-seunn) Pentecôte _f_

who (hoû) _pron_ qui

whoever (hoû-è-veu) _pron_ quiconque

whole (hôᵒᵘl) _adj_ complet, entier; intact; _n_ ensemble _m_

wholesale (hôᵒᵘl-séïl) _n_ vente en gros; ~ **dealer** grossiste _m_

wholesome (hôᵒᵘl-seumm) _adj_ sain

wholly (hôᵒᵘl-li) _adv_ entièrement

whom (hoûm) _pron_ à qui

whore (hoo) _n_ putain _f_

whose (hoûz) _pron_ dont; de qui

why (ᵒᵘaï) _adv_ pourquoi

wicked (ᵒᵘi-kid) _adj_ mauvais

wide (ᵒᵘaïd) _adj_ vaste, large

widen (ᵒᵘaï-deunn) _v_ élargir

widow (ᵒᵘi-dôᵒᵘ) _n_ veuve _f_

widower (ᵒᵘi-dôᵒᵘ-eu) _n_ veuf _m_

width (ᵒᵘidθ) _n_ largeur _f_

wife (ᵒᵘaïf) _n_ (pl wives) épouse _f_, femme _f_

wig (ᵒᵘigh) _n_ perruque _f_

wild (ᵒᵘaïld) _adj_ sauvage; féroce

will (ᵒᵘil) _n_ volonté _f_; testament _m_

*will (ᵒᵘil) _v_ *vouloir

willing (ᵒᵘi-linng) _adj_ disposé

willingly (ᵒᵘi-linng-li) _adv_ volontiers

will-power (ᵒᵘil-paouᵉᵘ) _n_ volonté _f_

*win (ᵒᵘinn) _v_ gagner

wind (ᵒᵘinnd) _n_ vent _m_

*wind (ᵒᵘaïnd) _v_ serpenter; remonter, enrouler

winding (ᵒᵘaïn-dinng) _adj_ serpentant

windmill (ᵒᵘinnd-mil) _n_ moulin à vent

window (ᵒᵘinn-dôᵒᵘ) _n_ fenêtre _f_

window-sill (ᵒᵘinn-dôᵒᵘ-sil) _n_ rebord de fenêtre

windscreen (ᵒᵘinnd-skriin) _n_ pare-brise _m_; ~ **wiper** essuie-glace _m_

windshield (ᵒᵘinnd-chiild) _nAm_ pare-brise _m_; ~ **wiper** Am essuie-glace _m_

windy (ᵒᵘinn-di) _adj_ venteux

wine (ᵒᵘaïn) _n_ vin _m_

wine-cellar (ᵒᵘaïn-sè-leu) _n_ cave _f_

wine-list (ᵒᵘaïn-list) _n_ carte des vins

wine-merchant (ᵒᵘaïn-meû-tcheunnt) _n_ négociant en vins

wine-waiter (ᵒᵘaïn-ᵒᵘéï-teu) _n_ sommelier _m_

wing (ᵒᵘinng) _n_ aile _f_

winkle (ᵒᵘinng-keul) _n_ bigorneau _m_

winner (ᵒᵘi-neu) _n_ vainqueur _m_

winning (ᵒᵘi-ninng) _adj_ gagnant; **winnings** _pl_ gains

winter (ᵒᵘinn-teu) _n_ hiver _m_; ~ **sports** sports d'hiver

wipe (ᵒᵘaïp) _v_ ôter, essuyer

wire (ᵒᵘaïᵉᵘ) _n_ fil _m_; fil de fer

wireless (ᵒᵘaïᵉᵘ-leuss) _n_ radio _f_

wisdom (ᵒᵘiz-deumm) _n_ sagesse _f_

wise (ᵒᵘaïz) _adj_ sage

wish (ᵒᵘich) _v_ désirer, souhaiter; _n_ désir _m_, souhait _m_

witch (ᵒᵘitch) _n_ sorcière _f_

with (ᵒᵘið) _prep_ avec; chez; de

*withdraw (ᵒᵘið-_droo_) _v_ retirer

within (ᵒᵘi-ðinn) _prep_ dans; _adv_ à

l'intérieur

without (⁰ᵘi-ðaout) *prep* sans

witness (⁰ᵘit-neuss) *n* témoin *m*

wits (⁰ᵘits) *pl* raison *f*

witty (⁰ᵘi-ti) *adj* spirituel

wolf (⁰ᵘoulf) *n* (pl wolves) loup *m*

woman (⁰ᵘou-meunn) *n* (pl women) femme *f*

womb (⁰ᵘoûm) *n* utérus *m*

won (⁰ᵘann) *v* (p, pp win)

wonder (⁰ᵘann-deu) *n* miracle *m*; étonnement *m*; *v* se demander

wonderful (⁰ᵘann-deu-feul) *adj* splendide, merveilleux; délicieux

wood (⁰ᵘoud) *n* bois *m*

wood-carving (⁰ᵘoud-kââ-vinng) *n* sculpture sur bois

wooded (⁰ᵘou-did) *adj* boisé

wooden (⁰ᵘou-deunn) *adj* en bois; ~ **shoe** sabot *m*

woodland (⁰ᵘoud-leunnd) *n* pays boisé

wool (⁰ᵘoul) *n* laine *f*; **darning** ~ laine à repriser

woollen (⁰ᵘou-leunn) *adj* en laine

word (⁰ᵘeûd) *n* mot *m*

wore (⁰ᵘoo) *v* (p wear)

work (⁰ᵘeûk) *n* travail *m*; activité *f*; *v* travailler; fonctionner; **working day** jour ouvrable; ~ **of art** œuvre d'art; ~ **permit** permis de travail

worker (⁰ᵘeû-keu) *n* ouvrier *m*

working (⁰ᵘeû-kinng) *n* fonctionnement *m*

workman (⁰ᵘeûk-meunn) *n* (pl -men) ouvrier *m*

works (⁰ᵘeûks) *pl* usine *f*

workshop (⁰ᵘeûk-chop) *n* atelier *m*

world (⁰ᵘeûld) *n* monde *m*; ~ **war** guerre mondiale

world-famous (⁰ᵘeûld-féï-meuss) *adj* de renommée mondiale

world-wide (⁰ᵘeûld-⁰ᵘaïd) *adj* mondial

worm (⁰ᵘeûmm) *n* ver *m*

worn (⁰ᵘoon) *adj* (pp wear) usé

worn-out (⁰ᵘoon-*aout*) *adj* usé

worried (⁰ᵘa-rid) *adj* soucieux

worry (⁰ᵘa-ri) *v* s'inquiéter; *n* souci *m*, inquiétude *f*

worse (⁰ᵘeûss) *adj* pire; *adv* pire

worship (⁰ᵘeû-chip) *v* adorer; *n* culte *m*

worst (⁰ᵘeûst) *adj* le plus mauvais; *adv* le pire

worsted (⁰ᵘou-stid) *n* laine peignée

worth (⁰ᵘeûθ) *n* valeur *f*; ***be** ~ *valoir; ***be worth-while** *valoir la peine

worthless (⁰ᵘeûθ-leuss) *adj* sans valeur

worthy of (⁰ᵘeû-ði euv) digne de

would (⁰ᵘoud) *v* (p will) *avoir l'habitude de

wound¹ (⁰ᵘoûnd) *n* blessure *f*; *v* offenser, blesser

wound² (⁰ᵘaound) *v* (p, pp wind)

wrap (ræp) *v* envelopper

wreck (rèk) *n* épave *f*; *v* *détruire

wrench (rèntch) *n* clé *f*; secousse *f*; *v* tordre

wrinkle (rinng-keul) *n* ride *f*

wrist (rist) *n* poignet *m*

wrist-watch (rist-⁰ᵘotch) *n* bracelet-montre *m*

***write** (raït) *v* *écrire; **in writing** par écrit; ~ **down** noter

writer (raï-teu) *n* écrivain *m*

writing-pad (raï-tinng-pæd) *n* bloc-notes *m*

writing-paper (raï-tinng-péï-peu) *n* papier à lettres

written (ri-teunn) *adj* (pp write) par écrit

wrong (ronng) *adj* impropre, incorrect; *n* tort *m*; *v* *faire du tort; ***be** ~ *avoir tort

wrote (rô⁰ᵘt) *v* (p write)

X

Xmas (*kriss*-meuss) Noël
X-ray (*èks*-réï) *n* radiographie *f*; *v* radiographier

Y

yacht (yot) *n* yacht *m*
yacht-club (*yot*-klab) *n* yacht-club *m*
yachting (*yo*-tinng) *n* yachting *m*
yard (yââd) *n* cour *f*
yarn (yâân) *n* fil *m*
yawn (yoon) *v* bâiller
year (yi^eu) *n* année *f*
yearly (*yi^eu*-li) *adj* annuel
yeast (yiist) *n* levure *f*
yell (yèl) *v* hurler; *n* cri *m*
yellow (*yè*-lô^ou) *adj* jaune
yes (yèss) oui
yesterday (*yè*-steu-di) *adv* hier
yet (yèt) *adv* encore; *conj* pourtant, cependant
yield (yiild) *v* rendre; céder
yoke (yô^ouk) *n* joug *m*
yolk (yô^ouk) *n* jaune d'œuf
you (yoû) *pron* tu; te; vous

young (yanng) *adj* jeune
your (yoo) *adj* votre; ton; vos
yourself (yoo-*sèlf*) *pron* te; toi-même; vous-même
yourselves (yoo-*sèlvz*) *pron* vous; vous-mêmes
youth (yoûθ) *n* jeunesse *f*; ~ **hostel** auberge de jeunesse
Yugoslav (yoû-gheu-*slââv*) *n* Yougoslave *m*
Yugoslavia (yoû-gheu-*slââ*-vi-eu) Yougoslavie *f*

Z

zeal (ziil) *n* zèle *m*
zealous (*zè*-leuss) *adj* zélé
zebra (*zii*-breu) *n* zèbre *m*
zenith (*zè*-niθ) *n* zénith *m*; apogée *m*
zero (*zi^eu*-rô^ou) *n* (pl ~s) zéro *m*
zest (zèst) *n* entrain *m*
zinc (zinngk) *n* zinc *m*
zip (zip) *n* fermeture éclair; ~ **code** *Am* code postal
zipper (*zi*-peu) *n* fermeture éclair
zodiac (*zô^ou*-di-æk) *n* zodiaque *m*
zone (zô^ou n) *n* zone *f*; région *f*
zoo (zoû) *n* (pl ~s) zoo *m*
zoology (zô^ou-o-leu-dji) *n* zoologie *f*

Lexique gastronomique

Mets

almond amande
anchovy anchois
angel food cake gâteau aux blancs d'œufs
angels on horseback huîtres enrobées de lard, grillées et servies sur toast
appetizer amuse-gueule
apple pomme
  ∼ **dumpling** sorte de chausson aux pommes
  ∼ **sauce** purée de pommes
Arbroath smoky églefin fumé
artichoke artichaut
asparagus asperge
  ∼ **tip** pointe d'asperge
assorted varié
avocado (pear) avocat
bacon lard à griller
  ∼ **and eggs** œufs au lard
bagel petit pain en forme de couronne
baked au four
  ∼ **Alaska** omelette norvégienne
  ∼ **beans** haricots blancs dans une sauce tomate
  ∼ **potato** pomme de terre en robe des champs cuite au four
Bakewell tart gâteau aux amandes et à la confiture

baloney sorte de mortadelle
banana banane
  ∼ **split** banane coupée en tranches, servie avec de la glace et des noix, arrosée de sirop ou de crème au chocolat
barbecue 1) hachis de bœuf dans une sauce relevée aux tomates, servi dans un petit pain 2) repas en plein air
  ∼ **sauce** sauce aux tomates très relevée
barbecued grillé au charbon de bois
basil basilic
bass bar
bean haricot, fève
beef bœuf
  ∼ **olive** paupiette de bœuf
beefburger bifteck haché, grillé et servi dans un petit pain
beet, beetroot betterave rouge
bilberry myrtille
bill addition
  ∼ **of fare** carte des mets, menu
biscuit 1) gâteau sec, biscuit (GB) 2) petit pain (US)
black pudding boudin noir
blackberry mûre sauvage
blackcurrant cassis

bloater hareng saur

blood sausage boudin noir

blueberry myrtille

boiled bouilli

Bologna (sausage) sorte de mortadelle

bone os

boned désossé

Boston baked beans haricots blancs au lard et à la mélasse dans une sauce tomate

Boston cream pie tourte à la crème en couches superposées, glacée au chocolat

brains cervelle

braised braisé

bramble pudding pudding aux mûres (souvent servi avec des pommes)

braunschweiger saucisson au foie fumé

bread pain

breaded pané

breakfast petit déjeuner

bream brème (poisson)

breast poitrine, blanc de volaille

brisket poitrine de bœuf

broad bean grosse fève

broth bouillon

brown Betty sorte de charlotte aux pommes et aux épices recouverte de chapelure

brunch repas qui tient lieu de petit déjeuner et de déjeuner

brussels sprout chou de Bruxelles

bubble and squeak sorte de galette de pommes de terre et choux, parfois accompagnés de morceaux de bœuf

bun 1) petit pain au lait avec des fruits secs 2) sorte de petit pain (US)

butter beurre

buttered beurré

cabbage chou

Caesar salad salade verte, ail, anchois, croûtons et fromage râpé

cake gâteau, tourte

cakes biscuits, pâtisseries

calf veau

Canadian bacon carré de porc fumé, coupé en fines tranches

caper câpre

capercaillie, capercailzie coq de bruyère

carp carpe

carrot carotte

cashew noix de cajou

casserole en cocotte

catfish poisson-chat

catsup ketchup

cauliflower chou-fleur

celery céleri

cereal céréale, cornflakes

   hot ~ porridge

check addition

Cheddar (cheese) fromage à pâte dure au goût légèrement acide

cheese fromage

   ~ **board** plateau de fromages

   ~ **cake** gâteau au fromage double crème

cheeseburger bifteck haché, grillé avec une tranche de fromage, servi dans un petit pain

chef's salad salade de jambon, poulet, œufs durs, tomates, laitue et fromage

cherry cerise

chestnut marron

chicken poulet

chicory 1) endive (GB) 2) (e)scarole, chicorée (US)

chili con carne hachis de bœuf aux haricots rouges et aux piments rouges

chili pepper piment rouge

chips 1) pommes frites (GB) 2)

pommes chips (US)

chitt(er)lings tripes de porc

chive ciboulette

chocolate chocolat

choice premier choix

chop côtelette
~ **suey** émincé de porc ou de poulet, de riz et de légumes

chopped émincé, haché

chowder bisque

Christmas pudding cake anglais aux fruits secs, parfois flambé; très nourrissant et servi à Noël

chutney condiment indien épicé à saveur aigre-douce

cinnamon cannelle

clam palourde

club sandwich double sandwich au *bacon*, poulet, tomate, salade et mayonnaise

cobbler compote de fruits recouverte de pâte

cock-a-leekie soup crème de volaille et de poireaux

coconut noix de coco

cod cabillaud

Colchester oyster huître anglaise très renommée

cold cuts/meat assiette anglaise, viandes froides

coleslaw salade de chou

cooked cuit

cookie biscuit

corn 1) blé (GB) 2) maïs (US)
~ **on the cob** épi de maïs

cornflakes flocons de maïs

cottage cheese fromage frais

cottage pie hachis de viande aux oignons recouvert de purée de pommes de terre

course plat

cover charge prix du couvert

crab crabe

cracker biscuit salé, craquelin

cranberry canneberge
~ **sauce** confiture de canneberges

crawfish, crayfish 1) écrevisse 2) langouste (GB) 3) langoustine (US)

cream 1) crème 2) velouté (potage) 3) crème (dessert)
~ **cheese** fromage double crème
~ **puff** chou à la crème

creamed potatoes pommes de terre coupées en dés dans une sauce béchamel

creole mets très relevé, préparé avec des tomates, des poivrons et des oignons, servi avec du riz blanc

cress cresson

crisps pommes chips

crumpet sorte de petit pain rond, grillé et beurré

cucumber concombre

Cumberland ham jambon fumé très réputé

Cumberland sauce sauce aigredouce; vin, jus d'orange, zeste de citron, épices et gelée de groseilles

cupcake madeleine

cured salé et parfois fumé

currant 1) raisin de Corinthe 2) groseille

curried au curry

custard crème anglaise, flan

cutlet sorte d'escalope, fine tranche de viande, côtelette

dab limande

Danish pastry pâtisserie ou gâteau riche en levure

date datte

Derby cheese fromage à pâte molle et au goût piquant, de couleur jaune pâle

devilled à la diable; assaisonnement très relevé

devil's food cake tourte au chocolat

devils on horseback pruneaux cuits dans du vin rouge et farcis d'amandes et d'anchois, enrobés de lard et grillés

Devonshire cream double crème, très épaisse

diced coupé en dés

diet food aliment diététique

dill aneth

dinner dîner, repas du soir

dish plat, assiette, mets

donut, doughnut boule de Berlin, beignet en forme d'anneau

double cream double crème, crème entière

Dover sole sole de Douvres, très réputée

dressing 1) sauce à salade 2) farce pour la volaille (US)

Dublin Bay prawn langoustine

duck canard

duckling caneton

dumpling boulette de pâte

Dutch apple pie tarte aux pommes saupoudrée de cassonade ou nappée de mélasse

eel anguille

egg œuf
   boiled ~ à la coque
   fried ~ au plat
   hard-boiled ~ dur
   poached ~ poché
   scrambled ~ brouillé
   soft-boiled ~ mollet

eggplant aubergine

endive 1) (e)scarole, chicorée (GB) 2) endive (US)

entrée 1) entrée (GB) 2) plat principal (US)

fennel fenouil

fig figue

fillet filet de viande ou de poisson

finnan haddock églefin fumé

fish poisson
   ~ **and chips** filets de poisson frits et pommes frites
   ~ **cake** galette de poisson et de pommes de terre

flan tarte

flapjack matefaim, crêpe épaisse

flounder flet, plie

forcemeat farce, hachis

fowl volaille

frankfurter saucisse de Francfort

French bean haricot vert

French bread baguette

French dressing 1) vinaigrette (GB) 2) sauce à salade crémeuse assaisonnée de ketchup (US)

french fries pommes frites

French toast croûte dorée

fresh frais

fried frit, grillé

fritter beignet

frogs' legs cuisses de grenouilles

frosting glaçage

fry friture

game gibier

gammon jambon fumé

garfish aiguille de mer

garlic ail

garnish garniture

gherkin cornichon

giblets abats, abattis

ginger gingembre

goose oie
   ~**berry** groseille à maquereau

grape raisin
   ~**fruit** pamplemousse

grated râpé

gravy jus de viande épaissi

grayling omble

green bean haricot vert

green pepper poivron vert
green salad laitue, salade verte
greens garniture de légumes verts
grilled grillé
grilse saumoneau
grouse petit coq de bruyère
gumbo 1) gombo (légume d'origine africaine) 2) plat créole à base d'*okra*, de viande, de poisson ou de fruits de mer et de légumes
haddock églefin
haggis panse de mouton farcie aux flocons d'avoine
hake colin
half moitié, demi
halibut flétan
ham jambon
  ~ **and eggs** œufs au jambon
hare lièvre
haricot bean haricot blanc
hash 1) émincé 2) hachis de bœuf recouvert de pommes de terre
hazelnut noisette
heart cœur
herb herbe aromatique
herring hareng
home-made fait maison
hominy grits bouillie de maïs, sorte de polenta
honey miel
  ~ **dew melon** variété de melon très doux à la chair vert-jaune
horse-radish raifort
hot 1) chaud 2) épicé
  ~ **cross bun** brioche aux raisins (se mange pendant le Carême)
  ~ **dog** hot-dog, saucisse chaude dans un pain
huckleberry myrtille
hush puppy beignet de farine de maïs
ice-cream glace
iced glacé

icing glaçage
Idaho baked potato pomme de terre en robe des champs cuite au four
Irish stew ragoût de mouton aux oignons et aux pommes de terre
Italian dressing vinaigrette
jam confiture
jellied en gelée
Jell-O dessert à la gélatine
jelly gelée de fruits
Jerusalem artichoke topinambour
John Dory Saint-Pierre (poisson)
jugged hare civet de lièvre
juice jus
juniper berry baie de genièvre
junket lait caillé sucré
kale chou frisé
kedgeree miettes de poisson au riz, aux œufs et au beurre
kidney rognon
kipper hareng fumé
lamb agneau
Lancashire hot pot ragoût de côtelettes, de rognons d'agneau, de pommes de terre et d'oignons
larded lardé
lean maigre
leek poireau
leg gigot, cuisse
lemon citron
  ~ **sole** limande
lentil lentille
lettuce laitue, salade verte
lima bean fève
lime lime, citron vert
liver foie
loaf pain, miche
lobster homard
loin filet, carré
Long Island duck canard de Long Island, très réputé
low-calorie pauvre en calories
lox saumon fumé

lunch déjeuner, repas de midi
macaroon macaron
mackerel maquereau
maize maïs
mandarin mandarine
maple syrup sirop d'érable
marinated mariné
marjoram marjolaine
marmalade confiture d'orange ou d'autres agrumes, marmelade
marrow moelle
   ~ **bone** os à moelle
marshmallow bonbon à la guimauve
marzipan massepain, pâte d'amandes
mashed potatoes purée de pommes de terre
meal repas
meat viande
   ~ **ball** boulette de viande
   ~ **loaf** rôti haché
medium (done) à point
melted fondu
Melton Mowbray pie croustade de viande
milk lait
mince hachis
   ~ **pie** tartelette aux fruits confits et aux épices
minced haché
   ~ **meat** viande hachée
mint menthe
mixed mélangé, panaché
   ~ **grill** brochette de viande
molasses mélasse
morel morille
mulberry mûre
mullet mulet
mulligatawny soup potage au poulet, très épicé, d'origine indienne
mushroom champignon
muskmelon sorte de melon

mussel moule
mustard moutarde
mutton mouton
noodle nouille
nut noix
oatmeal (porridge) porridge, bouillie d'avoine
oil huile
okra pousse de *gumbo* généralement utilisée pour lier les potages et les ragoûts
omelet omelette
onion oignon
ox tongue langue de bœuf
oyster huître
pancake crêpe, matefaim
parsley persil
parsnip panais (racine comestible)
partridge perdrix
pastry pâtisserie
pasty pâté, chausson, rissole
pea petit pois
peach pêche
peanut cacahuète
   ~ **butter** beurre d'arachide
pear poire
pearl barley orge perlé
pepper poivre
   ~ **mint** menthe (poivrée)
perch perche
persimmon kaki
pheasant faisan
pickerel brocheton (poisson)
pickle 1) légume ou fruit au vinaigre 2) cornichon (US)
pickled en saumure, au vinaigre
pie tarte, recouverte le plus souvent d'une couche de pâte, farcie ou garnie de viande, de légumes, de fruits ou de crème anglaise
pig porc
pike brochet
pineapple ananas

plaice plie, carrelet

plain nature

plate plat, assiette

plum 1) prune 2) pruneau 3) raisin sec
 ~ **pudding** cake anglais aux fruits secs, parfois flambé; très nourrissant et servi à Noël

poached poché

popcorn grains de maïs éclatés

popover petit pain au lait

pork porc

porterhouse steak épaisse tranche de filet de bœuf

pot roast bœuf braisé aux légumes

potato pomme de terre
 ~ **chips** 1) pommes frites (GB) 2) pommes chips (US)
 ~ **in its jacket** pomme de terre en robe des champs

potted shrimps crevettes au beurre épicé (fondu et refroidi)

poultry volaille

prawn grosse crevette rose

prune pruneau

ptarmigan perdrix des neiges

pudding pudding (mou ou consistant) à base de farine, garni de viande, de poisson, de légumes ou de fruits

pumpernickel pain de seigle complet

pumpkin potiron, courge

quail caille

quince coing

rabbit lapin

radish radis

rainbow trout truite arc-en-ciel

raisin raisin sec

rare saignant

raspberry framboise

raw cru

red mullet rouget

red (sweet) pepper poivron rouge

redcurrant groseille rouge

relish condiment fait de légumes émincés au vinaigre

rhubarb rhubarbe

rib (of beef) côte (de bœuf)

rib-eye steak entrecôte

rice riz

rissole croquette de viande ou de poisson

river trout truite de rivière

roast(ed) rôti(e)

Rock Cornish hen variété de poulet de grain

roe œufs de poisson

roll petit pain

rollmop herring filet de hareng mariné au vin blanc, enroulé sur un cornichon

round steak quasi de bœuf

Rubens sandwich corned-beef sur toast, avec choucroute, emmenthal et sauce à salade, servi chaud

rump steak rumsteak

rusk biscotte

rye bread pain de seigle

saddle selle

saffron safran

sage sauge

salad salade
 ~ **bar** choix de salades
 ~ **cream** sauce à salade crémeuse, légèrement sucrée
 ~ **dressing** sauce à salade

salmon saumon
 ~ **trout** truite saumonée

salt sel

salted salé

sauerkraut choucroute

sausage saucisse, saucisson

sauté(ed) sauté

scallop 1) peigne (coquille Saint-Jacques 2) escalope de veau

scone petit pain tendre à base de

farine de blé ou d'orge

Scotch broth soupe à base d'agneau ou de bœuf et de légumes

Scotch woodcock toast avec œufs brouillés et beurre d'anchois

sea bass loup de mer

sea kale chou marin

seafood poissons et fruits de mer

(in) season (en) saison

seasoning assaisonnement

service charge montant à payer pour le service

service (not) included service (non) compris

set menu menu fixe

shad alose (sorte de sardine)

shallot échalote

shellfish crustacé

sherbet sorbet

shoulder épaule

shredded wheat croquettes de froment (servies au petit déjeuner)

shrimp crevette

silverside (of beef) gîte (de bœuf)

sirloin steak steak d'aloyau

skewer brochette

slice tranche

sliced coupé en tranches

sloppy Joe hachis de bœuf dans une sauce relevée aux tomates, servi dans un petit pain

smelt éperlan

smoked fumé

snack repas léger, collation

soup potage, soupe

sour aigre

soused herring hareng au vinaigre et aux épices

spare rib côte de porc grillée

spice épice

spinach épinard

spiny lobster langouste

(on a) spit (à la) broche

sponge cake gâteau mousseline

sprat harenguet

squash courgette

starter hors-d'œuvre

steak and kidney pie croustade de viande de bœuf et de rognons

steamed cuit à la vapeur

stew ragoût

Stilton (cheese) fromage anglais réputé (blanc ou à moisissures bleues)

strawberry fraise

string bean haricot vert

stuffed farci, fourré

stuffing farce

suck(l)ing pig cochon de lait

sugar sucre

sugarless sans sucre

sundae coupe de glace aux fruits, noix, crème Chantilly et parfois sirop

supper souper, léger repas du soir

swede rutabaga

sweet 1) doux 2) dessert

~ **corn** maïs jaune

~ **potato** patate douce

sweetbread ris de veau

Swiss cheese emmenthal

Swiss roll biscuit roulé à la confiture

Swiss steak tranche de bœuf braisée avec des légumes et des épices

T-bone steak morceau de contre-filet et de filet séparés par un os en forme de T

table d'hôte menu fixe

tangerine orange-mandarine

tarragon estragon

tart tarte (généralement aux fruits)

tenderloin filet (de viande)

Thousand Island dressing mayonnaise aux piments ou au ketchup, avec des poivrons, des olives et des œufs durs

thyme thym

toad-in-the-hole morceaux de viande ou de saucisse briochés

toasted grillé
~ **cheese** toast au fromage

tomato tomate

tongue langue

treacle mélasse

trifle sorte de charlotte russe à l'eau-de-vie avec amandes, confiture, crème Chantilly et crème anglaise

trout truite

truffle truffe

tuna, tunny thon

turkey dinde

turnip navet

turnover chausson

turtle tortue

underdone saignant

vanilla vanille

veal veau
~ **bird** paupiette de veau

vegetable légume
~ **marrow** courgette

venison gros gibier

vichyssoise soupe froide aux poireaux, pommes de terre et crème

vinegar vinaigre

Virginia baked ham jambon cuit au four, piqué de clous de girofles, garni de tranches d'ananas, de cerises et glacé avec le jus des fruits

wafer gaufrette

waffle sorte de gaufre, chaude

walnut noix

water ice sorbet

watercress cresson de fontaine

watermelon pastèque

well-done bien cuit

Welsh rabbit/rarebit croûte au fromage

whelk buccin (mollusque)

whipped cream crème Chantilly

whitebait blanchaille

Wiener Schnitzel escalope viennoise

wine list carte des vins

woodcock bécasse

Worcestershire sauce condiment liquide piquant, à base de vinaigre, de soja et d'ail

yoghurt yaourt

York ham jambon (fumé) d'York

Yorkshire pudding sorte de pâte à choux cuite et servie avec le rosbif

zucchini courgette

zwieback biscotte

Boissons

ale bière brune, légèrement sucrée, fermentée à haute température

bitter ∼brune, amère et plutôt lourde

brown ∼brune en bouteille, légèrement sucrée

light ∼ blonde en bouteille

mild ∼brune à la pression, au goût prononcé

pale ∼ blonde en bouteille

angostura essence aromatique amère ajoutée aux cocktails

applejack eau-de-vie de pomme

Athol Brose boisson écossaise composée de whisky, de miel, d'eau et parfois de flocons d'avoine

Bacardi cocktail cocktail au rhum avec du gin, du sirop de grenadine et du jus de lime (citron vert)

barley water boisson rafraîchissante à base d'orge et aromatisée de citron

barley wine bière brune très alcoolisée

beer bière

bottled ∼ en bouteille

draft, draught ∼ à la pression

bitters apéritifs et digestifs à base de racines, d'écorces ou d'herbes

black velvet champagne additionné de *stout* (accompagne souvent les huîtres)

bloody Mary vodka, jus de tomate et épices

bourbon whisky américain, à base de maïs

brandy 1) appellation générique désignant les eaux-de-vie de vin ou de fruit 2) cognac

∼ **Alexander** mélange d'eau-de-vie, de crème de cacao et de crème fraîche

British wines vins «anglais» faits de raisins (ou de jus de raisin) importés en Grande-Bretagne

cherry brandy liqueur de cerise

chocolate chocolat

cider cidre

∼**cup** mélange de cidre, d'épices, de sucre et de glace

claret vin rouge de Bordeaux

cobbler *long drink* glacé à base de fruits, auquel on ajoute du vin ou une liqueur

coffee café

∼ **with cream** crème

black ∼ noir

caffeine-free ∼ décaféiné

white ∼au lait

cordial liqueur

cream crème

cup boisson rafraîchissante composée de vin glacé, d'eau gazeuse, d'un spiritueux et décorée d'une tranche d'orange, de citron ou de concombre

daiquiri cocktail au rhum, au jus de lime et d'ananas

double double dose

Drambuie liqueur à base de whisky et de miel

dry martini 1) vermouth sec (GB) 2) cocktail au gin avec un peu de vermouth sec (US)

egg-nog boisson faite de rhum ou d'un autre alcool fort avec des jaunes d'œufs battus et du sucre

gin and it mélange de gin et de

vermouth italien

gin-fizz gin avec jus de citron, sucre et soda

ginger ale boisson sans alcool, parfumée à l'essence de gingembre

ginger beer boisson légèrement alcoolisée, à base de gingembre et de sucre

grasshopper mélange de crème de menthe, de crème de cacao et de crème fraîche

Guinness (stout) bière brune légèrement sucrée, au goût très prononcé et à forte teneur en malt et houblon

half pint environ 3 décilitres

highball eau-de-vie ou whisky allongé d'eau gazeuse ou de *ginger ale*

iced glacé

Irish coffee café sucré, arrosé de whisky irlandais et nappé de crème Chantilly

Irish Mist liqueur irlandaise à base de whisky et de miel

Irish whiskey whisky irlandais, moins âpre que le *scotch;* outre l'orge, il contient du seigle, de l'avoine et du blé

juice jus

lager bière blonde légère, servie très fraîche

lemon squash citronnade

lemonade limonade

lime juice jus de lime (citron vert)

liquor spiritueux

long drink alcool allongé d'eau ou d'une boisson gazeuse, avec des glaçons

madeira madère

Manhattan whisky américain, vermouth et *angostura*

milk lait

~ **shake** frappé

mineral water eau minérale

mulled wine vin chaud aux épices

neat sans glace et sans eau, sec, pur

old-fashioned whisky, *angostura,* cerises au marasquin et sucre

on the rocks avec des glaçons

Ovaltine Ovomaltine

Pimm's cup(s) boisson alcoolisée mélangée à du jus de fruit ou du soda

~ **No. 1** à base de gin

~ **No. 2** à base de whisky

~ **No. 3** à base de rhum

~ **No. 4** à base d'eau-de-vie

pink champagne champagne rosé

pink lady mélange de blanc d'œuf, de Calvados, de jus de citron, de grenadine et de gin

pint environ 6 décilitres

port (wine) porto

porter bière brune et amère

quart 1,14 litre (US 0,95 litre)

root beer boisson gazeuse sucrée, aromatisée d'herbes et de racines

rum rhum

rye (whiskey) whisky de seigle, plus lourd et plus âpre que le *bourbon*

scotch (whisky) whisky écossais, généralement fait d'une combinaison de whisky d'orge et de whisky de blé

screwdriver vodka et jus d'orange

shandy *bitter ale* mélangée à une limonade ou une *ginger beer*

sherry xérès

short drink tout alcool non dilué

shot dose de spiritueux

sloe gin-fizz liqueur de prunelle avec soda et jus de citron

soda water eau gazeuse, soda

soft drink boisson sans alcool
spirits spiritueux
stinger cognac et crème de menthe
stout bière brune fortement houblonnée et alcoolisée
straight alcool bu sec, pur
tea thé
toddy grog
Tom Collins gin, jus de citron, sucre, eau gazeuse

tonic (water) eau gazéifiée, aromatisée de quinine
water eau
whisky sour whisky, jus de citron, sucre et soda
wine vin
   dry ~ sec
   red ~ rouge
   sparkling ~ mousseux
   sweet ~ doux (de dessert)
   white ~ blanc

Verbes irréguliers anglais

La liste suivante vous donne les verbes irréguliers anglais. Les verbes composés ou précédés d'un préfixe se conjuguent comme les verbes principaux : p. ex. *withdraw* se conjugue comme *draw* et *mistake* comme *take*.

Infinitif	Imparfait	Participe passé	
arise	arose	arisen	*(se) lever*
awake	awoke	awoken	*(se) réveiller*
be	was	been	*être*
bear	bore	borne	*porter*
beat	beat	beaten	*battre*
become	became	become	*devenir*
begin	began	begun	*commencer*
bend	bent	bent	*plier*
bet	bet	bet	*parier*
bid	bade/bid	bidden/bid	*ordonner*
bind	bound	bound	*attacher*
bite	bit	bitten	*mordre*
bleed	bled	bled	*saigner*
blow	blew	blown	*souffler*
break	broke	broken	*briser*
breed	bred	bred	*élever*
bring	brought	brought	*apporter*
build	built	built	*bâtir*
burn	burnt/burned	burnt/burned	*brûler*
burst	burst	burst	*éclater*
buy	bought	bought	*acheter*
can*	could	—	*pouvoir*
cast	cast	cast	*jeter*
catch	caught	caught	*attraper*
choose	chose	chosen	*choisir*
cling	clung	clung	*se cramponner*
clothe	clothed/clad	clothed/clad	*vêtir*
come	came	come	*venir*
cost	cost	cost	*coûter*
creep	crept	crept	*ramper*
cut	cut	cut	*couper*
deal	dealt	dealt	*conclure (marché)*
dig	dug	dug	*creuser*
do (he does)	did	done	*faire*
draw	drew	drawn	*dessiner*
dream	dreamt/dreamed	dreamt/dreamed	*rêver*
drink	drank	drunk	*boire*
drive	drove	driven	*conduire (auto)*
dwell	dwelt	dwelt	*habiter*
eat	ate	eaten	*manger*
fall	fell	fallen	*tomber*

* présent de l'indicatif

feed	fed	fed	*nourrir*
feel	felt	felt	*ressentir*
fight	fought	fought	*combattre*
find	found	found	*trouver*
flee	fled	fled	*fuir*
fling	flung	flung	*lancer*
fly	flew	flown	*voler*
forsake	forsook	forsaken	*abandonner*
freeze	froze	frozen	*geler*
get	got	got	*obtenir*
give	gave	given	*donner*
go	went	gone	*aller*
grind	ground	ground	*moudre*
grow	grew	grown	*croître*
hang	hung	hung	*pendre*
have	had	had	*avoir*
hear	heard	heard	*entendre*
hew	hewed	hewed/hewn	*couper*
hide	hid	hidden	*cacher*
hit	hit	hit	*frapper*
hold	held	held	*tenir*
hurt	hurt	hurt	*blesser*
keep	kept	kept	*garder*
kneel	knelt	knelt	*s'agenouiller*
knit	knitted/knit	knitted/knit	*tricoter/unir*
know	knew	known	*savoir*
lay	laid	laid	*étendre, placer*
lead	led	led	*guider*
lean	leant/leaned	leant/leaned	*s'appuyer*
leap	leapt/leaped	leapt/leaped	*sauter*
learn	learnt/learned	learnt/learned	*apprendre*
leave	left	left	*quitter*
lend	lent	lent	*prêter*
let	let	let	*permettre*
lie	lay	lain	*être couché*
light	lit/lighted	lit/lighted	*allumer*
lose	lost	lost	*perdre*
make	made	made	*faire*
may*	might	—	*pouvoir*
mean	meant	meant	*signifier*
meet	met	met	*rencontrer*
mow	mowed	mowed/mown	*faucher*
must*	—	—	*falloir*
ought (to)*	—	—	*devoir*
pay	paid	paid	*payer*
put	put	put	*mettre*
read	read	read	*lire*
rid	rid	rid	*débarrasser*
ride	rode	ridden	*monter (à cheval)*

* présent de l'indicatif

ring	rang	rung	*sonner*
rise	rose	risen	*se lever*
run	ran	run	*courir*
saw	sawed	sawn	*scier*
say	said	said	*dire*
see	saw	seen	*voir*
seek	sought	sought	*chercher*
sell	sold	sold	*vendre*
send	sent	sent	*envoyer*
set	set	set	*poser*
sew	sewed	sewed/sewn	*coudre*
shake	shook	shaken	*secouer*
shall*	should	—	*devoir*
shed	shed	shed	*verser*
shine	shone	shone	*briller*
shoot	shot	shot	*tirer*
show	showed	shown	*montrer*
shrink	shrank	shrunk	*rétrécir*
shut	shut	shut	*fermer*
sing	sang	sung	*chanter*
sink	sank	sunk	*couler*
sit	sat	sat	*s'asseoir*
sleep	slept	slept	*dormir*
slide	slid	slid	*glisser*
sling	slung	slung	*jeter*
slink	slunk	slunk	*s'esquiver*
slit	slit	slit	*fendre*
smell	smelled/smelt	smelled/smelt	*sentir (odeur)*
sow	sowed	sown/sowed	*semer*
speak	spoke	spoken	*parler*
speed	sped/speeded	sped/speeded	*accélérer*
spell	spelt/spelled	spelt/spelled	*épeler*
spend	spent	spent	*dépenser*
spill	spilt/spilled	spilt/spilled	*renverser*
spin	spun	spun	*filer*
spit	spat	spat	*cracher*
split	split	split	*fendre, séparer*
spoil	spoilt/spoiled	spoilt/spoiled	*gâter*
spread	spread	spread	*répandre, enduire*
spring	sprang	sprung	*jaillir*
stand	stood	stood	*se tenir debout*
steal	stole	stolen	*dérober*
stick	stuck	stuck	*coller*
sting	stung	stung	*piquer*
stink	stank/stunk	stunk	*empester*
strew	strewed	strewed/strewn	*joncher*
stride	strode	stridden	*marcher à grands pas*
strike	struck	struck/stricken	*frapper*
string	strung	strung	*ficeler*

---

* présent de l'indicatif

strive	strove	striven	*s'efforcer*
swear	swore	sworn	*jurer*
sweep	swept	swept	*balayer*
swell	swelled	swollen	*enfler*
swim	swam	swum	*nager*
swing	swung	swung	*se balancer*
take	took	taken	*prendre*
teach	taught	taught	*enseigner*
tear	tore	torn	*déchirer*
tell	told	told	*dire*
think	thought	thought	*penser*
throw	threw	thrown	*jeter*
thrust	thrust	thrust	*pousser*
tread	trod	trodden	*piétiner*
wake	woke/waked	woken/waked	*(se) réveiller*
wear	wore	worn	*porter (habit)*
weave	wove	woven	*tisser*
weep	wept	wept	*pleurer*
will*	would	—	*vouloir*
win	won	won	*gagner*
wind	wound	wound	*enrouler*
wring	wrung	wrung	*tordre*
write	wrote	written	*écrire*

---

* présent de l'indicatif

Abréviations anglaises

AA	*Automobile Association*	Automobile Club de Grande-Bretagne
AAA	*American Automobile Association*	Automobile Club des Etats-Unis
ABC	*American Broadcasting Company*	société privée de radio-diffusion et de télévision (US)
A.D.	*anno Domini*	apr. J.-C.
Am.	*America ; American*	Amérique ; américain
a.m.	*ante meridiem (before noon)*	avant midi (de minuit à midi)
Amtrak	*American railroad corporation*	société privée des chemins de fer américains
AT & T	*American Telephone and Telegraph Company*	compagnie privée des télé-phones et télégraphes (US)
Ave.	*avenue*	avenue
BBC	*British Broadcasting Corporation*	société britannique de radio-diffusion et de télévision
B.C.	*before Christ*	av. J.-C.
bldg.	*building*	immeuble
Blvd.	*boulevard*	boulevard
B.R.	*British Rail*	chemins de fer britanniques
Brit.	*Britain ; British*	Grande-Bretagne ; britannique
Bros.	*brothers*	frères
¢	*cent*	1/100 de dollar
Can.	*Canada ; Canadian*	Canada ; canadien
CBS	*Columbia Broadcasting System*	société privée de radiodiffu-sion et de télévision (US)
CID	*Criminal Investigation Department*	police judiciaire (GB)
CNR	*Canadian National Railway*	société nationale des chemins de fer canadiens
c/o	*(in) care of*	p.a., aux bons soins de
Co.	*company*	compagnie
Corp.	*corporation*	type de société
CPR	*Canadian Pacific Railways*	société privée des chemins de fer canadiens
D.C.	*District of Columbia*	District de Columbia (Washington, D.C.)
DDS	*Doctor of Dental Science*	dentiste
dept.	*department*	département

EEC	*European Economic Community*	CEE
e.g.	*for instance*	par exemple
Eng.	*England; English*	Angleterre; anglais
excl.	*excluding; exclusive*	non compris, exclu
ft.	*foot/feet*	pied/pieds (30,5 cm)
GB	*Great Britain*	Grande-Bretagne
H.E.	*His/Her Excellency; His Eminence*	Son Excellence; Son Eminence
H.H.	*His Holiness*	Sa Sainteté
H.M.	*His/Her Majesty*	Sa Majesté
H.M.S.	*Her Majesty's ship*	bâtiment de la marine royale de Grande-Bretagne
hp	*horsepower*	chevaux-vapeur
Hwy	*highway*	route nationale
i.e.	*that is to say*	c'est-à-dire
in.	*inch*	pouce (2,54 cm)
Inc.	*incorporated*	type de société anonyme américaine
incl.	*including, inclusive*	compris, inclus
£	*pound sterling*	livre sterling
L.A.	*Los Angeles*	Los Angeles
Ltd.	*limited*	type de société anonyme britannique
M.D.	*Doctor of Medicine*	médecin
M.P.	*Member of Parliament*	membre du Parlement britannique
mph	*miles per hour*	miles à l'heure
Mr.	*Mister*	monsieur
Mrs.	*Missis*	madame
Ms.	*Missis/Miss*	madame/mademoiselle
nat.	*national*	national
NBC	*National Broadcasting Company*	société privée de radiodiffusion et de télévision (US)
No.	*number*	numéro
N.Y.C.	*New York City*	ville de New York
O.B.E.	*Officer (of the Order) of the British Empire*	Officier de l'Ordre de l'Empire britannique
p.	*page; penny/pence*	page; 1/100 de livre sterling
p.a.	*per annum*	par année, annuel
Ph.D.	*Doctor of Philosophy*	docteur en philosophie
p.m.	*post meridiem (after noon)*	après midi (de midi à minuit)
PO	*Post Office*	bureau de poste

POO	*post office order*	mandat postal
P.T.O.	*please turn over*	tournez, s'il vous plaît
RAC	*Royal Automobile Club*	Automobile Club de Grande-Bretagne
RCMP	*Royal Canadian Mounted Police*	police royale montée canadienne
Rd.	*road*	route, rue
ref.	*reference*	voir, comparer
Rev.	*reverend*	pasteur dans l'Eglise anglicane
RFD	*rural free delivery*	distribution du courrier à la campagne
RR	*railroad*	chemin de fer
RSVP	*please reply*	répondez, s'il vous plaît
$	*dollar*	dollar
Soc.	*society*	société
St.	*saint ; street*	saint ; rue
STD	*Subscriber Trunk Dialling*	téléphone automatique
UN	*United Nations*	Nations Unies
UPS	*United Parcel Service*	service d'expédition de colis (US)
US	*United States*	Etats-Unis
USS	*United States Ship*	bâtiment de la marine de guerre américaine
VAT	*value added tax*	TVA
VIP	*very important person*	personne jouissant de privilèges particuliers
Xmas	*Christmas*	Noël
yd.	*yard*	yard (91,44 cm)
YMCA	*Young Men's Christian Association*	Union Chrétienne de Jeunes Gens
YWCA	*Young Women's Christian Association*	Union Chrétienne de Jeunes Filles
ZIP	*ZIP code*	numéro (code) postal

Nombres

Nombres cardinaux		Nombres ordinaux	
0	zero	1st	first
1	one	2nd	second
2	two	3rd	third
3	three	4th	fourth
4	four	5th	fifth
5	five	6th	sixth
6	six	7th	seventh
7	seven	8th	eighth
8	eight	9th	ninth
9	nine	10th	tenth
10	ten	11th	eleventh
11	eleven	12th	twelfth
12	twelve	13th	thirteenth
13	thirteen	14th	fourteenth
14	fourteen	15th	fifteenth
15	fifteen	16th	sixteenth
16	sixteen	17th	seventeenth
17	seventeen	18th	eighteenth
18	eighteen	19th	nineteenth
19	nineteen	20th	twentieth
20	twenty	21st	twenty-first
21	twenty-one	22nd	twenty-second
22	twenty-two	23rd	twenty-third
23	twenty-three	24th	twenty-fourth
24	twenty-four	25th	twenty-fifth
25	twenty-five	26th	twenty-sixth
30	thirty	27th	twenty-seventh
40	forty	28th	twenty-eighth
50	fifty	29th	twenty-ninth
60	sixty	30th	thirtieth
70	seventy	40th	fortieth
80	eighty	50th	fiftieth
90	ninety	60th	sixtieth
100	a/one hundred	70th	seventieth
230	two hundred and thirty	80th	eightieth
		90th	ninetieth
1,000	a/one thousand	100th	hundredth
10,000	ten thousand	230th	two hundred and thirtieth
100,000	a/one hundred thousand		
1,000,000	a/one million	1,000th	thousandth

L'heure

Les Britanniques et les Américains utilisent le système des douze heures. L'expression *a.m. (ante meridiem)* désigne les heures précédant midi, *p.m. (post meridiem)* celles de l'après-midi et du soir (jusqu'à minuit). Toutefois, en Grande-Bretagne, les horaires sont progressivement libellés sur le modèle continental.

I'll come at seven a.m.	Je viendrai à 7 h. du matin.
I'll come at one p.m.	Je viendrai à 1 h. de l'après-midi.
I'll come at eight p.m.	Je viendrai à 8 h. du soir.

Les jours de la semaine

Sunday	dimanche	*Thursday*	jeudi
Monday	lundi	*Friday*	vendredi
Tuesday	mardi	*Saturday*	samedi
Wednesday	mercredi		

GUIDES DE VOYAGE BERLITZ

Des petits guides de voyage qui couvrent le monde entier – discrets, puisqu'ils tiennent dans votre poche, et, de plus, économiques. 128 pages – illustrées de photos et de cartes en couleurs – qui vous disent que voir, que faire, comment acheter, que manger. Un compagnon indispensable.

Afrique
Algérie (256 p.)
Kenya
Maroc
Tunisie

Allemagne/Autriche
Berlin
Munich
Vallée du Rhin
Vienne

Amérique Latine
Mexico
Rio de Janeiro

Antilles
Antilles françaises
Bahamas
Caraïbes du Sud-Est
Jamaïque

Belgique/Pays-Bas
Bruxelles
Amsterdam

Chypre

Espagne
Barcelone*
Costa Blanca
Costa Brava
Costa del Sol
  et Andalousie
Costa Dorada et Barcelone
Ibiza et Formentera
Iles Canaries
Madrid
Majorque et Minorque
Séville

Etats-Unis/Canada
Californie

Floride
Miami
New York
USA (256 p.)
Canada (256 p.)
Montréal

Extrême-Orient
Chine (256 p.)
Hong Kong
Inde (256 p.)
Indonésie (192 p.) *
Japon (256 p.)
Singapour
Sri Lanka
Thaïlande

France
Côte d'Azur
Paris
Val de Loire

Grande-Bretagne
Ecosse
Iles Anglo-Normandes
Londres
Oxford et Stratford

Grèce
Athènes
Corfou
Crète
Iles grecques
Rhodes
Salonique et la Grèce
  du Nord

Hongrie
Budapest
Hongrie (192 p.)

Irlande

Italie/Malte
Florence
Italie (256 p.)
Riviera italienne
Rome
Sicile
Venise
Malte

Proche-Orient
Egypte
Jérusalem

Portugal
Algarve
Lisbonne
Madère

Scandinavie
Copenhague
Helsinki
Oslo
Stockholm

Suisse
Suisse (192 p.)

Tchécoslovaquie
Prague

Turquie
Istanbul/Côte égéenne
Turquie (192 p.)

URSS
Moscou et Leningrad
L'Ermitage, Leningrad*

Yougoslavie
Dubrovnik et Dalmatie
  méridionale
Istrie et Côte croate
Split et Dalmatie

1001 Adresses
Londres/New York/
  Paris/Rome

* en préparation